COMMERCIAL
BANKING

COMMERCIAL BANKING

Text and Readings

JOHN R. BRICK
Michigan State University

SYSTEMS PUBLICATIONS, INC.
P.O. Box 318
Haslett, Michigan 48840
(517) 349-4695

ISBN 0-912503-02-5
Library of Congress Catalog Information is available.

PRINTED IN THE UNITED STATES OF AMERICA

Designed and typeset by Publications Development Co. of
Crockett, Texas, Developmental Editor: Nancy Marcus Land,
Production Editor: Bessie Graham

Contents

Preface

In the early 1980s, major banking-related legislation began the restructuring of the entire system of depository-type financial institutions in the United States. Interest rate ceilings on deposits, competitive barriers, some usury laws, and restrictions on products and services that may be offered by such institutions were among the many cumbersome and out-dated regulations that were removed or phased out. Liability powers of depository institutions were expanded, especially for the non-bank institutions. Savings and loan associations, credit unions, and savings banks were empowered to offer accounts that are virtually identical to checking accounts, a service once offered exclusively by banks. So-called "money market accounts" were also authorized for the first time. On the asset side, new types of mortgage loans emerged making the mortgage lending process far more complex for both consumers and bankers. S&Ls and savings banks were empowered to offer commercial loans, consumer leases, trust services, credit cards, and commercial loans.

The removal of competitive restrictions and barriers has had widespread effects on the manner in which financial services are delivered. With much greater freedom to offer such services and technological advances in electronic delivery systems, the distinction between banks and nonbank depository institutions has become blurred. Rather than competing only against other banks in the markets for loans and financial services, commercial banks must now compete against an army of other depository-type financial institutions with similar powers. The changing competitive environment is not limited to depository institutions. Life insurance companies are also competing aggressively in lending markets once dominated by domestic commercial banks. Even nonfinancial firms are offering financial services.

The removal of interest rate ceilings on deposits coupled with a far more competitive market has resulted in narrower operating spreads and increased the cost of funds for banks. Equally important is that the cost of bank funds has become much more sensitive to changes in the general level of interest rates. This is a major management problem in a financial environment that has been characterized by a high degree of volatility in recent years.

Life is more complicated and challenging for bankers than at any time in the past. It is also more fun. Traditional policies and practices must be reexamined in light of the present competitive, regulatory, and financial environment. As new types of bank assets, liabilities, and financial services evolve, bank management concepts must keep pace to ensure continued growth, profitability, and in some cases, solvency. The objective of this book is to contribute to the evolution of the bank management process.

The book is divided into five major sections. In Part I—Introduction, the first chapter provides an overview to give the student of banking some perspective on how pieces of the banking puzzle fit together. A summary of the *Depository Institutions Deregulation and Monetary Control Act of 1980* in Chapter 2 provides additional perspective. The final chapter in this section deals with a topic that has received surprisingly little attention in the banking literature—financial mathematics in banking. This chapter provides the comprehensive mathematical framework necessary for decision-making in a depository-type financial institution.

In Part II—Asset Management, the chapters are divided into four sections covering the major asset management activities. The first chapter in the commercial lending section provides extensive coverage of that topic. Supplementary chapters cover lending-related activities leading to the collapse of the Penn Square Bank and certain aspects of foreign lending. The next section contains two chapters covering consumer lending and mortgage lending. These are supplemented by two chapters covering important and controversial aspects of consumer-related lending—usury laws and the Community Reinvestment Act. Few people, even within banks understand the next topic in Part II, the money position of a bank. Three short chapters introduce the background material necessary for a full understanding of this important function. A comprehensive management-oriented chapter completes the money position section. Part II concludes with a section covering the bank investment portfolio, an important source of liquidity, earnings, and in some banks, problems.

In Part III—Liability and Capital Management, several chapters cover specific types of liabilities arising in day-to-day banking operations. A chapter on bank capital concludes this section. Two of the most important aspects of modern banking are asset-liability management and the use of interest rate futures. Four chapters summarize the asset-liability management process. An introductory chapter on financial futures and a comprehensive chapter dealing with the use of futures in banks conclude Part IV.

In Part V, several topics involving cost, competitive, and regulatory issues are examined. The *Depository Institutions Act of 1982* (The Garn-St Germain Act) is summarized in this section because of its widespread effect on the competitive structure of depository institutions. The concluding chapter provides a thoughtful perspective on a sensitive topic—government intervention in the credit market.

The book is flexible. Although focused on commercial banking, most of the material is equally relevant to S&Ls, credit unions, and savings banks. Thus, the book may be used in courses dealing with the management of financial institutions as well as bank management. Most of the material has been used successfully at both the undergraduate and MBA levels. The book may also be used as a primary text or it may be used to supplement existing textbooks or casebooks. Practitioners will find the book useful as a reference or as an in-house training resource.

Several acknowledgements are in order. The authors of the articles used in this book have made significant contributions to the literature. We are indebted to these authors and the copyright holders for allowing the work to be reprinted. Thorough reviews of the author's chapters were provided by Eugene F. Drzycimski (University of Wisconsin-Oshkosh), Bruce Berlin (Ohio University), and Peter Gillespie (National Bank of Detroit). The author would also like to express his appreciation to the many finance students at Michigan State University, especially Kristina Tousley, who offered helpful comments and suggestions related to much of the work in this book.

John R. Brick
Michigan State University
East Lansing, Michigan
September 1983

PART I

INTRODUCTION

Commercial Banking– An Overview

Hardly a day goes by without the financial press or news commentators reporting major developments in the banking industry. This attention is not surprising for two reasons. The first is the banking revolution now taking place. In the past few years, more changes and dramatic developments have occurred in the banking industry than occurred in the preceding fifty years. Throughout the 1980s more changes will occur and competition will intensify. The second reason for the widespread interest in banking is the crucial role the industry plays in the country's economic and social systems. Management decisions and policies have pervasive effects. So important and widespread are these effects that banks and bank-related activities are monitored closely by regulators, labor unions, civil rights groups, law enforcement agencies, consumer activists, trade associations, narcotics dealers, and, of course, politicians. Only the KGB has not expressed much interest in banking, at least publicly.

Not all of these groups are well-informed about banking. In fact, at the rate changes are occurring in the industry, it is probably safe to say that many bankers are not well-informed about banking either. Even in the absence of the banking revolution now underway, banking is a complex business. The revolution, along with equally dramatic developments and changes in the financial markets, has complicated things for everyone, including bankers. Despite the increasing complexity of banking, it is essential for society to have a clear understanding of the bank management process. The purpose of this book is to help promote such an understanding.

In this chapter, the first step is taken by presenting a very brief overview of commercial banking. The economic functions of a commercial bank will be examined along with the implications of these functions. Then, to distinguish banks from manufacturing firms and provide an overview of the activities of banks, the financial statement of a bank is examined. Finally, the regulatory environment within which banks operate will be examined.

ECONOMIC FUNCTIONS OF COMMERCIAL BANKS

The commercial banking industry is made up of just under 15,000 banks with combined assets exceeding $2 trillion dollars. (This figure does not include trust assets of about $500 billion that are owned by others but managed by banks.) The industry is made up of individual institutions that are diverse, complicated, and require financial sophistication to understand their behavior. The diversity of banks stems from the fact that they provide a wide range of important financial services for domestic and foreign governments, commercial, and industrial businesses, farmers, consumers, and other financial institutions. In the process of meeting credit, depository, and other financial needs of such a broad clientele, commercial banks perform important economic functions in the financial system.

Before examining these functions, a distinction must be made between so-called *primary* and *secondary* claims. In their simplest form, primary claims are assets of the bank, and secondary claims are liabilities of the bank. When a bank accepts deposits for a checking account or savings account, it issues a secondary claim against itself. The funds may then be used to make a commercial loan, a primary claim. The distinction is important. The secondary claim issued by the bank is liquid, safe, and requires little or no administrative effort or technical expertise on the part of the depositor or saver. The bank loan, however, a *primary claim*, is risky, lacks liquidity, is longer-term, and requires considerable administrative and technical expertise. In light of the different properties of bank assets and liabilites, the question arises—how can a bank finance the acquisition of risky, illiquid, and longer-term assets by issuing liabilities that are safe, liquid, short-term, and convenient? The answer lies in an understanding of the economic functions of commercial banks. These are:

- Facilitating the formation and allocation of capital
- Transforming the risk of financial assets
- Promoting market efficiency.[1]

Formation and Allocation of Capital

By combining the deposits, savings, and invested funds of a large number of individuals, businesses, and other economic entities, commercial banks facilitate the formation of capital. Many savers are individuals with modest financial re-

---

[1] The functions discussed in this section pertain to nonbank financial institutions as well as commercial banks. These include credit unions, savings and loan associations, savings banks, life insurance companies, property-liability insurance companies, pension funds, and mutual funds.

sources. In the absence of banks and other financial institutions, minimum size requirements, high transaction costs, and the lack of technical expertise would discourage many individuals from saving at all. Since banks accept deposits—large or small—the resulting secondary claims of individuals are said to be highly divisible. It is this feature, *divisibility*, that enables banks to tap the market for small-scale savings, pool the funds, and generally stimulate savings that might not otherwise occur. The formation of capital is greatly facilitated by the existence of banks.

The formation of capital is only one side of the coin. Capital must also be allocated efficiently to users. There are two aspects of this process. First, the *physical allocation* of capital is facilitated by banks. Users of capital negotiate with the managers of the capital pools rather than attempting to locate and negotiate with a multitude of savers. In the absence of banks and other intermediaries, significant costs would be incurred in the search for capital by users as well as the search for opportunities by lenders.

The other aspect of the allocation process is the *economic allocation* of capital. This is accomplished by the continuous efforts of banks to finance economically feasible projects. Proper allocation of capital, an obviously scarce resource, requires that projects be evaluated in a risk-return context. This in turn requires information and managerial skill in evaluating the wide range of lending and investment opportunities available to banks. The benefits of professional management can be obtained at a low unit cost by spreading the costs of information and management expertise over a sizable base of pooled savings.

The economic allocation of capital is facilitated by the high degree of specialization in bank lending and investment activities. In many large banks commercial loan officers specialize in certain types of industries or companies. Similarly, specialists are involved in mortgage lending and management of the bank's investment portfolio. The existence of knowledgeable, specialized personnel enhances the effectiveness of the decison-making process in a risk-return context. In the process, capital is allocated more efficiently.

Risk Transformation

Most individual savers have a preference for financial assets that may be readily converted to cash without risk of loss, i.e., liquid assets. In addition, the assets should be free from the risk of loss resulting from default. This would seem to imply that financial assets such as savings accounts and other forms of bank deposits should be backed by loans and investments that are also default-free and short-term. While such assets would meet the needs of savers, most borrowers are understandably unwilling and even unable to issue such financial claims. It is in the best interest of borrowers to tailor the financing terms, especially the maturity, to their own needs. This impasse, or "maturity gap" between lenders and borrowers is bridged by banks and other financial institutions.

The creation of intervening assets and liabilities by banks has the effect of transforming longer-term primary claims into shorter-term, and in many cases, riskless secondary claims that appeal to a broad range of savers. The users of capital also benefit since the financing terms—especially the maturity—can also be tailored to meet their needs. How, then, is the maturity of financial claims transformed by banks?

Maturity Risk   Since commercial banks pool the resources of a large number of depositors and savers, there is a high degree of predictability associated with their behavior. Consider this in the context of a bank with a large number of checking accounts. The underlying funds are subject to immediate withdrawal and thus are very short-term from the standpoint of the individual. When checks are written, they are honored immediately when presented to the bank. But individual depositors behave differently. Not everyone writes checks against their account at the same time and deposits are made at different times by customers. Although there is considerable fluctuation in the day-to-day level of the aggregate demand deposit balance, the aggregate balance is far more stable, and thus more predictable, than individual balances. Because of the predictability of a large number of depositors, the underlying funds are often referred to as "core" deposits. Because of their collective stability, the funds may be placed in investments and loans that are longer-term than demand deposits and thus less liquid.

In this way, banks absorb the risks and lack of flexibility inherent in longer-term assets while issuing liquid and highly flexible liabilities. This is a critical point. Since longer-term loans and investments lack liquidity they provide returns that are usually higher than those available on shorter-term instruments. These returns not only pay for the intermediation process, but are also passed on to savers in the form of higher returns that would not otherwise be obtainable. Similar results are obtained when risky financial assets are transformed into safer financial claims through the process of reducing default risk through diversification.

Default Risk   Individual bank loans and some bank investments are subject to default risk. Through the careful selection of loans and investments, the risk level of a bank's pool of assets can be reduced such that the overall portfolio risk is substantially less than that of the individual, risky components. Stated another way, diversification enables the risk level of a bank's pool of assets to be reduced for a given expected return, or the expected return can be increased for a given risk level. This *portfolio effect* can be achieved with a relatively small number of holdings provided the asset returns are somewhat independent of each other. In turn, the beneficial effects of diversification enable the bank to issue liabilities that are considerably less risky than most of the bank's individual assets. In the absence of this diversifying effect, individuals would have little choice but to bear an unnecessary and uncompensated risk. Since many savers have modest financial resources it is difficult, if not impossible, for these individuals to invest directly in a cross section of loans and investments to obtain an adequately diversified portfolio.

The deposits of almost all banks are insured up to $100,000 by the Federal Deposit Insurance Corporation. A small number of banks have their deposits insured by an agency of the state in which they are chartered to operate. (A very small number of banks are uninsured.) For insured depositors, the underlying default risk, or any other bank-related risk, is not a major concern. Thus, deposit insurance is another link in the risk transformation process.

Market Efficiency

In the process of continuously evaluating and absorbing risks in the lending and investment markets, competing financial institutions contribute to the *efficiency* of financial markets. Such efficiency is important in a financial system because *both* borrowers and lenders benefit. This is accomplished in two ways. First, by virtue of their expertise and ability to diversify, banks and other financial institutions are able to obtain more favorable risk-return relationships than most individuals. The risk-adjusted net return to savers is higher with a system of intermediaries and borrower costs are lower than in absence of such a system. Second, with active competition in the financial markets, distortions in the pricing of financial assets are minimized.

Risk-Adjusted Net Returns   To see how banks and other intermediaries provide higher risk-adjusted net returns to savers and lower costs to borrowers, refer to Table 1. This table shows the hypothetical composition of a mortgage loan interest rate with and without intermediaries. In the absence of intermediaries individual savers might charge a gross rate of 14 percent. Of this return, 8 percentage points is consumed by search and information costs, administrative costs, and risk premiums for default and maturity risk. Deducting these costs from the gross rate results in a net risk-adjusted return of 6 percent for the saver. The spread between this net return and the gross rate is 8 percentage points. A system with financial intermediaries has much lower costs because of the intermediaries' scale of operations and their ability to diversify and absorb other risks. As shown in Table 1, the economic benefits of intermediaries— lower unit costs and reduced compensation for risk—may be translated into lower costs for the borrower and higher returns for the saver. The lender-borrower spread is reduced from eight to three percentage points.

Asset Pricing   The other related aspect of market efficiency is the manner in which banks and other financial institutions

Table 1   Hypothetical Composition of Mortgage Interest Rates

	Individual Savers	With Intermediaries
Gross mortgage rates	14%	12%
Search and information cost	−1	−½
Administrative costs	−3	−1½
Premium for		
Default risk	−2	−¼
Maturity risk	−2	−¼
Intermediary profit	—	−½
Saver's net risk-adjusted return	6%	9%
Lender-borrower spread	8%	3%

affect the pricing of financial assets. By competing in the financial markets for loans and investments, intermediaries tend to minimize pricing distortions. Prices of such assets tend to be reasonably good estimates of their "intrinsic value." To the extent that the price of a financial asset deviates from its "true" value, professional managers shift their portfolio emphasis in response. This is made possible through the collective efforts of intermediaries to monitor asset prices and to generate and interpret new information which affects prices. As a result, most financial markets are remarkably fair and competitive. This is, of course, the way it should be.

FINANCIAL STRUCTURE OF COMMERCIAL BANKS

Bank management can be described as two separate but related processes. The first is decision-making with respect to *individual* asset and liability accounts. Most of these accounts, in terms of their number and dollar amount, are financial in nature. That is, they are closely related to day-to-day events in the financial markets. In contrast, manufacturing firms have a much larger proportion of fixed assets in the form of plant, equipment, and working capital. The distinction between manufacturing firms and banks is important when highlighting the decision-making process in a bank. Virtually all bank asset and liability decisions must be made while monitoring the daily pulse of the many sectors of the money and capital markets.

The second aspect of the decision-making process relates to the *joint*, rather than individual, management of assets and liabilities. Since most of a bank's assets are closely related to the financial markets, bank revenues are affected by interest rate movements. Costs associated with bank liabilities are also closely related to conditions in the financial markets. In order to control the relationship, or spread, between revenues and costs, the overall asset structure must be managed in a way that is consistent with the interest rate sensitivity of the liability structure.

To provide a frame of reference for the asset-liability management process and the classes of assets and liabilities that must be managed, this section provides a brief overview of the financial structure of a commercial bank. This is like the initial step in assembling a puzzle. It is useful to have a picture from which to work in order to see how the pieces fit together. Viewed individually, the activities of commercial banks are analogous to the individual pieces of a puzzle—it may not be obvious how they fit together. Like working a puzzle, it is useful to get some idea how the end result looks before focusing on specific management activities, strategies, and policies that are covered in later chapters.

Banks have considerable latitude with respect to the management of their assets and liabilities. As a result, the financial structures of commercial banks vary from one bank to another. Also, the regulatory environment within which a bank operates has an impact on the composition of its asset and liability structures. Large banks are unlike small banks and city banks behave differently from their rural counterparts. Thus, it is difficult to characterize the financial structure of a "typical" commercial bank. With this in mind and at the risk of omitting important structural differences between banks, the Statement of Condition of the *Hypothetical National Bank*, shown in Table 2, is used as a reference point.

Asset Structure

With assets of $1 billion, the Hypothetical National Bank (HNB) is large enough to engage in the entire range of activities open to commercial banks. From Table 2, it is apparent that with loans making up 55 percent of assets, the lending function is the primary asset management activity. This proportion is representative of many banks under normal economic circumstances. Under tight credit conditions, —Why? the percentage of loans to total assets may increase to as much as 65 percent. Within the loan category the proportion of *Commercial and Industrial (C&I)* loans, usually referred to as *commercial loans,* tend to increase relative to consumer-related loans as the size of the bank increases.

Within the commercial loan category, the bank serves many industry classifications and in this respect HNB is reasonably well-diversified. The location of a bank affects the composition of its loan portfolio. The commercial loan portfolio of banks in the Plains states often have sizable proportions of agriculture-related loans. In the Southwest, energy-related loans play a key role in the portfolios of many banks. Some banks tend to be more consumer-oriented than others. Such CC considered a loan? banks have larger proportions of installment, credit card, and mortgage loans.

The amount or proportion of a particular class of loans shown on a bank financial statement is not always a precise indicator of the bank's lending emphasis. For example, residential mortgage loans make up 10 percent of HNB's assets. The bank could be much more active in this type of lending than the percentage suggests if many of the bank's mortgage loans were originated by the bank and then sold in the secondary mortgage market. The loans that show up on the financial statement are only those the bank has chosen to hold in its own portfolio. Similarly, many banks sell "participations" in commercial loans originated with their customers. The buying institutions are usually other banks with which the selling bank has a so-called *correspondent* relationship.

As shown in Table 2, the *Investments* account represents another important asset category. The primary purpose of the investment portfolio is to facilitate day-to-day cash management and cushion the effects of unexpected cash inflows and outflows resulting from changes in loan demand and deposit flows. In this respect, the investment portfolio functions as a shock absorber in the management process. Although the size of the investment portfolio of many banks is about 25 percent of assets, the proportion may vary from bank to bank for several reasons. The percentage may be somewhat lower for very large banks with access to the money markets. Also, to the extent that a bank has substantial deposits in *Money Market Accounts,* the investment portfolio may be larger than would otherwise be the case and the investment emphasis would be more heavily on short-term money market instruments. The size of a bank's *Trading Account,* if any, also affects the overall size of the portfolio. This account reflects a bank's activities as a dealer in bonds and money market instruments. The bank's traders attempt to

Table 2 Hypothetical National Bank Statement of Condition ($ in Millions)

ASSETS	Amount	Percent
Cash & Reserves		
Cash	$ 10	1.0%
Deposits—FR Bank	40	4.0
Deposits—Other Banks	35	3.5
Cash Items in Process of Collection	65	6.5
Total Cash & Reserves	150	15.0
Investments		
Funds Sold		
Federal Funds Sold	15	1.5
Securities Purchased Under Agreement to Resell	5	.5
Securities		
U. S. Treasury	95	9.5
U.S. Agency	5	.5
State and Local	120	12.0
Other	5	.5
Trading Account (at Mkt.)	5	.5
Total Investments	250	25.0
Loans		
Commercial & Industrial (C&I)		
Agriculture	10	1.0
Finance-Related	30	3.0
Industrial & Commercial	200	20.0
International	15	1.5
Lease Financing	35	3.5

LIABILITIES & CAPITAL	Amount	Percent
Deposits		
Demand Deposits	$ 200	20.0%
NOW and "Super" NOW Accounts	150	15.0
Money Market Accounts	100	10.0
Reg. Savings and Time Deposits	300	30.0
Foreign Deposits	50	5.0
Total Deposits	800	80.0
Borrowed Funds—Short-Term		
Funds Purchased		
Federal Funds Purchased	5	.5
Securities Sold Under Agreement to Repurchase	15	1.5
Federal Reserve Bank Advances	5	.5
Bankers' Acceptances Outstanding	15	1.5
Other Short-Term Borrowed Funds	10	1.0
Total Borrowed Funds—Short-Term	50	5.0
Borrowed Funds—Long-Term		
Capital Debentures	30	3.0
Mortgage Indebtedness	10	1.0
Total Borrowed Funds—Long-Term	40	4.0
Other Liabilities		
Interest Payable	10	1.0
Accounts Payable & Accrued Taxes	25	2.5
Miscellaneous Liabilities	15	1.5
Total Other Liabilities	50	5.0

Real Estate & Construction	40	4.0
Other	5	.5
Total Commercial Loans	335	33.5
Consumer Loans		
Installment	100	10.0
Credit Card	15	1.5
Mortgage (Residential)	100	10.0
Other	5	.5
Total Consumer Loans	220	22.0
Total Loans	555	55.5
Less: Reserve for Loan Losses	5	.5
Net Loans	550	55.0
Other Assets		
Interest Receivable	15	1.5
Due from Customers on Acceptances	15	1.5
Building & Equipment	15	1.5
Miscellaneous Assets	5	.5
Total Other Assets	50	5.0
Total Assets	$1,000	100.0%

Capital		
Preferred Stock	-0-	-0-
Common Shareholders' Equity		
Common Stock ($25 par)		
Authorized 1,200,000 Shares		
Issued 1,200,000 Shares	30	3.0
Capital Surplus	15	1.5
Retained Earnings	15	1.5
Total Common Equity	60	6.0
Total Capital	60	6.0
Total Liabilities & Capital	$1,000	100.0%

Key Ratios:
Loans/Deposits = 68.75%
Equity/Total Liabilities & Capital = 6.00%

take advantage of price swings in the financial markets.

Other than the funds "earmarked" for the Money Market Accounts, the Trading Account, and any securities pledged to collateralize deposits or bank borrowings, banks have considerable flexibility in selecting the types of investments, their maturity structure, and overall investment policy. Investment policies may vary from a passive "buy and hold" approach to a more aggressive or "active" style characterized by high turnover.

The *Cash and Reserves* position represents a sizable proportion of assets in most commercial banks. Since cash is a non-earning asset, this is kept to a minimum level sufficient to conduct daily operations. When the reserve requirements imposed by the *Depository Institutions Deregulation and Monetary Control Act of 1980* are completely phased-in by the late 1980s, banks and other depository institutions will be operating under uniform reserve requirements. The amount of reserves will depend on the size and composition of a bank's deposit structure. Until this phase-in is complete, the reserve position of a bank will vary depending on its size, location, and whether it is chartered by the federal government or a state government.

Liability Structure

On the liabilities and capital side, *Deposits* make up 80 percent of HNB's total. As is typical of most banks, *Demand Deposits* play a major role. Another transaction-type account is the so-called *Now Account.* NOW is an acronym for *negotiable order of withdrawal.* This is essentially an interest-bearing checking account but is legally classified as a savings account. A variation of this account, known as the *"Super" NOW Account,* was authorized for use by non-corporate depositors in January 1983. This account requires a higher minimum balance than a regular NOW Account and pays a higher rate of interest. *Money Market Accounts,* which were authorized for use in late 1982 to enable banks to compete with money market funds, are *investment-oriented* with the interest rate tied to the yield on short-term money market instruments. Although the funds underlying Money Market Accounts are subject to immediate withdrawal, the collective level of these funds may be quite stable as long as competitive market rates are paid on an on-going basis. In other words, the cost of these funds is extremely sensitive to changes in short-term interest rates. In order to achieve a similar degree of interest-rate sensitivity on the asset side, most banks invest all or most of the underlying funds in short-term money market instruments. Thus, the funds underlying money market accounts should *not* be considered as part of the bank's core deposits for fixed-rate lending purposes.

Regular Savings and *Time Deposits* are the usual passbook and certificate-type savings accounts. Although the maturity of Time Deposits may range from a few months to upwards of five to eight years, most time deposits mature within a few years. This account includes large denomination negotiable and non-negotiable certificates of deposit, most of which mature within one year. Most *Foreign Deposits* are also short-term.

Most bank assets are financed with short-term, interest rate-sensitive liabilities.

This has important managerial implications. Asset maturities must be correspondingly short-term and/or the interest rate on many loans must float with market rates to reflect a changing cost of funds. Failure to do this or otherwise hedge transactions in the futures market, exposes the bank to interest rate risk. Controlling this risk is one of the main objectives of the overall bank management process.

The lending and depository functions are the primary asset and liability activities of commercial banks. There is also a direct relationship between loans and deposits. A commonly used measure of this relationship is the *loan/deposit ratio.* This ratio reflects the extent to which the bank is "loaned up." In the case of HNB, the ratio is $550 million/$800 million = 68.75 percent. Most banks attempt to stay in the range of 65 to 75 percent. A ratio of 80 percent may indicate that a bank has limited ability to expand its loan portfolio.

Because of the uncertainty of flows into and out of banks, a high degree of liquidity must be maintained at all times. In addition to liquid assets in the investment portfolio, another source of this liquidity is short-term borrowing power. In Table 2, this shows up in several accounts. The *Funds Purchased* section is made up of overnight or otherwise very short-term borrowings known as *Federal Funds Purchased* and *Repurchase Agreements.* Other sources of short-term credit are *Federal Reserve Bank Advances* and the sale of *Bankers' Acceptances.* When coupled with the ability to sell time deposits in the form of *Certificates of Deposit* (CDs), the *Borrowed Funds—Short-Term* account is the bank's shock absorber on the liability side.

The capital position of commercial banks is usually equity capital although this base may be supplemented by preferred stock, a form of equity, or depending on the contractual features, long-term borrowings. The equity base may vary from just under 4 percent of total liabilities and capital for very large banks to 10 percent for smaller banks. This small equity base means that commercial banks are highly leveraged. Thus, they have limited ability to absorb sustained periods of operating losses or unusually large loan losses.

Since commercial banks are stockholder-owned, the financial objective of management is to maximize the value of the firm. This is accomplished by making decisions in a risk-return framework. Because of the social and economic importance of commercial banking, stockholder interests often are caught in a crossfire between the interests of consumer activists, politicians, and, notwithstanding deregulation, regulators. As a result, a complex regulatory maze has evolved around the banking industry.

BANK REGULATION

The Regulators

The regulatory framework engulfing the commercial banking industry is summarized in Table 3. As indicated, national banks and three categories of state banks make up four main classifications. National banks are chartered and examined by the office of the Comptroller of the Currency (COC), an agency of the federal government. These banks are subject to COC regulations. Since all national

Table 3   Primary Regulators of Commercial Banks

Regulatory Function	National Banks[a] (Member, Insured)	State Banks		
		Member, Insured	Non-Member, Insured	Non-Member, Non-Insured
Charter	Comptroller of the Currency	State	State	State
Examination	Comptroller of the Currency	FRB, State	FDIC, State	State
General Regulation	Comptroller of the Currency	FRB, State	FDIC, State	State

[a]National banks must be members of the Federal Reserve System and must carry FDIC deposit insurance. Although the Federal Reserve Bank and FDIC have the authority to examine national banks, this function is carried out by the Comptroller of the Currency. The Federal Reserve Bank is also responsible for examining bank holding companies.

banks must be "members" of the Federal Reserve System and must have their deposits "insured" by the Federal Deposit Insurance Corporation (FDIC), they may be examined by both the Federal Reserve Bank (FRB) and the FDIC. Thus, there is overlapping regulatory jurisdiction. As a practical matter, this regulatory authority is seldom exercised by the FRB or FDIC over national banks. Virtually all aspects of regulating national banks are performed by the Comptroller of the Currency. An exception arises when a national bank is in serious financial trouble. If a forced merger or liquidation is necessary, the FDIC plays a key role because of its position as an insurer of deposits. State banks that are "members" and "insured" are subject to examination by and the general regulations of, the FRB and the chartering state. Similarly, state agencies and the FDIC regulate and examine state chartered, non-member, insured banks. Again, there is overlapping authority. In the light of the potential duplication of effort that could result from this overlap, federal and state regulatory agencies often cooperate by exchanging information and conducting joint or concurrent examinations. The last category is the non-member bank whose deposits are not insured by the FDIC. The deposits of these banks may be insured by an agency of the state or simply uninsured. Since these banks are not involved with the Federal Reserve System or the FDIC, they are regulated solely by state agencies. They account for less than 1 percent of commercial bank assets.

The Examination Process

One of the most important aspects of bank regulation is the periodic examination conducted by the primary regulatory agency or agencies. The objectives of an examination are threefold: (1) to detect so-called "problem banks"; (2) to detect unsound policies and practices that could lead to financial problems; and (3) to ensure compliance with banking laws and regulations. To accomplish these objectives, examiners assess bank operations with respect to asset quality, level of liquidity, capital adequacy, managerial ability, earning power, and compliance with laws and regulations. Usually, a bank is examined about every twelve months. So-called "problem" banks are subject to more frequent examinations.

Although their legal authority differs, each regulatory agency has broad powers that may be used to impose sanctions and enforce bank regulations and laws. Consider the enforcement tools of the FDIC.

- *Moral Suasion.*   Problem areas are discussed with management and the bank's board of directors.
- *Cease and Desist Order.*   The FDIC may obtain a court order directing a bank's management to stop unsound or hazardous practices.
- *Removal of Officers and Directors.*   This sanction may be imposed for breach of duty, dishonesty, negligence, or incompetence on the part of officers and directors.
- *Termination of Insurance.*   Failure to comply with regulations or laws can be grounds for terminating a bank's deposit insurance.
- *Legal Action Against Officers and Directors.*   The officers and directors may be sued by the FDIC in order to recoup or minimize any losses incurred as a result of their negligence.
- *Merger or Liquidation.*   When an insured "problem" bank is declared insolvent, the FDIC may arrange a merger with a financially sound bank. An alternative is to liquidate the bank's assets and use the proceeds to pay off bank liabilities. Under either alternative the stockholders are usually wiped out.

Given the nature of regulatory sanctions, management decisions must be made with strict adherence to both the letter and spirit of banking laws, regulations, and directives. In the chapters that follow, many of the specific regulations that relate to commercial banking will be discussed.

CONCLUSION

The purpose of this chapter was to provide a brief sketch of the commercial banking process. This was accomplished by focusing on the economic functions performed by banks, their financial structure, and their regulatory environment. In this way, a frame of reference for subsequent topics, concepts, and chapters has been established.

2

The Depository Institutions Deregulation and Monetary Control Act of 1980*

Research Staff, Federal Reserve Bank of Chicago

On March 31, 1980, the President signed into law the *Depository Institutions Deregulation and Monetary Control Act of 1980* (the act). This legislation marked the culmination of many years of effort by members of the Congress, the regulatory agencies, and the financial industry to change some of the rules under which U. S. financial institutions have operated for nearly half a century. In many cases, these rules had been made obsolete by changes in the economy, the functioning of credit markets, technology, consumer demands for financial services, and the competitive environment.

At least five public and private studies, from the Report of the Commission on Money and Credit in 1961 to the FINE study in 1975, had recommended many of the reforms finally adopted in the act. In recent years the Federal Reserve Board has given strong support to two of them, the phase-out of deposit interest ceilings coupled with broader investment powers for thrift institutions and broader and more uniform application of reserve requirements. In adopting the new law, the Congress dealt with, or at least touched upon, most of the major issues that have been the subject of controversy over the years.

Several interacting factors finally precipitated legislative action on this massive set of reform measures. One was the high level of inflation and interest rates that magnified recognized problems under the old regulations and convinced participants that a piecemeal approach was unworkable. The attrition in Federal Reserve membership swelled from a trickle to a flood as high investment yields increased the penalty imposed on member banks by the requirement that they hold non-interest-bearing reserve deposits at the Federal Reserve; small savers were heavily disadvantaged in comparison with returns available to large investors; disintermed-

*Reprinted, with deletions, from *Economic Perspectives*, September/October 1980, pp. 3-23, with permission from the Federal Reserve Bank of Chicago.

iation again hurt the housing market as savers withdrew funds from mortgage lending institutions and invested them in high-yield money market mutual funds and other market instruments; the viability of thrift institutions was seriously threatened by the imbalance between the cost of funds and the return on long-term mortgage portfolios; and at times usury laws in some states effectively cut off credit to small businesses, farmers, and households.

Other factors were the promise of better customer service inherent in new technology such as electronic devices for funds transfer, the growing availability of payments services from depository institutions other than commercial banks, and the view that Federal Reserve credit should be available as an ultimate source of liquidity to all such institutions. Finally, increased emphasis on the monetary aggregates as intermediate targets of monetary policy focused attention on the need for changes that would permit better measurement and control of these aggregates. Under pressure due to the urgency of these problems, the Congress recognized the need for changing the ground rules for competition in the financial markets and for dealing with the many interrelated problems simultaneously in a coordinated and consistent manner.

The principal goals of the act include: (1) improving monetary control and equalizing its cost among depository institutions, (2) removing the impediments to competition for funds by depository institutions and allowing small savers a market rate of return, and (3) expanding the availability of financial services to the public and reducing competitive inequalities between financial institutions offering them. The major elements of the law that are expected to contribute to these goals are:

- Imposition of uniform federal reserve requirements on similar classes of reservable liabilities at all depository institutions—including commercial banks, savings banks, and credit unions.
- Authorization for collection of data needed to monitor and control the money and credit aggregates.
- Requirement that the Federal Reserve price its services and grant all depository institutions access to such services.
- Provision for the orderly phase-out of deposit interest rate ceilings.
- Preemption of state usury ceilings on certain types of loans.
- Nationwide authorization of NOW accounts and certain other interest-bearing balances at both banks and thrift institutions that can be used for transactions purposes.
- Broadening of the asset powers and permissible activities of thrift institutions.

The act will have far-reaching effects on financial markets for years to come. It calls for greater reliance on free market forces and less on regulatory decisions in the determination of interest rates and the distribution of financial services. It puts the burden on the Federal Reserve to prove its efficiency by forcing it to compete with alternatives available from the private sector. At the same time, the law will, to steal a phrase from the Senate Banking Committee Chairman, "create a level playing field" for competition between the various types of financial institutions. All depository institutions eventually will be subject to the same reserve requirements, will be permitted to pay competitive rates on savings and offer interest-bearing transactions accounts, and will have access to Federal Reserve services on equal terms. Thrift institutions will be permitted to provide a broader range of services to their savings customers—including transactions accounts, trust services, and nonmortgage credit—and to manage their assets in a more flexible way so as to offset the more volatile cost and changing effective maturity of their liabilities. Clearly, this means less functional specialization by various types of institutions.

But while the law opens many opportunities for both banks and thrift institutions to be more competitive, with attendant benefits to the consuming public, it also poses substantial challenges. With competition enhanced, less efficient instittutions may find it difficult to provide quality service at competitive prices. Depository institutions will have to assess carefully the costs and benefits of doing business in the new environment and reexamine their pricing policies and service levels. It seems likely that, eventually, some will be eliminated through liquidation or merger.

Some consolidation may result in economies of scale or integration and make possible improved service and a better return to savers. However, to minimize the near-term risks of a sudden change in the competitive environment, the act provides for a gradual transition from old to new rules, especially in the areas of reserve requirements and interest rate controls. Both the eight-year phase-in of reserve requirements for nonmember banks and thrift institutions and the six-year phase-out of deposit interest ceilings will allow the institutions time to develop their ability to meet market competition on a new bundle of services. In addition, the Congress was careful not to require a specific schedule for the interest ceiling phase-out and mandated regular reports on the impact of the program on the economic viability of the various depository institutions and on housing finance.

Transitional problems are inevitable as the thousands of depository institutions bring their operations into conformity with the new rules. The 1980s will be a period of adjustment. But the direction of change wrought by this historic legislation on the financial structure should be apparent long before the phase-ins and phase-outs are complete.

TITLE I—UNIVERSAL RESERVE REQUIREMENTS AND PRICING

Title I of the new legislation is designed to enhance the Federal Reserve's ability to implement monetary policy. The new legislation also ensures that all depository institutions share equally whatever burden is necessary for an effective national monetary policy.

There are three major parts to Title I—reporting requirements, reserve requirements, and pricing of Federal Reserve services. With respect to the first two, which are directly related to monetary control, Title I:

- Requires all depository institutions to report their assets and liabilities at such intervals as the Board of Governors of the Federal Reserve System (the Board) may prescribe.

- Extends reserve requirements imposed by the Board to all depository institutions, including all commercial, savings, and mutual savings banks, savings and loan associations, and credit unions that are federally insured or eligible to apply for federal insurance.[1]

- Requires each depository institution to maintain reserves of 3 percent on its transaction accounts of $25 million or less, plus 12 percent, or such ratio that the Board may set between 8 and 14 percent, on the amount over $25 million. This $25 million "tranche" is indexed to change each calendar year beginning in 1982 by 80 percent of the percentage change in total transaction accounts of all depository institutions during the previous year ending June 30.

- Requires each depository institution to maintain reserves of 3 percent, or such ratio that the Board may set between 0 and 9 percent, on its nonpersonal time deposits. The Board may vary the reserve requirements on nonpersonal time deposits according to maturity.

- Provides for an eight-year phase-in to the new reserve requirements on transaction accounts and nonpersonal time deposits for nonmember banks and thrift institutions and a four-year phase-down (in some cases, a phase-up) to the new requirements for members. However, requirements on new types of accounts or deposits authorized under federal law after April 1, 1980, such as NOW accounts outside New England, New York, and New Jersey, will not be phased in.

- Entitles any depository institution in which transaction accounts or nonpersonal time deposits are held to borrow from the Federal Reserve discount window on the same terms as member banks.

- Permits the Board to impose reserve requirements on certain borrowings from foreign sources, sales of assets by depository institutions in the United States to their foreign offices, and loans to U. S. residents made by foreign offices of depository institutions in the United States. Such Eurocurrency reserve requirements would apply to foreign branches, subsidiaries, and international banking facilities of member and nonmember institutions uniformly.

- Permits the Board, upon a finding by at least five members that extraordinary circumstances require such action and after consultation with the appropriate congressional committees, to impose any level of reserve requirements on any liability of depository institutions for up to 180 days.

- Specifies that reserve requirements may be satisfied by holdings of vault cash, reserve balances held directly at a Federal Reserve Bank, or, in the case of

---

[1] Reporting and reserve requirement provisions of the act also apply to industrial banks, cooperative banks, and homestead associations. In addition, under earlier amendements to the Federal Reserve Act, reporting and reserve requirements were applied to Edge Act and agreement corporations. The International Banking Act of 1978 extended them to the U. S. branches and agencies of foreign banks.

through a correspondent or other designated institution ("pass-through" balances).

- Permits the Board, upon an affirmative vote of five members and after consultation with certain federal financial regulatory authorities, to impose supplemental reserve requirements on every depository institution of up to 4 percent of its transaction accounts, but only if specified conditions are met, including that "the sole purpose of such requirement is to increase the amount of reserves maintained to a level essential for the conduct of monetary policy." The supplemental requirement is to be maintained either in an Earnings Participation Account at a Federal Reserve Bank, on which earnings will be paid quarterly at a rate not exceeding the rate earned on the Federal Reserve's securities portfolio during the previous calendar quarter, or in vault cash.

On August 15, 1980, the Board announced revisions in its Regulation D to implement the reporting and reserve requirement provisions of the act.[2]

Data Reporting

Accurate and timely information on the monetary and credit aggregates is essential to the effective discharge of the Federal Reserve's monetary policy responsibilities. Current data estimates rely heavily on reports submitted by banks that are members of the Federal Reserve System. In the past, however, it was often necessary to make large revisions when nonmember institution data, such as for quarterly "benchmark" dates, became available. Some improvement in the quality and timeliness of monetary and credit aggregates data has been made possible by voluntary reporting of certain nonmember institutions, as when the monetary aggregates were redefined in early 1980. But even with these improvements, current data estimates are imprecise and subject to revision as additional data become available, often with a significant time lag.

In order to remedy these deficiencies, the new law authorizes the Board to require all depository institutions to submit reports of their assets and liabilities as needed or desirable for monetary policy purposes. Under the Board's Regulation D, member banks, as well as other depository institutions that have transaction accounts or nonpersonal time deposits, will report certain deposits data directly to the Federal Reserve.

The Board's authority to require data reporting is not to be used indiscriminately. The new law stipulates that every effort should be made to avoid imposing unnecessary burdens and duplicate reporting requirements on depository institutions. This provision of the law is consistent with other congressional initiatives in recent years to reduce regulatory paperwork.

In its regulation implementing the reporting and reserve requirement provisions, the Board classified depository institutions by size for reporting purposes. Because the deposits of small institutions constitute such a small portion of the money

---

[2] Federal Reserve *Bulletin*, September 1980, pp. 758-773.

supply and frequent reporting could be a substantial burden to such institutions, the Board deferred reporting requirements and reserve maintenance for nonmember institutions with less than $2 million in total deposits until May 1981 and allowed certain institutions with total deposits of $2 million or more but less than $15 million to report and maintain reserves on a quarterly rather than a weekly basis.

Reserve Requirements

The reserve requirement provisions of the new law depart significantly from past U. S. experience. For the first time, all depository institutions will be subject to the same federally imposed reserve requirements. For many years, it had been argued that such universal extension of federal reserve requirements was needed both for monetary control purposes and to provide for greater competitive equality among financial institutions.

The Membership Problem
With few exceptions, only banks that were members of the Federal Reserve System were subject to federal reserve requirements before the new legislation was passed. Unlike nonmember commercial banks that could often satisfy state-imposed reserve requirements by holding interest-earning assets or compensating balances at correspondent banks, member banks were required to hold their reserves in non-interest-bearing balances at the Federal Reserve or in vault cash. The burden of holding these nonearning assets put member banks at a disadvantage relative to nonmember banks. This membership "tax" grew even more burdensome in recent years as interest rates rose to record levels. Consequently, an increasing number of member banks chose to withdraw from Federal Reserve membership, and most newly formed banks chose nonmember status. The proportion of deposits held by member banks, which had been declining for several decades, dropped at an accelerating rate in recent years.

The Federal Reserve argued repeatedly in recent years that the declining proportion of deposits subject to its reserve requirements weakened its ability to conduct monetary policy, in large part because of the greater difficulty in predicting the relationship between reserves and money. Considerable support was marshalled for the viewpoint that, besides helping to achieve competitive equality between depository institutions, universal application of federal reserve requirements would greatly enhance the Federal Reserve's ability to control the monetary aggregates.

The new reserve requirements, when fully implemented, will clearly reduce the burden on member banks. The Board's staff estimated earlier this year that, at current deposit levels and ignoring the transitional period, member bank required balances at the Federal Reserve would decline from about $32 billion to about $14 billion. In relative terms the burden on member banks would disappear as nonmember institutions will be subject to the same reserve requirements as member banks.

Money and   With membership no longer a problem, the focus will
Reserve Requirements   now be on the appropriateness of the new reserve re-
                              quirement structure for monetary control. Among the
features of an ideal structure would be a single—truly uniform—reserve requirement ratio applied only to those deposits included in the monetary aggregate to
be controlled. When more than one ratio applies to the deposits under control,
shifts in these deposits between institutions subject to different requirements affect required reserves even though there is no change in the total amount of these
deposits. Similarly, when reserve requirements apply both to deposits that are included in the targeted monetary aggregate and to some that are not, shifts between
the different types of deposits produce changes in the targeted aggregate that are
only partially reflected by changes in required reserves. In either case, the Federal
Reserve must predict the various types of deposit shifts in order to determine the
appropriate level of reserves consistent with desired money.

The requirements of the act fall short of an ideal reserve requirement structure
in several respects. Assume, for example, that the Federal Reserve seeks to control
a transactions measure of money such as M-1B (currency, demand deposits, and
other checkable deposits). The act imposes two reserve ratios on the deposits in
M-1B (3 percent on the first $25 million at each depository institution and 8-14
percent on those in excess of $25 million), as well as a separate ratio (0-9 percent)
on nonpersonal time deposits, which are not in M-1B.[3] The Board can eliminate
one of these problems by setting the nonpersonal time deposit ratio at zero. Nevertheless, the problem of predicting deposit shifts between institutions with more
and less than $25 million in transaction accounts, and therefore subject to differ-
ent ratios (at the margin), will remain.

In practice, this problem is likely to be far less serious than under the former
member bank reserve requirement structure. Under the former structure numerous ratios applied to transaction accounts, ranging from zero for nonmembers up
to 16¼ percent on demand deposits at the largest member banks. Thus, the new
requirements move closer to an ideal structure, assuming that M-1B is the monetary aggregate, because, once they are fully implemented, they will no longer
apply (except in an emergency) to personal time and nontransaction savings
deposits. In its conduct of monetary policy, though, the Federal Reserve has
generally placed considerable emphasis on the behavior of the narrower transaction aggregates, M-1A and M-1B. On balance, therefore, the new reserve requirement structure is a vast improvement over the old one.

Pricing Federal Reserve Services

In addition to improving monetary control, Title I of the new legislation is
designed to limit the loss to the Treasury resulting from the general lowering of

---

[3] Technically, there are some minor definitional differences between the transaction accounts included in
M-1B and those subject to reserve requirements. For example, U. S. government demand deposits, while subject to reserve requirements, are excluded from M-1B.

reserve requirements and to enhance the efficiency of the payments mechanism. To achieve these goals, it directs the Federal Reserve to impose explicit charges for services traditionally provided to member banks without charge. In brief, Section 107 of Title I:

- Requires the Board to publish no later than September 1, 1980, a set of pricing principles and a proposed schedule of fees based on those principles.
- Requires the Board to begin to implement the fee schedule no later than September 1, 1981.
- Specifies that the services to be priced include (1) currency and coin, (2) check clearing and collection, (3) wire transfer, (4) automated clearinghouse services, (5) settlement, (6) securities safekeeping, (7) Federal Reserve float, and (8) any new services which the Federal Reserve offers.
- Requires that all covered services be priced explicitly.
- Requires that all covered services be available to nonmember depository institutions on the same terms that they are available to member banks.
- Requires that fees be based on all direct and indirect costs of providing services, including interest at the federal funds rate on items credited prior to collection, overhead, and an allowance for the taxes that would have been provided had the services been furnished by a private business firm, "except that the pricing principles shall give due regard to competitive factors and the provision of an adequate level of such services nationwide."
- Requires the Board to reduce the operating budget of the Federal Reserve Banks, "commensurate with any actual or projected decline in the volume of services to be provided."

Background

Almost from its inception in 1913, the Federal Reserve has provided many services to member banks free of charge. Most of these, such as check clearing, the provision of coin and currency, etc., are basic payments services and their provision without charge was long defended as necessary to foster a more efficient payments system. However, many of these services can be supplied by private firms—indeed, some 60 percent of the dollar volume of all checks in the United States is cleared outside the Federal Reserve System—and it has been argued that pricing Federal Reserve services will increase the incentives for the private sector to offer similar services. The resulting competition should increase the efficiency with which these services are provided.

Pricing and Membership

The past reluctance of the Federal Reserve to price its services was largely attributable to the membership problem and the implications for monetary policy of the rapid erosion of the fraction of total deposits subject to federal reserve requirements. In this context, the provision of services without explicit charge partly offset the cost to member banks of holding noninterest-earning reserves and helped to prevent even more banks from leaving the Federal Reserve System.

The act eliminated this concern about pricing and its effect on the conduct of monetary policy. Member banks can no longer avoid the cost of holding sterile reserves by simply withdrawing from membership in the Federal Reserve System. Banks that withdraw must hold the same amount of reserves as member banks. Furthermore, the Federal Reserve is now legally required to charge for specific services and can no longer postpone this action. The issues of whether and when to price for services have been decided by the Congress. Nevertheless, as the discussion of the reserve requirement provisions of Title I made clear, the act does substantially reduce the burdens of membership.

Charging an explicit price will provide an incentive for the public to economize on the use of services that are now subsidized by the Federal Reserve. For example, the Federal Reserve processes without charge any number of checks that a member bank presents for collection. Aside from the fixed price of membership, the only costs to a member bank are the costs of presorting and encoding the checks before they are shipped to a Federal Reserve office. The Federal Reserve bears the costs of additional sorting and of any Federal Reserve float that is created.

This practice has had the effect of hiding the full costs of using checks for payments. Because member banks have not been required to pay an explicit price for check processing and because they must compete with other financial institutions for deposits, they have not charged their customers the full costs associated with paper checks. In turn, customers have had little economic incentive to economize their use of checks for payment. The results have been to encourage the "overconsumption" of the paper-based payments mechanism and to discourage the development of electronic payments systems.

TITLES II AND V—INTEREST RATE DEREGULATION

Title II of the act provides for interest rate ceilings on time and savings deposits at depository institutions to be phased out over a period of six years. Title V of the act overrides existing state usury laws limiting the interest rate that may be paid on a number of specified types of loans. In removing long-standing impediments to the paying and charging of market interest rates, the act introduces a new era in the long evolution of public policy toward competition in financial markets.

Interest Rates on Deposits

The first section of Title II states briefly the findings of the Congress and the purpose of the title:

   (a) The Congress hereby finds that—(1) limitations on the interest rates which
       are payable on deposits and accounts discourage persons from saving money,

create inequities for depositors, impede the ability of depository institutions to compete for funds, and have not achieved their purpose of providing an even flow of funds for home mortgage lending; and (2) all depositors, and particularly those with modest savings, are entitled to receive a market rate of return on their savings as soon as it is economically feasible for depository institutions to pay such rate.

(b) It is the purpose of this title to provide for the orderly phase-out and the ultimate elimination of the limitations on the maximum rates of interest and dividends which may be paid on deposits and accounts by depository institutions by extending the authority to impose such limitations for 6 years, subject to specific standards designed to ensure a phase-out of such limitations to market rates of interest.

Except for details, this section contains all the substantive provisions of the title. Considerable discretion in implementing the title was delegated to the *Depository Institutions Deregulation Committee,* consisting of the heads of the major federal financial regulatory agencies. Essentially the only specific actions mandated to the Deregulation Committee are that it:

- Shall work toward providing all depositors with a market rate of return on their savings with due regard for the safety and soundness of depository institutions.
- May not raise ceilings on all deposit categories above market rates during the six-year phase-out period.
- Must vote within 18 months after the date of enactment on whether to raise the ceilings on passbook savings by at least ¼ of 1 percentage point.
- Must vote before the end of each of the third through sixth years after enactment on whether to increase the ceilings on all time and savings deposits by at least ½ of 1 percentage point.

In addition, each member of the committee is required to report separately to the Congress each year regarding the economic viability of depository institutions. Each report must assess the effect of removing any differential between the rates payable on deposits by banks and thrift institutions on housing finance and the viability of thrift institutions and recommend measures to encourage saving, treat small savers fairly, and promote housing finance.

Origins and Rationale of
Interest Rate Ceilings

The prohibition of interest on demand deposits and the ceilings on interest rates on time and savings deposits established by Federal Reserve Regulation Q date from the passage of the Banking Act of 1933. That act declared that "[no] member bank shall, directly or indirectly, by any device whatsoever, pay any interest on any deposit which is payable on demand . . ." and empowered the Board of

Governors of the Federal Reserve System to "limit by regulation the rates of interest which may be paid by member banks on time and savings deposits."

Demand Deposits   The prohibition of interest on interbank demand deposits was originally proposed to prevent recurring liquidity crises that developed when rural banks attempted to withdraw temporarily surplus funds that they had deposited at large money center banks to take advantage of interest yields. When the prohibition of interest on demand deposits was finally adopted in 1933, however, it was largely for the same reasons that interest payments on time and savings deposits were limited.

The inequities and inefficiencies of the prohibition of interest on demand deposits of individuals (but not of corporations) were addressed in Title III of the act, which authorizes depository institutions to offer interest-bearing transaction accounts to individuals and nonprofit organizations. Because these new liabiity powers are so closely tied to the new asset powers authorized by Title IV of the act, they are considered together in the next section.

Time and   The need for interest rate ceilings on time and savings
Savings Deposits   deposits was perceived as being extremely urgent in 1933. In the wake of a decade in which the number of banks declined from a peak of over 30,000 in 1921 to about 24,000 in 1929, followed by an even more precipitous decline of over 9,000 between the end of 1929 and the Banking Holiday of March 1933, no stone was left unturned in the search for a villain.

The most widely accepted explanation of the failures was that excessive competition for deposits had forced banks to raise sharply the interest rates they paid on time and savings deposits. As the banks' costs rose and their profit margins were squeezed, they sought higher-yielding, but more risky, loans and investments to maintain their earnings. This made them more susceptible to failure when the economy weakened.

Though plausible and having a great deal of popular appeal, this explanation of the bank failures of the 1920s and 1930s has never been confirmed. In 1933 it was accepted largely on the basis of anecdotal evidence. Not until interest ceilings had been on the books for nearly 30 years did scholars finally get around to systematic and rigorous testing of the explanation. They found little evidence to support it.[4]

Whether valid or invalid, the original rationale for Regulation Q was a moot point during the next two and one-half decades. As economic activity continued weak after 1933, market interest rates continued to fall. They remained below the ceilings until the mid-1950s, held down by the depressed demand for credit during the 1930s and by the Federal Reserve's policy of supporting the government bond market during World War II. When rates finally pushed against the ceilings in the mid-1950s, the Federal Reserve responded by raising the ceilings, citing the desirability of increased competition.

[4] See, e.g., the study by Albert H. Cox, Jr., of 285 national banks, some of which survived and some of which did not survive the years 1930-33, *Regulation of Interest on Bank Deposits* (Michigan Business Studies. Vol. 17, No. 4, 1966).

The Credit Crunch of 1966

The policy of adjusting the ceilings to accommodate market forces continued until mid-1966. At that time, fueled in part by expenditures for the Vietnam War and more rapid monetary growth, inflation was accelerating from the 2-3 percent rates of the 1950s and early 1960s to a rate between 4 percent and 5 percent. The economy was overheated and was experiencing a boom led by investment expenditures financed, in large part, by loans from commercial banks.

To slow the investment boom without imposing further damage on interest-sensitive areas of the economy, the Federal Reserve refused to raise the rate ceilings established the previous December, precluding banks from selling new CDs and forcing them to cut back on their lending. The Board also sent to the Congress proposed legislation to broaden its powers to classify deposits for purposes of setting rate ceilings and to extend interest rate ceilings on deposits to savings and loan associations and mutual savings banks, to be administered by the Federal Home Loan Bank Board and the Federal Deposit Insurance Corporation, respectively.

The proposal was signed into law on September 21, 1966. The authorities moved quickly to implement their new powers. By setting ceilings on passbook savings at savings and loan associations and mutual savings banks higher than the 4 percent commercial banks were allowed to pay, they hoped to insulate thrift institutions and the mortgage market from commercial bank competition. This differential, which has since been narrowed to ¼ percentage point, became a major subject of controversy in the years preceding passage of the new act.

The events of 1966 constituted a landmark in the evolution of deposit interest rate ceilings. That year saw the first use of the ceilings as a tool of general monetary policy and also their first use as a means of influencing deposit flows between institutions in a selective way. These were major alterations, not only of the rationale of the ceilings, but of the way the ceilings were administered and the constituencies favoring their retention or elimination.

Evasion and Avoidance

Not foreseen either at the time the ceilings were first introduced or when they were revised and extended in 1966 were the great ingenuity and effort banks and other financial institutions would bring to their circumvention. During the last half of the 1960s and much of the 1970s, banks kept several steps ahead of the regulators in devising new liabilities that, because they were not defined to be deposits, were free of both reserve requirements and Regulation Q ceilings. Most of these were belatedly defined as deposits, thereby becoming subject to interest rate ceilings reserve requirements, or both.

Besides designing new forms of liabilities, financial institutions also sought other means to compete for deposits in the presence of interest rate ceilings. These included the establishment of more branch offices than would otherwise be built and offering depositors noncash premiums as an inducement to open accounts. The additional offices add somewhat to the convenience of the public, and the noncash premiums help to offset the loss in explicit interest due to the ceilings, but depositors would probably prefer to receive higher money interest returns. Although the Board long ago adopted regulations declaring that premiums did not constitute interest, their proliferation led the Board to place limitations on their cash value.

Cost of the Ceilings

Such aberrations would be merely funny were it not true that they involve serious social costs. Aside from the basic inefficiency of paying for deposits with premiums rather than money interest, the constant search for new ways to avoid Regulation Q and the efforts of the authorities to monitor and plug any resulting loopholes have both been responsible for considerable expenditure of time and effort.

Time and experience have led many depositors to search for outlets for their funds that do not involve public regulation of their realizable rates of return. When ceilings were binding, large depositors turned from the negotiable CD market to Treasury bills, commercial paper, and other unregulated financial instruments. Eventual recognition of this fact by the Federal Reserve and the FDIC led, in 1970, to the suspension of the ceiling on short-term CDs over $100,000 and, in 1973, to the elimination of the rate ceiling on longer-term large time deposits.

Even small savers have gradually been led to seek more remunerative uses for their funds. Such recently developed institutions as money market mutual funds have enabled them to share in the higher returns available on otherwise inaccessible large-denomination securities previously available only to large investors. To enable banks and thrift institutions to compete better, the supervisory agencies authorized them in June 1978 to begin issuing money market certificates, savings certificates whose yield is tied to the rate on Treasury bills.

To be sure, some small depositors, because of ignorance or the small size of their savings or the convenience of keeping them in a highly liquid form, have not seen fit to withdraw their deposits from passbook savings accounts. In nominal dollars, the losses to small savers from rate regulation have been estimated at $5.2 billion for the years 1968-70.[5] More recently, as inflation carried interest rates up to double-digit levels, the real, or price-adjusted, rate of return to such savers declined sharply. During the past several years, it has been strongly negative. This state of affairs is widely perceived as being inequitable, as well as providing a disincentive to saving at a time when productivity and investment have been lagging.

Some of the other undesirable side effects of the ceilings have been much more subtle and are wholly unknown to most of the public. For example, in carrying out monetary policy, the Federal Reserve monitors and influences the growth rates of several measures of the money supply. But when interest rates rise rapidly and the ceilings become binding, some of the broader measures of money—such as M-2, which includes savings and small time deposits—show weaker growth than they otherwise would. Eliminating the ceilings will remove this source of cyclical distortion in the various measures of the money supply.

[5] David H. Pyle, "The Losses on Savings Deposits from Interest Rate Regulation," *Bell Journal of Economics and Management Science*, V (Autumn 1974), 614-622.

Disintermediation and the Housing Market

Why would removal of ceilings cause disintermed.?

A primary obstacle to removal of the ceilings has been the fear that doing so would subject specialized mortgage lending institutions to repeated and severe bouts of disintermediation, with unfortunate consequences for the mortgage and housing markets. It has gradually become clear in recent years that it is not commercial bank competition—which the ceilings were designed to curb—that is the most serious threat to the mortgage and housing markets, but the competition of the open market and of the new, unregulated institutions like money market mutual funds. In the final analysis, the ceilings have fostered disintermediation from banks and thrift institutions alike by preventing them both from competing with the open market. Growing acceptance of this fact by the savings and loan industry, together with the greater flexibility offered by the enlarged asset powers for thrift institutions introduced by Title IV of the act, helped to overcome opposition to the elimination of the favorable treatment of thrift institutions under the present ceilings.

Usury Laws

Title V is much more specific in what it requires than Title II. It overrides state usury provisions, constitutional or otherwise, on types of loans specified in the several sections of the title. In particular, the title:

- Exempts from state limitations on interest and other charges loans made after March 31, 1980, that are secured by a first lien on residential real property, by a first lien on stock in a residential cooperative housing corporation where the loan, mortgage, or advance is used to finance the acquisition of such stock, or by a first lien on a residential manufactured home and that meet certain other criteria specified by Section 527(b) of the National Housing Act.

- Gives states until April 1, 1983, to reinstate usury ceilings by adopting a new law or allowing the voters to adopt a provision stating explicitly and by its terms that the state does not want to be subject to the provisions of the title.

- Overrides state limitations on the interest rates payable on deposits or accounts at depository institutions. This simply completes the deregulation of deposit interest rates provided for at the national level by Title II.

- Exempts business and agricultural loans of $25,000 or more from state usury provisions until April 1, 1983, replacing them with the restriction that interest rates on such loans may not exceed "5 per centum in excess of the discount rate, including any surcharge theron, on ninety-day commercial paper in effect at the Federal Reserve bank in the Federal Reserve district where the person is located."

- Provides for forfeiture of all interest on any loan on which the lender has knowingly charged a higher rate than allowed by the act and authorized persons paying interest in excess of the permitted rate to recover in a civil action twice the amount of interest paid.

- Allows state-chartered banks and both federally and state-chartered insured savings and loan associations and credit unions to disregard state interest ceilings on other types of loans in those cases where the maximum rate prescribed by the state is exceeded by "a rate of not more than 1 per centum in excess of the discount rate on ninety-day commercial paper in effect at the Federal Reserve bank in the Federal Reserve district where such State bank . . . is located. . . ."

- Allows small business investment companies to charge interest on business loans at a rate not exceeding the lowest of: the maximum rate prescribed by the Small Business Administration, the maximum rate authorized by state law which is not preempted by the act, and the Federal Reserve discount rate on ninety-day commercial paper plus 1 percentage point.

Although there have been few absolute prohibitions of the taking of interest since medieval times, most people retain strong convictions regarding the charging of what are seen as excessive or unfair rates of interest. State usury laws in the United States were patterned in many cases after the Massachusetts statute of 1641, which was repealed in 1867. The Massachusetts law, in turn, followed the English law of the early 17th century in prescribing a maximum lending rate of 8 percent.

Problems with Usury Laws

The problems with usury laws are fairly straightforward. First, the costs and risks of lending small amounts to poor credit risks make such lending unremunerative at the statutory levels. Consequently, such borrowers will not be accommodated at all at the statutory rate. Secondly, the profit opportunities inherent in lending to such borrowers at an unrestricted rate give rise to a variety of devices, legal and illegal, to circumvent the ceilings. Exceptions to the usury ceilings have proliferated, making a tangled web of the statutes governing lending in many states.

Finally, even usury ceilings that have appeared reasonable in normal times, in the sense of allowing lenders a modest but competitive rate of return, have become wholly unrealistic as market interest rates have risen sharply in recent years. The most dramatic effects have been observed in the mortgage markets, as some lenders in states with exceptionally restrictive ceilings on mortgage rates—e.g., New York—have at times virtually ceased to lend to borrowers within the state.

The disruption to housing markets induced by the ceilings has led to frantic efforts to amend the usury laws in these states, sometimes in the face of determined opposition. In some cases, changing the ceilings required amendment of the state constitution, an inherently difficult process. Nevertheless, a number of states have succeeded in liberalizing their usury laws, in some cases tying the ceiling rates to a market rate.

However, other states have encountered serious difficulties in obtaining revisions, and their consumers have suffered as a consequence. It was these difficulties that culminated in the adoption of Title V of the act, which overrides state usury laws with respect to the maximum allowable interest rates on a wide range of specified types of loans.

TITLES III AND IV—NATIONWIDE NOW ACCOUNTS AND NEW THRIFT INSTITUTION POWERS

New powers for banks and other depository institutions to extend and diversify their balance sheets are provided in Title III, designated the "Consumer Checking Account Equity Act of 1980," and Title IV. Title III provides the first permanent nationwide authorization for depository institutions to offer interest-bearing transaction accounts effective December 31, 1980, and expands other deposit offering and servicing capabilities of these institutions. Specifically, Title III:

- Authorizes most types of depository institutions to offer negotiable order of withdrawal (NOW) accounts.
- Authorizes banks to continue offering automatic transfer services (ATS) for shifting funds from savings to checking accounts.
- Authorizes all federally chartered credit unions to issue share drafts.
- Authorizes savings and loan associations to establish remote service units (RSUs) to facilitate debits and credits to savings accounts, loan payments, and related transactions.
- Increases deposit insurance from $40,000 to $100,000 at federally insured banks, savings and loan associations, and credit unions.

These provisions are designed to contribute to competitive equality among depository institutions by allowing all of them to offer interest-bearing transaction accounts. They are also designed to benefit individuals and nonprofit organizations by allowing them eventually to receive a market rate of return on their checking account balances. However, the 1933 prohibition of the payment of interest on transaction accounts of corporations and governmental units remains in effect.

Title IV of the act focuses primarily on the asset holdings of nonbank thrift institutions. It aims at overcoming the existing maturity imbalance between the predominantly long-term asset portfolios, mainly fixed-rate mortgage loans, and short-term deposit and nondeposit liability structures of these institutions. Among the new powers conferred on federally chartered savings and loan associations by Title IV are:

- Investment of up to 20 percent of their assets in consumer loans, commercial paper, and corporate debt securities.
- Investment in shares or certificates of open-end investment companies that are registered with the SEC and that restrict their portfolios to the same investment instruments that savings and loan associations are allowed to hold directly.
- Investment of up to 5 percent of their assets in loans for education and community development and unsecured construction loans.
- Issuance of credit cards and extension of credit in connection with credit cards.

- Provision of trust and fiduciary powers under restrictions and protections similar to those applicable to national banks.
- Inclusion of shares of open-end management investment companies among the assets eligible to satisfy liquidity requirements.
- Issuance of <u>mutual capital certificates</u> to be included as part of general reserves and net worth.   *← What?*

For mutual savings banks with federal charters, new powers include:

- Investment of up to 5 percent of total assets in commercial, corporate, and business loans within the home state of the bank or within 75 miles of the bank's home office.
- Acceptance of demand deposits in connection with commercial, corporate, and business loan relationships.

In addition to specific new powers for thrift institutions, Title IV mandated that the President convene an Interagency Task Force with representation from the Treasury, HUD, and various federal regulatory and insuring agencies for banks and thrift institutions. This task force studied the asset-liability management problems of the thrift industry and submitted its findings and recommendations in late June.

Why Thrift Institutions Need New Powers

The new powers for thrift institutions embodied in the act, and the recommendations of the Interagency Task Force, are aimed at alleviating the "thrift problem." Fundamentally, the thrift problem involves a maturity imbalance between the assets and liabilities of thrift institutions. The problem is rooted in the past high degree of specialization in mortgage lending by savings and loan associations and mutual savings banks.

Constrained by regulation, tax incentives, and management philosophy, thrift institutions have diligently marketed conventional and federally insured fixed interest rate loans with original maturities exceeding 20 years and an average effective life of more than ten years. For this to be profitable, the stable returns on outstanding fixed-rate loans had to exceed, over their effective lives, the costs of funding to support them. Until the mid-1960s, lenders were able to profit from the fairly stable spread between returns on their mortgage loan portfolios and interest costs on predominantly savings-account liabilities.

Since then, however, high rates of inflation, accompanied by rapidly rising and unpredictable market interest rates, have converted the advantage of a steady stream of interest and principal payments from fixed-rate mortgage loans into an overriding disadvantage. Several times in recent years the yield curve showing the relationship between yields and maturities on otherwise similar securities has been downward sloping. During these periods thrift institutions have had to pay more for some of their short-term funds than could be earned on mortgage loans, even at the margin. If such a situation were to prevail for a long period of time, thrift institutions would experience serious liquidity and solvency problems.

Thrift institutions suffered through their first major episode of financial disintermediation in 1966, as depositors shifted to higher-yielding alternative investments in the open market. As was noted in the discussion of Title III of the act, rate ceilings on thrift deposits precluded direct competition with the money market for funds. Even without rate ceilings, however, fixed returns on existing mortgage loans would have constrained the extent to which thrift institutions could compete for higher cost liabilities.

New Sources of Funds

More recently, thrift institutions have developed new funding sources to replace their eroded savings-deposit base for mortgage lending. The Federal Home Loan Bank Board (FHLBB) has greatly extended the borrowing privileges of member institutions.

Deposit liabilities of thrift institutions, have increasingly shifted into deposit instruments with market-related interest rates. Such deposits, which include six-month money market certificates, 2½-year certificates, and "Jumbo CDs" in denominations of $100,000 or more, accounted for almost half of the deposit liabilities of savings and loan associations as of September 1980. But while nondeposit liabilities and deposits with market-related rates of interest have helped to stabilize the flow of funds to thrift institutions, they do not solve the problem of increases in the average level of current funding costs or reduced predictability of future costs.

Pricing and Promoting NOWs

what?

The newly authorized NOW accounts are likely to be an important source of funds to thrift institutions in the future, as share draft accounts will be to credit unions. Indeed, the success of such institutions as full-service financial centers for consumers will largely depend on their ability to compete with commercial banks for NOW account-business. Some key features of these NOW offerings will be the level of interest payments, the level and distribution of charges between draft-clearing fees and monthly maintenance charges, and the size of minimum balance requirements.

I thought it was higher?

Interest Payments   Most banks and savings and loan associations are likely to pay the maximum legally allowed interest on NOW accounts—currently set at 5¼ percent per annum. Experience in New England has shown that customers prefer explicit service charges and minimum balance requirements for pricing NOW services rather than interest forfeitures or reductions in interest rates paid on NOW balances.

Draft-Clearing Fees   To give consumers an incentive to economize on the number of NOW drafts used, many banks and savings institutions probably will charge clearing fees of 5 cents to 10 cents or more per item, at least for customers carrying small average NOW balances. The likelihood of such charges is suggested by the New England NOW experience, recent reversals in the trend toward free checking at banks, and the fact that, under Title I of the act, institutions offering NOWs themselves will be subjected to explicit per-item charges for NOW drafts cleared by the Federal Reserve or by the Federal Home Loan Bank System.

Monthly Maintenance   Like per-item clearing fees, monthly charges will tend to
Charges   reduce the number of NOW account depositors. Unlike
                          per-item fees, however, monthly charges will not ration
individual account activity. The crucial consideration for the institution offering NOWs is determining whether per-item or monthly fees (or both) lead to the broadest base of customer appeal.

Minimum Balance   Requiring minimum account balances—either absolute
Requirements   minimums or on average over a month—is of course an
                      implicit method of pricing NOW services. Like explicit
clearing fees and monthly charges, minimum balances will tend to reduce the number of consumers using NOW services, but will raise profitability per account. To strengthen and emphasize the "total customer relationship," some banks are likely to include deposit balances other than NOW accounts in the minimum balance requirement. At least initially, there is a strong possibility of promotional pricing by some aggressive institutions resulting in short-term losses.

New Asset Powers

Title IV of the act is aimed at bringing the asset side of thrift institution balance sheets up to date with the regulatory and market-induced innovations on the liability side. By allowing greater latitude in the deployment of funds, Title IV will enable thrift institutions to shorten the effective maturities of their asset portfolios, more closely matching liability maturities. Such asset maturity reduction will assume even greater importance once thrift institutions begin competing for NOW accounts and when deposit interest ceilings eventually are removed.

Among the major advantages of the new lending and investment powers are the increased opportunities afforded thrift institutions for diversifying their earning-asset portfolios. As a general rule, diversification allows reduced risk-taking per dollar of return or, conversely, greater dollar returns for any particular overall level of risk borne.

Taken separately, consumer loans tend to yield somewhat higher returns net of administrative costs, but have somewhat greater risks of borrower default, than mortgage loans. At the same time, consumer loan maturities are only a fraction of those for fixed-rate mortgages. Diversification strategy to incorporate consumer loans into their portfolios will dictate that thrift institutions hold a sufficient dollar volume and variety of these loans so as to take advantage of reduced default risk-taking per dollar of return *within* the consumer loan portfolio itself. The second step in their strategy will be to manage their consumer loans, their other newly authorized short-term investments (of minimal default risk), and their longer-term mortgage loans as a unified portfolio to take advantage of diversification between short- and longer-term earning assets.

New Mortgage Instruments

In addition to seeking overall portfolio balance, thrift institutions must also look toward revising their basic mortgage instruments to make mortgage loan returns responsive to money-market conditions. State-chartered savings and loan associations in California for some years have issued variable-rate mortgages—instruments which allow periodic interest rate adjustments in response to changes in the lender's average funding costs. In January 1979 the FHLBB authorized variable-rate instruments for all federally chartered savings and loan associations in California, and in July 1979 extended these powers nationwide. In April 1980 the FHLBB also authorized federally chartered associations to issue renegotiable-rate, or "roll-over," mortgages which allow interest rate adjustments every three, four, or five years with up to a 5 percentage point maximum revision over the full term of the contract.

The report of the Interagency Task Force recommended continued development and use of these "more flexible, cost-responsive mortgage instruments." These mortgage instruments should dramatically improve the flow of mortgage credit and bolster thrift institution profitability in tight money periods. To improve the liquidity of these mortgages, the Task Force also recommended that adequate secondary markets be developed along the lines of those already pioneered for fixed-rate mortgages by the Federal National Mortgage Association and Government National Mortgage Association.[6]

Implications of New Powers
For Mortgage Lending

Clearly, one purpose of the new powers for thrift institutions was to increase the flow of funds to the mortgage and housing markets—or, at the very least, to prevent the wide countercyclical swings in mortgage activity and housing construction experienced in the past. However, one obvious effect of the thrift institutions' new lending powers will be to reduce the proportion of mortgages to total assets in their portfolios. Any net increase in the dollar volume of their mortgage lending must therefore be the result of growth in their total assets.

Under the new act, a federally chartered thrift institution can meet the consumer's transactions needs through a NOW account, provide investment outlets through regular savings and money-market instruments, and provide consumer credit for automobiles and home improvements and other purposes. The act also permits federal savings and loan associations to exercise trust and fiduciary powers.

To the extent that these new services attract new customers or help thrift institutions to retain deposits over the business and credit cycles, the benefits to these institutions should be enormous. In addition to more stability on the liability side, repayments on consumer installment loans and holdings of short-term investments—such as commercial paper and open-end investment funds—should provide a liquidity cushion for thrift institutions during period of tight credit. These cash flows can be used to help meet any deposit withdrawals that do occur or to add new

---

[6] The secondary mortgage market is discussed in Chapter III of *The Report of the Interagency Task Force on Thrift Institutions,* pp. 73-88.

mortgage loans to their portfolios. Conceivably, therefore, the effect of the new powers for thrift institutions could be both to expand and to stabilize their mortgage lending.

At present, there is no really convincing evidence bearing on this question. However, several of the deregulation provisions of the act—elimination of deposit rate ceilings, extension of third-party payment services and consumer lending powers to thrift institutions, and broadening of the thrift institutions' investment powers—were similar to those recommended by the Hunt Commission in 1971. In 1972 the effects of these changes on the mortgage and housing markets were simulated using a large-scale econometric model.[7] The overall conclusion was that the net effect of all the changes would be very small, on both mortgage lending and the housing market, with most of the positive impact attributable to the third-party payment and consumer loan services. Essentially similar conclusions were reached by another study done at about the same time.[8] Because of the many institutional changes that have occurred since the studies were carried out, these results must be taken with some reservations. But they do suggest that freeing thrift institutions to diversify their services is unlikely to have any disastrous effects on the mortgage and housing markets.

[7] Ray C. Fair and Dwight M. Jaffee, "The Implications of the Proposals of the Hunt Commission for the Mortgage and Housing Markets: An Empirical Study," in *Policies for a More Competitive Financial System,* Conference Series No. 8 (Federal Reserve Bank of Boston, 1972), pp. 99-148.

[8] Paul S. Anderson and Robert W. Eisenmenger, "Impact of the Proposed New Financial Structure on Mortgage Markets," in *Policies for a More Competitive Financial System,* Conference Series No. 8 (Federal Reserve Bank of Boston, 1972), pp. 149-172.

3

Financial Mathematics in Banking and the Capital Markets

A puzzling aspect of the financial markets is the manner in which interest rates and prices on financial instruments are quoted. Bonds, money market instruments, mortgage loans, commercial loans, consumer loans, and savings deposits are all quoted and priced differently. Quoted interest rates have different implications depending on the instrument in question. The quoted rate is usually *not* the instrument's actual cost or return. Even within a class of instruments pricing procedures vary, thus precluding a direct comparison of the cost or return on one instrument with the cost or return on another. The lack of comparability among quoted rates and pricing procedures is important to financial institutions because instruments held as assets generate income and instruments held as liabilities generate costs. An understanding of financial mathematics is essential if costs and returns are to be determined accurately and in a consistent manner.

The following section provides an overview of the role of financial mathematics and how the concepts are used in financial institutions. This is followed by a discussion of basic mathematical concepts. A number of banking-related applications and examples are then developed to highlight the nature of day-to-day financial problems and related policy issues.

ROLE OF FINANCIAL MATHEMATICS

The role of financial mathematics in banks and other financial institutions may be explained by examining the ways such concepts are used. They are used for decision-making, satisfying legal constraints, formulating competitive strategies, and solving miscellaneous problems that arise on a day-to-day basis.

Financial Decision-Making

Most financial institutions have access to a variety of sources of funds. Banks, for example, can create new liabilities by issuing certificates of deposit, selling bankers' acceptances, floating a bond issue, or purchasing federal funds. Funds may also be raised by selling assets like Treasury bills, commercial loans, or mortgage loans. Regardless of the source, the cost of funds is a crucial managerial consideration. By comparing alternatives, management can select the source of funds with the lowest cost. Some instruments are quoted on a *discount basis,* while others are quoted on a *coupon basis.* Interest may be accrued on a 360- or 365-day year. The compounding of interest may be continuous, daily, monthly, quarterly, semi-annually, or annually. Because of these variations, quoted rates are frequently not comparable nor are they indicative of the actual cost of the underlying funds.

The other side of the decision-making process is the return on loans, investments, and other financial assets. The same comments regarding the accuracy and comparability of returns are applicable.

The cost of funds is the basis for establishing an institution's *hurdle rate.* This is the standard against which the return on new loans and investments is evaluated. The resulting accept-reject decision is one of the most important aspects of financial decision-making. By providing the basis for developing accurate and comparable liability costs and asset returns, the decision-making process is improved with the use of mathematical concepts.

Legal Requirements

Almost all financial institutions are subject to a variety of laws that require the use of financial mathematics. Important legal requirements are contained in the federal *Truth-in-Lending Act* and the usury laws of many states.

Truth-in-Lending Act   Prior to the passage of the *Truth-in-Lending Act* in 1969, the lack of comparability between the quoted rate and the actual rate on consumer loans posed a serious problem. Consumers were often confused because the stated interest rate depended on the interest calculation method used. Among these methods are the *declining balance, add-on interest,* and *bank discount* methods. To complicate matters, front-end fees imposed on some loans also affected the borrower's cost and the lender's return. Because of the variety of ways of quoting interest rates and the front-end fees, borrowers had no basis for "comparison shopping."

The Truth-in-Lending Act, which applies only to consumer-related loans and not business-related loans, was implemented to enable consumers to compare interest costs regardless of the interest calculation method used. The Act requires that lenders inform consumers of the true interest rate on loans. This rate is called the *annual percentage rate,* or APR.[1] The APR is also the *internal rate of return,* a

---

[1] The APR is often referred to as an "effective rate." This usage is *incorrect* because the term "effective rate" has a specific meaning that is related to the frequency of compounding and the manner in which interest is accrued. This is discussed in detail later in the chapter.

widely used financial concept. The need for full disclosure of the true interest rate stems from the fact that, for example, an "8 percent add-on interest" loan payable monthly over three years has an APR of 14.55 percent! (The procedure for finding the APR is discussed later in this chapter.) The law as amended in 1980 requires that the stated APR be within 1/8 of 1 percentage point of the true APR for most transactions. The Act also requires that the total finance charges be prominently stated. These charges include interest and other fees charged such as origination fees, discount points, and mortgage insurance.

As a part of their periodic examination of banks, S&Ls, mutual savings banks, and credit unions, examiners from regulatory agencies conduct a *consumer compliance examination.* The purpose of this examination is to detect problems and ensure compliance with consumer protection laws and regulations. Among the most common violations are improper calculations of the APR and related finance charges. This is not surprising. These calculations can be confusing and difficult for individuals who lack a thorough understanding of financial mathematics.

Usury Laws   Many states have usury laws that limit the interest rate that may be charged on consumer-related loans. When the market rate is close to the usury limit, care must be exercised to avoid exceeding the limit. This can inadvertently happen if certain financial mathematics concepts are not understood. Consider the following example from the case of *Cagle vs. Boyle Mortgage Company.* [2]

> *Example.*   In December 1973, the Boyle Mortgage Company made a $28,000 mortgage loan to Lloyd Cagle bearing a 10 percent interest rate, then the legal maximum under Arkansas law. No payments were made and the borrower defaulted. The mortgage company sued to recover the loan balance by foreclosing the mortgage. The borrower argued that the manner in which the interest charges were computed and compounded resulted in an interest rate that exceeded the state usury limit. The borrower showed that the lender's computer programmer converted the 10 percent rate from a 360-day basis to a 365-day basis, i.e., (365/360) X 10% = 10.139%. Using this rate and monthly compounding, the resulting effective interest rate was 10.62 percent. Even though no payments were made by the borrower and the violation was unintentional, the Supreme Court of Arkansas, in a bizarre ruling, found that the loan was usurious. The "victim" fared rather well. The Court ordered that the note and mortgage be cancelled thus allowing the borrower to keep the property and avoid repaying the loan! The fate of the programmer is unknown.

Although state laws vary, the penalties for violating usury laws are usually harsh. In Florida, for example, if a loan is usurious the borrower can sue the lender for damages equal to three times the total amount of interest that would be payable over the life of the loan. Such a penalty can be staggering in the case of long-term loans. These problems can be avoided by understanding the nature of the mathematics underlying interest rate calculations.

[2] Cagle v. Boyle Mortgage Co. 549SW2d 474 1977.

Competitive Strategies

With the passage of the *Depository Institutions Deregulation and Monetary Control Act of 1980,* competition for savings became more intense. Although depository institutions like banks, S&Ls, and credit unions compete for these funds on the basis of service and convenience, most competitive strategies center around the *effective interest rate.* This rate reflects the impact of compounding and the manner in which interest is accrued, i.e. a 365-day year or a 360-day year. Suppose two competing banks offer the same base rate, or *nominal rate* as it is known, of 10 percent for a one-year deposit. Bank A compounds interest daily and uses a 360-day year. Bank B compounds interest semiannually and uses a 365-day year. The effective rate that Bank A would advertise is 10.67 percent and for Bank B the effective rate is 10.25 percent. The difference of 42 basis points would have a significant impact on each bank's competitive position and cost structure.[3]

In the mortgage lending process the tradeoff between a flat interest rate or a lower rate with front-end "points" must be evaluated. The decision has significant policy and competitive implications. Examples later in the chapter will demonstrate the nature of this type of problem.

"Nuts and Bolts" Applications

The discussion so far has focused on financial mathematics concepts as they relate to decision-making, legal issues, and competitive strategies. In the day-to-day management of financial institutions numerous other "nuts and bolts" applications arise. The seemingly straightforward task of pricing bonds can be complicated by the existence of a call provision. Proper pricing requires the use of financial mathematics. Understanding and being able to explain the complex assortment of new types of mortgage loans is possible only with a thorough understanding of mathematical concepts. The sale of loans through loan participations requires finding the present value or internal rate of return. Innovations in the area of mortgage-backed securities require that market values of mortgage loans be determined. The concepts discussed in this chapter are important in understanding the market behavior and price volatility of financial instruments.

Financial tables of the type found in most finance textbooks have limited use when dealing with the problem facing financial institutions. Although more extensive and specialized tables are available for certain types of transactions, the solutions are often approximations. It is virtually impossible to have tables that cover the entire spectrum of financial problems and all possible combinations of interest rates, compounding intervals, and accrual methods. Modern calculators or micro-computers are used to solve most problems facing financial institutions. Recognizing that the capacity of modern calculators and micro-computers eases the computational burden, the thrust of this chapter is on the formulation of problems, as well as understanding the solutions and managerial implications.

---

[3] The term *basis points* is often used when evaluating the spread between two interest rates. One hundred basis points is equal to one percentage point.

TIME VALUE OF MONEY

In the savings-investment process, a decision is made to forego current consumption with the expectation of enjoying greater consumption in the future. The compensation for waiting is the interest earned on the savings. If the interest rate is 8 percent, the investor has a choice of spending $1,000 now or having $1,080 to spend one year later. Similarly, if an individual is to receive $1,000 in one year, a smaller sum may be acceptable if the funds can be obtained now. Rather than a single lump-sum, the problem may involve a series of payments or a combination of a lump-sum and a series of payments. This section develops the framework for analyzing these and a variety of other time-value problems.

Single-Payment Problems

When approaching valuation or rate of return problems, the first step is to determine if the cash flows involve a single payment, a series of payments, or both. Then the issue is whether the problem involves a future value or present value. To begin, consider the procedure for finding the future value of a single payment.

Future Value (FV_{mn})   The *future value* is also called a *compound value* and results from an initial investment earning interest on both the principal and interest as it accumulates over time. Suppose $1,000 is invested for two years at 8 percent with interest paid at semiannual intervals. This means that there are four compounding periods with a periodic interest rate of 4 percent. The future value of this investment at the end of four periods (two years) is obtained by finding the accumulated value at the end of each of the preceding intervals and reinvesting the total at the period interest rate of 4 percent. The process is shown below.

$$FV_1 = \$1,000 + 1,000(.04)$$
$$= \$1,000(1 + .04)$$

$$FV_2 = FV_1(1 + .04)$$
$$= [\$1,000(1 + .04)](1 + .04)$$
$$= \$1,000(1 + .04)^2$$

$$FV_3 = FV_2(1 + .04)$$
$$= [\$1,000(1 + .04)^2](1 + .04)$$
$$= \$1,000(1 + .04)^3$$

$$FV_4 = FV_3(1 + .04)$$
$$= [\$1,000(1 + .04)^3](1 + .04)$$
$$= \$1,000(1 + .04)^4$$
$$= \$1,169.86.$$

The procedure shows that the future value of a single, lump-sum payment at the end of n years with interest paid m times per year is given by the expression

$$FV_{mn} = PV\left(1 + \frac{r}{m}\right)^{mn} \qquad [1]$$

where FV_{mn} = future value of an amount invested for mn periods
       PV   = present value or beginning amount of the investment
       r   = annual nominal or stated interest rate
       m   = number of times per year that compounding occurs
       n   = number of years.

The term $\left(1 + \frac{r}{m}\right)^{mn}$ is sometimes called the *future value interest factor,* or FVIF. Note that when interest is compounded annually, m = 1 and [1] becomes $FV_n = PV(1 + r)^n$, a familiar compounding expression. Equation [1] is more general because it is applicable to problems with different compounding intervals. The general model is necessary when dealing with financial institutions since their problems involve annual, semiannual, quarterly, monthly, and daily compounding. (The model for continuous compounding is developed later.)

Present Value (PV$_{mn}$)   The procedure for finding the present value of a future payment (or payments) is called *discounting.* This is a reversal of the compounding process. The general formulation for the present value of a lump-sum payment mn periods in the future is obtained by rearranging [1] as follows

$$PV = \frac{FV_{mn}}{\left(1 + \frac{r}{m}\right)^{mn}}$$

or

$$PV_{mn} = FV\left[\frac{1}{\left(1 + \frac{r}{m}\right)^{mn}}\right]. \qquad [2]$$

The term in the brackets is the *present value interest factor* or PVIF. Note that this term is the reciprocal of the FVIF. To see how this reverses the compounding process, consider the preceding problem in which $1,000 was invested for two years at 8 percent with interest compounded semiannually, and FV_{mn} = $1,169.86. Substituting these values into [2], the PV_{mn} is given by

$$PV_{mn} = \$1,169.86 \left[\frac{1}{\left(1 + \frac{.08}{2}\right)^{2(2)}}\right]$$

$$= \$1,169.86(.8548)$$

$$= \$1,000.00 .$$

Finding r   In some problems, both the beginning and ending values are known and it is necessary to find the interest rate.

This is accomplished by rearranging either equation [1] or [2] and algebraically solving for r. Using [1], the procedure is as follows

$$FV_{mn} = PV\left(1 + \frac{r}{m}\right)^{mn},$$

dividing both sides by PV results in

$$\left(1 + \frac{r}{m}\right)^{mn} = FV_{mn}/PV.$$

Taking the mnth root of both sides and subtracting 1 produces

$$\frac{r}{m} = \left(FV_{mn}/PV\right)^{1/mn} - 1.$$

Multiplying both sides by m, the model is

$$r = m\left[\left(FV_{mn}/PV\right)^{1/mn} - 1\right]. \qquad [3]$$

Most modern calculators are capable of solving this expression. Applications of this model are presented later in the chapter.

Annuities

An annuity is a series of equal payments or receipts occurring at the end of regular intervals and for a specified length of time.[4] Like single-payment problems, an annuity may involve either future value or present value calculations.

Future Value of an Annuity (FVA$_{mn}$)   The future value of an annuity is the sum of each payment or receipt compounded over time. Consider a semiannual annuity of $1,000 for two years with an annual interest rate of 8 percent per year. To see how the components of this problem fit together and how the compounding process works, refer to the time diagram shown in Figure 1. Note that the payments are received at the end of each compounding period and then reinvested at the original periodic interest rate of 4 percent. The last payment earns no interest while the first payment earns interest at the periodic rate of 4 percent for three periods. The future value of the annuity is the sum of the four payments and the accumulated interest.

The procedure demonstrated in this diagram works for equal or unequal payments since each one is compounded individually and then summed. When the payments are equal the problem is simplified because a general formulation can be developed. The problem shown in Figure 1 may be expressed numerically. Letting FVA$_4$ represent the future value of the four-period annuity, the problem may be formulated as

[4] Some annuities are payable at the beginning of the periods. Such an annuity is called an *annuity-due*. The focus here is on the more commonly used *regular annuity* in which equal payments occur at the end of the periods.

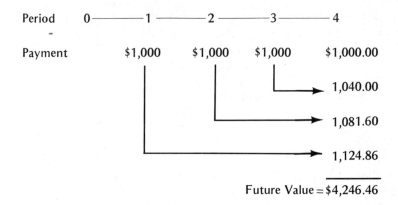

Figure 1   Future Value of a $1,000 Semiannual Annuity for 2 Years at 8%

$$FVA_4 = \$1,000\left(1 + \frac{.08}{2}\right)^3 + 1,000\left(1 + \frac{.08}{2}\right)^2 + 1,000\left(1 + \frac{.08}{2}\right)^1 + 1,000\left(1 + \frac{.08}{2}\right)^0$$

$$= \$1,124.86 + 1,081.60 + 1,040.00 + 1,000.00$$

$$= \$4,246.46.$$

Letting R represent the periodic receipt or payment, the pattern above indicates that the *general formulation* for an annuity is

$$FVA_{mn} = R\left(1 + \frac{r}{m}\right)^{mn-1} + R\left(1 + \frac{r}{m}\right)^{mn-2} + \cdots + R\left(1 + \frac{r}{m}\right)^1 + R\left(1 + \frac{r}{m}\right)^0.$$

Factoring the Rs results in

$$FVA_{mn} = R\left[\left(1 + \frac{r}{m}\right)^{mn-1} + \left(1 + \frac{r}{m}\right)^{mn-2} + \cdots + \left(1 + \frac{r}{m}\right)^1 + \left(1 + \frac{r}{m}\right)^0\right].$$

Since the term in the brackets is a geometric progression, the general formulation becomes

$$FVA_{mn} = R\left[\frac{\left(1 + \frac{r}{m}\right)^{mn} - 1}{\frac{r}{m}}\right]. \qquad [4]$$

The term in the brackets is the future value interest factor for an annuity (FVIFA). Referring to the problem in the time diagram, the values of R, n, m, and r may be substituted into [4] to obtain

$$FVA_4 = \$1,000\left[\frac{\left(1 + \frac{.08}{2}\right)^{2(2)} - 1}{\frac{.08}{2}}\right]$$

$$= \$1,000\left[\frac{1.169858 - 1}{.04}\right] = \$4,246.46.$$

This solution is the same as that obtained when each payment is compounded and then summed as shown in Figure 1.

Present Value of an Annuity (PVA$_{mn}$)   The nature of a present value problem involving an annuity may again be demonstrated by using a time diagram. Figure 2 shows how the present value of a two-year, $1,000 semiannual annuity is found assuming an annual interest rate of 8 percent. The diagram shows how each payment is discounted to the present. The pattern may be expressed as

$$PVA_{mn} = \$1,000\left[\frac{1}{\left(1 + \frac{.08}{2}\right)^1}\right] + 1,000\left[\frac{1}{\left(1 + \frac{.08}{2}\right)^2}\right] + 1,000\left[\frac{1}{\left(1 + \frac{.08}{2}\right)^3}\right] + 1,000\left[\frac{1}{\left(1 + \frac{.08}{2}\right)^4}\right]$$

$$= \$961.54 + 924.56 + 889.00 + 854.80$$

$$= \$3,629.90.$$

Like the preceding problem, the pattern underlying this numerical relationship suggests a general form. This is

$$PVA_{mn} = R\left[\frac{1}{\left(1 + \frac{r}{m}\right)^1}\right] + R\left[\frac{1}{\left(1 + \frac{r}{m}\right)^2}\right] + \cdots + R\left[\frac{1}{\left(1 + \frac{r}{m}\right)^{mn}}\right].$$

Again, factoring the Rs results in a geometric progression of the form

$$PVA_{mn} = R\left[\frac{1}{\left(1 + \frac{r}{m}\right)^1} + \frac{1}{\left(1 + \frac{r}{m}\right)^2} + \cdots + \frac{1}{\left(1 + \frac{r}{m}\right)^{mn}}\right].$$

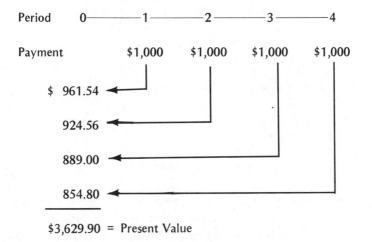

Period	0———1———2———3———4

Payment $1,000 $1,000 $1,000 $1,000

$ 961.54
   924.56
   889.00
   854.80

$3,629.90 = Present Value

Figure 2   Present Value of a $1,000 Semiannual Annuity for 2 Years at 8%.

Applying the formula for a geometric progression to the term in the brackets, the general model for the present value of an annuity may be written as

$$PVA_{mn} = R \left[\frac{1 - \dfrac{1}{\left(1 + \dfrac{r}{m}\right)^{mn}}}{\dfrac{r}{m}} \right].$$

[5]

The term in the brackets is the present value interest factor for an annuity (PVIFA). Substituting the numbers from the time diagram into [5] results in

$$PVA_{mn} = 1,000 \left[\frac{1 - \dfrac{1}{\left(1 + \dfrac{.08}{2}\right)^{2\,(2)}}}{\dfrac{.08}{2}} \right]$$

$$= 1,000(3.62990)$$

$$= \$3,629.90.$$

Finding R or r   If the annuity payment R is unknown, it may be found by rearranging equations [4] or [5]. If equal payments are to be made for the purpose of accumulating a known future amount, then equation [4], the future value formulation, is used. Rearranging [4] to solve for R results in

$$R = \frac{FVA_{mn}}{\left[\dfrac{\left(1 + \dfrac{r}{m}\right)^{mn} - 1}{\dfrac{r}{m}} \right]}.$$

[6]

If the problem involves the present value of an annuity, then equation [5] is solved for R. That is,

$$R = \frac{PVA_{mn}}{\left[\dfrac{1 - \dfrac{1}{\left(1 + \dfrac{r}{m}\right)^{mn}}}{\dfrac{r}{m}} \right]}.$$

[7]

This model would be used to find the payment necessary to pay off, or amortize, a mortgage loan and certain types of consumer loans.

Perhaps the most common problem facing financial institutions arises when the APR and/or the effective interest rate is unknown. It may seem unusual that an unknown interest rate is a common problem since an interest rate is virtually always quoted in a lending or investment transaction. But recall that the quoted interest rate on loans, mortgages, money market instruments, and many other financial instruments usually does not reflect the true interest cost or return. The quoted rate may simply reflect a standard pricing practice for a particular instrument or transaction.

Prior to the development of modern calculators, finding the interest rate on an annuity was a tedious "trial and error" process. To see why, suppose a $50,000 loan is to be repaid by monthly payments of $550 over 25 years. Since this problem involves a monthly annuity of $550 for 25 years and the present value ($50,000) is known, the interest rate r is found by using equation[5]. That is,

$$PVA_{mn} = R \left[\frac{1 - \dfrac{1}{\left(1 + \dfrac{r}{m}\right)^{mn}}}{\dfrac{r}{m}} \right]$$

$$\$50{,}000 = \$550 \left[\frac{1 - \dfrac{1}{\left(1 + \dfrac{r}{12}\right)^{12(25)}}}{\dfrac{r}{12}} \right].$$

Rearranging this expression to isolate the PVIFA (the term in the brackets)

$$90.9091 = \left[\frac{1 - \dfrac{1}{\left(1 + \dfrac{r}{12}\right)^{12(25)}}}{\dfrac{r}{12}} \right].$$

Since r cannot be solved by algebraic manipulation, an iterative search routine is built into many financial calculators. For example, letting r = .13, the PVIFA factor is 88.6654 which is too low. To increase the PVIFA, r must be reduced. Letting r = .12, the PVIFA factor is 94.9466 which is too high so the value of r is between 12 and 13 percent. Repeating the procedure and converging on the PVIFA value of 90.9091 would produce r = 12.629 percent. This is the nature of the search routine built into many calculators and computer programs. Later in this chapter, the formulation of other versions of this type of problem will be demonstrated.

Outstanding
Loan Balance
It is often necessary to find the future balance of an annuity-type loan. For example, an individual may be requesting a mortgage loan of $80,000 at a fixed rate of 12 percent with monthly payments based on a 30-year repayment schedule. After three years, the rate on the outstanding loan balance (OLB) will be renegotiated based on current interest rates. The borrower has the option to either repay or refinance the balance. The question arises—what will be the outstanding loan balance to be refinanced after 36 payments?

The OLB may be obtained in several ways. An amortization schedule may be prepared as shown in Table 1. The monthly payment of $822.89 is obtained using equation [7] and from this, the loan balance for each period may be obtained as shown. Since this is a cumbersome procedure, the following model may be used to find the OLB,

Table 1   Amortization Schedule for $80,000 Loan at 12%,
30-Year Term, Payable Monthly

Month	Beginning Balance	Monthly Payment	Portion of Payment to Interest	Portion of Payment to Principal	Ending Balance
1	$80,000.00	$822.89	$800.00[a]	$ 22.89[b]	$79,977.11[c]
2	79,977.11	822.89	799.77	23.12	79,953.99
3	79,953.99	822.89	799.54	23.35	79,930.64
4	79,930.64	822.89	799.31	23.58	79,907.06
5	79,907.06	822.89	799.07	23.82	79,883.24
—	—	—	—	—	—
—	—	—	—	—	—
—	—	—	—	—	—
34	79,110.29	822.89	791.10	31.79	79,078.50
35	79,078.50	822.89	790.78	32.11	79,046.39
36	79,046.39	822.89	790.46	32.43	79,013.96
37	79,013.96	822.89	790.14	32.75	78,981.21
38	78,981.21	822.89	789.81	33.08	78,948.13
—	—	—	—	—	—
—	—	—	—	—	—
—	—	—	—	—	—
178	68,968.20	822.89	689.68	133.21	68,834.99
179	68,834.99	822.89	688.35	134.54	68,700.45
180	68,700.45	822.89	687.00	135.89	68,564.56
181	68,564.56	822.89	685.65	137.24	68,427.32
182	68,427.32	822.89	684.27	138.62	68,288.70
—	—	—	—	—	—
—	—	—	—	—	—
—	—	—	—	—	—
356	3,993.84	822.89	39.94	782.95	3,210.89
357	3,210.89	822.89	32.11	790.78	2,420.11
358	2,420.11	822.89	24.20	798.69	1,621.41
359	1,621.42	822.89	16.21	806.68	814.74
360	814.74	822.89	8.15	814.74	—0—

[a]$80,000 × .12/12 = $800.00.
[b]$822.89 − $800.00 = $22.89.
[c]$80,000 − $22.89 = $79,977.11.

$$B_k = B_o \left[\frac{\left(1 + \frac{r}{m}\right)^{mn} - \left(1 + \frac{r}{m}\right)^k}{\left(1 + \frac{r}{m}\right)^{mn} - 1} \right] \qquad [8]$$

where B_k = outstanding loan balance (OLB) after the kth payment
B_o = original loan balance
r = interest rate on the loan
m = number of compounding periods per year
n = number of years on which payments are based.

In the example above, the OLB after 36 payments would be

$$B_{36} = \$80,000 \left[\frac{\left(1 + \frac{.12}{12}\right)^{12(30)} - \left(1 + \frac{.12}{12}\right)^{36}}{\left(1 + \frac{.12}{12}\right)^{12(30)} - 1} \right]$$

$$B_{36} = \$80,000 \left[\frac{35.949641 - 1.430768}{35.949641 - 1} \right]$$

$$B_{36} = \$80,000 \,(.9876746)$$

$$B_{36} = \$79,013.96.$$

Another approach is to find the present value of the remaining payments discounted at the contract rate. Equation [5] would be used for this purpose. The most expedient alternative is to use a modern financial calculator with the OLB problem preprogrammed.

Perpetuities

Another type of valuation problem involves perpetuities. As the name implies, these are financial instruments with payment streams that either continue indefinitely or are assumed to do so for valuation purposes. Such an assumption usually underlies the valuation of common stocks and many issues of preferred stock.

Banks, S&Ls, and most credit unions are prohibited from investing in common and preferred stock, but these instruments are important investments for pension funds, life insurance companies, property-liability insurance companies, and mutual savings banks. Bank trust departments are also active in these markets. Although not buyers for their own portfolio, banks have been issuers of common stock and preferred stock in recent years in order to increase their capital and facilitate growth.

Common Stock   To place the valuation procedure for common stock in perspective, it is useful to compare the cash flow characteristics of a bond to those of a stock. A bond represents a contractual obligation to pay specified interest at regular intervals and repay the principal at maturity. Valuing a bond involves finding the present value of an annuity and the lump-sum payment at maturity. The procedure for valuing a common stock differs in three respects. First, common stock has an assumed infinite life so there is no repayment of principal. Another difference is that the payments are not contractual. Finally, the payments are not necessarily constant over time.

Despite these differences, the price of a common stock is determined in the same manner as any other financial asset. That is, the price is the present value of the expected dividends. The fact that dividends may increase, remain constant, or decrease, may be reflected in a present value formulation. If the current dividend is expected to change at rate g, a general formulation may be written as

$$PV = \frac{D_0(1 + g)}{(1 + k)} + \frac{D_0(1 + g)^2}{(1 + k)^2} + \frac{D_0(1 + g)^3}{(1 + k)^3} + \ldots \qquad [9]$$

where D_o = current dividend
  g   = expected annual rate of change in dividends and earnings
  k   = required rate of return appropriate for the stock's risk class.

Implicit in this formulation are estimates of future dividends. If the current dividend is $2 and the estimated growth rate is 6 percent, the estimated third year dividend is $2(1 + .06)^3 = $2.38.

Equation [9] may be simplified if g is assumed to be constant and k is greater than g. Then it can be shown that [9] may be written as[5]

$$PV = \frac{D_o(1 + g)}{k - g} \qquad [10]$$

or

$$PV = \frac{D_1}{k - g}. \qquad [11]$$

An intuitive way to arrive at [11] is to assume the stock will be sold at the end of the first period when its price is $PV_1 = PV(1 + g)$ and the annual dividend is $D_o(1 + g)$. Discounting these values, the present price of the stock is

$$PV = \frac{D_0(1 + g) + PV(1 + g)}{(1 + k)}.$$

Rearranging this expression and algebraically solving for PV results in

$$PV = \frac{D_0(1 + g)}{k - g}$$

which is the same as [10] or [11].

Despite its theoretical origin, Equation [11] is consistent with the behavior of investors. The question may be asked—why own common stock? One might respond by saying—"capital gains, dividend yield, or a combination of both." Equation [11] says the same thing. This is evident when [11] is rearranged and solved for k, the required rate of return for stockholders. That is,

$$k = \frac{D_1}{PV} + g.$$

The first term on the right hand side is the dividend yield and g represents the expected capital gain resulting from the increasing dividends and earnings.

The use of equation [11] for decision-making involves several problems. If the growth rate is not constant or if g is initially greater than k, a common situation with growth stocks, a modified version of this approach must be used.[6] Other

---

[5] The derivation of equation [10] is demonstrated in most introductory finance books. For example, see: J. Fred Weston and Eugene F. Brigham, *Essentials of Managerial Finance*, 6th ed., Hinsdale, Ill.: Dryden Press, 1982, Chapter 18.

[6] For a discussion of modified versions of the basic stock valuation model, see J. Fred Weston and Eugene F. Brigham, op. cit., Chapter 18.

problems are more serious. The discount rate is subject to change over time as a result of changes in interest rates, inflationary expectations, or company policies. The future growth rate is also difficult to forecast accurately. Despite these limitations, the framework demonstrates that the principles underlying the valuation of common stock are the same as for other financial instruments. The current price is the discounted value of expected future cash flows.

Preferred Stock   Traditionally, preferred stocks have been valued on the assumption that they are perpetuities. However, many recently issued preferred stocks are callable so the perpetual life assumption is not always appropriate. For the preferred stocks that satisfy the perpetuity assumption, the valuation process is quite simple—they are valued as if they were zero-growth common stocks. Letting g = 0, equation [11] becomes

$$PV = \frac{D_0}{k}.$$ [12]

which is a commonly used valuation model for preferred stock.

Some preferred stocks are callable, usually at a premium, several years after they are issued. If such an issue has been outstanding for several years, it may be callable immediately. If the dividend rate on a callable preferred stock is below the market rate, the assumption may be made for pricing purposes that the issue is a perpetuity and equation [12] is appropriate. However, if the dividend rate is higher than the present market rate, an incentive may exist for the issuer to call the preferred stock and refinance it with a lower-cost issue. The price, therefore, depends on the estimated cash flows based on an expected call date. (The nature of this problem is discussed in a later section dealing with bond valuation.)

Compounding Intervals

Financial decision-making in banks and other financial institutions requires a thorough understanding of the impact of different compounding intervals. This is the interval over which interest is assumed to be paid and reinvested. The intervals used are annual, semiannual, quarterly, monthly, and daily. The process is called *discrete compounding* when one of these intervals is used. Another widely used approach is *continuous compounding.* Here, the compounding interest is infinitesimally small and the reinvestment process is assumed to be continuous rather than occurring at discrete intervals in time. The issue is important because the frequency of compounding affects the return on an asset or the cost of a liability. The more frequently interest is paid and reinvested, the higher the earnings, at least up to a point. To adjust for different compounding methods and place financial instruments on a comparable basis, the *effective yield* must be determined.

Discrete   The annual rate at which most financial instruments are
Compounding   quoted is the *nominal rate.* For example, a firm may sell 12 percent bonds at par to yield 12 percent with interest payable semiannually, as is standard practice with bonds. The nominal rate is the quoted market yield of 12 percent. A bank may also offer savers a deposit at a nominal rate of 12 percent but with interest compounded daily. To

compare the yields on these two instruments the effective yield must be determined. The linkage between the *effective rate* and the *nominal rate* is given by

$$1 + i = \left(1 + \frac{r}{m}\right)^m$$

or

$$i = \left(1 + \frac{r}{m}\right)^m - 1 \qquad\qquad [13]$$

where   i = effective annual rate of interest
        r = nominal annual rate of interest
      m = number of compounding intervals per year.

Note that when m = 1 (i.e., annual compounding), the effective rate is the same as the nominal rate. However, when compounding occurs more than once a year, r and i are not equal. Table 2 demonstrates the effects of various compounding intervals when the nominal rate is 12 percent.

Table 2 shows that the effective rate i depends on the nominal rate r and the compounding interval m. The 12 percent bonds cited above have an effective yield of 12.36 percent while the savings account has an effective yield of 12.747 percent, a difference of more than 35 basis points. The table also shows that the effect of increasing the frequency of compounding is limited. The effective yield increases only slightly when daily compounding (m = 365) is used rather than monthly compounding (m = 12). The last entry in the table shows that the highest possible effective yield is obtained with continuous compounding.

Continuous   One of the most obscure concepts in financial mathe-
Compounding   matics is *continuous compounding,* a method widely
used by banks and other depository institutions as they
compete for savings deposits. The pattern of effective yields shown in Table 2 provides insight into the continuous compounding process. The first five intervals shown in Table 2 are distinct, well-defined periods ranging from annual to daily. As the number of these intervals increases, the length of each interval becomes correspondingly smaller. For extremely large values of m the intervals become so small that they are virtually continuous rather than separate and distinct. The compounding is assumed to be taking place continuously. After studying the com-

Table 2   Effect of Compounding Intervals on a
Nominal Rate r = 12%

Compounding Interval	$i = \left(1 + \frac{.12}{m}\right)^m - 1$
Annual (m = 1)	12.000%
Semiannual (m = 2)	12.360
Quarterly (m = 4)	12.551
Monthly (m = 12	12.683
Daily (m = 365)	12.747
Continuously (m → ∞)	12.750

pounding process using discrete intervals this seems like a highly theoretical concept. But continuous growth is far more representative of most growth processes than is discrete compound growth. For example, trees grow continuously rather than in semiannual or monthly spurts. A savings account or investment may grow the same way.

Like other compounding problems, a distinction must be made between the nominal rate and the effective rate i. With continuous compounding, the relationship between the nominal rate r and the effective rate i is given by

$$1 + i = \lim_{m \to \infty} \left(1 + \frac{r}{m}\right)^m = e^r$$

or

$$i = e^r - 1. \qquad [14]$$

This simply means that when m is very large, the term in the parentheses may be expressed as the value e^r, where r is the nominal rate. But what is e? The term e has a (rounded) value of 2.71828. This is an important constant with many practical applications in the physical sciences as well as in financial mathematics.[7] The use of equation [14] may be demonstrated by referring to Table 2. The last entry shows the relationship between a 12 percent nominal rate and the effective rate i using continuous compounding. The effective rate was obtained using equation [14] as follows,[8]

$$
\begin{aligned}
i &= e^r - 1 \\
&= e^{.12} - 1 \\
&= 1.1275 - 1 \\
&= .1275 \text{ or } 12.75\%.[9]
\end{aligned}
$$

Most practical applications of continuous compounding involve savings accounts rather than loans, bonds, or other financial instruments. Like the discrete approaches, continuous compounding may be used for present value or future value problems involving single payments or annuities. Annuity formulations, however, have few practical uses in finance. Most financial applications involve single-payment problems.

Assuming continuous compounding at a nominal rate r, the valuation model used to determine the future value of a single payment in n years is

$$FV_n = PVe^{rn}. \qquad [15]$$

[7] A formal derivation of the constant e is available in most college calculus books.

[8] Problems involving the constant e are easily solved using a hand calculator with the built-in exponential, or "exp" function. Since e is a well-known constant it is written as "e" rather than its numerical value.

[9] If the continuously compounded effective rate is given and the nominal rate is unknown, the unique properties of e and the use of modern calculators enables the solution to be obtained quickly. For example, given the effective rate i = .1275 from the last entry in Table 2, the corresponding nominal rate r is obtained by finding the natural logarithm of (1 + i). That is,

$$
\begin{aligned}
r &= \ln(1 + i) \\
r &= \ln(1 + .1275) = .12 \text{ or } 12\%.
\end{aligned}
$$

If \$10,000 is invested for three and one-half years in a savings account paying a nominal rate of 10.7 percent compounded continuously, the future value is

$$FV_{3.5} = \$10,000e^{.107(3.5)}$$
$$= \$10,000(1.454264)$$
$$= \$14,542.64.$$

If annual compounding were used, the future value would be $\$10,000(1 + .107)^{3.5} = \$14,273.05$, a difference of \$269.59.

If the future value is known, the continuously discounted present value may be obtained by rearranging [15] to solve for PV. That is,

$$PV = FV_n \left[\frac{1}{e^{rn}} \right]$$

or

$$PV_n = FVe^{-rn}. \tag{16}$$

Again, this procedure is a reversal of the compounding process. Using Equation [16] to discount the future value obtained above results in

$$PV_{3.5} = \$14,542.64e^{-.107(3.5)}$$
$$= \$14,542.64(.687633)$$
$$= \$10,000.$$

In banks and other depository institutions, it is sometimes necessary to find the continuously compounded nominal rate r used in equations [15] or [16]. The model for r is obtained by algebraically rearranging either of the basic models. Using [15], the procedure is as follows:

$$FV_n = PVe^{rn}.$$

Dividing both sides by PV results in

$$e^{rn} = FV_n/PV.$$

Taking the nth root of both sides produces

$$e^r = (FV_n/PV)^{1/n}.$$

Now taking the natural logarithm of both sides results in

$$r = \ln \left[(FV_n/PV)^{1/n} \right]. \tag{17}$$

In a later section dealing with applications, a problem involving a withdrawal penalty shows how the model may be used.

Comment   The effective yield is usually stated when depository institutions are promoting or advertising savings-related instruments. When dealing with most other instruments such as bonds, mortgage loans, commercial loans, and borrowed funds, only the nominal rate is stated or considered. From a managerial standpoint the effective rate on all assets and liabilities should be used when evaluating costs and returns. Otherwise, important yield differences may be overlooked.

Interest Accrual Method

In the preceding discussion it was shown that the compounding interval has an important impact on the effective yield. It was also assumed that the nominal interest rate was earned by the saver and *accrued* by the payer on the basis of a 365-day year. This is called the *actual/365 accrual method.* Another approach—the *actual/360 accrual method*—is based on a 360-day year. This increases the effective yield to the saver or cost to the payer.

Under the *actual/360 method,* interest is earned on the basis of a 365-day year but the nominal rate is paid on the basis of a 360-day year. Consider the simple case of a "one-year" deposit of $1,000 at a nominal rate of 10 percent. Using the *actual/365 method,* the saver has $1,100 after 365 days. Under the *actual/360 method* the saver has $1,100 after 360 days. Reinvesting the original principal for the extra five days (or six days in a leap year) at 10 percent produces additional interest of $1,000(.10)(5/360) = $1.39. The total interest earned is $101.39. This increases the yield over that provided by the *actual/365 method.*

When calculating the future value of a deposit or its effective yield, the nominal rate must be adjusted when using the actual/360 method. Letting r represent the nominal rate, the *adjusted nominal rate* r* is given by

$$r^* = r(365/360).\qquad [18]$$

In the example above, the 10 percent nominal rate used in conjunction with the actual/360 method produces r* = .10(365/360) = 10.139%.

For discrete compounding and given the adjusted nominal rate r*, the effective rate i is obtained from

$$i = \left(1 + \frac{r^*}{m}\right)^m - 1.\qquad [19]$$

Assuming daily compounding, the effective rate in the example above is

$$i = \left(1 + \frac{.10139}{365}\right)^{365} - 1$$

$$= .10669 \text{ or } 10.669\%.$$

If continuous compounding were used, the effective yield would be

$$i = e^{r*} - 1$$
$$= e^{.10139} - 1$$
$$= .10671 \text{ or } 10.671\%.[10]$$

This is 15 basis points higher than the effective yield if continuous compounding is used with the actual/365 method. Note that the yield is 67 basis points higher than the quoted nominal yield of 10 percent.

APPLICATIONS OF FINANCIAL MATHEMATICS

In this section, applications of financial mathematics are discussed. These applications demonstrate the nature of various problems confronting banks and other financial institutions. The general applicability of basic concepts is highlighted by formulating different types of problems.

Deposit-Related Problems

Premiums   Prior to the passage of the *Depository Institutions Deregulation and Monetary Control Act of 1980,* the interest rate that could be paid on most savings deposits in banks and other depository institutions was subject to ceilings that were often below-market. To attract savers, depository institutions competed on a non-price basis by periodically offering new savers such items as toasters, blankets, radios, and stuffed animals. This enabled institutions to pay temporarily a higher return than permitted under regulations. With the gradual phase-out of interest rate ceilings in accordance with the deregulation act, increased emphasis was placed on paying market rates. Premiums continue to be offered by institutions as part of periodic promotional campaigns to attract new depositors. Consider the following example and its cost implications.

> *Example.* The Crocker National Bank offered stuffed dogs called "Crocker Spaniels" to any depositors who put $300 in a new or existing savings account. Suppose an individual opened an 8 percent savings account with a deposit of $500. If the stuffed dog cost $5, interest was compounded daily, the actual 365 method was used, and the funds stayed in the bank for six months, what was the cost of the funds to the bank?
>
> *Step 1*   Using the future value model, equation [1], find the future value of the deposit after one-half year.

---

[10] If interest is compounded daily using the actual/360 method, the effective rate may be obtained using a one-step procedure. That is,

$$i = \left(1 + \frac{r}{360}\right)^{365} - 1.$$

$$FV_{mn} = PV\left(1 + \frac{r}{m}\right)^{mn}$$

$$= \$500\left(1 + \frac{.08}{365}\right)^{365(.5)}$$

$$= \$520.40.$$

Step 2   Deduct the cost of the premium from the initial deposit to obtain the bank's net inflow, i.e., $500 − 5 = $495.

Step 3   Find the nominal rate r that equates the future value of the deposit from Step 1 with the net inflow from Step 2. That is,

$$\$520.40 = \$495\left(1 + \frac{r}{365}\right)^{365(.5)}$$

Equation 3 is used to solve for the nominal rate reflecting the combined effect of the interest and premium,

$$r = m[(FV_{mn}/PV)^{1/mn} - 1]$$

$$= 365\,[(\$520.40/495)^{1/(365)(.5)} - 1]$$

$$= .1001 \text{ or } 10.01\%.$$

This rate is 201 basis points higher than the stated nominal rate of 8 percent.

The additional cost of such a program depends on the combination of the cost of the premium and the deposit's size and term. In this example, if the deposit was only $300 and the term three months (n = .25), the bank's cost would be 14.73 percent even if the premium cost was kept at $5. From a policy standpoint consideration must be given to establishing appropriate combinations of deposit term, size, and premium cost.

Another type of promotion is the *in-lieu-of-interest* premium. The following example demonstrates the nature of the problem.

Example.   In 1978, the Bank of Columbia in Washington, D. C. offered an unusual savings plan as part of a promotional campaign. With a deposit of $65,000 for seven years the depositor would receive at the time of the deposit, a new Mercedes-Benz 450 SL Coupe with a tape deck. The Coupe had a value of $27,000 at that time. A reporter was quick to claim that the depositor would be better off if $65,000 was deposited in the bank's 7 percent, seven-year account with interest compounded daily. Using the actual/365 method, the account would accumulate interest of about $41,000, or $14,000 more than the value of the car. An understanding of financial mathematics would have led the reporter to a different conclusion.

Since the bank was paying interest *in advance*, the depositor's outlay was reduced by the value of the car. The depositor's net outlay was $65,000 − 27,000 = $38,000. Now the question is—what is the nominal rate if $38,000 is accumulated to $65,000 over seven years with daily compounding. Using equation [3] results in

$$r = m[(FV_{mn}/PV)^{1/mn} - 1]$$
$$= 365[(\$65,000/38,000)^{1/(365)(7)} - 1]$$
$$= .07669 \text{ or } 7.67\%.$$

This yield was higher than the savings rate of 7 percent.

Early Withdrawals   To reduce the risk of sudden withdrawals inherent in a short-term deposit structure, banks and thrift institutions (i.e., S&Ls, credit unions, and mutual savings banks) offer higher interest rates on longer-term deposits. If these higher-yielding deposits were freely withdrawable, financial planning would be complicated, excessive costs incurred, and the firm's risk increased. These withdrawal-related problems would be particularly serious during a period of rising interest rates. Savers would simply transfer funds to other higher-yielding instruments. To overcome these problems permission to withdraw the funds prior to maturity may be denied. A commonly used alternative is to impose a "substantial penalty" for early withdrawal.[11] On deposits with an original maturity of six months but less than one year, the penalty is usually the loss of 90 days' interest. If the original maturity is one year or longer, the penalty is a loss of 180 days' interest. In either case, *the penalty may invade the principal.*

Withdrawal penalties affect the institution's cost of funds and the saver's return. Consider the following example.

> ***Example.***   A saver deposits $10,000 in a bank savings certificate that has an original maturity of three years. The nominal interest rate is 10 percent with interest compounded continuously. The actual/360 accrual method is used. The funds are withdrawn after exactly four months and the penalty is the loss of six months' interest. The following steps may be used to determine the proceeds to the saver and the bank's cost of funds.
>
> ***Step 1.***   Find the future value of the certificate at the end of four months assuming no penalty. The *adjusted nominal rate* $r^* = .10(365/360) = .10139$. The actual term of the deposit is four months so $n = .333$. The future value is
>
> $$FV_n = PVe^{r^*n}$$
> $$= \$10,000e^{.10139(.333)}$$
> $$= \$10,000(1.034339)$$
> $$= \$10,343.39.$$
>
> ***Step 2.***   Find the proceeds to the saver. This is the future value of the certificate at the end of four months less the interest for six months. Letting p = the interest penalty period, .5 years in this case, the model is
>
> $$FV_{.333} = PVe^{r^*(n-p)}$$
> $$= \$10,000e^{.10139(.333-.5)}$$
> $$= \$10,000e^{-.016932}$$
> $$= \$9,832.10.$$
>
> Since n is less than p the proceeds to the saver are less than the initial deposit.

---

[11] In the event of death, the funds are paid to the saver's estate without a penalty.

Step 3.   The amount of the penalty is the difference between the values from steps one and two, i.e., \$10,343.39 − \$9,832.10 = \$511.29.

Step 4.   The bank's *actual* adjusted nominal rate is the value r* from equation [15]. That is,

$$\$9,832.10 = \$10,000e^{r*(.333)}$$

Using equation [17],

$$r* = \ln[(FV_n/PV)^{1/n}]$$

$$= \ln[(\$9,832.10/10,000)^{1/.333}]$$

$$= \ln(.95042)$$

$$= -.0508 \text{ or } -5.08\%.$$

In this example, the bank's negative cost means that a profit resulted because the penalty invaded the saver's principal. The saver may still benefit if market rates are high enough such that the additional income from reinvestment offsets the penalty within a short period. Thus, withdrawal penalties are not always sufficient to retain the funds. In situations involving discrete compounding, the same procedure is used with equation [3] in Step 4.

Valuing Bonds

Analyzing the yields or prices of bonds is a day-to-day activity in virtually all financial institutions. The price of a bond is the present value of the interest income and the principal repayment at maturity. Since the interest on bonds is paid semiannually, m = 2 and the bond valuation model is usually written as

$$PV_{mn} = \frac{C/2}{\left(1 + \frac{r}{2}\right)^1} + \frac{C/2}{\left(1 + \frac{r}{2}\right)^2} + \cdots + \frac{C/2}{\left(1 + \frac{r}{2}\right)^{2n}} + \frac{F}{\left(1 + \frac{r}{2}\right)^{2n}}$$

or

$$PV_{mn} = \sum_{t=1}^{2n} \frac{C/2}{\left(1 + \frac{r}{2}\right)^t} + \frac{F}{\left(1 + \frac{r}{2}\right)^{2n}}.$$

In this case C is the annual interest in dollars as specified by the coupon rate and F is the face or par value of the bond.[12] Since the interest payments represent an annuity and the repayment of principal is a known lump-sum future payment, equations [5] and [2] are used to find the present value. Letting C/2 = R the model may be written as

---

[12] If the bond is bought between coupon payment dates, the buyer pays the seller a pro rata portion of the accrued interest in addition to the present value of the future interest payments and principal. The quoted price of bonds does not include the accrued interest.

$$PV_{mn} = R \left[\frac{1 - \frac{1}{\left(1 + \frac{r}{2}\right)^{2n}}}{\frac{r}{2}} \right] + \frac{F}{\left(1 + \frac{r}{2}\right)^{2n}} .$$

Consider the following examples of a "discount" bond and a "premium" bond.

Example. Given a market interest rate of 12 percent, find the price of a 15-year bond with a coupon of 10 percent and interest payable semiannually. There will be 30 semiannual interest payments of $50 and a lump-sum payment of $1,000 at maturity. The present value is

$$PV_{mn} = \$50 \left[\frac{1 - \frac{1}{\left(1 + \frac{.12}{2}\right)^{2(15)}}}{\frac{.12}{2}} \right] + \frac{1000}{\left(1 + \frac{.12}{2}\right)^{2(15)}}$$

$$= \$50(13.76483) + 1000(.17411)$$
$$= \$688.24 + 174.11$$
$$= \$862.35 \text{ or } 86.235 \text{ (\% of par).}$$

Example. In 1972, the State of Minnesota sold an issue of tax-exempt bonds with maturities ranging from 1973 to 1992. The bonds maturing from 1973 to 1976 had coupons of 50 percent while the 1992 maturity had a coupon of only 1/10 of 1 percent. The 4-year 50 percent bonds were sold to yield 4 percent. Bearing in mind that the semiannual interest payment was $250, the price was

$$PV_{mn} = \$250 \left[\frac{1 - \frac{1}{\left(1 + \frac{.04}{2}\right)^{2(4)}}}{\frac{.04}{2}} \right] + \frac{1,000}{\left(1 + \frac{.04}{2}\right)^{2(4)}}$$

$$= \$250(7.3255) + 1000(.85349)$$

$$= \$2684.87 \text{ or } 268.49.$$

The two examples illustrate how a bond may sell at a discount from par value or a premium over par value. The discount results when the market rate is greater than the coupon rate and a premium occurs when the coupon rate exceeds the market rate. When the market rate equals the coupon rate the price equals the par value, or 100. The question may arise—isn't there a loss of capital when a premium bond matures since only $1,000 is returned? In a sense, this is true as shown in the second example. However, the loss is offset by the coupon rate which is in excess of the market rate.

An important aspect of bond valuation is the relationship between the price of a bond and its maturity. This relationship is shown graphically in Figure 3. The

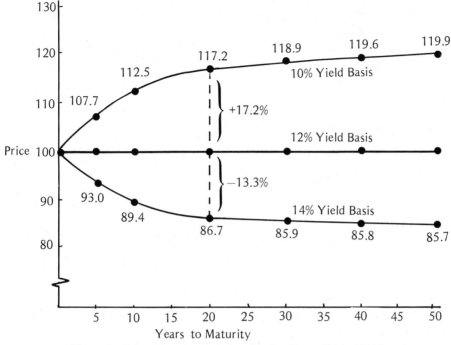

Figure 3   Price-Maturity Relationship for Noncallable 12% Bond

graph shows the price behavior of a 12 percent bond at various maturities when the market rate is 10, 12, and 14 percent. Note that the effect of a change in the interest rate from 12 percent to 14 percent is greater as the maturity increases. If the market rate increases from 12 percent to 14 percent the price of a five-year 12 percent bond would drop from 100 to 93.0, a decline of 7 percent. The same change in interest rates causes a 20-year bond to drop from 100 to 86.7, a decline of 13.3 percent. Similarly, when interest rates decrease, the prices of long-term bonds will increase more rapidly than the prices of short-term bonds. The greater price sensitivity of long-term bonds has important implications for banks and other financial institutions. To avoid the risk of selling bonds at a loss to raise funds to meet unexpected deposit outflows or loan demand, liquid assets must have short maturities.

Figure 3 demonstrates two other aspects of bond pricing. The flattening of the curves reflects the fact that the price sensitivity of long-term bonds diminishes as the maturity increases. There is little difference between the price risk of a twenty- or thirty-year bond. Figure 3 also shows that the effects of interest rates on bond prices are not symmetrical. An increase in the market rate from 12 to 14 percent on a twenty-year bond reduces the price by 13.3 percent; a decrease in the rate from 12 to 10 percent increases the price by 17.2 percent.

For the purpose of constructing Figure 3 and highlighting the relationship be- tween bond prices and interest rates, it was assumed that the bond was noncallable. That is, it could not be refunded by the issuer prior to maturity. However, many bonds are callable and this provision can alter the relationships characterized in Figure 3. Long-term U. S. Treasury and U. S. agency bonds are usually callable at par value five years prior to maturity. Most private sector bonds are callable ten years after the date of issuance at a premium equal to one year's interest. (After the first call date, the premium declines each year as the bond approaches maturity.)

The existence of a call provision means that the "maturity" is subject to change at the discretion of the issuer. If a call premium is involved, the lump-sum payment at maturity is also changed. The question arises—how are callable bonds priced? Are they priced on the basis of the yield-to-maturity, or the yield to the call date? To see the nature of the valuation process, refer to Figure 4.

The two curves shown in Figure 4 represent price-yield relationships for a 12 percent coupon bond with a 20-year maturity callable in 5 years at 112. The curve AEB shows the price-yield relationship at various yields assuming the bond runs to maturity. Curve CED represents the price-yield relationship assuming the bond is called in 5 years at 112. If the market yield is 15 percent, the price on a yield-to-maturity basis is 81.1. However, on a yield-to-call basis, the price is considerably higher at 95.5. If the market yield is 9 percent, the situation is reversed. The price on a yield-to-maturity basis is 127.6 which is considerably higher than the price of 119.6 based on the call assumption. The question arises—which method should be used? A simple bond pricing rule dictates the price to pay for callable bonds given a desired yield—*bonds should always be valued at the lowest price as determined by the yield to maturity or the yield to the first call date.*

Following this rule the valuation basis for the 12 percent callable bond is given by the curve CEB in Figure 4. To the right of point E, the yield-to-maturity is the pricing basis and to the left of this point the assumption is made that the bond will be called so the yield-to-first-call is the pricing basis. If interest rates decline significantly, the existence of a call provision has the effect of placing a lid on the price of the bond.

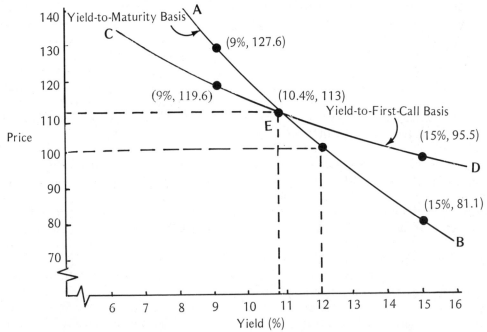

Figure 4   Price-Yield Relationship for 12% Coupon Bond with 20-Year Maturity and Callable in 5 Years at 112.

What if the pricing rule is violated? Suppose the bond in Figure 4 is incorrectly valued on the yield-to-maturity basis when the desired return is 9 percent. The price would be 127.6. If the bond is called at 112 after five years the realized yield is the value of r in the model

$$\$1{,}276 = \$60 \left[\frac{1 - \dfrac{1}{\left(1 + \dfrac{r}{2}\right)^{2(5)}}}{\dfrac{r}{2}} \right] + \frac{\$1{,}120}{\left(1 + \dfrac{r}{2}\right)^{2(5)}}$$

The value of r that satisfies this relationship is 7.336 rather than 9 percent. To ensure a yield of at least 9 percent, the price *must* be 119.6. Since the market rate of 9 percent is below the 12 percent coupon rate, it is more reasonable to assume that the bond will be called rather than allowed to mature. Conversely, if interest rates were 15 percent, the bond should be valued at 81.1 based on the assumption that it will mature. This is the most reasonable assumption since the market rate exceeds the coupon rate so it would not be advantageous for the issuer to call the bonds. If the bond is incorrectly valued at 95.5 based on the call assumption and the bond runs to maturity, the realized yield would be 12.62 percent rather than the required yield of 15 percent.

The nature of price-yield relationships for callable bonds is such that for a given market rate, the price of discounted bonds is *always* based on the yield-to-maturity. For premium bonds, the price must be calculated using *both* the yield-to-call basis and the yield-to-maturity basis. The market price is the *lower* of the two.

Consumer Loans

Consumer loans comprise an important class of loans made by banks and other depository institutions. These are loans made to individuals rather than businesses or governments and usually exclude mortgage loans. Some lending procedures are straightforward. A declining balance consumer loan is the same as the mortgage loan shown in Table 1 but with a much shorter term. Regular payments are made with the allocation of each payment depending on the loan balance at the beginning of the period.

Another method used for this type of loan is the so-called *add-on interest method.* Consider the following example.

> *Example.*   An individual borrows $6,000 from a bank to finance the purchase of an automobile. The quoted rate is "8% add-on" with 36 monthly payments. To find the monthly payment, the three-year finance charge is added to the original loan balance and the total is repaid in monthly installments. In this case, the finance charge is $6,000 X .08 X 3 = $1,440. The monthly payment is ($6,000 + 1,440)/36 = $206.67.
>
> A confusing aspect of this type of loan is that the actual rate charged is considerably higher than the stated add-on rate. This occurs because the approach does not reflect the fact that the loan balance decreases with each payment. Recognizing that the payments represent an annuity with a present value equal to the loan amount, the actual interest rate can be obtained by solving equation [5] for r. That is,

$$\$6{,}000 = \$206.67 \left[\frac{1 - \dfrac{1}{\left(1 + \dfrac{r}{12}\right)^{12(3)}}}{\dfrac{r}{12}} \right].$$

The value of r that satisfies the relationship is 14.55 percent.

This is also the APR that is revealed to the borrower. Although many consumer lenders are changing to the declining balance approach, the add-on method continues to be widely used.

Mortgage Lending

The mortgage lending process involves many aspects of financial mathematics. It is not uncommon for several "interest rates" to emerge in a mortgage loan transaction. Consider a 12 percent fixed-rate mortgage loan for $80,000 with monthly payments over 30 years. Using equation [7] the monthly payment R is

$$R = \frac{\$80{,}000}{\left[\dfrac{1 - \dfrac{1}{\left(1 + \dfrac{.12}{12}\right)^{12(30)}}}{\dfrac{.12}{12}} \right]}$$

$$= \frac{\$80{,}000}{97.2183}$$

$$= \$822.89.$$

The amortization schedule for this loan was shown earlier in Table 1.

The APR in this case is the same as the *contract rate* of 12 percent if no other finance charges are imposed. But if the lender charged a front-end fee of "3 points," the borrower would have to pay .03 × $80,000 = $2,400 up-front to get the loan. This reduces the lender's actual outlay to $80,000 − 2,400 = $77,600 and increases the return. Using equation [5] the APR is the value of r that satisfies the relationship

$$\$77{,}600 = \$822.89 \left[\frac{1 - \dfrac{1}{\left(1 + \dfrac{r}{12}\right)^{12(30)}}}{\dfrac{r}{12}} \right].$$

The APR is 12.41 percent which is 41 basis points higher than the contract rate of 12 percent. The APR calculation assumes the loan runs the full term. There is no prepayment.

Most mortgage loans are paid off prior to the full term of the loan. If no points are charged, such a prepayment does not affect the lender's yield. If a loan with points is prepaid, the lender's *realized yield* will exceed the APR. The sooner the prepayment, the higher the realized yield because the points will be earned over a shorter period.

Suppose that the lender wanted to calculate the return assuming that the balance on the above loan was paid off after five years or sixty payments. From equation [8], the OLB would be $78,130.57. Since the loan's cash flows are now made up of a 60-month annuity and a lump-sum payment of the OLB, the lender's realized return would be obtained by combining the present value annuity and lump-sum models, equations [5] and [2], and solving for r. The structure of this problem is the same as that of a bond bought at a discount. That is,

$$\$77{,}600 = \$822.89 \left[\frac{1 - \dfrac{1}{\left(1 + \dfrac{r}{12}\right)^{60}}}{\dfrac{r}{12}} \right] + \frac{\$78{,}130.57}{\left(1 + \dfrac{r}{12}\right)^{60}}.$$

The lender's *realized return* r is 12.82 percent. If the loan were prepaid after two years the OLB would be $79,382.57 and the *realized return* would be 13.73 percent. If a prepayment penalty were imposed, the return would be even higher.

To summarize, the following relationship holds when a loan with points is prepaid:

Contract Rate	<	APR	<	Realized Return
↓		↓		↓
Used to calculate payment		Assumes no Prepayment		Depends on timing of Prepayment

If no points are charged, the three rates are equal and prepayment has no effect on the yield.

In accordance with the Truth-in-Lending Act, lenders must reveal the total finance charges on a loan, assuming no prepayment. On a mortgage loan, the finance charges are the sum of points and interest. The interest is the difference between the total amount paid over the life of the loan and the face value of the note. In the mortgage loan example above, the finance charges are $2,400 + ($822.89 × 360) − $80,000 = $218,640.40. (This assumes no other finance charges such as mortgage insurance.)

Many other applications of financial mathematics stem from major developments and innovations in the mortgage market. The pooling and sale of mortgage loans require that they be valued by discounting the cash flows of each loan.

Some financial institutions issue bonds or commercial paper collateralized by mortgage loans. The collateral must be valued periodically and maintained at certain levels relative to the outstanding debt. The proliferation of different types of mortgage loans—graduated payment, adjustable rate, and growing equity mortgages—all require a thorough understanding of financial mathematics to formulate policy, evaluate loans, and properly administer portfolios.

Valuing Money Market Instruments

Money market instruments include Treasury bills, certain Federal agency issues, commercial paper, domestic negotiable certificates of deposit (CDs), Eurodollar certificates of deposit (ECDs), and bankers' acceptances (BAs).[13] Because of their generally high quality, short maturity (less than one year), and liquidity, these instruments are widely held as assets by financial institutions. CDs, commercial paper, and bankers' acceptances are also sources of funds for many financial institutions so they represent liabilities as well as assets. Money market funds, whose assets are comprised almost entirely of such instruments, play a key role in competing with banks and other financial institutions for savings. In response to this competition, banks, S&Ls, and credit unions are offering accounts based on or directly linked to money market instruments or their quoted rates.

Despite their importance and widespread use, the manner in which these instruments are priced is one of the most confusing aspects of the financial system. Valuation procedures differ depending on the type of instrument, the maturity, and the particular pricing convention used by practitioners. The rates quoted on different types of instruments are not comparable. In fact, quoted rates are often only rough approximations of the true rate.

In this section, the pricing methods used on Wall Street are examined. Then, alternative procedures are shown using the basic concepts developed earlier in the chapter. These procedures enable the cost or return on various instruments to be placed on a comparable basis known as the *bond-yield equivalent*.

Discounted When evaluating a money market instrument the first
Instruments step is to determine if the issue is *discounted* or *interest-bearing*. Treasury bills, most agency issues, commercial paper, BAs, and some CDs are sold at a discount from the face or par value. This discount, rather than a contractual rate, constitutes the investor's return or issuer's cost. The pricing model used by Wall Street for discounted instruments is

$$P = 1 - \frac{nd}{360} \tag{20}$$

where P = price per dollar of face value
       n = number of *days* to maturity
       d = quoted discount rate.

The model reflects the standard practice of accruing interest on the basis of a 360-day year for money market instruments. Using this model the dollar price of a 90-day Treasury bill quoted at 9.5 percent is

[13] These are the types of instruments of concern in this section. Other money market instruments are federal funds, repurchase agreements, the discount window, and U. S. Treasury and agency bonds that mature within one year.

$$P = 1 - \frac{90(.095)}{360}$$

$$= 1 - .02375$$

$$= .97625 \text{ or } 97.625 \text{ (\% of par)}.$$

The quoted discount rate of 9.5 percent in this example is an approximation of the true rate. To see why, equation [20] may be rearranged and solved for d. That is,

$$d = \left[\frac{1 - P}{1}\right] \frac{360}{n}.$$

Two problems emerge. The numerator of the term in the brackets is the interest earned on an investment of P per dollar of par value and not 1, the par value as indicated. Common sense suggests that the denominator should be P rather than 1. Another problem relates to the term 360/n. In order to annualize the return, it is assumed that the proceeds will be reinvested 360/n times per year at the same rate as that of the initial investment. Although the reinvestment rate is likely to be different, the "same-rate" reinvestment assumption is appropriate because of the uncertainty of future rates. However, reinvestment will occur 365/n times per year rather than 360/n times. A more accurate indication of the return is given by

$$r = \left[\frac{1 - P}{P}\right] \frac{365}{n}. \qquad [21]$$

where r is the Wall Street version of the *bond-yield equivalent.* From the preceding example,

$$r = \left[\frac{1 - .97625}{.97625}\right] \frac{365}{90}$$

$$= .0987 \text{ or } 9.87\%.$$

This is 37 basis points *higher* than the quoted discount rate. Another Wall Street version of the *bond-yield equivalent* model provides the same result. That is,

$$r = \frac{365d}{360 - nd}. \qquad [22]$$

From the example,

$$r = \frac{365(.095)}{360 - 90(.095)}$$

$$= .0987 \text{ or } 9.87\%.$$

It is important to note that the quoted discount rate *understates* the bond-yield equivalent. Equation [21] or [22] is used when the maturity is six months or less. The bond-yield equivalent models given by [21] and [22] remove the distortion caused by the improper use of par value in the discount model and also reflect the fact that bonds accrue interest on the basis of a 365-day year. The models do not reflect the semiannual compounding implicit in quoted bond yields. Since bond yields are the standard against which money market yields are evaluated, the bond-yield equivalents of money market instruments should be stated on a com-- parable semiannual compounding basis.

A more accurate measure of the bond-yield equivalent may be obtained by structuring the problem in the form of equation [1] developed earlier. That is,

$$FV_{mn} = PV\left(1 + \frac{r}{m}\right)^{mn}. \tag{1}$$

Recall that in this model n is stated in terms of years and not days. The preceding 90-day T-bill was quoted at 9.5 percent and priced at .97625. Assuming a par value of $10,000, and since m = 2, the problem may be formulated as

$$\$10,000 = \$9,762.50\left(1 + \frac{r}{2}\right)^{2(90/365)}$$

Using equation [3] the nominal rate r is

$$r = m[(FV_{mn}/PV)^{1/mn} - 1]$$

$$= 2[(\$10,000/9,762.50)^{1/[2(90)/365)]} - 1]$$

$$= 2[(1.024328)^{2.02778} - 1]$$

$$= .0999 \text{ or } 9.99\%.$$

This value of r is 12 basis points higher than the bond-yield equivalent obtained from [21] or [22]. The discrepancy becomes larger as the maturity decreases.[14]

When the maturity of a discounted instrument is greater than six months, a different procedure is used by practitioners to obtain the bond-yield equivalent. Suppose a nine-month or 270-day T-bill is quoted at 11 percent. Using the basic pricing model, equation [20], the price is .9175 or $9,175 for a $10,000 T-bill. The Wall Street version of the bond-yield equivalent is given by

$$FV = PV\left(1 + \frac{r}{2}\right)\left[1 + \frac{(n - 182.5)r}{365}\right] \tag{23}$$

where n is the number of days to maturity. From the example above, the formul- lation is

$$\$10,000 = \$9,175\left(1 + \frac{r}{2}\right)\left[1 + \frac{(270-182.5)r}{365}\right].$$

The value of r that satisfies this relationship may be found by trial and error or directly by the model,[15]

---

[14] For a discussion of the discrepancy, see: Bruce D. Fielitz, "Calculation of the Bond Equivalent Yield for Treasury Bills," *Journal of Portfolio Management*, Spring 1983, pp. 58-60.

[15] For a discussion of the derivation of this model, which is the solution to a quadratic equation of the form ax² + bx + c = 0, see: Marcia Stigum, *Money Market Calculations: Yields, Break-Evens, and Arbitrage*, Homewood, Ill.: Dow Jones-Irwin, 1981, pp. 34-35.

$$r = \frac{-\frac{n}{182.5} + 2\left[\left(\frac{n}{365}\right)^2 - \left(\frac{n}{182.5} - 1\right)\left(1 - \frac{1}{P}\right)\right]^{1/2}}{\frac{n}{182.5} - 1}. \qquad [24]$$

From the example,

$$r = \frac{-\frac{270}{182.5} + 2\left[\left(\frac{270}{365}\right)^2 - \left(\frac{270}{182.5} - 1\right)\left(1 - \frac{1}{.9175}\right)\right]^{1/2}}{\frac{270}{182.5} - 1}$$

$$= \frac{.057175}{.479452} = .11925 \text{ or } 11.925\%.$$

This bond-yield equivalent is well in excess of the quoted discount rate of 11 percent.

Again, present value concepts suggest that r may be derived using equation [3]. That is,

$$r = m[(FV_{mn}/PV)^{1/mn} - 1] \qquad [3]$$

with n stated in terms of years. Bearing in mind that $1/mn = 1/[2(270/365)] = .6759$, the formulation is

$$r = 2[(\$10,000/9,175)^{.6759} - 1]$$

$$= .11985 \text{ or } 11.985\%.$$

The difference between the values of r derived from [3] and [24] is only six basis points. Except at high discount rates (15 percent or higher), such differences are usually quite small. The difference stems from the fact that under the Wall Street method, equation [23], compounding occurs after six months and again after n − 182.5 days. If discounted money market yields are to be compared with bond yields, the bond-yield equivalent must be on the same basis as that of bonds, i.e., semiannual compounding. This is accomplished using equation [3].[16]

Interest-Bearing   Some federal agency money market issues and most cer-
Instruments   tificates of deposit issued by banks and other depository-
                          type institutions are interest-bearing. The instrument
specifies an annualized interest rate payable at maturity and based on a 360-day year. For example, a 90-day, $1 million CD issued at par value with a coupon rate of 10.5 percent would pay interest of $1,000,000 × .105 × (90/360) = $26,250 at maturity. On issues maturing in one year or less, there is no intervening interest payment. New CDs are issued at par value and the coupon rate is the same as the

---

[16] When the maturity of a discounted money market instrument is greater than 6 months, the discrepancy between the values of r from [3] and [22] depends on n as well as the level of rates. If n is such that the maturity is very close to six months or one year, the discrepancy ranges from zero to just a few basis points regardless of the level of rates. For a discussion of this point, see Fielitz, "Calculation of the Bond Equivalent Yield for Treasury Bills."

market rate. If the CD is subsequently sold in the secondary market, the market rate and the coupon rate are usually not equal so the price is not par. Also, some of the interest payable at maturity accrues to the seller. The amount of accrued interest is proportional to the time the instrument was held by the seller.

The pricing model used on Wall Street for secondary market trades of interest-bearing money market instruments is

$$\text{Price} = \text{Total Outlay} - \text{Accrued Interest}$$

$$P = \frac{cn_0 + 360}{yn + 360} - \frac{c(n_0 - n)}{360} \tag{25}$$

where P = price per dollar of par value
        c = coupon (or contractual) rate
     n_0 = original maturity in days
       y = quoted market rate
       n = remaining maturity in days.

Note that if a CD is bought on the original issue date, $n_0 = n$ so there is no accrued interest, and if $c = y$, $P = 1$.

Suppose an originally issued 90-day CD with a 10 percent contract rate now has sixty days remaining to maturity. If the CD is quoted at 11 percent, what is the price of the CD and what is its bond-yield equivalent? The price, total outlay, and accrued interest are obtained from equation [25]. That is,

$$P = \frac{.10(90) + 360}{.11(60) + 360} - \frac{.10(90\text{-}60)}{360}$$

$$= 1.00655 - .00833$$

$$= .99822 \text{ or } 99.822 \text{ (\% of par).}$$

The Wall Street version of the bond-yield equivalent is simply a conversion of the quoted CD rate to a 365-day basis. That is,

$$r = y(365/360). \tag{26}$$

In the example above, the bond-yield equivalent is

$$r = .11(365/360)$$
$$= .1115 \text{ or } 11.15\%.$$

If the remaining maturity of the CD is close to six months the adjustment given by [26] is reasonably accurate. Otherwise, the use of [26] distorts the bond-yield equivalent. Using equations [1] and [3] as in the earlier sections, a more accurate equivalent may be derived. In the preceding example, the future value is the par value of $1 plus interest of $1 \times .10 \times (90/360) = $.025 for a total of $1.025. The present value of the investment is the total outlay of $1.00655. (This is the first term on the right-hand side of equation [25].) The problem may now be formulated using [1]. That is,

$$\$1.025 = \$1.00655\left(1 + \frac{r}{2}\right)^{2(60/365)}$$

Now using [3] and bearing in mind that $1/mn = 1/[2(60/365)] = 3.0417$, the value of r is

$$r = 2[(\$1.025/1.00655)^{3.0417} - 1]$$
$$= .1136 \text{ or } 11.36\%.$$

This is 21 basis points higher than the Wall Street version of the bond-yield equivalent.

When the remaining maturity is greater than six months, the opposite effect occurs. The Wall Street version of r overstates the bond-yield equivalent.[17] Therefore, if the remaining maturity of an interest-bearing instrument in the secondary market is not six months, the bond-yield equivalent problem should be formulated using present value concepts discussed in this chapter.

CONCLUSION

The increasingly competitive environment resulting from deregulation requires that the managers of financial institutions have a thorough understanding of asset returns and the cost of funds. The task is complicated by the fact that many of the interest rates quoted in the financial markets lack uniformity and therefore are not directly comparable. In this chapter basic mathematical concepts that facilitate such comparisons were developed. To highlight the use of these concepts in the management of financial institutions, numerous examples and applications were presented. An understanding of these concepts and applications will enable management to cope with the day-to-day problems that arise. Equally important is the fact that such concepts underly the formulation of many policies and strategic operating decisions.

The models used in this chapter are listed and summarized in the Appendix for reference.

REFERENCES

Darst, David M., *The Complete Bond Book*, New York: McGraw-Hill Book Co., 1975.

Fielitz, Bruce D., "Calculation of the Bond Equivalent Yield for Treasury Bills," *Journal of Portfolio Management*, (Spring 1983), 58-60.

Glasgo, Philip W., William J. Landes, and A. Frank Thompson, "Bank Discount Coupon Equivalent, and Compound Yields," *Financial Management*, 11 (Autumn 1982), 80-84.

Spence, Bruce M., Jacob Y. Graudenz, and John J. Lynch, Jr., *Standard Securities Calculation Methods*, New York: Securities Industry Association, 1973.

---

[17] Consider a CD with a contract rate of 11 percent, an original maturity of 360 days, and a remaining maturity of 270 days. If the market yield is 10 percent, the Wall Street version of r is $.10(365/360) = 10.14$ percent. Using the present value procedure just discussed, the true bond-yield equivalent is 10.02 percent. The difference reflects the value of compounding associated with the bond.

Stigum, Marcia, *Money Market Calculations: Yields, Break-Evens, and Arbitrage*, Homewood, Illinois: Dow-Jones-Irwin, Inc., 1981.

Weston, J. Fred, and Eugene F. Brigham, *Essentials of Managerial Finance*, 6th ed., Hinsdale, Illinois: Dryden Press, 1982.

APPENDIX

Summary of Models

The following notation is used in the models presented in this chapter and summarized in this Appendix.

FV_{mn} = future value of a lump-sum amount invested for mn periods (may be written as FV)

PV_{mn} = present value of a lump-sum investment for mn periods (may be written as PV)

r = annual nominal or stated interest rate

m = number of times per year that compounding occurs

n = number of years; when dealing with models for money market instruments, n is the number of *days* to maturity

R = regular periodic annuity payment

FVA_{mn} = future value of an annuity for mn periods

PVA_{mn} = present value of an annuity for mn periods

B_k = outstanding loan balance (OLB) after the kth payment

B_o = original loan balance

D_o = current dividend on a common or preferred stock

k = discount rate on common or preferred stock dividends

g = growth rate of common stock dividends

i = effective annual interest rate

$r*$ = adjusted nominal rate (adjusted to reflect the actual/360 method, i.e., $r(365/360) = r*$)

P = price per dollar of par value for a money market instrument

d = discount rate on discounted money market instruments

c = contract rate on bond or interest-bearing money market instrument

n_o = original number of days to maturity for interest-bearing money market instrument

y = quoted market rate on an interest-bearing money market instrument.

1. Future value of a single payment:

$$FV_{mn} = PV \left(1 + \frac{r}{m}\right)^{mn}.$$

[1]

2. Present value of a single payment:

$$PV_{mn} = FV \left[\frac{1}{\left(1 + \frac{r}{m}\right)^{mn}}\right].$$

[2]

3. The value of r when future value and present value of a single payment is known:

$$r = m\left[\left(FV_{mn}/PV\right)^{1/mn} - 1\right].$$ [3]

4. Future value of an annuity:

$$FVA_{mn} = R\left[\frac{\left(1 + \frac{r}{m}\right)^{mn} - 1}{\frac{r}{m}}\right].$$ [4]

5. Present value of an annuity:

$$PVA_{mn} = R\left[\frac{1 - \frac{1}{\left(1 + \frac{r}{m}\right)^{mn}}}{\frac{r}{m}}\right].$$ [5]

6. Annuity payment given the future value:

$$R = \frac{FVA_{mn}}{\left[\frac{\left(1 + \frac{r}{m}\right)^{mn} - 1}{\frac{r}{m}}\right]}.$$ [6]

7. Annuity payment given the present value:

$$R = \frac{PVA_{mn}}{\left[\frac{1 - \frac{1}{\left(1 + \frac{r}{m}\right)^{mn}}}{\frac{r}{m}}\right]}.$$ [7]

8. Outstanding loan balance (OLB) after k^{th} payment:

$$B_k = B_0\left[\frac{\left(1 + \frac{r}{m}\right)^{mn} - \left(1 + \frac{r}{m}\right)^{k}}{\left(1 + \frac{r}{m}\right)^{mn} - 1}\right].$$ [8]

9. Present value of common stock dividends:

$$PV = \frac{D_0(1 + g)}{(1 + k)} + \frac{D_0(1 + g)^2}{(1 + k)^2} + \frac{D_0(1 + g)^3}{(1 + k)^3} + \ldots$$ [9]

10. Present value of common stock dividends (constant growth model):

$$PV = \frac{D_0(1 + g)}{k - g}.$$

[10]

11. Present value of common stock dividends (constant growth model):

$$PV = \frac{D_1}{k - g}.$$

[11]

12. Present value of preferred stock dividends:

$$PV = \frac{D_0}{k}.$$

[12]

13. Effective interest rate with discrete compounding and actual/365 method:

$$i = \left(1 + \frac{r}{m}\right)^m - 1.$$

[13]

14. Effective interest rate with continuous compounding and actual/365 method:

$$i = e^r - 1.$$

[14]

15. Future value of single payment with continuous compounding:

$$FV_n = PVe^{rn}.$$

[15]

16. Present value of single payment with continuous compounding:

$$PV = FV_n\left[\frac{1}{e^{rn}}\right]$$

or $$PV_n = FVe^{-rn}.$$

[16]

17. The value of r with continuous compounding and the present value and future value known:

$$r = \ln\left[(FV_n/PV)^{1/n}\right].$$

[17]

18. The adjusted nominal rate:

$$r* = r(365/360).$$

[18]

19. Effective rate given the adjusted nominal rate:

$$i = \left(1 + \frac{r*}{m}\right)^m - 1.$$

[19]

20. Price of a discounted money market instrument:

$$P = 1 - \frac{nd}{360} .$$ [20]

21. The Wall Street version of the bond-yield-equivalent for discounted money market instruments with a maturity of *six months or less:*

$$r = \left[\frac{1 - P}{P}\right]\frac{365}{n} .$$ [21]

22. The Wall Street version of the bond-yield equivalent for discounted money market instruments with a maturity of *six months or less:*

$$r = \frac{365d}{360 - nd} .$$ [22]

23. The Wall Street version of the bond-yield equivalent for discounted money market instruments with a maturity *greater than six months:*

$$FV = PV(1 + \frac{r}{2})\left[1 + \frac{(n - 182.5)r}{365}\right].$$ [23]

24. The bond-yield equivalent solution to [23]:

$$r = \frac{-\frac{n}{182.5} + 2\left[\left(\frac{n}{365}\right)^2 - \left(\frac{n}{182.5} - 1\right)\left(1 - \frac{1}{P}\right)\right]^{1/2}}{\frac{n}{182.5} - 1} .$$ [24]

25. The price per dollar of par value of an interest-bearing originally issued money market instrument:

$$\text{Price} = \text{Total Outlay} - \text{Accrued Interest}$$

$$P = \frac{cn_o + 360}{yn + 360} - \frac{c(n_o - n)}{360} .$$ [25]

26. The Wall Street version of the bond-yield equivalent for interest-bearing money market instruments:

$$r = y(365/360).$$ [26]

PART II

ASSET MANAGEMENT

A. COMMERCIAL LENDING

4

Commercial Lending

One of the most important functions of the commercial banking industry is lending to commercial and industrial (C&I) enterprises. Historically, this class of loans, often referred to as *commercial loans,* has distinguished commercial banks from other depository institutions such as savings and loan associations, mutual savings banks, and credit unions. Although recent legislation has empowered savings and loans and mutual savings banks to enter the commercial lending field, their role to date has been limited. Although it is likely that these institutions will increase their commercial loan activity, for the present, major commercial lenders are commercial banks, both domestic and foreign.

In this chapter, types of commercial loans and loan-related services are discussed along with the credit decision and loan pricing. This is followed by an overview of commercial lending regulations. The chapter concludes with a section on the elements of a commercial loan policy statement.

TYPES OF COMMERCIAL LOANS AND LOAN-RELATED SERVICES

One of the most fascinating aspects of commercial banking is the broad array of financial arrangements that are made between banks, borrowers, and "interested parties." Some of these financial arrangements are traditional in the sense that they represent standard banking practices. In recent years, banks have been expanding their scope of operations to include certain types of loan-related services. Some of these services are innovative financing techniques and represent departures from traditional banking practices.

Traditional Commercial Loans

The financial and contractual characteristics of traditional commercial loans have important managerial implications. It is in this context that the various types of traditional commercial loans are examined.

Open Line of Credit   One of the basic types of commercial loans is the *open line of credit.* Under an open line, the bank agrees to lend up to a certain amount as needed during a specified period, usually one year. Since borrowings under such an arrangement usually are unsecured, only the most creditworthy customers are given open lines of credit.

The promissory notes underlying open lines may be payable on demand by the bank or extend for short periods usually not exceeding ninety days. The interest rate usually "floats." That is, the rate is tied to the bank's prime lending rate. The interest rate may be fixed for the period of the note rather than floating. But because the period to maturity is so short, these fixed-rate arrangements are sensitive to changes in market rates. Thus, open lines are collectively considered *interest sensitive* even though some loans may be written on a fixed-rate basis.

The borrower may be given a choice between a flat rate (tied to prime or fixed) or a lower rate coupled with compensating balance requirements. For example, an open line, compensating balance requirement quoted on a "10 plus 5" basis means that the borrower will keep demand deposit balances equal to 10 percent of the entire line amount plus 5 percent of any borrowings or "takedowns" under the line. Thus, a takedown of $300,000 under an open line of $1 million would require compensating balances of $115,000 in addition to the interest on the borrowed funds. Another approach is to couple the interest rate with a compensating balance requirement tied only to the line amount.

Open lines of credit may be *informal* or *formal* arrangements. This distinction is important. Under an informal line, the borrower pays no direct fees and the bank has the legal right to refuse loan requests made under the line. Such a refusal may be brought about by a dramatic deterioration in the creditworthiness of the borrower or an extreme shortage of lendable funds resulting from tight credit conditions. Meeting informal line commitments is considered a strong moral obligation of the bank. Failure to do so would severely impair the bank's credibility in financial circles.

A *formal* open line of credit arises when the borrower pays a *commitment* or *availability fee* typically ranging from ¼ to ¾ of one percent (annualized) of the unused line amount. An alternative is to charge a commitment fee based on the entire line regardless of usage. When such a fee is imposed, the arrangement, in addition to being a "moral obligation" of the bank, has the basic components of a contract even in the absence of a written document. Failure to honor loan requests made under a formal line could precipitate a lawsuit and result in substantial damage claims against the bank.[1] From the bank's standpoint, formal agree-

---

[1] The *formal* open line of credit should not be confused with a revolving credit which is discussed later. Also, there is little agreement among bankers as to the contractual status of an open line of credit when a commitment fee is charged. Some bankers argue that they have the legal right to deny a loan request even if a

ments are desirable since a commitment fee is earned for doing something that is expected anyway—honoring loan requests under a line of credit. From the borrower's standpoint, an informal line arrangement may be satisfactory if the amount of funds involved is relatively small or the availablility of bank funds is not a major factor in the borrower's financial planning. If the amount of funds needed is sizable and alternative sources are not available, a borrower may prefer a more formal arrangement.

The amount of credit extended through open lines and the related usage must be monitored carefully by bank management because economic conditions may force many borrowers to use their lines simultaneously. The same economic conditions may make it difficult for banks to acquire new lendable funds or even retain existing funds. During normal credit conditions, line of credit takedowns usually range between 10 and 20 percent of the total amount outstanding. During tight credit conditions, takedowns often exceed 40 percent of the total amount outstanding. This problem can be particularly acute for regional banks whose borrowers often are tied to a particular line of business or industry. *Thus, the lack of a diversified commercial loan base limits the ability of a bank to extend open lines of credit.*

Working Capital Loans   Most firms have a production cycle that requires the acquisition and processing of raw material. Upon completion of the production cycle, the finished goods are converted to accounts receivable and ultimately to cash. This cycle requires that the firm expand its current assets. The expansion may be financed through *working capital loans.* When the entire production cycle is completed, the loans are repaid when current assets such as finished goods are converted to cash. The borrower's need for working capital depends on such factors as the length and complexity of the production cycle, credit terms, and seasonal factors.

Working capital loans are written on a short-term basis and in some cases they are payable on demand by the bank. Growth-oriented borrowers often attempt to obtain continuous working capital financing by constantly seeking a renewal of short-term loans. From a bank's standpoint, this may have the effect of extending intermediate- rather than short-term credit. This problem may be avoided by imposing a "clean-up" provision. For example, the borrower might be required to be out of debt to the bank for thirty consecutive days within a calendar year.

Working capital loans are short-term. Funds are constantly rolled over at rates of interest that are related to the bank's current cost of funds. Thus, changes in the level of interest rates pose no special problems with respect to these loans.

Transaction Loans   As its name implies, a *transaction loan* is one which is made to finance a specific and usually non-recurring transaction. A manufacturer may have the opportunity to obtain a piece of equipment or a large quantity of raw material at an unusually favorable or "distressed"

fee is paid while other bankers feel they are contractually obligated to meet loan requests. In light of this lack of agreement among practitioners, the distinction between *formal* and *informal* lines of credit is made in this chapter.

price. Usually such loans are secured, mature within one year, and have a fixed interest rate. Depending on the circumstances, a loan renewal or a conversion to a different type of loan is often appropriate.

Revolving Credit   A *revolving credit arrangement* is somewhat similar to an open line of credit. Like the open line, the bank agrees to make funds available up to a certain amount and for a specified period. The funds may be borrowed and repaid at any time at the discretion of the borrower. However, a revolving credit is a formal, contractual agreement that legally obligates the bank to provide funds on demand. The borrower pays a commitment fee typically ranging from ½ to ¾ of one percent of either the unused amount or the entire commitment.

Since funds must be provided on demand by the borrower, management must monitor the usage of revolving credits just as they should with open lines. Moreover, this arrangement usually involves a large amount of funds and represents an important part of a borrower's overall financial planning. As a result, the average usage of "revolvers" tends to be much higher than the usage of open lines. Usage averaging 50 to 75 percent of a total commitment is common. The usage could change dramatically depending upon economic conditions and create a financial strain on the bank.

Revolving credits usually extend over a three- to five-year period. They represent a form of intermediate- or longer-term credit. Because the funds may be taken down and repaid at the borrower's option, *revolving credits should always be made on a floating-rate basis.* To see why, assume a revolving credit is made at a fixed rate of 12 percent. If market interest rates increase to 15 percent during a period when the borrower has no need for credit, the funds will be taken down anyway and reinvested in money market instruments. Should market rates fall to 10 percent, the funds would be repaid. Thus, on a fixed-rate basis, the usage of a revolving credit often could be detrimental to the bank. (This problem does not arise with open lines written on a fixed-rate basis because of the short maturity of the underlying promissory notes.) Because the revolving credit is a longer-term credit facility, a floating rate is also essential to minimize the risk associated with changes in the bank's cost of funds brought about by rising interest rates.

Revolving credit financing is used when there is uncertainty with respect to one or more of the following: (1) the timing of the borrower's need for funds; (2) the amount of funds needed; (3) the method repayment; or (4) the future availability of credit. The following example demonstrates the kind of situation that calls for a revolving credit facility.

> *Example.*   A firm is embarking on an expansion program that involves the construction of several new plants. All construction is expected to be completed within three years. As the plants are being built, construction payouts will be required. The exact timing and dollar amounts of these payouts are unknown. As each plant is completed, outlays will be required for equipment and working capital. Management is concerned about the availability of credit to meet these substantial outlays. When the entire expansion program is completed and the plants are operational, the firm intends to sell an issue of long-term debt or equity on a public or private placement basis. The proceeds will be used to repay the borrowings under the revolving credit

arrangement. If market conditions are such that external financing is not possible, the firm has the option to convert the revolving credit to a longer-term, amortizing bank loan.

As this example demonstrates, the revolving credit arrangement is an ideal device for temporary or so-called "bridge financing" as fixed assets are acquired. The revolving credit may be used for a variety of other purposes such as financing acquisitions and takeovers, backing up commercial paper, or meeting the "permanent" portion of working capital needs. The borrower must be given considerable latitude with respect to the method of loan repayment. Although the sale of securities is one method of obtaining funds for repayment, many borrowers do not have access to the capital markets. For this reason, revolving credits often are convertible at the borrower's option into another type of arrangement known as a *term loan.*

Term Loans   A widely used form of intermediate- or longer-term bank credit is the *term loan.* These loans usually extend for periods of three to six years although loans with terms up to eight years are not uncommon. In addition to the longer term, a distinguishing aspect of term loans is that the borrowings, which are taken down on a lump-sum basis, are repaid regularly according to an installment schedule. Several variations of the term loan are possible. In its simplest form, the loan may be on a fixed-rate basis and completely amortized just like a conventional mortgage loan. For example, assume a firm requests a loan of $1 million under a four-year term loan agreement. If the interest rate is fixed at 14 percent and payments are made on a quarterly basis, the amount of each payment, R, may be obtained from the annuity model

$$R = \frac{PVA_{mn}}{\left[\dfrac{1 - \dfrac{1}{\left(1 + \dfrac{r}{m}\right)^{mn}}}{\dfrac{r}{m}}\right]} \qquad [1]$$

where PVA_{mn} is the present value or amount of the loan, m is the number of payments per year, n is the number of years and r is the interest rate. Substituting the values of PVA_{mn}, r, m, and n into [1] results in a quarterly payment R of

$$R = \frac{\$1,000,000}{\left[\dfrac{1 - \dfrac{1}{\left(1 + \dfrac{.14}{4}\right)^{4(4)}}}{\dfrac{.14}{4}}\right]}$$

$$R = \frac{\$1,000,000}{12.094117}$$

$$R = \$82,684.83.$$

If the loan in this example is consistent with bank policy and the quarterly payments do not jeopardize the borrower's financial condition, the term loan may be
made in this way. If the lending officer's analysis of the firm's earning power and
cash flow indicates that the borrower cannot carry such a large quarterly payment,
the loan may have to be restructured. One way to accomplish this would be to
lengthen the amortization period to eight or ten years and reduce the quarterly
payment. However, many banks are reluctant to make such extended fixed-rate
commitments. To overcome this problem and yet satisfy the borrower's needs,
the loan amortization may be linked with a *balloon payment.* The following example demonstrates the mechanics of a fixed-rate amortizing term loan with a
balloon payment.

> *Example.*   A loan officer has analyzed the loan request described above. On
> the basis of the borrower's current cash flow and earning power, the lending officer
> concludes that the quarterly payments on the term loan should not exceed $55,000
> to $60,000. Thus, a fully amortizing four-year loan with payments of $82,684.83 is
> not feasible. Substituting values of n into [1] the loan officer finds that a seven-
> year amortization period results in a more manageable quarterly payment of
> $56,602.65. But the bank's lending policy specifies a maximum term of six years
> on fixed-rate term loans. The lending officer then proposes a term loan with pay-
> ments based on a seven-year amortization schedule coupled with a *balloon payment*
> of the outstanding loan balance (OLB) after six years. The amount of the balloon
> payment is the present value of the remaining four quarterly payments of $56,602.65
> discounted at the loan rate of 14 percent. Since these payments represent an an-
> nuity, the balloon payment may be obtained by rearranging equation [1] to solve
> for the present value of the four remaining quarterly payments. That is,

$$PVA_{mn} = R \left[\frac{1 - \dfrac{1}{\left(1 + \dfrac{r}{m}\right)^{mn}}}{\dfrac{r}{m}} \right]$$

$$PVA_{mn} = \$56,602.65 \left[\frac{1 - \dfrac{1}{\left(1 + \dfrac{.14}{4}\right)^{4(1)}}}{\dfrac{.14}{4}} \right]$$

$$PVA_{mn} = \$56,602.65 \ (3.673079)$$

$$PVA_{mn} = \$207,906.01.$$

> The balloon payment also may be obtained by constructing an amortization table.

Under ordinary circumstances, the amount of the balloon should not exceed 15
to 20 percent of the original loan amount. A large balloon payment may require a
loan extension or some other arrangement for repaying the outstanding balance.

In this example, the balloon payment is at the upper end of the allowable range. If the balloon payment is considered excessive, it may be necessary to reduce the loan amount or increase the quarterly payment so the balloon payment will be smaller. Another alternative is to impose a *recapture clause* which requires the borrower to make principal repayments if earnings or cash flow exceed a certain amount.

Term loans may also be repaid on the basis of *level principal repayments* with interest paid on the declining balance. Under this method, the periodic payments are high in the early years of the loan and decrease over time. Recall that in the example given earlier, a $1 million, seven-year amortizing term loan with quarterly payments and an interest rate of 14 percent would require a constant payment of $56,602.65. However, with 28 level principal payments, the first quarterly payment would be $1,000,000/28 = $35,714.28 in principal plus interest of $1,000,000 X (.14/4) = $35,000 for a total of $70,714.28. Although this is considerably higher than the level payments made under an amortizing loan, the total payments decrease over time because of the fast loan repayment. This faster repayment also means that the average life of the level principal loan is shorter than that of the amortizing loan. A comparison of the two approaches is shown in Table 1 for a term loan of $100,000 for four years at 14 percent. Note that one-half the amortizing loan is repaid after 10 quarters while the level principal method repays one-half the loan in eight quarters. Although this faster repayment may be desirable from the bank's standpoint, the higher initial payments are likely to cause a strain on many borrowers.

If necessary, so-called *blind spots* can be arranged with term loans. Because they allow the postponement of loan payments during certain periods of the year, *blind spots* accommodate seasonal businesses. Since term loans usually involve a lump-sum takedown, no commitment fees are paid. Such fees should be imposed if the takedown is delayed several months or more, especially if it is a fixed-rate loan.

A special type of term loan is the so-called *bullet loan*. With this type of loan, only the interest is paid regularly and the entire principal is repaid at maturity in the form of one (big) balloon payment. The *bullet loan* is similar to a bond without a sinking fund. Because of the lack of any provision for loan repayment and the long average life, this type of term loan should be made only under very special circumstances.

An important aspect of term loans is that the loan repayment is based on estimated future earnings and cash flows rather than the near-term conversion of current assets. Since these estimates are uncertain and the borrower's creditworthiness may change over time, collateral may be required as a *secondary source of repayment*. Typically, term loans are used to acquire fixed assets or the permanent portion of working capital. Such assets may be pledged to secure the loan.

Term loans pose a dilemma for bankers because of their longer term. If they are written on a fixed-rate basis as in the example above, the bank may be assuming interest rate risk. If interest rates increase, the bank's cost of funds will tend to increase but the return on the loan remains constant. The result is reduced profitability. This problem can be overcome by writing such loans on a floating-

Table 1   Term Loan Repayment Schedules
$100,000, 4-Year Term, 14 Percent Rate, Quarterly Payments

Amortization Basis

Period	Outstanding Balance	Total Payment	Amount of Payment to: Interest	Principal	Loan Balance
1	$100,000.00	$8,268.48	$3,500.00[a]	$4,768.48[b]	$95,231.52[c]
2	95,231.52	8,268.48	3,333.10	4,935.38	90,296.14
3	90,296.14	8,268.48	3,160.36	5,108.12	85,188.02
4	85,188.02	8,268.48	2,981.58	5,286.90	79,901.12
5	79,901.12	8,268.48	2,796.54	5,471.94	74,429.17
6	74,429.17	8,268.48	2,605.02	5,663.46	68,765.71
7	68,765.71	8,268.48	2,406.80	5,861.68	62,904.03
8	62,904.03	8,268.48	2,201.64	6,066.84	56,837.18
9	56,837.18	8,268.48	1,989.30	6,279.18	50,558.00
10	50,558.00	8,268.48	1,769.53	6,498.95	44,059.05
11	44,059.05	8,268.48	1,542.07	6,726.42	37,332.63
12	37,332.63	8,268.48	1,306.64	6,961.84	30,370.79
13	30,370.79	8,268.48	1,062.98	7,205.51	23,165.29
14	23,165.29	8,268.48	810.79	7,457.70	15,707.59
15	15,707.59	8,268.48	549.77	7,718.72	7,988.87
16	7,988.87	8,268.48	279.61	7,988.87	0.00

[a]$100,000.00 \times (.14/4) = \$3,500.00$
[b]$\$8,268.48 - \$3,500.00 = \$4,768.48.$
[c]$\$100,000.00 - \$4,768.48 = \$95,231.52.$
[d]$\$100,000.00/16 = \$6,250.00.$
[e]$\$100,000.00 \times (.14/4) = \$3,500.00.$
[f]$\$100,000.00 - \$6,250.00 = \$93,750.00.$

rate basis. However, most borrowers prefer fixed-rate loans because such loans reduce uncertainty in their own cost structure. Many firms such as leasing and finance companies, require fixed-rate term loans and a bank's failure to accommodate these borrowers would result in the loss of business. Another alternative is to fund the loan with a long-term fixed-rate deposit. However, a substantial volume of such deposits is difficult for most banks to obtain.

A bank that is *relationship-oriented* will attempt to meet its borrowers' needs and develop risk management strategies that enable it to absorb or shift the interest rate risk associated with longer-term fixed-rate loans. A floating-rate loan may be written subject to a "cap" which limits rate increases. This shares a portion of the risk. Additional risk reduction may be achieved through the use of longer-term sources of funds or interest rate futures. When fixed-rate loans are written, prepayment penalties are an important part of the agreement. In the absence of such penalties, the bank would have little control over the actual term of the loan. Prepayments would occur during periods of falling interest rates and this would reduce the bank's earnings.

Table 2 summarizes the main characteristics of the loans discussed in this section.

Loan-Related Services

A direct bank loan is not always the best way to accommodate borrowers. As a result, many banks provide loan-related services such as leasing, arranging private

Table 1

Continued

	Level Principal Repayment			
Outstanding Balance	Principal Payment	Interest	Total Payment	Loan Balance
$100,000.00	$6,250.00[d]	$3,500.00[e]	$9,750.00	$93,750.00[f]
93,750.00	6,250.00	3,281.25	9,531.25	87,500.00
87,500.00	6,250.00	3,062.50	9,312.50	81,250.00
81,250.00	6,250.00	2,843.75	9,093.75	75,000.00
75,000.00	6,250.00	2,625.00	8,875.00	68,750.00
68,750.00	6,250.00	2,406.25	8,656.25	62,500.00
62,500.00	6,250.00	2,187.50	8,437.50	56,250.00
56,250.00	6,250.00	1,968.75	8,218.75	50,000.00
50,000.00	6,250.00	1,750.00	8,000.00	43,750.00
43,750.00	6,250.00	1,531.25	7,781.25	37,500.00
37,500.00	6,250.00	1,312.50	7,562.50	31,250.00
31,250.00	6,250.00	1,093.75	7,343.75	25,000.00
25,000.00	6,250.00	875.00	7,125.00	18,750.00
18,750.00	6,250.00	656.25	6,906.25	12,500.00
12,500.00	6,250.00	437.50	6,687.50	6,250.00
6,250.00	6,250.00	218.75	6,468.75	0.00

Table 2   Characteristics of Traditional Bank Loans[a]

Type of Loan	Interest Rate	Collateral[b]	Usual Term	Commitment Fee	Method of Loan Repayment
Open Line of Credit	Floating	None	1 year	1. Informal—no fee 2. Formal—¼ to ¾ of 1% of unused line or line amount	Conversion of current assets to cash
Working Capital Loan	Floating	A/R and/or inventory	6 mo. to 1 yr.	N/A	Conversion of current assets to cash
Transaction Loan	Fixed	A/R, Inventory, or equipment	3 mo. to 1 yr.	N/A	Conversion of current assets to cash
Revolving Credit	Floating	None	3 to 5 yrs.	¼ to ¾ of 1% of unused line or line amount	External financing or conversion to term loan
Term Loan	Floating, fixed, or floating w/ a cap	Fixed assets, Perm. work. cap.	3 to 6 yrs.	N/A[c]	Earnings and cash flow; amort., or level principal payments

[a]The characteristics shown are general and thus may vary among banks or borrowers.

[b]In the case of "workouts" and financially weak borrowers, substantial collateral may be required for any of the loans shown. This is often referred to as *asset-based lending*.

[c]A commitment fee may be imposed in the event of a delayed takedown of a term loan.

placements and project loans, and letter of credit financing. Indirect financing may be arranged through a loan participation. That is, a bank makes a loan and then sells it to another bank.

Leasing　　　　　　　　　　　An important adjunct to the commercial lending operation of many banks is the leasing function. Leasing may be conducted directly by banks or indirectly through a leasing subsidiary. Under a lease arrangement the *lessee* acquires the use of an asset which is owned by another firm known as the *lessor*. When acting as a lessor banks are restricted to *financial leases*. Such leases are also referred to as *full payout leases*. A financial lease is a noncancelable agreement that contractually enables the bank (as lessor) to recover all costs during the term of the *initial* lease. In contrast, an *operating lease* is cancelable, short-term, and does not enable the lessor to recover all costs during the initial lease. The asset must be re-leased, possibly several times in order to enable the lessor to recover its costs. Because of the uncertainty with respect to future leases and the recovery of all costs, banks are prohibited from writing *operating leases.*[2] Thus, the focus here is on *financial leases.*

The recovery of costs and any lease profits are generated by a combination of: (1) regular lease payments; (2) tax benefits to the lessor; and (3) the estimated residual value of the asset. The key to most leases is the differential tax effect for the lessor relative to the lessee. For example, in recent years many airlines needed new jet aircraft even though their earnings were insufficient to benefit from the investment tax credit or absorb the high depreciation and interest charges that result from direct ownership. Profitable banks (or leasing subsidiaries) can use the investment credit and shelter earnings by deducting interest charges and using accelerated depreciation. Since these tax benefits and the estimated residual value of the asset are factored into the lessor bank's rate of return, the airline's lease payments and overall financing costs are lower than if the planes were purchased outright. The user is usually given an option to purchase the asset at fair market value when the lease expires.

Aside from the tax implications and the bank's lack of legal standing as a creditor, the financial lease with an option to purchase is functionally equivalent to a term loan with a balloon payment. Leases are generally riskier than term loans because they tend to have longer payout periods than term loans and are written on a fixed-return basis. This risk may be offset by higher after-tax returns. Furthermore, during inflationary periods the residual value of leased assets often exceeds the original estimate so the realized return may be higher than expected.

A variation of the *financial lease* is the so-called *leveraged lease.* Under this arrangement, the bank as lessor-owner puts up about 20 percent of the purchase price of the asset as equity and borrows the remaining 80 percent from a third party such as an insurance company. Because the bank's equity position is highly leveraged, the realized return on the equity investment may be greatly magnified if the overall return on the lease exceeds the cost of the borrowed funds. These

---

[2] Bank-related *operating leases* may be written by a bank's leasing subsidiary or an affiliate of a bank's parent holding company.

transactions are legally complex and have a high acquisition cost. As a result, the minimum leveraged lease transaction is usually about $500,000.[3]

Private Placements   Many borrowers need long-term, fixed-rate loans. Because of their preference for shorter-terms and floating-rate loans, banks are unable to accommodate such borrowers, at least directly. However, some large banks actively assist borrowers by arranging private placements of debt securities.

> ***Example.***   In mid-1978, Citibank arranged the private placement of a $400 million bond offering of Middle South Utilities, Incorporated. The bonds had a maturity of 12 years, a fixed interest rate, and were placed with twelve life insurance companies. Citibank's fee for arranging this transaction was 1/5 of 1 percent, or $800,000. In contrast, the usual fee charged by Wall Street investment bankers is 1/2 of 1 percent.

As this example demonstrates, the terms desired by many borrowers often are more suitable for non-bank financial institutions. Rather than make loans on unsuitable terms to accommodate the client, the bank sells its financial expertise by arranging the appropriate financing.

Project Loans   One of the most risky, complex, and highest yielding types of bank-related financial transactions is the *project loan.* This arrangement is used to finance the construction of new capital-intensive projects with costs and risks beyond the financial or risk-bearing capacity of a single owner or creditor. The types of facilities financed by project loans include pipelines, harbors, refineries, mining facilities, and processing plants for natural resources. The cost of such projects is often in the multi-billion dollar category. Several users, or *sponsors,* contribute equity capital to form a new entity for the purpose of owning and operating the facility. The equity base is then heavily leveraged via *project loans* such that debt makes up 80 to 90 percent of the operating firm's total capital. The financial support for this debt stems from the contractual arrangements with the sponsor-owners. For example, in oil pipeline projects a "throughput and deficiency agreement" requires each of the sponsoring oil producers to transport a minimum amount of oil through the line for which they are charged a tariff sufficient to cover all costs and service the debt. The tariff is imposed even if the pipeline is not operating or the individual producer transports no oil.

From the *lender's* standpoint the risks of such financing may be substantial:

- *Credit Risk.* The credit risk of most commercial loans depends on a cross section of a firm's earning assets. The credit risk of a project loan hinges on the success of a *single* project. With no financial history associated with a new project, the analysis of credit risk is solely on the basis of long-range financial and economic forecasts which are subject to a high degree of uncertainty.

---

[3] For a discussion of leveraged leasing, see: James C. Van Horne, *Financial Management and Policy,* 5th ed., Englewood Cliffs, N. J.: Prentice-Hall, 1980, Chapter 19.

- *Completion Delays.* From the inception of a project to its completion, two to eight years can elapse depending on the scope of the project. During this period, bureaucratic red tape, environmental issues, or construction problems can result in a delayed completion date. This disrupts the financial timetable and results in cost overruns. At the extreme, the project may be abandoned!
- *Political Risk.* Many projects are located in foreign countries and thus are subject to adverse government action. Such action could include expropriation (i.e., a government takeover), increased taxes, or demands for higher royalties. To minimize this risk, foreign governments usually are one of the project's sponsors.
- *Interest Rate Risk.* Since the construction of these large projects takes several years, the earliest maturity loans are intermediate-term, i.e., three to five years. This, coupled with fixed interest rates, means that project loans are subject to interest rate risk.

In view of these sizable risks, the obvious question arises—what is the role of commercial banks in this type of financing? Before answering this question it is important to understand that much of the risk of a project loan can be shifted from the lenders. A project loan can be *recourse financing.* Most of the project's risk is shifted to its sponsors when they guarantee the payment of principal and interest. Since the guarantee affects their credit rating, sponsors prefer the *guarantee of completion* method. Under this approach, the sponsors agree to complete the project by providing additional equity capital if necessary. After the project is completed, lenders must rely on the success of the project. Finally, *non-recourse financing* has no backing or sponsor guarantees and thus is the riskiest type of loan. It is not used unless there is a sizable equity base.

Commercial banks play an important role in project loans. A number of large banks have the financial and engineering expertise necessary to evaluate and structure the loans and arrange for participation by insurance companies, pension funds, and other smaller banks. For this service, the lead bank is paid a fee of anywhere from 1 to 2 percent of the loan amount and is usually designated as the depository for the project. Participating banks, including the lead bank, confine their loans to the shortest maturities in order to minimize interest rate risk. The returns on such loans are, not surprisingly, among the highest in the commercial loan category.

Letter of Credit Financing

There are two types of financing based on the *letter of credit* (LOC). The *commercial letter of credit* underlies many transactions where the buyer and seller are unknown to each other. A bank may issue a letter of credit on behalf of a customer seeking to acquire equipment or merchandise. Upon receipt of the letter of credit and complying with its terms, the seller relies on the bank for payment. In effect, the bank substitutes its own reputation and creditworthiness for that of the buyer. When payment is made by the bank—and it is expected to be made—a loan is created. This type of arrangement is the basis of a banker's acceptance. Once limited to international transactions, the *commercial letter of credit* is becoming widely used to finance domestic sales.

The second type of LOC financing is the *standby letter of credit.* Under this arrangement, the issuing bank guarantees payment to a third party in the event the client is unable to meet its financial obligations or otherwise perform as expected. Unlike the commercial letter of credit, a payment by the bank is *not* expected to be made. Technically, banks are prohibited by law from guaranteeing the obligations of others. However, court rulings have held that the *standby letter of credit* is not a guarantee because the borrower is obligated to repay the bank if any payments are made. Despite the fine legal distinction, this type of LOC functions in the same manner as a guarantee.

The standby LOC is used to back commercial paper. In the event of nonpayment, the bank pays off the paper and the amount becomes a loan. Recently, banks have extended this type of financing to other classes of securities.

> *Example.*   In 1982, the Industrial Development Authority of Maricopa County Arizona authorized a 10-year, $75.3 million bond issue to finance low- to moderate-income housing. The Bank of America issued an irrevocable standby letter of credit promising to pay off the bonds in the event of default. The combined backing of the project's revenues and the B of A resulted in a triple-A rating for the bonds. For its role in the transaction, the B of A received an initial fee of .625 percent of the offering or $470,625, and an annual fee exceeding $400,000 each year through 1992 when the bonds mature. Such a transaction is shown as a "potential" liability in a footnote to the bank's financial statement.

The *standby letter of credit* has been used by large banks to guarantee performance of American firms entering contracts with foreign governments. For example, a foreign government may engage an American contractor to construct a dam, public utility system, or military installations. As a condition of the agreement, the contractor may be required to put up 10 percent of the contract amount to guarantee satisfactory completion of the project. This is often accomplished by the contractor obtaining a letter of credit from its bank callable on demand by the project's owner. If the contractor fails to comply with the terms of the agreement, the project owner presents the letter of credit to the bank and demands payment. Any payments made become loans to the contractor. For this service, the issuing bank collects a fee ranging from 1/8 of 1 percent to 1 percent of the contract amount depending on the risks involved. In foreign transactions, these risks can be substantial as the following example demonstrates.

> *Example.*   The Hughes Aircraft Company contracted with the government of Iran, then ruled by the Shah of Iran, to construct electronic warning systems. When the Shah was overthrown in 1979 Hughes Aircraft was unable to complete the project because of continuing civil strife. The new government presented the related *standby letter of credit* to the Bank of America as issuer and demanded payment of $1.5 million for the "non-performance" of Hughes Aircraft. B of A informed Hughes Aircraft that it would pay the claim. Hughes Aircraft in turn sued B of A to prevent payment on the grounds that the claim was a "forgery" since it was not made by representatives of the Shah's government. Subsequent rulings required that the payment be made to a frozen Iranian account for future litigation despite the objection of Hughes Aircraft.

Despite the risks inherent in some transactions, this type of financing appeals to banks because of the fee income and the fact that no funds are expected to be disbursed. Because of the temptation to generate fee income and of the ease with which these LOCs can be issued, the amount of contingent claims against a bank can be substantial.

Loan Participations   Small commercial banks have working relationships with larger banks usually referred to as *upstream correspondents.* The smaller banks are called *downstream correspondents.* Because of their size and expertise in certain areas, the large banks perform a number of important services for the smaller banks. These include computer services, investment counseling, executing money market transactions, and clearing checks. Another important aspect of the correspondent relationship deals with loan participations. This is the purchase or sale of commercial loans to other financial institutions, usually banks.

Banks become involved in loan participations for several reasons.

- *Lack of Liquidity.* A bank may be facing strong loan demand and be "loaned up" such that it cannot meet the credit needs of its service area. By making loans and selling them to a correspondent (upstream or downstream) the bank facilitates the acquisition of credit by its customers.
- *Slack Loan Demand.* When loan demand in a bank's service area is slack, lendable funds must be channelled into lower yielding investments. An alternative is to purchase loans in order to maintain desired loan and income levels.
- *Overlines.* Loans to a single borrower by national banks and many state chartered banks are limited to an amount equal to 15 percent of the bank's capital. The amount in excess of the legal limit is called an *overline.* The overline may be sold on a participating basis to the bank's upstream correspondent.
- *Diversification.* The loan portfolios of many banks tend to be concentrated in a few industries. The purchase or sale of loans enables banks to diversify their portfolios more effectively.
- *Risk Sharing.* Because of a borrower's weak financial condition, a bank may wish to extend asset-based credit on a shared basis with a specialist in this type of lending. The primary emphasis is placed on the marketability of collateral rather than earnings or financial strength. Extremely close control over the collateral is required.

The development of loan-participation relationships requires careful planning and a thorough understanding of the credit policies and requirements of other banks. Loans originated by other banks should be subjected to the same scrutiny as any other loan and evaluated by experienced lending personnel. This is not always done. In the aftermath of the collapse of the Penn Square Bank in July 1982, it was revealed that the bank, with assets of about $500 million, sold $2 billion of energy-related loans to some of the country's leading banks. The collapse of natural gas prices, and thus drilling activity, resulted in loan losses that wiped out Penn Square's equity and the bank was closed by the Comptroller of the Currency and the FDIC. Substantial losses were incurred on the loan participations that were acquired by other banks. Many of these loans were bought by the correspondent division of the acquiring banks and were not evaluated by experienced lending personnel. Since this episode, the policies of most banks involved in loan participations have been carefully reviewed and revised.

Loan participations do not always involve correspondent relationships. Some banks package large-scale loans for resale to other institutions such as pension funds and life insurance companies. For example, the Chemical Bank originates and sells real estate construction loans through a leading Wall Street investment banker. The bank backs the principal and interest with an irrevocable standby letter of credit. The LOC reduces the investor's risk so the rate at which the loan is sold is below the contract rate. The resulting difference in the borrower's payments is the bank's fee for originating, servicing, and guaranteeing the loan.

THE COMMERCIAL LENDING PROCESS

In this section the commercial lending process is examined. The credit decision is considered first. This is followed by a section dealing with commercial loan pricing, including the development of a loan pricing model.

The Credit Decision

Most banks have a large volume of loans relative to their capital base.[4] As a result, banks generally are unable to absorb prolonged periods of large-scale loan losses. Thus one of the primary risks facing commercial banks is the risk of default on the part of borrowers. It is not surprising that the credit-granting process is one of the keys to successful bank management. The implications of credit decison-making extend beyond simply avoiding bad loans. For pricing purposes, it is important that the borrower's default risk be properly assessed and its risk class established. Consider the following simplified example. Assume that a borrower applies for a one-year loan and submits the appropriate financial records. After examining the records, the credit analyst concludes that the borrower belongs in a particular risk class. From an analysis of past loans in the same risk class, the analyst is able to estimate the probability of full payment, as shown in Table 3.

In this table, two economic scenarios are shown along with their estimated probabilities of occurrence, i.e., .80 and .20 respectively. For this entire risk class, the analyst estimates that if a growth scenario prevails, 99 percent of the principal and interest will be paid; if a recession occurs, the estimated percentage drops to 90 percent. Multiplying these estimates by the probabilities of the economic scenarios yields the joint probability shown in column 4. The sum of these is .972

---

[4] Typically, the ratio of total loans to capital is about 10:1.

Table 3   Probability of Loan Repayment for a Given Class of Loans

1. Economic Scenario	2. Probability of Economic Scenario	3. Probability all Payments Made	4. Joint Probability (2 × 3)
Growth	.80	.99	.792
Recession	.20	.90	.180
		Probability of Full Payment =	.972

which means that the probability all payments will be made—regardless of the economy—is 97.2 percent. Stated another way, the bank expects to receive an average of 97.2 percent of the total principal and interest from a large pool of similarly classified loans. Thus, if a bank lends $1 at its prime, or virtually riskless rate of 12 percent, this is equivalent to lending $.972 at some higher rate. That is,

$$\$1(1 + .12) = \$.972(1 + r).$$

Solving for the loan rate r that is appropriate for the risk class yields

$$r = \frac{\$1.12}{.972} - 1$$

$$r = .152 \text{ or } 15.2\%.$$

The use of this numerical example is not to suggest that lenders actually go through such a process and think explicitly in terms of probabilities. Rather, the process is largely judgmental. The purpose of the example is to demonstrate the nature of the thought process and the pricing implications of the credit decision.[5]

In addition to pricing implications, the credit decision has growth implications as well. If a stringent credit policy is followed the bank's loan market will be smaller than if more relaxed credit standards are allowed. Furthermore, the analysis underlying the credit decision helps shape the structure of the loan agreement. A higher degree of risk may be offset by more stringent collateral requirements, protective covenants, loan restrictions, or a restructuring of the loan proposal.

Financial Analysis   The key to the credit decision lies in the analysis of the financial statements submitted by the borrower. From these statements, which are often less than adequate for smaller firms, relationships are developed in the form of ratios. These ratios provide insight regarding a firm's performance when trends are examined over a several-year period and they are compared to other firms in the same industry. A summary of the most commonly used ratios is provided in Table 4. Analysts are often required to develop their own ratios that are unique to a given industry. For example, when analyzing the loan request of an airline, the ratio of direct operating cost to revenue passenger miles provides insight as to the firm's ability to control costs.

Calculating ratios is a mechanical task; interpreting them is another matter. A firm's current ratio may be quite low, but this is usually the very reason the bor-

[5] Given a bank's prime lending rate, default probabilities are implicit in every loan rate set by a bank.

Table 4   Summary of Credit Ratios

1. Liquidity Ratios
   a. Current Ratio $= \dfrac{\text{Current Assets}}{\text{Current Liabilities}}$

   b. Quick Ratio $= \dfrac{\text{Current Assets-Inventories}}{\text{Current Liabilities}}$

2. Activity Ratios
   a. Inventory Turnover $= \dfrac{\text{Cost of Goods Sold}}{\text{Average Inventory}}$

   b. Average Collection Period (days) $= \dfrac{\text{Accounts Receivable}}{\text{Annual Credit Sales}/360}$

   c. Fixed Asset Turnover $= \dfrac{\text{Sales}}{\text{Fixed Assets}}$

3. Leverage Ratios
   a. Debt Ratio $= \dfrac{\text{Total Debt}}{\text{Total Assets}}$

   b. Debt to Equity $= \dfrac{\text{Total Debt}}{\text{Common Equity}}$

   c. Interest Coverage $= \dfrac{\text{Earnings Before Interest and Taxes}}{\text{Interest Charges}}$

   d. Debt Service Coverage[a] $= \dfrac{\text{Earnings Before Interest \& Taxes}}{\text{Interest} + \text{Principal}[1/(1-t)] + \text{Lease Payments}}$

4. Profitability Ratios
   a. Net Profit Margin $= \dfrac{\text{Net Profit}}{\text{Sales}}$

   b. Return on Equity $= \dfrac{\text{Net Profit}}{\text{Common Equity}}$

   c. Net Operating Profit Rate[b] $= \dfrac{\text{Operating Earnings}}{\text{Operating Assets}}$

---

[a]The term in the brackets in the denominator reflects the fact that principal payments are made on an after-tax basis.

[b]This ratio enables a firm's performance to be evaluated even in light of a changing capital structure. Also, the performance of firms with different capital structures may be compared.

---

rower is requesting a loan. The importance of specific ratios will vary depending on the type of loan involved. When analyzing a short-term working capital loan or open line of credit, more weight may be placed on activity and liquidity ratios than on the profitability ratios. Since longer-term loans are repaid through earnings and cash flow rather than the conversion of current assets to cash, profitability ratios become more important when analyzing term loans or revolving credits.

The projected cash budget also plays a key role in analyzing short-term loans. The purpose of this budget is to allow the analyst to trace all cash flows in order to determine the amount and timing of cash needs as well as the availability of funds for repayment of the loan. The process of tracing cash flows also enables usage estimates to be made for open lines and revolving credits. The estimated usage is a component of the pricing process as shown later in this section.

Credit Scoring Models   Some banks have attempted to expedite the credit analysis of commercial loans by using *credit scoring models*. With these systems key ratios and other variables are selected and weighted for the purpose of differentiating between "good" loans and "bad" loans. A simplified version of such a model is shown in Table 5. In this model the total scores indicate that Company A is in better financial condition than Company B. If the cutoff score for accepting a loan request is 30, no further analysis may be deemed necessary in the case of A. If the reject cutoff point is 15, Company B might be rejected outright. Firms with scores falling in between these cutoff points would be subjected to the usual credit analysis. The main advantage of such a scoring system is a reduction in the volume of applications requiring intensive analysis. More attention can be focused on firms falling in the "grey" area.

A problem arises with such a model when the variables are arbitrarily selected and weighted. The variables selected or their assigned weights may not be optimal. This problem can be overcome through the use of a sophisticated statistical technique known as multiple discriminant analysis, or MDA. Although predictive success has been achieved using MDA models, the lack of uniformity among commercial borrowers and the lack of adequate data for small-scale and defaulted borrowers has limited their use in the commercial lending sector.[6] However, such models have gained widespread acceptance in the consumer lending area.

Loan Review   The analysis of a borrower's creditworthiness and all other aspects of the loan agreement continue even after

Table 5   Hypothetical Commercial Loan Credit Scoring Model

Financial Ratios	Company A		Company B	
	Ratio	Score	Ratio	Score
Current Ratio	2.8	8	1.3	2
Average Collection Period (days)	28	6	45	3
Inventory Turnover (times)	3.4	4	5.3	5
Debt Ratio (%)	35	10	75	0
Return on Equity (%)	16	5	2	1
Score		33		11

Decision Rules:
1. If score $\geq$ 30, grant credit;
2. If score $\leq$ 15, reject credit;
3. If score is between 15 and 30, further analysis is required.

[6] See, for example, "ZETA^TM Analysis: A New Model to Identify Bankruptcy Risk of Corporations," by Edward I. Altman, Robert G. Haldeman, and P. Narayanan, *Journal of Banking and Finance*, Volume 1, June 1977, pp. 29-54.

a loan is made. Through an internal procedure known as the *loan review*, the overall quality of a bank's loan portfolio should be monitored on a continuous basis to ensure that all aspects of the loan agreement are in order. In this sense, the *loan review* process is a form of quality control. Updated financial statements should be examined for any dramatic changes that may require corrective action. Another function of the *loan review* is to ensure compliance with the bank's lending policy and regulations. Furthermore, a continuous assessment of individual loans enables the performance of lending officers to be evaluated.

An important aspect of the *loan review* process is the loan rating system. Loans may be classified using the following system.[7]

- *Excellent Risk.* There is a low degree of loss exposure. The probability of a rapid and serious deterioration in the firm's financial condition is very small.
- *Good Risk.* There is minor loss exposure. The probability of a significant financial deterioration is low. The loan is above-average in quality.
- *Satisfactory Risk.* There is a definite possibility of deterioration if adverse conditions prevail. The loan must be monitored on a regular basis. The loan quality is average or slightly below average.
- *Unsatisfactory Risk.* A significant probability of loss exists unless immediate corrective action is taken. Financial deterioration is already in evidence. The loan must be closely watched and the loan quality is below average.
- *Workout.* A high probability of loss exists. Corrective action must be taken to minimize the loan loss or maximize the recovery of funds.

Although all loans should be reviewed at least annually, it is clear from this classification that some loans require much more attention than others. The use of such a system enables management resources to be directed toward the most troublesome loans. The system also corresponds to that used by bank examiners as they perform an external loan review to assess the loan portfolio's quality.

"Chinese Wall"   Because of the nature of the credit decision, commercial banks have access to a large volume of confidential or *insider information* related to their borrowers. One type of problem this situation can create may be demonstrated by an example.

> **Example.**   In 1968 the Continental Illinois National Bank and Trust Company, acting as a trustee, acquired about 27,000 shares of the Penn Central Railroad common stock on behalf of several union pension funds. The bank itself was also a lender to the railroad. After Penn Central declared bankruptcy in 1970, the unions filed suit against the bank arguing that by virtue of its position as a lender to Penn Central, the bank "knew or should have known" of the railroad's deteriorating financial position. The suit further alleged that because of the bank's failure to reveal this information to the unions or act on the information by selling the stock, substantial losses were incurred as the stock's price collapsed.[8]

[7] P. Graham Conlin, *Commercial Loan Review Procedures*, Philadelphia, Pennsylvania.: Robert Morris Associates, 1978, p. 9.

[8] Ray F. Myers, "The Trust Wall—Or Stay Alive with 10b-5," *Trust Management Update*, Washington, D.C.: American Bankers Association, May 1976, p. 8.

Although this case was settled out of court, the underlying issues remain of concern to banks. As lenders, banks have access to material inside information and thus are usually aware of the fact that one of its customers is approaching the "unsatisfactory risk" or "workout" stage. The bank should use the information internally to monitor the loan and develop a program for corrective action. But a problem arises if the bank's trust department holds stock or other publicly traded securities of the troubled firm. As a trustee, the bank is legally obligated to act in the best interest of trust beneficiaries. Failure to do so could subject the bank to a civil suit and result in sizable damage claims. This seems to suggest that the bank should sell the stock on the basis of the insider information. However, federal securities laws require that anyone in possession of *material inside information* refrain from trading in or recommending the firm's securities while the insider information remains undisclosed. A violation of the law would subject the bank to civil damage suits and criminal proceedings. Thus, the bank appears to be on the horns of a dilemma. Acting in the best interest of trust beneficiaries would require the bank to commit an unlawful act while failure to act may be regarded as a breach of its duties as a trustee. The obvious quesiton is—what should the bank do?

In a number of lawsuits involving this question, the courts have made it clear that the use of insider information is strictly prohibited, notwithstanding a bank's obligation as a trustee. In short, the bank has an obligation as trustee that is paramount to everything except committing illegal acts.

Federal regulatory agencies have reinforced this view by declaring the use of insider information to be an "unsafe banking practice." As such, a violation would subject a bank to regulatory sanctions. Furthermore, federal regulatory agencies require that banks under their jurisdiction develop internal written policies that control the flow of insider information between the lending and trust departments. As a result of the court decisions and regulatory requirements, banks with trust departments must place an informational barrier, or "Chinese Wall" between the lending and trust departments. Some banks have gone so far as to physically relocate their trust departments in separate buildings.

The "Chinese Wall" concept may arise in another context as illustrated by the following example.

> *Example.* In early 1979, Talley Industries attempted a "hostile" takeover of the Washington Steel Corporation by means of a $70 million cash tender offer. The funds were to be obtained from a group of four banks headed by Chemical Bank, which was also Washington Steel's banker. Washington Steel filed suit contending that Chemical Bank should be prevented from financing the takeover. It was argued that the bank used confidential information related to Washington Steel when deciding whether or not to make the loan to Talley Industries. The bank argued that it had established a "Chinese Wall" *within* its loan department which prevented the Talley loan officer from obtaining any information about Washington Steel.
>
> Although the tender offer was ultimately withdrawn by Talley, an appeals court ruled in favor of the bank. By ruling that the bank was free to use the information when making its decision, the court dismissed the need for a "Chinese Wall" *within* the loan department.[9]

[9] "Chemical Bank Upheld in Takeover Role," *American Banker*, July 24, 1979, p. 1; and "Banks Get Free Hand in Takeovers," *American Banker*, July 25, 1979, p. 1.

It is important to understand the implications of this ruling. Although a bank is free to use internally any information in its possession, the dissemination of this information to others would violate securities laws. In other words, if Chemical Bank gave Talley Industries insider information regarding Washington Steel, a violation would have occurred. In a later section, the use of information and specific elements of the "Wall" as they relate to the trust department are discussed from a policy standpoint.

Pricing Commercial Loans

Commercial loan pricing is one of the most important aspects of bank management. For many banks, the income from these loans is the largest single contributor to earnings. This income is generated in several interrelated ways which are discussed in this section.

In recent years the pricing process has been complicated by several factors. Increased competition from life insurance companies and foreign banks has created other options for borrowers. Borrower attitudes are changing. Rather than being "loyal" to a single bank or group of banks and possibly paying a higher price for bank funds, more borrowers "shop around" in order to reduce costs. In this respect, it is not uncommon for major borrowers to solicit bids for the type of credit facility they need. Another change in recent years is the trend toward *unbundling*. That is, more borrowers are demanding that explicit fees be imposed for specific services. For example, rather than keeping compensating balances of 10 percent of a credit line, a borrower may want balances of zero and be willing to pay "hard dollars" for check clearing and other services ordinarily covered by a balance requirement. A volatile interest rate environment requires that extreme care be exercised when pricing commercial loans in order to minimize the adverse effects of costs rising more rapidly than returns on the loans. Because of these factors—increased competition, less "loyalty," unbundling, and risk control—the specific manner in which commercial loans are priced has become an increasingly important issue in recent years.

When discussing the various types of commercial loans offered by banks it was pointed out that a contractual loan rate was often used in conjunction with compensating balances and fees. Also, the issue of fixed-rate versus floating-rate loans was mentioned. Before looking at a loan pricing model these and several other aspects of pricing will be examined in more detail.

The Prime Rate   With a few exceptions, the prime rate is a bank's base lending rate. It is the contractual loan rate applicable to the most creditworthy customers of a bank. For those customers who are not prime borrowers, a *default risk premium* is added to the prime rate. Since the prime rate is for short-term loan commitments usually ranging from two months to one year, another risk premium is added to this base rate to compensate for longer-term commitments, particularly fixed-rate loans. This is referred to as a *term premium*. The prime rate is also the base for floating-rate loans. That is, changes in the prime rate trigger corresponding changes in the loan rate. Floating-rate loans involving large-scale firms with access to the international money market may be tied to the *lower* of the prime rate or the so-called *LIBOR*. This is the London interbank offer rate. At times, LIBOR is well below the domestic prime rate.

Floating-rate loans with a premium added for *default* and/or *term risk* may be tied to the prime in one of several ways. The *prime-plus* method is the most widely used. If the default and term risk require a two-percentage point premium over prime, the loan rate would be stated as "prime plus 2." Another approach gaining widespread acceptance is the *times-prime* method. That is, the rate is set at some percentage over the prime rate. A total risk premium of 20 percent over the base lending rate would result in a loan rate of "1.20 times prime." When the prime rate is 10 percent, the percentage change in the loan rate (and thus interest income) is the same for the *prime-plus* and the *times-prime* methods, but when the prime rate is other than 10 percent, differences emerge. For example, when the prime rate is 6 percent, "prime plus 2" equals 8 percent and "1.2 times prime" is 7.2 percent. When the prime rate is 14 percent, "prime plus 2" equals 16 percent while "1.2 times prime" equals 16.8 percent. Thus, when the level of interest rates is quite high, the loan rate increases faster using the *times-prime* method. Sometimes the two methods are combined. For example, the loan rate might be "1.10 times the sum of prime plus 1." If the prime rate is 12 percent, the loan rate in this case would be $(1.10)(.12 + .01) = 14.3$ percent.

The national prime rate is set by large money center banks. The rate is usually based on a three- or four-week average of 90-day CD costs plus several percentage points. The rate is reviewed weekly and usually changed in 25-basis point intervals. Other banks tend to follow the leaders but regional differences do emerge. The prime rate is a benchmark. The interaction of the rate, fees, compensating balances, and premiums for default risk and the term of the transaction interact to produce returns to the bank that vary widely from the nationally quoted prime rate. As a result, confusion surrounds the pricing process, especially a practice known as "below-prime pricing." This practice came to light in the late 1970s when it was revealed that large corporations were able to obtain bank financing at rates below the posted prime rate. Politicians and consumer advocates argue that the practice discriminates against small-scale businesses who pay the prime rate or higher.

Below-prime pricing can arise during a period of rising interest rates because of a "cap" or ceiling on the loan rate. This is discussed shortly. More often, such pricing arises because of competition between the commercial paper market and the market for bank loans. When a large corporation with access to the commercial paper market needs funds for a very short period of say one or two weeks, a short-term bank loan may be requested rather than incurring the cost of distributing commercial paper. Since the commercial paper rate is usually two to three percentage points lower than the prime rate, a prime rate loan would be unacceptable to the borrower. The borrower has the option of going into the paper market. If the loan is to be made, it must be below prime. The key to the below-prime pricing issue is the fact that for such a short term, the bank's only lending option is the overnight funds market, that is, federal funds and repurchase agreements. If rates in the overnight market are below the commercial paper rate, as is usually the case, it benefits the bank to make the loan at a rate that is higher than the overnight funds rate but lower than the prime rate. In effect, the bank is buying the borrower's very short-term commercial paper. The quoted prime rate, on the other hand, refers to loans or commitments that extend at least several months rather than several days. The two transactions involve completely different markets. This is reflected in the loan rates.

Compensating Balances

Although compensating balance requirements have been a traditional aspect of commercial loan pricing, corporate borrowers are becoming increasingly reluctant to hold a sizable amount of funds in the form of non-earning assets. This reluctance becomes stronger during periods of high interest rates because the opportunity cost of holding such deposits is correspondingly higher. Furthermore, it can be shown that because of reserve requirements, both the bank and the borrower could be better off without a balance requirement.[10] Despite these negative aspects of compensating balance requirements, they continue to be an important part of loan pricing. Rather than falling in the range of 10 to 20 percent of the loan amount as was once the case, most balances today are less than 10 percent. In some cases balances are maintained even without the requirement. In other cases the balances are sufficient only to compensate the bank for check clearing and other depository services.

Compensating balances allow banks to be more flexible in their loan pricing. If a borrower maintains high balances because of the nature of its business, this may be reflected in lower loan rates. Another borrower may be willing to pay a higher rate and maintain small balances. A bank that is flexible in its approach to pricing loans should be able to accommodate most borrowers.

Compensating balances appeal to bankers for two reasons. Since no interest is paid on demand deposits, they represent one of the lowest cost sources of bank funds. If a borrower gets into serious financial trouble and defaults on its loan, one of the remedies open to the bank is to seize the funds in the account and apply them to the loan balance. This *right of setoff* is obviously one of the final steps a bank would take to minimize its loan loss. A problem often arises when the bank and the IRS attempt to seize the same funds as a partial payment for bank loans and back taxes. Under the laws of some states, a bank's *right of setoff* is automatic and the funds may be seized by the bank upon default. In these states the bank's claim is superior to that of the IRS. In other states, a bank's claim is contingent upon other legal actions taken by the bank. Later in this section the pricing implications of compensating balances are examined.

---

[10] For example, assume a borrower needs $900,000 for one year and because of a 10 percent balance requirement, a loan of $1 million at 14 percent is made. The difference is the required balance of $100,000. Thus, the borrower pays $140,000 for the use of $900,000 which results in a cost of $140,000/900,000 = 15.56 percent. The bank's outlay is reduced by the lendable portion of the compensating balance. Assuming a 12 percent reserve requirement, the idle reserves would be $12,000 and the lendable portion of the compensating balance would be $88,000. Thus, the bank's income would be $140,000 on an outlay of $912,000. This is a return of 15.35 percent which is 21 basis points lower than the borrower's cost of 15.56 percent. If the bank loaned $912,000 at a flat rate of 15.56 percent and required no balances its net income would be $141,907. Alternatively, a lower rate could be charged to the borrower.

"Caps" and Other
Provisions[11]

Commercial borrowers seeking intermediate- or longer-term credit usually attempt to negotiate fixed-rate loans in order to reduce the uncertainty of their costs. On the other hand, banks as lenders have a preference for short-term loans or floating-rate loans because of their short-term liability structure. Some banks attempt to reach a compromise by offering term loans and revolving credits on a floating-rate basis subject to an upside limit or "average cap" on the rate. Under this arrangement the borrower pays interest based on a floating rate during the life of the loan. At the end of the loan's term, the bank calculates the interest based on the cap rate and payments in excess of this amount are refunded to the borrower. In some cases, the refund calculation is made annually.

If a term loan is priced to reflect both *default* and *term* risk, the use of an average cap may be appropriate. It is important that the cap be sufficiently high in order to prevent minor changes in the level of interest rates from converting a floating-rate term loan to a fixed-rate loan. In a volatile interest rate environment, a cap should be at least three or four percentage points above the initial loan rate. Whether competition would allow such a high cap rate may be another story.

The use of a cap with a revolving credit is inappropriate. As is the case with term loans, a cap may have the effect of converting a floating-rate loan to a fixed-rate loan during periods of high interest rates. Unlike a term loan which is taken down immediately and repaid according to a schedule, the revolving credit may be taken down and repaid solely at the borrower's discretion. In a volatile interest rate environment, this discretion means that the funds could be used and repaid only when it is disadvantageous for the bank. Consider the following actual case.

> *Example.* In May 1978, General Instrument Corporation negotiated a three-year, $50 million revolving credit arrangement with a group of four banks led by the Bankers Trust Company. The loan rate was tied to the prevailing prime rate of 8.5 percent. However, the loan was capped at 10.75 percent. The capped rate also included the commitment fee. Furthermore, the loan was convertible into a four-year term loan at the cap rate beginning in May 1981.
>
> In early 1980, a restrictive monetary policy resulted in money market yields of 18 percent. The prime rate was as high as 20 percent. Despite the "credit crunch," General Instrument's cash position was such that it had no immediate need for funds. However, in March 1980 the firm proceeded to borrow the entire $50 million at the capped rate of 10.75 percent. The funds were reinvested in money market instruments (such as Bankers Trust CDs) yielding 18 percent! When market rates fell below the cap rate the investments were allowed to mature and the funds were repaid.[12]

The example suggests that the use of caps, if at all, should be limited to term loans. Although they provide a bank with a competitive selling point, capped loans are usually one-way contracts in favor of the borrower. Since capped loans are usually written during periods of lower interest rates, it is more likely that the cap will work adversely against the bank rather than being inoperative. For these reasons

[11] The discussion in this section relates primarily to term loans and revolving credits.

[12] "General Instrument Finds a Rich Reward in High Interest Fees," *Wall Street Journal,* April 7, 1980, p. 10.

the use of capped term loans should be limited to special situations and their volume tightly controlled.

Longer-term, fixed-rate term loan agreements should restrict the borrower's ability to prepay the loan. In the absence of such a provision, borrowers could obtain alternative low-cost financing during a period of lower interest rates and prepay the loan. The bank would then be forced to reinvest its funds at a lower rate. If the term loan was initially funded with a correspondingly long-term fixed-rate liability, the cost of funds may then exceed the loan return. This problem may be resolved by prohibiting prepayments in the first several years or imposing prepayment penalties that decrease over time. For example, prepayments on a four-year term loan may be subject to a 4 percent penalty in the first year, 3 percent in the second year, and so forth.

Loan Pricing Model   In order to show how the loan rate, compensating balances, and other fees fit together to produce alternative prices or loan yields, it is useful to look at a numerical illustration. Assume a bank is analyzing a loan request for a three-year, $1 million revolving credit. A commitment fee of ½ of 1 percent per year will be imposed on the unused portion of the commitment. The borrower also agrees to maintain compensating balances of 7 percent of the commitment plus 5 percent of any borrowings. The interest rate on the loan will float with the prime rate which is 12 percent. However, the borrower's *default risk* and the *term risk* associated with a three-year commitment justify a price of 1.10 times prime. The initial contract rate on the loan is 1.1 × 12% = 13.2 percent. The bank uses the *actual/360* accrual method so the adjusted nominal rate is (365/360) × 13.2% = 13.38 percent. After analyzing the request and preparing detailed cash flow projections for the three-year period, the bank's credit analyst estimates that the usage will average 75 percent of the commitment, or $750,000, during the first year.

Because of compensating balances and the commitment fee, the bank's estimated yield on the loan will be higher than the contract rate and the adjusted nominal rate. In order to estimate this yield both the income and net outlay must be determined. In Table 6 the steps necessary to evaluate the loan are outlined. Given the estimated first-year usage of 75 percent, the interest is $100,350 and the commitment fee amounts to $1,250 for a total income of $101,600. The outlay necessary to obtain this income is the average loan amount less the usable net demand deposit balances provided by the borrower. The assumption here is that the firm borrows its own funds first. As shown, the average loan amount is reduced by net deposits of $94,600 resulting in a net outlay of $655,400. This produces an estimated yield of 15.50 percent. The effective yield is higher because interest payments are usually made monthly or quarterly with commercial loans. Since this is a floating-rate loan, the yield will change as the prime rate changes.

The procedure described in Table 6 may be expressed in the form of a loan pricing model as given by equation [2]:

$$y = \frac{ur + f(1 - u)}{u - [(b_1 + b_2 u)] \, (1 - R)} \qquad [2]$$

where y = estimated yield on loan
       u = estimated first-year commitment usage (.75)
       r = adjusted nominal rate (.1338)
       f = commitment fee (.005)
       b_1 = compensating balance requirement on total commitment (.07)
       b_2 = compensating balance requirement on borrowings (.05)
       R = reserve requirement on compensating balances (.12)

Table 6   Loan Pricing Example

Type of Loan . . . . Revolving Credit
Commitment ($) $1,000,000
Term . . . . 3 Years
Contract Interest Rate . . . . 1.10 × prime (initial prime is 12%) = 13.20%
Accrual Method . . . . actual/360 method
Adjusted Nominal Rate[a] . . . . 13.2% × (365/360) = 13.38%
Commitment Fee . . . . 0.5% on unused portion of commitment
Compensating Balances . . . . 7% of commitment + 5% of borrowings
Estimated Usage . . . . 75% (first year)
Reserve Requirement 12%
Options . . . . Convertible into 3-year, fixed-rate term loan
                                              at 1.1 × prime

A. Income
    1. Interest Income
        $1,000,000 (.75)(.1338)   = $100,350
    2. Fee Income
        $1,000,000 (1 − .75)(.005)   =   1,250
                                                          ─────────
           Total Income $101,600
B. Outlay
    1. Average Loan Amount
        $1,000,000 (.75)   = $750,000
    2. Less: Net Demand Dep. Balances
        $1,000,000 (.07)   = $ 70,000
        $1,000,000 (.05)(.75)   =   37,500
                                     ─────────
           Gross Demand Dep. $107,500
           Less: Res. Req. @ .12   =   12,900
                                     ─────────
           Net Demand Deposits   =   94,600
                                                          ─────────
           Net Outlay   = $655,400
C. Estimated Loan Yield (y)

$$y = \frac{\$101,600}{655,400} = .1550 \text{ or } 15.50\%$$

---

[a]When the *actual/365* accrual method is used the adjusted nominal rate is the same as the contract rate.

Substituting the example values into [2] results in

$$y = \frac{(.75)(.1338) + (.005)(1 - .75)}{.75 - [.07 + (.05)(.75)] \ (1 - .12)}$$

$$y = \frac{.10160}{.65540} = .1550 \text{ or } 15.50\%.$$

Assuming \$500,000 were borrowed continuously for an entire quarter (91 days), the borrower's interest expense in this example would be

$$\$500,000 \times .1320 \times (91/360) = \$16,683.33.$$

If the *actual/365* accrual method were used, the expense would be

$$\$500,000 \times .1320 \times (91/365) = \$16,454.79.$$

Note that the contract interest rate is used in this calculation and not the estimated yield or the adjusted nominal rate.

The model given by equation [2] enables equivalent pricing alternatives to be developed and the various tradeoffs analyzed. The borrower in the preceding situation may prefer to keep no balances and pay a higher contract interest rate on the loan. If so, both b_1 and b_2 equal zero and assuming the bank's desired loan yield remains 15.50 percent, equation [2] may be written as

$$y = \frac{ur + f(1 - u)}{u}$$

or

$$.1550 = \frac{.75r + .005(1 - .75)}{.75} \ .$$

Solving for the new adjusted nominal rate r results in

$$r = \frac{(.75)(.1550) - .005(1 - .75)}{.75}$$

$$r = .1533 \text{ or } 15.33\%.$$

Recall that the adjusted nominal rate is obtained by multiplying the contract rate by 365/360. That is,

$$\text{contract rate} \times (365/360) = 15.33\%.$$

Now solving for the loan's contract rate,

$$\text{contract rate} = (360/365) \times 15.33\% = 15.12\%.$$

Thus, with no balances, the borrower may pay a contract interest rate of 15.12 percent (using the *actual/360* method) rather than 13.20 percent (also using the *actual/360* method) with balances of 7 plus 5. In either case the bank's yield is 15.50 percent. If the borrower wanted to maintain balances only in relation to the commitment and not the usage, the model could be used to obtain a set of loan terms that provides an equivalent yield.

Since many commercial borrowers have different needs and alternative sources of financing, it is important from a service and competitive standpoint that banks be flexible in their pricing. The volatility that has characterized the financial markets in recent years has also complicated the loan pricing problem. A high level of interest rates increases the opportunity cost of holding idle balances. As a result borrowers have become more reluctant to maintain such balances. This has had an important effect on banks. To the extent that borrowers agree to maintain balances, the level is often sufficient only to compensate the bank for depository services such as check clearing. When balances are a part of the loan pricing process, a portion of the yield given by equation [2] may represent compensation for other banking services. Recall from the preceding example that balances of seven plus five were agreed upon. Assuming the bank estimates that balances of 4 percent of the commitment are necessary to cover the cost of depository services, the actual loan yield might be calculated using balances of three plus five rather than seven plus five. Using these values in equation [2] results in a yield of 14.71 percent rather than 15.50 percent.

The pricing model given by [2] may be used for pricing other types of loans as well. Since an open line of credit is identical to a revolving credit for modeling purposes, equation [2] may be used as shown. If no commitment fee is charged, the value of f is zero in the model. Term loans are fully utilized so u = 1 and, if there are no fees or balances required, the values of f, b_1, and b_2 are zero and thus y = r as expected.

The model given by [2] is a *variable-fee* model because the commitment fee varies with usage. However, if a revolving credit or an open line involves a fixed commitment fee based on the total commitment rather than the unused portion, the numerator of [2] must be changed. The *fixed-fee* model is

$$y = \frac{ur + f}{u - [(b_1 + b_2 u)](1 - R)} . \qquad [3]$$

Charging a fixed fee based on the total commitment makes more economic sense than does a fee tied to the unused portion of a commitment. During periods of tight credit conditions banks tend to raise both their base lending rate and the commitment fee. If the fee is tied to the unused portion of the commitment, an increase in the fee may actually lower the borrower's marginal rate on takedowns and thus increase usage. Assume a bank's loan rate is 12 percent which includes a commitment fee of ¼ of 1 percent of the unused portion. If the funds are taken down, the borrower pays 12 percent but "saves" ¼ of 1 percent for a marginal cost of 11.75 percent. Holding the loan rate constant, if the fee is increased to 1 percent this, in effect, reduces the borrower's marginal cost to 11 percent. Even if the loan rate is increased in order to reduce loan demand, an increase in the fee on unused commitments provides an offsetting incentive to borrow funds. For this reason, a fixed fee tied to the entire amount of the commitment is preferable from a pricing standpoint.[13]

The usage factor in revolving credits may vary from year to year. Usually the usage is lower in the earlier years than in the final year when the entire amount is taken down. This is typical of expansion-related revolvers. Since the usage affects the loan yield, it may be appropriate to estimate the usage for each of the years the loan facility is outstanding. In the example above, the estimated usage may average 75 percent in the first year, 85 percent in the second year, and 95 percent in the final year.

When compensating balances are involved in a loan arrangement, the bank's return as given by equations [2] and [3] is *lower* than the borrower's cost. The reason is the existence of legal reserve requirements which are not lendable and bear no interest. The borrower's cost may be derived easily from [2] or [3] simply by letting R = 0. In the example from Table 6, equation [2] was used to derive the bank's yield of 15.50 percent. Letting R = 0, the borrower's cost is 15.81 percent. The 12 percent reserve requirement lowers the bank's return by 31 basis points.

REGULATION OF COMMERCIAL LENDING

Commercial lending and related activities are governed by banking laws and regulatory directives. Other than the broad requirements that loans be made for a "legal purpose" and be "sound and prudent," most of the regulations relate to specific aspects of commercial lending. The more important of these regulations may be classified in two categories—portfolio constraints and legal constraints.

Portfolio Constraints

There are two major regulations that affect the commercial loan portfolio. Effective April 1983, the maximum loan a national bank may lawfully make to a single entity is an amount equal to 15 percent of the bank's capital plus another 10 percent for loans collateralized by marketable securities. (The limit was formerly 10 percent of capital.) This regulation forces loan diversification and prevents an excessive concentration of risk in a single borrower. Letters of credit are considered loans for the purpose of this calculation. Because of the importance of loan diversification many state chartered banks are subject to similar restrictions limiting single-entity loans to some percentage of capital. Such a regulation is not unduly restrictive because most banks diversify anyway. When faced with a loan request that exceeds its legal lending authority, a bank could arrange for an overline par-

[13] For a discussion of commitment fees, see: Randall C. Merris, "Loan Commitments and Facility Fees," *Economic Perspectives*, Federal Reserve Bank of Chicago, March/April 1978, pp. 14-21.

ticipation with another bank or group of banks. Violating the legal lending limit has serious implications for the directors of national banks. Consider the following actual situation.[14]

> ***Example.***   In 1979, a Los Angeles bank made a loan for $225,000 to the president of the Fame Furniture Company. This loan was within the bank's legal lending limit of $275,000. With the bank's knowledge, the funds were used by the company. Five months later, another loan for $225,000 was made to the company itself. One month after the second loan was made, a third loan for $125,000 was made to the company's treasurer. These funds were also used by the company and with the bank's knowledge.
>
> A bank examiner combined the three loans for lending limit purposes because the entire proceeds were being used in the company with the bank's knowledge. The combined loans totaled $575,000 and resulted in an overline of $300,000. When the company went bankrupt, losses totalling $243,000 were sustained by the bank on the three loans. Pursuant to 1978 amendments in the federal cease and desist statute, the Comptroller of the Currency ordered the bank's nine directors to indemnify the bank and correct the conditions resulting from a violation of the law. Specifically, the Comptroller ordered the following:
>
> - That the total recovery of $332,000 on the three loans be applied first to the legally made loan, with the directors *personally liable* for the remaining loan losses of $243,000.
> - That the directors pay the bank $72,000 for lost interest on the two illegal loans.
> - That the directors reimburse the bank for all legal costs incurred in attempting to collect the loans and in defending the directors against the Comptroller's action.
>
> The Comptroller's action was upheld by the U. S. Appeals Court. The directors resigned their positions.

The other major regulation affecting national banks results in an overlap between commercial and consumer-related loans. The aggregate amount of commercial real estate and residential real estate loans is limited to the greater of the bank's capital or the sum of time and savings deposits. This is not restrictive for most banks.

Legal Constraints

Usury Laws   The interest rate charged by state chartered banks on commercial loans may not exceed the usury limit of the chartering state. The *National Banking Act* enables national banks, all of which are federally chartered, to charge the *higher* of the usury limit of the state in which the bank is chartered or one percentage point over the Federal Reserve discount rate. Since the discount rate is an administered, below-market rate, this option is

---

[14] Linda W. McCormick, "Court Rules Officers May be Held Liable for Loan Losses," *American Banker*, August 4, 1982, p. 1, and C. Westbrook Murphy, "Liability Without Limit for Bank Officers, Directors," *American Banker*, September 13, 1982, p. 4.

rarely exercised by national banks. Usury laws related to commercial loans usually pose no problem because the laws of most states either exempt corporations or allow a commercial loan rate that is sufficiently high so as not to be restrictive. In those states where the limit may be a problem, some bankers have taken the unusual step of including a *recapture clause* in their loan agreements. During a period of high interest rates when the usury constraint is binding, the clause allows the bank to defer any interest in excess of the usury limit. The deferred interest is recaptured when interest rates fall below the usury limit. The legality of this provision has not been tested in court.

Securities Laws   The use of *insider information* was discussed earlier along with the need for a "Chinese Wall" to ensure compliance with securities laws. (The components of such a "Wall" are discussed in the next section dealing with commercial loan policy.) Loan officers may also violate securities laws by aiding and abetting the misrepresentation of a borrower's financial position. The most obvious way this could occur is through the use of a "window dressing" loan. This is a loan made to enhance the financial statement of a financially troubled borrower and mask a deteriorating situation while other financing is being sought. The point here is that a bank may be held responsible for a borrower's financial condition and its lack of disclosure. Extreme care must be exercised and legal advice sought when considering "bailout" loans or loans to distressed companies.

"Sweetheart" and   An area of bank lending that is of concern to regulators
Insider Loans   involves so-called "sweetheart" loans. These are loans made on unusually favorable terms to principals who control business directed to the bank. For example, a bank may have an important and highly profitable customer relationship with a large corporation. If a sizable loan were made to the president of that firm on an unsecured basis and at an interest rate several percentage points below the market rate, it is likely that examiners would construe this as an illegal "sweetheart" loan. The borrower in this case is entitled to credit like anyone else. However, it is extremely important that such loans be made on the same terms as for others in a comparable transaction.

An *insider loan* involves loans to executive officers, directors, and large shareholders (10 percent of ownership) of the bank either as individuals or companies they control. Since this self-dealing has been a primary cause of bank failures, insider loans are closely monitored by bank examiners. Under provisions of the *Depository Institutions Act of 1982,* federal regulatory agencies (the FDIC, Federal Reserve Board, and the Comptroller of the Currency) are empowered to establish reporting requirements and lending limits for such loans. Beyond the regulatory threshold, which is subject to periodic review and change by the agencies, loans must be approved by the bank's board of directors.

Tie-Ins and   As banks expand their services, care must be exercised
Gratuities   to avoid restricting a customer's right to select financial services. This could occur, for example, if a bank granted a loan conditional on the borrower agreeing to obtain trust, data processing, or

other services from the bank, a subsidiary, or the bank's parent holding company. Such a *tie-in* is illegal under 1970 amendments to the *Bank Holding Company Act of 1956*. However, certain standard bank practices such as requiring the maintenance of compensating balances are permitted.

Lending officers are legally prohibited from receiving *gratuities* such as money, gifts, services, or other considerations that result from a banking relationship. The reason for this restriction is obvious. Unless such a gift was clearly nominal in value, a bribe or "kickback" scheme could result or be inferred.

COMMERCIAL LENDING POLICY

One of the main objectives of a bank is to meet the credit needs of its service area. In order to meet these needs, a bank must have specific policies that guide both commercial and consumer lending activities. In this section, the various aspects of a commercial loan policy are examined. Such a policy is a subset of a bank's overall lending policy which also includes consumer lending.

A lending policy has four purposes. First, it is the basic framework within which lending decisions are made. Such a policy answers lending-related questions that arise on a day-to-day basis. Second, a well-conceived policy constitutes a working agreement between the Board and management. By defining the boundaries of lending-related decisions, such an agreement provides a degree of protection for both management and the Board and reduces the risk of "finger-pointing." The third purpose of a lending policy is to facilitate the examination of banks by examiners. One of the goals of bank examiners is to detect financially weak banks. Another goal is to detect unsound policies and practices that could lead to future problems. One of the first documents examiners request is the lending policy statement. Their concern stems from the fact that certain lending policies, or the complete lack thereof, have played major roles in the collapse of some banks and the financial impairment of others. Finally, the loan policy should serve as a control device. Since the total loan portfolio of most banks is about 55 to 60 percent of assets, it follows that the lending policies play a key role in controlling the bank's overall direction.

Because of its importance, a loan policy must be developed by the bank's top management working closely with the Board of Directors. In order to be effective and avoid any confusion between lending officers, management, and the Board, *it is absolutely essential that lending policies be in writing.* Against this background the more important elements of a written commercial lending policy will now be examined.

Organizational Structure

The ultimate responsibility for the development of a lending policy lies with the Board of Directors. To implement its policy the Board delegates authority to line personnel by establishing an organizational structure. Although such a structure will vary among banks, the basic elements of an organizational structure are similar. The starting point is to establish *loan limits* for the bank's lending officers.

Loan Limits   A loan limit represents the maximum loan amount that may be approved by an individual lending officer. For example, a bank may have limits similar to the following:

	Lending Limit
Commercial Loan Officer	$ 100,000
Assistant Vice President	200,000
Vice President	500,000
Senior Vice President	1,000,000

These limits may be combined to speed the processing of loan requests. That is, a loan request for $250,000 that was originated by a Loan Officer could be approved by the Assistant Vice President since their combined lending limit is $300,000. The exact limits for any bank will depend on its size and the experience of its lending officers. The limits may also vary for secured versus unsecured loans.

Loan Committee   When loan requests exceed the lending limits for individual loan officers, the *Loan Committee* must approve the loan. Such a committee meets frequently and should be made up of the President, one or two Board members, and the bank's senior lending officers. In addition to approving loans in excess of individual lending limits, this committee reviews *all* loans approved by lending personnel. The purpose of this review is to ensure that loans are "prudent" and consistent with bank policy.

Loan Review   The lending policy must provide for the *loan review function* within the commercial loan organizational structure. The individuals most qualified to perform this function are the lending officers. A sensitive situation arises if the appointed loan review officer is called upon to evaluate loans made by other lending officers who are senior in rank. This problem can be overcome by the Board appointing a high ranking officer to be in charge of the loan review process and having that officer report to the chairperson of the Loan Committee.

   Another loan review problem is not so easily resolved. The loan review process should be impartial and independent. The loan review officer should attempt to avoid making judgments on loans with which the officer was directly involved. Those loans may be reviewed by the Loan Committee or a subcommittee thereof. In any event, the manner in which the loan review process is carried out must be specified in the loan policy statement.

   In the event of extreme problem loans, or *workouts*, the Board may wish to specify how they are handled. In some banks, *workouts* are handled by specialists within the loan review area while in other banks that task falls on the officer specifically responsible for the loan.

Loan Characteristics and Terms

The various types of loans and loan-related services that are offered by banks were discussed in an earlier section of this chapter. Not all banks have the expertise or financial capacity to offer a complete array of these loans and services. Accordingly, a loan policy statement should indicate the types of loans and related services that the bank offers. Even acceptable types of loans may have qualitative features that are undesirable from a bank's standpoint. A bank may be willing to make six-year term loans but not if such loans constitute quasi-equity for the purpose of starting a new business. Real estate loans outside a bank's service area are usually not looked upon favorably. If the honesty or integrity of the principals is in question or if the principals are inexperienced, most bankers are understandably cautious. When certain loan characteristics are considered undesirable, they should be spelled out in the policy statement along with the fact that the loan in question would require approval of the Loan Committee.

The maximum length of term loans and revolving credit commitment periods should be specified in the policy statement. Regarding term loans, a distinction may be made between fixed-rate and floating-rate loans. The maximum term of a fixed-rate term loan may be four years while a floating-rate arrangement may span a six-year period. Because of competitive conditions, it may be necessary to exceed the stated limits in which case approval of the Loan Committee or the Board of Directors would be required.

It is not uncommon for policy statements to be vague in the area of pricing commercial loans. For example, a policy may state the following:

> Commercial loan pricing shall reflect the bank's prime lending rate as a base and a risk premium to reflect: (1) the borrower's *default risk;* (2) the *interest rate risk* associated with fixed-rate loans; and (3) the *term risk* associated with longer-term commitments, fixed or floating. The bank's cost of funds will be considered along with the overall profitability of the account.

The lack of definitive guidelines in such a statement is understandable. Because of changing market conditions and the interaction among the base interest rate, risk premiums, balances, and fees it is difficult to set forth precise pricing guidelines in a policy statement. For this reason, lending personnel are given considerable latitude depending on their experience. In many banks the Loan Committee handles the pricing of large loans.

Portfolio Composition

The desired composition of a loan portfolio is achieved by pricing loans to achieve certain goals or satisfy constraints specified in the policy statement. These goals and constraints play a key role in determining the overall direction of a bank. Several of the more important goals and constraints are the loan/deposit ratio, the mix of floating- and fixed-rate loans, and diversification requirements.

Loan/Deposit
Ratio

A commonly used constraint on the size of the total loan portfolio is the loan/deposit (or L/D) ratio. The manner in which this constraint is stated is important. Because both loans and deposits are subject to short-term variation, the L/D ratio should be expressed in the form of a *range* rather than a single figure. Since the L/D ratio of most banks is in the range of 65 to 75 percent, this is a reasonable starting point in the formulation of an individual bank's policy. As the ratio falls below 65 percent, for example, the target range becomes a goal; if the ratio approaches 75 percent, the upper limit acts as a constraint on further lending activity. An absolute limit of 80 percent may also be established in order to ensure that the portfolio size is under control. In this way, the ratio is a useful control device.

The L/D ratio applies to the total loan portfolio so the loan policy must specify the desired allocation between commercial and consumer-related loans. A bank oriented toward commercial lending might specify a target L/D ratio range of 65 to 75 percent with commercial loans falling in the range of 40 to 50 percent and the remainder in consumer loans. It is important to be flexible and allow a slack demand for commercial loans to be offset by a larger volume of consumer loans.

If a bank has ready access to the money markets, the L/D ratio may slightly understate the bank's lending capacity because short-term borrowings may be used rather than deposits to fund loans. However, the amount of such funds is usually a small component of liabilities so the ratio is not significantly understated.

The L/D ratio is often used inappropriately as a measure of liquidity. It is argued that a low ratio means that a larger proportion of a bank's other assets is held in the form of investments which are more liquid than loans. Such a conclusion may not be appropriate because the L/D ratio conveys no information regarding the maturity composition and liquidity of the investment portfolio. The ratio says nothing about the liquidity of the loan portfolio itself. Consider two banks. Bank A has an L/D ratio of 60 percent and a loan portfolio made up primarily of long-term fixed-rate consumer loans. Bank B has a ratio of 75 percent and a portfolio of short-term commercial loans. Because of the faster loan turnover resulting from the shorter maturity structure of its loan portfolio, the overall liquidity of Bank B may be greater than that of Bank A despite B's higher L/D ratio.

Floating vs.
Fixed-Rate Loans

The return on longer-term fixed-rate loans does not change commensurate with changes in market rates and the bank's cost of funds. In a volatile interest rate environment a large proportion of fixed-rate loans funded by interest sensitive liabilities will result in sizable swings in earnings. It seems reasonable for the loan policy statement to specify some limit on the volume of fixed-rate loans. However, specifying a meaningful limit on fixed-rate loans requires the joint analysis of both the asset and liability structure. The objective of such an analysis is to determine the bank's overall interest rate sensitivity.

To briefly sketch the problem and show how the mix of fixed-rate and floating-rate loans is part of a broader financial strategy, consider the following situation.

Example. A bank's total loan portfolio is $20 million and made up of $10 million in fixed-rate consumer loans, $3 million in longer-term fixed-rate commercial loans, and $7 million in rate-sensitive floating-rate and/or short-term commercial loans. If the bank has $13 million in fixed-rate deposits, the bank is in a hedged position because it has funded all the fixed-rate loans with fixed-rate liabilities. If such deposits were $15 million the bank would be in an unhedged position and have the capacity to increase the proportion of fixed-rate loans by $2 million. If the longer-term fixed rate deposits were only $11 million the bank may be forced to reduce the volume of fixed-rate loans to be in a hedged position, assuming this was one of its goals.

Reducing the proportion of fixed-rate loans by imposing a policy restriction may not be an ideal solution to this problem. Instead, interest rate futures may be used and additional long-term deposits obtained. Also, the interest rate risk of other assets and liabilities must be considered. The point is that the mix of floating-rate and fixed-rate loans is part of the overall financial policy of a bank. Once this policy is established, the optimum mix and any limits may then be established.

Loan Diversification   The commercial loan portfolio of a bank should be diversified across a variety of companies and industries that are affected in different ways by changing economic conditions. On the surface, it might appear that this could be accomplished by specifying an industry breakdown and limiting loans within geographical areas. In the case of small- and medium-sized banks, these types of limits work at cross purposes with one of the basic reasons for their existence—to meet the credit needs of their service areas.

It is not uncommon for the service area of smaller banks to be heavily dependent on a single industry or a few large employers. Rather than reducing risk through diversification effects, consumer loans may be risk-increasing if they are simultaneously affected by the same conditions impacting the commercial loan portfolio. For example, small banks located in the coal fields of West Virginia conduct virtually all of their lending business with mine operators and coal miners. During a strike in 1978, delinquent loans were as high as 25 percent of the portfolio in some banks. This, coupled with deposit outflows, put serious financial strains on the area's banks and regulators were understandably concerned.

Large banks may have a service area that is nationwide or even international, so they have much more ability to diversify their loan portfolio geographically and across industries. The question arises—what can the smaller banks do to minimize their risk? The development of a loan participation program is a partial solution to this problem. More stringent credit standards would reduce both the risk of loan losses and the size of the loan portfolio. This would also enable the bank to increase its cushion of liquid assets such as short-term government and agency securities.

Legal Issues

Prohibited   In recent years the legal risks associated with commercial
Transactions   lending activities have increased dramatically. Accord-

ingly, a loan policy should provide guidelines designed to minimize these risks and reflect the rising standards of legal and ethical conduct being demanded of bankers. Prohibited transactions or activities should be clearly specified. These would include usurious loans, "sweetheart" loans, tie-ins, and gratuities, all of which were discussed in the preceding section. Also, restrictions and limits on insider loans should be stated along with the procedure for making such loans.

The policy should also stress that loans must be made for a legal purpose. Even if a bank unknowingly finances an illegal activity, the legality of the loan may be jeopardized and the terms of the loan rendered unenforceable.

> *Example.*   A pilot obtained a bank loan to finance the purchase of an airplane for the purpose of hauling cargo to and from South America. The airplane was used to collateralize the loan. Unfortunately and unknown to the bank, one of the carrier's main products was marijuana obtained in Colombia and transported to the United States. One night while the crew was loading a new shipment, the Colombian police arrested them and confiscated the plane. The pilot went to jail, the police sold the plane, and the bank wrote off the loan.

The enforceability of a loan agreement may also be jeopardized unless there is full compliance with other relevant laws. Consider the following situation.[15]

> *Example.*   Between January 1977 and June 1978, a group of large international banks led by the Chase Manhattan Bank made loans totalling $1.3 billion to Iran, then under the control of the Shah of Iran. The loans were apparently made even though Chase was advised by its Iranian legal counsel that the loans appeared to be in violation of Iran's existing constitution and thus could be unenforceable claims. Specifically, the constitution required that state loans be approved by the Parliament. After the overthrow of the Shah in 1979, Iran defaulted on the loans. Exercising its *right of setoff*, Chase then seized $300 million of Iranian deposits, the legal issues surfaced, and lawyers began celebrating.

As these examples indicate there is a substantial risk of loss if the legal status of a loan is somehow jeopardized or unclear. For this reason, the loan policy should require that any doubts or legal uncertainty be resolved prior to the disbursal of funds.

Elements of
A "Wall"

Earlier in this chapter the use of *insider information* was discussed along with the need for a "Chinese Wall." Recall that the purpose of this barrier is to control the flow of material insider information between the commercial loan department and the trust department and avoid violating securities laws. The main elements of a "Wall" should be contained in the loan policy statement.

The factors to consider when developing a "Wall" will vary among banks. Small banks usually lack significant commercial loan relationships with larger, publicly held corporations. Since it is unlikely that such banks would have access to much material insider information, a simple policy statement prohibiting the use of insider information may suffice. Large banks usually have extensive relationships

---

[15] "Chase Bank and Others Face Court Challenge on Huge Loans in Iran," *Wall Street Journal*, March 28, 1980, p. 1.

with publicly held firms so a more comprehensive policy statement is required. Several of the more important factors to consider when building a "Wall" are summarized below.

- *Physical Separation.* The trust and commercial loan departments should be separated physically within the same building. Some banks go so far as to locate their trust activities and their loan departments in separate buildings.
- *Legal Separation.* Only very large banks are capable of legally separating the trust and loan functions by forming a separate corporation to engage in trust activities. The effectiveness of such a separation is questionable in view of the court's willingness to "pierce the corporate veil." However, such a move clearly signals a bank's intention to have a "Wall."
- *Authorized Communication.* A policy may specify that nonmaterial information may be exchanged. At the other extreme, an exchange of information of any kind may be prohibited. It may seem reasonable to allow a trust officer to see nonmaterial information in credit files or allow a loan officer to see industry reports in the trust department files. When such communications are allowed, the "Wall" loses credibility.
- *Committee Membership.* Trust personnel should not be members of any bank committee where credit matters are discussed, nor should loan officers play a role in the selection of trust investments.
- *Directors.* Bank officers and directors often serve as directors of other companies. This is a sensitive issue. Bank policy must prohibit the bank's use of information obtained in such a capacity. This prohibition should extend to both the loan and trust departments.

Depending on the bank, other aspects of a "Wall" may be necessary to ensure compliance. Regardless of how well the "Wall" is built, its success depends heavily on management's effort to educate the personnel involved.

The development of a well-conceived loan policy statement is no simple task. As should be clear from some of the guidelines presented previously, consideration must be given to a number of risk-return tradeoffs and interrelated issues. If such a policy is loosely written, unexpected and unpleasant surprises may result. If a policy is overly restrictive the bank's flexibility, earnings, and ability to meet customer needs will be adversely affected. The key point is that all banks must have a loan policy to avoid *ad hoc* decision-making and corresponding results.

CONCLUSION

This chapter focused on managing the commercial lending function of a bank. The types of loans and services offered, the credit decision, and loan pricing procedures were examined along with commercial lending regulations. The basic elements of a commercial lending policy statement were discussed. An understanding of these issues plays a key role in the success of a commercial bank. The banking industry's ability to perform in a socially and economically responsible manner is also affected by the commercial lending issues discussed in this chapter.

REFERENCES

Altman, Edward I., Robert G. Haldeman, and P. Narayanan, "Zeta^{TM} Analysis: A New Model to Identify Bankruptcy Risk of Corporations," *Journal of Banking and Finance,* June 1, 1977, pp. 29-54.

Carswell, Robert, "Construction of the Chinese Wall," *Trust Management Update,* Washington, D.C.: American Bankers Association, July 1977, pp. 1-6.

Castle, Grover R., "Project Financing—Guidelines for the Commercial Banker," *Journal of Commercial Bank Lending,* April 1975, pp. 14-30.

Conlin, Graham P., *Commercial Loan Review Procedures,* Philadelphia, Pa: Robert Morris Associates, 1978.

Cramer, Robert H. and William E. Sterk, "The Present Value Approach to Commercial Loan Pricing," *Journal of Bank Research,* 12 (Winter 1982), pp. 207-217.

Durden, Hugh M., "Legal Risks in Commercial Lending," *Journal of Commercial Bank Lending,* November 1973, pp. 11-18.

Maris, Brian A., "Irrationality of Compensating Balances," *Journal of Commercial Bank Lending,* October 1978, pp. 50-53.

Merris, Randall C., "Loan Commitments and Facility Fees," *Economic Perspectives,* Federal Reserve Bank of Chicago, March/April 1978, pp. 14-21.

——. "Business Loans at Large Commercial Banks: Policies and Practices," *Economic Perspectives,* Federal Reserve Bank of Chicago, November/December 1979, pp. 15-23.

Myers, Ray F., "The Trust Wall—Or Stay Alive with 10b-5," *Trust Management Update,* Washington, D. C.: American Bankers Association, May 1976, pp. 1-8.

Reed, Edward W., Richard V. Cotter, Edward K. Gill, and Richard K. Smith, *Commercial Banking,* 2nd ed., Englewood Cliffs, N. J.: Prentice-Hall, 1980.

Severson, Gary R., "Determining Pricing Alternatives," *Journal of Commercial Bank Lending,* November 1974, pp. 2-8.

Small, Thomas A., "Letters of Credit for the Commercial Lender," *Journal of Commercial Bank Lending,* August 1980, pp. 5-13.

Van Horne, James C., *Financial Management and Policy,* 5th ed., Englewood Cliffs, N. J.: Prentice-Hall, 1980, Chapter 19.

5

Penn Square, Upstream Lending, and the Bank Examination Dilemma*

Robert R. Dince†

What bank examiners do and how they do it is not a subject that is well known to the general public. A search of memory reveals only one bank examiner appearing as a character in American myth. Franklin Pangborn, the bank examiner in the famous W. C. Fields epic, "The Bank Dick," is portrayed as a sick, confused, drunken fool who was victimized by the bank dick and other bank employees. Forty years later, in Martin Mayer's study, *The Bankers*, we are exposed to another examiner. This one is a gum-chewing, rather silly young woman. Four decades separate these two portraits. Have examination techniques changed or improved in that time?

The traditional bank examination emphasized credit review and asset appraisal. Verification of items was another important function. Then came the failure of the Franklin National Bank in 1974, and that was the trigger for the first major overhaul of federal examination procedures. The then Comptroller of the Currency, James E. Smith, hired the "big-eight" firm of Haskin and Sells to review and revise national bank examination techniques. These revised procedures became operational in 1976. Creation of the Federal Inter-agency Examination Council resulted in partial acceptance of many of these new techniques by the other federal bank supervisory agencies, the Federal Deposit Insurance Corporation (FDIC) and the Federal Reserve Bank (FRB).

The revised techniques of the Office of the Comptroller of the Currency (OCC) emphasize processes and procedures. Devised with the help of auditors, the new

---

*Reprinted by permission from *The Bankers Magazine*, Volume 165, Number 6, November-December 1982, copyright © 1982, Warren, Gorham, and Lamont, Inc., 210 South Street, Boston, Mass. All rights reserved.

†The author is Professor of Finance at the University of Georgia.

methods emphasize that good audit procedures and management review practices be in place. Rather than looking only at asset quality, the traditional examination target, the new procedures find out how well the external and internal auditors do their job. Further, the new examination techniques insist on proper managerial review procedures and director review of managerial policies.

To quote directly from the current *OCC Examiner Handbook* (Sec. 1.1, p. 1), the functions of the examination are:

> (1) ... to provide an objective evaluation of a bank's soundness; (2) to permit the OCC to appraise the quality of management and directors; and (3) to identify those areas where corrective action is required to strengthen the bank, to improve the quality of its performance, and to enable it to comply with applicable laws, rulings, and regulations.

These resounding words are backed by a force of 2,500 OCC examiners, plus 3,000 other federal examiners and a larger number of state examiners. All this examination work costs approximately $500 million annually and cries out for a cost-benefit analysis. What are all these examiners really doing and are their efforts worth the cost?

The bank examination process does not prevent bank failures. The primary reason that bank failures occur is because of some form of fraud. Good management and good controls are the best defense against bank failure. As Professor Anthony Santomero of the Wharton School said:

> I think that the internal desire to run an orderly institutional structure and the internal desire to maintain profit growth is 90 percent of the reason we have very few bank failures. I think auditing is 6 percent and examination is 3 percent—and 1 percent is fraud. But the main factor is a viable management.[1]

In recent years, a major crisis occurred in the savings and loan industry. There, the traditional things examiners do had no effect on the viability of these institutions. Interest rate risk and not poor economic conditions or insider self-dealing laid the industry low. The regulators seemed to have been as unaware as management that a crisis was brewing, yet the S&L industry was sinking into oblivion before our eyes—and the eyes of regulators.

THE PENN SQUARE STORY

Since 1976, a number of banks with deposits exceeding $200 million have either failed or had serious financial difficulties. The bank examination process, revised or not, has not eliminated the severe risks faced by modern banking. For example, the difficulties with Penn Square Bank were uncovered in early 1980. A restraining memorandum was signed in September 1980. The bank was examined again in

---

[1] Personal interview, September 15, 1982.

October 1981 and its *improved* condition duly noted. Finally, in the Spring of 1982, the examiners came back and found the situation hopeless. Yet the Comptroller of the Currency stated that the bank had been under constant supervision of the Washington office, backed up by an elaborate computer surveillance system which was considered so good it was adopted by the Federal Reserve Bank for its monitoring activities.

The most revealing point about the Penn Square Bank, however, involved the "3" rating that the bank received after its 1980 examination. The bank maintained its "CAMEL" rating of "3" right up until the time the bank failed in the summer of 1982.[2] The "3" rating indicates a bank with some problems but serious loss or insolvency is not expected. So the bank was not in such a precarious situation as to tie up excessive examiner resources. What, then, were the examiners doing?

First, the OCC field examiners in Oklahoma were covering all the other Oklahoma national banks, the vast majority of which were in acceptable condition. On a national basis, for example, as of July 1982, only 37 out of about 4,375 national banks were in the worst categories 4 and 5, plus an additional 264 in the "poor" category "3." The examiners were out working the other 4,074 national banks. It takes a crew of five examiners two weeks to examine a bank with assets of $50 million. Roughly 5,000 examiners are needed for a single annual examination of all national banks with assets less than $100 million. Assuming 90 percent of these banks are in good condition, only 500 of these examiners were uncovering problem banks. Since, at most, there were only 2,500 national bank examiners to examine all national banks from Citibank to First National Bank of Alachua, something had to give. Either the examination schedule, the time in banks, or the thoroughness of the examination had to be allowed to slip.

Suppose a crew of five examiners had been placed for the whole 2½-year period in Penn Square. They would have missed examining 65 small banks, at least 60 of them in excellent shape. Instead of stopping Penn Square from selling $2 billion of questionable loan participations, the examination schedule was maintained.

But examiners complain that such criticism is unfair. It is argued that without examinations the 90 percent of banks in good condition might go bad. But this is the core of the problem; it is management, not examinations, which keeps banking a growing, viable, and scrupulously honest industry. The vast majority of all banks, then, are needlessly examined.

Under the so-called Lance Act of 1979, bank regulatory agencies have the right to remove bank officers and assess civil money penalties against wayward banks. Unless there are criminal acts, most regulators are reluctant to remove a bank officer. This is the crux of the examiner's dilemma—how tough should the examiners be and for what purpose?

What do the examiners do in the good banks? They check internal review procedures. They sample credit files looking for poor credits. They are particularly sensitive to evidence of officer or director self-dealing. They inspect files looking for violations of the Truth-in-Lending Act, Equal Credit Opportunity Act, and

---

[2] The acronym CAMEL was adopted by all Federal agencies in 1978. It refers to a uniform rating system in which captial, asset quality, management, earnings, and liquidity are all separately rated on a scale of 1 to 5. The overall rating is given by the regional administrator's office and not by the field examiners. About 93 percent of all national banks have a "1" or "2" rating.

anti-redlining regulations. These federal consumer protection laws are the creation of Congress responding to political pressures. These pressures are felt by regulators.

The bank examination process has changed so much that the old unannounced, surprise visit has been replaced by an announced visit in order that bank files and computer records can be ready for inspection. Surprise visits are supposed to be pointless if banks are under regular computer financial review.

The frantic activity in selling loans and buying money should have been a tip-off that something was wrong at the Penn Square Bank. Without examining the bank and working from public sources, David Cates, running a bank rating service, claimed that computer monitoring with available data revealed Penn Square's troubles. If the problems were visible to Cates, they surely should have been caught by the Comptroller's computer surveillance system. Perhaps a field examiner hears so many bells and whistles go off that there is a tendency to become bored and blasé about endless computer warnings.

The computer surveillance system using only financial data turns up about 12 to 15 percent of all national banks as being potential problem banks. But according to the OCC's official statement in July 1982, only 7 percent of all national banks were on the actual problem list as confirmed by actual bank examination, and less than one percent of all national banks were considered really serious cases.

UPSTREAM LENDING

There is an interesting aspect of the bank examination process that was revealed by the Penn Square collapse. Penn Square originated a high volume of energy-related loans which it promptly passed through to other banks. Why these other banks willingly purchased poor loans in such quantity is not apparent. But why the OCC, tracking the situation since 1980, did not ascertain where the Penn Square loans were going and severely criticize these loans at the buying banks as well as the selling bank, is another story.

It is common knowledge that where jurisdictional and geographical lines cross, the examination process tends to weaken. The fact is that for a variety of reasons— the turnover of top personnel, the rapidly changing character of banking, the lack of examiner training—the examining agencies have fallen technically far behind their clients.

Some regulators argue that the Penn Square affair was an aberration. Penn Square was *not* an aberration. It was the reaction of an over-zealous, middle-sized bank to a rapidly changing banking environment. If new high-risk assets are funded with high-cost purchased money, then trouble lies ahead. The examiner, the auditor, the officer, the director—they all knew the bank was in trouble. Yet no one blew the whistle.

One facet of OCC bank examination procedures reveals why bad loans made at Penn Square, the shopping center bank run amok, were not picked up by an examiner at Continental or Seafirst. Loans chosen for credit review come from a combination of sources, scheduled and random. In a general examination, the examiner looks at every loan criticized in the last examination, every loan criticized by the bank's own internal review staff, and every past due credit. In addition, the examiner looks at every loan that exceeds an amount equal to 1.4 percent of capital. From the remaining loans, all of which are less than this cutoff point, a random sample is selected for a detailed examination. The examination focuses on the loan's quality, documentation, and compliance with bank policy.

To obtain the sample, the examiner must establish a starting point and a sampling interval. Bank loans are numbered sequentially and are of a certain size. For a starting point the very first loan may be selected. A more sophisticated approach is to take the last digit of the serial number on a dollar bill as the number of the starting loan. The next step is to determine the dollar size of the sampling interval. This interval ranges from zero to an upper limit equal to about 7 percent of the bank's capital. Once the starting loan has been selected, the dollar amount of this loan and the amounts of the following, sequentially numbered loans are cumulatively added together until the total exceeds the upper limit of the sampling interval. The loan that causes the limit to be exceeded is then examined in detail, regardless of its size.

In the case of the Continental Illinois Bank, this examination and sampling procedure caused problems. Only those participated Penn Square loans in an amount exceeding 1.4 percent of the bank's capital, or $25 million, would have been examined. Apparently, none of the individual loans was this large. As a result, the Penn Square loans would have been examined only if randomly selected.

The chances of picking up one of the low-quality, oil-patch loans at a buying bank as large as Continental Illinois is quite remote.[3] Suppose the examiners in Oklahoma find bad loans and notify the regional office in Dallas. That office will notify all the Eleventh Region examiners to be on the lookout for participated loans flowing out of Penn Square. Unfortunately, the same warning flashed to Chicago rarely gets to the field examiner in the same agency. The Chicago office would not schedule a special examination of Continental based on what the examiners discovered in Oklahoma City.

Not only was there a serious lack of follow-up within the OCC, the other federal regulatory agencies apparently did nothing prior to the closing. Under the Bank Holding Company Act, the Federal Reserve Bank is responsible for the examination of bank holding companies. The chronology of events subsequently made public by the Comptroller of the Currency shows that the FRB took no special action either with the Penn Square holding company or the holding companies of the banks that bought Penn Square's loans. (Chase Manhattan, Continental, and Seafirst are all holding company banks.) The Fed could not claim they were unaware of the problems since they routinely receive examination reports on all member banks and this includes all national banks.

The FDIC represents a different story. This agency examines state chartered, non-member, insured banks. However, since national banks are examined by the

---

[3] According to rough estimates, the examiners would have looked at only 220 randomly selected loans at the Continental Illinois Bank. Since the number of loans booked at Continental was unknown, the probability of finding a Penn Square loan cannot be determined. But surely the odds are in excess of 100 to 1 against the examiners finding a Penn Square loan in the huge Continental portfolio—unless they were pointed to the loans. Since Continental continued to buy loan participation from Penn Square, one must deduce that the Dallas office of the OCC did not sufficiently warn the Chicago office that a serious problem was brewing.

OCC, these banks are outside the FDIC's examination jurisdiction. State chartered, member, insured banks are examined by the FRB. Thus, for those insured banks not under its jurisdiction for examination purposes, the FDIC is like a pathologist. It is called in when the patient is dying or dead.

Only when loans are over $20 million and known to be participated among many banks are they considered a "national credit." A committee of examiners from the three federal agencies determines a uniform credit rating for these loans. Thus every bank with a loan to Chrysler, for example, would have the loan classified the same way. But selling bundles of small commercial loans to larger banks all over the country is a situation which falls unnoticed between the examination cracks.

SECRECY OR DISCLOSURE?

After the 1980 examination of Penn Square, the OCC forced management of the bank to sign an *Administrative Order*. This formally put the bank and the OCC on record as to what the problems were and what action by the bank was required to correct the situation. Although this type of order is less formal than a *Cease and Desist Order* issued by a court, ignoring any aspect of an Administrative Order can lead to civil money penalties or the removal of recalcitrant officers and/ or directors.

But the key to any form of administrative action is secrecy—and this is another dilemma posed by the bank examination process. Secrecy permits the bank to get its house in order and reverse the tide before failure becomes inevitable.[4] The alternative is disclosure. Disclosure permits the financial markets to adjust to the risk, and the bank bears the brunt of its own mistakes. Letting the cat out of the bag would alert the large uninsured depositor, the buyer of loan participations, and generally make the community nervous, leading to deposit runoffs.

After the failure of the Penn Square Bank, the Comptroller of the Currency said that "not all failures are bad and some were needed to maintain the discipline of the market place."[5] Behind this statement is our modern concept of deposit insurance which covers deposits up to $100,000. An insured bank is able to use this insurance to shift some of its banking risk. Thus, insurance may be viewed as part of the bank's capital. If the government really insured all the deposits rather than just a portion, then we would totally eliminate the healthy effect of bank failures. If the government absorbs all the risks, managerial judgment is eliminated and the social cost might be very high. A system that is not allowed to fail cannot remain completely healthy.

We all agree that a bank buying bad loans should know better and a large depositor should use some discretion in placing large sums of money. But shouldn't everyone know the extent of the real risk? Do we want the slow lingering death

---

[4] The secret of Penn Square's problems was so well kept that when reading the anonymous versions of all the orders in the OCC's annual report, it is impossible to find the one covering Penn Square.

[5] *New York Times*, July 22, 1982, p. 34.

caused by the examining agency's penchant for secrecy? Or is the quicker, certain demise in the open marketplace the better way? The answer is not obvious. But at least the slow way gives you more time. The trouble may work itself out. Oil might reach $40 a barrel and some of those Penn Square loans might be good.

WHAT HAPPENS NEXT?

The perplexing question of where the examination fits into the scheme of things was addressed by Comptroller C. T. Conover in his first interview after taking office. He said:

> We will continue to examine banks. I should say that we will continue to obtain information about their activities, and the examination process will be one of the ways that we will obtain that information. Then we will interpret it and take action where it's appropriate to do so.[6]

With the failure of Penn Square and the involvement of so many other banks, coupled with a rapidly changing banking environment, it appears that the regulators have their work cut out for themselves.

Ed. Note. Subsequent to the collapse of the Penn Square Bank and the original publication of this article, the Comptroller of the Currency revised its examination procedure. So-called "problem banks" are now examined more frequently while banks with a high examiner rating are examined less frequently.

---

[6] Richard B. Miller, "Conversations with the Reagan Regulators," *The Bankers Magazine*, March/April 1982, p. 35.

A Supervisory Approach to Foreign Lending[*]

Roger M. Kubarych

International lending activities by United States commercial banks have increased greatly in size, complexity, and geographical scope during recent years. International credits now make up a significant portion of major bank loan portfolios and represent an important source of bank earnings. Foreign lending, of course, involves special kinds of risk that are not ordinarily found in domestic lending, although banks' loss experience from foreign loans has in fact been better than from domestic loans in recent years. Nevertheless, the rapid growth of international banking activities has created the need for improved techniques on the part of both banks and bank supervisors for defining, monitoring, and controlling those special risks.

The Federal Reserve System responded by reviewing existing bank examination procedures for foreign credits. It also made a survey in early 1977 of risk management practices by United States banks. Drawing on these reviews, a System Committee on Foreign Lending recommended changes in Federal Reserve procedures to strengthen supervision of international banking. The Federal Reserve Bank of New York has adopted these procedures on a trial basis in its current examinations of international loan portfolios. Systemwide implementation would follow final approval by the Board of Governors.

The other Federal bank supervisory agencies—the Office of the Comptroller of the Currency (OCC) and the Federal Deposit Insurance Corporation (FDIC)—were in the meantime studying their respective systems for supervising foreign lending. The three agencies joined together in an effort to develop principles for a common approach to international bank supervision. The aim is an effective supervisory system to ensure that foreign lending does not have adverse effects on the safety and soundness of the United States banking system.

*Reprinted from the *Quarterly Review*, Spring 1978, pp. 1-6, with permission from the Federal Reserve Bank of New York.

A broad measure of agreement has now been reached on the essentials of a new Federal supervisory approach to foreign lending. An important element is the development of a common reporting form, which measures overall international exposure and its components for each bank. Most banks in this country with international operations have been asked to provide information on their foreign exposure twice a year. That information would enable bank supervisors to evaluate the exposure by country of individual banks and of the United States banking system as a whole.

A further element involves changes in procedures for examination of bank international loan portfolios. The emphasis would be on identifying concentrations of lending that seem large relative to bank capital and country conditions. In addition, examiners would pay particular attention to a bank's own procedures for monitoring and controlling its exposure in each country where it does business.

This article provides some of the details of how the new approach was developed and how it is expected to work.

DEFINING THE SPECIAL RISKS OF INTERNATIONAL LENDING

Much of the risk in foreign lending is no different from that in domestic lending. The present and future standing of individual borrowers must be appraised and monitored in light of changes in economic and financial conditions. Well-managed companies may be adversely affected by a general economic slowdown in a country or by problems in a particular industry. Poorly managed companies may have difficulties even in a strengthening economy. Banks and bank examiners have found it useful to analyze *credit risk* in loan portfolios in terms of traditional risk categories.[1] These same categories are applied to individual international credits as well as to domestic credits.

In addition, international lending involves *country risk*. It is a principal factor that differentiates international lending from domestic lending. Country risk can be and has been defined in various ways. But, broadly speaking, it encompasses the whole spectrum of risks that arise from the economic, social, legal, and political conditions of a foreign country and that may have potentially favorable or adverse consequences for loans to borrowers in that country. More concretely, country risk includes the risks of political or social upheaval, nationalization or expropriation, government repudiation of external debts, exchange controls, or foreign exchange shortfalls that might make it impossible for a country to meet external obligations on time. In some cases, payment of interest or principal on loans may be delayed or loan terms may have to be restructured. In rare cases, the result may be actual loan defaults.

Events such as these might materially affect the condition of the United States banks that make loans to a foreign country. Consequently, the potential risks must

---

[1] Three classifications of loans with above-normal risk are used by examiners: substandard, doubtful, and loss. In addition, some loans which are superior to those in the substandard class are specially mentioned as warranting more than usual management attention.

be carefully considered by banks and bank examiners. The examiners are responsible for alerting bank management to those risks that might be difficult for a bank to absorb and might therefore jeopardize the liquidity or soundness of the bank.

THE FEDERAL RESERVE'S REVIEW OF INTERNATIONAL LENDING

In view of the growth of international lending by United States banks and the enlarged role of commercial banks in financing international payments imbalances, the Federal Reserve undertook a comprehensive review of the System's supervisory approach in this area. An *ad hoc* Committee on Foreign Lending was appointed in late 1976 to study procedures and techniques used by member banks in making foreign loans and by Federal Reserve examiners in appraising state-chartered member bank foreign lending.

The committee initially conducted a survey of the existing foreign lending practices of member banks. The survey took the form of detailed discussions with senior bank officers by representatives of Federal Reserve Banks and the staff of the Board of Governors. In addition, an OCC examiner attended each meeting with a national bank. In all, discussions were held with 46 banks across the country, including the 25 largest banks, to obtain a broad cross section by bank size and location.

The discussions were structured around questions concerning a bank's procedures for appraising, monitoring, and controlling foreign credit exposure. Each bank was asked how it defined country exposure, how it distinguished between different types and maturities of credits, and how it treated such factors as guarantees, collateral, and contingencies. The bank was asked whether limits on credits or commitments to a country were established and how they were reviewed as a country's economic and financial conditions changed. Questions were posed on how economic projections for a country were considered in individual lending decisions. Finally, each bank was asked about its policy toward diversification of country credits.

The survey revealed that all banks visited had in place internal systems for monitoring and controlling foreign lending, although practices varied considerably from bank to bank. The range of procedures largely reflected differences in bank size and organization as well as the kinds of international business conducted by individual banks. But they also reflected the relative inexperience of some banks in defining country risk and in measuring exposure to that risk. As a result, the detailed measurement of country exposure differed among banks, both in the types of credits considered subject to country risk and in the methods for consolidating the exposure to a country of different offices of a bank.

Although banks would naturally wish to emphasize particular aspects of their country exposure depending upon their business, the survey suggested that a greater uniformity in measuring exposure would be useful. It would allow bank supervisors to compare banks and let individual banks compare their foreign loan portfolios with averages for others. But, given the diversity of bank size and organization, it would not be desirable to impose a uniform set of procedures for all banks to use in evaluating, monitoring, and controlling foreign lending. Instead, the survey suggested aspects of an effective risk management system could be drawn from the experience at a wide range of banks.

WHAT A NEW SUPERVISORY APPROACH SHOULD INCLUDE

From this review, it became clear that a restructured supervisory approach to appraising foreign lending should incorporate several features.

It should provide for uniform measurement of a bank's country exposure and a systematic basis for calling bank management's attention to any relatively large exposure which might be potentially troublesome. There is no precise way of measuring country risk, *per se*, or of assigning probabilities to potentially adverse developments in a country. However, a bank's country exposure, the sum of its credits and commitments to a country, can be quantified. A consistent measure of exposure would allow examiners to compare portfolio management among different banks and to formulate standards for appropriate diversification within portfolios.

It should ensure that banks themselves have adequate internal systems for appraising, monitoring, and controlling country exposure. A bank supervisor can assess a bank's country exposure only at periodic intervals, but a bank's exposure may change from day to day. An effective internal control system is essential for maintaining continuous management oversight of international lending.

It should keep the appraisal of country exposure separate from the traditional risk classification system used for evaluating individual credits.

It should be capable of uniform application throughout the System. In the past, individual examiners had differing approaches to appraising international loan portfolios, and their individual judgments could vary.

It should provide a mechanism by which Federal Reserve Bank examiners would draw upon the knowledge and expertise of specialists within the System about country conditions to help identify potentially adverse developments in a country.

It should not give credit ratings to countries. Nor should it establish a list of particularly risky countries to which banks would be told not to lend. Bank supervisors are concerned with the condition of individual institutions as the components of a sound banking system. Actions of bank supervisors are not intended to result in the channeling of credit flows toward or away from specific countries or to lead to large disruptions of credit flows. In any case, there is no reason to believe that assessments about countries by bank supervisors would always be better than those of commercial banks.

It should recognize the great uncertainties that exist in any assessment of country risk and should stress that banks are best protected against adverse developments through diversification within their foreign loan portfolios.

Based on those criteria, new examination procedures and techniques were developed that would assist examiners in making more professional evaluations of individual loans and country exposures. They were field tested at state-chartered member banks in the New York, Chicago, and San Francisco Districts in the course of regular examinations. In addition, examination concepts and proposed techniques were discussed with senior officers of several other member banks.

Concurrently, work was in progress by the OCC and the FDIC to review their respective examination procedures for international lending. Discussions among the Federal Reserve and these other agencies suggested that a new Federal supervisory approach would provide the most effective and most equitable basis for examining United States banks' foreign lending portfolios. A broad measure of consensus has been reached on the basic elements of that approach. These are outlined in the following section.

THE NEW SUPERVISORY APPROACH

Under the new supervisory approach to international lending, credit risk would continue to be appraised using standard examination procedures and techniques. Individual credits would be reviewed to determine the creditworthiness of the borrowers. Credits identified as having an above-normal credit risk element would be classified by the examiner using the traditional groupings of substandard, doubtful, and loss.

Where the new examination approach would differ from previous procedures is in the treatment of country risk. The new approach would consist of three parts:

1. Measurement of exposure in each country where a bank has a business relationship. In turn, individual bank exposure would be consolidated to show the overall exposure of the United Stated banking system to each country abroad.
2. Analysis of exposure levels and concentrations of exposure in relation to the bank's capital resources and the economic and financial conditions of each country in which the bank has outstanding credits.
3. Evaluation of the risk management system used by the bank in relation to the size and nature of its foreign lending activities.

The end product would be an examination report that reviews internal management systems and identifies certain concentrations of credit within the foreign loan portfolio that warrant management attention.

MEASUREMENT OF EXPOSURE

The Federal Reserve survey of United States commercial banks' foreign lending practices showed that there was no standard or uniform banking industry approach to measuring country exposure and no single best method among those used by different banks. Similarly, the Federal supervisory authorities had been defining country exposure differently.

The Federal supervisory authorities have now agreed on a uniform method for measuring exposure. It is based on a common reporting system for international lending information. That system benefited from earlier exercises in collecting international lending data conducted by the major central banks under the auspices of the Bank for International Settlements (BIS). But it goes further by measuring international exposure on a consolidated bank basis. Thus, loans to each foreign country would be included whether made by a bank's head office or by a branch or affiliate abroad. Information about foreign claims is provided by each reporting bank in a semiannual country exposure report, beginning with data for end-December 1977.[2] The report breaks down the bank's claims for each country by type of borrower and by maturity. Loan commitments and other contingencies are also detailed. Activities of a bank's foreign offices with local residents in local currencies are shown separately.

One feature of the country exposure report takes account of an important distinction in international lending. The location of a borrower may not coincide with the location of the ultimate country exposure. If, for example, a United States bank has made a loan to a borrower in country X and the loan is guaranteed by another institution in country Y, then the ultimate country exposure is allocated to country Y.

In its exposure report, a bank is asked to reallocate credits and commitments to the country where the ultimate risk appears to reside. The examiner would then be able to analyze the foreign loan portfolio by this more comprehensive treatment of country exposure, as well as by country of location of borrower. The reallocation of exposure takes into account external guarantees or realizable collateral outside the country of the borrower. In the case of claims on foreign branches of other banks, ultimate exposure is reallocated to the location of those banks' head offices.

By consolidating the data for all reporting banks, the supervisory authorities also get a clearer picture, by location of credit and by country of ultimate risk, of the United States banking system's exposure to each country abroad. These aggregates allow the authorities to compare one bank's foreign loan portfolio with those of other United States banks.

In the examination process, the examiner would use the information from the country exposure report in analyzing a bank's international exposure. In particular, the examiner would express the overall measure of exposure for each country where a bank has outstanding credits as a ratio of the bank's capital funds. These ratios would give a picture of the bank's concentrations of lending relative to its own ultimate resources to absorb risk. They would serve also as an indicator to the examiner of which parts of a bank's international portfolio deserve a deeper look.

In summary, the country exposure data would enable the examiner: (1) to evaluate the amounts, location, maturities, and types of claims a bank has abroad, (2) to evaluate the amounts of claims reallocated to country of ultimate risk, and

---

[2] The country exposure report is filed by all United States banks and bank holding companies with international activity above a specified level. For a description of the report see the Box.

COUNTRY EXPOSURE REPORT

A semiannual country exposure report (FR 2036, CC 7610-88, or FDIC 6502/03) is filed by all United States banks and bank holding companies with international activity above a specified level. The report consolidates exposure for all domestic and foreign offices of an institution. Aggregate data from the country exposure report will be made public. The initial report provides data for end-1977. Results of a preliminary survey for June 1977 were released in Janauary 1978.

Country exposure includes both outstanding claims on foreign residents and contingencies. Foreign claims are defined under three categories: (1) *Cross-border claims* are those of bank offices located in one country on residents of other countries. A loan to a company in Britain by a New York bank's head office is a cross-border claim. (2) *Nonlocal currency claims* are those of a bank's foreign offices on local residents denominated in currencies other than the local currency. A loan in dollars to a company in Britain by a New York bank's London branch is a nonlocal currency claim. (3) *Local currency claims* are those of a bank's foreign offices on local residents denominated in the local currency. A loan in pounds sterling to a company in Britain by a New York bank's London branch is a local currency claim.

On the report, cross-border and nonlocal currency claims are combined and shown by country of residence of the borrower. The total for each country is broken down by type of borrower: banks, public borrowers, and all other borrowers. The totals are also broken down by estimated time remaining to maturity. Four maturity categories are used: one year and under, one to two years, two to five years, and over five years.

Contingencies are shown separately. They are contractual commitments to extend credit, such as letters of credit and undisbursed portions of loans that are not subject to further bank approval. Contingencies are broken down into two categories: (1) public borrowers and (2) banks and other nonpublic borrowings.

Total cross-border and foreign office nonlocal currency claims are adjusted for each country to take account of external guarantees, collateral, and interbank placements that shift the ultimate country risk to another country. The reporting bank makes a separate tally by reallocating the claims from the country of the borrower to that of the guarantor. A similar reallocation is made for contingencies. The adjusted data show exposure by country of ultimate risk.

Guarantees are narrowly defined to include only formal and legal obligations by residents of countries other than the borrowers'. Claims collateralized by tangible and liquid assets (*e.g.,* cash, certificates of deposit, gold, marketable securities) are reallocated to the country where the pledged assets are held or where their value can be fully realized. In the case of marketable securities, for instance, the exposure would usually be shifted to the country where the security was issued. Interbank claims on a branch abroad are shifted to the country in which the head office is located. Claims on subsidiary banks are adjusted to the country of the parent only if formally guaranteed or collateralized in that country.

Local currency claims of a foreign office, the third category of claims noted above, are treated as a country exposure only to the extent that they are not offset by local currency liabilities. To provide a broader picture, local currency assets and liabilities by country are shown separately.

As a final entry, each reporting institution shows for each country in which it has offices the net amount "due to" or "due from" those offices. This reflects the cross-border flows of funds within a banking organization.

(3) to compare the exposure levels with the bank's capital and to suggest areas for further analysis.

ANALYSIS OF EXPOSURE LEVELS AND CONCENTRATIONS

The second part of the new examination approach would involve analysis of country exposure levels and concentrations of exposure. The objective would be to identify high concentrations of exposure relative to the bank's capital funds and relative to the economic and financial conditions of borrowing countries.

The analysis of country exposure levels would involve three steps:

1. An evaluation of country conditions by research economists and country specialists. These evaluations would be made available to bank examiners for use as background to their analyses of foreign loan portfolios.
2. Disaggregation by the examiner of aggregate exposure by referring to a bank's internal records. Particular attention would be paid to the types of borrowers and the maturity distribution of the bank's foreign claims.
3. Examiner comments on the results of the analysis.

Countries that warrant in-depth review would be identified through simple statistical screening techniques. The techniques would be used to pick out countries which have, in relation to other countries, large current account deficits or heavy external debt service or low international reserve positions relative to the size of their own economies and their external trade. The aim is to base a screening mechanism on objective criteria. But the statistical indicators themselves are not designed to be, nor would they be used as, predictors of potential debt repayment difficulties.

For this limited screening purpose, indicators have been computed from reported balance-of-payments statistics and other financial data. One is a measure of short-term current account imbalance, while another is an indication of medium-term current account imbalance and the rate of external debt-accumulation. Other indicators measure countries' debt interest burden in terms of such factors as current receipts (exports of goods and services) and international reserves. The indicators would be regularly computed for the major borrowing countries in which United States banks have exposure.

The screening mechanism is intended to be suggestive only and not exhaustive. But its obvious advantage is its objectivity and relative simplicity. System research economists, moreover, continue assessing available economic statistics which could improve the screening process.

Countries identified through the screening process would be thoroughly reviewed. Comprehensive studies would be prepared for the examiner's use in raising questions with the bank under examination and in appraising country risk in portfolio concentrations. On the economic side, the focus would be on a country's balance of payments and its international reserves, both current and prospective. The review would also include an analysis of the country's domestic economic situation and government policies, foreign exchange rate behavior, and structural trends in the economy. In addition, conditions affecting political and social stability would be noted, especially as they may have a bearing on the overall economic environment.

These reviews of country conditions would provide background for the examiner's analysis of exposure concentrations in a bank's international loan portfolio. All country concentrations which appeared high would be looked at in detail. A bank's outstanding credits in a country would be examined by type of business (loans, acceptances, investment, placements, etc.), by maturity (short-term versus long-term), and by class of borrower (government, nonbank private sector borrowers, and banks).

Drawing on this analysis of exposure levels and the assessment of country conditions, the examiner would comment on those country exposures which appeared high in relation to the bank's ability to absorb risk and to the country's condition. Certain norms would be established to guide examiners in making critical comments on high concentrations by country. These would not be hard and fast rules. But the approach would ensure a reasonable level of uniformity, while allowing the examiners to exercise judgment and discretion in framing their comments.

Examiner comments might include references to a country's status with the International Monetary Fund or adherence to conditions imposed by the IMF on credit drawings. Comments might also be made where a bank's outstanding loans to a country represent a disproportionate share of the total lending by United States banks to that country, or where information maintained by the bank on a country or group of countries is deemed inadequate.

The objective of any critical commentary would be to encourage appropriate diversification in a bank's international lending portfolio. Diversification remains a bank's best protection against risk in an uncertain world.

EVALUATION OF RISK MANAGEMENT SYSTEMS

The third part of the new examination approach would involve an evaluation of the risk management systems used by banks in appraising and controlling their foreign credit exposure. All banks engaging in international business should have the capability to analyze their customers and risks independently. No bank should lend to a particular borrower, for example, simply because other banks are extending credits to that borrower.

As the Federal Reserve survey of bank foreign lending practices confirmed, banks involved in international business have already set up internal systems for controlling foreign lending. There are notable differences in approach among banks, although these mostly reflect differences in the size and organizational structure of banks as well as the composition of their business.

Whatever the differences of detail, certain general characteristics should be found in all internal control systems. The examiner would need to be satisfied that a bank's risk management system is comprehensive and covers all aspects of the bank's international business. The examiner would evaluate the bank's internal system for measuring exposure to each country where the bank does business. The bank's methods for assessing country conditions would be evaluated to see whether risk assessments are based on reliable and up-to-date information, reviewed with reasonable frequency, and kept separate from marketing considerations. The bank's procedures for monitoring and controlling country exposure would be analyzed. The analysis would consider how the bank limits its lending to individual countries. It would also focus on how and at what stage country risk assessments are considered by bank officers in making lending decisions and in modifying country exposure limits. Any inadequacies found by the examiner in the bank's country risk management system would be brought to management's attention in the examination report.

CONCLUDING REMARKS

The new approach to appraising international lending outlined in this article has several advantages. It emphasizes diversification of risk in individual bank portfolios. By doing so, it avoids any implications of official credit ratings of foreign countries. It underlines the role of bank managements in seeking diversified portfolios and in maintaining adequate internal mechanisms for monitoring and controlling country exposure. Details of this supervisory approach are still being developed, and discussions among the Federal supervisory agencies are continuing. There is every reason to hope that before long the technical groundwork will be completed and a new approach fully implemented.

B. CONSUMER AND MORTGAGE LENDING

7

Consumer Lending

Lending activities of commercial banks are usually divided into three categories—commercial lending, mortgage lending, and the topic of this chapter, consumer lending. The term *consumer loans* refers to specific types of loans made to individuals rather than corporations, partnerships, or governments. Although mortgage loans are also made to individuals, they are separately classified because of their highly specialized nature and characteristics. Like other aspects of banking, decisions related to consumer loans are constrained by a variety of legal, regulatory and self-imposed policy constraints. And, like commercial loans, the related management decisions have important risk-return implications with short- and long-term consequences. In the following sections, these issues are examined by focusing on the types of loans, lending policies and practices, managerial issues, and the regulation of consumer-related lending.

TYPES OF CONSUMER LOANS

One of the most important issues facing the top management of a bank is the extent to which that bank will be oriented toward consumer loans. A consumer-oriented bank tends to have a larger proportion of its loan portfolio in consumer and mortgage loans and a correspondingly smaller proportion in the form of commercial loans. Generally, the *consumer loans* made by banks are installment loans, credit card loans and several types of personal loans.

Installment Loans

Installment loans usually represent the largest component of a bank's consumer loan portfolio. As the name implies, installment loans are repaid with regular installments, usually monthly, over terms ranging from one to four or five years. Such loans are made to finance automobiles, boats, appliances, furniture, and certain types of services. Usually expensive items such as mobile homes and motor homes are financed with longer terms. The asset acquired by the borrower usually collateralizes the loan. If an installment loan is used to finance the acquisition of services such as travel, medical, or educational expense, some other form of collateral or a co-signer may be required.

Installment loans made by banks are usually "closed-end." The entire amount is borrowed at the inception of the agreement rather than over time and at the option of the borrower. Compared to commercial loans, installment loans have a high servicing cost per dollar loaned. Servicing costs are fixed and the size of most consumer installment loans is relatively small, that is, less than $10,000. As the loan size decreases, the unit servicing cost increases. The net return on such loans can be considerably less than the quoted gross yield.

Although most installment loans are made directly by the bank to the borrower, some lenders purchase a sizable volume of loans initiated by the sellers of durable goods. However, when acquiring installment loans indirectly, extreme care must be exercised by the bank. At one time, under the provision of the *holder in due course doctrine*, banks had the legal right to collect on loans purchased from dealers or other loan originators even if the goods or services were defective. But in 1976, the Federal Trade Commission issued a regulation that had the effect of eliminating this doctrine as it relates to consumer loans. As a result, consumers can withhold payment to the bank for defective goods or services provided by the dealer. Thus, banks should only acquire the paper of reputable, well-established, and responsible dealers.

Credit Card Loans

Many commercial banks extend lines of consumer credit by issuing credit cards. These are "open-end" or revolving credit arrangements in that loans are made at the cardholder's discretion subject to some limit. Since these limits typically range from $1,000 to $2,000, credit cards are more suitable for smaller retail purchases than for "big-ticket" items such as cars, boats, or furniture. It is also possible to obtain small cash advances with credit cards.

Most bank credit card business is conducted under a franchise arrangement with VISA and/or MasterCard. In order to see how a bank provides a line of credit through a credit card, consider the following simplified example.

> *Example.* An individual holds a credit card issued by a bank in East Lansing, Michigan. On June 1st, while in Chicago, the individual purchases a suit and accessories for $450. After using the card to imprint a sales draft, the merchant sends the draft to its own bank which is also a franchised issuer of the same credit card. As

such, the bank is obligated to credit the merchant's account immediately. The credit is for $436.50, which is the face amount of the sales draft less a discount of 3 percent in this case, or $13.50. If the merchant had a credit card clearing agreement with the bank but not a deposit account, the bank would pay the merchant by check within a few days. The merchant's bank is reimbursed by the card-issuing bank in East Lansing. Three weeks later on the billing date of June 21st, the customer's credit card bill is mailed by the card-issuing bank. The customer then has the choice of paying the bill of $450 in full or making a partial payment and carrying the balance as a revolving credit loan. The payment must be made within 25 days, or by July 16th in this example.

Assuming a full payment of $450 is made, no interest would be charged even though the cardholder had a "free ride" for over six weeks. Assuming a payment of $50 is made, the July 21st statement will show a "previous" balance of $400 plus interest based on the average daily loan balance from June 1st to July 21st. Assuming no other purchases and an interest rate of 18 percent on the average daily loan balance, the interest charged for 51 days would be $400 × .18 × (51/365) = $10.06.[1]

Several aspects of this transaction should be noted. From a merchant's standpoint, the discount will range from 1 to 5 percent depending on the type of business and volume generated. In return, the merchant does not have to operate its own credit department and losses from bad checks are eliminated. From the customer's standpoint, the credit card represents a convenient alternative to carrying cash or checks. Furthermore, the customer has an instant line of credit, subject to the imposed limit.

Credit card operations pose a number of problems for banks. As shown in the example, when the entire balance is paid by the due date, the customer has use of the funds during a grace period. Therefore, unless "convenience-users" pay a fixed fee of some kind, these cardholders are subsidized by those who carry balances and pay an interest rate that is higher than would otherwise be the case. The significance of this problem was revealed in a study by Robert W. Johnson who found that approximately one-half the users of credit cards pay their balances in full and thus avoid interest charges.[2] This finding has important pricing implications which are discussed later in the chapter. In addition to the costs incurred because of the grace period, credit card operations are subject to losses resulting from bad debts, theft, and fraud. Furthermore, a little known provision of the *Fair Credit Billing Act (1975)* enables consumers to avoid paying for defective merchandise or services purchased with a credit card. When this occurs it is necessary for the bank to charge back the merchant to recoup the disbursed funds.

Since credit card operations have high fixed costs, a high volume of credit card transactions is necessary to achieve profitability. As a result, this banking function often incurs sizable losses in early stages. To complicate matters, the interest rate that banks can charge is subject to state usury laws. During periods of high interest

---

[1] Several methods are available for computing the interest charges on credit cards. For a thorough discussion of these approaches and their effects on profitability see: Ray McAlister and Edward DeSpain, "Credit Card Yields under Alternative Assessment Methods," *Journal of Retail Banking*, September 1980, pp. 56-75.

[2] Robert W. Johnson, "Pricing of Bank Card Services," *Journal of Retail Banking*, June 1979, pp. 16-22.

rates, the ceilings imposed by such laws often prevent banks from charging a suf-ficiently high rate to cover their cost of funds and other operating costs.

Other Consumer Loans

There are several other types of consumer loans made by commercial banks. The *single-payment* loan is usually a short-term arrangement in which the loan is repaid contingent upon some future event such as the sale of an asset, or the receipt of funds from, for example, a tax refund or inheritance. The personal *line of credit* is widely used to avoid the high front-end cost of making small individual loans. These loans may be created by writing a check drawn against a special account or by the bank automatically creating a loan when a regular checking account is overdrawn. The limits on such accounts depend on the relationship between the bank and the consumer. Such loans are repaid on an installment or lump-sum basis.

Although technically not a loan, *leases* are used to finance some "big ticket" consumer durable goods, particularly automobiles. Despite legal distinctions and different tax effects, consumer-related leases and installment loans are similar transactions from a cash flow standpoint. Until and unless the residual value is realized, the lessor bank will not recover its investment, to say nothing of a profit. In order to minimize this risk with leasing automobiles, many banks write "open-end" leases. Under this arrangement, the bank is responsible for selling the car at the end of the lease period and if the sale price is less than the previously agreed-upon residual value, the customer pays the difference; if the sale price exceeds the residual value, the customer keeps the difference. Under a "closed-end" lease the customer may or may not benefit from a higher resale value but the bank assumes the risk of a lower residual value. The payments are higher under this arrangement than with the open-end lease.

On a typical open-end lease involving an automobile, for example, the user pays only one or two monthly payments in advance. This "downpayment" is usually much less than that necessary for an outright purchase. The user also pays all maintenance, insurance, and operating expenses. Since the monthly payments are based on depreciation over a three-year period rather than recovery of the full cost, the monthly lease payments are usually lower than the payments under an outright purchase. As owner of the asset, the bank benefits from depreciation charges and the investment tax credit.

THE CREDIT DECISION

The consumer loan credit decision is unlike that of commercial loans. When evaluating a commercial loan request, the credit analysis goes beyond the decision to grant the loan. For pricing purposes, it is also essential to determine the risk class of the commercial borrower. In contrast, the consumer loan credit decision only involves the decision to grant or reject the loan request. For a given type of loan, such as an installment loan to finance a new car, all consumers pay the same rate even though some borrowers are more creditworthy than others. An exception is the single-payment personal loan where the circumstances of the individual borrower and the purpose of the loan are taken into account when determining the rate.

A number of factors are taken into account when examining a consumer loan request. These usually include the individual's income, employment characteristics, assets, other debts, and credit rating. Collateral and the size of a downpayment relative to the amount of the loan and the borrower's overall relationship with the bank are other factors taken into account. The credit decision involves using readily available information that has the same meaning across all borrowers. This enables credit scoring models to be used in the credit decision process.

Credit Scoring Model

The objective of a credit scoring system is to make an accurate assessment of an individual's creditworthiness and use the results to draw inference regarding the probability of full repayment of the loan. In order to understand credit scoring, consider the development and use of such a system by a medium-sized bank.

A Scoring Model   This example of a credit scoring model was designed specifically for a bank by the General Electric Credit Corporation (GECC), itself a major consumer lender. The first step was for the bank to select randomly from its files 500 "good" accounts, 125 "seriously delinquent" accounts, 250 "rejected" accounts, and 125 "charge-off" accounts. As a result of a statistical analysis of the information provided on the loan applications, certain characteristics emerged as having predictive value regarding the likelihood of problems related to the loan repayment. Many variables were evaluated before the final credit criteria were determined on the basis of statistical significance. In this example, seven characteristics were selected as being the most significant from a predictive standpoint. These are shown in Table 1.

The regression procedure used to select these characteristics also produces coefficients or weights for each of the factors. By transforming these coefficients, the point values shown in Table 1 are determined. For example, in this case if the applicant owns a residence, eight points are assigned whereas a renter is assigned five points. Most of the characteristics shown in Table 1 are straightforward; an exception is the occupational breakdown which is a proxy for job and income stability. Based on this lender's experience, little trouble has been encountered with individuals in certain occupations collectively comprising "Group I." This group includes architects, chemists, teachers, physicians, engineers, registered nurses, managers, and of course, college professors, to name a few. At the other extreme, borrowers in Groups III and IV have been associated with a higher incidence of problem loans. These occupations include, among others, bartenders, construction workers, truck drivers, contractors, welders, and factory workers.

The decision rules for using this particular model are also shown in Table 1.

Table 1   Credit Scoring Model for Consumer Loans

Evaluation Characteristics		Point Value				
1. Residence	Own 8	Rent 5				
2. Co-Applicant Employed	Yes 13	No 0				
3. Occupation[a]	Group I 38	Group II 35	Grp. III/IV 8			
4. Years on Present Job	Less than 1 yr. 8	1-5 19	6-9 32	10+ 35		
5. Age	18-24 21	25-29 23	30-34 20	35-39 8	40-49 25	50+ 30
6. Applicant's Gross Monthly Income	$0-799 18	$800-999 16	$1000-1299 10	$1300-1599 15	$1600-1999 20	$2000+ 23
7. Debt Service Ratio[b]	0-19% 16	20-29% 14	30-39% 12	40-49% 18	50-59% 13	60%+ 11

[a]Self-employed applicants require investigation.
[b]Total monthly payments on all debts (including mortgage loan) divided by the applicant's gross monthly income.

Decision Rules
- If score ≥ 130, grant loan request
- If score < 90, reject loan request
- If score is 90-129, investigate further
- Investigate self-employed applicant

If the score is 130 or higher, no further investigation is necessary and the borrower may be informed that the loan will be granted. Applicants scoring less than 90 are rejected outright. For applicants with scores of 90 to 129, further investigation is required. This includes obtaining a credit rating, checking credit references and verifying employment information.

From a management and control standpoint, an important part of the system described above is the *risk analysis* and *volume analysis* shown in Table 2. The risk analysis shows the probability of getting a "good" loan at various credit score intervals. These are loans with no serious delinquency problems (90 days or more) and result in a full payoff of the loan. In the example, applicants with scores in the range of 70-74 have only a 22.5 percent chance of repaying the loan in full and without any problems or major delinquency. In contrast, a score of 110 to 114 indicates a 75 percent chance of full payment and no problems. This analysis enables management to control the quality of the loan portfolio and to assess the tradeoff between credit scores and loan losses.

The *volume analysis* enables management to estimate the volume effects of various cutoff scores. Again, tradeoffs exist. In this example, the cutoff score of 90 would result in 2.7 percent of the "good" accounts being incorrectly rejected and 26.6 percent of the "bad" accounts being properly rejected. As the cutoff score is raised, the volume of "bad" accounts rejected increases but so does the incorrect

Table 2   Risk and Volume Analysis

A. Risk Analysis		B. Volume Analysis			
Credit Score	% Probability of a Good Loan[a]	Cutoff Score	% of Good Accts. Rejected	% of Bad Accts. Rejected	% of Total Loan Requests Rejected
Below 60	0.0%	Below 60	0.0%	4.9%	1.2%
60-64	0.0	65	0.0	7.1	1.8
65-69	14.3	70	0.2	11.0	2.9
70-74	22.5	75	0.9	17.9	5.1
75-79	32.4	80	1.8	23.5	7.2
80-84	45.0	85	2.4	25.9	8.3
85-89	50.0	90	2.7	26.6	8.7
90-94	55.6	95	6.0	34.6	13.2
95-99	60.0	100	9.1	40.9	17.1
100-104	65.7	105	15.8	51.3	24.7
105-109	69.5	110	23.6	61.6	33.1
110-114	75.0	115	24.0	62.0	33.5
115-119	78.0	120	34.1	70.5	43.2
120-124	80.6	125	42.1	76.3	50.7
125-129	82.2	130	54.8	84.6	62.2
130-134	84.8	135	68.8	92.1	74.7
135-139	87.5	140	70.4	92.8	76.0
140-144	89.2	145	80.9	96.6	84.8
145-149	91.5	150	84.9	97.8	88.1
150-154	93.8	155	93.8	99.5	95.2
155-159	95.3	160	95.3	99.8	96.5
160-164	98.2	165	99.3	100.0	99.5
165+	100.0	170	99.8	100.0	99.8

[a]A "good" loan is one that results in a full payoff with no serious delinquency experience, i.e., 90 days or more.

rejection of "good" accounts. The last column of the volume analysis shows the proportion of the total loan applications that will be rejected at given cutoff scores. When the cutoff score is 90, the bank will reject loans representing approximately 8.7 percent of the volume of all loan requests; increasing the cutoff score to 95 results in a rejection rate of 13.2 percent of all loan requests. This is useful information when it becomes necessary to alter credit standards in response to changes in loan demand, the availability of loanable funds, or both. Similarly, the analysis of changes in a bank's performance objectives such as size, growth, or market share, can be made more effectively with such information.

In addition to being a useful management tool, a well-conceived credit scoring model provides a number of other benefits. By approving more "good" loans and rejecting more "bad" loans, the quality of the loan portfolio is improved. This results in a lower level of loan losses and reduced collection expenses. Since loan applicants above and below certain scores require no further investigation, lending personnel may channel their investigative efforts toward the borrowers falling in the middle range of the scoring scale. This group typically accounts for about two-thirds of loan requests. Thus, the expenses associated with credit analysis can be reduced by about one-third. Faster turnaround and uniform handling of loan requests are other advantages of scoring systems.

Some Caveats   Constructing a statistically reliable credit scoring system
                                        is not a simple task. The system must comply with all
aspects of Regulation B of the Federal Reserve Board. This regulation implements
the *Equal Credit Opportunity Act* which prohibits discrimination in the granting
of credit on the grounds of sex, marital status, age, race, and religion.[3] Even seemingly neutral characteristics may have the effect of being discriminatory and thus
violate the law. For example, at one time some scoring systems included zip codes
as one of the characteristics. Since zip codes correlate with race this was held to
be a discriminatory tactic.

Since a scoring system must be developed on the basis of the user's own past
experience, the models are not general. If a bank has geographically dispersed
branches, each branch may require a different scoring model that reflects its experience with borrowers in the branch's service area. For this reason, scoring
models can be expensive to build. The cost must be weighed against the benefits.
The model should also be updated annually to reflect changing conditions. Furthermore, the system should not be publicly disclosed since knowledge of how it
works would facilitate fraud or enable poor credit risks to falsify their applications
to get a passing score.

The numerical weights assigned to particular categories in a credit scoring model
may not always agree with a lender's *a priori* beliefs. For example, note that in
Table 1 the point values for monthly income initially decrease as income rises.
Also, individuals with a debt service ratio in the 40-49 percent range statistically
appear to handle their debt load more effectively than others with lower debt loads.
Again, this simply reflects the characteristics of a particular class of borrowers
served by a specific lender.

Bankruptcy

Some borrowers find themselves overwhelmed with debt. In an attempt to get
a fresh start some seek to have their debts discharged by filing for bankruptcy.
The resulting loan losses are considered a normal element in the consumer lending
process. However, in October 1979 when the *Bankruptcy Reform Act of 1978*
was implemented, serious problems for consumer lenders began emerging from
the bankruptcy courts. The Act made it remarkably easy and advantageous for
individuals to avoid repaying debts by declaring bankruptcy. About the same time
the Act was implemented, advertising by lawyers was permitted. As a result of the
Reform Act and extensive promotion of bankruptcy services by lawyers, consumer
lenders experienced a dramatic increase in loan losses directly related to bankruptcy.

Chapter VII   There are two forms of personal bankruptcy. The *Chap-*
                                         ter VII proceeding is often called a *liquidation* or *straight*
bankruptcy; a *Chapter XIII* bankruptcy is a rehabilitation proceeding under the

---

[3] In the model shown in Table 1 age is a factor in the analysis. This is permissible if the numerical score
given to those over age 62 is no lower than the other lowest score. For example, if an age group category of
"62+" were assigned a numerical value of say 5 points, this would have to be raised to 8 points because this
is the lowest of the other categories. As a practical matter, age tends to be a highly positive factor in most
scoring systems.

Adjustment of Debts section of the law. Under a Chapter VII bankruptcy, certain assets of the debtor are "exempt" and the remaining assets are used to pay as much of the indebtedness as possible. The debtor is then discharged from any further obligations on the unpaid debts. *No consideration is given to the debtor's earning power.* The Chapter VII section of the law created several problems for lenders. The first was the establishment of federal exemptions. The debtor may choose to exempt either the property described in the new law or property exempted by state law. In most cases the federal exemptions are far more lenient so this alternative is usually selected. Federally exempted property includes up to $7,500 of equity in a home, $1,200 of equity in a motor vehicle, $500 in jewelry, life insurance contracts, and for all practical purposes, all furniture, household goods, and clothing. In addition, a "wild card" exemption—$400 plus any unused part of the real estate equity exemption—may be applied to other assets in any way the debtor chooses.

To see what these exemptions mean, assume a bank has a secured car loan of $6,000 and the car is worth $7,200. The debtor has no real estate. The debtor in this case has $1,200 in equity, all of which is exempt. The debtor may keep the car free of all claims of the bankruptcy Trustee and all creditors except the bank. If the car is worth say $8,000, it would appear that the Trustee has the right to sell the car in order to obtain the non-exempt, excess equity of $800 and use the proceeds to satisfy some creditors. But now comes the wild card exemption. Since the debtor owns no real estate the exemption is $400 + $7,500 = $7,900, of which $800 may be used to shield the excess equity of $800 in the car. The remaining $7,100 may be used to shield other assets from creditors—including cash in the bank or securities!

Another problem for consumer lenders resulted from the *Reform Act's* establishment of *redemption right.* This gives the debtor the right to cancel any security interests in exempt goods by paying the creditor the *lesser* of the amount of the loan or the value of the collateral. For example, if the car loan of $6,000 cited above were secured by a car worth $3,500, the debtor may pay the bank $3,500 and own the car free of any lien.

Before enactment of the new law, consumer lenders were often able to collect discharged debts through a process known as reaffirmation. That is, after bankruptcy the debtor voluntarily entered into a binding agreement to repay an obligation which would otherwise be unenforceable because of the bankruptcy. The present law makes a valid reaffirmation extremely difficult to obtain. It must be negotiated through the debtor's attorney and it must also be shown to the bankruptcy court that the reaffirmation is in the best interest of the debtor. It is difficult for a creditor to show how the re-assumption of debt, which led to the bankruptcy in the first place, can benefit the debtor. Usually reaffirmations are allowed when the loan is fully secured and the debtor wants the asset. For example, if a car loan of $6,000 is secured by a car worth $7,000 the loan may be reaffirmed. However, if the car is worth $3,000, this would be the reaffirmed amount, assuming the debtor wants the car. Unless a loan is validly reaffirmed, a creditor may make no attempt to collect a discharged debt.

Voluntary repayments may be accepted by the bank but extreme care must be exercised. If the debtor received a new loan from the creditor bank shortly before or after the voluntary payment, an unscrupulous borrower could claim that the new loan was contingent upon repayment of the discharged debt. If the claim is upheld, the new loan will be unenforceable and the bank has another loan charge-off.

Chapter XIII   The Chapter XIII proceeding is somewhat similar to a debt consolidation plan in that it provides for the adjustment of debts of an individual with a regular income. A debtor is allowed to keep all or most property and a portion of the debtor's income is turned over to the Trustee. The income is disbursed periodically to creditors according to a plan filed by the debtor's attorney. If the debtor completes the plan, which usually spans three to five years, the balance of remaining debts is discharged. If the debtor fails to meet the obligations of the plan but makes a good faith effort, the court may discharge the debts anyway.

The repayment plan must ensure that each creditor receives at least as much as the creditor would get in a liquidation proceeding. For unsecured loans such as credit card balances, this is often zero, or close to it. For secured claims the plan must provide for either (1) the secured party retaining its lien and receiving at least the value of the collateral, or (2) the surrender of the collateral to the lender. In effect, a Chapter XIII bankruptcy allows the debtor to achieve a *redemption* under an "easy payment" arrangement. The *exemptions* provided under a Chapter VII proceeding also apply to Chapter XIII proceedings.

Other Issues   What makes the bankruptcy problem so vexing for lenders is that many individuals who should not be filing bankruptcy are doing so. Since many of these individuals have substantial earning power and a high degree of creditworthiness, these bankrupts are "atypical" in that there is no indication of impending financial problems. Thus, it is virtually impossible to reject their loan requests using any type of credit analysis, judgmental or statistical. The resulting losses pose a dilemma for bankers. Raising credit standards to counter the adverse effects of a larger volume of bankruptcy-related losses may reduce the charge-offs resulting from the more "typical" bankruptcies, but at the same time curtail the volume of "good" loans and have no effect on the level of "atypical" bankruptcies. This explains why some problem loans are associated with the higher credit scores shown in Table 2.

A bankruptcy filing becomes a part of an individual's credit record for ten years. Also, the law requires that six years elapse before another Chapter VII bankruptcy is filed. It could be argued—and is argued by attorneys specializing in bankruptcy—that with a "clean slate" and no opportunity for bankruptcy in the near term, extending new credit to bankrupts makes economic sense. There are two problems with this reasoning. The bankruptcy filing may indicate an absence of one of the key ingredients of most good loans—a willingness to pay. This is a particularly relevant concern for the atypical bankrupts discussed above. The second problem is the fact that personal bankruptcy is often the result of an ongoing behavioral or mismanagement problem that persists despite bankruptcy. Even though another Chapter VII bankruptcy would not be allowed for six years, this does not ensure that a new loan will be repaid or trouble-free. These concerns, coupled with only a one-year waiting period for another Chapter XIII filing, require that special care be exercised when lenders are considering loan requests from the rapidly increasing population of bankrupts.

The law allows lenders to apply different credit criteria to such requests provided the criteria are uniformly applied. Because of this uniformity requirement, no distinction can be made by lenders between the loan requests from the atypical bankrupts with earning power but who lack the willingness to repay, and those individuals whose bankruptcy resulted from unfortunate events such as an illness or accident. If loan requests are granted out of compassion, the lender may then be forced to make loans to other bankrupts whose unwillingness to pay is well-known. To avoid this problem, many consumer lenders have adopted a simple policy regarding loans to bankrupts—no loans until ten years have elapsed since bankruptcy. Because of this widespread policy, bankrupts are often surprised to find that their action had serious long-term implications.

INTEREST CALCULATIONS

Declining Balance Methods

Several procedures are used by commercial banks in the financial mathematics related to consumer loans. Two variations of the declining balance approach are among those used. The first is a *standard amortization* procedure used with fixed-rate mortgage loans. Under this approach, a periodic payment, usually monthly, is calculated such that the loan is repaid with interest over a specified period. Each payment is assumed to be made on the same day such as the 1st or 15th of the month. A portion of the payment is applied to the interest with the remainder applied to debt retirement. For example, assume a loan of $10,000 is made at a rate of 15 percent with equal monthly payments over a two-year period. The payment R is given by the following annuity model in which m is the number of payments per year, n is the number of years, r is the interest rate, and PVA_{mn} is the present value of the loan. That is,

$$R = \frac{PVA_{mn}}{\left[\dfrac{1 - \dfrac{1}{\left(1 + \dfrac{r}{m}\right)^{mn}}}{r/m}\right]}$$

$$\$484.87 = \frac{\$10,000}{\left[\dfrac{1 - \dfrac{1}{\left(1 + \dfrac{.15}{12}\right)^{12(2)}}}{.15/12}\right]}$$

The interest portion of the first payment is based on the beginning balance, that is, $\$10,000 \times .15 \times (1/12) = \$125.00$. The portion allocated to the principal is $\$484.87 - 125.00 = \$359.87$, so the month-end loan balance is $\$10,000 - 359.87 = \$9,640.13$. This ending balance is the next period's beginning balance and the process is repeated. If the loan is repaid early, the amount of the prepayment would be the balance as of the month-end in question. Late payments made after a 10- or 15-day grace period are subject to late payment charges, typically $5 or $10.

Another version of the declining balance approach which is gaining widespread use is the *simple interest method*. This procedure is similar to the standard amortization approach except that interest is paid on the basis of the exact number of days between payments. In the loan cited above, suppose the first payment is made thirty-seven days after the loan is made. The monthly payment, which is computed in the same manner shown above, is allocated to interest and principal in a slightly different way. The interest for the first month is $10,000 × .15 × (37/365) = $152.05. The portion of the payment allocated to debt reduction is $484.87 − 152.05 = $332.82 so the "month-end" loan balance is $10,000 − 332.82 = $9,667.18. If the next payment occurs say twenty-three days later, that month's interest would be $9,667.18 × .15 × (23/365) = $91.37. The debt reduction would be $484.87 − 91.37 = $393.50 so the loan balance at the end of the second month would be $9,667.18 − 393.50 = $9,273.68.

The *simple interest* method has several advantages. It is easy to understand and administer. The method is fair to both the borrower and the lender because interest is paid for the exact number of days the funds are used; late payments result in higher interest charges for the borrower and early payments reduce the interest cost. Like the regularly amortized loan, if the simple interest loan is prepaid, the amount due is the outstanding loan balance at the time. This is not the case with another widely used procedure.

Add-On Interest Loans

The *add-on interest* approach used on some consumer loans is a questionable practice still followed by some commercial banks and other consumer lenders. At one time lenders would promote loans on the basis of the add-on rate which is deceptively low relative to the true rate. Although this problem was remedied with the passage of the *Truth-in-Lending Act* (1969) which requires full and prominent disclosure of the *annual percentage rate* (APR) and the dollar amount of all finance charges, another problem remains in the form of a hidden prepayment penalty.

An Illustration   In order to see the nature of the prepayment penalty and how an *add-on interest* loan works, consider once again the 24-month, $10,000 loan cited above. Recall that the rate on this loan under the standard amortization or the simple interest approaches was 15 percent. This rate is also the APR, assuming no other finance charges. Now assume that this loan is made at the *add-on* rate of 8.1844 percent. As will be shown, this add-on rate produces an APR of 15 percent.

To find the monthly payment for an add-on interest loan, the first step is to find the total interest payable over the life of the loan, in this case, two years. This amount, I, is given by

$$I = \$10,000 \times .081844 \times 2$$
$$= \$1,636.88.$$

The periodic payment R is the sum of the total interest plus the original principal divided by the number of payments. That is,

$$R = \frac{\$1,636.88 + 10,000.00}{24}$$

$$= \$484.87.$$

The APR for this loan is the value of r in the annuity model

$$PVA_{mn} = R \left[\frac{1 - \frac{1}{\left(1 + \frac{r}{m}\right)^{mn}}}{r/m} \right]$$

$$\$10,000 = \$484.87 \left[\frac{1 - \frac{1}{\left(1 + \frac{r}{12}\right)^{12(2)}}}{r/12} \right]$$

The value of r, or the APR, that satisfies this relationship is 15 percent. This is also the familiar *internal rate of return.*

Rule of 78s

When the add-on approach is used and the loan is prepaid, the hidden prepayment penalty arises because of the *Rule of 78s* which is used to compute the allocation of each payment to interest and principal. To demonstrate how this occurs and the extent of the overpayment relative to the declining balance approach, Table 3 was prepared.

In Table 3 the regularly amortized declining balance loan that was discussed above is compared with the same loan made on the *add-on* basis in conjunction with the *Rule of 78s.* It is important to note that the two loans are identical, including the APR of 15 percent; they differ only in the interest calculation method used. In Panel A, the standard amortization procedure is shown. The APR is constant regardless of when or if the loan is prepaid. Using the *Rule of 78s,* the interest earned by the lender is found by first summing the digits from one through the number of payments (n), or twenty-four in this case.[4] The sum of the digits is given by

$$\frac{n(n + 1)}{2} = \text{Sum of the Digits}$$

$$\frac{24(25)}{2} = 300.$$

Recall that the total interest payable on the add-on loan over its life is $1,636.88. The first payment of $484.87 will include 24/300's of this total interest, or

[4] The term *Rule of 78s* arises from the fact that on a one-year loan with monthly payments, the sum of the digits 12 + 11 + 10 + ... + 2 + 1 = 78.

Table 3 Comparison of Declining Balance and Rule of 78s Approaches
Loan Arrangement

Assumptions:

1. Standard Amortization used in declining balance approach
2. Original Loan = $10,000
3. Term = 2 years with monthly payments
4. APR = 15%
5. Monthly Payment = $484.87
6. The *add-on* rate used with the Rule of 78s is 8.1844%

Month	Payment	A. Declining Balance—15% APR			B. Rule of 78s				
		Interest	Principal	Ending Balance	Interest[a]	Principal	Ending Balance	Overpayment[b]	APR if Prepaid
1	$484.87	$125.00	$359.87	$9640.13	$130.95	$353.92	$9646.09	$ 5.96	15.71%
2	484.87	120.50	364.36	9275.77	125.49	359.38	9286.71	10.94	15.66
3	484.87	115.95	368.92	8906.85	120.04	364.83	8921.88	15.03	15.62
4	484.87	111.34	373.53	8533.32	114.58	370.29	8551.59	18.27	15.57
5	484.87	106.67	378.20	8155.12	109.13	375.74	8175.85	20.73	15.52
6	484.87	101.94	382.93	7772.19	103.67	381.20	7794.65	22.46	15.48
7	484.87	97.15	387.72	7384.47	98.21	386.66	7407.99	23.52	15.44
8	484.87	92.31	392.56	6991.91	92.76	392.11	7015.88	23.97	15.39
9	484.87	87.40	397.47	6594.44	87.30	397.57	6618.31	23.87	15.35
10	484.87	82.43	402.44	6192.00	81.84	403.03	6215.28	23.28	15.32
11	484.87	77.40	407.47	5784.53	76.39	408.48	5806.80	22.27	15.28
12	484.87	72.31	412.56	5371.97	70.93	413.94	5392.86	20.89	15.24
13	484.87	67.15	417.72	4954.25	65.48	419.39	4973.47	19.22	15.21
14	484.87	61.93	422.94	4531.31	60.02	424.85	4548.62	17.31	15.18
15	484.87	56.64	428.23	4103.08	54.56	430.31	4118.31	15.23	15.15
16	484.87	51.29	433.58	3669.50	49.11	435.76	3682.55	13.05	15.12
17	484.87	45.87	439.00	3230.50	43.65	441.22	3241.33	10.83	15.10
18	484.87	40.38	444.49	2786.01	38.19	446.68	2794.65	8.64	15.08
19	484.87	34.83	450.04	2335.97	32.74	452.13	2342.52	6.55	15.06
20	484.87	29.20	455.67	1880.30	27.28	457.59	1884.93	4.63	15.04
21	484.87	23.50	461.37	1418.98	21.83	463.04	1421.88	2.90	15.02
22	484.87	17.74	467.13	951.85	16.37	468.50	953.38	1.53	15.01
23	484.87	11.90	472.97	478.88	10.91	473.96	479.42	.54	15.001
24	484.87	5.99	478.88	-0-	5.45	479.42	-0-	-0-	15.00

[a] Interest is calculated according to the Rule of 78s.

[b] The overpayment is the difference between the ending monthly balance under the declining balance approach and the balance resulting from the Rule of 78s.

$1,636.88 × (24/300) = $130.95. Thus, the amount allocated to the principal is $484.87 − 130.95 = $353.92, and the ending balance is $10,000 − 353.92 = $9,646.08. Note in Table 3 that this balance is $5.96 higher than the ending balance that results from the declining balance approach. In the unlikely event the loan is prepaid at the end of the very first month, the resulting APR would be 15.71 percent rather than 15 percent. In the second month, the interest allocation is 23/300's of the total interest or $1,636.88 × (23/300) = $125.49, and if the loan is prepaid the overpayment would be $10.94. The resulting APR is the value of r that satisfies the relationship

$$\$10,000 = \frac{\$484.87}{\left(1 + \frac{r}{12}\right)^1} + \frac{\$484.87 + 9,286.71}{\left(1 + \frac{r}{12}\right)^2}.$$

The APR is 15.66 percent.

Several aspects of the overpayment and APR columns in Table 3 should be noted. First, when the loan is prepaid the dollar amount of the overpayment reaches a maximum at about one-third of the loan's term. This is typical of add-on loans. If no prepayment occurs, there is no hidden penalty and the APR is the same as that on a declining balance loan. However, note that the sooner the prepayment, the higher the APR.

It may be argued that the prepayment penalty is a proper adjustment of the loan yield to compensate for the unrecovered acquisition costs associated with prepaid loans. Such compensation might be reasonable in the example shown in Table 3. However, in addition to being related to the size of the loan, the magnitude of the prepayment penalty increases as the term of the loan increases and as the interest rate increases. Consider the following example.

Example.   A borrower obtains a 12-year, 10 percent add-on loan for $15,000 to finance a home improvement. Payments will be made monthly and the APR is 15.417 percent. The total interest payable over the life of the loan is

$$\$15,000 \times .10 \times 12 = \$18,000.$$

The monthly payment is

$$\frac{\$18,000 + 15,000}{144} = \$229.17.$$

Since the sum of the digits is

$$\frac{144(145)}{2} = 10,440,$$

the interest allocation for the first payment is

$$\$18,000 \times (144/10,440) = \$248.28.$$

However, this interest allocation exceeds the monthly payment and thus there is *negative amortization*. That is, the loan balance is increasing. This occurs the entire first year. Thus, if this loan were repaid at any time during the first year, the borrower would have to repay more than the original amount of the loan! If this loan were repaid after four years or forty-eight months, the hidden prepayment penalty would be $1,263.

This example demonstrates the potential inequity and deceptiveness of the *add-on* approach when used in conjunction with the *Rule of 78s*. The problem exists despite the *Truth-in-Lending Act* because no one knows when or if a specific loan will be prepaid. The stated APR is accurate only if the loan runs its full term. Even if full disclosure is made regarding the potential effects of prepayment, it is unlikely that many consumers would fully understand all the implications. Since many consumer loans are prepaid, the actual return on a portfolio of such loans is higher than the portfolio's average APR. Although banks in general are shifting from this approach to the simple interest procedure, it continues to be widely used by banks and other lenders. One reason for its continued use is that a number of states have laws that *require* some state chartered institutions to use this procedure for certain types of loans, particularly those for mobile homes and home improvements.

MANAGERIAL ISSUES

Administering a consumer loan portfolio involves a number of policy issues, especially in a volatile interest rate environment. The most significant of these issues is the extent to which consumer loans affect a bank's risk with respect to changes in interest rates.

Interest Rate Risk

A high concentration of consumer loans can result in a correspondingly higher degree of interest rate risk for banks. Such risk manifests itself in a more volatile earnings stream. This occurs because most consumer loans are on a fixed-rate basis and have terms extending for several years. Thus, when interest rates increase, the cost of funds tends to rise but the return on the assets financed with those funds remains the same; when rates decline, profit margins expand as the asset return remains constant and interest costs decline. One way to overcome this problem is to fund such fixed-rate loans with deposits that have a similar maturity or average life. For example, a four-year amortizing car loan with an interest rate of 15 percent has an average life of about 28 months. Taking prepayments into account, the average life of a portfolio of such loans may be about two years. That is, it takes this long for one-half the principal to be repaid. If deposits with a matching maturity are used to fund the loans, the bank will be insulated against the swings in profit margins caused by changing interest rates. A problem with this strategy is that the supply of such longer-term, fixed-rate deposits is limited thus making it impractical to fund a sizable volume of consumer loans in this way. Furthermore, the trend in recent years has been toward a shorter and more interest-sensitive liability structure for banks and other depository-type situations. As interest rate ceilings are phased out in accordance with the *Depository Institutions Deregulation and Monetary Control Act of 1980*, the interest sensitivity of bank liability structures will increase.

Floating-Rate Loans   In the absence of an adequate volume of fixed-rate deposits to fund installment loans, the bank must absorb the interest rate risk or seek alternative solutions to the problem. One strategy gaining increased acceptance as a partial solution is the use of *floating rate* installment loans. The objective of a floating-rate program is to reflect the lender's cost of funds in the loan rate. There are two ways this may be done. The first is to tie the loan rate to the lender's cost of funds. There are several problems with this approach. If the loan agreement is vague, indefinite or otherwise gives the lender excessive discretion to change the rate, the contract laws of some states may render the agreement void. The cost of funds may be computed in a number of ways so unless the procedure is described in detail, excessive discretion may be presumed to exist. A major problem with this approach is that the effects of managerial errors may be passed on to borrowers. If a bank locks in high cost deposits at the peak of the interest rate cycle, and then rates decline, borrowers on a floating-rate basis would bear the burden.

To avoid these problems, and minimize adverse political fallout, the rate should be tied to an index that is easy to define, readily verifiable by the borrower, and beyond the control of the lender. The auction rates on six-month and one-year Treasury bills or the market rates on intermediate-term Treasury notes and bonds are ideally suited for this purpose. Different indexes may be used for different classes of loans. The Federal Reserve discount rate and the bank prime rate should not be used because both are administered rates and often the subject of political controversy.

A floating rate program involves a number of policy issues. The manner in which loan rates are linked to the index must be specified. For example, the loan rate may be adjusted semiannually such that it is five percentage points over the six-month Treasury bill rate. Any limitations such as caps and/or floors must also be spelled out. The manner in which rate changes are effected must be clearly explained. To avoid placing a financial burden on borrowers, it is common practice to hold the payment constant when interest rates increase. This creates a balloon payment at the end of the term. Several additional payments are necessary to retire the balloon.

An example of such a loan under different interest rate scenarios is shown in Table 4. In each instance the loan is for $10,000 with an initial interest rate of 15 percent, an initial term of 36 months, and constant monthly payments of $346.65. Standard amortization is used. In Panel A, it is assumed that interest rates increase one percentage point at six-month intervals. After 36 months, the loan balance is $343.56 which could be paid off in a lump-sum payment or through two additional monthly payments of $346.65 and $3.01. In Panel B, a more dramatic increase in interest rates is assumed. Here, rates increase five percentage points after only six months and stay at that level. After the initial term of 36

Table 4   Floating-Rate Installment Loan Under Alternative Interest Rate Scenarios

Loan Arrangement
$10,000 original loan
Constant monthly payments of $346.65
Standard Amortization
15% initial loan rate
36-month initial term

A. Interest Rate Increases One Percentage Point at Six-Month Intervals

Months	Interest Rate	Monthly Payment	Ending Loan Balance[a]
1-6	15%	$346.65	$8,627.82
7-12	16	346.65	7,190.99
13-18	17	346.65	5,669.32
19-24	18	346.65	4,039.60
25-30	19	346.65	2,274.89
31-36	20	346.65	343.56
37	20	346.65	2.96
38	20	3.01	—0—

B. Interest Rate Increases Five Percentage Points After the First Six Months

Months	Interest Rate	Monthly Payment	Ending Loan Balance
1-6	15%	$346.65	$8,627.82
7-36	20	346.65	814.64
37-38	20	346.65	142.95
39	20	145.33	—0—

[a]This is the loan balance at the end of the intervals or months shown.

months, the ending balance is $814.64. This requires two additional regular payments of $346.65 and one final payment of $145.33 to amortize the loan. Despite a dramatic increase in the level of interest rates, the effect on the borrower is mitigated by a small number of additional payments. If interest rates decrease, the term of the loan could be kept constant and the payment reduced. Alternatively, the payment could be kept the same and the number of payments reduced by shortening the term of the loan. Unless the term of the loan is at least nine or ten years, the constant payment does not result in *negative amortization.* This arises when the payment is insufficient to cover the interest.

Although the interest rate on a floating rate loan portfolio will track market rates, the lender's actual cost of funds will not necessarily move in lockstep. In fact, the portfolio return and cost of funds could move in opposite directions as banks become deregulated on the liability side. If interest rates are falling while banks are becoming more interest-sensitive in their deposit structure, a floating-rate program would call for lowering loan rates at a time when the cost of funds continues to rise, or at least does not fall with market rates. However, once the liability structure stabilizes, changes in loan rates will track the cost of funds.

Because of their risk-reducing effects, the initial interest rate on floating-rate installment loans should be somewhat lower than the rate on fixed-rate loans. Another inducement would be the use of the *simple interest* or *standard amortization* procedure for interest calculations. In fact, the nature of this type of loan requires that a declining balance approach be used. Because of possible rate increases, borrowers must have the right to prepay all or a portion of the loan without incurring a prepayment penalty, hidden or explicit.

Portfolio Composition   Because of interest rate risk implications, the mix of fixed-rate and floating-rate consumer loans represents an important managerial issue. When properly implemented in the consumer loan portfolio, the floating-rate concept helps ensure a positive spread between the cost of funds and the return on the underlying assets. To the extent that fixed-rate loans are funded with interest-sensitive liabilities, the magnitude of the imbalance, or *gap* as it is called, is an indication of the interest rate risk being incurred. Managing the consumer loan *gap* by altering the mix of fixed-rate and floating-rate loans is limited by traditional consumer preferences for fixed interest costs. Thus, the floating-rate consumer loan is only a partial solution to the overall interest rate risk problem. This is not to say such risk is uncontrollable. Rather, the interest rate risk resulting from a *gap* in the consumer loan portfolio must be viewed as a part of a broader financial problem involving commercial loans, mortgage loans, investments, and the entire liability structure of the bank. In this broader context, the overall gap can be monitored and controlled more effectively by supplementing floating-rate loan policies with certain financing policies and the use of interest rate futures. Depending on management's attitude and policy toward interest rate risk, the overall gap may require changes in the policies guiding individual operating components of the bank such as consumer lending. For example, changes may have to be made in the mix of fixed- versus floating-rate consumer loans or in the overall size of the consumer loan portfolio. Such changes in the loan mix may be supplemented by alternative liability policies or hedging strategies involving interest rate futures.

Consumer Loan Pricing

Price Discrimination   One of the characteristics of consumer loans is the limited degree of price discrimination exercised by banks and other consumer lenders. For example, a bank's loan rate for new cars usually applies to all borrowers with no rate distinction for differences in creditworthiness, down payment, or the term of the loan. Rates often differ, however, depending on the *purpose* of the loan. For instance, new car loans may be 15 percent, used car loans 17 percent, and credit card balances 18 percent. Although questionable from a risk-return standpoint, the lack of price discrimination on the basis of individual creditworthiness is expedient politically in that it minimizes the risk of allegations that the lender is discriminating on grounds prohibited by law. However, there is nothing discriminatory about other forms of price differentiation based on the risk associated with the terms of a loan agreement.

Loan Terms   In recent years inflation and high interest rates have
                                                made the acquisition and financing of consumer durable
goods more difficult. In response, many banks have altered their loan terms only
to find that additional uncompensated risks are being assumed. An example is
provided by new car loans. At one time, the maximum financing period for new
cars was three years and the down payment requirement was 20 percent. Although
such loans continue to be made, in recent years many banks have extended the maximum period to four or even five years while lowering downpayment requirements
to 10 percent and in special cases, zero. Despite the fact that these longterm
low-downpayment loans are far riskier than the shorter-term, higher-downpay-
ment loans, there is usually no risk premium in the form of a higher rate.

Since the longer-term fixed-rate loans contribute to the interest rate risk of a
bank or other type of depository institution, it is reasonable that a risk premium
be reflected in the bank's rate structure as it is with most commercial loans. For
example, to induce borrowers to accept a three-year fixed-rate car loan the offering
rate should be lower than the rate on four- and five-year loans.

Low-downpayment loans also contribute to a bank's risk. The risk of default
on a low-downpayment secured loan is greater than a corresponding high-down-
payment loan. A low downpayment results in a smaller equity base and thus there
is more incentive for the borrower to default. Furthermore, if default should occur,
the value of the collateral may be less than the loan balance. In a study of the relationship between consumer loan terms, borrower characteristics, and defaults,
Peterson and Peterson found that when the downpayment was less than 20 percent, the default rate was about two and one-half times the default rate on loans
with downpayments of 20 percent or more.[5]

The added risk associated with longer terms and lower downpayments on certain
types of consumer loans means that banks should price loans on the basis of the
underlying risk as well as the purpose of the loan. Competitive forces may limit
the extent to which an individual bank can alter consumer preferences, but failure
to address the problem results in uncompensated risks.

Usury Laws   During periods of high interest rates, usury laws pose
                                               serious problems for consumer lenders in many states.
When such laws are binding and prohibit the charging of market rates, lenders
respond in several ways. First, to the extent that loans are made, they are made
only to the most creditworthy customers of long standing. Lenders may impose
stringent terms such as very short repayment periods and high downpayments.
Even more disruptive to local economies is the practice of diverting lendable funds
to unregulated markets such as commercial loans and investments. Thus, during
periods of high interest rates, the volume of consumer lending contracts sharply.
Although legislators in many states are aware of the perverse effects of usury laws,
special interest groups in many states effectively lobby against their repeal.

[5] Carol M. Peterson and Richard L. Peterson, "Downpayments, Borrower Characteristics, and Defaults,"
Journal of Retail Banking, March 1981, pp. 1-6.

Credit Cards—Special Problems

Credit card operations pose special problems for banks. The magnitude of these problems depends on the individual bank's commitment to consumer lending in general and credit cards in particular. Once a credit card has been issued, the decision to borrow is at the option of the cardholder. The bank has lost some degree of control over the size of its loan portfolio. The resulting line of credit is similar to the open line of credit or revolving credit used by commercial borrowers. Because of the latent loan demand that must be met, the bank must monitor the unused portion of these lines. An unexpected surge in credit card balances could occur simultaneously with other cash flow pressures such as increased commercial loan demand or deposit outflows. Accommodations must be made to handle such contingencies.

Another problem relates to the pricing of credit cards. Because cardholders have a grace period of four to six weeks to pay their bill in full and avoid any finance charges, significant carrying costs are incurred when individuals pay their bills in full. The impact of the grace period was revealed in the study by Robert W. Johnson that was cited earlier. In a sample of seventeen California banks, the gross yields on credit card operations ranged from 12.3 percent to 15.3 percent, far below the APR of 18 percent.[6] To offset the lower yields, many banks impose an annual fee, typically $10 to $20. In light of the convenience of a credit card and the line of credit it provides, such a fee is reasonable and makes economic sense.

Another problem with credit card operations relates to the usury laws discussed earlier. Like other consumer loans, the interest rate on credit card balances is subject to a ceiling in most states. Despite the widespread imposition of an annual fee, individuals who carry balances continue to bear a disproportionate share of the cost of such systems in the form of higher interest rates. However, during periods of high interest rates, usury laws often prevent banks from charging an adequate rate to cover the the total cost of a credit card operation. Furthermore, since the option to carry a balance lies with the cardholder, the bank is unable to divert loanable funds to unregulated markets or impose more stringent terms to ration its funds. Thus, the profitability of credit card operations is closely related to the interest rate cycle. In the event of substantial losses because of high interest rates and binding usury laws, a bank has few options. The credit card operation may be sold or the credit cards recalled and the operation closed.

Another tactic used to cope with usury laws is to relocate the bank's credit card operation to a state that has less restrictive laws. Some states actively solicit banking activities by promoting their favorable business and regulatory climate. For example, in 1980, the state of Delaware passed the *Financial Center Development Act* in order to induce banks to relocate credit card and other banking activities in Delaware. The Act eliminated usury ceilings, allowed credit card fees, and provided tax incentives for banks. Responding to stringent usury ceilings in their own states, many banks moved their credit card processing subsidiaries to Delaware. Among the banks with "foreign" subsidiaries in Delaware are the Chase Manhattan Bank, J. P. Morgan & Company, Philadelphia National Bank, and the First Mary-

---

[6] Johnson, "Pricing of Bank Card Services," p. 21.

land Bancorp. Similarly, Citibank moved its credit card operations to South Dakota from New York. Most bankers simply hope for lower interest rates.

REGULATION OF CONSUMER-RELATED LENDING

Regulatory Overview

One of the most heavily regulated and closely monitored aspects of banking is consumer lending. Since most consumers are unsophisticated in the ways of banking and finance, consumer-related regulations primarily focus on consumer protection. The main federal laws are summarized below, including those that are specifically related to mortgage loans.

- *Truth-in-Lending.* This act requires full and prominent disclosure of the annual percentage rate (APR) and the total finance charges. An error factor of plus or minus 1/8th of one percentage point is allowed for loans with regular payments. For loans with multiple advances or irregular payments a broader error tolerance is allowed.

- *Equal Credit Opportunity Act (ECOA).* This act prohibits discrimination on the grounds of race, color, sex, marital status, religion, age, or national origin. Lenders may not discount or refuse to consider reliable alimony, child support, or public assistance payments.

- *Home Mortgage Disclosure Act.* In order to detect possible discrimination, mortgage lenders must maintain a detailed register of loan applications and loans actually made. It is argued by the law's proponents that when a bank's mortgage lending activity is broken down by census tract, it is possible to detect *redlining,* or *disinvestment* as it is called. This is the arbitrary denial of mortgage financing to creditworthy borrowers because of a property's geographic location. Such a practice tends to discriminate against minorities. However, the absence of mortgage loans in an area may simply reflect the lack of loan demand resulting from the fact that many qualified borrowers prefer to live elsewhere.

- *Community Reinvestment Act (CRA).* This is an anti-discrimination law requiring that lenders implement certain policies and practices. The law states that federally insured banks, S & Ls, and mutual savings banks have a "continuing and affirmative obligation" to help meet the credit needs of the local communities that make up their service area. Thus, the burden is on the bank or other lenders to uncover any latent or unmet loan demand from qualified borrowers.

- *Real Estate Settlement Procedures Act (RESPA).* This Act requires that on real estate transactions, the lender must provide the borrower with a complete breakdown of the costs that will be incurred. RESPA disclosures also satisfy Truth-in-Lending disclosure rules.

- *Fair Credit Billing Act.* This Act requires creditors to correct errors promptly and without damaging the borrower's credit rating. Errors include such things as mathematical mistakes and failure to reflect payments or credits to an account. The Act also enables consumers to settle disputes arising from credit card transactions involving defective merchandise.

- *Fair Credit Reporting Act.* This Act enables individuals to examine the information contained in their credit files maintained by credit reporting agencies. Erroneous information must be removed or corrected. The purpose of the law is to ensure that credit agencies conduct their affairs with accuracy, fairness, and respect for an individual's privacy. If a bank or other type of consumer lender denies a loan request because of information contained in a credit report, the nature of the information and the name of the credit reporting agency must be revealed to the applicant.

On the surface, the intent of these laws seems reasonable and straightforward. However, regardless of management's intentions, total compliance can be a problem because of regulatory and legal interpretations of laws that are often vague, and frequently confusing.

Regulatory Compliance

Because of the difficulty of total compliance with consumer protection laws, banks and other consumer lenders should designate a *compliance officer* to oversee regulatory aspects of consumer lending activities. The main responsibility of the compliance officer is to ensure that the appropriate operating policies and procedures are in place so that compliance is possible. This involves policy formulation, employee training, and the development of a system for detecting deviations from policies, procedures, and regulations.

The objective of a well-conceived compliance system is to ensure regulatory compliance and avoid unpleasant surprises. Such surprises may arise in the course of a regulatory examination conducted by the bank's primary regulator. If violations are found, even if unintentional, the bank may be cited in the examiner's report, depending on the severity and other circumstances. Minor technical violations usually result in verbal suggestions for corrective action. However, the laws also provide that the affected consumers can bring legal action against the bank and sue for damages. The laws relating to the *Truth-in-Lending Act, ECOA,* and the *Fair Credit Billing Act* also allow class action suits. (This is a suit filed on behalf of a group with similar claims.) Even if a lender is innocent of wrongdoing, the adverse publicity of such suits, individual or class action, extracts a heavy toll. Similarly, violation of the *Community Reinvestment Act* can result in serious economic sanctions such as the denial of expansion plans, mergers, or acquisitions. For these reasons, full compliance with the letter and spirit of consumer lending regulations must be given a high priority by management.

CONCLUSION

The importance of consumer lending varies from bank to bank depending on its emphasis. At one end of the spectrum are a few of the very large, so-called "wholesale" banks that deal primarily with other banks and large corporations. For these banks, consumer lending is on a small-scale basis and such loans are usually made as an accommodation rather than a primary business activity. However, for most other banks, such lending constitutes a major activity in the asset management process. For this reason, the policies and practices guiding consumer lending play a central role in the overall bank management process. The development of these policies and practices requires an understanding of the various types of consumer-related loans along with an understanding of the credit decision, interest calculations, managerial implications, and regulations. These issues were examined in this chapter.

REFERENCES

Dyl, Edward A., and Michael D. Joehnk, "Prepayment Penalties Inherent in the Rule of 78s—A Truth-in-Lending Issue," *Journal of Bank Research*, 9 (Spring 1977), 16-21.

Johnson, Robert W., "Pricing of Bank Card Services," *Journal of Retail Banking*, 1 (June 1979), 16-22.

Kramer, Susan W., "An Analysis of the Rule of 78s," *Journal of Retail Banking*, 3 (September 1981), 46-55.

McAlister, Ray, and Edward DeSpain, "Credit Card Yields Under Alternative Assessment Methods," *Journal of Retail Banking*, 2 (September 1980), 56-75.

Peterson, Carol M. and Richard L. Peterson, "Downpayments, Borrower Characteristics, and Defaults," *Journal of Retail Banking*, 3 (March 1981), 1-6.

Sale, Alvin T., "Floating Rate Installment Loans: An Option for Increased Profitability," *Journal of Retail Banking*, 2 (September 1980), 1-6.

Savage, Donald T., "CRA and Community Credit Needs," *Bankers Magazine*, 162 (Jan.—Feb. 1979), 49-53.

Von der Ohe, Robert, William Hampel, *An Overview of Variable Rate Consumer Lending for Credit Unions*, Madison, Wisconsin: CUNA Supply Corporation, 1982.

Warren, John C., "An Evaluation of Truth-in-Lending Simplificiation," *Issues in Bank Regulation*, 5 (Summer 1981), 7-14.

Mortgage Loans and Related Securities

8

In recent years some of the most significant innovations in the financial system have occurred in the mortgage loan market. Because of the importance of mortgage loans in the country's social and economic system, these innovations have widespread implications for individuals, financial institutions, and society as a whole. Rather than a single type of mortgage loan, consumers are now confronted with a broad and often confusing assortment of mortgage instruments. These include *adjustable-rate, rollover, graduated payment, growing equity,* and *balloon* mortgages. These are in addition to the fixed-rate *conventional mortgage loan.* Similarly, the lending policies of financial institutions have changed dramatically. The development of new types of mortgage loans, collectively known as *alternative mortgage instruments,* has been coupled with important developments in the secondary mortgage market. Mortgage loans originated by banks, savings and loan associations, credit unions, and savings banks may be "packaged" in the form of mortgage-backed securities with bond-like characteristics. These securities are then sold in the national capital markets to other financial institutions that traditionally have avoided direct investment in mortgage loans. This enables funds to be recycled by local mortgage lenders. Today, it is difficult to imagine a financial institution that is not somehow involved in the mortgage market.

To understand the contemporary mortgage market, it is necessary first to examine the characteristics of the so-called *conventional mortgage loan* and the concept of *mortgage insurance.* Then the *average life concept* will be discussed. The importance of this concept will become clear in the subsequent discussion of alternative mortgage instruments and mortgage-backed securities.

CONVENTIONAL MORTGAGE LOANS

From the days of the Great Depression in the 1930s until the early 1980s, the main instrument of mortgage financing in the United States was the *conventional mortgage loan,* or CML.[1] This type of loan has a periodic payment based on a fixed interest rate. Both the payment and the interest rate are constant over the 25- or 30-year term of the loan. The payment, usually monthly in the case of residential mortgages, is sufficient to repay the loan with interest over the term of the contract. The repayment procedure is known as *amortization.* Since alternative mortgage instruments are created by altering the standard amortization procedure, it follows that a thorough working knowledge of amortization mechanics is essential.

The Amortization Process

Loan amortization is a fundamental financial concept that is not limited to mortgage loans. It is used for many other types of loans and investments by banks and other financial institutions. An example demonstrating the procedure will highlight the main ideas underlying the procedure.

Suppose an individual wants to buy a home valued at $100,000. A local bank is willing to make a conventional mortgage loan for an amount equal to 80 percent of the value, or $80,000. The downpayment is $20,000 and the fixed interest rate is 12 percent. Monthly payments of $822.89 are required over a term of 30 years.[2] Using this monthly payment, the amortization process is demonstrated in Table 1. Note how the payment is allocated to interest and principal. At the end of the first month the interest due is 1/12th of the annual rate times the loan balance at the beginning of the month, i.e., (.12/12) × $80,000 = $800.00. The rest of the payment, $822.89 − 800.00 = $22.89, is applied to the loan balance. The loan balance at the end of the first month is $80,000 − 22.89 = $79,977.11. This is also the beginning balance for the next month and the process is repeated.

In the early years the rate of loan reduction is very slow. As the loan balance decreases, the amount of the fixed payment that is allocated to interest decreases and the allocation to principal increases. As shown in Table 1, this process accelerates over time and in later years most of the payment is allocated to principal as the loan balance is more rapidly reduced. At the end of the term the outstanding balance is zero.

The monthly payment is sensitive to both the interest rate and the terms of the loan. This is demonstrated in Table 2 which shows the monthly payments for a loan of $80,000 with various terms and interest rates. As one would expect, the payment increases substantially as the interest rate increases. Also note that an increase in the term from 15 to 20 years has a much greater effect on the monthly payment than an increase from 30 to 35 years. This is an important point. The ex-

---

[1] The term "mortgage" is often used when referring to a "mortgage loan." Strictly speaking, the terms are not interchangeable. A mortgage is evidence of property securing a loan whereas a loan is evidenced by a note.

[2] For a discussion of the procedure used to calculate the periodic payment for an annuity such as a stream of mortgage loan payments, see the chapter dealing with financial mathematics in this book.

Table 1   Amortization Schedule for $80,000 Loan at
12%, 30-Year Term, Payable Monthly

Month	Beginning Balance	Monthly Payment	Portion of Payment to Interest	Portion of Payment to Principal	Ending Balance
1	$80,000.00	$822.89	$800.00[a]	$ 22.89[b]	$79,977.11[c]
2	79,977.11	822.89	799.77	23.12	79,953.99
3	79,953.99	822.89	799.54	23.35	79,930.64
4	79,930.64	822.89	799.31	23.58	79,907.06
5	79,907.06	822.89	799.07	23.82	79,883.24
.	.	.	.	.	.
.	.	.	.	.	.
.	.	.	.	.	.
34	79,110.29	822.89	791.10	31.79	79,078.50
35	79,078.50	822.89	790.78	32.11	79,046.39
36	79,046.39	822.89	790.46	32.43	79,013.96
37	79,013.96	822.89	790.14	32.75	78,981.21
38	78,981.21	822.89	789.81	33.08	78,948.13
.	.	.	.	.	.
.	.	.	.	.	.
.	.	.	.	.	.
178	68,968.20	822.89	689.68	133.21	68,834.99
179	68,834.99	822.89	688.35	134.54	68,700.45
180	68,700.45	822.89	687.00	135.89	68,564.56
181	68,564.56	822.89	685.65	137.24	68,427.32
182	68,427.32	822.89	684.27	138.62	68,288.70
.	.	.	.	.	.
.	.	.	.	.	.
.	.	.	.	.	.
356	3,993.84	822.89	39.94	782.95	3,210.89
357	3,210.89	822.89	32.11	790.78	2,420.11
358	2,420.11	822.89	24.20	798.69	1,621.42
359	1,621.42	822.89	16.21	806.68	814.74
360	814.74	822.89	8.15	814.74	—0—

[a]$80,000 × .12/12 = $800.00
[b]$822.89 − $800.00 = $22.89
[c]$80,000 − $22.89 = $79,977.11

tent to which the effects of rising interest rates can be blunted by extending the term of new loans is quite limited since most mortgage loans are written for 30-year terms. An extension of the term is also an important aspect of some of the alternative mortgage instruments discussed later in this chapter.

Table 2   Monthly Payment Required to
Amortize an $80,000 Loan

Payment Period	Interest Rate				
	8%	10%	12%	14%	16%
15 yrs.	$764.52	$859.68	$960.13	$1,065.39	$1,174.96
20 yrs.	669.15	772.02	880.87	994.82	1,113.00
25 yrs.	617.45	726.96	842.58	963.01	1,087.11
30 yrs.	587.01	702.06	822.89	947.90	1,075.81
35 yrs.	568.21	687.74	812.44	940.54	1,070.78
40 yrs.	556.25	679.32	806.80	936.91	1,068.52

Loan Provisions

Prepayment Penalty   Most conventional mortgage loans are not repaid strictly according to an amortization schedule. The loan may be repaid earlier at the option of the borrower by making payments in excess of the regularly scheduled payments. The excess portion of any payment, which is usually called a *prepayment*, is applied to the principal and the loan balance decreases at a faster rate. As long as such prepayments are modest, no prepayment penalty is assessed. But a large, lump-sum loan prepayment resulting from the refinancing of a fixed-rate mortgage is another story.

If market interest rates increase over the contract rate, the borrower simply repays according to the amortization schedule. But, if interest rates fall well below the mortgage loan rate, the borrower may attempt to refinance the loan by borrowing elsewhere at a lower rate. The lender is then forced to reinvest the funds at a lower rate. Unless some penalty is imposed, the CML would be a one-way contract in favor of the borrower. As a result, most conventional mortgages are subject to a prepayment penalty of 1 to 3 percent of the prepaid amount if the prepayment takes place within the first three or four years and is in excess of a specified amount. The provision is similar to the call premium on bonds. Although not severe, such penalties are often a deterrent when combined with the cost of obtaining a new mortgage loan from another lender. However, if the loan is prepaid because the underlying property is sold, a prepayment penalty is not usually assessed. The main concern of lenders is lump-sum refinancing during a period of low interest rates.

Due-on-Sale Clause   In 1976 the Federal Home Loan Bank Board, the regulator of federally chartered savings and loan associations, issued a regulation permitting S&Ls under its jurisdiction to enforce a *due-on-sale clause* on mortgage loans. This provision enables the lender to demand repayment of the outstanding loan balance if the mortgaged property is sold. Enforcement of this provision resulted in litigation which was resolved by the U. S. Supreme Court in 1982. The Court ruled that by authorizing enforcement of the due-on-sale clause, the FHLBB acted within its regulatory powers and that the FHLBB regulation preempts state laws prohibiting such enforcement. The *Depository Institutions Act of 1982* extended the federal preemption to state chartered S&Ls, banks, and mutual savings banks. This extension remains in effect unless overriding state legislation was passed within three years of the 1982 Act. As a result of this act and the Supreme Court ruling, virtually all mortgage lenders may enforce the *due-on-sale clause.*

To see why this clause is so important to mortgage lenders, consider the following situation. The seller of a property valued at $100,000 has a mortgage loan of $60,000 at 8 percent at a time when the market rate is 14 percent. The seller's equity is $40,000. If the buyer had a downpayment of $20,000 and obtained regular financing from a mortgage lender for the remaining $80,000, the low-rate $60,000 loan would be paid off and the seller would receive $40,000. However, using so-called "creative financing" techniques, the old low-rate loan could remain outstanding to the detriment of the lender. The seller may accept a downpayment of $20,000 and take back a second mortgage of $40,000. The buyer makes monthly payments to the seller that are sufficient to cover payments on the low-rate first mortgage loan and to partially amortize the second mortgage loan. After several years, presumably after a decline in the level of interest rates, the buyer refinances the property with a new loan and both mortgage loans are repaid. Such financing prevents low-rate loans from being rolled over at current rates, or "brought to market." If a lender is forced to carry such loans, which benefit only a few, and at the same time must pay market rates to savers, a negative spread develops. Mortgage money is diverted to other markets with higher rates and mortgage loan rates are higher than would otherwise be the case.

Under some mortgage loan arrangements discussed later in this chapter, the loans need not be repaid when the property is sold. That is, a *formal assumption* of a mortgage loan may be made by the buyer of the property with the approval of the lender. However, these assumable mortgages usually involve floating-rate loans rather than fixed-rate loans such as the CML.

INSURED MORTGAGE LOANS

When assessing default risk, one of the most important aspects of a mortgage loan is the relationship among the downpayment, the loan amount, and the value of the underlying property. Because of regulations or self-imposed lending policies, most banks and other mortgage lenders require a downpayment, or equity, of at least 20 percent of the property's value. Usually, such equity will safely support an 80 percent loan. Stated another way, lenders are willing to assume the risk inherent in a loan with a *loan-to-value ratio*, or *L/V ratio*, of 80 percent or less. If the L/V ratio were say 90 or 95 percent, the smaller downpayment provides some incentive for the borrower to "walk away" from the property in the event of financial adversity or a decline in the property value. Thus, high L/V ratio loans have a higher probability of default. The magnitude of default-related losses also tends to increase as the L/V ratio increases because the smaller equity base reduces the ability to absorb default-related losses and costs.[3] The burden then falls on the lender unless arrangements have been made to shift the default risk. This is possible by acquiring private mortgage insurance or backing from a government agency.

Private Mortgage Insurance

One of the most common problems facing homebuyers, especially first-time homebuyers, is their inability to make a 20 percent downpayment. The existence of private mortgage insurance companies (PMIs) enables borrowers to buy homes with a downpayment as low as 5 percent and at the same time shift the added risk

---

[3] George M. von Furstenberg, "Default Risk on FHA-Insured Home Mortgages as a Function of the Terms of Financing: A Quantitative Analysis," *Journal of Finance*, June 1969, pp. 459-477.

of such loans from the lender to the PMI. To see why low downpayment loans possess a high degree of risk and how private mortgage insurance works, consider the following example of a claim settlement.

A Numerical Example   The buyer of a home valued at $80,000 obtained a 30-year, 12 percent mortgage loan for $72,000. The down-payment was $8,000 or 10 percent. Since the loan had a loan-to-value ratio of 90 percent, the lender required private mortgage insurance with, in this case, "20 percent coverage." After making all payments for one year, the borrower was laid off because of the closing of a large plant in the area. No further payments were made for nine months and the borrower refused to seek other employment or discuss the matter with the lender. The lender then foreclosed on the defaulted mortgage loan. The following amount was owed the lender:

Outstanding loan balance	$71,739
Accumulated interest (9 mo.)	6,457
Attorney fees	1,000
Property taxes	2,150
Property insurance premium	450
Total claim	$81,796

This claim may be settled in one of two ways at the option of the insurer. Under one option, the private mortgage insurer would pay the lender $81,796 in return for clear title to the property. The insurer ultimately sells the property. Under the second option, the lender would retain the title and dispose of the property. If the property were sold for $80,000 less a sales commission of 7 percent, or $5,600, the net proceeds would be $74,400. The insurance claim is determined as follows:

Amount due lender	$81,796
Net proceeds from sale	74,400
Actual loss	$ 7,396

Insurance claim—lower of
(a) 20% of $81,796
    = $16,359

                    or $ 7,396

(b) Actual loss of $7,396

Balance   0

Several aspects of this example should be noted. Since 20 percent coverage was carried, the portion of a loss in excess of 20 percent of $81,796 would be borne by the lender. This might occur if the resale value of the property fell because of a depressed real estate market. Except in very unusual circumstances this coverage is adequate with 90 percent L/V ratio loans. For loans in the 91 to 95 percent range, the required coverage is usually 25 percent because of the higher probability of loss and the increased magnitude of potential losses.

Cost of Private   The cost of private mortgage insurance depends on the
Mortgage Insurance   policy. Most policies are annually renewable at the dis-
                        cretion of the lender. If the L/V ratio is 81 to 90 per-
cent, the required coverage is usually 20 percent. The first-year cost of such a policy is ½ of 1 percent of the outstanding loan balance. Thereafter, the annual premium is ¼ of 1 percent of the loan balance. The first-year premium cost for loans with L/V ratios of 91 to 95 percent and 25 percent coverage is 1 percent of the OLB and ¼ of 1 percent of the OLB thereafter. The premium is paid by the borrower along with the regular monthly payments. Annually renewable policies may be terminated when a combination of a lower loan balance and higher property value lowers the L/V ratio to an acceptable risk level, typically 75-80 percent. A variety of insurance plans are available including multiple-year policies extending from four to ten years.

Although quite reasonable, the cost of private mortgage insurance to the borrower is not limited to the cost of the premiums. Most mortgage lenders increase the base loan rate by about 25 basis points and charge a higher number of front-end points for insured mortgages. For example, assume an uninsured loan is quoted at a rate of 12 percent plus an origination fee of 2 points, or 2 percent of the loan amount. An insured mortgage might be quoted at 12.25 percent, plus 3 points, plus the cost of the insurance. The borrower's cost is higher than it appears at first glance.

Government-Backed Mortgages

In addition to shifting the risk of default on high L/V ratio loans to private mortgage insurance companies, lenders can obtain government backing on certain types of mortgage loans. These are FHA-insured and VA-guaranteed loans.

FHA-Insured Loans   From a lender's standpoint, loans insured by the *Federal
                        Housing Administration* (FHA) involve considerably
more paperwork than other mortgage loans. For this reason many mortgage lenders avoid making FHA-insured loans even though these loans are completely riskless with respect to default. Unlike private mortgage insurance which covers the top 20 or 25 percent of the loan and default-related costs, FHA insurance covers the entire loan. The coverage remains in force throughout the life of the mortgage loan. In addition to the paperwork involved with these loans, there are other problems especially for the seller of the property. For political reasons, the interest rate that lenders may charge is set by the Government at a rate 1 to 1.5 percentage points below prevailing market rates for mortgage loans. To induce lenders to make loans at the below-market rates, front-end points must be paid in order to increase the yield. Since regulations prohibit charging the borrower more than one

point, the seller of the property must pay any additional points. This could be anywhere from two or three points on the low side to eight to ten points on the high side depending on the disparity between the market rate and the FHA rate.[4] Understandably, most sellers resent having to subsidize the borrower's below-market rate. Depending on the state of the real estate market and the sellers' bargaining power, the cost of the points may be added to the selling price of the property. The seller must also make any necessary repairs and take the property off the market for the four to six weeks that it takes for the buyer to get approval from the FHA. Approval from private mortgage insurers is usually obtained within 24 hours and the property is sold "as is."

From the borrower's standpoint, the downpayment requirement for FHA loans is only 3 percent of the first $25,000 and 5 percent of any excess. The maximum loan amount is $100,000. At ½ of 1 percent, the insurance premium is higher than the private sector premium.

VA-Guaranteed Loans   Veterans and their families are eligible to obtain a mortgage loan guaranteed by the Veterans Administration. Such loans may be obtained with little or no downpayment, depending on the lender's policy, and in an amount up to $100,000. The loans are riskless from the lender's standpoint. Like FHA loans, the maximum interest rate that may be charged is administratively set below the prevailing market rate. Thus, VA loans are subject to the unpopular practice of charging the seller points. Unlike privately insured or FHA-insured mortgages, there is no premium or guarantee fee.

THE "AVERAGE LIFE" CONCEPT

One of the foremost concerns of the managers of banks and other financial institutions is the maturity structure of assets and liabilities. The maturity structure is important because it provides an indication of the interest-rate sensitivity of the asset or liability. If a class of liabilities is short-term, for example, their cost is interest-rate sensitive because they will be rolled over at prevailing market rates at maturity. Long-term liabilities with fixed interest rates are not interest-rate sensitive with respect to cost because the cost will remain the same until maturity. The same comments apply to assets. Thus, one of the primary functions of the managers of banks and other financial institutions is to control the firm's overall interest-rate sensitivity.

One approach to this problem is to match the maturities of various classes of assets and liabilities. By funding short-term assets with short-term liabilities, asset returns and liability costs move in the same direction with similar magnitudes when interest rates change, preserving the lender's interest rate spread. Similarly, the spread is maintained when long-term assets are funded with long-term liabilities.

---

[4] Each "point" is worth about 12 basis points in yield on a 30-year, 10 percent loan if the loan runs its full term. If the loan is fully prepaid after 5 years, each point would be worth 26 basis points in yield.

The word "maturity" is misleading when dealing with mortgage loans. Such loans are repaid gradually rather than on a lump-sum basis. Similarly, the "term" of a mortgage loan simply indicates when the last scheduled payment is to be made. To overcome this problem, the concept of *average life* is often used as an approximate measure of the investment period and hence the mortgage loan's interest-rate sensitivity. This expression refers to the estimated time it takes for the lender to get back one-half the principal amount invested. The term "half-life" is often used in this context.

Determinants of Average Life

The factors that determine the average life of a mortgage portfolio can be grouped into several categories that affect the loan repayment pattern. One of these categories is the loan amortization process which specifies the contractual or scheduled payments. The other factors—economic conditions and changes in family status—relate to unscheduled loan repayments.

Loan Amortization   In a previous section, the amortization process was explained in detail. To see how this process affects the average life of a mortgage loan portfolio, refer to Figure 1. The "amortization only" curve shows how the scheduled payments decrease the outstanding loan balance over the entire term for a pool of 12 percent, 30-year, fixed-rate loans. Note that one-half the original principal is repaid in the twenty-fourth year. This is called the *mathematical life* and it is always less than the term of the contract. As the term of the loan decreases, the mathematical life decreases. For example, if the pool consisted of 25-year loans the mathematical life would be about 18 years. Also, the interest rate on the loan affects the mathematical life. If the loan rate were 8 percent the life would be shorter.

Economic Conditions   The actual *average life* of a mortgage pool is less than the mathematical life because of unscheduled payments made prior to the due dates. One of the factors that affects the level of these prepayments is economic conditions—especially the level of interest rates. If interest rates are high, prepayments diminish. During such periods, individuals with low-rate mortgages tend to invest surplus funds in higher yielding investments instead of making higher or additional payments to reduce their mortgage loan balance. In addition, job-related transfers or relocations usually require the sale of property and the prepayment of existing mortgages. When interest rates are high and mortgage money is scarce, however, mobility in the labor market is reduced. Conversely, low interest rates encourage individuals to prepay high-rate mortgage loans and increased mobility in the labor market stimulates real estate turnover. Thus, prepayments tend to be higher during periods of low interest rates and fall during periods of high rates.

The severity of adverse economic conditions affects the average life of a mortgage pool in conflicting ways. A severe recession may increase the default rate on mortgage loans and this increases the average life by slowing down the payment

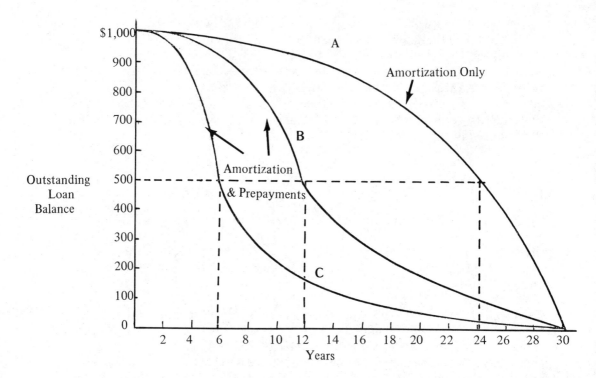

Figure 1   Outstanding Balance Per $1,000 for a 12%, 30-Year Mortgage Loan Portfolio.

stream. If defaults persist, foreclosures may result and the ensuing sale of the property and loan repayment decreases the average life.

Change in   The housing needs of most families change over time.
Family Status   Children are born, later demand separate bedrooms,
                                   and then leave home. Alternatively, in-laws may move
in or the children may return. Job transfers or promotions, divorce, and retirement are other factors that alter housing needs or desires and bring about prepayments of mortgage loans. Inheritances or a sizable change in the family income
level also play a role. Illness, disability, or death are other factors affecting the
family status and thus the average life of a mortgage loan portfolio.

Managerial Implications

   Although the effect of amortization on the average life can be determined easily,
the combined effects of economic conditions and changes in family status must
be estimated. In Figure 1, curves B and C illustrate the combined effects of both
amortization and prepayments. When prepayments are considered, the average life
drops significantly. If a lender's actual loan repayment pattern for a portfolio is
approximated by curve B, the average life would be about twelve years rather
than the mathematical life of 24 years. This does *not* mean that the entire invest-

ment will be returned through loan repayments by that time. In a mortgage port-folio, some loans are repaid very early and others remain outstanding over the entire term. Similarly, curve C demonstrates a repayment pattern that would pro-vide a six-year average life.

The experience of most lenders lies between curves B and C so the average life of most fixed-rate mortgage loan portfolios is between six and twelve years. A six-year life means that about 1/6, or 16.7 percent, of the portfolio will be turned over each year and re-invested at current interest rates. (The repayment rate is assumed to remain constant.) A twelve-year life means that only about 8.3 percent of the portfolio will be available for reinvestment at current rates each year. The shorter the average life, the greater the portfolio cash flow. This increases the portfolio's interest-rate sensitivity in that a larger proportion of the portfolio may be repriced at current interest rates. Conversely, a long average life reduces the portfolio's interest-rate sensitivity.

It is important to recognize that the average life of a portfolio is simply a proxy for its interest-rate sensitivity. With fixed-rate loans, the lender has virtually no control over prepayments so the average life of a portfolio has extremely important implications. But if interest-rate sensitivity can be achieved in other ways, such as periodically adjusting the interest rate, lenders would have little concern over the length of time the funds are tied up. This rationale—increasing the interest-rate sensitivity—underlies the development and increasingly widespread use of many so-called *alternative mortgage instruments*.

ALTERNATIVE MORTGAGE INSTRUMENTS

In the late 1970s and early 1980s, two major developments dramatically changed the mortgage lending process. First, the inflationary environment that characterized this period was accompanied by high and unusually volatile interest rates. Since the mortgage loan portfolios of banks, S&Ls, and mutual savings banks were made up almost entirely of conventional, fixed-rate mortgage loans, the cost of funds for mortgage lenders increased more rapidly than the returns generated by the loans. Spreads narrowed and operating losses on mortgage loan portfolios were common. Although serious, the effects of rising interest rates on costs were miti-gated somewhat by the interest rate ceilings on many of the accounts offered by banks and other depository lenders. Then the other shoe fell when the *Depository Institutions Deregulation and Monetary Control Act of 1980* was enacted. The Act required the phase-out of interest rate ceilings on previously regulated deposits. As the phase-out began in the early 1980s, the liability structure of depository in-stitutions became more interest-rate sensitive. This, in turn, compounded the basic problem associated with funding long-term fixed-rate mortgage loans with short-term rate-sensitive deposits during a period of rising interest rates.

To overcome the problems associated with fixed-rate mortgage loans, the use of adjustable-rate instruments was authorized by federal regulatory agencies shortly after passage of DIDMCA. Not all innovations in the mortgage market were designed solely to protect lenders from the adverse effects of rising interest rates. The high cost of housing coupled with high interest rates during the late 1970s and early 1980s created an "affordability" problem for homebuyers. New instruments emerged to cope with this problem. In this section these and other innovations in the mortgage market are examined.

Adjustable-Rate Mortgage Loans

There are two broad types of mortgage loans with loan rates that are adjustable depending on market conditions. One is officially designated as the *adjustable-rate mortgage*, or ARM, by the office of the Comptroller of the Currency which regulates all national banks. The Comptroller has issued regulations empowering national banks to offer ARMs. Under provisions of the *Depository Institutions Act of 1982*, often referred to as the Garn-St Germain Act, the Comptroller's regulations also apply to state chartered banks unless subsequent state legislation overrides the federal regulations. The other adjustable loan is designated as the *adjustable mortgage loan*, or AML, by the Federal Home Loan Bank Board. The Board has authorized federally chartered S&Ls to offer AMLs. Again, the *Depository Institutions Act of 1982* extends these powers to state chartered S&Ls. The regulations surrounding the ARM and AML are so broad that each type should be viewed as a class of loans rather than a single instrument. Loans may be structured with very few restrictions. Regulations, or the lack thereof, reflect the regulatory attitude that lenders should be given latitude to design instruments that allow market forces to determine the optimal methods and terms of mortgage financing. Although their own liability structures heavily influence the specific types of mortgage loans they offer, lenders cannot be indifferent to borrower preferences.

Among the most important market forces at work in shaping the design of mortgage instruments are the requirements imposed by buyers of mortgage loans in the secondary market. These requirements have resulted in the development of several standard loan arrangements. Before discussing these, the characteristics of ARMs and AMLs are examined.

ARMs   Banks may offer ARMs with an interest rate that is adjustable at any interval provided the borrower receives 30 to 45 days notice in advance. The loan rate may be tied to any interest rate index as long as it is verifiable by the borrower and beyond the control of the lender. The most commonly used indexes are the interest rate series for six-month Treasury bills, and Treasury securities with maturities of one, three, and five years. Weekly or monthly averages are usually used. Another index used is the National Average Mortgage Contract Rate as computed monthly by the Federal Home Loan Bank Board.

When market rates increase, the loan rate is automatically adjusted at the repricing date. The magnitude of the adjustment depends on the manner in which the loan rate is linked to the index. For example, the loan rate might be set at 250 basis points above the rate on one-year Treasury notes. At the time of each adjustment, the spread is simply added to the index rate. Most ARMs and AMLs work this way. The spread depends on competitive pressures and market conditions.

There are no regulatory limitations on the size of the interest rate adjustment. In the event of an increase in the interest rate, the payment may be increased, the term of the loan extended, or a combination of both adjustments may be made in order to blunt the adverse effect of the increase on the borrower. The only major limitation on the ARM is that the term may not exceed 30 years. With ARMs, if interest rates increase and the payment is kept constant to accommodate the borrower, *negative amortization* may result. Assume an ARM for $80,000 is made at a rate of 12 percent with a term of 30 years and an adjustment period of one year. The monthly payment during the first year is $822.89 and the loan balance after one year is $79,709.69. If interest rates increase such that the new rate is 14 percent, the new payment should be $946.66 in order to fully amortize the loan over the remaining term of 29 years. The interest due after the thirteenth month would be $79,709.69 $\times$ (.14/12) = $929.95. If the payment is held constant an interest deficiency of $929.95 - 822.89 = $107.06 would result. This deficiency is added to the loan balance so after the thirteenth payment, the loan balance is $79,709.69 + 107.06 = $79,816.75. The loan balance increases each month until the payment is increased to a level such that regular amortization begins. When ARMs were initially authorized, limits were placed on the amount by which the loan balance could increase. Although banks are now free to impose their own limits on the extent to which negative amortization can occur, secondary market considerations influence the decision. These considerations are discussed later in this section.

To provide borrowers with some degree of protection against rising interest rates, lenders usually do not impose a prepayment penalty on ARMs. Rather than contending with a higher interest rate, the borrower may repay the loan. When interest rates are adjusted downward, the incentive to refinance the loan at a lower rate with another lender is reduced. The ARM may also contain a due-on-sale clause or be assumable. If the loan is assumed the lender usually reserves the right to reset the loan rate immediately to reflect market conditions.

AMLs   Regulations governing the use of *adjustable mortgage loans* (AMLs) by S&Ls are virtually the same as those surrounding the use of ARMs by banks. Since the regulations are so broad, virtually any type of adjustable-rate mortgage loan may be offered by S&Ls. One difference is that the term of AMLs may be as long as 40 years. The loans usually have no prepayment penalty and they may be assumable or contain a due-on-sale clause. Although regulations provide regulated banks and S&Ls with flexibility in designing mortgage loans, competition and secondary market considerations have had a major impact in the design of standard ARM and AML plans.

Standard   Among the most important considerations in the design
ARM/AML Plans   of specific ARMs and AMLs by mortgage lenders are the
                      requirements imposed by buyers of mortgage loans in the secondary market. The major participants in this market are the Federal National Mortgage Association, or Fannie Mae, and the Federal Home Loan Mortgage Corporation, or Freddie Mac. When designing and making mortgage loans, most

lenders follow the guidelines established by these agencies in order to ensure that their portfolio, or a portion thereof, is marketable. A summary of the three standard mortgage loan plans that are acceptable to *Fannie Mae* is shown in Table 3.

Several aspects of Table 3 should be noted. In all three loan plans the interest rate index is an observable, externally verifiable index of interest rates on government securities. The indexes are beyond the control of the lender. End-investors such as federal agencies or other financial institutions prefer external indexes because the return on the loan is automatically adjusted to reflect the current cost of funds for a given maturity. In the case of ARMs and AMLs the corresponding "maturity" is the interest rate adjustment period, that is, one, three, or five years in the case of the standard plans. In contrast, if an internal cost-of-funds index is used, the end-investor has no assurance that the return on the loan will be adjusted to reflect current market conditions. Internal indexes are also ambiguous since a cost-of-funds index may be calculated several ways. The use of external indexes also enables federal agencies such as Fannie Mae and Freddie Mac to tailor the terms of their own borrowing specifically to the terms of the mortgage pools they are buying. For example, three-year securities may be sold to finance the purchase of ARMs or AMLs with a three-year interest adjustment period. For this reason the interest adjustment period coincides with the term of the Treasury security used as an index.

Each of the standard plans gives the borrower the right to limit the amount of any annual increase in monthly payments to 7.5 percent, even if an increase in the interest rate would normally call for a greater increase in the payment. The borrower may elect to cap the payment increase at anywhere between 7.5 percent and the full indicated payment, or to pay the full indicated amount.

If a capped payment is insufficient to cover all the interest owed, negative amortization results. For the plan with a one-year adjustment period, the cap is 7.5 percent at each adjustment date. For the plans using the three- and five-year adjustment periods, the cap is 7.5 percent at the time of the adjustment and 7.5

Table 3　Summary of Standard ARM/AML Plans Purchased by the Federal National Mortgage Association[a]

Plan Number	Interest Rate Index	Interest Rate Period	Payment Adjustment Period	Maximum Interest Rate Change Per Adjustment Period	Maximum Payment Increase[b]
1	1-yr. T-Sec.	1 year	1 year	no limit	7.5%
2	3-yr. T-Sec.	3 years	3 years	no limit	7.5%
3	5-yr. T-Sec.	5 years	5 years	no limit	7.5%

[a]Effective May 9, 1983. In addition to the plans shown, other loans may be purchased on a case-by-case basis in blocks of $5 million. The plans shown are available with a graduated payment option. The standard plans purchased by FNMA are subject to change.

[b]At the borrower's option, an increase in the monthly payment may be limited to the indicated percentage, or cap. If the payment is insufficient to cover the interest due, the deficiency is added to the outstanding loan balance. The extent of this *negative amortization* is limited by FNMA guidelines. For the three- and five-year plans, the 7.5 percent cap is in effect at the time of the adjustment and at annual intervals thereafter until regular amortization begins. In no case is the loan balance allowed to exceed 125 percent of the original loan amount as a result of negative amortization. In the unlikely event this limit is reached, the payment cap may not be used until the loan is brought below the limit.

percent annually thereafter until the loan begins amortizing normally again. Under FNMA regulations, the outstanding loan balance is not allowed to exceed 125 percent of the original loan amount as a result of negative amortization. In the unlikely event this limit is reached, the payment cap may not be used until the loan is brought below the limit.

Each of the plans may be combined with an optional "graduated payment" feature, which starts monthly payments at a reduced level and increases the payments gradually during the following years. On the plan using the one-year Treasury security index, the initial payment adjustment period is extended to three years when the graduated payment feature is used. During the graduated payment period, mortgage payments increase by 7.5 percent per year for a specified number of years. The amount of the normal interest payment not paid is added to the outstanding principal amount. The graduated payment provision is examined in more detail later in this section. There are no prepayment penalties for any of the Fannie Mae ARM/AML plans, and all loans are assumable by qualified buyers.

Comments   Although the preceding discussion focused on the Fannie Mae ARM/ AML plans, Fannie's cousin, Freddie Mac, purchases loans that are identical to, or very similar to, those shown in Table 3. The combined secondary market influence of these two agencies has been a major force in shaping the types of loans offered by lenders.

The question may arise—what is the average life of ARMs or AMLs? Strictly speaking, the ability to adjust interest rates periodically to reflect market conditions does not affect the average life of an adjustable-rate loan portfolio. However, the repricing of such loans has the same effect as the prepayment of an old loan and the simultaneous granting of a new loan at the current rate. If a repricing interval is one year, the "average life" would be about one year, or slightly less because of amortization. Since the purpose of the average life concept is to convey information regarding the interest-rate sensitivity of a loan portfolio, it is appropriate to view the interest rate adjustment period as the *de facto* average life of an ARM or AML.

Renegotiable Mortgage   Another instrument gaining widespread use is the *re-*
Loan (RML)   *negotiable mortgage loan,* or RML. It is also referred to
                                  as a *rollover mortgage loan.* This type of loan is similar to Plans 2 and 3 in Table 3. The RML is written for a 25- or 30-year term and at three-, four-, or five-year intervals the loan rate is brought to market. The new payments are sufficient to amortize the loan over the remaining term. The RML is simply a series of renewable mortgage loans. The main difference between the RML and the ARM/AML Plans 2 and 3 in Table 3 is that the new rate is renegotiated rather than being automatically set according to a verifiable, external index. The lack of this contractual linkage substantially reduces the marketability of these loans in the secondary market. The renegotiated rate offered by lenders is usually the same as the offering rate on comparable new loans. Usually the loans are assumable and no prepayment penalty is charged.

Balloon Mortgage Loan

The *balloon mortgage loan* is similar to the RML except that there is no commitment by the lender to renew the loan after the initial period of three to five years. Payments are based on a 25- or 30-year amortization period and a fixed interest rate. At the end of the specified initial period the loan balance is due and payable in one lump-sum, balloon payment. The borrower must refinance the loan. The lender has no obligation to provide such refinancing. Although once used only to finance income and commercial property, balloon mortgages are used on a limited basis in residential financing.

Call-Option Mortgage

A variation of the conventional fixed-rate loan and the balloon loan is the *call-option mortgage*. This is the same as a conventional mortgage loan except that at the end of a three- to five-year period, the lender has the option to call the loan or let the loan run its full term at the original loan rate. If the loan is called, refinancing at current market rates is necessary in order to meet the balloon payment. The lender is not obligated to provide such refinancing. If the loan is not called, the borrower in effect has a conventional fixed-rate loan.

Growing Equity Mortgage (GEM)

An increasingly popular instrument in residential financing is the *growing equity mortgage*, or GEM.[5] To see the nature of this fixed-rate loan, consider the example shown in Table 4. This loan is for $80,000 with a fixed interest rate of 12 percent and an "initial" amortization period of 30 years. The monthly payment is $822.89. During the first year the GEM is identical to the conventional fixed-rate loan. However, at the beginning of the second and each subsequent year, the monthly payment increases by 4 percent. The monthly payment during the second year is $855.81. All of the excess payment is applied to the principal so the loan balance is reduced at a faster rate than that of a conventional mortgage. Although the increase in the monthly payment is only 4 percent per year, the effect on the average life of this loan is dramatic. Note that one-half the loan is repaid during the eleventh year. If this were a conventional loan, this would not occur until the twenty-fourth year. (See the loan repayment profile of a conventional loan in Figure 1 shown earlier in this chapter.)

The GEM has important advantages for both borrowers and lenders. From the borrower's standpoint, the fixed-rate feature is appealing. The increases in the payment are known with certainty and because they are nominal in size, the increases should pose no problem. The shorter average life also results in lower

---

[5] The term GEM is a registered service mark of GEM Savings, Dayton, Ohio.

Table 4   Example of a Growing Equity Mortgage

Amount of Loan $80,000

Interest Rate 12%

Initial Amortization Basis . . . . 30 Years

First-Year Payments $822.89

Annual Increase in Payments 4%

Year	Borrower's Monthly Payments	Increase in Monthly Payments	Loan Balance at Year-End
1	$ 822.89	—	$79,709.70
2	855.81	$32.92	78,965.07
3	890.04	34.23	77,691.88
4	925.65	35.61	75,805.60
5	962.67	37.02	73,210.58
6	1,001.18	38.51	69,798.05
7	1,041.23	40.05	65,444.79
8	1,082.88	41.65	60,011.20
9	1,126.20	43.32	53,339.09
10	1,171.25	45.05	45,249.44
11	1,218.10	46.85	35,539.64
12	1,266.82	48.72	23,980.51
13	1,317.49	50.67	10,312.77
14	1,370.19	52.70	—0—[a]

[a] The loan is paid off after the eighth payment in year 14.

total interest paid over the life of the loan. Assuming the loan runs its full term, the total interest that would be paid on the loan shown in Table 4 is $94,962. If this were a conventional loan, the total interest would be $216,240, a difference of $121,278. From the lender's standpoint, the lower average life means that the earning rate on this loan is more interest-rate sensitive than that of a conventional loan. However, since most mortgage loans are paid off early, the difference in average life is not as significant as it appears. Despite this, the shorter life of GEMs has considerable appeal to mortgage lenders and investors in the secondary market.

Graduated Payment Mortgage (GPM)

Another fixed-rate instrument that has attracted considerable attention in recent years is the *graduated payment mortgage,* or GPM. The monthly payments on a GPM initially are lower than the standard amortization schedule would require. The payments increase each year at a specified rate and for a fixed number of years, and then level off at a higher amount than would have been paid under the regular amortization schedule. Thus, the term and the interest rate are constant but the payment increases each year according to a predetermined schedule. For example, a "7½ and 5" plan would call for the below-normal, first-year payments to increase 7½ percent each year for 5 years. To see how this affects the borrower's monthly payment, consider a fixed-rate mortgage loan of $80,000 at 12 percent with a 30-year term. The normal monthly payment would be $822.89. Under the "7½ and 5" plan, the payments would be as follows:

Year	Monthly Payment
1	$660.00
2	709.50
3	762.71
4	819.91
5	881.40
6-30	947.51

Note that the monthly payment during the first year is considerably lower than the normal payment of $822.89 required by the standard amortization schedule. The difference decreases each year and by the fifth year the payments exceed the normal payment for the remainder of the term. The procedure for calculating monthly payments for a GPM is complex so tables are used for this purpose.[6]

Benefits and Risks for Borrowers   The GPM can be tailored to meet a common problem— insufficient income. One of the lending guidelines used by mortgage lenders is that the borrower's monthly income should be at least three or possibly four times the borrower's "monthly housing expense" which is defined as the sum of principal, interest, property taxes, and insurance. If the monthly payment for taxes and insurance is $250, the monthly housing expense for a 30-year conventional mortgage loan of $80,000 at 12 percent would be $822.89 + 250 = $1,072.89. Assuming a borrower's income must be three times this amount, the gross monthly income requirement is $3,218, or $38,616 annually. Under the "7½ and 5" GPM plan shown above, the annual income requirement is reduced to $32,760. Thus, a borrower may obtain housing that otherwise might be out of reach financially. This is an important consideration, especially for younger first-time homebuyers.

The loan repayment pattern can be tailored to the expected income pattern of the borrower. For example, the payment pattern can be structured to increase at 2 percent per year for a ten-year period, 5 percent per year for five years, or some other combination.

The main risk of the GPM for borrowers is that the rising payments may be a financial burden if the expected income on which the loan is based does not materialize. However, the fact that the increases are known with certainty and nominal in size should reduce any financial problems.

Lender Risk   From the lenders' standpoint, the GPM is a riskier instru- ment than most others with respect to default risk and interest rate risk. The added default risk arises because the below-normal payments in the first few years are insufficient to cover the interest so negative amortization

---

[6] See, for example, *FHA Graduated Payment Mortgages Table*, Publication No. 540 (Revised), Boston: Financial Publishing Company, 1981.

results. The "7½ and 5" plan cited above would call for payments of $660.00 in the first year (rather than a constant payment of $822.89). At the end of the first month the interest due is $(.12/12) \times \$80,000 = \$800.00$. The deficiency of $140.00 is added to the loan balance. In effect, the deferred interest constitutes another loan. Each month thereafter the amount of the deficiency increases until the payment increases sufficiently to begin the amortization process. After several years of such monthly deficiencies, the loan balance is well in excess of the original amount of the loan. The increasing loan balance increases the L/V ratio in the earlier years of the mortgage. It is difficult to offset this effect by requiring a higher downpayment because most of the borrowers who use this type of financing are only capable of making a small downpayment. Thus, to shift the added default risk associated with small downpayments and negative amortization, most GPMs must be insured and the downpayment must be at least 10 percent.

Since the GPM is a fixed-rate loan and the loan balance is increasing in the early years of the loan, the average life is longer than a conventional loan with a corresponding term. Thus, its interest-rate risk is greater. This risk may be shifted to long-term investors by selling the loans in the secondary market. However, the interest rate on these loans must be 50 to 100 basis points higher than that on conventional loans. Also, to be marketable the loans should contain a due-on-sale clause and a prepayment penalty. The penalty partially protects the lender or end-investor against the adverse effects of refinancing the loan at a lower rate if market interest rates fall.

It is difficult for lenders to price GPMs to be compensated for the risk involved and at the same time satisfy borrowers. When a high risk premium and mortgage insurance premium are added to the base mortgage loan rate, the resulting payment may be only slightly lower than the payment on the other mortgage instruments discussed earlier.

Other Types of Mortgage Loans

Several other types of mortgage loans exist although their use is limited or confined to special situations. Despite pricing problems and the inherent lender risks associated with fixed-rate GPMs, there is a need for this instrument in an era of high-cost housing and high interest rates. To make this type of instrument more appealing to lenders, the Federal Home Loan Bank Board, regulator of federally chartered S&Ls, has authorized the use of *graduated payment adjustable mortgages*, or GPAMs. Although not widely used, the GPAM combines features of both the ARM and GPM. A below-normal early payment stream is established but the rate is adjusted periodically to keep pace with changing interest rate conditions. Not surprisingly, the complexity of this instrument has limited its use by lenders and its acceptance by borrowers.

During periods of rampant inflation and high interest rates the so-called *shared appreciation mortgage*, or SAM as it is known, has been used by a few lenders to obtain an inflation hedge. In return for a below-market interest rate, the borrower agrees to give the lender a portion of the capital appreciation on the underlying property at the end of a specified period, usually five years.

Because of its extreme complexity, along with disclosure, accounting, and regulatory problems, the SAM is not commonly used in residential mortgage financing. However, the sharing concept is used in financing commercial real estate ventures involving financially sophisticated participants.[7]

The *reverse annuity mortgage* (RAM) enables elderly people whose home is paid off to live off their equity without selling the underlying property. Rather than making a lump-sum loan at the inception of the agreement, the lender pays the borrower a specified amount each month in a manner similar to an annuity. The loan balance grows each month and the interest at the end of each month is added to the loan balance. When the elderly person or couple moves or dies, the property is sold and the loan is repaid. One problem with this type of loan is the assumption that the owner's equity, which is being consumed, will outlast the owners. This may not happen. Also, if the property value declines, the loan may be too large relative to the collateral value. These problems have limited its use.

MORTGAGE-BACKED SECURITIES

Until the mid-1970s the major sources of capital for the residential mortgage market were S&Ls, banks, and mutual savings banks. Financial institutions such as life insurance companies, pension funds, endowments, and trust funds tended to avoid direct investments in residential mortgages because of the cumbersome nature of the instrument and its high cost. Much paperwork is required for each mortgage loan. Physical facilities and a trained staff are needed to administer a mortgage loan portfolio. Compounding the problem is the fact that residential loans are usually made in relatively small denominations. The result is that residential mortgages have a high administrative cost per dollar of investment. In contrast, bonds require considerably less administrative effort and have low transactions costs. The costs related to a bond portfolio may be spread over large denominations so the administrative cost per dollar invested is quite low.

A related impediment that affected the flow of capital to the mortgage market was simply the inaccessibility of large institutions such as insurance companies and pension funds to borrowers, and vice-versa. Unless such an institution had a decentralized investment operation with geographically dispersed outlets, it was virtually impossible for these types of institutions to channel a significant amount of funds into the residential mortgage market. It is unlikely that someone in Detroit would seek a residential mortgage from the New York Life Insurance Company. It is equally unlikely that the company would make the loan because it lacks familiarity with the local market and its minimum investment is well in excess of the size of most residential mortgage loans. Through mortgage-backed securities, New York Life may be financing homes not only in Detroit, but through-

---

[7] For a discussion of the shared appreciation concept and related policy implications, see: Thomas J. Parliment and James S. Kaden, "The Shared Appreciation Concept in Residential Financing," in *Financial Markets: Instruments and Concepts*, edited by John R. Brick, Reston, Virginia: Reston Publishing Co., Inc., 1981, pp. 285-300.

out the country. Many other types of financial institutions that once avoided direct investment in the mortgage market are now active participants via mortgage-backed securities.

The basic concepts underlying these instruments were developed by federal agencies in an attempt to overcome market impediments and stimulate the flow of capital into the mortgage market. The widespread acceptance of the mortgage-backed securities in the financial markets has led to dramatic changes in both the mortgage market and financial management practices of many financial institutions. The three instruments underlying these changes are the *pass-through certificate*, the *mortgage-backed bond*, and a hybrid of the first two, the *pay-through bond*.

Ginnie Mae Pass-Through Certificates

One of the most innovative and popular capital market instruments is the *pass-through certificate*. These certificates represent direct ownership of a portfolio of mortgage loans. The portfolio is created when a mortgage lender assembles a pool of mortgage loans that are alike in their term, interest rate, and quality. The portfolio is then placed in trust with a bank and certificates of ownership are sold to investors. The ownership of loans in the pool lies with the holders of the certificates and not the original lender. Since the pass-through arises through the sale of the issuer's assets, pass-through certificates are not debt obligations of the issuer. They do not show up on the issuer's financial statement.

Although the holders of pass-through certificates own the mortgage loans, the loan originator "services" the mortgage pool. That is, the originator collects monthly payments, handles the accounting, and disburses the principal and interest payments to the pool owners. All interest, principal, and prepayments on the underlying mortgage loans, less the servicing fee, are passed through monthly and in a single payment to the owners—hence the name "pass-throughs." The payment is accompanied by an itemized statement showing the proportions of principal and interest. The holder of a certificate owns a portion of a mortgage portfolio by holding an instrument with convenient, bond-like characteristics.

A moment's reflection on the pass-through concept raises several questions. If some of the underlying mortgages default, how are the certificate-holders protected? What are the characteristics of the mortgages in the pool? Since the actual payment stream is unknown because of prepayments, how are these capital market instruments priced in the market? To address these and several other issues, a distinction must be made between the pass-throughs issued by federal agencies and those issued by private sector lenders. Although the underlying concept is similar in both the agency and private sector, the resulting instruments differ in their details.

The pass-through concept was developed in 1970 by the Government National Mortgage Association (GNMA), a direct agency of the federal government. The most important characteristic of these GNMA issues, commonly referred to as *Ginnie Mae pass-throughs*, is that they are riskless with respect to default. This stems from three sources of financial backing.

- The securities are collateralized by mortgage loans held in trust for the holders of the certificates.

- The mortgage loan portfolio underlying the Ginnie Mae pass-through is comprised entirely of government-backed FHA and VA loans.
- The GNMA, an arm of the federal government, guarantees the prompt monthly payment of both principal and interest—*regardless of whether or not it has been collected.*

The guarantee of the monthly payments has the effect of "modifying" the actual stream of mortgage payments. If a mortgage loan is in a nonpaying or even a foreclosure status, it is irrelevant to the holder of the pass-through certificate since principal and interest are paid by Ginnie Mae. If a foreclosure results and the loan is repaid by the FHA or VA, this constitutes a prepayment and it is passed through to the owners of the pool.

In light of the collateral, FHA and VA backing, and the Ginnie Mae guarantee, it is difficult to imagine a security with more financial backing than a Ginnie Mae pass-through. Because of this backing, the securities are considered direct obligations of the U. S. Government. As such, they may be held in any amount by regulated financial institutions such as banks, S&Ls, and credit unions.

Pricing Pass-Throughs   The importance of these instruments requires an understanding of the manner in which they are priced in the market. The pricing process is more complicated than that of bonds. Before looking at two examples that illustrate the pricing process, several points should be made. First, the loans in the pool should be similar in their quality, interest rate, and term. This facilitates the pricing process since the entire portfolio may be viewed as a single loan. Unless the pool is made up of riskless FHA and/or VA mortgages, it should contain a large number of loans that are geographically diversified.

When offering a new pass-through security made up of new 30-year loans, the yield is estimated (or the price determined) by assuming that the cash flows stem only from the scheduled amortization payments for twelve years and at the end of this period all loans are fully prepaid. This assumption is used because on new pools made up of new loans, there is no prepayment experience available. Since it is known that most loans will be prepaid, some prepayment assumption must be made. The yield produced by the twelfth-year prepayment assumption corresponds to the yields historically generated by pools of FHA-insured loans. However, specific pools may prepay at a much faster or slower rate than the general FHA experience. If the certificate was bought at a discount or premium rather than par value, as is usually the case, the rate of repayment and changes in the rate affect the buyer's yield. After a Ginnie Mae pass-through has been outstanding, information is published regarding the speed at which the specific issue is being prepaid. This speed determines the average life of the portfolio. The information can then be used to obtain a better estimate of the yield. The numerical examples that follow demonstrate the pricing process and show how the FHA repayment experience is used as a benchmark when evaluating specific pass-through issues.[8]

---

[8] The examples are adapted from: *Pass-Through Yield and Value Tables*, Publication No. 715, 8th ed., Boston: Financial Publishing Co., 1982.

Example.   GNMA mortgage pool No. 22021 was issued January 1, 1978 and has a term that extends to January 15, 2008. This is a period of 30 years and 15 days. The additional 15 days, when coupled with the first month, provide a total of 45 days to pass-through the initial payment. The interest rate on the mortgage loans is 8.5 percent and the net pool rate is 8 percent after deducting servicing and guarantee fees. As of March 1, 1982, the pool had been outstanding for 4 years and 2 months. How is the price determined for a particular yield? What is the average life of the investment? The following steps outline the pricing process.

The Decimal Balance Table.   Periodically, GNMA publishes the unpaid loan balance for each pool and a decimal representing the outstanding proportion of each pools' original loan amount. The outstanding balance of pool No. 22021 on March 1, 1982 was $1,420,146 and the decimal was .7073. The loan balance is the par value at a point in time. Using this information and the fact that the pool had an elapsed time of 4 years 2 months, the *Decimal Balance Table* shown in Table 5 may be used to determine the *payoff speed*. This affects the value of the pool.

The Payoff Speed.   To determine the payoff speed using the 8 percent *Decimal Balance Table* shown in Table 5, find the row for the elapsed time of 4 years and 2 months. Reading across this row, note that the reported decimal of .7073 is between .6824 in the "200% FHA" column and .7439 in the "150% FHA" column. The term "200% FHA" means that the pool is repaying the principal at a rate that is twice as fast as the overall FHA experience. A "0% FHA" experience means that the only source of repayment is through amortization. By interpolation the experience of pool number 22021 is about "180% FHA." In practice it may be desirable to examine the reported decimal balance for a several-month period prior to the purchase. The pool's payoff speed may be increasing or decreasing and the investor may wish to project the payoff speed rather than using the most recently reported figure. Different assumptions produce different yields. In this case, the reported decimal balance was declining so it is assumed that the payoff speed will be "150% FHA."

The Yield-Value Table.   Using the payoff speed of "150% FHA" and assuming a desired yield of 12.50 percent, the price may be obtained from the *Yield and Value Table* shown in Table 6. This table is for an 8 percent pool with approximately four years elapsed and 26 years remaining. Reading down the yield column to 12.50 percent and across to the "150% FHA" column, a price of 81.17 is obtained. Because of loan repayments a certificate representing an original loan balance (or par value) of $100,000 now has a loan balance (or par value) of .7073 × $100,000 = $70,730. The dollar price of this certificate is .8117 × $70,730 = $57,411.

At the bottom of the Yield and Value Table is the *half-life*, or the *average life* as discussed earlier. Recall that this is the time it takes for the investor to receive one-half the principal. This value is based on the repayment experience to date and the remaining term. As the payoff speed increases, the average life decreases and vice-versa. In this example, if the "150% FHA" experience is realized over the term of the pool, the average life of this investment will be only 5.8 years. In the unlikely event that all the loans are repaid only through regularly scheduled payments, the average life would be 19.1 years. Like a bond, if a pass-through certificate is bought at par value, i.e., 100, the investor's return is unaffected by prepayments, assuming no prepayment penalties. However, if a pass-through is bought at a price above or below par value and the expected repayment speed changes, the investor's yield is affected. The next example illustrates this point.

8% POOL RATE

Table 5
Decimal Balance Table

POOL RATE **8%**

The mortgage rate for borrower is ½ % greater because of service charge.
The decimal is the proportion of original pool still unpaid according to assumptions as
to experience for elapsed time. It thus corresponds to decimal published by GNMA

DECIMALS BASED ON FHA MORTGAGE MORTALITY EXPERIENCE

Elapsed Yrs Mos	1000% FHA	800% FHA	600% FHA	400% FHA	300% FHA	200% FHA	150% FHA	125% FHA	100% FHA	75% FHA	50% FHA	0% FHA
0 1	9900	9919	9938	9956	9966	9975	9980	9982	9985	9987	9989	9994
0 2	9801	9838	9875	9913	9931	9950	9960	9964	9969	9974	9978	9988
0 3	9703	9758	9814	9869	9897	9925	9939	9946	9953	9961	9968	9982
0 4	9606	9679	9752	9826	9863	9900	9919	9929	9938	9947	9957	9976
0 5	9510	9600	9691	9783	9829	9876	9899	9911	9922	9934	9946	9969
0 6	9415	9522	9630	9740	9795	9851	9879	9893	9907	9921	9935	9963
0 7	9320	9444	9570	9697	9761	9826	9859	9875	9891	9907	9924	9957
0 8	9227	9367	9510	9654	9727	9801	9838	9857	9875	9894	9913	9950
0 9	9134	9291	9450	9612	9694	9776	9818	9839	9860	9881	9902	9944
0 10	9043	9215	9390	9569	9660	9752	9798	9821	9844	9867	9891	9937
0 11	8952	9140	9331	9527	9626	9727	9778	9803	9828	9854	9880	9931
1 0	8862	9065	9272	9485	9593	9702	9757	9785	9813	9840	9868	9924
1 1	8577	8830	9090	9358	9495	9634	9704	9739	9775	9810	9846	9918
1 2	8301	8601	8911	9233	9398	9566	9651	9694	9737	9780	9824	9911
1 3	8034	8377	8735	9109	9302	9498	9598	9649	9699	9750	9801	9904
1 4	7775	8160	8563	8987	9206	9431	9546	9604	9662	9720	9779	9898
1 5	7525	7948	8395	8866	9112	9365	9494	9559	9624	9690	9757	9891
1 6	7283	7742	8229	8747	9019	9298	9442	9514	9587	9660	9734	9884
1 7	7048	7540	8067	8630	8926	9233	9390	9469	9550	9630	9712	9877
1 8	6821	7345	7908	8514	8835	9167	9338	9425	9512	9601	9690	9870
1 9	6602	7154	7752	8400	8744	9102	9287	9381	9475	9571	9667	9863
1 10	6389	6968	7599	8287	8654	9038	9236	9336	9438	9541	9645	9856
1 11	6183	6787	7449	8176	8565	8974	9185	9292	9401	9511	9623	9849
2 0	5984	6610	7302	8066	8477	8910	9134	9249	9364	9482	9600	9842
2 1	5721	6376	7105	7919	8359	8825	9067	9191	9316	9443	9572	9835
2 2	5469	6149	6914	7774	8243	8741	9001	9133	9268	9405	9544	9828
2 3	5228	5931	6728	7632	8128	8657	8934	9076	9220	9367	9516	9820
2 4	4998	5720	6547	7492	8015	8574	8869	9019	9173	9329	9488	9813
2 5	4778	5517	6370	7355	7903	8493	8803	8963	9126	9291	9460	9806
2 6	4568	5321	6199	7221	7793	8411	8738	8907	9078	9253	9431	9798
2 7	4367	5132	6031	7088	7685	8331	8674	8851	9031	9215	9403	9791
2 8	4174	4950	5869	6959	7577	8251	8610	8795	8985	9178	9375	9783
2 9	3991	4774	5711	6831	7472	8172	8546	8740	8938	9140	9347	9776
2 10	3815	4604	5557	6706	7367	8094	8483	8685	8891	9103	9319	9768
2 11	3647	4440	5407	6583	7264	8016	8420	8631	8845	9066	9291	9760
3 0	3486	4282	5261	6463	7163	7939	8358	8576	8799	9028	9264	9753
3 1	3316	4114	5104	6332	7052	7855	8290	8516	8749	8988	9233	9745
3 2	3154	3952	4951	6203	6943	7772	8222	8457	8699	8948	9203	9737
3 3	3000	3796	4803	6077	6836	7689	8155	8399	8649	8907	9173	9729
3 4	2854	3647	4660	5954	6730	7608	8089	8340	8600	8867	9143	9721
3 5	2715	3503	4520	5833	6626	7527	8022	8282	8550	8827	9113	9713
3 6	2582	3365	4385	5715	6524	7447	7957	8225	8501	8787	9083	9705
3 7	2456	3232	4254	5598	6423	7368	7892	8167	8452	8748	9053	9697
3 8	2336	3105	4127	5485	6323	7290	7827	8110	8404	8708	9023	9688
3 9	2222	2982	4003	5373	6225	7212	7763	8054	8355	8669	8993	9680
3 10	2113	2865	3883	5264	6129	7135	7699	7997	8307	8629	8964	9672
3 11	2010	2752	3767	5157	6034	7059	7636	7941	8259	8590	8934	9664
4 0	1912	2643	3654	5052	5940	6984	7573	7886	8212	8551	8904	9655
4 1	1811	2531	3536	4941	5840	6904	7506	7826	8161	8509	8873	9647
4 2	1715	2423	3421	4832	5742	6824	7439	7767	8110	8468	8841	9638
4 3	1625	2319	3310	4726	5646	6746	7373	7709	8060	8426	8810	9629
4 4	1539	2220	3203	4622	5551	6668	7308	7651	8009	8385	8778	9621
4 5	1457	2125	3099	4520	5458	6591	7243	7593	7960	8344	8747	9612
4 6	1380	2035	2999	4420	5366	6515	7179	7535	7910	8303	8715	9603
4 7	1307	1948	2902	4323	5276	6440	7115	7478	7860	8262	8684	9594
4 8	1238	1864	2807	4227	5188	6366	7052	7422	7811	8221	8653	9585
4 9	1173	1785	2716	4134	5100	6292	6989	7365	7762	8181	8622	9576
4 10	1111	1709	2628	4043	5014	6219	6926	7308	7714	8140	8591	9567
4 11	1052	1635	2543	3954	4930	6147	6865	7254	7665	8100	8560	9558
5 0	0996	1566	2460	3866	4847	6076	6803	7199	7617	8060	8529	9549
5 1	0938	1492	2373	3773	4758	5999	6737	7139	7565	8017	8495	9540
5 2	0884	1422	2288	3682	4670	5924	6671	7080	7514	7974	8462	9530
5 3	0833	1356	2207	3593	4584	5849	6606	7021	7462	7931	8429	9521
5 4	0785	1292	2129	3506	4500	5775	6542	6963	7411	7888	8396	9512
5 5	0739	1232	2053	3421	4417	5702	6478	6905	7360	7846	8363	9502
5 6	0696	1174	1980	3338	4335	5629	6415	6848	7310	7803	8330	9492
5 7	0656	1119	1909	3258	4255	5558	6352	6791	7260	7761	8297	9463
5 8	0618	1067	1841	3179	4176	5487	6290	6734	7210	7719	8264	9473
5 9	0582	1017	1776	3102	4099	5418	6228	6678	7160	7677	8232	9463
5 10	0548	0969	1712	3027	4024	5349	6167	6622	7111	7636	8199	9453
5 11	0516	0924	1651	2953	3949	5281	6107	6567	7062	7594	8166	9444
6 0	0486	0880	1593	2882	3876	5214	6047	6512	7013	7553	8134	9434

Source: Pass-Through Yield and Value Tables for GNMA Mortgage-Backed Securities, Pub.
No. 715, 8th ed., Boston: Financial Publishing Company, 1982, p. 112, reproduced with
permission.

Table 6

8%   Yield-Value Table

Mortgage Net Rate to Pool

Years Elapsed 4
Years Remaining 26

VALUES BASED ON FHA MORTGAGE MORTALITY EXPERIENCE, BOTH FASTER AND SLOWER

YIELD	1000% FHA	800% FHA	600% FHA	400% FHA	300% FHA	200% FHA	150% FHA	125% FHA	100% FHA	75% FHA	50% FHA	0% FHA
10.00	96 99	96 50	95 73	94 42	93 35	91 71	90 55	89 84	89 02	88 08	86 98	84 17
10.25	96 67	96 11	95 26	93 81	92 61	90 80	89 52	88 74	87 84	86 80	85 60	82 51
10.50	96 35	95 73	94 79	93 20	91 89	89 91	88 51	87 66	86 69	85 56	84 25	80 91
10.75	96 03	95 35	94 33	92 59	91 18	89 04	87 53	86 61	85 56	84 35	82 94	79 36
11.00	95 71	94 98	93 87	92 00	90 47	88 18	86 56	85 58	84 46	83 16	81 66	77 85
11.25	95 39	94 61	93 42	91 41	89 78	87 34	85 62	84 58	83 38	82 01	80 42	76 39
11.50	95 08	94 24	92 97	90 83	89 10	86 51	84 69	83 59	82 34	80 89	79 22	74 98
11.75	94 76	93 87	92 53	90 26	88 43	85 70	83 78	82 63	81 31	79 80	78 04	73 62
12.00	94 45	93 51	92 08	89 69	87 77	84 90	82 90	81 69	80 31	78 73	76 90	72 29
12.10	94 33	93 36	91 91	89 47	87 50	84 58	82 55	81 32	79 92	78 31	76 45	71 77
12.20	94 20	93 22	91 73	89 24	87 24	84 27	82 20	80 95	79 53	77 89	76 01	71 26
12.30	94 08	93 07	91 56	89 02	86 98	83 96	81 85	80 59	79 14	77 48	75 57	70 75
12.40	93 96	92 93	91 39	88 80	86 73	83 65	81 51	80 22	78 76	77 08	75 14	70 25
12.50	93 83	92 79	91 21	88 58	86 47	83 35	81 17	79 87	78 38	76 67	74 71	69 76
12.60	93 71	92 64	91 04	88 36	86 22	83 04	80 84	79 51	78 00	76 27	74 28	69 27
12.70	93 59	92 50	90 87	88 14	85 96	82 74	80 50	79 16	77 63	75 88	73 86	68 79
12.80	93 47	92 36	90 70	87 92	85 71	82 44	80 17	78 81	77 26	75 49	73 44	68 31
12.90	93 35	92 22	90 53	87 71	85 46	82 14	79 84	78 46	76 89	75 10	73 03	67 84
13.00	93 23	92 08	90 36	87 49	85 21	81 85	79 52	78 12	76 53	74 71	72 62	67 38
13.10	93 11	91 94	90 19	87 28	84 96	81 56	79 19	77 78	76 17	74 33	72 22	66 92
13.20	92 98	91 80	90 02	87 07	84 72	81 26	78 87	77 44	75 82	73 96	71 82	66 46
13.30	92 86	91 66	89 85	86 85	84 47	80 97	78 56	77 11	75 46	73 58	71 42	66 01
13.40	92 74	91 52	89 68	86 64	84 23	80 69	78 24	76 78	75 11	73 21	71 03	65 57
13.50	92 62	91 38	89 52	86 43	83 99	80 40	77 93	76 45	74 77	72 85	70 64	65 13
13.60	92 51	91 24	89 35	86 22	83 75	80 12	77 62	76 12	74 42	72 48	70 26	64 70
13.70	92 39	91 10	89 18	86 01	83 51	79 84	77 31	75 80	74 08	72 12	69 88	64 27
13.80	92 27	90 96	89 02	85 81	83 27	79 56	77 00	75 47	73 74	71 77	69 50	63 85
13.90	92 15	90 83	88 86	85 60	83 03	79 28	76 70	75 16	73 41	71 41	69 13	63 43
14.00	92 03	90 69	88 69	85 40	82 80	79 00	76 40	74 84	73 08	71 06	68 76	63 02
14.10	91 91	90 55	88 53	85 19	82 56	78 73	76 10	74 53	72 75	70 72	68 39	62 61
14.20	91 79	90 42	88 37	84 99	82 33	78 46	75 80	74 22	72 42	70 38	68 03	62 20
14.30	91 68	90 28	88 20	84 79	82 10	78 19	75 51	73 91	72 10	70 03	67 67	61 80
14.40	91 56	90 14	88 04	84 58	81 87	77 92	75 21	73 60	71 78	69 70	67 32	61 41
14.50	91 44	90 01	87 88	84 38	81 64	77 65	74 92	73 30	71 46	69 36	66 97	61 02
14.60	91 33	89 87	87 72	84 18	81 41	77 39	74 63	73 00	71 14	69 03	66 62	60 63
14.70	91 21	89 74	87 56	83 99	81 19	77 12	74 35	72 70	70 83	68 70	66 28	60 25
14.80	91 09	89 61	87 40	83 79	80 96	76 86	74 06	72 40	70 52	68 38	65 94	59 87
14.90	90 98	89 47	87 24	83 59	80 74	76 60	73 78	72 11	70 21	68 06	65 60	59 50
15.00	90 86	89 34	87 08	83 40	80 51	76 35	73 50	71 81	69 91	67 74	65 26	59 13
15.10	90 75	89 21	86 93	83 20	80 29	76 09	73 22	71 52	69 60	67 42	64 93	58 77
15.20	90 63	89 07	86 77	83 01	80 07	75 83	72 95	71 24	69 30	67 11	64 60	58 41
15.30	90 52	88 94	86 61	82 81	79 85	75 58	72 67	70 95	69 01	66 80	64 28	58 05
15.40	90 40	88 81	86 46	82 62	79 64	75 33	72 40	70 67	68 71	66 49	63 96	57 70
15.50	90 29	88 68	86 30	82 43	79 42	75 08	72 13	70 39	68 42	66 18	63 64	57 35
15.60	90 18	88 55	86 14	82 24	79 20	74 83	71 87	70 11	68 13	65 88	63 32	57 00
15.70	90 06	88 42	85 99	82 05	78 99	74 59	71 60	69 83	67 84	65 58	63 01	56 66
15.80	89 95	88 29	85 84	81 86	78 77	74 34	71 34	69 56	67 55	65 28	62 70	56 32
15.90	89 84	88 16	85 68	81 67	78 56	74 10	71 07	69 29	67 27	64 99	62 39	55 99
16.00	89 72	88 03	85 53	81 48	78 35	73 86	70 81	69 01	66 99	64 70	62 08	55 66
16.10	89 61	87 90	85 38	81 30	78 14	73 62	70 55	68 75	66 71	64 40	61 78	55 33
16.20	89 50	87 77	85 23	81 11	77 93	73 38	70 30	68 48	66 43	64 12	61 48	55 00
16.30	89 39	87 64	85 07	80 93	77 72	73 14	70 04	68 22	66 16	63 83	61 19	54 68
16.40	89 27	87 51	84 92	80 74	77 52	72 90	69 79	67 95	65 89	63 55	60 89	54 37
16.50	89 16	87 38	84 77	80 56	77 31	72 67	69 54	67 69	65 62	63 27	60 60	54 05
16.60	89 05	87 26	84 62	80 38	77 11	72 44	69 29	67 43	65 35	62 99	60 31	53 74
16.70	88 94	87 13	84 47	80 19	76 90	72 21	69 04	67 18	65 08	62 72	60 03	53 44
16.80	88 83	87 00	84 32	80 01	76 70	71 98	68 80	66 92	64 82	62 44	59 74	53 13
16.90	88 72	86 88	84 18	79 83	76 50	71 75	68 55	66 67	64 56	62 17	59 46	52 83
17.00	88 61	86 75	84 03	79 65	76 30	71 52	68 31	66 42	64 30	61 90	59 19	52 53
17.25	88 34	86 44	83 66	79 21	75 80	70 96	67 71	65 80	63 66	61 24	58 50	51 80
17.50	88 06	86 12	83 30	78 77	75 31	70 40	67 12	65 19	63 03	60 59	57 83	51 09
17.75	87 79	85 81	82 93	78 33	74 82	69 86	66 54	64 59	62 41	59 95	57 18	50 40
18.00	87 52	85 51	82 58	77 90	74 34	69 32	65 97	64 01	61 81	59 33	56 53	49 72
18.25	87 25	85 20	82 22	77 47	73 87	68 79	65 41	63 43	61 21	58 72	55 91	49 06
18.50	86 99	84 90	81 87	77 05	73 40	68 27	64 86	62 86	60 63	58 12	55 29	48 41
18.75	86 72	84 60	81 52	76 63	72 94	67 76	64 32	62 31	60 06	57 53	54 69	47 79
19.00	86 46	84 30	81 17	76 22	72 49	67 25	63 78	61 76	59 50	56 96	54 10	47 17
19.25	86 20	84 00	80 83	75 81	72 04	66 75	63 26	61 22	58 94	56 39	53 52	46 57
19.50	85 94	83 71	80 49	75 41	71 59	66 26	62 74	60 69	58 40	55 84	52 96	45 99
19.75	85 68	83 41	80 15	75 01	71 15	65 78	62 23	60 17	57 87	55 30	52 40	45 42
20.00	85 42	83 12	79 81	74 61	70 72	65 30	61 73	59 66	57 35	54 76	51 86	44 86
Half Life Years	1 1	1 3	1 7	2 4	3 1	4 5	5 8	6 7	8 1	10 0	12 7	19 1

Mortgages always 30 Years Original Term, at Rate ½% greater than Net of Pool

Source: Pass-Through Yield and Value Tables for GNMA Mortgage-Backed Securities, Pub. No. 715, 8th ed., Boston: Financial Publishing Company, 1982, p. 117, reproduced with permission.

> *Example.*   Assume the pass-through certificate of pool number 22021 was pur-
> chased at 81.17 to yield 12.50 percent on the basis of the "150% FHA" assumption.
> If the actual repayment experience over the remaining life of this pool turns out to
> be "75% FHA," what is the investor's realized yield and the average life?
>
>   Given the prepayment experience of "75% FHA" and the purchase price of
> 81.17, the realized yield can be obtained from the Yield and Value Table. Reading
> down the "75% FHA" column, note that the price of 81.17 is between the prices
> corresponding to yields of 11.25 and 11.50 percent. The yield is lower than 12.50
> percent because the return of principal is taking longer than initially expected. The
> new average life is 10 years rather than 5.8 years.

    The prepayment experience of mortgage pools change over time and differs
from one pool to another. One of the main factors to consider is the changing level
of interest rates relative to the pool rate. If current rates are high or rising, low-
rate pools tend to have slower repayment speeds. When interest rates are low or
falling, the loan repayment process accelerates in high-rate pools.

    When pricing pass-throughs, one other factor should be kept in mind. Since in-
terest is paid monthly on pass-throughs and semiannually on bonds, the compounding intervals are different. A bond and a pass-through with the same quoted
yield will have different effective yields. Assuming a quoted rate r of 10 percent,
the effective rate i on the pass-through resulting from monthly compounding is

$$i = \left(1 + \frac{.10}{12}\right)^{12} - 1$$

$$= .1047 \text{ or } 10.47\%.$$

The bond's effective rate resulting from semiannual compounding is

$$i = \left(1 + \frac{.10}{2}\right)^{2} - 1$$

$$= .1025 \text{ or } 10.25\%.$$

In this example, monthly compounding increases the effective yield by 22 basis
points over that of a bond.

Other Characteristics   New issues of Ginnie Mae pass-throughs are available in
minimum denominations of $25,000 and with terms of
28 to 30 years. Because of the loan reduction through amortization and prepayments, older issues are available in smaller denominations and with shorter terms.
The interest income is taxable at federal, state, and local levels. Although lacking
liquidity because of their price sensitivity resulting from changes in interest rates,
an active and well-developed secondary market provides a high degree of marketability for these securities.

Freddie Mac Pass-Throughs

The success of Ginnie Mae pass-throughs prompted the Federal Home Loan Mortgage Corporation (FHLMC)—or *Freddie Mac* as it is known—to develop its own version of the pass-through. This indirect federal agency was chartered by Congress in 1970 for the purpose of increasing the flow of capital to the mortgage market. Unlike Ginnie Mae, which only purchases FHA-VA loans primarily from mortgage bankers, Freddie Mac purchases conventional and privately insured mortgage loans, primarily from S&Ls and banks. To finance this activity and support an active secondary market for conventional and privately insured mortgages, the agency issues several types of securities. The most important of these is a pass-through security called a *participation certificate*, or PC.

PCs are similar in concept to the Ginnie Mae pass-through. The PC represents ownership of a portion of a mortgage portfolio. However, there are some important differences. The mortgage loans underlying the PCs are either uninsured loans with L/V ratios of 80 percent or less, or privately insured loans if the L/V ratio exceeds 80 percent. The loans are not government-backed so PC mortgage loan pools are geographically diversified and considerably larger than the Ginnie Mae mortgage pools. Each pool usually contains between 2,000 and 5,000 loans.

As with the Ginnie Mae pass-throughs, mortgage loans constitute the source of repayment and back the PC. The financial risk of these loans is minimized by the owner's equity or private mortgage insurance. In addition, the PCs are guaranteed by Freddie Mac as to the "timely payment of interest and the full return of principal." This means that the monthly interest is guaranteed but the principal is passed through as collected. Although the full repayment of principal is guaranteed, there may be slight delays in the event of default by borrowers. Since the loans are high quality, there are few such defaults so delays are relatively few. When such delays do occur the effect on the total monthly payment is small because of the large number of loans in each pool.

Although Freddie Mac's guarantee does not constitute formal backing by the federal government, the guarantee coupled with well-secured loans results in a security of exceptionally high quality. In fact, PCs are like Ginnie Mae pass-throughs in that they are exempt from any "percent of asset" limitations imposed by regulators of banks, S&Ls, and credit unions. This means that PCs may be held in unlimited amounts.

Although the pricing of PCs is similar to that of Ginnie Maes, there is a tendency for conventional and privately insured mortgages to repay at faster rates than FHA loans. The result is a shorter average life of about 7 to 9 years for the PCs rather than 10 to 12 years for Ginnie Maes. The experience of individual pools may differ considerably.

Because of a large minimum denomination, $100,000, the market for PCs is dominated by financial institutions. An active secondary market provides reasonably good marketability. Generally, the yields on PCs are about 15 to 25 basis points higher than yields on comparable term Ginnie Mae pass-throughs. The spread varies depending on market conditions.

Private Sector Pass-Throughs

In September 1977, the Bank of America successfully issued the first private sector pass-through security. This offering was backed solely by conventional mortgages. There were no government or agency guarantees and as pass-throughs the securities were *not* debt obligations of the BofA. However, the imaginative use of private mortgage insurance and special hazard insurance substantially reduced the risk of loss to the holders of the pass-throughs. This landmark financing had an immediate and widespread impact on both the mortgage market and the management policies of many financial institutions. Before discussing the managerial implications, the characteristics of private sector pass-throughs and the rating process must be clarified.

BofA Pass-Through   In May 1978, the Bank of America publicly issued another pass-through security which was rated AA by Standard & Poor's. In light of this high rating and the fact that the issue became a model for other private sector pass-throughs, the main features of the BofA offerings are summarized below.

- *The Issue.*   The Bank of America pass-through was comprised of $201 million of Mortgage-Backed Certificates with a 9 percent pass-through rate. The minimum denomination was $25,000.
- *Mortgage Pool.*   The pool consisted of 3,443 conventional mortgage loans originated by the BofA. The loans had interest rates ranging from 9 to 9.25 percent with remaining terms of 25 to 30 years. Although all loans were secured by property dispersed throughout California, mortgages on second homes or rental properties were excluded. The mortgages were assigned without recourse to the Wells Fargo Bank as trustee.
- *Average Life.*   At the time of the offering, the bank's recent experience indicated that the prepayment experience, or payoff speed, of their 30-year conventional loans was about 200 percent of the FHA rate. If this experience continued, the average life of the portfolio would be about 7 years, given its range of loan rates.
- *Private Mortgage Insurance.*   To minimize the financial risk to the holders of the pass-throughs, a private mortgage insurance policy was obtained. The coverage was limited to 5 percent of the original principal balance of the pool. If claims exceeded this amount the policy then lapsed and additional losses would have been borne by the certificate holders. Like ordinary private mortgage insurance policies, the coverage required that a property be restored to its original condition before a claim could be paid. This requirement posed a potential risk for the certificate holder that was reduced by a "Special Hazard Policy."
- *Special Hazard Insurance.*   Each of the underlying properties was covered by standard hazard insurance policies that insured against losses resulting from various causes such as fire, lightning, and windstorms. Certain other risks which were not otherwise insured against such as floods, mud flows, and earthquakes were covered under a Special Hazard Policy. To see why

such a policy was required to protect the certificate holders, assume one of the mortgaged properties in the pool was destroyed by an earthquake. Since this loss would be uninsured, the owner could simply walk away from the debris and the mortgage loan. The resulting default would not be covered by private mortgage insurance unless the property was restored to its original condition. This restoration was the main purpose of the Special Hazard Policy. The maximum liability payable under this policy was 1 percent of the original pool balance. Losses in excess of this amount were to be absorbed by the pass-through holder.

- *Voluntary Advances.*   The bank intended to use its own funds to cover late payments of principal and interest. This action had the effect of stabilizing the cash flow to the certificate holders. Such advances, however, were voluntary and limited to amounts that were recoverable under the insurance contracts.
- *Service and Other Fees.*   The bank's service fee was the difference between the weighted average interest rate on the mortgages, 9.12 percent in this case, and the 9 percent pass-through rate. The bank also retained any prepayment penalties, late payment penalties, and front-end points.

The BofA pass-through shows how mortgage loans coupled with the innovative use of mortgage and hazard insurance combined to create a high-quality instrument. This is evident from the high rating given this and most other pass-through securities.

Quality Rating   The key to a private sector pass-through offering by a financial institution is the quality of the security as measured by the bond rating services such as Standard & Poor's and Moody's. The rating plays a role in several ways. First, from the standpoint of many regulated financial institutions as buyers of such securities, the purchase of an unrated issue must be justified to examiners. As a result, most institutions simply avoid buying unrated issues or issues with ratings lower than BBB or Baa. From the issuer's standpoint, the sale of pass-throughs constitutes a sale of assets. The price received by the selling institution depends on the rating. In fact, the entire pass-through concept depends on the quality rating. If the BofA pass-through issue cited above were rated BBB rather than AA, the required yield to investors may have been 10 percent which was greater than the average interest rate on the pool. The mortgages would have to be sold at a discount and the capital loss absorbed by the bank. This would inhibit the use of the pass-through as a financing device. As it was, the BofA issue was sold at a profit because the default risk related to each loan was minimized by careful underwriting, special hazard insurance, and mortgage insurance.

To obtain a high rating on a pass-through security, several criteria must be satisfied. Loans underlying the pass-through must be secured by first mortgages on single-family, owner-occupied, primary residences. The loan-to-value ratio must be no greater than 80 percent. The mortgage insurance and special hazard policies must provide ample protection as illustrated in the BofA example. The financial strength of the loan servicer, trustee, and insurance companies are other important elements in the rating process.[9] Although the BofA pass-through involved conventional fixed-rate mortgage loans, this need not always be the case. Adjustable-rate pass-through certificates rated AA have been sold in the public debt markets.

Some Variations   In an attempt to further reduce both the cost and default risk of pass-throughs and at the same time increase the price at which they may be sold, some commercial banks back their issues with an irrevocable letter of credit. The LOC replaces the mortgage insurance and special hazard insurance policies as well as the bank's agreement to make voluntary advances. When there is a delinquency on any loans in the pool, the trustee calls on the bank to make payments under provision of the LOC. Since the issuing bank has a binding obligation to make such advances, the bank has parted with the assets but retains some of the risk. To limit this risk and comply with legal restrictions on borrowings, the Comptroller of the Currency, the regulator of national banks, has ruled that the amount of LOC backing is limited to 7 percent of the principal balance in the pool.

Another innovative approach to the risk reduction problem is to divide the mortgage pool into senior and subordinated certificates. The senior certificates have a priority claim on the principal and interest payments made on mortgage loans in the pool. The holders of subordinated certificates receive no payments until the holders of senior certificates have been completely satisfied for a specified period. Because of the added backing of the loans underlying the subordinated certificates, the senior certificates usually obtain a very high rating. Correspondingly, the rating of the subordinated certificates is lower unless some other form of protection is provided.

Managerial   The ability to package and sell conventional and alterna-
Implications   tive mortgage loans in a convenient, bond-like form
                           enables mortgage lenders to obtain capital from nontraditional sources such as pension funds, life insurance companies, trust funds, and endowments. The ready acceptance of pass-throughs by financial institutions carries over to the private placement market where large, complex transactions can be negotiated quickly between a small number of financial institutions.

The existence of an active private placement market for pass-throughs has important implications for smaller mortgage lenders. Since the minimum size for a public offering is about $20 million, many smaller institutions are unable to package a sufficiently large portfolio. A logical alternative is to place smaller issues privately with other financial institutions. Issues as small as $5 million have been placed in this manner. Another approach for smaller institutions is to sell their individual mortgage loans to so-called conduits. Several private mortgage insurance companies, for example, act as an intermediary and buy small blocks of mortgage loans from lenders and then pool the loans for resale as a pass-through security in the national markets.

The pass-through concept has enhanced the financial flexibility of mortgage

---

[9] For a discussion of the rating process for mortgage-related securities, see *Credit Overview: Corporate and International Ratings*, New York: Standard & Poor's Corporation, 1982, pp. 64-70.

lenders and this is accomplished without incurring additional liabilities. The capital structure, and thus the financial risk of the lender, is unchanged when pass-through securities are sold. This is not the case with *mortgage-backed bonds.*

Mortgage-Backed Bonds

The *mortgage-backed bond* (MBB) is a debt obligation of a mortgage lending institution and is collateralized by mortgage loans.[10] Unlike pass-throughs, the issuer retains ownership of the loans. From the investor's standpoint these instruments are like other bonds in that they have a stated maturity with the interest usually paid semiannually. Typically, bonds in the private sector have a maturity ranging from five to twelve years. This maturity range corresponds to the average life of a portfolio of fixed-rate conventional mortgage loans. Since these bonds do not have long maturities, they are usually not callable. However, bonds with maturities toward the longer end of the spectrum may have a sinking fund to provide for an orderly repayment schedule.

Although federal agencies issue mortgage-backed bonds, the focus of this section is on private-sector issues. Since these bonds lack direct federal or agency guarantees, the indenture provisions and certain aspects of the collateral mortgage loan portfolio assume added importance. Despite the lack of any direct government backing, the private-sector mortgage-backed bond is an unusually high-quality instrument. This is a result of three sources of financial strength. First, the bonds are direct liabilities of the issuer and, as such, the bonds are backed by the creditworthiness of the issuing mortgage lender. The second source of financial strength is the quality of the underlying mortgage loans that are held in trust as collateral for the bondholders. If the loans are FHA or VA backed, the collateral is riskless from a credit standpoint. Although not riskless in this respect, uninsured and privately insured mortgages represent high quality collateral. Finally, the quality of a bond hinges on a key indenture provision—the required *collateral level.*

Collateral Level   When structuring a mortgage-backed bond, a collateral level is specified in the indenture. In order to obtain the highest possible bond rating, AAA or Aaa, the collateral must be at least 180 percent of the par value. Thus, a $50 million offering would require that mortgage loans with a *market value* of at least $90 million be placed in trust to collateralize the bonds. The market value of the collateral pool is the present value of the loans discounted at the prevailing mortgage loan rate. The pool is valued quarterly. If the value falls below 180 percent of the bonds outstanding, the issuer must add additional mortgage loans or other securities to the pool to bring the collateral up to the required amount. If the amount of bonds outstanding declines because

---

[10] There are two types of *bonds* backed by mortgage loans and they should not be confused. This section deals with the *mortgage-backed bond* while the *pay-through bond* is covered in the next section. The *pass-through certificate,* although backed by mortgage loans, is not a bond because it arises through the sale of assets and thus it is not an obligation of the issuer.

of debt retirement, the amount of collateral may decline subject to the 180 percent constraint.

The question may be asked—why is so much collateral required? There are three reasons. Since the outstanding balance of any mortgage pool declines over time and the cash flows go to the issuer, the pool must have excess collateral that is "used up" between valuation dates. The second reason for the high collateral requirement is to provide additional credit protection for the bondholders. Since uninsured and privately insured mortgage loans are not riskless, foreclosures could result in losses and reduce the value of the collateral. Finally, the high collateral level protects the bondholders against declines in the market value of the collateral resulting from rising interest rates.

Although held in trust for the bondholders, the mortgage loans continue to be owned by the issuer of the bonds. In the event of a default, the trustee can sell the mortgage loans in the secondary market in order to redeem the bonds with full interest. For this reason, only high quality, marketable loans are acceptable as collateral.

Quality Rating   Like pass-throughs, the quality rating of MBBs is a major factor in the feasibility of such financing. Most publicly offered MBBs are rated AAA by Standard and Poor's because of the "overcollateralization" feature. The key factors involved in the rating process are the amount of collateral as indicated by the collateral level, the quality of collateral, and the creditworthiness of the issuer. Because of the need for marketability, certain types of loans such as balloon loans, second mortgage loans, and loans underlying nonowner occupied properties are excluded in order to get the higher bond rating. Usually loans in the collateral pool are written in conformance with standards required by the secondary mortgage market, especially the Federal Home Loan Mortgage Corporation and the Federal National Mortgage Association.

Because of the high collateral requirements underlying these bonds, an issue of MBBs may have a rating of AAA even though unsecured debt of the same issuer may be rated only BBB. If the general creditworthiness of an issuer is a concern the collateral level may be increased to offset the added risk.

Managerial   The MBB is an important financing device for S&Ls and
Implications   mutual savings banks. However, it is unclear whether
                     federally chartered (national) banks and some state chartered banks have the authority to issue collateralized bonds.[11] With the exception of public deposits, federally chartered banks are prohibited from collateralizing deposits and thus giving preferred status to any depositors. The Federal Reserve Bank defines "deposit" as

---

[11] This and a subsequent discussion of the legality of collateralized bonds draws from: Richard B. Foster, Jr., "Pay-Through Bonds—How Financial Institutions Can Increase Their Profits on Long-Term, Low-Yielding, Real Estate Mortgages," a paper presented at the Midwest Finance Association Meeting, St. Louis, Missouri, April 8, 1983.

... any member bank's liability on a note, acknowledgment of advance, due bill, or similar obligation (written or oral) that is issued or undertaken by a member bank primarily as a means of obtaining funds to be used in its banking business.[12]

This definition is sufficiently broad to cast doubt on the ability of national banks to issue MBBs. The uncertainty has inhibited their use. Similarly, with the exception of public deposits, the laws of some states prohibit state chartered banks from pledging assets to secure any depositors or creditors. However, a bank may be actively involved in this market as a trustee for the bondholders.

MBBs enable a medium-grade issuer to obtain low-cost, triple-A money. Raising funds in the national capital markets also avoids or minimizes adverse effects on the issuer's cost of local deposit-related funds. For example, a savings and loan association may decide to raise funds by increasing the rate paid on a certain type of deposit from, say, 9 percent to 10 percent. This may seem preferable to offering MBBs at 11 percent. However, the marginal cost of obtaining the incremental funds by raising the deposit rate may exceed the cost of MBBs. This occurs because the S&L will have to pay the higher deposit rate on both new and old deposits. Thus, "old" 9 percent money may now cost 10 percent so the increase in interest costs might be much greater proportionally than the increase in deposits. An offering of MBBs would leave the existing deposit cost structure unaffected. The marginal cost of the new funds would be the MBB offering rate.

The use of MBBs has two opposite effects on the financial risk of the issuer. Since these bonds are direct obligations of the issuer, their use increases leverage and thus the financial risk of the firm. (Increasing the deposit level has the same effect.) On the other hand, MBBs have a risk-reducing impact in that they allow the mortgage lender to lengthen the maturity of a portion of its liability structure. These bonds represent one of the few sources of longer-term, fixed-rate funds available to mortgage lenders. Financing mortgage loans with MBBs enables financial institutions to reduce the adverse effects of financing a long-term, fixed-rate loan portfolio with short-term funds during a period of rising interest rates.

Pay-Through Bonds

The *pay-through bond* combines features of both the mortgage-backed bond and the pass-through security. Like the MBB, the pay-through is a bond collateralized by mortgage loans so it appears on the issuer's financial statement as debt. The cash flow from the mortgage loan pool is "dedicated" to servicing the bonds in a manner quite similar to that of pass-throughs. Unlike the pass-through, however, an issuer can "liquify" low-yielding mortgage loans without selling the loans and realizing substantial losses.

---

[12] Regulation Q, 12 CFR 217.1(f).

A Numerical Example   In Table 7 a numerical example of a pay-through bond is shown. A $25 million pay-through issue is fully amortized over a twelve-year period at 12 percent with monthly payments. The monthly payment, R, is given by the present value annuity model

$$R = \frac{\$25 \text{ million}}{\left[\dfrac{1 - \dfrac{1}{\left(1 + \dfrac{.12}{12}\right)^{12\,(12)}}}{.12/12} \right]}$$

$$= \$328,355.$$

To generate these payments and support the pay-through bond, the issuer assembles a large pool of mortgage loans that have a combined, remaining loan balance of $35 million, a remaining average term of 14 years, and an average interest rate of 8 percent. This collateral pool generates a monthly cash flow of $346,961. This is sufficient to cover the monthly debt service requirements of $328,355. Each month the balance of $18,606 is added to a reserve fund until it reaches an amount equal to 10 percent of the outstanding bonds. When the reserve reaches this level, excess cash flows and interest income earned on the funds revert to the issuer. The nature of this reserve is discussed below.

Table 7   Example of Fully Amortizing Pay-Through Bond

Bond Characteristics	
Par value	$25 million
Coupon rate	12%
Amortization term	12 years
Monthly bond payments	$328,355
Cash reserve requirement	10% of outstanding bonds
Mortgage Collateral Characteristics	
Remaining loan balance	$35 million
Average loan rate	8%
Average remaining term	14 years
Monthly cash flow	$346,961
Monthly contribution to cash reserve	$18,606 [a]
Present value of cash flows	$28,175,465 [b]
Over-collateralization	$3,175,465 [c]

[a]The monthly contribution to the cash reserve fund is the difference between the monthly bond payments and the cash flow from the collateral pool. When the reserve requirement is reached, 10 percent of the outstanding bonds in this example, the excess cash flow reverts to the bond issuer.

[b]The present value is found by discounting the collateral cash flows at the pay-through rate, 12 percent in this example.

[c]Over-collateralization is the difference between the par value of the bonds and the present value of the collateral cash flows.

Using the pay-through bond rate as the discount factor, the present value of the cash flow from the collateral pool is about $28.2 million. Since it is unlikely that any of the loans could be sold at the pay-through bond rate, this present value is somewhat overstated and thus it is only an approximation. This is sufficient because the emphasis of a pay-through bond is on the cash flow rather than the liquidation value. The main point, however, is that the amount of collateral necessary for a pay-through bond is considerably less than that required for a mortgage-backed bond. Assuming a collateral requirement of 180 percent, a $25-million issue of MBBs would require collateral with a present value of $45 million rather than $28.2 million.

It is unlikely that the cash flow pattern of a collateral pool will precisely coincide with the bond's payout requirements. Prepayments are usually required to be passed through to the bondholders in the form of additional principal. Temporary cash shortfalls or permanent losses may result from delinquencies and foreclosure proceedings. However, the timely payment of principal and interest payments by the trustee can be assured by drawing on the reserve fund. To the extent that permanent losses are incurred in the collateral portfolio, the excess cash flow that reverts to the issuer is reduced. As owner of the loans, the issuer absorbs credit-related losses. Mortgage insurance and bank letters of credit are other approaches that may be used along with, or in lieu of, the cash reserve to reduce the risk of loss to the pay-through bondholders.

Pay-Through Advantages

Since a pay-through bond is the functional equivalent of a pass-through security it has all the advantages of a pass-through. However, since the mortgage loans are not actually sold, low-rate mortgage loans may be used, without realizing capital losses. Unlike pass-throughs, lower quality mortgage loans may also be used provided the added credit risk is offset with a combination of additional collateral, a larger cash reserve, a letter of credit, or mortgage insurance.

When forming a pass-through pool, all loans must be similar with respect to their interest rate, term, and quality for pricing purposes. Depending on the size of the issue and the issuer, up to several months may be needed to form a sufficiently large pool of similar loans. In a volatile interest rate environment changing market conditions could disrupt the formation process and possibly result in the sale of loans at a loss. This problem does not arise with pay-through bonds.

The pay-through also has a number of important advantages over mortgage-backed bonds. Since the emphasis is on the collateral's cash flow rather than its marketability, an issuer's less marketable, non-homogeneous loans may be used effectively to reduce borrowing costs rather than lying dormant. Less marketable loans might include those with high L/V ratios, large loan balances, low interest rates, or a junior lien position. Again, to the extent that these loans increase the credit risk of the pool, additional collateral can be pledged or other arrangements made. This flexibility greatly expands the list of loans that may be used as collateral.

Since the collateral pool of a pass-through is fixed at the time of the offering, the pool need not be "marked-to-market" on a quarterly basis like the collateral of the MBB. The pool is self-supporting so it does not have to be replenished for any reason, even defaults.

Quality Rating   Like pass-throughs and MBBs, the quality rating of a pay-through is crucial because it determines the issuer's cost of funds. Because of their flexibility in the way they may be structured to reduce the bondholder's risk, pay-through bonds are usually rated AA or AAA by Standard & Poor's. Credit risk of the collateral pool, cash flow coverage of scheduled bond payments, the extent of over-collateralization, and external sources of protection such as mortgage insurance or a bank letter of credit are among the factors evaluated.

Since the pay-through bond is self-supporting, the financial strength of the issuer is not a major factor in the rating analysis. However, the issuer's servicing and loan underwriting capabilities are evaluated. Since federally insured S&Ls, savings banks, and commercial banks are not subject to bankruptcy laws, pay-throughs issued by these institutions are considered "bankruptcy-proof." That is, the failure of these types of institutions would not disrupt the collateral pool and its cash flow. Other issuers, such as mortgage bankers and homebuilders, can achieve the same result by forming a single-purpose financing subsidiary to own the collateral and issue the bonds.

Legality of   Regulators and governing statutes allow most savings
Pay-Throughs   and loan associations and savings banks to pledge their assets and issue pay-through bonds. However, many commercial banks are restricted by the same regulations limiting their use of MBBs. Recall that some states prohibit state chartered banks from pledging assets to secure deposits or any other borrowings except public deposits. Federally chartered (national) banks are not allowed to pledge collateral to secure "deposits." As pointed out earlier, the Federal Reserve's definition of the term "deposit" is so broad that sufficient doubt is raised regarding the ability of a national bank to pledge collateral and issue pay-throughs, at least directly.

A bank could issue such bonds indirectly through a wholly-owned subsidiary. The mortgage loans would be transferred to the subsidiary in return for all of the capital stock of the subsidiary. The subsidiary, as owner of the loans, then pledges the loans to secure pay-throughs without recourse to the subsidiary or the bank. The proceeds of the financing are then loaned to the bank by the subsidiary. Using this approach, the bank has not pledged its assets and neither the subsidiary nor the bank have any further financial obligation.

CONCLUSION

The mortgage loan market has been characterized by dramatic innovations in recent years. Starting with the cornerstone of mortgage financing, the conventional mortgage loans, this chapter also examined the new types of loans collectively referred to as alternative mortgage instruments. Understanding their contractual features and cash flow patterns is essential if risk and return relationships are to be fully understood by both mortgage lenders and consumers alike.

Using the discussion of the various mortgage loans as a base, the chapter then examined three types of mortgage-backed securities. The pass-through, mortgage-backed bond, and the pay-through bond offer low-cost financing options to issuers that traditionally lacked access to the national capital markets. These securities, along with the alternative mortgage instruments, characterize the dynamic changes in a once stodgy sector of the capital markets. It is likely that more changes in the mortgage market are on the way.

REFERENCES

Credit Overview: Corporate and International Ratings, New York: Standard & Poor's Corporation, 1982.

Foster, Richard B., "Pay-Through Bonds—How Financial Institutions Can Increase Their Profits on Long-Term, Low-Yielding, Real Estate Mortgages," a paper presented at the Midwest Finance Association Meeting, St. Louis, Missouri, April 8, 1983.

Parliment, Thomas J., and James S. Kaden, "The Shared Appreciation Concept in Residential Financing," *Financial Markets: Instruments and Concepts,* edited by John R. Brick, Reston, Virginia, Reston Publishing Co., Inc., 1981, 285-300.

Senft, Dexter E., *Inside Pass-Through Securities,* New York: The First Boston Corporation, 1978.

Sivesind, Charles M., "Mortgage-Backed Securities: The Revolution in Real Estate Finance," *Quarterly Review,* Federal Reserve Bank of New York, Autumn 1979, pp. 1-10.

von Furstenberg, George M., "Default Risk on FHA-Insured Home Mortgages as a Function of the Terms of Financing: A Quantitative Analysis," *Journal of Finance,* June 1969, pp. 459-477.

9

The Effects of Usury Ceilings*

Donna Vandenbrink

Regulations designed to prevent usury, or the taking of "excessive" interest, have been debated from the time of Moses. Today, as a result of a prolonged period of high inflation, record interest rates, and sluggish economic growth, the usury ceilings in effect in many states are the center of controversy. Are the critics of these usury ceilings simply speaking out of self-interest when they argue that interest rate ceilings work to consumers' disadvantage by restricting credit flows and distorting financial markets? Do usury ceilings protect consumers from abusive lending practices and enable them to obtain loans at reasonable rates, as their advocates claim?

Recent legislation, at both the federal and state levels, has been in the direction of relaxing interest rate controls. The 1980 *Depository Institutions Deregulation and Monetary Control Act* overrode state interest ceilings on some categories of loans, and additional federal action may be forthcoming. At the same time, many state legislatures have revised their usury statutes. In large part, these recent changes in usury regulation have been in response to the current economic situation. But is deregulation of usury ceilings desirable? And if it is desirable, should it be left to the states or is it best accomplished by federal preemption? This article surveys the economic research on usury ceilings in order to help answer these questions.

USURY CEILINGS IN A COMPETITIVE MARKET: THE THEORETICAL ARGUMENTS

In economic theory, the credit market is viewed like any other market.[1] There are buyers (borrowers) and sellers (lenders) of credit; the price of credit is the in-

*Reprinted from *Economic Perspectives*, Midyear 1982, pp. 44-55, with permission from the Federal Reserve Bank of Chicago.

[1] For a simple theoretical treatment of usury ceilings see Chapter 9 in James Van Horne [25]. For a more advanced discussion see Rudolph C. Blitz and Millard F. Long [2].

terest rate. The credit market is easily represented in a conventional supply and demand diagram (see figure). The demand curve indicates the amount of credit borrowers are willing to purchase at various prices (interest rates). The supply curve indicates how lenders' marginal cost of funds varies with the amount of credit supplied and, thus, the amount of credit they are willing to grant at various interest rates, assuming the market is competitive. According to theory, borrowers and lenders will eventually establish an equilibrium in the market at a price which just balances the supply and demand for credit. We can call this price the market rate of interest. Such a rate is shown as r_m.

Usury laws stipulate a maximum rate of interest which lenders may legally charge. When a usury law is introduced, it may alter the way in which both price and quantity are determined in the credit market. Exactly what happens depends on the level of the usury ceiling relative to the market rate. When the legal ceiling is above the market rate of interest (r_m), the law has no effect at all. The market forces of supply and demand are unconstrained by the usury ceiling, and the equilibrium price and quantity of credit are unchanged. However, when the legal ceiling is below r_m, the regulation does affect the market outcome. Such a usury ceiling, like the rate r_u in the figure, is said to be binding or effective.[2] A binding ceiling obviously alters the price of credit—the ceiling rate becomes the rate of interest charged. Therefore, if the market rate r_m were considered too high, a usury ceiling of r_u would lower the rate of interest for those borrowers who were able to obtain credit.

However, establishing a lower-than-market interest rate by means of a usury ceiling will also bring about a decrease in the quantity of credit supplied. Given lenders' costs (as reflected in the supply curve shown in the figure), the most credit which they will provide when the interest rate is held down to r_u is Q_u. Therefore, the binding usury ceiling will lead to a reduction from Q_m to Q_u in the amount of credit supplied. Furthermore, in contrast to the situation in the unregulated market, this amount of credit will not satisfy all those who are willing to borrow

The Effects of a Binding Usury Ceiling

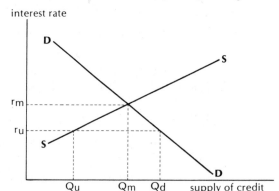

[2] What has happened in many states over the last decade is that for various economic reasons market interest rates have risen above what were initially nonbinding statutory ceilings. While the ceilings always existed, only recently have they begun to impinge on the market.

at the ceiling price. The usury ceiling creates a situation of excess demand with borrowers seeking an amount of credit, Q_d, that exceeds the amount supplied by lenders, Q_u. Borrowers are prevented by the ceiling from bidding to obtain more credit and lenders will not provide any more credit at the legal maximum interest rate. Thus, at the legal ceiling price the reduced amount of credit must be rationed among borrowers by some means other than price.

The important implication of this straight-forward supply-demand analysis is that usury laws can succeed in holding interest rates below their market levels only at the expense of reducing the supply of credit to borrowers.

THE EFFECT OF USURY CEILINGS ON
THE QUANTITY OF CREDIT SUPPLIED: THE EVIDENCE

Potential borrowers would surely find it less than desirable if binding interest rate ceilings did have the predicted effect on the supply of credit. In order to test this predicted relationship and to measure its importance, investigators have examined a number of different credit markets.

Because commercial loans are usually exempt from state usury ceilings, there have not been many studies of the effects of usury ceilings on commercial lending. In one of the few such studies, Robert Keleher of the Federal Reserve Bank of Atlanta [9] determined that banks in Tennessee extended fewer commercial loans the further market interest rates rose above the state's 10 percent usury ceiling.[3]

More widely studied has been the mortgage market, where binding usury ceilings also have been found to have very restrictive effects on credit supplies. The Federal Reserve Bank of Minneapolis [3, 20] analyzed Minnesota's experience with an 8 percent usury ceiling on conventional home mortgages. In this case, the usury ceiling had a significant impact on the composition of mortgage credit even though the total volume of mortgage lending apparently was unaffected. The Minneapolis study found that when market rates climbed to between 9 and 10 percent in 1973-74, home financing in Minnesota shifted substantially from conventional mortgages that were subject to the ceiling to FHA or VA loans that were exempt from the ceiling. About 40 percent of all new mortgage loans issued in the state in late 1974 were FHA-insured, almost double the usual share, and conventional mortgages were virtually unavailable in the Twin Cities.

More formal analyses of the effect of usury ceilings on the supply of mortgage credit were carried out by James Ostas [16], Philip Robins [19], and James McNulty [12]. Ostas and Robins approached the issue indirectly, looking at the impact of ceilings on homebuilding rather than on mortgage lending. Ostas estimated that the number of authorized housing permits fell by 11 to 19 percent for every one percentage point that the market rate was above the usury ceiling. Robins found that for each percentage point by which market rates exceeded usury limits,

---

[3]The exceptions were loans to nondurable and durable manufacturing and loans to service industries. Keleher speculates that these loans were not adversely affected by the ceiling because of previous commitments, strong customer relationships, and nonprice rationing.

single-family housing construction was reduced by 16 percent. Looking directly at mortgage lending, McNulty found that usury ceilings have an impact on the supply of credit even before the average market rate hits the ceiling. He estimated that as the average market rate rose from a point below, but still close to the ceiling, mortgage lending was lowered 7.5 to 12.5 percent for each 1 percentage point rise in the market rate relative to the ceiling.[4]

Usury ceilings appear to have some adverse effect on the supply of consumer credit as well. In a technical study for the National Commission on Consumer Finance (NCCF), Robert Shay [21] found that state usury ceilings had a small but statistically significant negative effect on the number of consumer loans extended. Each 1 percentage point decrease in the usury ceiling on small loans was associated with 18 fewer loans per 10,000 families.[5] In addition, Shay found that lower rate ceilings were associated with fewer new auto loans. However, he found no significant effect on the supply of credit to purchase other consumer goods (mobile homes, boats, aircraft, and recreational vehicles).

The Credit Research Center (CRC) at Purdue University has conducted several studies of usury ceilings and consumer credit. In one such study, Johnson and Sullivan [8] found that a 1977 change in Massachusetts law which lowered the usury ceiling on small loans was an important factor in the 12.5 percent drop in the amount of such loans outstanding in that state between 1975 and 1979.

In another study for the CRC, Richard Peterson [17] compared urban consumer credit markets in Arkansas, which had a 10 percent comprehensive usury ceiling, with similar credit markets in Illinois, Wisconsin, and Louisiana, which had less restrictive ceilings. Although he found that residents of Arkansas obtained as much (or more) credit overall as consumers in the other states studied, he also found that consumers in Arkansas obtained significantly less cash credit and more point-of-sale credit (retail credit and credit cards) than their counterparts in the states with less restrictive ceilings. Here, as in the Minnesota mortgage market, the usury ceiling apparently did not reduce the total supply of credit, but it did cause consumers to substitute one type of credit for another—and, importantly, the change in the mix of credit favored lenders rather than consumers. Merchants and dealers who issue point-of-sale credit can compensate for the reduced profitability of their credit operations by raising prices on the goods they sell.

NONINTEREST CREDIT CONDITIONS:
USURY CEILINGS AND CREDIT RATIONING

Altogether, the empirical research on the effects of usury ceilings largely substantiates the argument that binding usury ceilings lead to a reduction in the

---

[4] Despite finding this impact on the number of loans extended, McNulty did not find that Georgia's ceiling had a significant impact on housing construction. McNulty believed this was because Georgia's ceiling was only moderately, and briefly, restrictive during the period under study.

[5] Shay also found a positive but insignificant relationship between the dollar volume of loan extensions and usury ceilings. If the average size of each loan were to rise while the number of loans fell, the usury ceiling might not affect the total dollar volume of loans extended.

amount of credit provided by lenders. But credit transactions involve a number of terms other than the interest rate. Usury ceilings determine the price that lenders can charge, but they do not constrain the other conditions that lenders may choose to offer. Faced with a binding usury ceiling, lenders may be expected to alter these noninterest conditions in order to achieve a higher effective return on the smaller amount of credit they will offer. For example, by such means as strengthening loan terms, adjusting borrower-screening criteria, or increasing noninterest fees and charges, lenders may be able to skirt the impact of usury ceilings on their overall profitability. It is important to consider how these strategies affect the borrowing public.

As pointed out above, under binding usury ceilings borrowers demand more credit than lenders are willing to provide. This requires lenders to rely on nonprice means to allocate credit among potential borrowers. Many of the strategies lenders are likely to follow in this situation can be expected to concentrate the impact of usury ceilings on certain borrowers. For example, making loan terms more stringent reallocates credit away from those who are unable to afford larger downpayments or the larger monthly payments necessitated by shorter maturities and higher minimum loan size. Determining credit-worthiness according to individual borrower characteristics rations credit away from high-risk consumers who might be willing to pay higher-than-ceiling rates. Finally, adding noninterest charges eliminates from the market those for whom these extra costs are too great.

By encouraging these lending practices, usury ceilings may fail to give consumers the protection and benefits which they were intended to provide. For example, usury laws may work against the goal of ensuring that credit is available to small, inexperienced borrowers. When lenders ration credit by some means other than price, small borrowers, low-income borrowers, and high-risk borrowers are likely to find it more difficult to obtain credit. Prime borrowers, on the other hand, may obtain even more credit than they would have at normal market interest rates. Furthermore, when lenders institute noninterest charges to compensate for interest rate ceilings, they effectively raise the cost of credit for the successful borrower. This means that, while a ceiling may reduce the explicit price of credit (the interest rate), it may not result in lower overall costs of borrowing even for those able to obtain loans. The noninterest charges also make it more complicated for customers to comprehend the total cost of borrowing and make it more difficult to make well-informed credit decisions.

These lending practices and their undesirable consequences may exist in the absence of interest rate ceilings. However, some empirical studies have found that the extent to which these devices are used is influenced by the restrictiveness of usury laws. Several studies have established that loan terms do become less favorable to borrowers when usury ceilings become more restrictive. For example, the Minneapolis Federal Reserve Bank [3, 20] found that during one period when Minnesota's ceiling on mortgage loans was binding, the average maturity of conventional mortgages in the Minneapolis-St. Paul SMSA fell significantly. The same study found that required downpayments increased much more sharply in the Twin Cities compared with SMSAs not subject to binding usury ceilings. Similarly, according to the New York State Banking Department [10], downpayment requirements increased and maximum maturities decreased during the

1974 credit crunch when market interest rates rose above New York's 8.5 percent ceiling on mortgage loans.

Phaup and Hinton [18] actually measured the magnitudes of the changes in noninterest mortgage terms due to New York's usury ceiling. Using data on new mortgage lending for single-family dwellings in Schenectady, New York for 1961 through 1976, they estimated that for each 1 percentage point the market rate rose above the usury ceiling, there was a 4 percent shortening of mortgage maturities and an 8 percent decline in loan-to-value ratios.[6]

Peterson's study [17] indicated that usury ceilings have similar impacts on noninterest loan terms in the consumer credit market. This study found that maturities of auto loans in Arkansas were shorter than in states with less restrictive usury laws. In addition, the average minimum size for personal loans at commercial banks and credit unions was 2.5 times larger in Arkansas than in other states covered by the study. Peterson found that Arkansas lenders charged higher fees for mortgage credit investigations and appraisals than did lenders in other states with less restrictive interest rate ceilings. Arkansas residents also paid higher charges for checking accounts and overdrafts. (Moreover, retailers faced bigger discounts and less desirable terms when selling their retail credit contracts to other creditors.)

Empirical research has also tended to confirm the expectation that the burden of usury ceilings falls unevenly on the borrowing public. The availability of credit to certain groups of borrowers appears to depend on the restrictiveness of usury ceilings. Peterson, for example, found that cash credit was significantly less available to low-income and high-risk borrowers when usury ceilings were more restrictive. The lowest income group and the three highest risk groups of consumers in Arkansas obtained a larger proportion of their credit from point-of-sale sources than in other states in the study with more liberal interest rate ceilings. In their study of the Schenectady, New York mortgage market, Phaup and Hinton [18] found that lower income areas felt the impact of usury regulations on mortgage lending activity more than other areas. They found that mortgage activity in census tracts of the lowest economic stratum was more sensitive to the usury ceiling and to noninterest credit terms than mortgage lending in tracts characterized by higher economic status. Johnson and Sullivan [8] found that Massachusetts' lowered ceiling had a greater impact on the availability of small regulated loans than of large ones, particularly at small, local finance companies. They concluded that less prosperous consumers who needed and could afford only small loans "were progressively excised from this portion of the legal cash loan market" (p. 14).

The survey data collected by the National Commission on Consumer Finance (NCCF) have been used in several studies of the impact of usury ceilings on consumer credit markets. Greer's [7] analysis showed that differences in finance company rejection rates were closely related to differences in state usury ceilings. The lower were rate ceilings, the higher was the rate of rejection for personal loan applicants. Greer concluded from this study that, with higher allowable interest rates, lenders are more willing to accept risky borrowers and, consequently, binding ceilings make it more difficult for riskier borrowers to obtain credit. Finally,

---

[6] Ostas also found mortgage downpayments were larger and maturities shorter, the more binding the usury ceiling. The maturity effect, however, was not statistically significant.

using the same NCCF data, Shay [21] found additional evidence that high-risk borrowers are most affected by usury ceilings. Generally, higher-risk borrowers obtain credit through auto dealers and finance companies rather than banks. The fact that the higher rate ceilings specifically applicable to auto dealers and finance companies were found to be responsible for curtailed credit in the new auto and personal loan markets led Shay to conclude that the burden of the ceilings falls largely on those whose credit standing is weakest.

The broad conclusion that emerges from these empirical studies is that usury ceilings create a climate in which lenders are able to pursue practices unfavorable to some or all borrowers. On balance, usury ceilings appear to be a type of regulation whose benefits to borrowers are extremely questionable. The primary benefit is a lower-than-market interest rate. But, depending on lenders' actions, borrowers may end up facing higher noninterest credit charges and less favorable terms as a result of usury ceilings. Moreover, attached to the lower-interest benefit of usury ceilings is a direct cost to the borrowing public in the form of a reduced supply of credit. Furthermore, it is likely that the cost of restricted credit availability falls disproportionately on high-risk, low-income borrowers—those whom usury ceilings are usually designed to protect.

Thus far, usury ceilings have been discussed in terms of their effect on individual borrowers. Usury ceilings also affect consumers and the economy in a more general way. This broader impact is a consequence of the particular way in which interest rate regulation has been implemented in the United States.

Diversity of Usury Ceilings

Since colonial times, the responsibility for regulating interest rates on credit has rested with the states. As credit markets have evolved since that time, states have developed complex sets of statutes which apply to specific types of lenders and specific types of credit, often with different limits depending on the size of the loan. As a result, there is great diversity in the coverage of interest rate ceilings within individual states.[7] Furthermore, there is also great diversity in ceiling rates and coverage across states.

These legal arrangements have important implications for the economic impact of usury ceilings. Lack of uniformity of limits and coverage means that some forms of credit are constrained by ceilings while others are not. Under these circumstances, lenders will want to shift their portfolios into loan categories which are not subject to binding ceilings.[8]

---

[7] A 1981 listing by the Financial Institutions Bureau of the Michigan State Department of Commerce contains 25 different loan categories subject to interest rate ceilings imposed by state law. The effective maximum rates ranged from 5 percent on personal loans by individuals for nonbusiness purposes to 36 percent on loans by pawnbrokers. A 1980 survey of Iowa usury laws summarized that state's current interest rate ceilings under nine categories, with maximum permitted rates ranging from 5 percent (the legal rate) to 36 percent (the maximum rate on the first $500 of a loan by a chattel loan licensee).

[8] For example, according to an article in *Business Week*, March 22, 1982, finance companies are switching emphasis from consumer lending to commercial lending in part because commercial loans are generally exempt from usury regulation while consumer loan charges are not.

State-imposed usury laws establish interest rate ceilings on credit extended to borrowers within a particular state. But, since credit markets are not confined by state boundaries, lenders may find it more attractive to extend credit across state lines to borrowers in states which offer less constraining usury laws. Thus, inter-state differences in limits and coverage will distort the geographic distribution of credit and alter the allocation of funds to credit-sensitive economic activities.

Many of the studies cited previously provide implicit support for the notion that the diversity of usury ceilings among states affects the geographic distribution of credit. Studies comparing loan volumes across states with different usury ceilings suggest also that credit availability varies among states depending on the restrictiveness of their usury ceilings.

A study by the staff of the New York State Banking Department [10] shows somewhat more directly how credit flows away from states with restrictive usury ceilings. The study found that during the period 1966 to 1974, when national mortgage market rates were almost continuously above New York's usury ceiling, savings and loans in New York increased their proportion of out-of-state mortgage holdings from 6.5 percent to over 18 percent. Over the same period, in-state conventional mortgage holdings by these institutions fell from 67 percent of total assets to 47 percent and from 75 percent of total mortgages to 57 percent. Clearly, New York State S&Ls responded to the ceiling which bound in-state conventional mortgage rates by increasing their relative holdings of uncovered loan categories, including out-of-state mortgages.[9]

In the long run, state differentials in usury ceilings may even influence the location of suppliers of credit and of credit-sensitive economic activities. Arkansas, which had a low, comprehensive 10 percent usury ceiling, provides several examples of the locational effects. There are no consumer finance companies located in Arkansas and that state has a much larger number of pawnbrokers than Illinois, Wisconsin, or Louisiana, which have more lenient ceilings on consumer credit. In addition, a survey of merchants in the adjacent cities of Texarkana, Texas and Texarkana, Arkansas [1] revealed that there were many more automobile, furniture, and appliance dealers on the Texas side of the border than on the Arkansas side. Furthermore, 84 percent of the merchants interviewed indicated that Arkansas' usury ceiling had been an important factor in their decision to locate in Texas.

Differences in state usury regulations also were cited in recent decisions to relocate the credit card operations of Citibank, First National Bank of Maryland, Philadelphia National Bank, and the First National Bank of Chicago.[10] In addition,

---

[9] Savings banks and state-chartered commercial banks did not exhibit the same large, steady increase in the proportion of out-of-state mortgage holdings. However, New York State savings banks already held almost one-half of their mortgages on out-of-state properties. Furthermore, in-state conventional mortgages, those subject to the ceiling, comprised very small proportions of the total assets of savings banks (approximately 12 percent) and commercial banks (approximately 2 percent) compared with S&Ls.

[10] See *Wall Street Journal*, December 5 and 15, 1981 and *The American Banker*, September 30 and October 30, 1981. The ability of banks to take advantage of interstate differences in ceilings on credit card lending derives from a 1978 Supreme Court ruling. In Marquette National Bank v. First of Omaha Service Corporation, the Court determined that national banks may charge out-of-state credit customers the rate permitted by the law of the bank's home state. See *Federal Reserve Bulletin*, vol. 67 (February 1981), p. 181 fn. The same option does not apply to department stores, gasoline companies, or other issuers of retail or sellers' credit cards.

How Ceilings Vary Among Seventh District States

	First mortgage	New auto loan	Bank credit card	Unsecured personal instalment loan*
Illinois	No limit by state law	No limit	No limit	No limit
Indiana	No limit by state law ←———————		21% or	{ 36% on unpaid balance to $540 18% on unpaid balance to $1,800 15% on unpaid balance over $1,800
Iowa	No limit by state law	21%	18% on unpaid balance to $500 15% on remainder	31% of unpaid balance to $150 24% of unpaid balance to $300 · 18% of unpaid balance to $700 12% of unpaid balance to $2,000
Michigan	No limit due to federal	16.5%	18%	18% or 31% of unpaid balance to $500 13% of unpaid balance to $3,000
Wisconsin	No limit by state law	Greater of 18% or 6-month T-bill rate + 6%	18% or no limit when 2-year T-bill rate remains above 15% for 5 consecutive Thursdays**	Greater of 23% or rate on 2-year or 6-month T-note + 6%

*Rate limits often vary by type of lender. Limits shown are highest permitted for any lender. Under the 1980 Monetary Control Act, banks, S&Ls, and credit unions may charge the greater of the Federal Reserve discount plus 1 percent or the highest rate permitted any state lender for the type of loan in question.

**The operative limit has been 18% since the law became effective November 1, 1981.

banks in Seattle and Detroit are reported to be considering relocating credit card operations to other states because of usury limits.[11]

The Macroeconomic Impacts of Usury Ceilings

When usury ceilings make it unattractive to make loans in a particular state, the adverse impact of the ceilings falls most heavily on the credit-sensitive sectors of the state's economy. The health of a state's residential construction industry, for example, can be seriously affected by its usury regulations. As Ostas and Robins showed, housing starts and permits are sensitive to ceilings on mortgage rates. Furthermore, the New York State Banking Department concluded that New York's restrictive usury ceiling contributed to the depressed condition of the housing market in that state during the late 1960s and early 1970s.

Similarly, there is evidence that restrictive usury ceilings on automobile loans and other forms of consumer credit can affect the level of consumer purchases and retail trade. The survey of merchants in Texarkana, Arkansas, and Texarkana, Texas [1] revealed that approximately 38 percent of credit sales among merchants on the Texas side of the border were to customers from Arkansas. This substantial out-of-state shopping, which is presumably due to the 10 percent usury ceiling in

[11] See *The American Banker*, May 6, 1982.

Arkansas, represents a significant loss of potential business revenues for Arkansas-based retailers. Furthermore, as the authors of the study concluded, it represents a loss of jobs and local tax revenues.

A state's usury ceiling is likely to have far-reaching consequences for the state's real economy. Its effects can be expected to show up first in the level of credit-financed expenditures and eventually in levels of state employment and income. A study by Richard Gustely and Harry L. Johnson, described by Harold Nathan [14], used an econometric model of Tennessee to examine the impact of the state's comprehensive 10 percent usury ceiling. According to Nathan, the authors found that Tennessee's economy grew faster than the national economy except at times when market interest rates exceeded the state usury ceiling. The ceiling was estimated to have cost the state annually between 1974 and 1976 $150 million in output, $80 million in retail sales, and 7,000 jobs. This study indicates how restrictive usury ceilings may deprive a state of the credit needed to keep its economy expanding. All residents of the state are affected, not only those borrowers who find credit difficult to obtain.

USURY CEILINGS AND COMPETITION

As the foregoing discussion has shown, the impacts of usury ceilings extend well beyond simply holding a lid on interest rates. The adverse effects on the economy as a whole may even be sufficient to outweigh the benefit to those who are able to borrow at below-market interest rates. However, a common argument is that without usury laws borrowers would be forced to pay exorbitant interest rates, or at least rates that were unreasonable in relation to the cost of supplying credit. Thus, evaluation of usury laws is not complete without a consideration of the consequences of not having usury ceilings.

According to economic theory, a competitive market is sufficient to prevent lenders from exercising power over pricing or earning more than a normal return. The price established in a competitive market reflects suppliers' costs of providing the given amount of the good. To be sure, removing a binding usury ceiling will result in higher interest rates. However, if credit markets are competitive, the resulting market rate of interest will not exceed lenders' cost of providing credit. It is when competition is absent that consumers may face unreasonable interest rates. Thus, the consequences of not having usury ceilings depend importantly on the competitiveness of credit markets. Indeed, the absence of competition is the only clearly defensible theoretical reason for imposing a usury ceiling.

We might argue that U. S. credit markets today are fairly competitive. Many types of institutions—banks, finance companies, credit unions, thrift institutions, and retailers—make up the supply side of the credit market and frequently offer credit in closely substitutable forms. Moreover, in many (but not all) local market areas, consumers can choose among several lenders of any particular institutional type. However, competition in credit markets may be hampered by the fact that lending institutions have become specialized according to the types of credit they offer and/or the types of borrowers they serve. In the area of personal consumer credit, for example, banks and other depository institutions primarily offer cash credit to lower risk borrowers while finance companies specialize in servicing higher risk customers. Thus, the question of whether credit markets are sufficiently competitive to protect consumers from unreasonable interest charges is one which must be answered empirically. Unfortunately, studies of the extent of competition in credit markets do not provide a definitive answer to the question.

Smith [22] concluded from a study of the structure of rates on personal loans at commercial banks that there is a considerable degree of interbank competition for the more profitable type of loans, but that this does not extend to the small high-risk loan where the social problems of credit regulation are most acute (p. 524). He also found evidence of interinstitutional competition in the influence of consumer finance companies on bank loan rates and portfolio composition. On the other hand, Geer's analysis of the NCCF data on personal loan rates [5] did not allow him to conclude firmly that finance companies and commercial banks compete vigorously.

The NCCF Report provided some evidence of the existence of competiton in its findings regarding the pattern of interest rates across states. The Commission's 50-state survey revealed that rates on auto loans and unsecured loans at banks clustered within a rather narrow range (the market rate?) regardless of state usury ceilings.[12] Also, average observed interest rates for these loans were in the same range even in states with no ceiling at all.[13] In contrast, in the finance company loan market, the Commission noticed a much closer correspondence between observed rates and the state usury ceilings.

The conflicting findings of these few studies illustrate the difficulty in reaching a definitive conclusion about the extent of competition in credit markets. The studies described here suggest that competitive behavior may vary considerably among different segments of the credit market. Rates on finance company personal loans, for example, appear to be set less competitively than rates on auto loans or personal loans extended by banks. Another factor which makes an overall assessment of competition difficult stems from the potentially great differences in local market conditions. Lending institutions located in urban areas may face much greater competitive pressures than lenders in smaller cities or towns.

What can be stated definitively, however, is that from the point of view of protecting borrowers from unreasonable interest charges, competition is desirable, and the more the better. To the extent that competitive pressures arise from the presence and ready entry of many firms into the market, consumers are best served by policies that foster these conditions in credit markets.[14]

---

[12] Of course, it could simply be that the state usury ceilings were above the optimum price for an oligopolistic competitor. Even if that were the case, however, the situation indicates that the rate oligopolist lenders establish is below what most legislatures consider usurious.

[13] In addition, an investigation by the Federal Reserve Bank of St. Louis revealed that mortgage rates in the Chicago, Minneapolis, and Pittsburgh SMSAs did not rise to state ceilings when these usury limits were allowed to float. See Lovati and Gilbert [11].

[14] The literature on the structure of banking markets has established that firm entry and concentration have highly significant, although quantitatively small, effects on competitive pricing behavior. See Stephen Rhoades, *Structure-Performance Studies in Banking: A Summary and Evaluation*, Staff Economic Studies 92

There is some evidence that usury ceilings, rather than fostering these conditions, tend to restrict competition in some parts of the credit market. The NCCF found, for example, a strong inverse relationship between statewide finance company concentration ratios and the average level of legal rate ceilings on personal loans. (Higher concentration ratios are usually associated with lower levels of competition.) The relationship was even stronger within the group of states having low rate ceilings. The finding that lending firms tend to be more highly concentrated in states with lower rate ceilings can be attributed to several factors. First, low usury ceilings drive inefficient firms out of the market, thereby increasing concentration [6, p. 1377]. In addition, low usury ceilings create barriers to entry making it difficult for new firms to compete during the start-up phase [15, p. 137].

Rate ceilings may impede competition in various other ways. The NCCF argued that different rate ceilings for different types of consumer lenders tend to segment the market artificially and restrict interinstitutional competition [15, p. 147 and 5, p. 60]. A recent study by Sullivan for the CRC [23] supports this argument. She found that the extent of competition between banks and finance companies for consumer loans depended on whether the two types of lenders operated under the same or different rate ceilings. In a local personal loan market in Illinois, which differentiates ceilings by type of institution, borrowers from banks had significantly different risk characteristics than borrowers from finance companies. Such segmentation was not found in a comparable local loan market in Louisiana where all lenders are treated equally.

Another difficulty with usury ceilings, suggested by Shay's findings, is that rate ceilings may offer convenient focal points for setting rates higher than they might otherwise be set, when lenders already have some power to set prices [21, p. 457]. Finally, the Treasury Department's Interagency Task Force on Thrift Institutions [24] recently argued that very low usury ceilings discourage thrift institutions from adding consumer loans to their portfolios and from actively competing with finance companies by offering consumer loans. According to all of these arguments, the removal or easing of usury ceilings would tend to make credit markets more competitive.

Knowledgeable, informed borrowers also foster competition in credit markets. When consumers do not know or cannot compare rates being charged by various lenders, each lender has more scope to charge whatever rate he chooses. Thus, a high level of borrower awareness can place a natural constraint on interest rates, in lieu of the external constraint of a usury ceiling. Indeed, as the NCCF pointed out, "Not all consumers need be aware of the APR [annual percentage rate] or shop for credit to bring about effective price competition. A significant marginal group of consumers who are aware and do shop is sufficient to 'police' the market" [15, p. 175].

It is difficult to say exactly what the size of that group needs to be, but the Commission suggested that one-third to one-half of all borrowers is certainly sufficient. By this criterion, today's consumers seem to exert a rather effective pressure

(Board of Governors of the Federal Reserve System, 1977); Harvey Rosenblum, "A Cost-Benefit Analysis of the Bank Holding Company Act of 1956," *Proceedings of a Conference on Bank Structure and Competition* (Federal Reserve Bank of Chicago, 1978); and George Benston, "The Optimal Banking Structure: Theory and Evidence," *Journal of Bank Research*, vol. 3 (Winter 1973), pp. 220-37.

on lenders. A 1977 Consumer Credit Survey sponsored by the Board of Governors of the Federal Reserve System [4] classified 65 percent of consumers as aware of APRs on revolving credit. The awareness level on bank credit cards was 71 percent, and on closed-end credit it was 55 percent.

Consumer awareness levels were not always this high. Surveys comparable to the 1977 one were conducted in 1970 and 1969. Only 38 percent of credit users were found to be aware of APRs on closed-end credit in 1970 and only 15 percent in 1969.[15] Awareness levels on retail revolving credit and bank credit cards were only 35 and 27 percent, respectively, in the 1969 survey, although they stood at 56 and 63 percent by 1970.

At least some of the improvement in consumer awareness since 1969 revealed by these surveys is probably attributable to the consumer protection legislation enacted in the late 1960s and 1970s. The Truth-in-Lending Act (Title I of the 1968 Consumer Credit Protection Act) was passed only shortly before the 1969 survey, and its impact seems evident in the 1970 survey results. This association of improved consumer awareness with the passage of Truth-in-Lending suggests that, in the absence of usury ceilings, such legislation could effectively ensure consumers of reasonable interest rates by fostering more intense price competition in the credit market.

POLICY ACTION AND OPTIONS

Over the past few years there has been a spate of legislative activity affecting usury regulations at the national and state levels. Probably all of these legislative changes have helped to ease the adverse economic effects of binding usury ceilings during the recent period of high market interest rates. However, the specific policies implemented have differed greatly in the extent of their move toward deregulation; not all have involved completely removing legal price constraints.

For example, some states have acted to raise, but not eliminate, ceilings when they have impinged on credit availability and economic activity. This approach preserves fixed statutory interest rate limits and whatever protection they might afford consumers from outrageously high interest charges. But, if state legislatures intend to avert the negative economic impacts of fixed usury ceilings, they must act deliberately and quickly to adjust ceilings limits in response to changes in market rates—a task made more difficult by the increased volatility of rates in recent years.

A second approach, tying ceiling limits to market interest rates, avoids this problem and at the same time preserves the protection afforded by statutory limits. Some states have instituted legislation to allow ceilings to float, usually by stipulating limits several percentage points above certain specified interest rates—such as Treasury bill yields or the Federal Reserve discount rate—over which neither

---

[15] In analyzing the results of the 1970 survey, the NCCF found awareness levels in the "general market"—the market comprised mainly of higher income, more highly educated, white, homeowning borrowers who live in nonpoverty areas and use mostly cash credit—sufficient to police the market. The high-risk market, on the other hand, had disturbingly high levels of unawareness.

borrowers nor lenders have control. These usury ceiling limits, then, adjust auto-matically at frequent intervals to changes in the market interest rate. While floating rate ceilings are designed to be nonbinding with respect to the rates charged on the vast majority of loans, they prevent lenders from charging rates which are out of line with the market.

The difficulty with floating ceilings is in choosing a tie-in formula which will keep the ceiling above the average market rate over time. In a 1979 study of float-ing ceilings in the mortgage market, the Federal Reserve Bank of St. Louis [11] concluded that ceiling rates set 2.5 percentage points above yields on ten-year U. S. Treasury bonds or 5 percentage points above the discount rate were high enough not to distort the flow of credit to housing. Other floating rate schemes, however, continued to bind mortgage rates and impede housing activity.

Action by state legislatures has not been limited to partial easing of controls, by raising limits or implementing floating ceilings. Many other states have com-pletely eliminated their usury ceilings. These states can and still do regulate lenders in other ways, of course.

In addition to these changes on the state level, the federal government has also acted recently to remove legal constraints on interest rates. The 1980 Monetary Control Act temporarily preempted state usury limits on mortgage loans and on large business and agricultural loans. The same act also overrode state interest ceil-ings on loans by national and state banks, S&Ls, and credit unions when the state ceiling is below the local Federal Reserve discount rate plus 1 percent. Proposals to extend federal preemption to include consumer credit were considered during the 1981 Congressional session.[16]

This move by the federal government to supplant state usury regulations raises an important and difficult issue. From an economic point of view federal action has an advantage over states acting individually. It would impose uniformity on credit markets, eliminating legislatively created differentials in interest rates that artificially distort credit flows among states. (Uniformity could be achieved, of course, whether the federal government imposed its own fixed usury ceiling, in-stituted floating ceilings, or eliminated ceilings altogether.) From another point of view, however, federal action may not be so desirable. The economic advantage of uniform treatment needs to be weighed against the political implications of the federal government stepping into an area—usury regulation—which has traditionally been under the jurisdiction of the states. Thus, the question whether deregulation of usury ceilings should be left to individual states or whether it is best accomp-lished by federal preemption should not be answered on the basis of economics alone.

SUMMARY

Economic research clearly supports the current legislative moves toward dereg-ulation of usury ceilings. The evidence on the impact of usury ceilings shows that

---

[16] A Senate bill was introduced by Senator Lugar and incorporated in S. 1720 by Senator Garn: House bills were sponsored by Representatives John La Falce and William Alexander.

they have not achieved their objectives. According to the empirical studies surveyed, usury ceilings have significantly reduced the availability of credit and created hardships for those who were supposed to be protected. Ceilings have encouraged lenders to use such credit rationing devices as higher downpayments, shorter maturities, and higher fees for related noncredit services, which increase the effective interest rate. They have curtailed the amount of credit available to lower income and higher risk borrowers, harming primarily those individuals whom the ceilings are intended to benefit. Finally, the lack of uniformity of usury laws across states has distorted credit flows and economic activity, favoring those states and regions which are less regulated.

REFERENCES

1. Blades, Holland C., Jr. and Gene C. Lynch. *Credit Policies and Store Locations in Arkansas Border Cities: Merchant Reactions to a 10 Percent Finance Charge Ceiling.* Monograph 2, Krannert Graduate School of Management, Purdue University, 1976.
2. Blitz, Rudolph C. and Millard F. Long. "The Economics of Usury Regulation," *Journal of Political Economy,* vol. 73 (December 1965), pp. 608-19.
3. Dahl, David S., Stanley L. Graham, and Arthur J. Rolnick. "Minnesota's Usury Law: A Reevaluation," *Ninth District Quarterly,* vol. 4 (Spring 1977), pp. 1-6.
4. Durbin, Thomas A. and Gregory E. Ellichauser. *1977 Consumer Credit Survey.* Washington: Board of Governors of the Federal Reserve System, 1978.
5. Greer, Douglas F., Jr. "An Econometric Analysis of the Personal Loan Credit Market," in Douglas F. Greer and Robert P. Shay, eds. *An Econometric Analysis of Consumer Credit Markets in the United States.* Technical Studies Volume IV. Washington: The National Commission on Consumer Finance, 1974.
6. Greer, Douglas F. "Rate Ceilings, Market Structure, and the Supply of Finance Company Personal Loans," *Journal of Finance,* vol. 29 (December 1974), pp. 1363-82.
7. Greer, Douglas, "Rate Ceilings and Loan Turndowns," *Journal of Finance,* vol. 30 (December 1975), pp. 1376-83.
8. Johnson, Robert W. and A. Charlene Sullivan, *Restrictive Effects of Rate Ceilings on Consumer Choice: The Massachusetts Experience.* Working Paper No. 35, Credit Research Center, Krannert Graduate School of Management, Purdue University, 1980.
9. Keleher, Robert E. *State Usury Laws: A Survey and Application to the Tennessee Experience.* Processed. Working Paper Series, Federal Reserve Bank of Atlanta, January 1978.
10. Kohn, Ernest, Carmen J. Carlo, and Bernard Kaye. *The Impact of New York's Usury Ceiling on Local Mortgage Lending Activity.* Processed. New York State Banking Department, January 1976.
11. Lovati, Jean M. and R. Alton Gilbert. "Do Floating Ceilings Solve the Usury Rate Problem?" *Federal Reserve Bank of St. Louis Review,* vol. 61 (April 1979), pp. 10-17.
12. McNulty, James E. "A Reexamination of the Problem of State Usury Ceilings: The Impact in the Mortgage Market," *Quarterly Review of Economics and Business,* vol. 20 (Spring 1980), pp. 16-29.
13. Mors, Wallace P. *Consumer Credit Finance Charges.* New York: National Bureau of Economic Research, 1965.
14. Nathan, Harold C. "Economic Analysis of Usury Laws," *Journal of Bank Research,* vol. 10 (Winter 1980), pp. 200-11.

15. National Commission on Consumer Finance. *Consumer Credit in the United States.* Washington: Government Printing Office, 1972.

16. Ostas, James R. "Effects of Usury Ceilings in the Mortgage Market," *Journal of Finance,* vol. 31 (June 1976), pp. 821-34.

17. Peterson, Richard L. "Effect of a Restrictive Usury Law on the Consumer Credit Market." Processed. 1981.

18. Phaup, Dwight and John Hinton. "The Distributional Effects of Usury Laws: Some Empirical Evidence," *Atlantic Economic Journal,* vol. 9 (September 1981), pp. 91-98.

19. Robins, Philip K. "The Effects of State Usury Ceilings on Single Family Homebuilding," *Journal of Finance,* vol. 29 (March 1974), pp. 227-36.

20. Rolnick, Arthur J., Stanley L. Graham, and David S. Dahl. "Minnesota's Usury Law: An Evaluation," *Ninth District Quarterly,* vol. 11 (April 1975), pp. 16-25.

21. Shay, Robert P. "The Impact of State Legal Rate Ceilings Upon the Availability and Price of Credit," in Douglas F. Greer and Robert P. Shay, eds., *An Econometric Analysis of Consumer Credit Markets in the United States.* Technical Studies Volume IV. Washington: National Commission on Consumer Finance, 1974.

22. Smith, Paul F. "Pricing Policies on Consumer Loans at Commercial Banks," *Journal of Finance,* vol. 25 (May 1970), pp. 517-25.

23. Sullivan, A. Charlene. *Effects of Consumer Loan Rate Ceilings on Competition Between Banks and Finance Companies.* Working Paper No. 38. Credit Research Center, Krannert Graduate School of Management, Purdue University, 1981.

24. U. S. Congress. Senate. Committee on Banking, Housing, and Urban Affairs. *Report of the Interagency Task Force on Thrift Institutions.* Washington: Government Printing Office, July 1980.

25. Van Horne, James C. *Financial Market Rates and Flows.* Englewood Cliffs, New Jersey: Prentice-Hall, 1978.

10

CRA and Community Credit Needs[*]

Donald T. Savage[†]

Legislation, such as the Community Reinvestment Act (CRA) and regulatory actions in states, such as Massachusetts, have placed new emphasis on the responsibility of financial institutions to meet the credit needs of their communities. These new laws and regulations have been applauded by community antiredlining groups and attacked by many financial institutions as both unnecessary and as a move toward a credit allocation system. Regardless of how one feels, it seems that the "convenience and needs" analysis involved in regulatory decisions on bank charters, branches, mergers, and holding company formations and bank acquisitions is being modified to give greater weight to the community lending record of financial institutions.

STATE DEVELOPMENTS

A small, but increasing, number of states have adopted rules requiring financial institutions to make greater efforts to serve the credit needs of all segments of their community. Perhaps the most far-reaching of these state regulations are in Massachusetts. Massachusetts' state-chartered institutions seeking approval to establish or relocate a branch, merge, or form or expand a holding company must file an affidavit attesting to their commitment to serving the credit needs of the community. Included in the affidavit are factors such as: willingness to provide

[*]Reprinted by permission from the *Bankers Magazine*, January-February 1979, pp. 49-53. Copyright © 1979, Warren, Gorham, and Lamont, Inc., 210 South Street, Boston, Massachusetts. All rights reserved.

[†]Donald T. Savage is an Economist in the Financial Structure Section, Division of Research and Statistics, Board of Governors of the Federal Reserve System.

loan application forms and accept applications for all types of loans at all offices; maintenance of a loan inquiry register, including telephone inquiries; local media advertising; communication of lending policies to real estate brokers; willingness to discuss lending policies with community groups; and, for mutual institutions, governing bodies that are representative of the community.

In addition to regulator-initiated actions, formal loan agreements have been formulated between community groups and financial institutions in New York and the District of Columbia. In several instances, community groups have intervened in the branch office approval process and have gained pledges of greater community lending as a condition for withdrawing their protest of the application.

FEDERAL LEGISLATION

New federal action in the area of stressing credit needs in the total analysis of convenience and needs is contained in Title VIII of the Housing and Community Redevelopment Act of 1977. Title VIII was introduced by Senator Proxmire and is generally known as the Community Reinvestment Act of 1977.

The CRA instructs the federal financial supervisory agencies—the Federal Reserve System, the Comptroller of the Currency, the Federal Deposit Insurance Corporation and the Federal Home Loan Bank Board—to encourage financial institutions to help meet the credit needs of their entire communities, including low- and moderate-income neighborhoods, consistent with the safe and sound operation of the institutions. Under regulations effective in November 1978, the agencies are required, in the course of regular bank examinations, to assess each institution's record of meeting community credit needs. This record is to be taken into account when evaluating applications for branches, mergers, bank holding company formations and acquisitions, and other changes in financial institution structure.

The federal agencies responsible for administering the law held public hearings in Spring 1978 in Washington, D. C. and six other cities. The hearings produced conflicting suggestions from consumer groups and financial institutions. Most consumer groups perceived the law as necessary to prevent redlining and to require institutions to reinvest deposits in home-mortgage, home-improvement, and small-business loans in older urban neighborhoods. Financial institution representatives, in general, argued that they were already meeting all reasonable credit needs and that the law would require banks to make high-risk unsound loans and be a move toward credit allocation.

The Unmet Credit Needs Question

The basic premises behind the CRA seem to be that (1) there are many credit-worthy people, especially in low- and moderate-income neighborhoods, who are unable to obtain credit from financial institutions; and (2) moreover, the financial regulatory agencies have not given sufficient attention, in assessing convenience and needs, to whether institutions were meeting the credit needs of their entire community. Numerous consumer group studies have concluded that there are unmet credit needs resulting from redlining, but methodological problems make it difficult to reach unambiguous conclusions on this issue.

The first analytical problem is the definition of "credit needs." Neither the CRA nor the regulatory agencies have attempted to define "credit needs." Indeed, credit needs may be undefinable. In a quantitative sense, credit needs are significantly different from credit demands, given that the former may be based on social objectives and the latter are based on willingness and ability to pay. In a market system, needs are important only as they create a basis for, and are reflected in, demands. A low-income neighborhood may have a need for housing rehabilitation credit, but most property owners may lack the income necessary to be considered demanders of credit. Thus, needs would remain even though demands were being met at the going market price of credit. Even the quantity demanded at a zero interest rate would not fill all credit needs, given that even interest-free loans have to be repaid. Credit needs for housing rehabilitation, for example, would be based on the total quantity of credit required to rehabilitate all homes in a specified neighborhood or banking market. With repayment ability limited, this standard would not be workable; the CRA recognized this limitation and requires only that institutions *"help meet* the credit needs . . ."* (emphasis added). Meeting all credit needs is not feasible for a free enterprise banking system; only a government subsidized banking program could possibly meet all credit needs.

Are financial institutions meeting the credit demands of low- and moderate-income neighborhoods? While the banks argue that they are answering all reasonable demands for credit, allegations of unreasonable credit denials continue; most frequently these allegations are associated with charges of redlining on home mortgages and home-rehabilitation and improvement loans.

The Question of Redlining

The economic theory against redlining is presented persuasively by George Benston.[1] Basic microeconomic theory would not allow for the existence of redlining. If there is a profitable lending opportunity and perfect flow of information, some institution should be willing to make the loan, regardless of the geographic location of the property used as collateral. Given the persistence and widespread nature of redlining charges, however, one wonders whether the market is working as efficiently as Benston suggests.

Perhaps there is a possible reconciliation of microtheory, the very limited empirical evidence, and the redlining allegations. Consider the following line of reasoning: First, rather than establishing a unique set of loan terms—interest rate, down payment and maturity—for each loan, lenders may establish one set of loan terms for a given type of loan, and then accept or deny individual applications for loans on those terms. The Benston findings in Rochester, New York would tend to sup-

[1] Benston, *The Anti-Redlining Rules: An Analysis of the Federal Home Loan Bank Board's Proposed Nondiscrimination Requirements* 2-7 (Law and Economics Center, University of Miami School of Law, 1978).

port the one-set-of terms argument, because the terms on mortgage loans made in the central city were not significantly different, except for average maturity of loans, from terms on loans in the suburb used as a control area.

Second, lenders may either overestimate the risk of urban lending, or that risk may be significantly higher than the risk of suburban lending. While many bank representatives testifying at the CRA hearings indicated that lending in older neighborhoods was very risky, no one presented any evidence to support these assertions. Consumer groups, on the other hand, argued that careful appraisal and lending policies could produce urban loss rates equal to those of other areas. Systematic empirical evidence is needed to resolve this issue; studies of loan loss experience of institutions that do extensive lending in urban areas would contribute to resolution of this question.

Third, the costs associated with lending in older areas may be higher. General mortgage servicing costs are relatively fixed; on a small mortgage, such as would be associated with a lower-priced urban dwelling, the cost per dollar of mortgage debt would be higher than the comparable cost for a large mortgage on a suburban home. If, in addition, there are special costs associated with urban lending, such as the need for more detailed property appraisal, urban lending costs are increased relative to those of lending on standardized suburban tract homes.

A possible rationale for the existence of what seems to be redlining can be developed from the above points. Assume that risk and lending costs are higher in urban areas and that lenders make all loans at the market-determined equilibrium interest rate. Given that lenders will accept lowest-risk lowest-cost applications first, the proportion of accepted suburban applications will be higher than the proportion of accepted urban applications. At the market-clearing interest rate, the quantity of loans demanded in the urban area is greater than the quantity supplied, and there is an unmet credit demand. To eliminate the excess quantity demanded in the urban portion of the market, interest rates would have to be higher in that portion of the market than in the total market.

Why don't lenders charge different prices in the urban area than in the suburban portion of the market to account for any higher risks and lending cost? Or, why isn't there a unique interest rate for each loan to reflect the specific level of risks and costs associated with that loan? A number of reasons could be suggested, including the hypothesis that the setting of a unique interest rate for each loan would be more expensive than simply making all loans at one rate. In the present setting, it is likely that a dual pricing system for urban and suburban areas or individual loan pricing would encounter strong objections from urban consumer groups. In addition, in some states, usury ceilings might preclude establishing an urban lending rate at the market-clearing level.

How would the quantity of credit demanded by potential urban borrowers be reduced to the quantity institutions were willing to supply at the below-market-clearing interest rate? This could be accomplished by various prescreening techniques such as discouraging formal applications, not operating branches in low-income areas, or any of the other practices alleged by antiredlining groups. The Benston *et al.* study does not really account for this type of demand reduction. Benston's groups contacted prospective sellers, rather than prospective buyers;

the sellers could not be expected to have full information on the availability of mortgages to prospective buyers for their homes.

The above analysis, while consistent with theory, Benston's analysis, and anti-redlining groups' charges, like most of the work in the area, has not been tested empirically. If, for whatever reason, there is some failure to lend in urban areas, what effect could one expect the CRA to have on this phenomenon?

HOW THE CRA CAN HELP

The major contribution of the CRA and similar state regulations may lie in the area of requiring institutions to be aware of, and consider plans for helping to meet, the credit needs of the entire community. Under the regulations, each institution's Board of Directors will approve a CRA statement outlining the institution's community or communities and the types of loans that the institution will be willing to provide within the community. Agency examiners will review these statements for reasonableness and to ascertain that low- and moderate-income neighborhoods have not been excluded.

The factors to be examined by the agencies in assessing the institution's record do not require any specific lending pattern or loan standards for types of loans, but rather examine the institution's stated lending policies and conformance to those policies. Does the institution do those things that would be expected of an institution dedicated to service to the entire community in which it operates?

Some of the questions to be considered by the examiners reflect the concern with service to the entire community. For example, does the institution attempt to assess community credit needs? Does it discourage formal loan applications? Is it willing to meet with interested community groups? Does it advertise its willing-ness to consider applications for various types of loans? Does it maintain offices throughout its community and provide credit services at all its offices? Does it participate in loans to, or purchase securities issued to finance community devel-opment projects?

From the consumer group point of view, the CRA statement provides an indi-cation of what services the financial institution will make available in its commun-ity. The antiredlining groups can check the CRA statement and the bank's definition of its "community" and can register any opposition with both the institution and the appropriate regulatory agency. Members of the antiredlining groups can test whether or not the institution is living up to its CRA statements.

For the regulatory agencies, the CRA statement provides a measure against which the institution's performance can be examined over time; this information will be available when the agency is considering an application from the institu-tion. Public comments on the CRA statement and/or the institution's performance also will be available for examiner review.

The CRA may also reduce one aspect of the total risk of lending in older urban neighborhoods. Assume that one institution is willing to lend on a given piece of property, but knows that no other institution will be willing to supply financing when this property is resold in the future. This institution is accepting a higher degree of risk than would be required if it could assume that many lenders would be willing to lend to subsequent purchasers of the property. The institution, fearing the possible negative impact on its position of the actions of other institutions, may decide not to accept the risk. If the CRA has the effect of encouraging many institutions to lend in urban areas, the risk to any given institution may be reduced by the greater assurance of the availability of credit for future purchasers in that area.

WHAT THE CRA WILL NOT DO

The CRA is not a panacea for the ills of urban areas. The problems of the cities are much more far-reaching than merely a possible lack of credit. Credit alone will not improve the tax base, upgrade municipal services, attract new employment-creating investments, or reverse years of economic decline.

The CRA is not an income-redistribution measure. It does not require institutions to subsidize loans to low-income borrowers. While institutions may become more willing to lend to low- and moderate-income individuals, it is unlikely that the credit standards required to maintain the lender's safety and soundness will be relaxed. Thus, those without the income necessary to repay loans will not benefit directly by any change resulting from the CRA.

It also seems unlikely that the CRA will result in lower interest rates in urban areas. In fact, assuming that there is an unmet demand for loans in the urban portion of the market, the CRA could have the effect of increasing urban interest rates. If, in compliance with the CRA, the alleged demand reduction or prescreening devices are eliminated, separate urban and suburban loan rates, reflecting different cost and loss experiences would be a reasonable lender response. It would then be incumbent upon the lenders to justify this interest rate difference to protesting urban consumer groups by reference to its lending cost and loan loss data.

The impact of the CRA on the provision of convenient banking services in low- and moderate-income neighborhoods is questionable. On the one hand, the Act may encourage banks to establish branches in these areas; on the other hand, the law does not require banks to maintain unprofitable office locations. Naturally, the CRA does not change the branching prohibitions which may limit the ability of banks to provide convenient offices in those areas which could generate enough business for a profitable branch but not enough business to justify the establishment of a *de novo* bank.

CRA RISKS AND POTENTIAL

The risk mentioned most often in the testimony at the public hearings held by the agencies was that enforcement would become a form of credit allocation. Other witnesses, however, quoted Senator Proxmire to the effect that the measure was not an attempt to create an agency-managed credit allocation system. The regulatory agencies have not indicated any desire or tendency to use this law as a credit allocation device.

Possible loss of the benefits of institutional specialization is another risk presented by the CRA. The extent to which the regulations permit specialization by financial institutions is unclear. Although institutions would seem to be free to specialize, all institutions do have a continuing and affirmative obligation to help meet the credit needs of their entire community. A bank that made only yacht loans to people residing outside of its geographic community would probably be hard pressed to convince its regulator that it was meeting the credit needs of its entire community, including low- and moderate-income neighborhoods.

While not a panacea for the problems of urban areas and carrying some risks, the CRA does have some promise in the area of increasing the flow of funds to creditworthy low- and moderate-income borrowers. Even if it merely ensures that all potential borrowers are granted the opportunity to apply for credit and have their application appraised on its merits, the CRA will have contributed to the more equitable treatment of all customers of financial institutions.

C. THE MONEY POSITION

11

The Money Market[*]

James Parthemos

Economic units, such as financial institutions, other business firms, governmental units, and even individuals, find, as a rule, that their inflow of cash receipts does not coincide exactly with their cash disbursements. The typical economic unit finds that on some days its cash holdings build up because receipts exceed outlays. On other days, it might experience a sharp reduction in cash balances because spending outstrips cash inflow.

One of the most important reasons for holding cash reserves is to bridge the gap between receipts and outlays and to insure that a planned stream of expenditures can be maintained somewhat independently of cash inflow. There are, of course, other reasons for holding reserves. In particular, depository institutions must meet legal reserve requirements.[1]

Maintenance of cash reserves involves cost, either in the form of interest paid on borrowed balances, or in the form of interest foregone on nonborrowed balances which have not been lent out. For many economic units, especially large firms, these costs can be significant, particularly in periods of high interest rates. To minimize such costs, economic units usually seek to keep their cash holdings at a minimum consistent with their working capital needs and, in the case of depository institutions, with their reserve requirements. This may be done by holding low risk and highly marketable income-bearing assets instead of cash and by maintaining access to the market for short-term credit. The *money market* has evolved to meet the needs of such economic units.

[*]Reprinted, with deletions, from *Instruments of the Money Market*, 5th Edition, edited by Timothy Q. Cook and Bruce T. Summers, 1981, with permission from the Federal Reserve Bank of Richmond.

[1] As a result of the Depository Institutions Deregulation and Monetary Control Act of 1980, all depository institutions must meet Federal reserve requirements on reservable liabilities, i.e., transactions accounts and nonpersonal time deposits. These requirements are prescribed in Regulation D of the Federal Reserve System.

THE MONEY MARKET

The term "money market" applies not to one but rather to a group of markets. In the early part of the United States' financial history, the term was frequently used in a narrow sense to denote the market for call loans to securities brokers and dealers. At other times in the past, it has been employed broadly to embrace some long-term as well as short-term markets. In current usage, the term "money market" generally refers to the markets for short-term credit instruments such as Treasury bills, commercial paper, bankers' acceptances, negotiable certificates of deposit (CDs), loans to security dealers, repurchase agreements, and federal funds.

In general, money market instruments are issued by obligors of the highest credit rating, and are characterized by a high degree of safety of principal. Maturities may be as long as one year but usually are of 90 days or less, and sometimes span only a few days or even one day. The market for money market instruments is extremely broad and on a given day it can absorb a large volume of transactions with relatively little effect on yields. The market is also highly efficient and allows quick, convenient, and low cost trading in virtually any volume. Unlike organized securities or commodities markets, the money market has no specific location. Like other important financial markets in this country, its center is in New York, but it is primarily a "telephone" market and is easily accessible from all parts of the nation as well as foreign financial centers. No economic unit is ever more than a telephone call away from the money market.

At the center of the money market are numerous "money market banks," including the large banks in New York and other important financial centers; about 34 government securities dealers, some of which are large banks; a dozen odd commercial paper dealers; a few bankers' acceptance dealers; and a number of money brokers who specialize in finding short-term funds for money market borrowers and placing such funds for money market lenders. The most important money market brokers are the major Federal funds brokers in New York.

MARKET PARTICIPANTS

Apart from the groups that provide the basic trading machinery, money market participants usually enter the market either to raise short-term funds or to convert cash surpluses into highly liquid interest-bearing investments. Funds may be raised by borrowing outright, by selling holdings of money market instruments, or by issuing new instruments. The issue and sale of new money market instruments is, of course, a form of borrowing.

Generally, money market rates are below the prime lending rates of the large money market banks. Consequently, borrowers who have the ability to do so find it advantageous to tap the money market directly rather than obtaining funds through banking intermediaries. The U. S. Treasury, many commercial banks, large sales finance companies, and well-known nonfinancial corporations of the highest credit standing borrow regularly in the money market by issuing their own short-term debt obligations. Short-term loans to government securities dealers, loans of reserves among depository institutions and Federal Reserve discount window loans to depository institutions are also money market instruments although they do not give rise to negotiable paper.

Suppliers of funds in the market are those who buy money market instruments or make very short-term loans. Potentially, these include all those economic units that can realize a significant gain through arranging to meet future cash requirements by holding interest-bearing liquid assets in place of nonbearing cash balances. The major participants on this side of the market are commercial banks, state and local governments, large nonfinancial businesses, nonbank financial institutions, and foreign bank and nonbank businesses. In recent years individuals have also become a significant supplier of funds to the money market both indirectly through investment in short-term investment pools such as money market mutual funds and directly through the purchase of Treasury bills and short-term Federal agency securities.

By far the most important market participant is the Federal Reserve System. Through the Open Market Trading Desk at the New York Federal Reserve Bank, which executes the directives of the Federal Open Market Committee, the system is in the market on a virtually continuous basis, either as a buyer or as a seller, depending on financial conditions and monetary policy objectives. The System's purpose in entering the market is quite different from that of other participants, however. As noted in greater detail below, the Federal Reserve buys and sells in certain parts of the money market not with the objective of managing its own cash position more efficiently but rather to supply or withdraw bank reserves in order to achieve its monetary policy objectives. In addition, the Federal Reserve enters the market as an agent, sometimes as a buyer and sometimes as a seller, for the accounts of foreign official institutions and for the U. S. Treasury. Overall, the operations of the Federal Reserve dwarf those of any other money market participant.

INTERRELATION AND SIZE
OF THE VARIOUS MARKET SECTORS

While the various money market instruments have their individual differences, they nonetheless are close substitutes for each other in many investment portfolios. For this reason the rates of return on the various instruments tend to fluctuate closely together. For short periods of time, the rate of return on a particular instrument may diverge from the rest or "get out of line," but this sets in motion forces which tend to pull the rates back together. For example, a large supply of new commercial paper may produce a rapid run-up of commercial paper rates, resulting in a relatively large spread between these rates and rates on CDs. Sophisticated traders note the abnormal differential and shift funds from CDs into commercial paper, causing CD rates to rise and commercial paper rates to fall. In this way, a more "normal" or usual rate relation is restored. This process, known as interest arbitrage, insures general conformity of all money market rates to major interest rate movements.

THE MARKET'S SIGNIFICANCE

The money market provides an important source of short-term funds for many borrowers. In addition, since there is a continuous flow of loan funds through the market, it is possible for borrowers, through successive "roll-overs," or renewals of loans, to raise funds on a more or less continuous basis and in this fashion to finance not only their immediate cash requirements but also working capital and some long-term capital needs as well. By bringing together quickly and conveniently those units with cash surpluses and those with cash deficits, the market promotes a more intensive use of the cash balances held in the economy.

The market is especially important to commercial banks in managing their money positions. Banks in the aggregate are large-scale buyers and sellers of most money market instruments, especially federal funds. The money market permits a more intensive use of bank reserves and enhances the ability of the commercial banking system to allocate funds efficiently. By allowing banks to operate with lower excess reserves, it also makes the banking system more sensitive to central bank policy actions.[2]

Finally, conditions in the money market provide an important guide for monetary policy. The money market is an eminently free and competitive market, and the yields on money market instruments react instantaneously to changes in supply and demand. As a result, the behavior of the market provides the most immediate indication of the current relationship between credit supplies and credit demands.

THE FEDERAL RESERVE
AND THE MONEY MARKET

The Federal Reserve System influences the money market not only through open market operations but also through the discount windows of the 12 Federal Reserve Banks. Commercial banks may borrow short-term from the Federal Reserve to meet temporary liquidity needs and to cover reserve deficiencies as an alternative to selling money market securities or borrowing federal funds. Similarly, banks with cash or reserve surpluses can repay outstanding borrowings at the Federal Reserve rather than invest the surpluses in money market instruments.

---

[2] As the phase-in of required reserves for nonbank depository institutions, mandated by the Monetary Control Act of 1980, progresses, it is likely that these institutions will also become active in the market for reserve funds.

Reserve adjustments made by individual institutions using the discount window differ in one important respect from alternative adjustment techniques. Trading in such instruments as federal funds, negotiable certificates of deposit, and Treasury bills among commercial banks or between banks and their customers involves no net creation of new bank reserves. Rather, existing reserves are simply shifted about within the banking system. On the other hand, net borrowings or repayments at the discount window result in a net change in Federal Reserve credit outstanding and, consequently, they affect the volume of bank reserves. Thus, the choice by individual institutions between using the discount window or alternative means of reserve adjustment may influence the supply of money and credit in the economy. Decisions to use the discount window or raise funds elsewhere in the money market depend importantly upon the relation of the Federal Reserve's discount rate to yields on money market investments and on the legal and administrative arrangements surrounding use of the discount window. Both sets of factors are determined primarily by Federal Reserve actions.

The daily operations of the Federal Open Market Trading Desk occupy a central role in the money market. For many years the Desk has conducted transactions in U. S. Government securities and in bankers' acceptances and in December 1966 it was authorized to conduct operations in Federal Agency issues also. The Federal Reserve enters the market frequently either to provide new depository institution reserves through purchases or to withdraw reserves through sales. To a large extent, Federal Reserve operations are undertaken to compensate for changes in other factors that affect the volume of reserves, such as float, Treasury balances, and currency in circulation. Such operations are undertaken primarily to insure the smooth technical functioning of the market mechanism. But the operations of the greatest importance from the standpoint of the economy are those undertaken by the Federal Reserve to achieve its policy objectives. Since the early 1970s these objectives have centered on achieving targeted growth rates of the money supply. Thus, in addition to its other functions, the money market serves as the mechanism for implementing the Federal Reserve's objectives.

12

Federal Funds and Repurchase Agreements

It is often necessary for banks and other depository institutions to obtain or invest funds on very short notice and for short periods, even one day. To meet these borrowing and lending needs, two different and yet closely related money market instruments—*federal funds* and *repurchase agreements*—have emerged. The market for federal funds, or *fed funds* as they are known, is monitored closely by market participants, economists, and forecasters for clues to the future direction of monetary policy and interest rates. Since fed funds are closely related to the banking system's reserve position, the fed funds interest rate is extremely sensitive to changes in supply and demand conditions in the credit market and to changes in monetary policy by the Federal Reserve. Repurchase agreements, or *repos*, have many of the same features as fed funds transactions. In fact, they are close substitutes for each other. One of the common features of both instruments is that the funds obtained are free of reserve requirements. Another common feature and the key to federal funds transactions and repurchase agreements is that they both involve *immediately available funds.*

IMMEDIATELY AVAILABLE FUNDS

When lending or investing funds for periods as short as overnight, the funds must be transferred immediately and be available for use without delay. To accomplish this, *immediately available funds* are used to settle federal funds transactions, repurchase agreements, and certain other transactions in which immediate payment is essential. Immediately available funds take two forms—deposits of banks and other depository institutions held in Federal Reserve banks as reserves, and certain "collected liabilities" of depository institutions. When a bank receives a check drawn on another bank, the depositor is given a tentative, or provisional credit until the funds are collected. Once collected, the funds become immediately available for use by the bank until the customer makes use of the funds. A depositor may receive credit in the form of immediately available funds by depositing cash or having such funds wire transferred to the account. Usually such a transfer is made over the Federal Reserve's wire transfer network (Fedwire) and through a member bank's reserve account. For transfers involving nonmember banks a clearing account is often used. Although immediately available funds are a means of making payment, not all transactions using such funds are related to fed funds or repo transactions.[1] However, the nature of fed funds and repos does require immediate funds availability.

FEDERAL FUNDS

Federal funds are very short term loans made with immediately available funds. These loans are usually unsecured. The funds are free of the reserve requirements imposed on banks and other depository institutions provided the funds are obtained from a depository institution, a U. S. Government agency, or a domestic branch or agency of a foreign bank. Although fed funds transactions usually mature in one to three days, transactions with longer maturities known as *term fed funds* are common. These transactions may extend as long as 90 days.

Nature of Transactions

Transactions involving excess reserves and reserve deficiencies of commercial banks make up an important segment of fed funds activity. Banks are required to maintain specified percentages of their deposits in the form of reserves on deposit with the Federal Reserve. Sufficient funds must also be kept on deposit to cover withdrawals, loan takedowns, securities purchases, and other outflows. Often these outflows are sizable and unexpected. It is important that the actual reserves held be as close as possible to the required amount because excess reserves are nonearning assets and deficiencies are subject to penalties. To avoid such costs, banks buy and sell fed funds to bring their reserve positions in line with requirements.[2] Reserve adjustments using fed funds are made by transferring funds from the selling bank's reserve account at the Federal Reserve to the buying bank's reserve account.

Although the use of fed funds to make adjustments in the reserve position of

---

[1] Market participants often use the term *fed funds* very broadly. For example, the Treasurer of an insurance company may specify that fed funds be used to pay for securities. Although the transaction involves immediately available funds, it is not technically a fed funds transaction.

[2] For a comprehensive discussion of the reserve management problem, see the chapter entitled "Managing the Bank Money Position," elsewhere in this book.

banks accounts for a large number of fed funds transactions, it is deficient to describe the market simply as an interbank market involving reserves held at the Federal Reserve Bank. The fed funds market is much broader, encompassing other types of nonbank depository institutions. Credit unions, S&Ls, and savings banks are now active participants in this market as are several large government agencies and U.S. Government securities dealers.

Many of the transactions conducted by depository institutions go beyond adjusting reserve positions. Large banks tend to be net buyers of fed funds as an ongoing part of their liability management, regardless of their reserve position. For these banks, fed funds are quasi-permanent and supplement other forms of "purchased funds" such as large-scale CDs. Smaller banks and smaller nonbank depository institutions tend to be net sellers of fed funds. Thus, the fed funds market plays a key role in the asset management of these institutions, especially when loan demand is slack. Smaller depository institutions usually sell their fed funds to a larger bank with which they have a working relationship. The larger bank, usually known as an *upstream correspondent*, pools funds obtained from the smaller *downstream correspondents* and resells the funds in the national market. When acting in this capacity, the upstream bank simultaneously buys and sells fed funds. Thus, it operates on *both* sides of the market, and, as far as this activity is concerned, without regard for its reserve position.

The role of both parties in a fed funds transaction must be understood. If a bank buys fed funds for its own account or acts as a *principal* and resells the funds in the national market, the seller's only concern is for that bank's creditworthiness. However, if the bank that purchases the funds acts as an *agent* and sells the funds to a third institution, the credit risk is borne by the seller of the funds and not the agent bank. To control the use of its funds in an agency relationship, the seller of fed funds should provide the agent bank with an approved list of buyers. Otherwise, the seller may be absorbing an unknown risk.

The mechanics of a fed funds transaction are quite simple. In a transaction involving correspondents, bookkeeping entries reflect the conversion of a non-interest bearing demand deposit to a federal funds account. The banks' reserve positions at the Federal Reserve are unaffected. The next day, or at maturity, the transaction is reversed with both principal and interest being credited to the seller's account. For a transaction between noncorrespondent institutions within a Federal Reserve district, the seller of the funds authorizes the district bank to debit its reserve account and credit the reserve account of the institution that is purchasing the funds. When an interdistrict transfer occurs, the seller of funds has its Federal Reserve Bank debit its account and wire transfer funds to the buyer's Federal Reserve Bank. That bank then transfers the funds to the buyer's reserve account. The next day, or at maturity, the transaction is reversed.

The Fed Funds Market

There is no central, organized exchange for fed funds transactions. Telephone lines and other electronic communications equipment link fed funds brokers, traders, and the major financial institutions. Fed funds brokers match buyers and sellers and receive a commission when a transaction is completed.

The fact that smaller financial institutions can be accommodated in this market by working through upstream correspondent banks is important because in the national fed funds market, most trades are in round lots of $5 million. Trades may be made in smaller amounts but only at a lower price (or higher yield) on the selling side or a higher price (lower yield) on the buying side. The interest rate on fed funds is quoted in multiples of 1/16ths and on the basis of a 360-day year. The interest cost or return on fed funds is given by the model

$$I = Ar(n/360)$$

where I = the cost or return in dollars
       A = the amount of funds
       r = the quoted fed funds rate
       n = the number of days the funds are loaned.

For example, a round lot of $5 million at 9 3/16 percent for one day would cost

$$I = \$5,000,000(.091875)(1/360)$$
$$= \$1,276.04.$$

Because of its very short maturity and the sensitivity of fed funds to changes in credit conditions, the interest rate is extremely volatile. During periods of tight credit, it is not uncommon for the rate to swing several percentage points in the course of one day. Major swings in the rate occur most often on Wednesday, the last day to make any final adjustments in a depository institution's reserve position.

Fed funds transactions may be made late in the day when the markets for other instruments are closed. This is important to financial institutions because last minute flows can create serious cash management problems.

REPURCHASE AGREEMENTS

As pointed out in the preceding section, a number of factors can suddenly change a bank's reserve position. Thus, the ability to borrow or lend large amounts on very short notice is an essential aspect of banking. This need was partially met as the fed funds market developed. But a fed funds transaction is unsecured so credit risk remained a concern of market participants. The *repurchase agreement*, often called a *repo*, or *RP*, emerged to minimize this risk and eliminate the need for a time-consuming credit analysis when time is of the essence.

Like the fed funds market, the repo market plays an extremely important role in the financial system. The instrument is used extensively by banks, other financial institutions, non-financial corporations, government securities dealers, state and local governments, and the Federal Reserve. After examining the nature of the repo and its variations, the role of the major market participants and the flexibility of the instrument are examined.

Types of Repurchase Agreements

Strictly speaking, a repurchase agreement is not a money market instrument or a security, but rather it is a type of transaction. The transaction can take several forms.

Standard Repo   A repurchase agreement is a means of executing a short-term, secured loan through the purchase of securities (by the lender) with a simultaneous commitment from the seller (the borrower) to repurchase the securities on a specified date and at a specified price. If the borrower defaults, the lender has the securities as collateral. Thus, unlike fed funds, the repo is a collateralized transaction. The loan is usually equal to the value of the securities. This value is the sum of the market price and the accrued interest. A margin in the form of additional securities may be required depending on the nature of the transaction and the creditworthiness of the parties involved.

Like most fed funds transactions, repos are usually made to cover overnight needs or needs extending over a weekend. Repos for longer periods are referred to as *term repos.* These may extend for as long as several months. A *continuous repo* remains in effect until cancelled by either party. The *term repo* and the *continuous repo* reduce the administrative costs associated with daily transactions. All repo transactions involve immediately available funds.

The flexibility of the repo arises from several factors. Transactions may be arranged late in the day when the markets for most other money market instruments are closed. Also, the maturity may be arranged to meet the needs of both the borrower and lender without regard to the maturity of the underlying security. Although any security that is acceptable to the lender may be used as collateral in a repo, the most commonly used securities are U. S. Treasury and agency issues. This eliminates default risk with respect to the collateral. The price risk of the collateral is usually not a concern because of the seller's commitment to repurchase. The seller's creditworthiness does affect its ability to honor the repurchase commitment. If creditworthiness is a factor or the repo extends for several months, an additional margin in the form of securities may be required. Such a margin protects the lender in event of a decline in the value of collateral.

When properly executed, the repo is a remarkably flexible, convenient, liquid, and safe money market instrument. This does not mean that the repo, or its variations, is riskless. Some caveats are discussed later in this section.

Reverse Repo   Every short-term loan under a repurchase agreement involves a counterparty that borrows the funds by selling securities. From the borrower's standpoint the transaction may be called a *reverse repo.* One firm's repo is another firm's reverse repo. Although the terms *repo* and *reverse repo* are often used interchangeably, it is often necessary to make a distinction between the lender and borrower. When analyzing the potential risks involved in the transaction and the manner in which the repurchase agreement is used by market participants, the distinction is essential.

Dollar Repos   A variation of the repo discussed above is the *dollar repurchase agreement.* This is the same as the standard repo except that the seller agrees to repurchase securities that are of the same name or agency but not necessarily identical to the securities sold. The maturity or coupon may be slightly different. This gives the lender somewhat more flexibility. Again, from the borrower's viewpoint, this is called a *dollar reverse repo.*

Although they are used sparingly, the boundaries of such transactions must be understood clearly by both parties. The use of these transactions is limited to government securities dealers with well-established trading relationships. Regulated depository institutions must treat the transaction as an outright sale and purchase of securities. Thus, gains or losses would have to be realized and reflected on the financial statement. This limits their use in such institutions.

The Repo Market

The repo market is similar to the fed funds market in that it consists of a telephone network linking the major participants—large banks, government securities dealers, and fed funds brokers. The fed funds brokers arrange transactions between lenders and borrowers whereas the major banks and government securities dealers are continuously lending and borrowing using repos and reverse repos.

Most transactions in the national market are in blocks of $1 million or more. Transactions involving smaller amounts may be made but at a yield concession. Although the repo rate is negotiated, it closely tracks the fed funds rate and it is extremely volatile because of its short maturity. Since this is a secured transaction, the repo rate is usually slightly lower than the fed funds rate. Like the fed funds rate, the repo rate is quoted in 1/16ths and on a basis of a 360-day year. The model given earlier for determining the dollar cost of fed funds is used to compute the dollar cost of a repo.

Market Participants

The flexibility of repurchase agreements has spawned a broad cross section of market participants. Often the manner in which the repo is used depends on the participant and its objectives.

Commercial Banks   Like fed funds, the funds obtained under a repo are immediately available and are classified as *funds purchased.* If the underlying security is a Treasury or agency issue, the funds are nonreservable, regardless of the source. As a result, the repo is used extensively in managing the day-to-day money position of commercial banks. In fact, from a bank's standpoint a repo may be viewed as a secured fed funds transaction. The large holdings of Treasury and agency securities facilitates the use of repos by large banks. Because they deal in large repos, typically $1 million to $5 million, the large banks are able to obtain the best rates on both the lending and borrowing sides of the market. This enables these banks to arbitrage immediately available funds. This is done by borrowing through a repo and immediately reselling the funds in the fed funds market at a higher rate. Another approach is to sell the funds under a repo at a higher rate.

Government
Securities Dealers

Government securities dealers hold sizable positions in U. S. Treasury and agency issues. Most of the funds used to acquire the securities are borrowed, primarily under repurchase agreements. These dealers also act as brokers by arranging repo transactions on behalf of other parties. Another use of the instrument by dealers is the "matched repo." Here the dealer arbitrages by borrowing under a repo and reselling the funds under another repo with the same maturity. The dealer profits by obtaining funds at a cost that is slightly lower than the return on the funds the dealer supplied. A more speculative approach is to enter an unmatched transaction. For example, a dealer may borrow funds under an overnight repo and simultaneously lend under a term repo for ten days. If rates fall, the dealer's cost of funds will fall faster than the return on the funds loaned, thus generating a speculative profit as well as an arbitrage profit. The transaction can be reversed in anticipation of rising interest rates.

In their role as a market maker for U.S. Government and agency securities, dealers often sell such securities short. Rather than borrowing the securities from a bank or other investor in order to make delivery, dealers execute a repo. This lowers the cost of acquiring the securities for delivery.

Nonfinancial

Nonfinancial corporations accumulate funds in anticipation of large payouts for dividends, payrolls, taxes, and other major expenditures. High interest rates and improved technology for collecting, concentrating, and investing funds has resulted in greater emphasis on the management of these cash balances. An important aspect of this *cash management*, as it is known, is the investment of overnight funds. Using overnight, term, and continuous repos, nonfinancial corporations are major suppliers of funds in the one- to thirty-day maturity range. Beyond this range, non-financial corporations invest in CDs, T-bills, commercial paper, and bankers' acceptances.

Arranging repos is one of the cash management services offered to nonfinancial customers by some commercial banks. Late in the day, demand deposit balances in excess of a specific amount are automatically converted into an overnight repo. The next morning, the funds are returned to the demand deposit account for use that day. This service ensures that cash balances are held to a minimum level.

NonBank Financial
Institutions

In recent years, S&Ls, savings banks, and credit unions have become more active in the repo market. Although primarily suppliers of funds, the role of these institutions is expanding as they become more familiar with the repo and its flexibility. Increasingly, nonbank institutions engage in a form of arbitrage. Securities in an institution's portfolio are sold under a reverse repo. The funds are then reinvested in higher yielding securities, such as CDs, with the same maturity as the reverse repo.

Federal Reserve

The Federal Reserve conducts monetary policy in a variety of ways. When a long-lasting effect is desired, the outright purchase or sale of government securities will expand or reduce bank reserves and thus affect the money supply. However, short-term adjustments are often necessary to offset changes in float and Treasury balances at the Federal

Reserve, as well as to accommodate seasonal needs. Temporary reserves are supplied when the Federal Reserve enters repurchase agreements with banks and securities dealers while reserves are temporarily withdrawn through reverse repos. Thus, the repo and reverse repo play an important role in the implementation of monetary policy.

Repos—Some Caveats

Certain precautions must be taken by lenders and borrowers in order to minimize the risks involved with repos and in the case of depository institutions, to avoid incurring the wrath of regulators.

Credit Risk

Despite the fact that it is a collateralized transaction, legal aspects of the repo should be understood and certain procedures must be followed. One procedure is to include the accrued interest in the price of the underlying security. To see why, consider the case of Drysdale Government Securities.

Prior to its collapse in 1982, Drysdale Government Securities Inc., was a thinly capitalized government securities dealer. To supplement its small capital base, Drysdale used repurchase agreements in a novel manner. Assume for example, that a $5 million block of 12 percent bonds was selling at par and paid interest of $300,000 semiannually. Five months elapsed since the last interest payment so the accrued interest on the bond was five-sixths of $300,000 or $250,000. Drysdale acquired such bonds from a bank under a repurchase agreement and paid only the price of the bonds, $5 million, but not the accrued interest. These securities were then sold short in the market in anticipation of falling prices. The price received in an outright short sale included the accrued interest of $250,000. Drysdale had, in effect, wrung the accrued interest out of the securities and used the funds as capital. When the semiannual interest payment came due, the funds were to be paid to the original owner of the securities. Because of its huge short position in bonds, rising prices in the bond market caused substantial losses. When the semiannual interest payment on the short bonds came due, Drysdale was unable to pay the original owners a total of $160 million in accrued interest. The firm collapsed.

Credit risk is usually associated with the borrower. In this case it was the *lender's* failure that caused the problems. As a result of the Drysdale affair, the inclusion of accrued interest is now an essential aspect of repurchase agreements to reduce this source of credit risk.

The failure of another government securities dealer had major implications in the repo market. Traditionally, market participants operated on the assumption that a repo was a set of independent contracts for the sale and purchase of securities rather than representing a collateralized loan. The distinction is important. If a repo is a set of independent contracts and the borrower defaults on its repurchase commitment, the lender, as "owner" of the securities, could sell the securities to recoup its funds. However, when Lombard-Wall, Inc., went bankrupt in 1982, a bankruptcy judge ruled that a repo was a collateralized loan. This meant that the holders of securities obtained under a repo could not sell the securities without court approval. Thus, if the securities are tied up in a bankruptcy proceeding and interest rates rise, the value of the collateral may deteriorate.

The ruling in the Lombard-Wall case blunted the effectiveness of the repo. But because of the importance of this instrument to the Federal Reserve in implementing monetary policy, it is likely that legislation will be enacted to protect repurchase agreements in a bankruptcy proceeding.

The legal standing of the parties in a repurchase agreement can also be clouded if the documentation is not in proper order. This problem is easy to overcome but often overlooked.[3]

Pyramiding   It is a common practice for an institution to borrow funds by selling bonds to dealers under a reverse repo and reinvesting the proceeds in higher yielding securities. If the transaction ends at this point, it is not an inherently speculative practice. The nature of the transaction quickly changes if the newly acquired securities are sold under another reverse repo and the proceeds are used to purchase another security. By repeating the process several times—a practice known as *pyramiding*—a high degree of leverage results. A slight change in the value of the underlying securities can result in huge profits or losses depending on the magnitude of the pyramid. As a result, this is considered an unsound financial practice by examiners of depository financial institutions.

"Repo-to-Maturity"   Financial institutions usually hold some securities that management would like to sell but are reluctant to do so because the realized loss would have an adverse effect on earnings. Some managers attempt to get around the problem by using a *repo-to-maturity*. The security is sold under a reverse repo but never bought back. This is considered a deceptive practice by the regulators of depository institutions because it is a way of masking losses on the sale of securities. If discovered by examiners, national banks will have to file adjusted earnings statements to reflect the losses.

CONCLUSION

Federal funds and repurchase agreements provide lenders and borrowers with a remarkable degree of flexibility in managing day-to-day cash flows. Although once relatively obscure segments of the market for immediately available funds, these

---

[3] The documentation problem came to light after a small bank in Mt. Pleasant, Iowa collapsed in 1982. Papers that related to "retail repurchase agreements" were not in proper order so a number of the bank's small-scale savers were left in an unsecured position. Since the repos were not deposits, the saver's funds were also uninsured. These retail repos were used by some depository institutions to circumvent interest rate ceilings that were on deposits at the time.

money market instruments are becoming more widely used by a broader spectrum of market participants. It is likely that the use of fed funds and repos will expand further in the future.

REFERENCES

1.   Bowsher, Norman, N., "Repurchase Agreements," *Review,* Federal Reserve Bank of St. Louis, September 1979, pp. 17-22.
2.   Jones, Marcos T., Charles M. Lucas, and Thom B. Thurston, "Federal Funds and Repurchase Agreements," *Quarterly Review,* Federal Reserve Bank of New York, Summer 1977, pp. 33-48.
3.   Maerowitz, Seth P., "Federal Funds," *Instruments of the Money Market,* 5th ed., edited by Timothy Q. Cook and Bruce J. Summers, Richmond, Virginia: Federal Reserve Bank of Virginia, 1981, pp. 42-51.

13

The Discount Window*

James Parthemos and Walter Varvel

Adjustments in bank reserve positions are accomplished through purchase and sales of financial instruments in the money market. In addition to reliance on money market instruments, member banks have long had the "privilege" of acquiring reserves by borrowing at the discount window of their regional Federal Reserve Bank. By arranging an advance at the Federal Reserve, a bank suffering an unexpected reserve loss can bring its reserve position back to the desired or required level. Similarly, an institution experiencing a temporary buildup of reserves beyond desired levels may, before placing funds in the money market, pay off any borrowings it may owe at the window. In any event, the discount window affords an additional recourse in working out reserve adjustments and may be properly viewed as an operational part of the money market.

Following passage of the Depository Institutions Deregulation and Monetary Control Act of 1980 or Monetary Control Act as it is often called, nonmember banks and thrift institutions can also choose to adjust reserve positions through the discount window. The new legislation requires nonmembers to maintain reserves balances against transaction and nonpersonal time deposits. In addition, all institutions issuing reservable deposit liabilities are authorized access to the discount window.

Reserve adjustments made by individual institutions using the discount window differ in one important respect from alternative adjustment techniques. Trading in such instruments as Federal funds, negotiable certificates of deposit, and Treasury bills among commercial banks or between banks and their customers involves no net creation of new bank reserves. Rather, existing reserves are simply shifted about within the banking system. On the other hand, net borrowings or repayments at the discount window result in a net change in Federal Reserve credit outstand-

---

*Reprinted, with deletions, from *Instruments of the Money Market*, 5th edition, edited by Timothy Q. Cook and Bruce J. Summers, 1981, with permission from the Federal Reserve Bank of Richmond.

ing and, consequently, affect the volume of bank reserves. Thus, the choice by individual institutions between using the discount window or alternative means of reserve adjustment may influence the availability of money and credit in the economy. Policy decisions of the Federal Reserve affecting discount window borrowing, therefore, have ramifications for the conduct of monetary policy.

Decisions to use the discount window relative to other segments of the money market for making reserve adjustments depend importantly upon the relation of the Federal Reserve's discount rate to yields on money market investments and on legal and administrative arrangements regarding use of the discount window. Neither of these factors are determined by the competitive interaction of market forces, but rather by administrative decision. Adjustments in interest rates on window. borrowings are recommended by the Boards of Directors of the regional Reserve Banks in accord with current economic and money market conditions, with final approval required by the Board of Governors. In addition, the legal requirements and administrative guidelines for extensions of credit through the window are embodied in Federal Reserve Regulation A.

EARLY DISCOUNTING PRINCIPLES

An important principle underlying creation of the Federal Reserve System was providing a pool of funds which could be drawn on by banks experiencing reserve shortages. The ability of banks to draw on this pool, however, was not envisaged as an absolute right. Rather, it was linked to a widely held theory of commercial banking which is known as the commercial loan of "real bills" doctrine. According to this doctrine, commercial banks should borrow only against short-term, self-liquidating paper arising from the normal conduct of production and trade. Member banks were initially permitted to borrow from the Federal Reserve Banks only by rediscounting customer loans which met certain carefully specified conditions based on the commercial loan theory. Promissory notes and other credit instruments meeting these specifications were defined as "eligible paper," that is, paper eligible for rediscount at the Federal Reserve. By and large, the real bills doctrine dominated member bank use of the discount window until the banking crisis of 1933.

During the 1920s, trading in such money market instruments as short-term government debt and Federal funds was not nearly so well developed as at present. Consequently, the discount window was a primary tool of adjustment for member banks. While banks made extensive use of bankers' acceptances, commercial paper, and call loans against stock exchange collateral for reserve adjustment purposes, they also relied heavily on the discount window. Many bankers made it a regular practice to hold a supply of eligible paper which would be readily available for reserve adjustment through the discount window. Throughout the 1920s, average daily borrowings at the discount window usually exceeded $500 million and at times amounted to more than twice that figure.

FROM THE 1930s TO THE ACCORD

The banking reforms of the 1930s incorporated features designed to encourage use of the discount window by banks. In some measure, these features were related to a growing conviction that the real bills doctrine and discount window eligibility requirements unduly restricted banks seeking central bank assistance in times of stress. The effect of the reforms was to sweep away the real bills basis for discounting, although the concept of eligible paper was retained in the language of Federal Reserve discount regulations.

At an early stage in Federal Reserve history, member banks were allowed to borrow on their own notes, secured by eligible paper or government securities, instead of by rediscounting customer paper. Since 1933 direct advances against government securities have accounted for most Federal Reserve lending. In addition, banking legislation of the 1930s incorporated a new section, 10(b) into the Federal Reserve Act authorizing loans to member banks against any collateral satisfactory to the lending Reserve Bank.

Despite the encouragement of these changes and low discount rates, banks used the discount window sparingly between 1933 and 1951. From 1935 to 1940 daily borrowings generally averaged below $10 million. For the most part, banks held large amounts of excess reserves and were under little pressure to borrow. Even after the business recovery of the early 1940s, borrowing remained at low levels. By that time, banks held large quantities of government securities and the Federal Reserve's practice of pegging the market for these securities, instituted in 1942, eliminated the market risk of adjusting reserve positions through sales of governments. The Treasury-Federal Reserve Accord of 1951, however, ended the pegged market for government securities and began a new chapter in the history of the discount windows.

DISCOUNTING SINCE THE ACCORD

Prices of government securities fluctuated over a broader range after the Accord, and it became riskier for banks to rely on these securities as a source of reserves when adjustments were necessary. Consequently, banks began to reassess the relative attractiveness of the discount window. Partly for this reason, borrowings jumped sharply, reaching the $1 billion level in mid-1952 for the first time in more than 20 years. For most of the 1950s borrowings were at levels comparable in absolute terms (although smaller relative to required reserves) with those of the 1920s.

The renewed importance of the discount window, coming in an overall economic and credit environment quite different from that prevailing in the 1920s, suggested the need for a general review of the principles on which the discount privilege was based. In 1955, after an extended inquiry, the Board of Governors promulgated a major revision in its Regulation A. As embodied in Regulation A, administrative restrictions on use of the discount window relate to the broader aspects of the Federal Reserve's operations rather than to any particular banking theory. For example, Regulation A recognizes that discount borrowing creates new reserves and, unless subject to some restraint, could conflict with policy goals such as economic and price stability. It also recognizes the necessity for insuring that the public resources administered by the Federal Reserve are not used to support questionable banking practices, but rather to insure the continuity of banking services provided to the public.

Generally, Regulation A envisages use of the discount window primarily as a temporary expedient open to institutions requiring reserve adjustments resulting from unanticipated shortages of funds. Indeed, short term adjustment credit represents the great bulk of window borrowings. In addition, two other categories of borrowing have been considered "appropriate." Reserve needs of smaller institutions occasioned by seasonal swings in credit demand and in deposits may give rise to appropriate borrowing. Similarly, reserve problems associated with emergency situations affecting a community or a region, or with local or regional secular change, provide appropriate reasons for borrowing. Within the constraints embodied in Regulation A, the discount window is open to depository institutions in a variety of situations that may be considered more or less normal commercial banking operations. As long as an institution demonstrates in its overall performance its intention to operate within the limits of its own resources, it can usually arrange temporary accommodation to cover a variety of needs.

Continuous borrowing at the discount window is considered "inappropriate" whatever its cause since it implies that the borrowing bank has permanent reserve difficulties that should be corrected through basic portfolio adjustments. Extended use of central bank funds would supplement an institution's capital resources as a permanent base for investment in bank assets. The Federal Reserve has enumerated specific purposes for which use of the discount window is deemed inappropriate. These include borrowing to profit from interest rate differentials, to substitute Federal Reserve credit for normal sources of short-term interest-sensitive funds, and to support increases in loan or investment portfolios [2].

In April 1973, Regulation A was revised to permit greater use of the discount window for seasonal borrowing. Short-term access to the discount window had previously been available to member banks experiencing unusually strong seasonal reserve needs. The revision in Regulation A was designed explicitly to assist those member banks, especially small institutions, that lacked access to the national money markets in meeting seasonal needs arising out of predictable patterns in deposits and loans.

Under the 1973 revision, a member bank could obtain Federal Reserve credit to meet seasonal needs exceeding 5 percent of its average annual deposits. In order to qualify for the seasonal borrowing privilege, the bank had to provide the Federal Reserve with advance evidence indicating that the seasonal need would persist for at least eight consecutive weeks. The seasonal borrowing program initiated in 1973 was available only to banks with deposits of less than $250 million. Furthermore, member banks were not permitted to use the seasonal borrowing privilege and at the same time be net sellers of Federal funds.

In August 1976, Regulation A was further revised to liberalize the seasonal borrowing privilege. Under the revised regulations member banks could use the seasonal borrowing privilege to meet that part of their seasonal need for funds exceeding 4 percent of the first $100 million of the previous years average deposits; 7 percent of the second $100 million; and 10 percent of any deposits over $200 million. The period over which the seasonal need must persist was lowered from eight weeks to four weeks, and banks with deposits up to $500 million were made eligible for the seasonal borrowing privilege. In practice, however, the increasing deductible makes it unlikely that institutions with deposits in excess of $250 million will qualify for seasonal credit. In addition, the revision permits net sales of Federal funds while banks are engaged in seasonal borrowing from the Federal Reserve, as long as the sales represent the institution's normal operating pattern of Federal funds sales—including its usual seasonal and cyclical variation in sales and allowance for growth. This change was made in recognition of the growing number of small banks that were continuous net sellers of Federal funds. Since the initiation of the seasonal borrowing program in 1973, seasonal borrowing has generally been heaviest in the period from July through October. The magnitude of average monthly seasonal borrowing has varied over subsequent years from a low of $18 million in 1974 to a high of $145 million in 1979.

Emergency credit assistance at the discount window has been infrequently extended to institutions facing liquidity crises. Such assistance is sometimes necessary to minimize potentially serious adverse impacts of failure on financial flows in the economy and to provide federal banking agencies sufficient time to work out a satisfactory permanent solution. In the case of Franklin National Bank in 1974, deteriorating earnings and massive withdrawals of deposits induced the Federal Reserve, in its role as "lender of last resort,"[1] to advance funds to Franklin, peaking at $1.75 billion just prior to takeover of the bulk of the bank's assets and deposits by the European American Bank. More recently, large discount window borrowings played a key role in alleviating liquidity problems at First Pennsylvania Bank. Regulation A permits emergency credit extensions to nondepository institutions when alternative sources of credit are not available and failure to obtain such credit would adversely affect the economy. Such credit, however, will be at a higher rate of interest than that applicable to depository institutions.

THE MONETARY CONTROL ACT: A NEW ERA

The Depository Institutions Deregulation and Monetary Control Act of 1980 gives all nonmember banks, savings and loan associations, savings banks, and credit unions holding transaction accounts or nonpersonal time deposits the same discount

---

[1] For a discussion of the classical concept of the role of the central bank as lender of last resort, see [5].

and borrowing privileges as member banks. The Act directs the Federal Reserve to administer the window taking into consideration "the special needs of savings and other depository institutions for access to discount and borrowing facilities consistent with their long-term asset portfolios and the sensitivity of such institutions to trends in the national money markets." The impact of this legislation on the administration of the discount window is far-reaching.

In September 1980, the Federal Reserve revised Regulation A to implement the provisions of the Act. The revision establishes an additional lending category to provide credit for an extended period of other than seasonal needs. "Other extended credit" can now be arranged for individual depository institutions experiencing financial strains due to exceptional circumstances such as sustained deposit drains, impaired access to money market funds, or sudden deterioration in loan repayment performance. Depository institutions with investment portfolios composed of primarily longer-term assets and experiencing difficulties adjusting to changing money market conditions, particularly during periods of deposit disintermediation, may also borrow under the other extended credit provision.

The revised lending provisions do not, however, alter the Federal Reserve's expectation that depository institutions are to rely primarily on their usual sources of funds before turning to the discount window for assistance. Discount window credit will generally be made available only after alternative sources have been exhausted. In the case of thrift institituions, alternative sources of funds include special industry lenders such as the Federal Home Loan Banks, the National Credit Union Administration's Central Liquidity Facility, and corporate central credit unions. Before extending credit, the Reserve Banks will consult with the borrowing institution's supervising agency to determine why funds are not available from other sources.

The September 1980 revision in Regulation A made discretionary use of a discount rate surcharge a permanent addition to the Federal Reserve's discount lending policy. Such a surcharge can be made applicable to both adjustments and extended credit. In March 1980, as part of the special credit restraint program, the System briefly instituted a 3 percent surcharge on adjustment credit of member banks with over $500 million in deposits when such borrowings occurred successively in two reserve statement weeks or more, or when the borrowing occurred in more than four weeks in a calendar quarter. The surcharge which did not apply to seasonal borrowings or emergency loans, was designed to discourage frequent use of the discount window. The surcharge was eliminated in May but was reinstated on adjustment credit extended to frequent borrowings of large depository institutions in late 1980.

ADMINISTRATION OF THE WINDOW

Currently, most Federal Reserve loans are made under the provisions of Section 13 of the Federal Reserve Act and are in the form of direct advances secured by U. S. Government securities. Advances under Section 13 can also be made against

Federal agency securities. Loans under Section 10(b) may be secured by any collateral satisfactory to the lending Reserve Bank, including State and local government securities, mortgage notes covering 1-4 family residences, and business and other customer notes. The use of these additional types of collateral has been relatively unimportant in recent discount activity, in part, because the rate charged on 10(b) loans was ½ of one percentage point higher than on Section 13 loans. Moreover, depending on the collateral offered, 10(b) loans may involve some delay before funds are made available. Banks borrowing under this Section usually offered municipal securities as collateral. The Monetary Control Act authorized the Federal Reserve to eliminate the ½ of one percentage point differential required on 10(b) loans, a change that became effective in September 1980. With the removal of the penalty rate, institutions may choose to increase use of municipals and residential mortgages as collateral for window borrowings.

Maturities of up to 90 days are authorized on Section 13 loans, while the statutory limit on 10(b) maturities is four months. In practice, however, Reserve Banks encourage borrowers to limit maturities to shorter periods. Large institutions with broad access to money market funds are expected to make necessary adjustments in their portfolios faster than smaller banks. Consequently, adjustment credit extended to money market banks will normally be only to the next business day. Smaller institutions may borrow with somewhat longer maturities.

Adjustment credit is available on a short-term basis to assist depository institutions "in meeting temporary requirements for funds, or to cushion more persistent outflows of funds pending an orderly adjustment of the institution's assets and liabilities."[2] It is the responsibility of the Reserve Bank discount officer to ensure that adjustment borrowing is for appropriate purposes and not simply a substitute for regular sources of funds. Borrowing requests from institutions that are not presently in the window or that have not in the recent past relied heavily on the window are normally accommodated immediately. When the size or frequency of borrowing increases, however, an institution may be asked to provide information justifying continued use of discount credit. If the borrowing is judged to be inappropriate, the borrower is asked to discontinue use of the window. Such administrative pressure represents nonprice rationing of discount credit.

To assist in the determination of the appropriateness of window borrowing, heavy reliance is placed on analysis of balance sheet trends, especially flows in loans and deposits, net positions in Federal funds, and changes in liquid assets. Balance sheets are examined to determine the extent of liquidity pressures and to see if appropriate adjustments are taking place.

An extensive review of discount window policy conducted by the Federal Reserve in the late 1960s [2] reported that some differences existed among Regional Banks in the determination of what constituted appropriate borrowing. To help achieve uniformity in discount administration, numerical guidelines for the size and frequency of borrowing by an individual institution have been established. Such guidelines, used as a secondary measure by the discount officer, provide a norm for the amount of borrowing a typical bank is likely to require, the amount of time usually needed to adjust the bank's position, and a measure of how frequent-

---

[2] Regulation A, Section 201.3(a).

ly a bank is likely to need adjustment credit. Borrowing that exceeds the guidelines does not necessarily mean that the borrowing will be considered inappropriate.

Since large institutions generally have greater access to alternative sources of funds than smaller institutions, the guidelines are more stringent for large borrowers. Borrowings as a percentage of domestic deposits are generally expected to be lower than for smaller institutions, and less frequent. Some variation in the size classifications included in the guidelines exists among the regional Reserve Banks.

MECHANICS OF BORROWING

In order to borrow, an institution must furnish the Federal Reserve Bank a resolution adopted by its Board of Directors specifying which of its officers are authorized to borrow on its behalf. A *Continuing Lending Agreement* is normally executed facilitating prompt extension of discount credit upon telephone requests from borrowing institutions.

Advances secured by government obligations can be made up to the face amount of the collateral. The collateral must be held by the Federal Reserve Bank unless prior arrangements have been made permitting another institution to hold the securities under a custody receipt arrangement. Under such an arrangement, the securities may be held by a "custody" bank which in the usual course of business performs correspondent bank services, including the holding in custody of government securities, for the borrower. While institutions may also borrow on their promissory note secured by eligible paper, this procedure can be more time consuming since the Reserve Bank must verify the eligibility of the collateral, then analyze and value it. Institutions, therefore, often submit collateral in advance of the date of the borrowing. Applications processing is prompt when municipal securities are offered as collateral, but delays may result when customer notes are offered. In addition, 10(b) collateral may be valued at less than the face amount.

Once an application for Federal Reserve credit is approved by the Reserve Bank, borrowings are normally credited directly to the institution's reserve account. Unless the Federal Reserve is notified to the contrary, the principal plus interest due on the note is automatically charged against the borrower's reserve account on the maturity date. Notes may, of course, be paid in part or in full before maturity. Nonmember institutions may (a) decide not to hold reserves directly with the Federal Reserve but hold them with a correspondent institution on a "pass-through" basis or (b) have reserve liabilities that can be met with vault cash. In these instances, three-party arrangements may be made among the Federal Reserve, borrower, and a correspondent institution providing for credits and debits to be charged against the correspondent's reserve account.

BORROWING LEVELS

The volume of borrowings at the discount window fluctuates over a wide range. Borrowings generally increase in periods of high or rising market interest rates and decline in periods of low or falling rates. To a large extent, this is because changes in the discount rate lag behind movements in money market rates. Consequently, in periods of rising rates, the cost of borrowing at the discount window frequently becomes relatively more attractive compared to the cost of raising funds in the money market.

There is a strong relationship between total member bank borrowing and the differential between the Federal funds rate and the discount rate. The 1950s and early 1960s were generally characterized by periods of relatively stable interest rates. Throughout this period, the discount rate was usually maintained at or above market rates, providing little financial incentive for discount borrowing. The latter 1960s and much of the 1970s, however, saw large swings in the interest differential. Borrowing averaged well over $1 billion throughout most of 1969 and early 1970 when the Federal funds rate exceeded the discount rate, at times, by over 3 percentage points. Throughout 1973 and 1974 member bank borrowings averaged nearly $2 billion and exceeded $3 billion in June through September 1974 when the interest differential approached 5 percent. Borrowings fell rapidly with the onset of the recession and the related drop-off in loan demand in late 1974 and early 1975. Market rates fell dramatically and were generally below the discount rate from early 1975 through mid-1977, when window borrowing was minimal.

From 1977 through most of 1979, the Federal Reserve demonstrated a desire to keep the discount rate more closely in line with increasing market rates. Discount rate increases were more frequent but still lagged behind market rates resulting in a general increase in borrowing levels. Borrowing grew rapidly, approaching a level of $3 billion following the Federal Reserve's shift to a reserve targeting procedure (described below) in October 1979 which resulted in large differentials between the funds rate and the discount rate. The imposition of the credit restraint program with its temporary three percentage point surcharge on large bank borrowings and the reduced economic activity beginning in early 1980, contributed to the subsequent sharp drop in market rates (relative to the discount rate) and the lower level of discount borrowing. Considering the low level of the discount rate relative to the cost of alternative sources of reserve adjustment funds during periods of high interest rates, the volume of borrowings would undoubtedly have been much greater without the use of discount administration as a rationing device.

During periods of high interest rates, the discount rate has usually remained below market rates and, in effect, subsidized member bank borrowing from the Federal Reserve. In such times, reduced interest expenses from borrowing at below market rates provided a partial offset to the opportunity costs associated with maintaining non-earning reserve balances with the Federal Reserve [1].

Both small and large banks use the discount window, but in most years large banks have accounted for the greater dollar volume of borrowings. Banks that manage their reserve positions closely usually meet short-run reserve deficiencies either by borrowing from the Federal Reserve or by buying Federal funds. Large banks tend to incur reserve deficiencies more frequently than small banks. Thus, they tend to rely more heavily on borrowed funds. The tendency to use both the discount window and Federal funds increases with bank size.

Since large banks are more frequent users of discount window credit than small banks, most savings on interest expenses resulting from borrowing at below-market discount rates would seem to accrue to large banks. A study analyzing member bank borrowing in the Eighth Federal Reserve District from 1974 to 1977 confirms that the dollar amounts of such benefits are disproportionately concentrated among the largest banks. Measures of the interest savings per dollar borrowed and interest savings as a percentage of average reserve balances held at the Federal Reserve, however, show that relatively small banks which borrowed heavily "benefited as much or more than the large banks" when market rates were substantially above the discount rate [4].

ROLE OF THE DISCOUNT WINDOW
IN MONETARY POLICY

The role of discount rate administration in the making of monetary policy has changed somewhat since the October 1979 shift in Federal Reserve operating strategy. Prior to October 1979, the Federal Reserve attempted to achieve its money supply objectives by manipulating the Federal funds rate. Because in that policy setting the Federal Reserve chose to fix the Federal funds rate in the short-run, increases in the discount rate reduced the differential between the Federal funds rate and the discount rate, and decreased the demand for borrowed reserves. To keep the federal funds rate steady following an increase in the discount rate, the Federal Reserve had to increase the supply of nonborrowed reserves. Consequently, increases in the discount rate did not directly affect the level of short-run interest rates; they simply changed the mix of nonborrowed and borrowed reserve. At most, under the old regime, discount rate changes were used by the monetary authorities to signal changes in policy through what was referred to as the "announcement effect."

The importance of discount window policy has been enhanced under the reserve targeting strategy adopted by the Federal Open Market Committee in October 1979. Under this strategy, the Federal Reserve attempts to achieve its money supply objectives by setting targets for nonborrowed and borrowed reserves. The demand for borrowed reserves is largely dependent on the spread between the Federal funds rate and the discount rate. Consequently, a given borrowed reserve objective will, roughly speaking, produce a particular spread between the funds rate and the discount rate. The more the Federal Reserve makes the banking system borrow, the higher the funds rate will be in relation to the discount rate. Under the new operating procedure, then, given a specific borrowed reserves objective, a rise in the discount rate is immediately transmitted to the Federal funds rate and to other short-term interest rates. For this reason in all instances from October 1979 through the end of 1980, increases in the discount rate resulted in increases in the Federal funds rate of at least equal magnitude.

The change in the effect of discount rate movements on short-term interest rates since the October 1979 change in operating strategy illustrates an important point, namely, that the effect of discount rate movements on market interest rates depends on the operating strategy of the Federal Reserve.

REFERENCES

1.   George J. Benston, *Federal Reserve Membership: Consequences, Costs, Benefits, and Alternatives,* Association of Reserve City Bankers, 1978, p. 34.
2.   Board of Governors of the Federal Reserve System, "Operation of the Federal Reserve Discount Window Under the Monetary Control Act of 1980," September 1980.
3.   Board of Governors of the Federal Reserve System, *Reappraisal of the Federal Reserve Discount Mechanism: Volume I,* August 1971.
4.   R. Alton Gilbert, "Benefits of Borrowing From the Federal Reserve When the Discount Rate is Below Market Interest Rates," *Review,* Federal Reserve Bank of St. Louis, March 1979, pp. 25-32.
5.   Thomas M. Humphrey, "The Classical Concept of the Lender of Last Resort," *Economic Review,* Federal Reserve Bank of Richmond, January/February 1975, pp. 2-9.

14

Managing the Bank Money Position

Each day, a large volume of payments flow through the typical commercial bank. Since these flows are uncertain and claims against the bank must be honored without delay, special problems arise in the management of day-to-day bank funds, or the *money position* as it is called. An integral part of the *money position* is the bank's legal reserve position. Legal reserves are funds that must be held in a non-interest-bearing form against certain classes of deposits. Since excess reserves result in a loss of income and reserve deficiencies result in penalties, the reserve account must be managed efficiently to comply with regulations and minimize the cost of holding reserves. Problems arise in managing the money position because the large volume of uncertain flows are through, and thus affect, a bank's reserve account. The reserve account is constantly changing because of these flows so corrective adjustments in the bank's money position must be made continuously. In this chapter, the nature of these adjustments is examined after providing an overview of the *money position* of a commercial bank.

THE MONEY POSITION—AN OVERVIEW

In Table 1, a financial statement for the Hypothetical National Bank (HNB) is presented. The purpose of this statement is to place specific money position assets and liabilities of banks in perspective in terms of their roles and relative size. The bank's money position is embedded in a number of accounts on both the asset and liability sides of the financial statement. Note that *Cash and Reserves* amount to 15 percent of assets. Although this total and the individual components will

Table 1 Hypothetical National Bank Statement of Condition ($ in Millions)

Assets	Amount	Percent
CASH AND RESERVES		
Cash	$ 10	1.0%
Deposits—FR bank	40	4.0
Deposits—other banks	35	3.5
Cash items in process of collection	65	6.5
Total Cash and Reserves	$ 150	15.0
INVESTMENTS		
Funds sold		
Federal funds sold	$ 15	1.5
Securities purchased under agreement to resell	5	.5
Securities		
U. S. Treasury	95	9.5
U. S. Agency	5	.5
State and local	120	12.0
Other	5	.5
Trading account (at market)	5	.5
Total Investments	$ 250	25.0
LOANS		
Commercial and Industrial (C&I)		
Agriculture	$ 10	1.0
Finance-related	30	3.0
Industrial and commercial	200	20.0
International	15	1.5
Lease financing	35	3.5
Real estate and construction	40	4.0

Liabilities and Capital	Amount	Percent
DEPOSITS		
Demand deposits	$ 200	20.0%
NOW and "Super" NOW accts.	150	15.0
Money Market Accounts	100	10.0
Reg. savings and time deposits	300	30.0
Foreign deposits	50	5.0
Total Deposits	$ 800	80.0
BORROWED FUNDS—SHORT-TERM		
Funds purchased		
Federal funds purchased	$ 5	.5
Securities sold under agreements to repurchase	15	1.5
Federal Reserve Bank advances	5	.5
Bankers' Acceptances outstanding	15	1.5
Other short-term borrowed funds	10	1.0
Total Borrowed Funds—Short-Term	$ 50	5.0
BORROWED FUNDS—LONG-TERM		
Capital debentures	$ 30	3.0
Mortgage indebtedness	10	1.0
Total Borrowed Funds—Long-Term	$ 40	4.0
OTHER LIABILITIES		
Interest payable	$ 10	1.0
Accounts payable and accrued taxes	25	2.5
Miscellaneous liabilities	15	1.5
Total Other Liabilities	$ 50	5.0
CAPITAL		
Preferred stock	—0—	—0—

Other	5	.5
Total Commercial Loans	$ 335	33.5
Consumer Loans		
Installment	$ 100	10.0
Credit card	15	1.5
Mortgage (residential)	100	10.0
Other	5	.5
Total Consumer Loans	$ 220	22.0
Total Loans	$ 555	55.5
Less: Reserve for loan losses	5	.5
Net Loans	$ 550	55.0
OTHER ASSETS		
Interest receivable	$ 15	1.5
Due from customers on acceptances	15	1.5
Building and equipment	15	1.5
Miscellaneous assets	5	.5
Total Other Assets	$ 50	5.0
TOTAL ASSETS	$1,000	100.0%

Common shareholders' equity		
Common stock ($25 par)		
Authorized 1,200,000 shares		
Issued 1,200,000 shares	30	3.0
Capital surplus	15	1.5
Retained earnings	15	1.5
Total common equity	$ 60	6.0
Total Capital	$ 60	6.0
TOTAL LIABILITIES AND CAPITAL	$1,000	100.0%

Key Ratios:
Loans/Deposits = 68.75%
Equity/Total Liabilites & Capital = 6.00%

vary from bank to bank because of size, location, regulatory, and other factors, the figures shown provide an indication of the relative size of some of the money position components on the asset side.

The overall money position depends on the interaction of the *Cash and Reserves* components, several other accounts usually classified within the *Investments* section of the financial statement, and certain liability accounts. Before looking at the nature of this interaction, it will be useful to describe the components of the *Cash and Reserves* account and clarify the terminology used. A bank's cash, or *vault cash* as it is known, is the amount of coin and currency on hand to meet the day-to-day transaction needs of its customers. The cash on hand is subject to a high degree of seasonal variation. Prior to Christmas and other holidays, holdings of vault cash are increased to accommodate a higher level of withdrawals. After the holiday, the cash position is reduced as customers become net depositors of cash. Cash is a non-earning asset and it requires costly storage space so it is kept to a minimum level. However, vault cash is used to satisfy a portion of a bank's *legal reserve requirements.*

Legally required reserves are funds that banks must keep in a specified form. In addition to vault cash, deposits in a district Federal Reserve Bank are used for reserves. Like cash, these deposits are non-earning assets so they are kept at a minimum level, as discussed in the next section.

Most banks have deposits in other commercial banks. These may be in the form of demand deposits or interest-bearing accounts. Often such deposits are reciprocal. For example, HNB may have deposits in the "Other Banks" that have accounts with HNB. Such balances enable banks to conduct business in different parts of the country or even internationally. Money center and large regional banks tend to hold a larger volume of deposits from other banks because of their *correspondent relationships* with smaller institutions. That is, by holding deposits in a larger money center bank, smaller outlying banks, often called *downstream correspondents,* broaden their operating scope in terms of having the ability to transfer funds. Such a correspondent relationship enables smaller banks to obtain other services offered by the larger *upstream correspondent.* These services include investment counseling, participating in the purchase or sale of loans, data processing, and executing securities transactions. One form of compensation for these services is deposit balances. These "Deposits—Other Banks" affect the reserve computations as shown later.

The account *Cash Items in Process of Collection* (CIPC) represents items drawn on other banks and that have been credited to customers' accounts but not yet paid. The funds represented by this account are often referred to as *float.* This account also plays a role in the reserve calculations.

In the *Investments* section of HNB's asset structure, three categories are shown. One of these accounts, *Funds Sold,* plays a key role in managing the money position. These are funds that are loaned to other institutions through repurchase agreements (repos) and the sale of federal (fed) funds. Repos and fed funds are referred to as *overnight funds.* Most transactions involving overnight funds are for one to three days, although longer-term arrangements are often made. The counterpart of *Funds Sold* is on the liability side of HNB's statement. Under the *Funds Purchased* section, fed funds purchased and securities sold under repo agreements represent nonreservable funds borrowed by the bank for overnight purposes. As will be shown in this chapter, the lending and borrowing of overnight funds play a key role in managing the cash position and legal reserve position of a bank. Management of the overall money position is also facilitated by Federal Reserve borrowings or the sale of bankers' acceptances. These accounts are shown on the liability side of HNB's financial statement.

MANAGING THE MONEY POSITION[1]

The problems associated with managing a bank's money position are best understood by first explaining the manner in which payments are made through the banking system. On a typical business day well over $100 billion is transferred through the banking system in the form of checks and check-type drafts such as negotiable orders of withdrawal (NOWs) and share drafts drawn against credit unions. In addition, over $500 billion is transferred daily by means of electronic wire transfers. In the check-clearing process, when a bank is presented with a check drawn on a customer's demand deposit account, the transfer of funds to another institution is made by debiting the bank's reserve account at the Federal Reserve, or *Fed* as it is called. When checks drawn on other banks are deposited by its customers, the bank's reserve balance at the Fed increases when the check clears and the funds are "collected" by means of a book entry crediting the receiving bank's reserve account and debiting the paying bank's account.

Most of the funds transferred through the reserve account of larger banks, especially money center banks, result not from check-related transfers but from electronic payments and collections for customers. A customer instructs its bank by telephone, cable, or computer linkup to pay a specified party with an account at another bank. The bank's "money transfer" computer then sends an electronic transfer message usually through one of three commonly used systems. The *Fedwire* is the Federal Reserve System's electronic funds transfer network. Using this system, the paying bank's computer instructs a computer at the Fed to (1) transfer funds from the sending bank's reserve account to the receiving bank's reserve account; and (2) inform the receiving bank of the payment. The payment is made immediately in the form of entries on the books of the Federal Reserve. Thus, funds transferred via *Fedwire* are *immediately available funds*. Most other electronic transfers, including those related to international payments, are made through the New York Clearing House Interbank Payment System, or CHIPS, as it is known. The procedures for a CHIPS payment are similar to those for a Fedwire transfer. The funds are on a "same-day" basis, that is, they are available for use that day. However, rather than being immediately available, the funds are not available until late in the day. At 4:30 p.m. eastern time, the CHIPS system stops accepting payment instructions and transfers are balanced between banks. Between

---

[1] The first part of this section draws from "Life at a Bank's Money Desk," *The Morgan Guaranty Survey*, November 1981, pp. 11-15.

5:30 and 6:00 p.m banks owing money to other banks settle their CHIPS position by transferring funds from their reserve accounts at the Fed via the *Fedwire* to CHIPS. Banks owed money have their reserve accounts credited by CHIPS. Since non-member banks do not have reserve accounts at the Fed, wire transfers and other forms of payment are handled through a clearing account with the Fed or a member, upstream correspondent bank. The third system is the *Cash Wire*. This funds transfer network, which is privately owned by a consortium of banks, provides domestic banks with same-day settlement.

Handling the huge volume of payments flowing through a commercial bank involves much more than simply processing checks, making computer entries and keeping records. Sufficient funds must be maintained to cover net deposit outflows, loans, purchases of securities, and the bank's reserve requirements. Keeping funds in excess of these needs is costly because of the loss of interest income. At larger regional and money center banks, the uncertainty of these flows makes this balancing act even more difficult. The customers of these banks include large corporations, financial institutions, domestic and foreign correspondent banks, and securities firms. These depositors conduct many large-scale financial transactions. The total dollar volume of these payments far exceeds their overnight deposit balances. The size, volume, and day-to-day uncertainty of these flows coupled with late-in-the-day changes and wire transfer/settlements can create a serious money position problem. At the hub of this problem is the bank's legal reserve position.

Reserve Requirements

The Monetary Control Act   Until March 1980, the reserve requirements imposed on a commercial bank depended on the origin of its charter. Since all states had their own reserve requirements and these differed from those imposed on Federally chartered national banks by the Federal Reserve Board, there was little uniformity among banks. In addition to requiring that reserves be in the form of noninterest-bearing cash and Federal Reserve deposits, requirements of the Federal Reserve tended to be higher than those imposed on state chartered banks. Furthermore, many states allowed a portion of their requirements to be satisfied by holding certain interest-bearing securities. Thus, for national banks the combination of higher reserve requirements and the reserves being held as non-earning assets imposed a "cost" in the form of reduced earnings.

The opportunity cost of Federal Reserve membership increased dramatically in the late 1970s as interest rates reached record levels. In order to reduce this cost, many national banks switched to a state charter and enhanced their profitability. It soon became apparent to regulators that a continuation of this trend would reduce the Federal Reserve's ability to control the money supply by altering reserve requirements.

In response to bank defections from the Federal Reserve System and a number of other problems facing financial intermediaries, the *Depository Institutions Deregulation and Monetary Control Act of 1980* became law in March of that year. One of the provisions of this Act imposed uniform reserve requirements on *all* depository institutions offering transaction accounts, regardless of their charter. The Act also authorized banks, S&Ls, and mutual savings banks to offer NOW accounts, and credit unions were able to offer their equivalent *share drafts.* The entire spectrum of depository institutions became subject to the uniform reserve requirements.

Since depository-type financial institutions were subject to diverse requirements at the time the *Monetary Control Act* became law in 1980, an eight-year phase-in period was established to allow an orderly transition to the uniform system. Exceptions were NOW accounts and share drafts which were subjected immediately to the new reserve requirements.

The Requirements   The *Monetary Control Act* imposes reserve requirements on transaction accounts and certain other deposits. Transaction-type accounts include demand deposits, NOW accounts, automatic transfer accounts, and certain other accounts subject to telephone or pre-authorized transfers. For reserve calculations, *net demand deposits* are used rather than the gross amount. Net demand deposits are defined as gross demand deposits less the sum of cash items in process of collection and demand balances due from domestic commercial banks. Time deposits that are transferable (such as negotiable CDs) and have a maturity of 2½ years or less are also subject to reserve requirements. Such deposits may be *personal* or *nonpersonal.* The latter is a deposit held by a party other than a natural person. Finally, the Act requires that reserves be held against Eurodollar liabilities. The reserve requirements related to these *reservable liabilities* are summarized in Table 2.

Table 2   Reserve Requirements

Deposit Category	Reserve Requirement (%)
Transaction Accounts[a]	
First $25 million	3%
Amount over $25 million[b]	12
Nonpersonal Time Deposits	
Maturities less than 2½ years	3
Maturities of 2½ years or more	0
Personal Time Deposits	
Nontransferable	0
Transferable	
Maturities less than 2½ years	3
Maturities of 2½ years or more	0
Eurodollar Liabilities	3

[a]These accounts include demand deposits, NOW accounts, automatic transfer accounts, share draft accounts, and accounts subject to telephone or pre-authorized transfers.

[b]The Federal Reserve Board may vary this percentage from 8 to 14 percent.

Purpose of   Bank reserves serve three purposes. The primary role is
Reserve Requirements   to enable the Federal Reserve to control the supply of
                                                  money. Raising the requirement from 12 to 14 percent,
for example, decreases the banking system's loanable funds; decreasing the requirement increases the system's lending capacity. It is argued that reserve requirements
also act as a tax on banks. Bank reserves on deposit with the Fed are non-interest
bearing but the funds earn interest for the Fed. Not surprisingly, Federal Reserve
Banks are very profitable institutions. Their profits however, are remitted to the
U. S. Treasury which usually needs all the help it can get. The third purpose of
reserves is to play a minor role in the liquidity management of a bank. The term
"reserves" implies a hoard of funds kept aside to meet contingencies, but only a
small portion of legally required reserves may be viewed this way. For example,
assuming a demand deposit withdrawal of $1 million and reserve requirements of
12 percent, a release of the related reserves would cover only $120,000 of the
outflow. The balance must come from other sources.

Managing the Reserve Position

In September 1982, the Federal Reserve Board made a major change in the procedure for managing the reserve position of many banks and other depository
institutions. Beginning February 2, 1984, banks and other depository institutions
with total deposits of $15 million or more must use the *contemporaneous reserve
accounting* system for transaction accounts. This change was a departure from the
so-called *lagged reserve accounting* system. Under the lagged system used by most
banks, the one-week period beginning every Thursday and ending the following
Wednesday was the *reserve computation period*. The seven-day average of reservable
liabilities during this period was the base for calculating the daily average of the
legal reserves to be held during the one-week *reserve maintenance period* beginning
two weeks hence. In other words, there was a two-week lag between the ends of
the *reserve computation period* and the *reserve maintenance period*. For example,
assume that for the one-week *reserve calculation period* beginning Thursday, June
1 and ending Wednesday, June 7, reservable deposits were such that a bank's average daily required reserves were $4.8 million. If the bank's vault cash averaged
$600,000, the average daily balance the bank had to maintain at the Federal Re-
serve during the one-week *reserve maintenance period* beginning June 15 and ending June 21 would be $4.2 million.

The advantage of the lagged system was that the manager of the money position
knew the average required reserves with certainty. What the manager did *not*
know was the amount of funds that would be available on a day-to-day basis during the reserve maintenance week to meet the requirement. The reserve position
had to be watched closely and last minute adjustments made to bring the average
reserves in line with the requirements.

Prior to initiating the new procedure, the lagged system described above was
used by most banks. However, banks with total deposits of less than $15 million
reported deposits and maintained reserves on a quarterly basis rather than weekly.
Under the new regulations, these banks have the option to continue using the lagged

system on a quarterly basis or switching to the new *contemporaneous reserve accounting* system required of all banks with deposits of $15 million or more.

The *contemporaneous reserve accounting* system differs from the lagged system in two respects. The reserve computation period and the reserve maintenance periods were increased from one week to two weeks. Thus, the average daily required reserves and the actual reserves represent 14-day averages. (The required and actual reserves may also be viewed as 14-day totals rather than daily averages.) The most significant change however, is that the lag between the ends of the computation and maintenance periods is only two days rather than two weeks. The nature of this approach is shown in Figure 1.

Under the contemporaneous approach banks have only two days to determine their final deposit balances, compute the required reserves, and make final adjustments in the bank's actual reserve position. In light of the size, volume, and uncertainty of day-to-day flows into and out of the reserve account, this is no simple task for most banks.

It is important to note that the contemporaneous reserve accounting system applies only to transaction-type accounts. These include demand deposits, NOW accounts, and automatic transfer accounts. Reserve computations based on savings deposits, time deposits, Eurodollar liabilities (borrowings by domestic banks from foreign branches), and vault cash continue to be on a lagged basis. (Vault cash is used to satisfy a portion of the requirements.) The two-week computation period for these accounts ends seventeen days before the two-week maintenance period. Since this provides ample time to determine deposit balances and reserve requirements are small relative to those required on transaction accounts, most reserve management problems relate to transaction accounts.

Reserve Strategy[2]   Since a penalty is imposed on reserve deficiencies and interest income is lost on excess reserves, it is important the actual reserve position be as close as possible to the required reserves or *reserve target*. This requires that some degree of flexibility be built into the reserve procedures and the resulting management strategies. Some flexibility stems from the fact that reserves are based on a two-week daily average. Thus banks do not have to meet the reserve requirements each day. A shortage early in the reserve computation period can be offset by an excess later in the period, and vice-versa.

[2] In the remainder of this section it is assumed that *contemporaneous reserve accounting* is used.

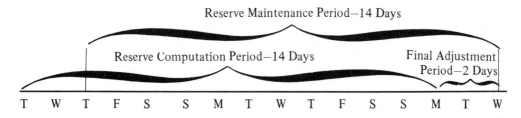

Figure 1 Contemporaneous Reserve Accounting System for Transaction Accounts

Recognizing the difficulty of hitting the reserve target because of the uncertainty of daily flows and the short two-day adjustment period for transaction accounts, the regulations provide flexibility in the form of a *carry-over* provision. This feature plays a key role in determining the reserve target.

The carry-over provision enables a bank to carry a reserve deficiency or excess reserves forward to the next reserve period. Under the new rules the amount of the carry-over is limited to the greater of (a) $25,000 or (b) 2 percent of the reserves required during the current reserve maintenance period before any adjustments for earlier carryovers.[3] This means that a bank which has excess reserves during its maintenance period is permitted to incur a reserve deficit the following period subject to the carryover limitation. If a reserve deficiency is carried forward, the bank must hold excess reserves that are at least equal to the deficiency. During the carry-over period, if more reserves were held than necessary to cover the deficiency, the additional excess could be carried-over to the next period, the amount being subject to the 2 percent limit. The nature of the carry-over provision is demonstrated in the following example.[4]

> *Example.* Suppose a bank's average daily required reserves for the current reserve period are $6.5 million. The maximum daily average carry-over the bank would be allowed is 2 percent of $6.5 million or $130,000. Assume further that the bank has a zero carry-over from the previous period and that it experiences an actual reserve excess averaging $110,000 daily in the current reserve period. The bank would then have a carry-over excess of $110,000 to the following reserve period.
>
> During the next reserve period, three possibilities exist. First, the bank could have a reserve deficiency precisely equal to $110,000. Under this possibility, full use would have been made of the carry-over from the previous period and the carry-forward to the next period would be zero.
>
> Second, the bank could realize a reserve deficiency of less than $110,000 or even have excess reserves. In this event, the bank would not have fully utilized its carry-over allowance. If the bank had a reserve deficiency of less than $110,000, no carry-over would be allowed to the following period since reserves cannot be carried forward more than one period. If the bank had excess reserves, the carry-over would be limited to the size of the excess, provided it did not exceed the 2 percent maximum allowable carry-over.
>
> Third, if the bank experienced a reserve deficiency in excess of $110,000, the bank could, within the 2 percent limit, establish a deficit carry-over to the next period. Full use would have been made of the $110,000 carry-over excess and the bank should offset the additional deficiency in the following reserve period. Thus, a bank entering a reserve maintenance period with an excess carry-over would obtain full use of all reserves by establishing a deficit carry-forward to the following period.

From a strategy standpoint, *the maximum benefit from the carry-over provision is obtained when reserve excesses and deficiencies are alternated from one reserve period to the next and the carry-over amounts are kept within the allowable 2*

---

[3] For simplicity, the remainder of the discussion focuses only on the 2 percent carry-over limitation. Also during the first six months in which the new contemporaneous procedure is used, the percentage carry-over is 3 percent. During the next six months the limit is 2.5 percent, and after one year the limit is 2 percent as indicated in the text.

[4] This example is adapted from: Robert E. Knight, "Guidelines for Efficient Reserve Management," *Monthly Review*, Federal Reserve Bank of Kansas City, November 1977, p. 14.

percent range. If a bank had excess reserves for two consecutive periods, this means that the first period's excess was unused and interest income was foregone. Two consecutive periods of reserve deficiencies would result in a penalty on the first period's deficiency and on any part of the second period's deficiency that was not offset in the following reserve period.

Reserve Target   Managing the reserve position of a bank requires contin-
uous adjustments. To ensure that money managers are zeroed-in on this target, most banks establish a *target range.* The boundaries of this range depend on the bank's carry-over position. When there is a *carry-over deficiency* from the previous period, the *lower boundary* is the sum of the required reserves for the current period plus the amount needed to offset the reserve deficiency. A smaller amount would subject the bank to a penalty because the carry-over deficiency was not offset with an equal amount of excess reserves. The *upper boundary* is such that reserves should exceed the minimum level by not more than 2 percent of the current period's requirement. Reserves in excess of this level would result in an opportunity cost since these funds earn no interest and may not be carried forward to the next period because of the one-period carry-over limitation.

When there is a *carry-over excess,* the boundaries of the reserve target range change. The upper boundary is the amount that would result in the complete utilization of the carry-over excess. Additional balances would not be utilized. The *lower boundary* would be an amount that is less than the maximum level by 2 percent of the required reserves. A smaller reserve position would mean that there was a deficiency in excess of the carry-over amount. Some examples will clarify the nature of reserve targets.[5]

> *Example.* Suppose a bank's total reserves required for the current period are $5,000,000, that its vault cash was $500,000, and that it has a reserve *carry-over deficiency* from the previous period of $60,000. The *lower limit* of reserves the bank could carry at the Federal Reserve without incurring a reserve deficiency would be $5,000,000 − 500,000 + 60,000 = $4,560,000. A reserve balance of this amount would meet the requirement for the current period and would make up the deficiency of the previous period.
>
> The bank would have a maximum carry-forward allowance to the next period of 2 percent of $5,000,000 or $100,000. The *upper limit* of the target range, therefore, would be $4,560,000 + $100,000 = $4,660,000. Any larger amount would mean that the bank had held more in excess reserves than could be carried forward to the next period.
>
> *Example.* Instead of a deficiency, assume the bank in the previous example has an *excess carry-over* of $60,000. All other figures remain the same. In this case, the *upper limit* of the target range is $5,000,000 − 500,000 − 60,000 = $4,440,000. The *lower limit* of this range is $4,440,000 − 100,000 = $4,340,000.

Because the reserve computation period and the reserve maintenance period overlap by twelve days, the establishment of a reserve target is tentative until the

---

[5] The examples are adapted from: Robert E. Knight, "Guidelines for Efficient Reserve Management," *Monthly Review,* Federal Reserve Bank of Kansas City, November 1977, p. 18.

exact reserve requirement is known at the end of the reserve computation period. If the daily reserve position within a maintenance period is such that it is too high relative to the reserve target range, reserves can be reduced by selling federal funds, purchasing securities outright, or the purchase of securities through repurchase agreements. Rapid adjustments are possible because fed funds and repo transactions involve *immediately available funds*. Similarly, if the reserve position is too low, reserves may be obtained through the purchase of federal funds, the outright sale of securities, the sale of securities through a repo, or borrowing at the Federal Reserve discount window.

When a bank keeps its actual reserves within the appropriate target range and alternates its carry-over excesses and deficiencies, the bank will be able to count all its reserves toward reserve requirements. The bank is then in a *zero net reserve position*. Banks that have not made full use of their reserves are in a *non-zero net reserve position*. This could arise if a bank had an excess or deficiency carry-over for two consecutive periods or the bank failed to utilize an excess carry-over from a preceding period.

Reserve Management Problems

Late Adjustments   Despite the flexibility built into the reserving procedures, problems arise. One of these problems usually surfaces on Wednesday, the last day of the settlement week. Since reserve positions must be settled that day, efficient reserve management requires that reserve positions be brought into each banks' target range. Thus, banks with reserve positions outside their target range *must* buy or sell funds regardless of the cost or return in order to avoid penalties or loss of interest. As a result of these last-day adjustments, conditions in the fed funds market on Wednesday are sometimes chaotic and swings of several hundred basis points in the fed funds rate are not uncommon. As Wednesday wears on the situation can become even more hectic for large money center banks where last-minute inflows or outflows can exceed a bank's entire reserve position. For example, assume that at 4:45 P. M. a bank's reserve position is within its target range. A large *Fedwire* outflow suddenly reduces the bank's account at the Fed. If the bank does nothing, a reserve deficiency may result if the outflow is not offset by later inflows. Alternatively, the bank may buy funds immediately in the fed funds market, only to find that large inflows arrived later but before the close of the *Fedwire* at 6:30 P. M. The bank is then in the position of having to sell fed funds in the final minutes of the reserve period. At this time, the reserve positions of most other banks are settled and there is little incentive for any banks to borrow additional overnight funds. If the funds can be sold at all, the rate may be substantially lower, perhaps by as much as several hundred basis points, than the cost at which the funds were acquired only minutes before. If funds have to be acquired very late in the day, the cost of overnight funds may be far higher than the rate at which funds could have been acquired earlier in the day.

A similar problem can arise on Friday. Many banks are closed on Saturday and Sunday so their reserve balances on these days are the same as the closing balance on Friday. A sizable late-in-the-day inflow on Friday can create a reserve excess that reduces the bank's flexibility in the management of its reserve account during the remaining working days of the maintenance period. When the following Monday is a holiday and the bank is closed, the problem is even more serious as the following example shows.

> *Example.*   For the first eight days of a reserve computation period, Thursday through Thursday, a large money center bank has daily average reserves of $400 million. This was also the bank's closing balance on Thursday and the bank's tentative reserve target. On Friday, the day before a three-day holiday weekend, the bank's reserve balance was about $400 million throughout the day and there was no indication that the closing balance would be far from this level. Then, just before the close of the *Fedwire*, inflows of $250 million increased the reserve balance to $650 million. If this excess is unsold because of the late timing, the bank's actual reserve position would average $400 million for eight days, and $650 million for four days (Friday through the Monday holiday). This is a 12-day average of $483.3 million. Now assume the late inflows were reversed on Tuesday, but had the effect of increasing the bank's reserve requirements to a daily average of $409 million for the 14-day maintenance period. To achieve this 14-day average, the bank would have to carry a *negative* reserve position of $37 million for Tuesday and Wednesday, the last two days of the maintenance period. In other words, the bank would have to overdraw its Federal Reserve account. In the event of such an overdraft, a monetary penalty in the form of interest at an above-market rate is imposed. The bank must make up the overdraft the next day. In effect, the bank would be paying interest on funds that may not be used to meet reserve requirements. Unless the excess reserves can be sold, the bank's flexibility in managing its reserve account is reduced and added costs are incurred.
>
> In this situation a problem might still exist if Monday were a business day and the $250 million inflow was reversed. Since the entire inflow was held for three days, the actual average daily reserves would be inflated. To reduce the 14-day average and avoid excess reserves, it may be necessary to carry extremely low balances in the reserve account for the last three days of the maintenance period. However, the volume of flows through the bank may make it difficult to maintain such a low balance and avoid costly overdrafts.

As this example illustrates, the timing and magnitude of flows through a large bank can be such that corrective action in the management of reserves is difficult, costly, and sometimes impossible. A similar problem can arise when the transfer of funds is prevented by a malfunctioning computer on the part of the sending or receiving bank. These problems and complications arise even when the reserve position is closely monitored and well-managed on a day-to-day basis.

Trading Blocks   In contrast to money center banks, smaller banks are not usually subject to large unexpected inflows and outflows. Thus, adjusting the reserve position of smaller banks is generally an easier task. One problem that is unique to small banks relates to the size of reserve adjustments that must be made. Assume that a small bank has excess reserves of $40,000, $60,000, $50,000 and $50,000 for the period Thursday through Monday. On Thursday and Friday, the bank could attempt to sell its excess reserves in the fed funds market through its upstream correspondent. Such small amounts may be difficult to sell and the rate offered may be lower to reflect the small block size. An alternative is to offset the excess by selling $200,000 in overnight fed funds on Monday. Another approach would be to sell $100,000 on Monday for two days. Similarly, the purchase of fed funds is facilitated when larger trading blocks are involved. Thus, by letting small excesses or deficiencies accumulate, the maneuverability of smaller banks is improved.

The Discount Window   The discount window provides short-term "adjustment credit" that may be used to meet reserve requirements. Although the below-market interest rate is favorable, window borrowings should be viewed as a last resort and not as a substitute for regular sources of overnight or other short-term funds. Excessive use of the window to meet recurring reserve deficiencies may be viewed by the Fed as a sign of mismanagement. Just what constitutes "excessive use" depends on the size, term, and frequency of borrowings as well as certain characteristics of the bank. Large banks with access to the money market are expected to make money position adjustments faster than smaller banks and with funds provided by the money market. Thus, adjustment credit is usually extended only on an overnight basis to large banks whereas smaller institutions may borrow for longer periods.

In order to discourage continuous use of the window, a surcharge in the form of a higher interest rate is imposed on frequent borrowers. At the extreme, borrowing privileges may be withdrawn. Thus, the window should be used with considerable discretion.

Non-Compliance   If a bank has a reserve deficiency in excess of the 2 percent limitation discussed earlier, a penalty is assessed on the deficiency. The penalty is a rate that is two percentage points above the Federal Reserve discount rate. However, persistent reserve deficiencies raise the possibility of serious regulatory action. If a state chartered member bank has persistent deficiencies, the Federal Reserve may suspend membership privileges. In the case of national banks, all of which are members of the Federal Reserve System, the Fed could direct the Comptroller of the Currency to begin legal action to remove the bank's charter. In light of these sanctions, a modest degree of pressure by the Fed is usually sufficient to induce more effective reserve management.

OTHER ASPECTS OF MANAGING OVERNIGHT FUNDS

When a bank has excess overnight funds or needs such funds to meet reserve requirements or other cash needs, several options exist. As pointed out earlier, these include the outright purchase or sale of securities, the purchase or sale of fed funds, or the purchase or sale of securities under a repo agreement. The return on or cost of funds under these options can vary widely depending on the circumstances under which they are used. Thus, each alternative must be evaluated by the money position manager. In this section, a framework for analyzing the cost or returns of overnight funds is presented along with borrowing and lending limits.

Cost of Overnight Funds

The necessity of making adjustments in the money position coupled with the very short maturity of overnight funds transactions results in a volatile interest rate. For those banks that are net purchasers of such funds, this means that the cost of continuous overnight positions is highly uncertain. Similarly, the returns to net sellers of funds can vary widely from day to day. Fed funds transactions are usually unsecured so the fed funds rate is ordinarily higher than the repo rate. The spread varies with market conditions but a spread of 25 to 50 basis points is common. Occasionally market distortions result in a higher repo rate. Fed funds rates are quoted in the daily financial press.

The dollar cost or return on overnight funds is given by the model

$$I = Ar(n/360) \qquad\qquad [1]$$

where I = interest cost or return in dollars
A = amount of funds
r = quoted fed funds or repo rate (quoted in 1/16ths)
n = number of days to maturity.

If a bank needed $500,000 in fed funds for one day and the fed funds rate was 12.50 percent, the dollar cost from equation [1] would be

$$I = \$500,000 \, (.1250)(1/360)$$
$$= \$173.61.$$

When evaluating the cost or return on overnight funds in terms of the rate, the money position manager should be aware of subtle but important yield effects. Like other money market instruments, the quoted or nominal rate r in equation [1] is in terms of a 360-day year. To reflect a 365-day year, the nominal rate is multiplied by the factor 365/360. The model is

$$r^* = r(365/360) \qquad\qquad [2]$$

where r^* is the adjusted nominal rate. In the example above, this adjustment adds 17 basis points to the cost or return. That is, 12.50 percent $\times$ (365/360) = 12.6736 percent.

Another yield effect relates to the fact that most overnight funds transactions are for only one day. Thus, if interest is assumed to be compounded daily, the *effective rate* on the funds, denoted i, is given by the model

$$i = \left(1 + \frac{r^*}{365}\right)^{365} - 1 \qquad\qquad [3]$$

where r^* is the *adjusted nominal rate*. In the example above, the effective rate is

$$i = \left(1 + \frac{.126736}{365}\right)^{365} - 1$$
$$= 1.13509 - 1$$
$$= .13509 \text{ or } 13.51\%.$$

Because of weekends and the fact that some fed funds and repo transactions are for extended periods of several days or even weeks, the daily compounding assumption slightly overstates the effective rate.[6] Nonetheless, the rate computed on this basis is a more accurate measure of the cost than the quoted rate. Note that in the example above the effective rate is 101 basis points higher than the quoted rate. At higher levels of interest rates, the discrepancy is greater. As an asset a net funds sold position represents one of the ways a bank can improve its return through daily—or "almost daily"— compounding. On the liability side, banks evaluate their cost of funds in terms of a 365-day year and the effective yield. A continuous net funds purchased position should be evaluated in the same manner. The importance of the discrepancy between the quoted rate and the effective rate depends on the magnitude of the bank's net overnight funds position. It may be a factor in analyzing alternative short-term investments or alternative sources of funds.

Turnaround Cost

When securities are sold outright to obtain funds when managing the money position, short-term Treasury bills are usually the instruments involved. Treasury bills have excellent marketability and low transactions costs. However, when funds are needed for short periods ranging from one to four or five days, a fed funds or repo transaction is usually arranged rather than the outright sale of securities. The outright sale of securities and repurchase one to several days later can result in a prohibitively high *turnaround cost*. This is the cost of selling securities to a dealer at a "bid" price which is lower than the "asking" price at which the securities are repurchased. The difference between these prices is measured in terms of the *spread* between the corresponding yields. For example, 85-day bills may be quoted "10.31 bid—10.25 ask" for a spread of 6 basis points. (In terms of dollars, the "bid" price is lower than the "ask" price.) This is a typical spread for Treasury bills in the three-month maturity range. The spread tends to increase for shorter term bills. A bill maturing in 30 days might have a bid-ask spread of 10 to 15 basis points, while a 15-day bill usually has a slightly higher spread.[7] The spreads vary depending on market conditions.

Assuming a 360-day interest accrual basis, as is common in the money market, the annualized *turnaround cost* related to the outright sale and repurchase of securities is given by the model

$$TC = \frac{sn}{d}$$

where TC = annualized turnaround cost (in decimal form)
      s = spread between bid and ask yields in decimal form (e. g., 8 basis points = .0008 in decimal form)
     n = number of days to maturity
    d = number of days the funds are needed.

[6] The expression "term fed funds" is often used to describe a fed funds transaction involving an extended term. Similarly, a "continuous repo" stays in effect until canceled by either party.

[7] The dealer's cost of processing a Treasury bill transaction is the same regardless of the maturity. To cover these costs, the spread must be higher on shorter maturity bills to generate the same dollar spread that results from a longer-term Treasury bill transaction.

Although the spread is important, the turnaround cost is most heavily influenced by the maturity of the instrument (n) and the number of days the funds are needed (d). To see this and how the model is used, consider the following example.

> *Example.*   A bank needs overnight funds for one day. The options open to the money position manager are the outright sale of 85-day Treasury bills or 15-day Treasury bills, the purchase of fed funds, or the purchase of funds through a repo agreement. The 85-day bills are quoted by dealers at "12.28 bid–12.23 offered" for a spread of 5 basis points. The 15-day bills are quoted "11.92 bid–11.78 offered" for a spread of 14 basis points. Using equation [4] the turnaround costs, TC, for the Treasury bill transactions are as follows:
>
> 1. The 85-day Treasury bill
>
> $$TC = \frac{(.0005)(85)}{1}$$
>
> $$= .0425 \text{ or } 4.25\%$$
>
> 2. The 15-day Treasury bill
>
> $$TC = \frac{(.0014)(15)}{1}$$
>
> $$= .021 \text{ or } 2.1\%.$$

These turnaround costs are in addition to the loss of interest for one day on the Treasury bills. Using the bid price to calculate this loss, the total cost of overnight funds generated by the sale the 85-day bill would be 12.28% + 4.25% = 16.53%. The total cost related to the sale of 15-day bills is 11.92% + 2.10 = 14.02%. Clearly, this alternative is preferable to the sale of the longer-term bills. If the fed funds rate or repo rate is lower than 14.02 percent, then one of these alternatives may be preferred.

If a bank needs overnight funds for five or six days, the turnaround cost is reduced because it is spread over a longer period. For example, when d = 6, the turnaround costs are .71 percent and .35 percent for the two alternatives.[8]

This example demonstrates that in addition to considering the bid-ask spread, the turnaround cost can be minimized by: (1) limiting the outright sale of securities to those issues with very short maturities, or (2) selling securities only when the funds are needed for extended periods. Otherwise, the turnaround cost is such that fed funds and repos usually represent lower cost sources of funds. Furthermore, last minute changes in the money position may occur late in the day when the securities markets are closed. Thus, the money position manager may have no choice but to obtain funds via repos or fed funds.

Repos vs. Fed Funds

Since a fed funds transaction is usually an unsecured loan and a repo is secured by the underlying securities, there is more paperwork associated with the repo.

---

[8] It is assumed that interest rates do not change between the time of the sale and repurchase of the securities and that the spread remains constant as the maturity shortens.

Despite the additional paperwork, it is advantageous for a bank to acquire most of its purchased funds through repos. The reason is that the interest rate on repos is usually lower than the fed funds rate. The spread between the two rates will vary depending on market conditions, but as pointed out earlier, a spread of 25 to 50 basis points is not unusual.

In order to see the effects of proper funds management, consider the purchased funds position of HNB as shown earlier in Table 1. Since the bank has sold $15 million in fed funds and purchased $5 million in fed funds, its net position is $10 million in fed funds sold. Assuming the rate on these funds is 12 percent, the annualized earnings on this net position would be $1.2 million. The repo position shows $5 million in funds sold and $15 million in funds purchased for a net purchased position of $10 million. Assuming the rate on these funds is 11.50 percent, the annualized cost of this net position is $1.15 million. Thus, by acquiring most of its purchased funds via lower cost repos, the bank earns a spread worth $50,000 on annualized basis even though its net purchased funds position is zero.[9] Since most banks prefer to sell funds in the fed funds market rather than via repos, it may be necessary for the money manager to develop working relationships with the cash managers of non-financial corporations in order to obtain a sufficient volume of the lower-cost repo funds.

Borrowing Limits

The ability of an individual bank to borrow sizable amounts in the overnight funds market is constrained by several factors. Since fed funds transactions represent unsecured loans, borrowing banks must be well-managed and in a strong financial position. A record of consistent profitability, tight controls, adequate capital, a quality loan portfolio, and liquidity are some of the key factors that indicate a bank's financial strength and the quality of its management. Although repos are secured transactions, providers of funds under this alternative are equally concerned about the strength of the borrowing bank. When determining the overnight borrowing capacity of an individual bank, fed funds and repo borrowings are viewed collectively rather than as separate categories.

Assuming a bank is financially strong and well-managed, the question arises— how much can a bank borrow in the overnight funds market? A commonly used constraint on such borrowings is 50 percent of equity capital. That is,

$$\frac{\text{Net fed funds purchased} + \text{Net repo borrowings}}{\text{Equity Capital}} \leqslant 50\%$$

The financial statement of the Hypothetical National Bank shown in Table 1

[9] No special significance should be attributed to HNB's net purchased funds position of zero. The fact that HNB is simultaneously buying and selling funds simply reflects its activities as a funds dealer or a conduit for its smaller correspondent banks. In practice, large banks tend to show a net funds purchased position while small banks tend to be net sellers of overnight funds. To the extent that HNB's overnight funds position is affected by its role as a dealer or conduit for downstream correspondent banks, the overall spread on its overnight funds position would be slightly higher. Rather than buying and selling fed funds at 12 percent as cited in the example, the bank might sell fed funds at 12 percent and buy some of its fed funds from correspondents at 11 15/16 percent. A similar spread of 1/16 of 1 percent might be earned on a portion of the bank's repo position.

indicates an equity position of $60 million. The bank's limit on net overnight borrowed funds is 50 percent of this base, or $30 million. Since the bank's *Funds Sold* position of $20 million is offset by a *Funds Purchased* position of $20 million, the net position is zero. Thus, the bank's additional borrowing capacity as of the statement date is the full $30 million.

When the overnight funds position shows net borrowings in excess of 50 percent of equity capital on a *continuous* basis, the bank may encounter resistance in the money market because of its excessive reliance on a volatile source of funds.[10] A high net borrowed position means that the bank has reduced liquidity by exhausting its overnight borrowing capacity. In order to maintain such a position without eroding the market's confidence, the bank should increase the liquidity of its assets by shortening the maturity structure of its investment portfolio and possibly increasing its emphasis on marketable loans.

Because of their extreme need for market acceptance in the overnight market, money managers must resort to other sources of funds as market limits are reached. The discount window may be used only sparingly so the money manager must consider the sale of securities from the investment portfolio to reduce the amount of purchased funds and restore liquidity to the money position.

Lending Limits

The sale of overnight funds constitutes a loan and should be viewed accordingly. As indicated above, the creditworthiness of the borrowing institution is of paramount importance, especially since fed funds are unsecured transactions. At the first sign of financial trouble on the part of a borrower, a lending bank should minimize its exposure by reducing the size of its commitment, requiring collateral for fed funds, placing more emphasis on repos, or some combination of these. To achieve diversification most banks limit the amount of overnight funds they will sell to a single bank. This limit is usually 10 percent of the selling bank's capital. In the case of HNB, such a constraint would limit the sale of overnight funds to $6 million for a single borrower. This is not a troublesome constraint in most banks.

CONCLUSION

This chapter addressed the nature of the management process underlying one of the most obscure aspects of banking—the *money position*. This term refers to a bank's position at a point in time with respect to its legally required reserves and day-to-day cash position. The management task is complicated by the volume, magnitude, and uncertainty of the daily flow of payments through a typical bank.

---

[10] The question might arise—how do market participants know when a bank is relying too heavily on overnight funds? Money position managers monitor periodic financial statements of banks. To prevent the possibility of "window dressing" for statement purposes, financial statements are often based on daily averages for all the accounts. Thus, excessive reliance on purchased funds shows up where it is most visible—in the numbers.

Contributing to this management problem is the fact that longer-term liquidity stresses resulting from changing economic conditions and changes in monetary policy are first felt in the money position of a bank. Thus, the money position is the bank's first line of defense when coping with a volatile financial environment. The importance of this activity in a commercial bank or other types of depository institutions cannot be over-emphasized.

Managing the money position should not be viewed as an isolated activity that is unrelated to other aspects of banking. It is an integral part of the overall funds management process. In most banks, the money position is managed jointly with the investment portfolio. The investment portfolio provides backup liquidity for short- and intermediate-term needs and serves as a temporary and longer-term haven for funds. Although there are functional and operational differences in the management of the money position and investments, their overlap and interaction requires an integration of management activities.

REFERENCES

Bowsher, Norman N., "Repurchase Agreements," *Review*, Federal Reserve Bank of St. Louis, September 1979, p. 17-22.

Knight, Robert E., "Guidelines for Efficient Reserve Management," *Monthly Review*, Federal Reserve Bank of Kansas City, November 1977, p. 11-23.

Lucas, Charles M., Marcos T. Jones and Thom B. Thurston, "Federal Funds and Repurchase Agreements," *Quarterly Review*, Federal Reserve Bank of New York, Summer 1977, p. 33-48.

Maerowitz, Seth P., "The Market for Federal Funds," *Economic Review*, Federal Reserve Bank of Richmond, July/August 1981, p. 3-7.

Morgan Guaranty Trust Company of New York, "Life at a Bank's Money Desk," *The Morgan Guaranty Survey*, November 1981, p. 11-15.

D. INVESTMENTS

15

Treasury Bills and Federal Agency Money Market Instruments

Treasury bills are the most well-known and popular of all the money market instruments. The investment characteristics of T-bills are such that this instrument is a benchmark against which the characteristics and yields of other debt securities are evaluated. Certain short-term securities issued by federal agencies have investment characteristics that are very similar to those of T-bills. Because of this similarity, investors, especially financial institutions, view these instruments as interchangeable and ready substitutes for each other.

Both T-bills and short-term agency securities have several important functions in banks and other depository institutions. One of these functions is to help satisfy safety and legal requirements. When evaluating the financial soundness of banks, for example, examiners focus on their liquidity. This is the ability to convert assets to cash on very short notice with little risk of loss. Because they have this feature, T-bills and agency securities are an institution's primary base of liquid assets. The federal government and most states have so-called "pledging requirements." Securities must be pledged as collateral for deposits involving public funds. T-bills and agency securities are acceptable securities for this purpose. They may also be used as collateral for Federal Reserve borrowings by depository institutions.

These instruments are also used as an investment base for the money market accounts offered by most depository institutions. This account, which was authorized by the *Depository Institutions Act of 1982*, enables banks and thrift institutions (S&Ls, credit unions, and savings banks) to compete directly with money market funds. The rate paid on these insured accounts is linked to interest rates in the money market. Most of the funds underlying this type of account are, or should be, invested in short-term, rate sensitive assets such as T-bills and agency securities. Earnings, less a management fee, should be passed through to the account holders. In effect, the bank or other depository institution is operating like a money market fund manager.

Treasury bills and agency securities, along with other money market instruments, are also used in the asset-liability management process. This is the joint or simultaneous management of assets and liabilities for the purpose of controlling interest rate risk. This risk arises when there is an imbalance between the interest-rate sensitivity of assets and liabilities. For example, if a bank funds long-term, fixed-rate assets with short-term, interest-rate sensitive liabilities, a common practice in depository institutions, the cost of liabilities would increase faster than the return generated by assets when interest rates increase. This could result in lower profit margins, operating losses, or even the financial collapse of the bank. This risk can be reduced by realigning the assets and liabilities to match more closely their interest-rate sensitivity. This is easier said than done because most borrowers have a strong preference for longer term, fixed-rate loans while depositors prefer shorter maturities. Hence, a structural imbalance exists in most depository institutions. A partial solution to the problem, and one that does not require a realignment of the asset-liability structure, is to keep the bank's investment portfolio invested in money market instruments such as T-bills and agency securities with very short maturities. In this way, interest insensitive assets are offset by a smaller proportion of assets with an extremely high degree of rate sensitivity. The bank's borrowers and depositors are unaffected by the decision.

In the following section, Treasury bills are examined with particular attention focused on their investment characteristics, the auction procedure, and pricing. This is followed by a section covering federal agency money market instruments.

TREASURY BILLS

Investment Characteristics of T-Bills

Treasury bills have four important investment characteristics that affect the investment decision-making process of financial institutions. These characteristics—the lack of default risk, favorable tax status, liquidity, and a low minimum denomination—distinguish T-bills from other money market instruments.

Lack of Default Risk   Since T-bills are direct obligations of the U. S. Treasury, they are riskless with respect to default. Because they lack default risk, T-bills almost always sell at the lowest yield of any money market instrument for a given maturity. The T-bill yield represents a "pure" interest rate and is the base to which a risk premium is added for risky investment. The riskless nature of T-bills allows the instruments to be held without limit in banks and other depository institutions. They may also be pledged to secure federal, state, and local deposits.

Favorable Tax Status   The interest income earned on T-bills is exempt from state and local income taxes. This feature is important in states with a high income tax rate. For a given state tax rate, t, and ignoring any difference in default risk, the relationship between a Treasury bill yield r_{TB}

and a commercial paper rate r_{CP}, that leaves an investor indifferent between the two rates is given by the model

$$r_{TB} = r_{CP}(1 - t),$$

or

$$r_{CP} = r_{TB}/(1 - t).$$

Assuming a marginal state tax rate of 6 percent and a Treasury bill rate of 8 percent, the corresponding commercial paper yield at which the investor would be indifferent is

$$r_{CP} = .08/(1 - .06)$$

$$= .0851 \text{ or } 8.51\%.$$

Ignoring other factors, the exemption from state taxes is worth 51 basis points in this example.[1] If interest rates were considerably higher such that the T-bill rate was 15 percent, the spread would increase to 96 basis points.

The exemption from state and local income taxes is important only to investors subject to the tax. In many states, commercial banks are subject to either an excise tax or a franchise tax that has the effect of taxing interest income from Treasury bills.

Liquidity   The term *liquidity* refers to the ability to convert an asset to cash quickly and with a minimum risk of loss. To be liquid, a security must have three characteristics. First, the instrument must have a low degree of price risk resulting from changes in interest rates. T-bills have this trait because of their short maturities. Second, the instrument must be readily marketable.[2] Since the T-bill market is well organized and efficient, very large transactions can be absorbed without distorting the price. This characteristic, marketability, must be accompanied by the third characteristic, low transaction costs. This is reflected by the narrow spreads between the bid-ask prices. The narrow spreads are a result of intense competition among dealers in the Treasury bill market.

The liquidity of T-bills is enhanced by so-called *book-entry* accounting. Rather than issuing cumbersome paper certificates to investors, ownership of T-bills is simply recorded on computer tapes that are maintained by the Federal Reserve Bank. This procedure reduces transactions costs and facilitates the transfer of ownership. Several other money market instruments including agency securities, also use this efficient procedure.

Small Denomination   The minimum denomination in which T-bills may be purchased is $10,000 and increments of $5,000 over this amount. This is well below the minimum denomination of other money market

---

[1] There are 100 basis points in one percentage point.

[2] A non-marketable security may be considered liquid if it matures within a very short period.

instruments with the exception of some federal agency issues. Thus, Treasury bills represent one of the few money market instruments available for direct investment by small institutions or individuals. The minimum denomination of other instruments like commercial paper or certificates of deposit is usually $100,000. The minimum denomination should not be confused with the "round-lot" which is the usual trading block. The round lot for T-bills and most other instruments is $1 million. Usually, the maximum yield is obtained by buyers of round lots.

The Treasury Bill Auction

New offerings of 91- and 182-day Treasury bills are announced each Tuesday with an auction held on the following Monday. Bills maturing in 360 days are auctioned on the fourth Thursday of each month. Bids may be made on a *competitive* or *non-competitive* basis. When a competitive bid is made, a subscriber indicates the amount and price of the bills willing to be purchased. These bids are usually submitted by dealers and large financial institutions that are very active in the market. Typically, about 85 percent of an offering is sold on a competitive basis. Treasury rules limit the amount of a single bidder's purchase to less than 35 percent of the bills offered for sale.

When making a non-competitive bid, the investor indicates the amount of bills desired, subject to a Treasury limit of $1 million, and agrees to purchase the bills at the average price of the accepted competitive bids. By bidding on a non-competitive basis, investors avoid the risk of paying a high price or the risk of not getting any T-bills because of a low bid. The limit of $1 million prevents large-scale investors from dominating the non-competitive bidding process. Thus, small-scale investors and institutions are assured of being able to participate in the auction.

The significance of the auction extends beyond its use as a means of distributing Treasury securities. The amount of securities auctioned is closely monitored by all sectors of the financial community for clues regarding supply and demand conditions in the financial markets. Auction yields are closely watched as barometers of market yields. These yields are also widely used as indexes for adjustable-rate consumer loans and mortgage loans. The rates that banks and other depository institutions pay on certain types of deposits or accounts are often linked directly or indirectly to the auction yields.

Cash Management Bills

The government's cash inflows tend to be concentrated around the main tax payment dates—March, April, June, September, and December. Outflows are more stable so the sale of Treasury securities must cover the expected, temporary shortfalls. For this purpose, the Treasury will supplement the sale of regular T-bills with an auction of so-called *cash management bills*. These are simply additional amounts of regular T-bills that are already outstanding. The maturity of these bills ranges from a few days to several weeks rather than the standard 91-, 182- or 360-

day maturities. These bills usually mature shortly after one of the five tax payment dates mentioned above.

Discount Pricing

   Treasury bills, like most other money market instruments, are traded and quoted in the market on a *discount yield basis*. Rather than having a contractually stated interest or coupon rate payable to the holder, bills are issued at a discount from the face or par value, the amount due at maturity. This discount is the holder's interest income. In addition, Treasury bills, like *all* other original issue money market instruments, accrue this interest on the basis of a *360-day* year. In contrast, the benchmark *bond-yield equivalent* is based on semi-annual coupon payments with the interest accruing on the basis of a *365-day* year. Thus, *the quoted yields on Treasury bills and all other money market instruments are not directly comparable to the bond-yield equivalent*. Given the discount rate, however, the bond-yield equivalent may be estimated very easily.
   The price of a discounted money market instrument is given by the model

$$P = 1 - \frac{nd}{360} \tag{1}$$

where P = price per dollar of par or face value
       n = number of days to maturity
       d = discount rate.

The Wall Street version of the bond yield r that is equivalent to the discounted yield d is estimated by the model

$$r = \frac{365d}{360 - nd}. \tag{2}$$

Another version of the bond-yield equivalent is given by equation [3] and provides the same result.[3] That is,

$$r = \left[\frac{1 - P}{P}\right]\frac{365}{n}. \tag{3}$$

An example will demonstrate the pricing approach.

   Example.   A 91-day Treasury bill is quoted on a discount basis at 8.76 bid—8.65 asked. This means that dealers are offering to buy these bills at a price to yield 8.76 percent and to sell the bills to yield 8.65 percent. (The higher bid yield relative to the asked yield results in a lower bid price.) Using equation [1], the purchase price of the bill is

$$P = 1 - \frac{(91)(.0865)}{360} = .9781 \text{ or } 97.81 \text{ (\% of par)}.$$

---

[3] Both models for the bond-yield equivalent provide an approximation. A discussion of the problems with these models is in the chapter dealing with financial mathematics. More accurate procedures for finding the bond-yield equivalents are demonstrated in that chapter for both discounted and interest-bearing money market instruments.

Since it is understood that the price of a fixed income security is quoted in terms of percent of par value, the percent sign is not used. Using equation [2], the bond-yield equivalent is

$$r = \frac{365(.0865)}{360 - (91)(.0865)}$$

$$= .0897 \text{ or } 8.97\%.$$

Note that the bond-yield equivalent is 32 basis points higher than the quoted discount rate.

This pricing procedure is used for other discounted money market instruments including most federal agency issues.

FEDERAL AGENCY MONEY MARKET INSTRUMENTS

In 1974, the Federal Financing Bank (FFB) was established as an arm of the U. S. Treasury to consolidate the borrowing activities of over a dozen direct federal agencies. Rather than issuing their own securities on Wall Street, agencies were authorized to borrow from the FFB at a rate 1/8 of 1 percentage point over the Treasury borrowing rate. The FFB borrows its funds from the Treasury at the Treasury's cost. The purpose of this conduit is to lower the cost of agency borrowing and reduce the confusion resulting from a large number of government agencies continually flooding the market with securities. As a result of this consolidation, only a few so-called "sponsored" agencies now issue money market instruments and other securities on a regular basis. In contrast to "direct" agencies, which are arms of the government and whose securities are guaranteed by the government, sponsored agencies are generally owned by the market participants they serve and their securities are guaranteed by the issuing agency. This section focuses on four sponsored agencies that are the primary issuers of agency-related money market instruments.

Primary Issuers

Farm Credit Banks (FCBs)   The system of Farm Credit Banks is made up of 12 Federal Intermediate Credit Banks, 12 Federal Land Banks, 12 Banks for Cooperatives, and one Central Bank for Cooperatives for a total of 37 financial institutions. These federally sponsored institutions provide short-, intermediate-, and long-term credit to farmers, ranchers, commercial fishermen, cooperatives, and other agriculture-related businesses. At one time, each group of banks obtained its funds by borrowing separately in the credit markets. To consolidate this borrowing, eliminate confusion, and reduce costs, the banks now borrow jointly through "consolidated systemwide" issues of discounted notes and bonds backed by the 37 banks. The characteristics of

Table 1   Characteristics of Money Market Instruments Issued by Federally Sponsored Agencies

Issuer	Type of Investment	Maturity or Range	Offering Schedule	Minimum Denomination	Tax Exemption
Farm Credit Banks	Consolidated System Discount Notes	5 to 270 days	Daily	$ 50,000	State & local
	Consolidated System Bonds	6 and 9 months	Monthly	$ 5,000	State & local
Federal Home Loan Banks	Consolidated System Discount Notes	30 to 270 days[a]	Daily	$100,000	State & local
Federal Home Loan Mortgage Corp.	Discount Notes	5 to 360 days[a]	Varies	$ 5,000[b]	No exemption
Federal National Mortgage Assoc.	Discount Notes	30 to 270 days	Daily	$ 5,000[b]	No exemption

[a]Exact maturity specified by the investor.
[b]Minimum purchase is $50,000.

money market instruments issued by the FCBs are shown in Table 1, along with the characteristics of other agency-related instruments. Note that the interest income from some agency issues is tax-exempt whereas in other cases it is not exempt.

Federal Home Loan Banks (FHLBs)

To assist the housing market, 12 regional Federal Home Loan Banks provide credit to mortgage lending institutions. These are savings and loan associations, mutual savings banks, cooperative banks, and homestead associations. Loans to these institutions, or *advances* as they are called, are made to offset deposit outflows, to meet seasonal mortgage loan demand, or to meet day-to-day needs on a short-term basis. The ability to borrow from FHLBs during periods of financial stress enables mortgage lenders to adjust their asset and liability structures in an orderly way and with less disruptive effects on the housing market. The backup liquidity provided by the FHLB coupled with deposit insurance are two key reasons for the public's trust and confidence in thrift institutions.

In performing its function, the FHLB issues several types of securities with a wide range of maturities. The money market instruments are called *Consolidated System Discount Notes* and are offered with maturities ranging from 30 to 270 days at the discretion of the investor. The minimum denomination is $100,000 and the notes are backed by the 12 Federal Home Loan Banks. Like most other agency securities, the notes are actively traded in the secondary market. The interest income is exempt from state and local income taxes.

Federal Home Loan Mortgage Corporation (FHLMC)

The *Federal Home Loan Mortgage Corporation*—often called *Freddie Mac*—purchases mortgage loans from originating institutions whose deposits are insured by an agency of the federal or state governments. These include banks, S&Ls, and mutual savings banks. Although the agency owns the acquired mortgages, the originating institution continues to service the mortgages for a fee. The agency "pools" the acquired mortgages, and after adding its own guarantee, sells interests in the pool to long-term investors.

To finance its activities and facilitate the flow of capital to the mortgage market, Freddie Mac issues securities with various maturities. Its money market instruments are available with maturities ranging from 5 to 360 days and are sold on a discounted basis. The interest income is not tax exempt at the state and local levels.

Federal National
Mortgage Association
(FNMA)

This agency, also known as *Fannie Mae*, is unusual in that it is a government-sponsored agency that is owned entirely by the private sector. Its stock is listed on the New York Stock Exchange. The agency plays an important role in the residential mortgage market by raising capital in the financial markets through the sale of short-term securities and mortgage-backed bonds. The funds are used to purchase mortgage loans from S&Ls, banks, mortgage companies, and life insurance companies, especially during tight credit conditions. The proceeds received by the selling institutions may be recycled into the mortgage loan market. When mortgage money is plentiful, the agency sells mortgage loan portfolios to institutions with excess funds.

Fannie Mae issues securities with maturities ranging from one month to twenty-five years. The agency's money market instruments are discount notes with original maturities of 30 to 270 days at the option of the investor. The minimum purchase is $50,000 and secondary markets provide excellent marketability. These notes, like all Fannie Mae issues, are taxable at the federal, state, and local levels.

Investment Characteristics

The agency securities shown in Table 1 compare very favorably with Treasury bills in their investment characteristics. Although backed by the issuing agency rather than directly by the U. S. Government, the securities are considered virtually riskless. Because of the importance of these agencies in the country's economic and social systems, market participants perceive an implied backing of these securities by the U. S. Government. Because of their high quality, these money market instruments may be held in unlimited amounts by regulated financial institutions.

A number of government securities dealers also make markets for agency securities. Since bid-asked spreads tend to be slightly wider for these securities relative to Treasury bills, their marketability is somewhat less than that of T-bills. Despite this, the marketability of agency issues is considered excellent. Large transactions can be absorbed by the market without affecting the price. Although some agency securities are issued in certificate form, most agency securities are in book-entry form.

CONCLUSION

Since the Treasury bills are a benchmark in the financial markets, it is important for market participants to understand the nature of these instruments. In particular, an understanding of the investment characteristics, auction procedure, and pricing of T-bills is essential. These aspects of the T-bill market and the parallels with certain federal agency securities were highlighted in this chapter.

an understanding of the investment characteristics, auction procedure, and pricing of T-bills is essential. These aspects of the T-bill market and the parallels with certain federal agency securities were highlighted in this chapter.

REFERENCES

Cook, Timothy Q., "Treasury Bills," *Instruments of the Money Market*, 5th ed., edited by Timothy Q. Cook and Bruce J. Summers, Richmond, Virginia: Federal Reserve Bank of Richmond, 1981, pp. 7-19.

Howell, Donna, "Federally Sponsored Credit Agency Securities," *Instruments of the Money Market*, 5th ed., edited by Timothy Q. Cook and Bruce J. Summers, Richmond, Virginia: Federal Reserve Bank of Richmond, 1981, pp. 20-29.

Stigum, Marcia, *The Money Market*, Homewood, Illinois: Dow Jones-Irwin, 1983.

16

Managing the Bank Investment Portfolio

The primary functions of a commercial bank are to act as a depository for its customers' funds and to meet the credit needs of its service area. But deposit flows and loan demand are subject to a high degree of uncertainty with respect to their direction, magnitude, and timing. A commercial bank must have backup sources of liquidity to cope with these uncertain flows if it is to meet its legal and social responsibilities as a depository and a lender. In this chapter, the primary source of this backup liquidity, the investment portfolio, is covered from a decision-making standpoint.

In the following section, the relationship between bank liquidity and the investment portfolio is examined with special emphasis on the *term structure of interest rates*. In subsequent sections, portfolio management policies and concepts are considered in the context of a bank's liquidity needs and conditions in the financial markets. At the end of the chapter, two case studies are provided along with a discussion of an investment policy statement.

BANK LIQUIDITY AND INVESTMENTS

This section explores the relationship between bank liquidity and the investment portfolio of a commercial bank. The investment portfolio has two primary functions. Because of the portfolio size, approximately 25 percent of assets in most small and medium-size banks, it is a major contributor to earnings. Its management has an important impact on profitability. The other function of the portfolio, excluding the trading account, is to provide the bank with liquidity to meet expected or unexpected cash needs. The investment portfolio is the primary element in the liquidity management process.

These two investment functions—generating earnings and providing liquidity—often work at cross purposes with each other and pose a dilemma for bankers. As a result, investment decisions involve an important tradeoff, the nature of which will become clear after examining bank liquidity needs.

Bank Liquidity

One of the most important considerations in managing a bank is the liquidity position. Liquidity refers to the ability of a bank to obtain funds internally and externally to meet immediate or short-term cash needs. Internally generated liquidity is obtained through the conversion of assets to cash with little or no risk of loss and with low transactions costs. Externally generated liquidity refers to the issuance of new liabilities to meet cash needs. The need for liquidity arises from a number of sources whose effects can vary in magnitude. Unexpected outflows resulting from withdrawals must be met on demand and uncertain loan takedowns under revolving credit arrangements, lines of credit, and credit cards must be honored without delay. The cumulative effects of these and other sources of liquidity pressures are felt initially in the bank's money position.

The money position of a bank is subject to considerable day-to-day variation. Although sizable, these variations are often offset by cash flows in the opposite direction. Offsetting flows could occur anywhere from several minutes to several weeks later. But what happens if sizable outflows are not reversed? Suppose that a stable interest rate environment is followed by a period of rapid economic expansion. Such expansion is usually followed by strong loan demand and this in turn drives up interest rates. In its attempt to minimize the potentially inflationary effects of such expansion, the Federal Reserve may then increase interest rates further by reducing the money supply. Under this "tight money" scenario, a bank's money position would be under intense pressure because of the increasing loan demand and contraction in the supply of loanable funds. The day-to-day cash shortfalls would persist and ultimately increase to a point beyond the bank's ability to finance the shortfalls by using a combination of overnight funds and discount window borrowings. At this point, other sources of liquidity must be tapped.

External sources of liquidity are new liabilities, or in general, borrowing power. In addition to the purchase of overnight funds, these liabilities arise through the issuance of domestic and Eurodollar CDs, and the sale of bankers' acceptances. However, few banks have access to the entire spectrum of such instruments as continuous and reliable sources of funds.

Internally generated liquidity may be derived from a loan portfolio with a short maturity distribution and thus a rapid loan runoff. That is, loan repayments may be used to fund loan demand, deposit outflows, or other cash needs. In most banks loan runoff makes only a small contribution to liquidity needs. During periods of financial stress when liquidity is most needed, loan renewals blunt the effectiveness of a short maturity distribution as a major source of readily available funds. Because of the limitations on external funds and loan runoff, these sources should be viewed as supplements to the cornerstone of bank liquidity—the investment portfolio.

When intense liquidity pressure arises from a "tight credit" policy, the liquidity provided by the investment portfolio must enable a bank to meet immediate, sizable commitments. If such pressures persist for extended periods, the bank, by drawing down the investment portfolio, is able to make orderly adjustments in its asset structure, liability structure, or both. A sizable decrease in the level of deposits may be temporary or long-term. Until this uncertainty is resolved with the passage of time, the bank can fund the outflows by selling investments. This avoids a sudden curtailment in lending operations and the resulting hostility on the part of commercial borrowers who rely on bank funding. As it becomes clear that the decreased level of deposits will be long-lasting, lending operations can be curtailed gradually through a change in loan pricing policy, or the lower level of deposits can be supplemented, at least partially, with other sources of funds.

Most liquidity management problems stem from not having enough liquidity. But excess liquidity can also arise. Large inflows can result from a sudden increase in the level of deposits. The investment portfolio absorbs these cash inflows until the funds can be more effectively deployed. That is, the funds would initially be invested in short-term securities. If the higher deposit level persists over time, the funds would be gradually shifted from the investment portfolio to higher yielding loans. The lower level of earnings resulting from excess liquidity is minimized as the loan portfolio is brought in line with the deposit structure in an orderly manner.

The question might arise—why not put the funds to work immediately in commercial or consumer loans? The answer is twofold. First, as pointed out earlier, it is not always clear that a sudden sizable change in the level of loanable funds is long-lasting. This uncertainty is resolved with the passage of time. Second, it takes time to expand the loan portfolio. In the same way that it enables the bank to cope with liquidity pressures, the existence of the investment portfolio enables a bank to "buy time" as it copes with excess liquidity.

The investment portfolio also enables a bank to cope with seasonal deposit flows with known peaks and troughs. The seasonal inflows are invested in money market instruments with maturities coinciding with seasonal outflows. This is another aspect of the liquidity management process.

Bank liquidity needs may be classified as immediate, short-term, and intermediate-term. Hence, the terms *primary, secondary,* and *tertiary reserves* are often used when examining the liquidity position of a bank. Using these classifications, the various components of bank liquidity are shown in Table 1.

Primary Reserves   It is necessary to combine the money position, investment portfolio, and the short-term borrowing capacity when structuring the liquidity position of a bank. From these categories, several levels of liquidity may be defined. The most liquid sources of funds are referred to as *primary reserves*, not to be confused with the *legal reserves* which are maintained against certain classes of deposits. Primary reserves are used to meet the day-to-day liquidity demands incurred when managing the entire money position. These reserves are made up of cash, deposits in other banks, Federal Reserve

Table 1   Components of Bank Liquidity

Primary Reserve	Secondary Reserve	Tertiary Reserve	
Cash	Short-term Treasury and Agency	Intermediate-Term In-	
Deposits in FR Bank	Securities (mat. <1 yr.)	vestments (1-5 yr.)	
Deposits in Other Banks	Maturing Municipal Bonds	Loan Runoff	Asset-
Cash Items in Process of Col.	(mat. < 3 mo.)	Sale of Loans	Related
Funds Sold	Loan Runoff		
Federal Funds Sold			
Securities Purchased Under			
Agreement to Resell			
Federal Reserve Borrowings	Issuance of CDs		
Funds Purchased	Sales of Bankers' Accept.		Liability-
Federal Funds Purch.			Related
Securities Sold Under			
Agreement to Repurch.			

Bank deposits, cash items in process of collection, and the bank's borrowing capacity in the overnight funds market. The legal reserves of a bank are buried in several of these accounts. With the exception of the legal reserves released because of deposit withdrawals, the legal reserve portion of a bank's primary reserves are not liquid.

To clarify the nature of primary reserves, refer to the Financial Statement of the Hypothetical National Bank shown in Table 2. The *Cash and Reserves* component of HNB's asset structure is $150 million. In a well-run bank the amount of funds in this category is kept to a minimum level that is only sufficient to cover legal reserve requirements and daily working balances. For simplicity, suppose that the bank's $10 million in the Cash account and the $40 million in the account *Deposits—Federal Reserve Bank* cover HNB's legal reserve requirements of approximately $50 million. If HNB's deposits of $800 million decline by say 10 percent, this would create a need for $80 million. Assuming the same percentage reduction in the legally required reserves, the release of reserves would provide only about $5 million to meet the deposit outflow. It is unlikely that much more than $5 million of the $35 million in the account *Deposits—Other Banks* could be used to meet the outflow. Most of these funds are balances maintained on a continuing basis in correspondent banks. Similarly, most of the funds in the $65 million CIPC account are needed for daily working balances to clear checks and manage the money position. In a well-run bank most of the funds in the *Cash and Reserves* accounts should be viewed as necessary working balances. Such balances are essential to meet *daily* liquidity needs. The "free" proportion of such funds that are available to meet longer term liquidity needs is quite small.

The limited amount of such "free" funds in the *Cash and Reserves* accounts may be supplemented by *Funds Purchased*. Like most banks, HNB's borrowing capacity in this overnight funds market (fed funds and repos) is 50 percent of its $60 million equity base, or $30 million. The bank's net position is presently zero because the $20 million in *Funds Purchased*, or borrowed, via fed funds and repos is offset by a like amount of *Funds Sold* to other institutions. When the bank's "free" portion of *Cash and Reserves* is depleted and its overnight borrowing capacity is exhausted, the bank would then draw on its *secondary reserves* if additional liquidity is needed.

Secondary Reserves   The most significant and reliable source of bank liquidi-
                            ty is in the form of short-term, high-quality investments.
These investments, when coupled with borrowing capacity in the CD and
banker's acceptance markets, make up the secondary reserve. Like primary
reserves, this is a management concept rather than an accounting classification
that is readily identifiable on the financial statement. Although there is no precise
definition, it is generally agreed that U.S. Treasury and agency securities make up
most of the secondary reserves. These instruments are of the highest quality and
are readily marketable. However, in order for these investments to be *liquid* their
maturity must be short-term, typically less than one year.

When managing the bank liquidity position it is important to understand the
distinction between *liquidity* and *marketability*. A 20-year Treasury bond is
marketable but lacks liquidity because its price is sensitive to changes in interest
rates. If this bond must be sold to meet outflows, a substantial loss may be incurred because of an increase in the level of interest rates between the time of
purchase and the need for the funds. Also, higher transactions costs are imposed
on long-term issues. A six-month Treasury bill is both marketable and liquid
because of low transactions costs, and its short maturity minimizes the risk of
selling the security at a sizable loss in periods of rising interest rates. In order to be
liquid, a security should be both marketable and have a relatively short-term. That
is, it should mature within one year. An exception to this statement arises when
less marketable issues such as municipal bonds mature within a few months.
Such investments may be considered liquid because of their rapidly approaching
maturity. While they may lack marketability, municipal bonds with a very short
term may properly be viewed as a component of *secondary reserves*. Maturing
loans, or runoff, and short-term borrowing capacity may be viewed as supplementary components of the secondary reserves.

The perplexing question often arises—what is the appropriate amount of secondary reserves for a bank? There is no single answer to this question. For the
individual bank, the size of the secondary reserve depends on such factors as the
volatility of loan demand and deposits, customer diversification, maturity distribution of the loan portfolio, access to the money market, and management's attitude toward safety and liquidity. After assessing these factors management may
decide that its secondary reserve should be approximately 10 to 12 percent of its
assets or about one-half of its investment portfolio. But what about the remainder
of the portfolio?

Tertiary Reserves   After satisfying itself that the bank's primary and sec-
                           ondary reserve positions are adequate and that loan de-
mand is being met, management must then make decisions regarding the balance
of investable funds. In the HNB example, this balance is about 12 percent of the
bank's total assets. Since immediate and short-term liquidity needs are covered by
the combination of primary and secondary reserves, additional investments are
often viewed as an intermediate-term source of liquidity. These *tertiary reserves*
as they are called, should be available to meet liquidity needs that may arise
from one to several years in the future. As these future liquidity needs materialize with the passage of time, the investments making up the tertiary reserves become shorter-term and thus they become more liquid. In this way, tertiary reserves supplement the bank's primary and secondary reserves. Should this supple-

Table 2 Hypothetical National Bank—Statement of Condition ($ in Millions)

ASSETS	Amount	Percent
CASH AND RESERVES		
Cash	$ 10	1.0%
Deposits—FR Bank	40	4.0
Deposits—Other Banks	35	3.5
Cash Items in Process of Collection	65	6.5
Total Cash & Reserves	$ 150	15.0
INVESTMENTS		
Funds Sold		
Federal Funds Sold	$15	1.5
Securities Purchased Under Agreements to Resell	5	.5
Securities		
U. S. Treasury	95	9.5
U. S. Agency	5	.5
State and Local	120	12.0
Other	5	.5
Trading Account (at Mkt.)	5	.5
Total Investments	$ 250	25.0

LIABILITIES AND CAPITAL	Amount	Percent
DEPOSITS		
Demand Deposits	$ 200	20.0%
NOW and "Super" NOW Accts.	150	15.0
Money Market Accounts	100	10.0
Reg. Savings and Time Deposits	300	30.0
Foreign Deposits	50	5.0
Total Deposits	$ 800	80.0
BORROWED FUNDS—SHORT-TERM		
Funds Purchased		
Federal Funds Purchased	$ 5	.5
Securities Sold Under Agreements to Repurchase	15	1.5
Federal Reserve Bank Advances	5	.5
Bankers' Acceptances Outstanding	15	1.5
Other Short-Term Borrowed Funds	10	1.0
Total Borrowed Funds—Short-Term	$ 50	5.0
BORROWED FUNDS—LONG-TERM		
Capital Debentures	$ 30	3.0
Mortgage Indebtedness	10	1.0
Total Borrowed Funds—Long-Term	$ 40	4.0

LOANS

Commercial and Industrial (C&I)

Agriculture	$ 10	1.0
Finance-Related	30	3.0
Industrial and Commercial	200	20.0
International	15	1.5
Lease Financing	35	3.5
Real Estate and Construction	40	4.0
Other	5	.5
Total Commercial Loans	$ 335	33.5

Consumer Loans

Installment	$ 100	10.0
Credit Card	15	1.5
Mortgage (Residential)	100	10.0
Other	5	.5
Total Consumer Loans	$ 220	22.0
Total Loans	$ 555	55.5
Less: Reserve for Loan Losses	5	.5
Net Loans	$ 550	55.0

OTHER ASSETS

Interest Receivable	$ 15	1.5
Due from Customers on Acceptances	15	1.5
Building and Equipment	15	1.5
Miscellaneous Assets	5	.5
Total Other Assets	$ 50	5.0
TOTAL ASSETS	$1,000	100.0%

OTHER LIABILITIES

Interest Payable	$ 10	1.0
Accounts Payable and Accrued Taxes	25	2.5
Miscellaneous Liabilities	15	1.5
Total Other Liabilities	$ 50	5.0

CAPITAL

Preferred Stock	–0–	–0–
Common Shareholders Equity		
Common Stock ($25 par)		
Authorized 1,200,000 Shares		
Issued 1,200,000 Shares	$ 30	3.0
Capital Surplus	15	1.5
Retained Earnings	15	1.5
Total Common Equity	$ 60	6.0
Total Capital	$ 60	6.0
TOTAL LIABILITIES AND CAPITAL	$1,000	100.0%

Key Ratios:

Loans/Deposits = 68.75%

Equity/Total Liabilities and Capital = 6.00%

mental liquidity prove to be unnecessary, the maturing funds can be rolled over into new intermediate-term securities.

Managing this portion of the investment portfolio raises a number of issues. What maturity range is appropriate for this component of the investment account? What is the role of tax-exempt state and local (municipal) bonds relative to taxable securities? What is an acceptable quality level for municipal bonds? These are important policy questions and will be addressed in subsequent sections. In order to place the maturity decision in proper perspective, it is first necessary to understand how the *term structure of interest rates* affects a bank's need for liquidity and the investment decision-making process.

Term-Structure Implications[1]

When making investment decisions for a bank or other depository-type institution, the portfolio manager must examine conditions in the financial markets. Is the level of interest rates low, or is it high? Are credit conditions "tight" or "easy?" Are short-term bonds more appealing from a risk and return standpoint than long-term issues? Which way are interest rates headed? These are some of the questions facing portfolio managers each day. It is also important for the portfolio manager to bear in mind that loan demand, deposit flows, the cost of funds, and bank liquidity needs are simultaneously affected by conditions in the financial markets. Thus, there is an important linkage among market conditions, investment decisions, and bank liquidity needs. The nature of this linkage may be clarified by focusing on a framework known as the *term structure of interest rates,* or the *yield curve,* as it is also known. This framework also provides insight into the specific questions raised above.

The term structure is a graph of bond yields on a specific date plotted against the maturity of the bonds. The graph visually shows the yield-maturity relationships that exist across the entire spectrum of short-term, intermediate-term, and long-term bonds. When constructing a term structure, U. S. Treasury securities are used because they are risk-free. This eliminates distortions in the shape because of the differences in default risk within most other classes of securities. The shape of the yield curve provides considerable information about prevailing conditions in the financial markets.

Term Structure
Shape

Four shapes of the term structure are shown in panels A through D in Figure 1. Market participants refer to these shapes as *upsloping, flat, downsloping,* and *humped.* Each of these four shapes are related to certain phases of the economic cycle. An *upsloping* yield curve generally characterizes a period of low interest rates brought about by the interaction of a number of factors. These include monetary ease on the part of the Federal Reserve, deposit inflows, slack loan demand, rapid loan runoff, and a reduced level of business activity. The economy may even be in a

---

[1] The material in this section draws from: Burton G. Malkiel, *The Term Structure of Interest Rates: Theory, Empirical Evidence, and Applications,* Silver Burdett Company, 1970; and Kelly Price and John R. Brick, "The Term Structure: Forecasting Implications," *Financial Markets: Instruments and Concepts,* edited by John R. Brick, Reston, Virginia: Reston Publishing Co., 1981, pp. 379-395.

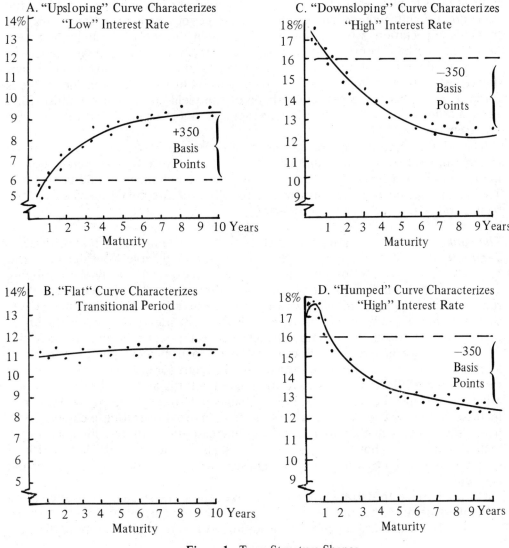

Figure 1 Term Structure Shapes

recession. The cumulative effect of these conditions is an increase in bank liquidity. The *flat* yield curve is observed during transitional periods such as when interest rates recede from high levels or increase from low levels. Usually this shape is short-lived. The *humped* and *downsloping* yield curves, often referred to as *inverted* yield curves, are associated with a high level of interest rates stemming from monetary restraint, strong demand for new loans and loan renewals, and a high level of economic activity. Bank liquidity tends to be under heavy pressure when the yield curve is inverted.

Since an upsloping yield curve characterizes a period of low interest rates, it seems reasonable to conclude that the market expects the next major move in interest rates to be upward. Indeed, this *is* the market's implied forecast. Since the *downsloping* and *humped* curves characterize periods of high interest rates, the market's expectation is for falling interest rates in the future.[2] The market's expectations are based on information as it becomes available so they are subject to change. Since information arrives in an unsystematic manner and with different degrees of economic importance, there is uncertainty surrounding the market's forecast as implied by a particular shape of the yield curve. Thus, implied forecasts should be used as a guide in developing a "most probable" future interest rate scenario.

The relationships among the various shapes of the term structure and conditions in the financial markets are summarized in Table 3. Note that monetary policy, interest rates, loan demand, and deposit flows exert simultaneous liquidity pressure. The manner in which the investment portfolio is structured plays a key role in the bank's ability to cope with such pressure.

The Bankers'   Bankers must cope with a temptation that is directly
Temptation   linked to the shape of the yield curve. Consider a scenario
                        of low interest rates as characterized by the upsloping
yield curve shown in Panel A of Figure 1. As pointed out, slack loan demand, loan runoff, deposit inflows, monetary ease, and excessive bank liquidity characterize such a period. Equally important from an investment standpoint is that the prices of bonds tend to be considerably higher than the prices prevailing under other shapes of the term structure. Because of slack loan demand, the proportion of loans in the asset structure of banks tends to decline (or at least not grow) under such a scenario. Because loans have the highest returns and risk, both gross operating income and the general risk level of banks tend to decline. (Net income may increase if the cost of funds declines faster than gross operating income.) Some bankers would argue that to maintain or increase gross interest income, investments in long-term bonds are essential. It is also argued that the higher risk of such bonds is offset by the smaller loan base resulting from the slack loan demand and runoff.

On the surface this strategy seems to make sense. The strategy is also tempting to bankers because the long-term bonds have a higher current income than short-term bonds when the yield curve is upsloping. In Figure 1, Panel A, note that ten-

Table 3   The Term Structure and Conditions in the Financial Markets

Shape of the Term Structure	Monetary Policy	Present Level of: Interest Rates	Bond Prices	Loan Demand	Deposit Flows	Cost of Funds	Bank Liquidity	Implied Forecast
Upsloping	Easy Credit	Low	High	Slack	Inflows	Decreasing	Increasing	Rising Rates
Flat				—Transitional Structure—				
Downsloping	Tight Credit	High	Low	Strong	Outflows	Increasing	Decreasing	Falling Rates
Humped	Tight Credit	High	Low	Strong	Outflows	Increasing	Decreasing	Falling Rates

[2] For a discussion of the manner in which implied forecasts are derived from the prevailing term structure, see: Kelly Price and John R. Brick, "The Term Structure: Forecasting Implications," *Financial Markets: Instruments and Concepts,* edited by John R. Brick, Reston, Virginia: Reston Publishing Co., Inc., 1981, pp. 379-395.

year bonds yield about 9.5 percent, which is 350 basis points higher than the 6 percent yield on one-year bonds. So the dilemma arises—should management forego the liquidity of a short-term bond and invest in the long-term bond in order to increase its current income?

If long bonds are purchased and then interest rates increase, the value of the bonds will fall. If the increase in rates is moderate such a policy may still be successful despite the bond losses. Suppose that the 9.5 percent bond was bought at par and after one year the market rate on this bond increased from 9.5 percent to 9.9 percent. The ten-year bond now has a maturity of nine years and with a coupon rate of 9.5 percent, its price would be $976.53. The loss in value of $23.47 is more than offset by the high current income of $95 per bond. The *holding period return* (HPR), which is a combination of the income and the gain or loss on the bond, is

$$\frac{\$95.00 \; + \; (-23.47)}{1,000} = 7.15\%.$$

This exceeds the HPR of 6 percent on the one-year bond. But one year later, what is the situation if interest rates are much higher such that a *humped* or *downsloping* yield curve prevails as indicated in Panels C or D.

One year hence, if the market interest rate is 12.5 percent, the 9.5 percent, long-term bond with its remaining nine-year maturity would have a value of $840.59. The resulting loss in value of $159.41 far exceeds the higher interest income provided by the long-term bond. The HPR is

$$\frac{\$95.00 \; + \; (-159.41)}{1,000} = -6.44\%$$

which is far less than the 6 percent HPR on the one-year bond. The one-year bond is now worth par because it is maturing and the funds are available for reinvestment or liquidity needs.

The problem with acquiring long-term bonds when the yield curve is upsloping is that bond prices tend to be high relative to prices prevailing when the term structure is inverted. As interest rates rise and the term structure becomes inverted, long-term bond prices fall sharply and losses result. Such losses create special problems for banks because they occur at an inopportune time. Recall that during periods characterized by an inverted yield curve most banks face serious liquidity problems stemming from increased demand for new loans, requests for loan renewals, and deposit outflows. During such periods a bank should be able to sell securities from its portfolio to meet these needs. If bond prices are depressed, many bankers are reluctant to sell bonds at a loss because of the adverse effect of such losses on the bank's net income.[3] When this happens the invested funds are unavailable to cope with the economic conditions that brought about the inversion of the yield curve in the first place. If management invested in short-term bonds and not yielded to the temptation of the yield curve, the bank would have additional capacity to cope with stressful economic conditions.

[3] Some bankers argue that earnings are affected only if the long-term bonds are sold. Even if the bonds are held, earnings are adversely affected because the return on the bonds is fixed while the cost of funds used to acquire the bonds increases rapidly as the yield curve becomes inverted. Other aspects of bond losses are discussed later in this chapter.

Although short-term bonds are less risky than long-term bonds in terms of price sensitivity, it may be argued that short-term bonds possess reinvestment risk. That is, the income stream is uncertain because the rate at which the funds will be reinvested is unknown. When bonds are viewed individually, the argument has merit. However, in a portfolio theory context, this "risk" characteristic of short-term securities is actually risk reducing! Consider the situation given above. Assume the bank bought the one-year bond to yield 6 percent and one year later, interest rates are considerably higher with the yield curve inverted as shown in Panel C of Figure 1. If the funds are reinvested in another one-year security, the annualized income would increase from 6 percent to about 16 percent. This dramatic increase offsets, at least in part, the escalating cost of bank funds brought about by the higher interest rates and the inversion of the yield curve. If interest rates fall, the lower rate at which reinvestment occurs is offset by a lower cost of funds. This portfolio effect arises because the liability structure of most banks is short-term and therefore interest-sensitive. A short-term investment portfolio provides offsetting rate-sensitivity on the asset side and thus interest income changes in the same direction as interest expense. This portfolio effect produced by short-term securities minimizes swings in earnings that can occur in a volatile interest rate environment.

When interest rates are high as characterized by an inverted yield curve, the same kind of temptation arises and leads bankers to make inappropriate investment decisions. Assuming that a bank has funds for investment when the yield curve is inverted, that is, short rates exceed long rates, the short-term bonds would now be more tempting because of their higher current income. In Panel C of Figure 1, one-year bonds yield 16 percent and ten-year bonds yield 11 percent. Recall that the inverted yield curve characterizes a period of monetary restraint, high interest rates, and depressed bond prices. If a bank is planning to hold long-term bonds in its investment portfolio, this would be an appropriate time to acquire such bonds despite their lower current income. When rates fall, and falling rates is the implied forecast when the yield curve is inverted, short rates will fall faster and more dramatically than long rates. Thus, the rate at which reinvestment takes place will be much lower. If long bonds were purchased, the high rate would be contractually fixed.

Even though interest rates are high when the yield curve is inverted, the acquisition of long-term bonds at this time could prove later to be ill-timed. Rates may increase further. However, the potential magnitude of such an error is considerably less than when long bonds are acquired during a low interest rate scenario as characterized by an upward sloping yield curve.

Few banks actually buy long bonds when an inverted yield curve exists. The fear of illiquidity, the lack of investable funds, and succumbing to the current income temptation are among the reasons for this portfolio behavior.

Managerial   The various shapes of the yield curve provide bank man-
Implications   agers with considerable information regarding condi-
                        tions in the financial markets. The relationship between
economic forces underlying the shapes and overall bank operations must be fully understood. A lack of such understanding results in many bankers being tempted to invest in long-term bonds when short bonds are more appropriate, and vice-

versa. It is not uncommon for the same shortsighted policies to be followed in managing the commercial loan portfolio.

The investment portfolio is an important contributor to earnings. But because the portfolio also represents the bastion of liquidity, bank investment decisions must be made in a multi-period context. That is, investment decisions must reflect potential liquidity needs in future periods. If they do not, the ability of a bank to cope with rapid changes in economic conditions can be impaired.

MANAGING THE INVESTMENT PORTFOLIO

Having examined the relationship between bank liquidity and investments, this section focuses on specific aspects of managing the investment portfolio. The maturity structure, investment implications of the "money market account," role of tax-exempt bonds, investment quality, yield spreads, and the trading portfolio are among the topics covered.

The Maturity Structure

One of the most important aspects of managing the investment portfolio is the maturity structure. In light of a bank's need for liquidity and the term structure implications discussed in the preceding section, it is clear that most of a bank's portfolio should be made up of short- and intermediate-term securities. Short-term securities are those maturing within one year and intermediate-term maturities are those in the one- to five-year range. Bonds with a maturity in excess of five years are usually considered long-term bonds. Ignoring, for the moment, the maturity implications of "money market accounts," the maturity schedule of the bond portfolio may be structured in one of three ways—the *laddered, barbell,* or *buffer* approach.

Laddered Portfolio   In a laddered investment portfolio, bond maturities are staggered such that approximately the same amount matures each year. In Table 4, two versions of a laddered portfolio are shown for a $10 million portfolio. In the absence of liquidity demands, the proceeds of maturing issues are invested in the longest maturity. It is argued that this approach enables a bank to earn average market returns over an interest rate cycle. This claim may have merit if bonds are bought consistently over a cycle. However, as discussed in the preceding section, liquidity demands are most pressing when interest rates are high and the yield curve is inverted. These demands usually prevent the purchase of bonds at higher levels of interest rates. In the absence of liquidity demands, interest rates are likely to be low and this is when most bonds will be purchased. Thus, the average yield on a laddered portfolio may be lower than the average interest rate over a complete interest rate cycle.

Another problem with the laddered portfolio relates to its liquidity. In the case

Table 4   Alternative Maturity Structures for a $10 Million Investment Portfolio

Year of Maturity	1. Laddered Portfolio		2. Barbell Portfolio		3. Buffer Portfolio	
	5-Year	8-Year	5-Year	8-Year	5-Year	8-Year
1	$2,000,000	$1,250,000	$3,000,000	$3,000,000	$3,500,000	$3,000,000
2	2,000,000	1,250,000	2,000,000	1,000,000	3,000,000	2,000,000
3	2,000,000	1,250,000	—0—	1,000,000	2,000,000	1,500,000
4	2,000,000	1,250,000	2,000,000	—0—	1,000,000	1,250,000
5	2,000,000	1,250,000	3,000,000	—0—	500,000	1,000,000
6		1,250,000		1,000,000		750,000
7		1,250,000		1,000,000		250,000
8		1,250,000		3,000,000		250,000
Weighted Avg. Maturity[a]	2.5 yrs.	4.0 yrs.	2.5 yrs.	4.0 yrs.	1.7 yrs.	2.475 yrs.

[a]For the purpose of this calculation, it is assumed that bonds mature at the mid-point of the year of maturity. For example, bonds maturing within the first year are assumed to mature in .5 years, bonds in the second year mature in 1.5 years, and so on. The weighted average maturity for the 5-year laddered portfolio is calculated as follows:

$$[\$2,000,000(.5) + \$2,000,000(1.5) + \ldots + (4.5)\$2,000,000]/\$10,000,000 = 2.5 \text{ years.}$$

The average maturity is used to show the similarity between two seemingly different portfolio strategies. However, care must be exercised when using the average life as a measure of risk. Depending on the specific maturities and weights of securities, two portfolios with the same average maturity may be affected differently by changes in interest rates. In practice it may be useful to value alternative portfolios under different interest rate assumptions in order to examine the effects of interest rate changes. For an excellent discussion of the limitations of average maturity as a risk proxy, see: Jess B. Yawitz, George H. Hempel, and William J. Marshall, "The Use of Average Maturity as a Risk Proxy in Investment Portfolios," *Journal of Finance*, May 1975, pp. 325-333.

of the five-year ladder shown in Table 4, it is questionable that a one-year runoff of only 20 percent of the portfolio, or $2,000,000, is sufficient in a volatile interest rate environment. Even more questionable is the liquidity provided by the eight-year laddered portfolio. Depending on a bank's characteristics and need for liquidity, a four-year ladder may be more appropriate. Despite its drawbacks, the laddered approach is simple and requires little managerial expertise. The approach is widely used.

Barbell Portfolio   Examples of the *barbell approach* are also shown in Table 4. Note that maturities are lumped at both ends of the maturity spectrum. This approach requires that securities be sold as they approach the mid-point of the maturity schedule and the proceeds reinvested in the longest maturity. However, liquidity demands can disrupt the "shape" of such a portfolio.

The runoff of investments within the first year is considerably higher than the runoff of the corresponding laddered portfolios. For this reason, it is argued that the barbell approach provides greater liquidity than the laddered approach. It is also argued that the current return on the portfolio is higher because of the high concentration of longer-maturity bonds which tend to be higher yielding than the short-term bonds. Both arguments are flawed.

What appears to be additional liquidity provided by the faster first-year runoff relative to the laddered approach is offset by the lower degree of liquidity in the long end of the barbell portfolio. Since the longer-term issues are more price-sensitive than short-term issues, higher bond losses will result from this portion of the portfolio if interest rates increase and liquidity demands intensify. A higher concentration of long-term bonds will produce a higher level of current income only if the yield curve is upsloping when the bonds are purchased and stays that way. The higher income on the long portion of the portfolio is offset by the lower income on the higher concentration of short-term securities. Also, recall from the preceding section that bank purchases of long-term issues is a questionable practice when the yield curve is upsloping.

The laddered and barbell approaches appear to be different strategies. When the portfolios are examined in terms of their overall contribution to liquidity rather than the contribution of individual maturities, the approaches are similar. A measure of this similarity is given by the average maturity of the portfolios as shown in Table 4. Note that the five-year laddered and barbell portfolios have the same average maturity, 2.5 years. The eight-year laddered and barbell portfolios also have the same average maturity, 4 years. The difference between the two strategies is less than it appears.

Buffer Portfolio   The third strategy shown in Table 4 is the *buffer portfolio*. Under this strategy, most of the securities are concentrated in the short end of the maturity schedule. This results in an average maturity that is considerably shorter than the average maturities of the corresponding laddered and barbell portfolios.

As its name implies, this portfolio acts as a buffer enabling a bank to absorb the kinds of shocks that characterize a volatile financial environment. With a high concentration of securities in the short end of the maturity spectrum the bank has greater liquidity with which to cope with tight credit conditions, strong loan demand, deposit outflows, or a sharply rising cost of funds. As pointed out in the preceding section, short-term securities are risk-reducing in the context of overall bank operations.

Comment   Despite the importance of the maturity distribution, there are no regulatory constraints imposed on this aspect of the portfolio. But as pointed out earlier, rising interest rates can result in sizable losses on long-term bonds. Such losses usually occur at inopportune times and are as serious as loan losses or default-related investment losses. Thus, while there are no legal maturity restrictions, bankers should exercise caution when formulating the maturity structure of the investment portfolio. The buffer portfolio structure reflects such caution.

When interest rates were stable and deposit costs regulated, the *laddered* and *barbell* approaches may have had merit. In recent years the combination of volatile interest rates and deregulated rates on deposits has increased the interest-rate sensitivity of bank liabilities. The acquisition and retention of rate-sensitive deposits is possible only by paying competitive market rates. During a period of high interest rates when the yield curve becomes inverted and deposit costs rise sharply, the shorter-term *buffer portfolio* provides the necessary shock absorbing capability far more effectively than the alternative strategies. The approach is more consistent with the times, in particular, the financial environment and the deregulation of depository-type financial institutions.

Implications of "Money Market Accounts"

When a bank issues liabilities, the underlying funds are usually comingled with other bank funds and invested in a cross-section of assets. Although many banks attempt to match the maturities and/or interest-rate sensitivity of assets and liabilities, there is usually no attempt to link a specific liability to a specific asset. However, unless such a linkage is established for *money market accounts*, serious investment-related problems could arise.

These insured accounts are designed to compete with money market funds by offering money market yields, liquidity, safety, and convenience. The underlying funds are immediately withdrawable and extremely interest-rate sensitive. Unless competitive yields are paid on a continuous basis, the funds will be withdrawn by customers and reinvested elsewhere. If the funds in the account are invested solely in a portfolio of money market instruments with a weighted average maturity comparable to that of the money market fund industry, competitive yields can be paid on a day-to-day basis.

When interest rates are high as characterized by an inverted yield curve, most banks would keep their money market fund investments in the short sector of the market to obtain the high yields. However, during a period of lower interest rates as characterized by an upsloping yield curve, a temptation exists to invest in longer-term instruments to obtain the higher yield. If the weighted average maturity of the portfolio were, say, 220 days at a time when the average maturity of the money market fund industry was only 40 days, rising interest rates would cause the earnings rate on the invested funds to lag far behind competing rates. If the bank continued to pay competitive rates substantial losses could result from this account. The failure to pay competitive rates could result in massive outflows. The same problem would arise if the underlying funds were used to make fixed-rate loans.

Policy Constraints   To avoid this risk, funds underlying the *money market account* should be segregated, or earmarked, for control purposes and subject to specific policy constraints. One such constraint is to require that the funds be invested only in short-term money market instruments such as Treasury bills, certain agency securities, CDs, bankers' acceptances, commercial paper, fed funds, and repurchase agreements. Some banks allocate a portion of these funds to floating-rate loans. This may be appropriate if the loans are subject to immediate re-pricing such as some prime-rate loans, or the loans have a short re-pricing interval such as three months. To the extent that a re-pricing interval is longer, such as six months, the allocation should be correspondingly smaller in order to keep the overall interest-rate sensitivity of the portfolio in line with competing money market funds.

Another policy constraint should link the average maturity of the money market account's investments to the industry average for money market funds. For example, a constraint might require that the weighted average maturity be maintained within an interval equal to the latest industry average plus or minus 10 days. If floating-rate loans are included in this portfolio, the "maturity" is the re-pricing date for the purpose of computing the average maturity. Loans tied to the prime rate and subject to immediate re-pricing may be viewed as extremely short-term investments for computational purposes.

Because of the nature of this account and the fact that the bank acts as a conduit, the money market account should *not* be considered as a part of the bank's core deposits, especially for fixed-rate lending purposes. Similarly, investments related to the account should *not* be considered a part of the bank's secondary reserves or general liquidity position. Written policies should reflect the fact that the investments relate only to a particular offsetting liability account that has special characteristics.

The Earnings Rate   The earnings generated by the investments underlying money market accounts may be allocated to depositors in several ways. One approach is to link the offering rate to some well-known money market rate such as the weekly auction rate for three-month Treasury bills. If this rate is, say, 8.85 percent, any return above this rate (or the rate plus some increment) may be kept by the bank to cover the cost of management, administration, and FDIC insurance. The difference is the bank's *operational spread*. Another approach is to pass through the portfolio yield less an operating spread to cover management, administration, and insurance costs. For example, assume that on a particular day the weighted average annualized return on the funds is 9.80 percent. If the bank's annualized operating spread is say 75 basis points, the account's annualized rate for that day would be 9.05 percent. Regardless of the allocation method used, the important point is to structure the earmarked portfolio so that competitive rates may be paid and the bank's spread maintained over all phases of the interest rate cycle.

Taxable vs. Tax-Exempt Securities

Another decision in managing the investment portfolio relates to the mix of taxable and tax-exempt securites. Like other investors in tax-exempt securities, the primary purpose of bank investments in these securities is to reduce income taxes and maximize after-tax income. Assuming no other tax shields, *the net income of a commercial bank is maximized when the size of the taxable investment portfolio is such that the combined taxable investment income and other taxable income is offset by tax deductible expenses, and the balance of the investment portfolio is invested in tax-exempt securities.* This may result in a zero-tax position and the resulting portfolio is optimal, at least in a financial sense. For political and other reasons discussed later, some banks do not hold an optimal mix of taxable and tax-exempt securities. Before looking at these issues, the nature of the decision-making process is examined by focusing on a numerical example using the optimal-mix portfolio as a benchmark.

A Numerical Example   In Panel A of Table 5, a condensed financial statement is given for a commercial bank. Given this statement and the revenues and costs generated by the assets and liabilities of the bank, the question arises—how should the investment portfolio of $25 million be allocated between taxable and tax-exempt securities if net income is to be maximized? In

Table 5   Taxable vs. Tax-Exempt Securities in the Bank Investment Portfolio

A. Financial Statement

Assets		Liabilities & Capital	
Cash & Reserves	$ 15,000,000	Demand Deposits	$ 20,000,000
Investments		Interest-Bearing Dep. (@ 9%)	60,000,000
$25,000,000 { (Taxable @ 12%)	13,333,333	Borrowed Funds (@ 10%)	9,000,000
{ (Tax-Exempt @ 8%)	11,666,667^c	Other Liabilities	5,000,000
Loans	55,000,000	Equity Capital	6,000,000
Other Assets	5,000,000		
	$100,000,000		$100,000,000

[($1,600,000/.12) = $13,333,333]

B. Income Statements (Estimated)

	1. All Taxable Securities	2. All Tax-Exempt Securities	3. Optimal Portfolio
Loan and Fee Income	$ 7,700,000	$ 7,700,000	$ 7,700,000
Expenses			
Operating (3% of Assets)	3,000,000	3,000,000	3,000,000
Interest Expense			
Interest Bearing Dep. ($60,000,000 × .09)	5,400,000	5,400,000	5,400,000
Borrowed Funds ($9,000,000 × .10)	900,000	900,000	900,000
Income Before Invest. Income & Taxes	(1,600,000)	(1,600,000)	(1,600,000)
Taxable Investment Income	3,000,000^a	-0-	1,600,000
Taxable Income	1,400,000	(1,600,000)	-0-
Income Tax @ 46%	644,000	-0-	-0-
After-Tax Income	756,000	(1,600,000)	-0-
Add: Tax-Exempt Income	-0-	2,000,000^b	933,333^c
Net Income	$ 756,000	$ 400,000	$ 933,333

a $25,000,000 × .12 = $3,000,000
b $25,000,000 × .08 = $2,000,000
c Since $13,333,333 is invested in taxable securities, the balance of the investment portfolio is $11,666,667. When invested in tax-exempt bonds at 8%, this balance of the portfolio generates income of $933,333.

Panel B of Table 5, estimated income statements are shown for three different portfolio mixes. Each statement is identical through the *Income Before Investment Income and Taxes*. The first column shows the effects of investing the entire $25 million portfolio in taxable securities yielding 12 percent. Net income is $756,000. As shown in the second column, the net income falls to $400,000 when the entire portfolio is invested in tax-exempt securities at 8 percent. In column 3, note that tax deductible expenses are $9.3 million. Taxable income from loans is $7.7 million or $1.6 million less. Thus, in order for taxable income to completely offset tax deductible expenses, the taxable portion of the portfolio must be such that it produces taxable income of $I.6 million. Assuming a taxable rate of 12 percent, the size of the portfolio necessary to generate this amount is $1.6 million/.12 = $13,333,333. The balance of the portfolio is $11,666,667. When invested in tax-exempt bonds at 8 percent, this balance generates income of $933,333. In this instance, the bank is in a zero-tax position. The bank's net income is considerably higher than the net income generated by other portfolio combinations.

Some Caveats

In practice, there are a number of reasons why bank managers may hold a sub-optimal mix of taxable and tax-exempt securities. Bankers must weigh the benefits of an optimal portfolio against the adverse political reaction that may result from a zero-tax position. It is not uncommon for politicians or the press to make an issue of the fact that some banks pay no federal income taxes. To avoid this kind of publicity, many banks deliberately hold sub-optimal portfolios. Another problem arises from the fact that the portfolio must be structured on the basis of *estimated* income and expenses. If the estimates are inaccurate, the original portfolio is no longer optimal. It may be evident early in the tax year that the income and expense forecasts are inaccurate. Appropriate portfolio adjustments may then be made. Suppose that early in the tax year management structures its portfolio in the optimal manner shown in Table 5. Shortly thereafter, management revises its forecast of loan income to $8.1 million with expenses remaining the same. This would require that taxable investment income be about $1.2 million. This would be generated by investing approximately $10 million in taxable securities. The exact amount of taxable income needed and the portfolio size will depend on the amount of taxable income already generated in that tax year. If a sizable forecast error arises late in the year, it may be impossible to make the necessary portfolio adjustments.

In a volatile interest rate environment, rapidly changing loan income and/or cost of funds can result in frequent and large forecast revisions. To make the necessary switches from taxable to tax-exempt securities, or vice versa, *the maturity distribution of both taxable and tax-exempt securities must be tilted toward the short end*. If a large portion of the portfolio is invested in longer maturity bonds and interest rates increase, switching the portfolio is difficult because of the resulting bond losses and their impact on the bank's earnings and capital position.

If the loan income shown in column 3 of Table 5 were say $9.8 million with expenses remaining the same, the *Income Before Investment Income and Taxes* would be $500,000. In this case, the bank would pay income taxes of $500,000 x .46 = $230,000, and the optimal strategy would be to invest the entire portfolio in tax-exempt securities. Since many municipal bonds are not readily marketable, such a policy may not be prudent because of a lack of liquidity and flex-ibility.

In many banks, the actual portfolio mix of taxable and tax-exempt securities is affected by other tax-related factors. Leasing operations generate tax credits and depreciation charges while foreign tax payments are credited against U.S. taxes. For these and the other reasons cited above, not all banks hold what appears to be an optimal mix of taxable and tax-exempt securities. Thus, the framework shown in Table 5 should be viewed as a benchmark in the overall tax planning process.

State Taxation   Although income from tax-exempt bonds is exempt from Federal income tax, the income may be taxed by the state. Several possibilities exist. In a number of states, municipal bond income is not taxed because the states either do not have an income tax or such income is specifically excluded from taxation. Most states with an income tax impose a tax on the income from out-of-state- bonds while exempting the income from in-state municipal bonds. For example, a Michigan bank would pay taxes on the income earned from New York City bonds, but not on the income from bonds issued by Detroit or by the state of Michigan. For this reason, the tax-exempt holdings of many banks are weighted toward in-state issues. Finally, several states impose a tax on all forms of municipal bond income. A summary of state taxation of municipal bond interest is shown in Table 6.

Investment Quality and Regulation

Investment activities are constrained by regulations. For most banks these regulations are not overly restrictive. Since the main regulatory objective is to minimize default-related losses, the most important regulations center around the quality of investments. Specific regulations affecting a bank vary depending on the bank's charter and whether it is a member of the Federal Reserve System. Since state regulations vary among states, the general nature of quality constraints can be examined by focusing on the regulations issued by the Comptroller of the Currency. These regulations apply to national banks and all state banks which are members of the Federal Reserve System. They guide the investment activities of most of the country's banks. For the purpose of controlling the quality of bank investments, the Comptroller's regulations specify three classes of *investment grade* securities eligible for bank investment—Type I, Type II, and Type III.

Type I Securities   Securities in the Type I class include U.S. Treasury obligations, debt issues of Federal agencies, and general obligation bonds of any state or political subdivision thereof. (General obligation bonds are backed by the taxing power of the issuing state or local government.) *A bank may deal in, underwrite, or hold such securities with no limitation as to the amount.*

In recent years the creditworthiness of many cities and some states has deteriorated. Thus, the Comptroller's regulation that such securities may be held without

Table 6   State Taxation of Municipal Bond Interest[a]

States With No Income Tax	States With a Tax On Income From Out-of-State Bonds
Connecticut	Alabama
Florida	Arizona
Nevada	Arkansas
South Dakota	California
Texas	Delaware
Washington	Georgia
Wyoming	Hawaii
	Idaho

States With No Tax On Municipal Bond Income	
Alaska	Kentucky
Indiana	Maine
Louisiana	Maryland
Nebraska	Massachusetts
New Mexico	Michigan
Utah	Minnesota
Vermont	Mississippi
	Missouri
	Montana

States With a Tax On Income From Bonds of In- and Out-of-State Issuers	
Colorado	New Hampshire
Illinois[b]	New Jersey
Iowa[b]	New York
Kansas	North Carolina
Oklahoma	North Dakota
Wisconisn	Ohio
	Oregon
	Pennsylvania
	Rhode Island
	South Carolina
	Tennessee
	Virginia
	West Virginia

[a]Bonds issued by the District of Columbia, Guam, Puerto Rico, and the U. S. Virgin Islands are exempt from Federal, State, and local income taxes.

[b]The income from certain in-state bonds is exempted by statute.

Source: Standard and Poor's Corporation, *The Outlook,* September 4, 1978, p. 572.

limit appears to be overly permissive. The regulations do emphasize that even with Type I securities, banks must exercise "prudent judgment" in their decision-making. Since U.S. Treasury and agency securities are riskless, or virtually so, this caveat is directed toward the municipal bonds in the Type I category.

Types II and III   Securities in the Type II classification include those issued by "quasi-agencies" such as the International Bank for Reconstruction and Development, Asian Development Bank, Inter-American Development Bank, and the Tennessee Valley Authority. Also included in the Type II category are bonds issued by state agencies for housing, dormitory, or university purposes. Banks may deal in and underwrite such securities. The maximum holding of an individual issuer of a Type II security is an amount equal to 10 percent of bank's capital and surplus.

Securities in the Type III category include other marketable bonds and notes for which there is adequate evidence that the issuer will be able to meet its obligations. Such a judgment may be made on the basis of an issuer's historical operating record or on the basis of reliable estimates in the case of new projects. Securities in this category include state and local revenue bonds and corporate bonds. Ordinarily, if a bond is rated Baa/BBB or higher by Moody's or Standard and Poor's, this is sufficient evidence that the security is *investment grade* and may be held. Most bankers rely on these ratings in their decision-making. Many unrated bonds are investment grade and may also be held by banks. Although a complete credit file must be maintained on all bonds not backed by the U.S. government, it is especially important to maintain a complete file on unrated bonds. Only by maintaining such a file can the investment officer and bank examiners determine that a security is investment grade.

Individual Type III securities are subject to the same limitation, 10 percent of capital and surplus, as applied to Type II securities. In addition, the bank may not deal in or underwrite such securities.

Ineligible Securities Other than the common stock of the Federal Reserve Bank, national banks are not permitted to hold equities or preferred stock. If such securities are used to collateralize a loan and ultimately are acquired by the bank, the securities must be sold within a reasonable period, usually several years. It is possible for a bank to invest in equities indirectly via investment grade convertible bonds or bonds with warrants attached. At the time of purchase, the value of the security must be written down to reflect its value independent of the conversion feature or the value of the warrants. This usually results in a large charge-off, so most bankers are reluctant to acquire such securities.

Yield Spreads and Relative Yields

The absolute level of interest rates plays an important role in all aspects of bank management. Interest rates affect the cost of a bank's funds and the return on its assets, including investments. When managing investments, the portfolio manager must also consider the *relative yields* of alternative investments. Some investments are close substitutes for one another but sell at different yields. Thus, relative yields are as important as the absolute level of bond yields from a decision-making standpoint.

A commonly used measure of relative bond values is the *yield spread*. The yield spread is simply the difference in yield (in basis points) between two securities that are alike in all respects except one. For example, a five-year Aaa-rated general obligation (GO) bond may be selling at par to yield 8.25 percent. A Baa-rated, five-year GO may be yielding 10.20 percent for a spread of 195 basis points. The bonds are alike in all respects except quality, so the spread is attributable to the difference in quality. The significance of this spread is that it changes, often dramatically.

Depending on the yield spread, a bond may be underpriced or overpriced relative to another security. This affects the relative price performance of the securities. Although numerous spreads can be monitored, two spread relationships are particularly important to the bank portfolio manager. These are quality spreads and the spread between taxable and tax-exempt securites.

Quality Spreads   Bonds at the lower end of the investment grade spectrum possess a higher degree of default risk. Like other bonds, the market prices of these issues are also sensitive to changes in the level of interest rates. However, their higher default risk often magnifies the interest rate sensitivity of lower grade bonds. Consider the following example.

> *Example.*   A bond portfolio manager is considering the purchase of a five-year, Aaa-rated general obligation bond at par to yield 6 percent, or a five-year, Baa-rated GO at par to yield 6.4 percent. The spread is somewhat narrow at 40 basis points. The portfolio manager is seeking to increase the portfolio's yield so the decision is made to purchase the Baa-rated bond and pick up the additional 40 basis points in yield.
>
> Six months later the economic climate has changed dramatically. Tight credit conditions, high interest rates, and economic uncertainty have depressed bond prices. The market rate on the Aaa-rated bond, which was *not* purchased, is 6.75 percent, resulting in a price of 97.13. (The bond now has a maturity of four and one-half years.) This represents a decline of 2.87 percent in value. Because of the economic uncertainty and increased likelihood of default under such conditions, the Baa-related bond is now yielding 8.25 percent, resulting in a price of 92.44. This represents a decline of 7.56 percent in value. This decline resulted from the dual effect of an increase in the general level of interest rates and an increase in the yield spread from 40 to 150 basis points. Despite the fact that both bonds declined in value, the changing yield spread caused the higher quality bond to outperform the lower grade bond by declining less in value.

Most bank investment managers have considerable latitude when structuring the quality distribution of the portfolio. Rather than purchasing different quality bonds in a haphazard fashion, quality spreads should be used by the portfolio manager to determine which area of the quality spectrum merits attention in both the purchase and sale of securities. In the example above, the narrow spread of 40 basis points favored the purchase of the higher quality bond despite its lower yield. When the spread widens, the lower grade bond may be more attractive. A return to normal economic circumstances would cause interest rates to fall and the spread to narrow. The price of the lower grade bond would increase relative to the higher grade bond. Thus, a more effective strategy in the example would have been to buy the higher quality bond when the spread was 40 basis points and when the spread increased to 150 basis points, shift to the lower grade bond.[4]

Taxable vs.   Since banks are actively involved in the municipal bond
Tax-Exempt Spreads   market, the spread between taxable and tax-exempt bonds is another aspect of relative yields. Care must be exercised when interpreting this spread. The spread must be evaluated in terms of

---

[4] A source used by many practitioners to monitor yield spreads is: Salomon Brothers, *An Analytical Record of Yields and Yield Spreads*, New York: Salomon Brothers, published periodically.

the level of interest rates as well as its magnitude. Suppose that the yield on a taxable bond is 9 percent and the tax-exempt yield on a bond with a similar maturity and quality rating is 5.40 percent for a spread of 360 basis points. When evaluated historically, this spread may be quite wide so the taxable bond may appear to be a better relative value. However, given a taxable yield and the marginal tax rate at which investors are indifferent between taxable and tax-exempt yields, the equilibrium spread can be determined. The prevailing spread is then compared to the equilibrium spread to determine the relative attractiveness of the bonds in question. The following example demonstrates the procedure.

> **Example.**   A portfolio manager is considering the purchase of a taxable bond yielding 9 percent or a comparable but tax-exempt bond yielding 5.40 percent. These yields are linked together by the marginal tax rate t in the model
>
> $$r_{TE} = r_T(1-t)$$
>
> where r_{TE} is the tax-exempt rate and r_T is the taxable rate. Assuming a marginal tax rate of 35 percent and given the taxable rate of 9 percent, the equilibrium tax-exempt rate is
>
> $$r_{TE} = .09(1-.35)$$
> $$= .0585 \text{ or } 5.85\%.$$
>
> The actual tax-exempt rate is 5.40 percent, so the taxable bond is a better relative value. Viewed another way, the yield spread should be 9% − 5.85 = 3.15%, or 315 basis points. The actual spread is 360 basis points. If the actual spread were less than 315 basis points, the tax-exempt bond would be a better relative value.

As interest rates change, the spread between taxable and tax-exempt yields also changes. As shown in Table 7, the spread should increase as interest rates increase and vice versa. This is why it is inappropriate to simply look at the spread without considering the level of interest rates. If taxable rates were 14 percent and tax-exempt rates 10.10 percent, the spread of 390 basis points may be very high by historical standards. Taxable bonds seem to be the better relative value. But as shown in Table 7, at this level of interest rates, the spread should be 490 basis points so the tax-exempt bond is a better relative value.[5] Thus, the spread must be evaluated in terms of the level of interest rates *and* the magnitude of the spread.

The Trading Portfolio

In many larger banks, a trading account is established. On HNB's financial statement shown earlier, this account amounted to only $5 million. This figure reflects the bank's holdings at a point in time and not the volume of transactions

---

[5] Underlying this analysis is the assumption that the marginal tax rate remains constant at 35 percent. For a discussion of the rationale for this assumption and the behavior of the marginal tax rate over time, see: Timothy Q. Cook, "Some Factors Affecting Long-Term Yield Spreads in Recent Years," *Economic Review,* Federal Reserve Bank of Richmond, September 1973, pp. 2-14.

Table 7   Taxable Versus Tax-Exempt Yield Spreads
When the Marginal Tax Rate is 35%

Taxable Yield	Equivalent Tax Exempt Yield[a]	Equilibrium Spread in Basis Points
8.00%	5.20%	280
9.00	5.85	315
10.00	6.50	350
11.00	7.15	385
12.00	7.80	420
13.00	8.45	455
14.00	9.10	490
15.00	9.75	525

[a]The equivalent tax-exempt rate r_{TE} is determined from the model

$$r_{TE} = r_T(1 - t)$$

where r_T is the taxable rate and t is the marginal tax rate.

within the account or its contribution to profits or losses. Its small size may not be an indication of its impact on the bank. In this account, the bank may trade U.S. Treasury, agency, or municipal securities to take advantage of expected changes in interest rates. In anticipation of falling interest rates, the trading account may show a *long position*, or ownership of bonds with an intermediate- or long-term maturity. If interest rates fall, the prices of such bonds would rise faster than the prices of shorter-term bonds. If rates are expected to rise and thus depress bond prices, the trading account may show a *short position* in these types of bonds. That is, they have been sold in anticipation of buying them back later at a lower price.

On the financial statement, long and short trading positions are carried on a net basis and, unlike investment securities, all positions are carried at market value. This means that trading gains or losses are reflected immediately in the income statement. Depending on its ability to forecast interest rates and the scope of its trading activities, a bank can show sizable gains or losses from a trading operation. This account also includes securities held as inventory for the bank's activities as a dealer in money market instruments, municipal bonds, or U.S. Treasury and agency issues.

OTHER ASPECTS OF PORTFOLIO MANAGEMENT

The portfolio manager must be aware of other factors or constraints that affect investment operations. Among these are pledging requirements, inappropriate investment practices, certain accounting issues, and the impact of investment-related losses.

Pledging Requirements

When the deposit level of a bank changes, the asset composition will also change. When these deposits involve federal or local governments, the related asset changes take on an added dimension. Federal laws and the laws of most states require commercial banks to hold certain types of securities to collateralize government deposits in excess of the amount insured by the Federal Deposit Insurance Corporation. Changes in the level of such deposits may induce immediate changes in the investment portfolio.

The Requirements   The portfolio manager must be familiar with pledging requirements at the federal, state, county, and local levels. For federal government deposits, eligible collateral must at least equal the amount of uninsured deposits. Such collateral consists of U. S. Treasury and agency securities at par value, state obligations at 90 percent of par value, and obligations of other political subdivisions at 80 percent of par value. Securities collateralizing federal government deposits must be held by a district Federal Reserve Bank, one of its branches, or an approved custodian.

Most states have pledging requirements that vary widely in their details. The disparity among states shows up in Table 8 which lists the requirements of seven states located in the Tenth Federal Reserve District. The required amount of pledged securities ranges from 50 to 110 percent of the deposits. In each of these states, the requirements are uniform for state, county, and municipal deposits. This is not always the case in other states. In some states the requirements apply to state deposits but not county or municipal deposits.[6]

U.S. Treasury and agency securities are acceptable collateral in all states with pledging requirements. It is common practice for states to limit eligible state and local bonds to in-state issues. The use of market value is the most common valuation method used. Usually, the physical transfer of securities must be made to a designated custodian.

Role of Pledging   It is argued that pledging requirements ensure the safe-
Requirements   ty of public deposits in the event the depository bank should fail. Whether this is an efficient way to obtain such safety is open to question. It is also argued that such requirements strengthen the market for U.S. Treasury, agency, and state and local securities. With the existence of pledging requirements, banks tend to hold more of these securities than would otherwise be the case. A study showed that this is the case but at a cost—bank holdings of private sector loans were reduced.[7] The lower cost of government borrowing is offset by the reduced availability and higher cost of credit in the private sector. By virtue of holding more government securities than would otherwise be the case, bank portfolios are more liquid. Bank liquidity may be reduced if the bank holds a smaller proportion of non-pledged short-term securities as a result of pledging requirements. Such an effect was found in the study cited above.

---

[6] For a summary of pledging requirements, see, "Pledging Assets for Public Deposits," Appendix C, American Bankers Association, Washington, D. C., 1976. A discussion is also provided in: Ronald A. Ratti, "Pledging Requirements and Bank Asset Portfolios," *Economic Review*, Federal Reserve Bank of Kansas City, September/October 1979, pp. 13-23.

[7] Ratti, *ibid.*

Table 8   Pledging Requirements of Tenth District States

| | Pledging Ratios | | | | |
	State	County	Municipal	Eligible Collateral	Valuation Method
Colorado	100%	100%	100%	U. S. Treasury and Agency, In-state Municipals, First Mortgages	Market
Kansas	70	70	70	Same as Colorado	Par
Missouri	100	100	100	U. S. Treasury and Agency, In- and Out-of-State Municipals	Market
Nebraska	110	100	100	Same as Missouri	Market
New Mexico	50	50	50	U. S. Treasury and Agency, In-State Municipals	Mixed[a]
Oklahoma	110	110	110	Same as New Mexico	Par
Wyoming	100	100	100	Same as New Mexico	Market

[a]Par value is used for New Mexico and other in-state obligations; market value is used for other obligations.
Source: Ronald A. Ratti, "Pledging Requirements and Bank Asset Portfolios," *Economic Review,* Federal Reserve Bank of Kansas City, September/October 1979, p. 15.

Managerial
Implications

When securities are pledged, they may not be sold to meet liquidity needs unless the needs relate to an outflow of the underlying deposits. From a managerial standpoint, pledged securities should be earmarked as a separate and distinct segment of the investment portfolio. That is, pledged securities should *not* be viewed as components of the primary or secondary reserves discussed earlier.

From a strategy standpoint, the securities pledged should be the least marketable and least liquid in the bank portfolio. Regardless of their underlying characteristics, pledged securities lack marketability or liquidity by virtue of being pledged. When the term structure is upsloping and a bank is holding short-term Treasury bills for liquidity purposes, the bank is accepting a lower yield because of the high quality and short maturity of the Treasury bills. If these are then pledged, the bills are no longer liquid. Since they lack liquidity anyway, intermediate-term municipal bonds are the most appropriate securities for the bank to pledge.

There is another reason to pledge municipal bonds. Most laws require dollar-for-dollar backing of deposits so the underlying funds are not loanable. But federal tax laws allow a "tax arbitrage." The interest paid on CDs is tax-deductible but if the CD proceeds are invested in municipal bonds, the interest income is tax-exempt. Thus, if a bank pays a municipality 12 percent for its funds and its tax rate is 46 percent, the after-tax cost of these funds is $.12(1 - .46) = .0648$, or 6.48 percent. If municipal bonds yield in excess of 6.48 percent, a profitable tax arbitrage is possible. In order to be true arbitrage, the maturity of the deposit and the securities should be matched. This is a desirable strategy if the bank is sporadic in its competition for public deposits and it is unsure of its tax position. If the bank is consistently competing for public funds and holds intermediate-term municipal bonds anyway, the maturities of the deposits and securities need not be matched.

Inappropriate Practices

Large banks usually have in-house investment expertise. As shown later in this chapter, such expertise is not always combined with good judgment. In small- and many medium-size banks, the degree of investment expertise is not always up to the task of managing the investment portfolio. Thus, smaller banks are often the target of unscrupulous securities dealers and inappropriate investment practices often result. Consider the following example of one such practice known as an *adjusted trade*.

> *Example.* A salesman representing a municipal bond dealer calls on a small-town banker with a proposal for a bond trade. The bank holds $100,000 par value of 4 percent, Baa-rated municipal bonds maturing in five years. The bonds were purchased at par value to yield 4 percent. The bonds are selling at 85 so the bank has an unrealized loss of $15,000.
>
> The sales representative offers to buy these bonds at par value, a ficticiously high price. No loss would be recorded on the bank's books. Simultaneously, the bank would purchase another overpriced municipal bond from the same dealer. This bond would be purchased at its par value of $100,000. The bond has a coupon rate of 6 percent so the bank's yield would be 6 percent. The bond matures in 10 years and is unrated. The representative explains that since no loss is recorded and no additional funds are required, the bank has simply swapped a 4 percent yield for a 6 percent yield.
>
> This deal sounds too good to be true—and it is. It appears that the bank has increased its income by simply replacing a low-yielding 4 percent bond with a higher yielding 6 percent bond. If the banker accepts this proposal, the bank will end up with a bond that has a longer term and lower quality. The bank will be trading bonds with a market value of $85,000 for bonds that could be bought in the market for $80,000. thus, a loss of $15,000 grows to $20,000 while no loss shows up on the books. The dealer pockets the difference of $5,000 between the market values of the two securities.

Placing newly purchased bonds on the books at an inflated price is not only an irregular accounting practice, it is considered an *unsound banking practice* by regulatory agencies. If detected during an examination, an immediate write-down to market value would be ordered. When securities are sold, transactions must be reflected at market value and any losses recorded immediately. Failure to do so overstates a bank's earnings and financial position. These problems can be avoided by dealing only with reputable securities firms and obtaining third-party verification of the market prices of securities. Such policies would have prevented a swindle that federal investigators referred to as the "Kansas Bank Robbery."[8]

> *Example.* A bond salesman approached the owner of two small Kansas banks. One of the salesman's clients was a "snuff-dipping old lady from Dallas" who had a tax

---

[8] "How Country Banker Bought a Bond Deal that Didn't Pay Off," *Wall Street Journal*, January 28, 1976, p. 1.

problem. She has to raise $330,000 immediately. The salesman proposed that the bank purchase the woman's $1 million par value California water revenue bonds for $330,000. Since these bonds had very low coupons, they sold at a deep discount from par. In fact, the bonds were worth less than the "price" of $330,000. Acknowledging this, the salesman assured the banker that the "snuff-dipper" would buy the bonds back in 90 days for $330,000. In return, the bank would earn the tax-exempt interest on the bonds plus a sizable "fee." The next day, the banker gave the salesman two cashier's checks totalling $330,000 and drawn against his two banks. The salesman then left after promising to deliver the bonds. Several days later, the bonds arrived. Shortly thereafter, the salesman induced the banker to invest an additional $215,000 in another batch of overpriced bonds.

Several weeks later the Dallas police found evidence of these transactions while investigating the salesman's role in various swindles. The police notified the FBI which in turn notified the FDIC. Examiners from the FDIC descended on the two banks to investigate the purchases and found that the bonds purchased for $330,000 had a market value of only $190,000. The second block purchased for $215,000 had a value of $129,000. Unless the bonds were sold at their purchase price, the bonds would have to be written down to their market value.

When the repurchase date arrived, a part of the first block of bonds was repurchased by the salesman, ostensibly on behalf of the little old lady. The salesman then disappeared with approximately $175,000 in bank funds. The two banks then sold the remaining bonds and took losses totalling $185,000. The losses impaired the solvency of the banks and the owner was forced to add capital.

This situation could have been much worse. Payment for securities should only be made *against delivery*, that is, when the securities are actually delivered. By receiving payment in advance of delivery, the swindler could have disappeared at that point. If the bonds were stolen or counterfeit, other tricks of the trade, the two banks' losses would have been greater.

Although adept at making loans, many bankers lack familiarity with sound investment practices. Thus, there are many ways by which unsuspecting bankers can be relieved of investment-related funds. To avoid the kinds of problems cited above, a written investment policy should guide day-to-day investment operations. The elements of such a policy are discussed later in this chapter.

Accounting Issues

Several accounting issues affect the investment portfolio. For accounting purposes, a distinction must be made between securities held for investment purposes and trading securities. As pointed out earlier in this chapter, trading securities are carried at market value for financial statement purposes. When these securities are marked-to-market as the practice is known, the resulting gains or losses are reflected "above the line" in the bank's operating results even though the securities have not been sold. For investment securities, only gains or losses that are actually realized affect bank earnings. These gains or losses are shown "below the line." That is, they are not a part of operating earnings. These gains or losses are reflected in net income and earnings per share.

When purchased at par value, investment securities are carried at par value. When investment securities are bought at a discount from or premium over par value, they are carried on the books at *amortized value.* That is, the premium or discount is written off or absorbed into income over the life of the bond. Assume an 8 percent bond due in five years is bought at 92.28 to yield 10 percent. One year later, the bond would have a four-year maturity and its carrying value would be 93.54 using a discount rate of 10 percent. The difference of 1.26 (percent of par) is reflected as income. By the time the bond reaches maturity, the discount will be completely amortized. The discount rate used for valuation purposes is the yield at which the bond was purchased even though the market rate may be much higher or lower. The same procedure is used to amortize the premium on bonds bought above par value.

Bankers should understand the implications of using amortized value. Since price fluctuations are ignored, the carrying value of bonds may not reflect their value. The use of amortized value, and the notion that interim price fluctuations can be ignored, is based on the assumption that the bonds will be held until maturity. It follows that the risk of forced liquidation to meet deposit outflows, loan demand, or other cash needs is assumed to be quite low. This is a questionable assumption since one of the main functions of the investment portfolio is to meet such liquidity needs.

As a practical matter, the use of amortized value usually poses no special problems for short- or intermediate-term issues. The rapid approach of maturity blunts the potentially distorting effects of rapidly changing interest rates. Distortions are unlikely to be significant. Long-term bonds are another matter. Assume an 8 percent, ten-year bond is purchased at 87.54 to yield 10 percent. One year later, the amortized value will be 88.31. However, if market interest rates are 12 percent the market value of the bond will be 78.34. The value of the bond has increased on the bank's books while its market value has decreased. When securities are sold, all gains or losses are treated as ordinary income or losses for tax purposes.

Investment Losses

The need for liquidity to meet loan demand or deposit outflows usually arises during periods of high interest rates and depressed bond prices. If most of the investment portfolio is in short-term securities as suggested by the *buffer strategy,* the liquidity needs of most banks could be met without incurring investment losses on the sale of the bonds. But what if the short-term portfolio is insufficient to meet liquidity stresses and other sources of liquidity have been exhausted? The bank is then faced with the question—should intermediate- or long-term bonds be sold at a loss in order to make loans?

Like other investors, bankers prefer to avoid selling securities at a loss. But there may be sound economic reasons for doing so. After explaining how to analyze this problem, several decision-making barriers are examined.

Loss-Recovery Period   There are several reasons why bankers are reluctant to sell securities at a loss to obtain funds to meet loan demand. Investment losses reduce earnings and this in turn reduces the bank's retained earnings. Since retained earnings are the primary source of bank capital, the rate of capital growth is reduced by investment losses. When properly evaluated, however, the sale of securities at a loss can have favorable long-term implications for a bank's capital position. The problem may be addressed by focusing on the *loss-recovery period*. Suppose a bank is considering the sale of $1 million par value 9 percent, five-year Treasury bonds. The price is 92.46 to yield 11 percent. The bonds were purchased at par so a loss of $75,400 will be incurred. The proceeds of $924,600 will be reinvested in fixed-rate loans at a yield of 14 percent. An analysis of this problem using the *loss recovery period* as a guide is shown in Table 9.

The first step is to find the after-tax loss. Since losses are deductible from ordinary income, the loss of $75,400 is reduced by the tax savings. The savings are 46 percent of the loss or $34,684, so the after-tax loss is $40,716. The funds available for reinvestment are the sum of the proceeds of the sale and the tax savings. This totals $959,284 as shown in Part B of Table 9. The incremental income is the difference between the reinvestment of the after-tax proceeds and the income from the existing bonds, or $44,300. The after-tax loss of $40,716 must be recovered by this incremental income within a reasonable period. In this example, the loss recovery period is .92 years. The after-tax loss is completely recovered in less than one year and the impact on the bank's reported capital position is offset. After this rapid loss recovery, the bank's capital will grow more rapidly because of the increased earnings on the reinvested funds. The bank will be in a stronger financial position and its relationship with borrowers improved. If the loss-recovery period were say two or three years as might be the case with longer-term bonds, it would be more difficult to justify taking the loss using this approach.

The loss-recovery approach shown in Table 9 assumes that the reinvestment is at a fixed-rate and for a term equal to the maturity of the bond. In this way, the indicated recovery period is assured. If the funds are reinvested in floating-rate

Table 9   Analysis of Loss-Recovery Period

A. After-tax Loss
Cost of 9% bonds	$1,000,000
Proceeds of sale (@ 92.46)	924,600
Loss	$ 75,400
Tax saving (@ 46%)	34,684
After-tax loss	$ 40,716

B. Proceeds for Reinvestment
Proceeds of sale	$ 924,600
Plus: Tax savings	34,684
After-tax proceeds	$ 959,284

C. Incremental Income
Reinvestment of after-tax proceeds (.14 × $959,284)	$ 134,300
Income from old bonds (@ 9%)	90,000
Incremental income	$ 44,300

D. Loss-Recovery Period

$$\frac{\text{After-Tax Loss}}{\text{Incremental Income}} = \frac{\$40,716}{\$44,300} = .92 \text{ years}$$

loans and interest rates increase, the loss recovery is faster. If rates decline, the recovery is slower and the switch may prove to be disadvantageous for the bank. Thus, the manner in which the funds are reinvested will depend on management's interest rate expectations and risk preferences.

Some Barriers   Despite the economic merits of taking losses, many bankers are reluctant to do so because the losses may be construed by the public as a sign of mismanagement. Also, when analyzing a bank's capital adequacy, examiners usually ignore unrealized bond losses and focus on the reported capital.[9] This discourages the sale of bonds at a loss.

The unwillingness of bankers (and other investors) to sell bonds at a loss is often traceable to the misguided notion that a loss can be avoided by holding the bonds to maturity. From an accounting standpoint this is true. From an operational standpoint, a loss is incurred regardless of whether the securities are sold or held to maturity. Assume a five-year, 10 percent bond was bought at par to yield 10 percent. One year later, the market yield on this bond is 12 percent and the price is 93.79 based on a remaining life of four years. If the bonds are sold, a loss of $62.10 per bond will be recorded; if the bonds are held to maturity no such loss is recorded. However, having made the initial investment, the bank must now forego an annuity represented by the difference between the semi-annual income of $60 on a new 12 percent bond and $50 on the existing 10 percent bond. This annuity is $10 semi-annually for four years. The present value of this foregone income stream discounted at the prevailing market rate of 12 percent is

$$\text{Present Value} = \sum_{t=1}^{8} \frac{\$10}{(1 + \frac{.12}{2})^t}$$

$$= \$62.10.$$

This is exactly the same as the accounting loss that would be realized if the bonds were sold! This example demonstrates that losses cannot be avoided by simply holding the bonds until maturity. The issue is not whether the losses are realized or unrealized, but whether the funds can be more effectively redeployed without significantly impairing the bank's reported capital position.

EXAMPLES OF INVESTMENT MISMANAGEMENT

Periodically, classic examples arise that demonstrate how *not* to run a bank or other financial institution. In this section, two such investment-related examples are discussed. The purpose of these examples is not to point fingers, but to emphasize the importance of the concepts developed in this chapter and highlight the crucial role of effective investment management.

***

[9] If unrealized bond losses are substantial and could ultimately impair the solvency of a bank, examiners consider such losses in their analysis. A key factor is whether the bank has sufficient earning power to continue operating as a going concern.

The First Pennsylvania Bank Case[10]

During the early 1970s, the First Pennsylvania Bank was an aggressive lender to marginal credits. As a result of the 1974-75 economic recession, the bank suffered large loan losses during the mid-1970s. Despite these losses, the bank was not in danger of failing. Its assets were $8.5 billion and its equity exceeded $300 million. To offset these loan losses and restore its earning power, management zeroed-in on the investment portfolio.

During 1976 and 1977 an upward sloping yield curve prevailed with long-term rates exceeding short-term rates by a wide margin. Tempted by this spread and anticipating a sharp decline in the level of interest rates, management implemented a two-part strategy. First, almost $1 billion of long-term Treasury bonds were purchased in anticipation of selling the bonds at substantial profits when interest rates declined. (Recall from the earlier discussion of the term structure that when the yield curve is upsloping this is *not* the time to go long.) The second phase of the strategy was to finance the bond purchases using low cost, short-term funds obtained through the sale of CDs and the purchase of fed funds. If interest rates fell, the bank's positive spread would increase as the carrying cost of the bonds decreased while the return on the bonds remained constant.

The bank was perfectly positioned for a major decline in interest rates. In 1978, the major move in rates began—but upward! The portfolio of long-term bonds became an albatross. As interest rates increased, the value of the bond portfolio plunged. As the yield curve became inverted the cost of the short-term funds used to finance the bonds increased rapidly resulting in a negative spread and sizable operating losses. Rumors of the bank's financial problems started circulating and a *silent run* began. That is, large-scale depositors and providers of funds quietly began withdrawing their funds and refusing to purchase new CDs or provide additional fed funds. The investment portfolio was illiquid because of the huge losses so it could not be used to cope with the outflows. By March 1980, unrealized bond losses totalled $315 million, an amount that exceeded the bank's equity by $8 million. The bank was virtually wiped out by the investment decisions!

Through an unusual bailout effort engineered by the FDIC, new management, and the financial assistance of a group of other commercial banks, the First Pennsylvania Bank survived this investment-related debacle. The Franklin National Bank was not so fortunate.

The Franklin National Bank Case[11]

The collapse of the Franklin National Bank in 1974 sent shock waves through the country's financial system. With assets of about $5 billion in the early 1970s, the Long Island based bank was one of the nation's largest at that time. Studying its collapse is useful for two reasons. First, the Franklin National Bank—or its

---

[10] This section draws from: Linda Snyder Hayes, "The Bet That Almost Broke a Bank," *Fortune*, June 2, 1980, pp. 48-50.

[11] This section draws from: Sanford Rose, "What Really Went Wrong at Franklin National Bank," *Fortune*, October 1974, p. 118.

debris—may be viewed as a monument to mismanagement. Students of banking find it hard to believe that so many mistakes could be made and so many things could go wrong in a bank. The second reason the case merits attention is that it demonstrates the linkage between investments and other aspects of bank operations. Of particular concern is the manner in which investment decisions contributed to Franklin's collapse.

Some Background   In the late 1960s and early 1970s, the Franklin National Bank began an aggressive expansion program by invading New York City. Seeking to expand its loan portfolio, marginal credits were readily accepted. These loans resulted in sizable loan losses. Even high quality loans were unprofitable because the bank used the average cost of funds rather than the marginal cost of funds when pricing loans. With interest rates rising, the average cost of funds lagged behind the marginal cost so loans were under-priced. Excessive branching and elaborate physical facilities made the bank's occupancy costs excessive. Personnel expenses were far above the industry norm. Expecting interest rates to fall, the bank funded a large volume of long-term fixed-rate loans with short-term interest-sensitive funds. Interest rates then increased with the usual results—a negative spread on loans. By the early 1970s, the bank's financial condition began deteriorating. The negative spread on many of the bank's loans reached 400 to 500 basis points in late 1973 and early 1974.

Role of the   Although not center-stage, the investment portfolio did
Investment Portfolio   its part in bringing about the bank's collapse. Throughout the 1960s, Franklin National aggressively sought low-cost demand and time deposits of Long Island municipalities. To induce public officials to place funds in the bank, it bought a large amount of tax-exempt Long Island school-district bonds yielding an average of about 4 percent. (Interest rates were much lower in the 1960s than in later years.) Most of the bonds had maturities ranging from ten to twenty years. As a result of these purchases, a sizable amount of public deposits flowed into the bank.

The bank made no attempt to determine its optimal mix of taxable and tax-exempt securities. Because of the heavy purchases of municipal bonds and operating losses, the bank had too much tax-exempt income and insufficient taxable income. It made sense for the bank to switch from tax-exempt to taxable securities. The income from taxable bonds would be offset by operating losses so the income would not be taxed. By offsetting operating losses, the higher level of income resulting from the switch would have reduced the hemorrhaging that was taking place. But the bank was unable to execute such a switch. Rapidly rising interest rates coupled with the long bond maturities caused bond prices to fall sharply. The sale of these bonds and the realization of losses would have further impaired the bank's deteriorating capital base.

By holding tax-exempt bonds, operating at a loss, and exhausting its ability to take advantage of loss carryback and carryforward provisions of the tax laws, the bank could not benefit from the tax-exemption provided by municipal bonds. In this situation, the cost of the funds used to carry the bonds is *not* reduced by the tax savings. This can be devastating. In the late 1960s, the bank held $300 million in tax-exempt bonds with an average yield of 4 percent. This yield was approximately 3.5 percentage points below the bank's marginal pre-tax cost of funds at the time. Thus, the bank was losing money at a rate of about $10.5 million ($300 million × .035) annually on its tax-exempt portfolio.

Although the bank continued to hold its oversize tax-exempt portfolio, the bank stopped buying municipal bonds. Ignoring the bank's heavy bond purchases earlier, public officials were annoyed that Franklin National was no longer buying their new bond offerings. Throughout the early 1970s, low-cost public demand and time deposits began flowing out of the bank, thus contributing to the on-going nightmare.

In late 1973, management was convinced that interest rates were about to decline sharply. About $200 million of five- to ten-year maturity Government and agency bonds were acquired with interest-sensitive short-term funds raised in the money market. Interest rates increased causing another negative spread and additional unrealized bond losses. Since some of these purchases were in the bank's trading account, the bonds were supposed to be *marked-to-market* and the losses reflected in operating results. A Federal investigation later revealed that when the bond market deteriorated, bank records were falsified as some of the bonds were illegally switched to the investment account in order to avoid showing the bond losses on the income statement. (Such a switch may be made only within 30 days after the purchase date.)

As rumors of Franklin's problems became more ominous, a silent run began in late 1973. But management was not finished, at least not yet. In a final attempt to recoup its staggering losses, the bank gambled heavily in the foreign exchange market. Losses exceeding $45 million were incurred within a few months and by May, 1974 the bank was declared insolvent. In the fall of 1974, after futile attempts to merge the bank with another institution, the FDIC administered the *coup de grâce* by liquidating the bank. The stockholders were wiped out, criminal trials followed an extensive Federal investigation, and students of banking gained considerable insight into how *not* to run a bank.

THE INVESTMENT POLICY STATEMENT

Bank investments must be closely monitored and controlled. This may be accomplished by having a written investment policy statement. The development of such a policy statement is not a simple task. If loosely written, it is likely to raise more questions than it answers and result in unpleasant surprises. If the policy statement is too restrictive, investment opportunities may be lost with adverse effects on earnings. The task is further complicated by the fact that no two banks are alike. Differences in investment expertise, amount of capital, location, size, regulatory jurisdiction, diversification of the customer base, and risk preferences interact to shape the policies of individual banks. An investment policy must also reflect an interaction with other bank operations such as the money position and lending. Also, the policy should reflect the risks assumed in other activities. For example, the risk associated with a large volume of interest-sensitive fixed-rate loans may be partially offset by a higher concentration of short-term interest-sensitive investments. Similarly, the investment policy of a bank with a large volume of open lines of credit and revolving credits outstanding should reflect a more cautious approach than the policy of a bank with limited exposure to sudden loan takedowns.

Although most banks have an investment policy, it is not always in writing. Before looking at the elements of a policy, the need for a *written* policy is examined.

Why a Written Policy?

There are several reasons why a bank should have a written, board-approved policy statement. A well-defined and carefully prepared statement constitutes a working agreement between management and the Board of Directors. Such an agreement minimizes confusion by defining the boundaries within which day-to-day investment decisions are made. In the absence of a written statement, investment policy is often vague, known only to a few people, and a complete mystery to the Board. This situation is inconsistent with the fact that the Board is responsible for the development of investment policy and overseeing investment decisions.

A written policy promotes efficiency by answering investment-related questions. By making the policy statement available to all investment personnel, securities dealers, and other banks with which investment-related business is conducted, everyone knows the bank's investment guidelines and operating constraints. This reduces the time wasted on matters that are outside the investment department's scope of operations.

A written policy statement also facilitates the bank examination process. In addition to detecting "problem banks," another goal of bank examiners is to detect unsound policies and practices that could lead to financial problems. To assess the potential riskiness of a bank's investment portfolio, examiners usually request a copy of the policy statement. This provides the examiner with insight as to where to look for potential problems. The lack of such a statement is grounds for a critical comment in the examiner's written report.

Components of a Policy Statement

Since investment policy cannot be made on the spur of the moment, the details of a policy statement must be thought out in advance. The statement must cover all critical aspects of investment decision-making. In this section, the components of a policy statement are summarized.

Investment Objective   The first step in formulating an investment policy is to state the investment objective. Such an objective may be stated in the following way:

> The investment objective is to facilitate management of the money position and provide immediate, short-term, and longer-term liquidity to meet loan demand, deposit outflows, or other contingencies. The investment portfolio will also be consistent with tax considerations and pledging requirements.

This objective reflects the interaction and overlap between the money position and the investment portfolio. In the context of primary and secondary reserves, which collectively provide funds for immediate and short-term needs, the statement emphasizes liquidity rather than earnings. For those securities making up tertiary reserves, which help meet longer term needs, more emphasis may be placed on earnings but without losing sight of longer-term liquidity needs.

A statement of the investment objectives is important because investments must be consistent with the objective. The objective affects the portfolio composition by constraining the types and characteristics of securities that may be held by the bank. The investment objective stated above might have prevented the kinds of investments and related activities that contributed to the collapse of the Franklin National Bank and near-collapse of the First Pennsylvania Bank.

Decision-Making The Board of Directors is responsible for the develop-
Process ment of investment policy. The policy statement must indicate a delegation of decision-making authority to line personnel who implement the policy and carry out day-to-day activities. Investment decisions must then be consistent with the policy statement.

In many smaller banks, investment decisions are concentrated in the hands of one individual. This can create problems. Policy violations and illegal activities such as theft and embezzlement are facilitated when all investment-related matters are handled by one person. If an error in judgment is made by an individual, an attempt may be made to "recoup the losses." The importance of this activity requires that backup personnel be familiar with investment operations. One person should not be allowed to dominate the entire investment process.

The policy statement should authorize the formation of an investment committee to oversee the decision-making process. This committee has three functions. The first is to review investment decisions to ensure compliance with board policy. Second, the committee assists management in coping with policy-related problems or special situations. Finally, this committee integrates investment activities with other bank operations. This may be accomplished by having line officers from investments, lending, and funds acquisition on the committee. Ideally, the Board of Directors should be represented on this committee with at least one member.

Portfolio Composition To control investment risk, the policy statement must specify the types of investments that are authorized, the quality levels, maturity structure, and diversification requirements. Authorized investments would include Federal funds sold, repos, U. S. Treasury and agency securities, domestic and Eurodollar CDs, bankers' acceptances, commercial paper, tax anticipation notes, municipal bonds, and corporate bonds.

Specifying quality levels is handled in two ways. In the case of rated securities such as commercial paper, most municipal bonds, and corporate bonds, the lowest acceptable rating may be specified along with a range for each rating category. In the case of unrated securities such as CDs and bankers' acceptances, an "approved list" of acceptable banks should be included in the policy statement. Such a list should also be prepared for fed funds and repo transactions.

The maturity structure of the portfolio is controlled by specifying the general strategy (*ladder, barbell,* or *buffer*), maximum maturity, and possibly a weighted average maturity.[12] For the purpose of specifying or evaluating the maturity structure, fed funds and repos should usually be omitted.

Diversification requirements are imposed by limiting the amount of funds that may be invested in a single, risky investment. It is difficult for most small banks to diversify their entire portfolio because size constraints result in lower yielding small blocks, or "odd-lots" as they are called. In the money market, a "round-lot" is usually $1 million. In the municipal bond market, small blocks are readily obtained without foregoing yield.

Other Procedures   Because of the close relationship between the money position and investments, short-term borrowing policies should also be specified. Such policies would include constraints on the amount of purchased funds (fed funds and repos) as well as limitations on borrowings at the discount window. An "approved list" of financially strong and reputable securities dealers can minimize the potentially adverse effects resulting from a dealer that fails while executing a transaction. Special constraints on the investment of funds underlying money market accounts should also be specified, along with safekeeping guidelines for all securities. Finally, a statement should have a provision calling for the periodic review of the policy by the investment committee. This review is essential in a period of rapid change both in banking and the financial markets.

CONCLUSION

The purpose of this chapter was to examine the nature of the investment management process within a commercial bank. It was first necessary to examine the linkage between the need for bank liquidity on the one hand, and the money position and investments on the other. Investment policies, strategies, and operational constraints were explained. Examples demonstrated the far-reaching implications of investment decisions. The need to integrate investment activities with other bank functions was also explained. The significant role played by the portfolio manager should now be better appreciated.

REFERENCES

Brick, John R., "A Model Investment Policy," *Credit Union Executive,* (Winter 1981-82), pp. 18-23.

[12] See the footnote in Table 4 for a caveat regarding average maturity as a measure of risk.

Cook, Timothy Q., "Some Factors Affecting Long-Term Yield Spreads in Recent Years," *Economic Review,* Federal Reserve Bank of Richmond (September 1973), pp. 2-14.

Hayes, Linda Snyder, "The Bet That Almost Broke a Bank," *Fortune,* 101 (June 2, 1980), pp. 48-50.

Hempel, George H., "Basic Ingredients of Commercial Banks' Investment Policies," *The Bankers Magazine,* 155 (Autumn 1972), pp. 50-59.

Hoffland, David L., "A Model Bank Investment Policy," *Financial Analysts Journal,* 34 (May/June 1978), pp. 64-67.

Price, Kelly and John R. Brick, "The Term Structure: Forecasting Implications," *Financial Markets: Instruments and Concepts,* edited by John R. Brick, Reston, Virginia: Reston Publishing Co., Inc., 1981, pp. 379-395.

Ratti, Ronald A., "Pledging Requirements and Bank Asset Portfolios," *Economic Review,* Federal Reserve Bank of Kansas City (September/October 1979), pp. 13-23.

Rose, Sanford, "What Really Went Wrong at Franklin National," *Fortune,* 90 (October 1974), p. 118.

Yawitz, Jess B., George H. Hempel, and William Marshall. "The Use of Average Maturity as a Risk Proxy in Investment Portfolios," *Journal of Finance,* XXX (May 1975), pp. 325-333.

PART III

LIABILITY AND CAPITAL MANAGEMENT

17

Certificates of Deposit and Eurodollar Deposits

A *certificate of deposit*, or CD, represents evidence of a large-scale deposit for a specified period in a commercial bank, S&L, or mutual savings bank. In recent years, CDs have become one of the main sources of funds for these institutions, especially the large, domestic, money center banks. Like other segments of the money market, the CD market has undergone dramatic changes in recent years. Emerging from the simple concept of a bank deposit, contemporary CDs can be tailored to meet a wide range of financial needs of investors and issuers, both domestic and foreign. In this chapter, *domestic CDs, Eurodollar Deposits* and so-called *Yankee CDs* are examined. The market structure and pricing of CDs are also covered.

DOMESTIC CDs

The most important segment of the CD market is the domestic market. Until recently only short-term, large denomination, negotiable CDs of well-known, U.S. money center banks were considered money market instruments. Because of deregulation, increased competition for funds, and changes in the CD market structure, the CD has been redefined as a money market instrument. In addition to the large denomination negotiable CDs mentioned above, the market now includes the CD offerings of small- and medium-size banks, S&Ls, and savings banks. To distinguish these and other money market CDs from small-denomination, savings certificates issued to small-scale individual savers, a denomination of $100,000 is used as a breakpoint.

Most CDs offered by smaller institutions are non-negotiable because the issuers lack the national recognition and, in some cases, the creditworthiness necessary to sell negotiable CDs. The obvious question arises—why are these CDs considered money market instruments? Before addressing this question, it is necessary to examine the investment characteristics of domestic CDs and the market structure for these instruments.

Investment Characteristics

CDs of domestic depository institutions are offered in negotiable and non-negotiable form with maturities ranging from as short as 14 days to as long as 8 to 10 years. The concern here is for those CDs issued with an original maturity less than one year, the arbitrary maturity limit for a money market instrument classification. Since a CD is a deposit, it is insured up to $100,000 by the Federal Deposit Insurance Corporation (FDIC) in the case of banks, and the Federal Savings and Loan Insurance Corporation (FSLIC) in the case of S&Ls and savings banks. Any amount over $100,000 is uninsured.

The interest on CDs accrues on the basis of a 360-day year. Although most CDs are issued on an interest-bearing basis, the nature of which is discussed later, some banks offer CDs on a discounted basis. Buyers of CDs prefer discounted instruments because the yields are directly comparable with other discounted money market instruments such as T-bills, agency securities, and commercial paper. Dealers in CDs also prefer discounted instruments because there is no accrued interest to be paid when the CDs are purchased in the secondary market. The payment of accrued interest to the seller of interest-bearing CDs increases the capital needs of dealers.

A major change in the CD market in recent years is the use of floating-rate CDs. A one-year CD, for example, may be subject to repricing at quarterly or semiannual intervals. The rate during each "leg" of the CD is tied to a highly visible, external index such as the three- or six-month Treasury bill auction rate. The variable-rate CD provides the investor with the interest-rate sensitivity of a short-term instrument. Because the funds are tied up for longer periods, the rate on each leg of the CD is usually higher than the yield on CDs with a maturity that corresponds to the leg being adjusted. The yield premium usually depends on the maturity of the CD.

Market Structure

CD transactions are conducted through dealers, brokers, in-house efforts of issuers, money finders, and an automated exchange. The dealer market, which handles large-denomination negotiable CDs, is made up of about 25 firms located in New York and other money centers. These dealers buy CDs for their own inventory from issuing banks and resell the CDs to investors. The dealers also make a secondary market by buying and selling existing CDs.

One of the keys to a successful CD program for a financial institution is the ability to acquire funds from outside the issuer's geographical service area. Brokers such as Merrill Lynch and Dean Witter Reynolds help smaller issuers accomplish this by marketing CDs the same way stocks and bonds are sold. When going through a broker, the CDs of a particular issuer may be divided into small blocks for resale to individuals or packaged with the CDs of other issuers and sold as part of a large block to institutional investors. Since all the CDs are in blocks of $100,000 or less, and each CD retains its identity, the investor has the safety of a fully insured deposit even though the amount purchased may be well in excess of the insurance limit. Equally important is that the brokers maintain a secondary market for the CDs even when the denomination is $100,000 or less. Thus, these CDs offer competitive rates, safety, marketability, and depending on the maturity, liquidity. They are also available in floating- and fixed-rate form. From the issuer's standpoint, the use of brokers greatly facilitates the acquisition of funds, especially on short notice. The issuer's cost is a fee to the selling broker.

So-called *money finders* play a much more limited role. These are specialized solicitors whose sole function is to bring CD issuers and buyers together. The use of brokers and money finders is more common among the smaller institutions. As institutions become larger, they tend to develop their own in-house distribution capability. Examples of in-house approaches are a weekly auction of CDs by Citibank or the development of a network of potential buyers similar to that used in the direct placement of commercial paper.

Another aspect of the CD market is an automated exchange known as *CDx*. Issuers list their CDs in a central computer by maturity and rate. The minimum purchase is $1 million but this is made up of at least ten different CDs, none of which exceed $100,000. The program is such that no more than $100,000 will be placed in any one institution, thus resulting in a fully insured instrument regardless of size.

Non-Negotiable CDs

It is appropriate to view non-negotiable CDs as money market instruments if they meet certain criteria regarding creditworthiness and liquidity. A fully insured CD for $100,000 is riskless from a credit standpoint so the creditworthiness of the issuer is not a major factor to be considered. As the size of the CD increases, the creditworthiness becomes increasingly important. Although nonnegotiable CDs may not be sold, they may possess sufficient liquidity if the maturity is short and tailored to meet specific needs of the buyer. A three-year, $500,000 CD of a medium-grade issuer would hardly qualify as a money market instrument whereas a three-month CD for $100,000 from the same issuer is riskless and reasonably liquid because of its near-term maturity. Thus, it could properly be viewed as a money market instrument despite its lack of marketability.

EURODOLLAR DEPOSITS

Most large banks in foreign countries deal in several currencies on an on-going basis. Since the dollar is widely recognized as a strong and stable currency, many international transactions are conducted in dollars. When a foreign bank or a foreign branch of a United States bank needs dollars, it simply enters the money market and purchases the funds in dollar form that it needs. Thus, *Eurodollar deposits are defined as dollar-denominated deposits in foreign banks and foreign branches of U. S. banks.* These deposits may be in the form of negotiable certificates of deposit known as *Euro-CDs* or in the form of time deposits known as *Euro-TDs.*

Euro-CDs

These CDs have the same basic characteristics as the CDs of domestic banks. They are negotiable instruments with most maturities falling in the range of one to six months. Interest is paid at maturity on the basis of a 360-day year. The primary and secondary market for Euro-CDs is very active. Most of the trading activity takes place in London, Nassau, and Grand Cayman Island. Trading also takes place in Luxembourg, Singapore, and Hong Kong.

Issuers of Euro-CDs are very large banks with extensive international banking operations. Purchasers are usually sizable institutional investors. Since most transactions are in blocks of $5 million or more, the Euro-CD market is considered a wholesale market. Transactions of $1 million are possible but they are usually made at a yield concession. Despite the international scope, Euro-CD transactions are as easily made as domestic transactions. Access to the primary market may be through the issuing bank, the U. S. parent bank, or a CD dealer. In the secondary market many of the domestic CD dealers also make a market in Euro-CDs.

Euro-TDs

Eurodollar time deposits are nonnegotiable so ownership may not be transferred. This is also a wholesale market with transactions in blocks of $5 million or more. Contact must be made with the issuing bank or a broker acting as an intermediary since there is no secondary market.

Return vs. Risk

The return on Eurodollar deposits tends to be about 50 to 100 basis points above the yield on comparable quality, domestic CDs with the same maturity. Depending on market conditions and the level of interest rates, the spread may fall outside this range. When evaluating the spread, the risk of Eurodollar deposits must be considered. The term *sovereign risk* refers to the possibility of unfriendly or hostile action by the foreign host government. For example, the assets may be frozen and the funds prevented from leaving the country. As a practical matter, any hint of political instability that would lead to such action would dry up the market overnight. The imposition of exchange controls would cause economic chaos within a country and destroy it as an international money center. Politicians are not oblivious to such a result. The sovereign risk, therefore, is real but in most cases is rather small in well-established, international money centers.

Eurodollar deposits are uninsured and the issuing banks are not monitored or regulated by U. S. regulatory agencies. Thus, the credit standing of the issuer is of prime importance. But credit risk may be difficult to estimate in the case of foreign banks. The strength of foreign subsidiaries of U. S. banks and especially foreign branches of U. S. banks depends on the parent, domestic bank. In many cases these domestic parents are among the premier U. S. banks.

YANKEE CDs

Another rapidly growing CD instrument is the *Yankee CD*. These are *dollar-denominated deposits in foreign bank branches and agencies located in the U. S.* For example, like Citibank, the New York City branch of the Sumitomo Bank may sell CDs in the domestic market to obtain dollar-denominated deposits. Banks from Japan, Canada, England, Germany, Switzerland, and the Netherlands are active in U. S. branch and agency operations.

It is important to distinguish between branches, subsidiaries, and agencies. Branches of foreign banks are established to conduct international banking activities. They are subject to the banking laws and regulations of the United States. Deposits in branches are obligations of the foreign bank. However, U. S. subsidiaries of foreign banks are actually domestic banks because they are separately chartered, legal entities. CDs of these subsidiaries, which often have the same name as the parent bank, are domestic CDs rather than Yankee CDs since they are not obligations of the foreign bank. U. S. agencies of foreign banks are similar to branches but they are more restricted in their ability to accept deposits. Agencies based in New York may issue Yankee CDs.

These CDs are very similar to negotiable Euro-CDs and domestic CDs. FDIC insurance is available to foreign branches and agencies but since this is a wholesale market with most transactions in $5 million blocks, deposit insurance is not a factor for investors. Transactions are easily arranged directly with issuers or in the secondary market through dealers. Sovereign risk is usually not an issue with Yankee CDs but the issuer's credit risk is an important factor.

PRICING CDs

Although some banks issue CDs on a discounted basis like Treasury bills and commercial paper, most CDs are priced on an interest-bearing basis. A stated annualized rate is paid at maturity in the case of instruments maturing in one year or less. Newly issued CDs have a contractual rate that is equal to the market rate at the time of the offering so the price is par. With the passage of time and as money market rates change, the market value of an existing negotiable CD will change. To conduct transactions involving interest-bearing, negotiable CDs in the secondary market, the mechanics of CD pricing must be understood.

The outlay for an existing CD reflects both the price of the CD and the contractual interest that accrues to the seller for the interval the seller held the CD. The model is

$$\text{Price} = \text{Total Outlay} - \text{Accrued Interest}$$

$$P = \frac{cn_o + 360}{yn + 360} - \frac{c(n_o - n)}{360}.$$

where P = price per dollar of par value
    c = contractual rate
    n_o = original maturity in days
    y = quoted CD market rate
    n = remaining maturity in days.

An example will demonstrate the process.

> *Example.* A negotiable, interest-bearing 10 percent CD had an original maturity of 90 days and now has sixty days remaining to maturity. The market rate quoted for this CD is 11 percent. What is the price of the CD and the accrued interest?
> Substituting the values of c, n_o, y, and n into the model results in
>
> $$P = \frac{.10(90) + 360}{.11(60) + 360} - \frac{.10(90 - 60)}{360}$$
>
> $$= 1.00655 - .00833$$
>
> $$= .99822 \text{ or } 99.822 \ (\% \text{ of par}).$$

The Wall Street version of the bond-yield equivalent is a simple conversion of the quoted CD rate to a 365-day basis. Letting r represent the bond-yield equivalent, the conversion model is

$$r = y(365/360).$$

In the example above, the bond-yield equivalent is

$$r = .11(365/360)$$
$$= .1115 \text{ or } 11.15\%.$$

This yield adjustment is accurate if the remaining maturity of the CD is close to six months. Otherwise it is an approximation and a more refined approach should be used.[1]

---

[1] See the chapter dealing with financial mathematics in this book for such an approach.

CONCLUSION

CDs have been and continue to be one of the main sources of funds for large commercial banks. Because of deregulation, increased competition for funds, and a changing market structure, the market is no longer limited to large domestic money center banks issuing negotiable CDs. Smaller depository institutions as well as foreign banks have added other dimensions to this market. As a result, the role of the CD market in the management of banks and other depository institutions will become more prominent, especially as the competition for funds intensifies.

REFERENCES

Goodfriend, Marvin, "Eurodollars," *Instruments of the Money Market*, 5th ed., edited by Timothy Q. Cook and Bruce J. Summers, Richmond, Virginia: Federal Reserve Bank of Richmond, 1981, pp. 123-133.

Melton, William C., "The Market for Large Negotiable CDs," *Quarterly Review*, Federal Reserve Bank of New York, Winter 1977-78, pp. 22-34.

Stigum, Marcia, *The Money Market*, Homewood, Illinois: Dow Jones-Irwin, 1983.

Summers, Bruce J., "Negotiable Certificates of Deposit," *Instruments of the Money Market*, 5th ed., edited by Timothy Q. Cook and Bruce J. Summers, Richmond, Virginia: Federal Reserve Bank of Richmond, 1981, pp. 73-92.

18

Bankers' Acceptances

One of the least understood money market instruments is the *banker's acceptance* (BA). Despite this lack of understanding, acceptances have become increasingly important to commercial banks, institutional investors, and firms involved in international trade. Although increasingly used to finance domestic trade and the domestic storage of goods, most BAs arise through the financing of United States imports or exports. In recent years about one-third of the total export-import trade of the U. S. has been financed with acceptances. The BA market is centered around U. S. banks, but foreign banks are increasing their use of the instrument to finance transactions between different countries. The importance of bankers' acceptances in international trade stems from the fact that they are a form of trade credit like accounts receivable or direct bank loans. But unlike these forms of credit, acceptances enable buyers and sellers who are unknown to each other and located in different parts of the world to conduct business with the financial arrangements guaranteed by banks. In the absence of such arrangements, exporters might be unwilling to extend trade credit to a buyer in a foreign country because of difficulty in obtaining credit information. Also, if the foreign buyer simply refused to pay after receiving the goods, the seller may have little recourse. Similarly, buyers would be reluctant to pay for goods in advance without assurance that the merchandise will actually be shipped. Since BAs overcome these obstacles, they facilitate the shipment of goods and stimulate trade.

NATURE OF BANKERS' ACCEPTANCES

Acceptances are short-term instruments with maturities usually ranging from 30 to 180 days. They have an extraordinary record of safety with no known losses of principal to investors since their use began in the early 1900s. The banker's acceptance is similar to an ordinary check drawn on a bank in that it is an order to pay a specified amount to a particular party such as an exporter of goods. Unlike a check, however, an acceptance is payable in the future rather than immediately. For this reason, an acceptance is called a *time draft.* The bank's obligation to pay the draft at maturity is formally acknowledged when the word "accepted" is stamped on the draft. The acceptance of the draft by the bank has the effect of substituting the bank's credit standing for that of the buyer of the goods underlying the transaction. The bank may then hold the acceptance, sell it on a discounted basis to a BA dealer, or discount it directly to an end-investor.

Life-Cycle of an Acceptance

In order to gain insight regarding the BA, its market, and the role of commercial banks, it is useful to trace the life-cycle of an acceptance. The creation and disposition of BAs can take several forms. After examining the following example and the accompanying flowchart, some variations will be discussed.[1]

> *Example.*   A buyer of office equipment in Brussels, Belgium wishes to purchase office equipment from a seller located in Chicago. The equipment has a cost of $825,000 and is to be financed by a banker's acceptance. The sequence of steps is shown in Figure 1 and explained below.
>
> 1. The buyer applies for a *letter of credit* (LOC) from its Brussels bank. After examining the creditworthiness of its customer, the bank issues a letter of credit "in favor of" the seller in Chicago. The LOC is often the key to an acceptance transaction. It specifies the details of the transaction, the responsibilities of all parties, and authorizes the seller in Chicago to draw a draft on the Brussels' correspondent bank in Chicago. The draft is for $825,000 and is payable at the end of the financing period, in this case 90 days from the date of shipment.
> 2. Upon approval of the LOC application, the buyer places an order for the equipment.
> 3. The Brussels bank sends the LOC to the Chicago bank.
> 4. The Chicago bank authenticates the LOC and sends it to the seller, along with the draft.
> 5. The seller ships the goods to the buyer in Brussels and then presents the shipping documents, LOC, and draft to the Chicago bank for payment.
> 6. After satisfying itself that the documents are in compliance with the terms of the LOC, the Chicago bank then discounts the acceptance, charging the discount to the Brussels bank, and pays the seller the face value. Assuming the banker's acceptance discount rate, d, is 9.4 percent, the price for this n-day instrument is obtained from the discounting model.

$$P = 1 - \frac{nd}{360}$$

$$= 1 - \frac{90(.0940)}{360}$$

$$= .9765 \text{ or } 97.65 \text{ (\% of par).}$$

[1] The example is adapted, with modifications, from Jack L. Hervey, "Bankers' Acceptances," *Business Conditions,* Federal Reserve Bank of Chicago, May 1976, pp. 3-11.

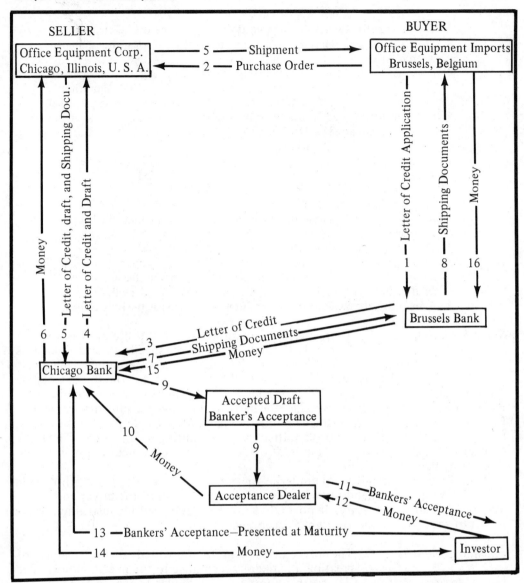

Figure 1   A Bankers' Acceptance Is Created, Discounted, Sold, and Paid at Maturity. Figure adapted from Jack Hervey, "Banker's Acceptances," Federal Reserve Bank of Chicago, *Business Conditions*, May 1976, p.5.

The value of the acceptance is

$$\$825,000 \times .9765 = \$805,612.50$$

and the discount is $19,387.50. An acceptance fee usually ranging from ½ of 1 percent to 1 percent of the face amount is also charged to the Brussels bank. Assuming a fee of 1 percent, this would be $8,230. The fee and discount are paid immediately by the Brussels bank rather than at maturity.

7. The Chicago bank sends the shipping documents to the Brussels bank.
8. The Brussels bank sends the documents to the buyer to clear the equipment when it arrives.
9. After paying the seller and stamping the draft "accepted," the Chicago bank then sells it to an acceptance dealer at a discount. An additional profit may be made by the bank if the BA can be sold to the dealer at a lower yield than that which was used to calculate the original discounted value when the seller was reimbursed (in step 6).
10. The dealer pays the Chicago bank.
11. The acceptance dealer marks up the price of the BA (or lowers the yield) and sells it to an end-investor. This investor has provided the financing for the office equipment.
12. The investor pays the dealer.
13. At maturity, 90 days after the shipment, the investor presents the BA to the accepting bank for payment.
14. The investor receives the face value of the acceptance.
15. At maturity the Brussels bank wire transfers the face amount of the acceptance to the Chicago bank. (The discount and acceptance fee were paid earlier after the draft was presented to the Chicago bank by the seller.)
16. At maturity, the buyer pays or makes arrangements to pay the Brussels bank.

Some Variations

There are several variations of the life-cycle shown in Figure 1. If the letter of credit specifies that the seller is to pay the discount, the face value of the BA may be correspondingly higher. If the seller receives the discounted value, the seller may decide to hold the acceptance until maturity. If so, the seller then provides the financing and earns the discount. Payment at maturity is guaranteed by the bank. If the seller presents the acceptance for immediate payment as in the example, the bank may decide to hold the instrument and earn the discount itself rather than discounting it to a dealer. The bank then provides the financing. About 10 percent of all acceptances are held in the originating bank's portfolio.

A letter of credit need not underlie the transaction as it did in the life-cycle diagram. An agreement between banks, as representatives of the buyer and seller, may be all that is necessary. If no LOC is involved, the resulting instrument is referred to as a "clean" or "outright" acceptance.

Financing Imports

The preceding example illustrated the mechanics of creating a banker's acceptance to finance an export. The use of an acceptance to finance an import is quite similar as demonstrated in the following example.

Example.   A U. S. retailer—the importer—wishes to finance the purchase of television sets from Japan on an acceptance basis. The retailer arranges for a letter of credit to be issued by its commercial bank in New York in favor of the Japanese exporter. The letter authorizes the exporter to draw a time draft for a specified amount on the New York bank. The exporter then presents the draft to its local bank in Japan and receives immediate payment. The Japanese bank then forwards the draft to the New York bank that issued the letter of credit. The bank stamps the draft "accepted" and thus acknowledges its obligation to pay the draft at maturity. The banker's acceptance is then either returned to the Japanese bank or sold to an acceptance dealer and the proceeds credited to the account of the Japanese bank. The shipping documents are released to the American importer thus allowing the retailer to obtain and distribute the television sets. The proceeds of the sales will be deposited by the retailer in the accepting bank in time to honor the acceptance. At maturity, the acceptance is presented to the New York bank for payment and the transaction is completed.

It should be noted that in both of the examples above, the accepting banks were in the United States. This occurs because the secondary market for acceptances is primarily in the U. S. The examples also enable the advantages and disadvantages of acceptances to banks, investors, and borrowers to be placed in perspective.

Advantages and Disadvantages of BAs

The Bank's Viewpoint   BAs provide the accepting bank with a high degree of flexibility. At the bank's option, an acceptance may or may not involve an outlay of funds. If the bank chooses to discount the acceptance in the money market, the end-investor supplies the funds. The bank has simply lent its name to the transaction and collects a fee in the process. This is an important consideration during periods of tight credit and strong loan demand. By using acceptance financing, a bank is able to accommodate customer demands for credit without expanding its loan base. Depending on its liquidity and loan position, the accepting bank may, as pointed out, hold the acceptance rather than discounting it to a dealer or end-investor. This is an extension of bank credit much like a commercial loan. Unlike most bank loans, however, acceptances are readily marketable. After deciding to hold the acceptance, the bank may experience heavy loan demand. Since BAs may be sold to raise funds, they can be an important element in a bank's liquidity position.

As discussed shortly, an acceptance may be classified as *eligible for discount* if certain conditions are met. When such an acceptance is sold in the secondary market by a member bank, the outstanding acceptance is *not* included as part of the bank's normal lending limit for individual customers. This limit is an amount equal to 15 percent of capital and subordinated debentures plus 50 percent of the bank's loan loss reserve. Thus, the ability to sell acceptances provides the bank with flexibility in extending credit beyond the statutory limit. This additional extension of credit is limited to 10 percent of the bank's capital. Another aspect of BAs that are *eligible for discount* is that when such instruments are sold in the secondary market, the funds obtained are *not* subject to reserve requirements. This lowers the cost of such funds relative to deposits such as CDs.

BAs have a high administrative cost. Since a specialized staff with international experience is essential, this activity is conducted primarily by large banks. However, in recent years medium-size regional banks have increased their share of the BA market.

The Investor's   From the investor's standpoint, BAs are well-secured in-
Viewpoint   struments. In addition to the backing of the accepting
                     bank, BAs are usually secured by either direct title to
the merchandise underlying the transaction, or indirect title through a warehouse or trust receipt. The drawer of the investment is also contingently liable for pay-

ment. Because of their high quality, the yields on acceptances of well-known banks closely parallel the yields on prime CDs and prime commercial paper. An active secondary market provides investors with a high degree of marketability. There are, however, some drawbacks for investors.

BAs are not always available in a specific maturity or amount needed by an investor. Acceptances in amounts smaller than $500,000 are considered odd-lots. A yield concession is necessary to execute an odd-lot transaction in the secondary market. For this reason, the market is dominated by large-scale institutional investors. Some banks attempt to overcome this problem by selling to end-investors "participations" in BAs held by the bank in their own portfolio.

The Borrower's   The borrower's cost of acceptance financing is usually
Viewpoint   quoted at an "all-in" rate. This includes the discount
                         rate and the acceptance fee. Further adjustments may
be made to reflect documentation costs or to convert the discount rate to a simple interest rate or bond-yield equivalent. Even with such adjustments, the cost of acceptance financing usually compares favorably with alternatives such as bank loans. However, only special types of transactions may be financed using acceptances. Furthermore, it is essential that the borrower know the precise term for which the funds are needed. A prepayment may raise the borrower's cost substantially.

REGULATION OF BANKERS' ACCEPTANCES

The Federal Reserve has the authority to regulate the creation of acceptances by depository institutions. Under provisions of the *Depository Institutions Deregulation and Monetary Control Act of 1980* the Federal Reserve also has reserve requirement authority over all depository institutions. The reserve status of funds obtained by the sale of acceptances is affected by this authority.

Many of the present regulations affecting BAs stem from current practices of the Federal Reserve as well as the earlier use of acceptances in open-market operations. Like Federal Reserve open-market operations involving U. S. Treasury securities, acceptances were bought and sold to expand and contract the banking system's reserves. This form of direct involvement in the acceptance market ended in 1977. Current practices by the Federal Reserve include using BAs in repurchase agreements to make short-term adjustments in the money supply, purchasing BAs for its own account, and holding acceptances to collateralize advances to banks. These current practices, coupled with the Federal Reserve's earlier use of BAs in open-market operations, have resulted in the specification of so-called "eligibility" standards. These standards have a significant impact on the acceptance market and they are now viewed as quality benchmarks in the secondary market.

Eligible for Discount

An important Federal Reserve classification for BAs is the *eligible for discount* category. Acceptances in this category qualify for outright purchase by the Federal

Reserve, repurchase agreements, and collateral for member advances. The reserve status and *eligible for discount* requirements are covered by separate regulations. However, as a practical matter, almost all acceptances that are *eligible for discount* are also reserve-free if sold.

Generally, to be eligible for discount, acceptances related to both international and domestic transactions must have an original maturity not exceeding six months and represent marketable goods. If it is a foreign transaction, the shipment of goods must be between countries (rather than *within* a foreign country). Domestic transactions may involve the shipment of goods or the storage of readily marketable goods secured by a warehouse receipt.[2] The acceptance must also be endorsed by at least one member bank.

Eligible for Purchase

Another class of acceptances as defined by the Federal Reserve is the *eligible for purchase* category. The term is misleading because under present Federal Reserve procedures it refers to the use of particular acceptances in repurchase agreements rather than outright purchases for the Federal Reserve's own portfolio. Such BAs also qualify as collateral for advances to banks. Any acceptance that is *eligible for discount* is also *eligible for purchase,* but the reverse is not true. The requirements for the *purchase* category are slightly less stringent than the *discount* category. The main difference is that the maturity of the acceptance is six to nine months rather than six months or less. When these longer maturity acceptances are sold in the secondary market, the funds are subject to reserve requirements.

BAs that do not qualify as *eligible for discount* or *eligible for purchase* are called *ineligible* acceptances. In addition to "long maturity" acceptances, those with an original maturity exceeding nine months, this category includes so-called *finance bills,* or *working capital bills* as they are also known.

Market Implications

The classification of acceptances by the Federal Reserve has important implications in the secondary market. Bankers' acceptances are distributed through the in-house efforts of major banks and through acceptance dealers. Although some investors do not care if an acceptance is eligible or ineligible, the latter are generally not as well received in the secondary market as are eligible issues. Thus, some dealers will not trade ineligible issues. Banks are somewhat reluctant to originate such instruments because of the lower degree of marketability, reserve requirements, and the reduced flexibility relative to eligible acceptances. When these instruments do arise, they tend to be held in the originating bank's own portfolio or they are sold directly to end-investors through in-house distribution efforts.

---

[2] For a summary of the different types of transactions underlying acceptances, their eligibility characteristics, and reserve status, see: Jack L. Hervey, "Bankers' Acceptances Revisited," *Economic Perspectives*, Federal Reserve Bank of Chicago, May/June 1983, pp. 21-31.

Other Aspects of Regulation

The *Export Trading Company Act of 1982* limits the aggregate amount of a bank's outstanding acceptances to 150 percent of its paid-in capital and surplus. With permission from the Federal Reserve, the limit may be raised to 200 percent. The same restriction applies to U. S. branches or agencies of foreign banks. The Act also limits BAs related to domestic shipping and storage to 50 percent of a bank's allowable outstanding acceptances. The law allows banks to "participate out," or sell, a portion of its acceptance liability to another institution. The participated portion is not a part of the bank's outstanding acceptances for the purpose of computing the ceiling on outstanding BAs. Another aspect of the Act affects domestic transactions. It is no longer necessary for title documents to accompany an acceptance related to domestic shipments to qualify as *eligible for discount*. The removal of this barrier will stimulate the domestic use of these instruments.

Like other market participants, the Federal Reserve is concerned about the quality of the bankers' acceptances in which it deals. In addition to imposing eligibility standards on acceptances, the Federal Reserve limits its activities to "prime" acceptances. Such a designation is based on such factors as the creditworthiness of the accepting bank, marketability of the bank's instruments, and the bank's volume of acceptance transactions. Bank size is not necessarily a critical factor.[3] A "prime" designation by the Federal Reserve enhances a bank's ability to conduct a successful acceptance operation.

CONCLUSION

Although highly specialized and not well-known outside of international banking circles and the money market, bankers' acceptances are ideally suited to finance certain types of transactions, both international and domestic. Agricultural products, oil, food, trucks, machinery, computers, and appliances are just a few of the commodities underlying bankers' acceptances. These instruments offer important advantages for commercial banks, investors, and borrowers. Because of these advantages, the use of acceptances to finance trade has expanded in recent years. Further expansion is likely as these benefits become more widely recognized.

REFERENCES

Helfrich, Ralph T. "Trading in Bankers' Acceptances: A View from the Acceptance Desk of the Federal Reserve Bank of New York," *Monthly Review*, Federal Reserve Bank of New York, LVIII (February, 1976), 51-57.

Hervey, Jack L. "Bankers' Acceptances," *Business Conditions*, Federal Reserve Bank of Chicago, (May 1976), 3-11.

———. "Bankers' Acceptances Revisited," *Economic Perspectives*, Federal Reserve Bank of Chicago, (May/June 1983), 21-31.

Melton, William C., and Jean M. Mahr. "Bankers' Acceptances," *Quarterly Review*, Federal Reserve Bank of New York, VI, No. 2 (Summer, 1981), 39-55.

[3] For a discussion of the manner in which "prime banks" are designated see: Ralph T. Helfrich, "Trading in Bankers' Acceptances: A View from the Acceptance Desk of the Federal Reserve Bank of New York, *Monthly Review*, Federal Reserve Bank of New York, February 1976, pp. 56-57.

19

Commercial Paper

Commercial paper represents unsecured, short-term promissory notes issued by industrial firms, finance companies, public utilities, bank holding companies, insurance companies, S&Ls, mortgage companies, and municipalities. In recent years many foreign issuers have sold commercial paper in the domestic market. Industrial firms sell paper to meet day-to-day working capital and seasonal needs while public utilities often rely on commercial paper as interim or "bridge financing" between the sale of long-term securities. Bank holding companies use commercial paper to finance banking-related activities of subsidiaries involved in mortgage banking, factoring, leasing, and consumer finance. Finance companies borrow continuously in the paper market to support their business and consumer lending activities. S&Ls have used commercial paper to offset deposit outflows and finance the "warehousing" of mortgage loans until they are packaged and sold. Municipalities, whose paper is tax-exempt, use the paper market to offset the uneven cash inflows resulting from periodic property tax payments.

The original maturity of newly issued paper ranges from a few days to not more than 270 days. The maturity restriction arises because paper with a maturity greater than 270 days must be registered with the Securities and Exchange Commission, a time-consuming and expensive process.

Most paper is issued with maturities ranging from 30 to 120 days but the market is such that maturities may be tailored to meet specific needs of investors. Like Treasury bills and most agency instruments, commercial paper is issued on a discounted basis and interest accrues on the basis of a 360-day year. The minimum purchase of commercial paper is typically $100,000 although a round lot is $1 million. The investment side of the paper market is dominated by large-scale investors such as money market funds, large corporations, endowments, and financial institutions.

Table 1 Commercial Paper Ratings

	Rating Service		
	Standard & Poor's	Moody's	Fitch's
Highest Investment Grade	A-1	Prime-1	F-1
High Investment Grade	A-2	Prime-2	F-2
Medium Investment Grade	A-3	Prime-3	F-3

DEFAULT RISK

In 1970, the financial markets were shaken when Penn Central was unable to refinance $82 million in commercial paper and went into bankruptcy. As a result, investors became more concerned about the creditworthiness of issuers. Since commercial paper is unsecured, only those issuers with an excellent credit standing are able to sell paper. To assist investors in making such a judgment, financial ratings are provided for issuers of paper by Moody's, Standard & Poor's and Fitch's. The rating classifications are shown in Table 1.

BANK SUPPORT

Although commercial banks do not issue commercial paper, they are actively involved in the paper market. Banks are buyers of paper for their own portfolios or on behalf of trust accounts. Banks also act as paying and collection agents for issuers. More importantly, commercial banks provide essential financial support for the issuers of commercial paper.

Backup Lines of Credit

The market requires that issuers back their commercial paper dollar-for-dollar with *backup lines of credit* maintained with commercial banks. Under these lines, issuers may borrow on a short-term basis, usually 90 days, to pay off maturing paper. This backup is important for both investors and the issuer. At times, tight credit conditions in the financial markets are such that even strong, creditworthy issuers find it difficult to refinance or "roll over" outstanding paper. The backup provides an interim source of financing until the market stabilizes. The cost of the backup lines usually ranges from 3/8ths of 1 percent to 3/4ths of 1 percent of the line amount depending on the issuer's creditworthiness.

In addition to the standard backup lines, many issuers have so-called *swing lines of credit*. Under this arrangement bank funds are provided for very short periods to cover shortfalls in the sale of paper on a given day. Another form of bank support for commercial paper is provided by a *revolving credit*. This arrangement is functionally similar to the backup line except that it extends for several years, is highly formal, and enables an issuer to use bank financing or commercial paper interchangeably.

LOC-Backed Paper

Issuers that lack market recognition or the creditworthiness necessary to issue paper in the national markets can obtain a high rating and lower their interest cost by backing their paper with an irrevocable, *standby letter of credit* from a commercial bank. In effect, the bank guarantees repayment of the commercial paper at maturity. The credit standing of the bank supplements the issuer's creditworthiness. Usually such paper, often referred to as a *documented discount note,* has the highest rating. The cost of such backing is higher than the cost of backup lines. However, the LOC cost is usually more than offset by lower interest costs on the paper.

DEALER VS. DIRECT PAPER

The commercial paper market is usually classified according to the manner in which the paper is distributed by issuers to investors, that is, through dealers or directly placed by the issuer. Directly placed paper accounts for about 60 percent of the total. To place paper directly, an issuer must have its own facilities, staff, and distribution network. The direct placement of paper is economically feasible only for those firms with substantial and continuous needs for commercial paper financing. Finance companies and bank holding companies are the dominant issuers of directly placed paper.

In contrast to the direct placement approach, paper may be issued through dealers who purchase the paper from the issuer for inventory and proceed to market the paper through their own distribution network. To compensate the dealers for these efforts and for bearing the added risk of price changes while selling the paper, dealers receive a fee, typically 1/8 of one percent (annualized). For example, if the market discount rate for paper is 9.25 percent, the dealer would buy the paper from the issuer at a discount rate of 9.25 + .125 = 9.375 percent. Since commercial paper is discounted, the price paid by the dealer is given by the model

$$P = 1 - \frac{nd}{360}$$

where P is the price in decimal form, n is the number of days to maturity, and d is the discount rate in decimal form. If 90-day paper is bought by a dealer at a discount rate of 9.375 percent, the price is

$$P = 1 - \frac{90(.09375)}{360}$$

$$= .9765625 \text{ or } 97.65625 \text{ (\% of par)}.$$

From an offering of $10 million, the issuer's proceeds from the dealer would be $9,765,625. The dealer would sell the paper (assuming the same day) for $9,768,750. The difference of $3,125 is the dealer's fee.

There is an important aspect of this market structure that should be kept in mind by investors. The two methods of distribution—direct and dealer placement—constitute *the* market. There is no established secondary market as is the case for most other money market instruments. This means that commercial paper usually cannot be sold prior to maturity to meet an unforeseen demand for funds. Should an investor find unexpectedly that the funds are needed, the investor may contact the issuer or the dealer to determine if either party would be willing to redeem or repurchase the paper prior to maturity. In order to maintain good relations, many issuers and dealers attempt to accommodate the investor. However, such a request should not be a standard procedure. Although the need to liquidate paper prematurely is minimized by its usually short maturity, the lack of a secondary market requires that the maturity be carefully timed to coincide with cash needs. *As a matter of policy, investors should plan to hold commercial paper until maturity.* If the ability to do this is questionable, the portfolio manager should either shorten the maturity or consider a money market instrument that has an active secondary market.

PAPER VS. BANK BORROWINGS

Firms with access to the commercial paper market are able to borrow at an interest rate that is well below the national prime lending rate quoted by banks. The spread between the two rates varies depending on market conditions, but a difference of 100 to 300 basis points is common. When the bank borrowing cost is adjusted for compensating balances and other fees, and the paper rate is adjusted for the cost of bank support, the spread is usually greater than it appears. In light of the cost savings, the commercial paper market has grown rapidly in recent years in terms of the number of issuers and the volume of paper outstanding. Much of this growth has been at the expense of commercial banks in the form of lower loan volume. Ironically, banks contribute to their own loss of market share for loans by writing letters of credit and providing other forms of support that enable firms to tap the paper market rather than borrow from banks. The fee income from this activity does provide some measure of comfort for banks.

When market interest rates are increasing, bank lending rates tend to increase more slowly than commercial paper rates and money market rates in general. As a result, the cost advantage of commercial paper usually diminishes during cyclical upswings in interest rates. During such periods, the volume of outstanding paper tends to decrease as some issuers shift the focus of their financing from paper to bank loans to reduce their reliance on the paper market. When interest rates are declining, the "sticky" bank lending rates result in commercial paper becoming relatively more advantageous. The volume of paper then expands as some issuers shift emphasis from bank loans to paper.

To remain competitive with commercial paper over all phases of the interest rate cycle, some banks make so-called *below-prime* loans. These loans are usually for very short periods such as a week or two, rather than several months. The interest rate usually approximates the commercial paper rate. The borrower benefits by avoiding the high cost of issuing paper for a very short period. Although the rate is below the prime rate, the bank benefits because the return is higher than that available on comparable alternatives such as term fed funds. In effect, banks are buying commercial paper when making below-prime loans in this manner.

CONCLUSION

In recent years, commercial paper has emerged as an important financing option for a variety of borrowers, both domestic and foreign. Like other money market instruments, it is essential that market participants understand the characteristics of commercial paper, its pricing, and the nature of the paper market. Because of the impact of the commercial paper market on the demand for commercial loans, bankers must be particularly cognizant of developments in this market. As major issuers of commercial paper, bank holding companies are also actively involved on the borrowing side.

With expanding bank support, especially the letter of credit, it is likely that this financing device will become even more widely used in the future, particularly by the "less-than-prime" borrowers. The recent trend toward the formation of bank holding companies will further develop this rapidly expanding market.

REFERENCES

Abken, Peter A., "Commercial Paper," *Economic Review*, Federal Reserve Bank of Richmond, March/April 1981, pp. 11-22.

Haag, Leonard H., *Cash Management Short-Term Investments for Colleges and Universities*, Washington, D. C., National Association of College and University Business Officers, 1977.

Hurley, Evelyn M., "The Commercial Paper Market," Federal Reserve Bulletin, March 1976.

Stigum, Marcia, *The Money Market*, Homewood, Illinois: Dow Jones-Irwin, 1983.

20

Banking's Capital Shortage: The Malaise and the Myth*

Ronald D. Watson

Is it possible that bank capital—like oil— is a scarce resource whose supply is in danger of being exhausted? To read the financial industry's trade journals a person might conclude that capital is a rare substance whose supply can grow only at a strictly limited rate. However, the current presumption that banks can't raise the funds they want for strengthening their capital positions and expanding deposits needs a lot of rethinking. Banks must have capital to inspire public confidence and absorb losses.[1] If they can't get the capital required to support their operations, maybe banks aren't serving the economy as effectively as is generally assumed.

Clearly, the banking industry must raise additional capital if it is to grow. Growth without new capital is possible, but only if bank regulators are willing to allow risks to increase, and that isn't likely. The "shortage" is occurring because banks are expanding their assets more rapidly than reinvested profits can boost capital. The obvious supplement to retained earnings is new capital from public issues of long-term debt and equity securities. But bankers claim that declining stock prices and higher interest rates have made the cost of this new money (especially the equity) too high. The problem is compounded by generally weak markets for bank securities, especially in the wake of several failures of large banks in recent years. Most banks resort to outside financing only when other sources of funds are no longer readily available.

Restricting the industry's growth to the rate at which it can generate capital internally has been suggested, but most banks are reluctant to accept a policy that might mean losing ground to other financial intermediaries or even slowing the

---

*Reprinted from *Business Review*, September 1975, pp. 3-13, with permission from the Federal Reserve Bank of Philadelphia and the author.

[1] Ronald D. Watson, "Insuring Some Progress in the Bank Capital Hassle," *Business Review* of the Federal Reserve Bank of Philadelphia, July-August 1974, pp. 3-18.

whole economy's growth. Yet, further growth for banking appears to be stymied. Internal generation of new capital is too slow, outside capital seems too costly, and the regulators are closing off the alternative of expanding without additional capital.

This should not—and need not—be an impasse. If the problem looks insurmountable, it may be that we are zeroing in on the wrong target. The issue should not be one of "how to get capital for future expansion," but "are the profit opportunities of this expansion great enough to justify raising new capital at today's prices?" If the profits are there, banks can afford to pay the going rate for capital. If they aren't, then the capital should go to industries that have better opportunities to use it. Bank capital markets may be in poor shape, but that alone shouldn't change the way the decision to expand is made.

THE CAPITAL CHASM

The bank capital "shortage" has been brewing for several years, but recent projections of enormous capital shortfalls over the next decade have significantly pepped up discussions of the problem. Projections have intensified the industry's awareness that the methods used for financing growth in the 1960s may not be equal to the task in the 1970s.

Bankers have normally considered it impractical to try to close this gap with outside sources of funds. Data on bank financing is very sketchy, but the industry has a long history of depending heavily on earnings retention for additional long-term funds (as have most corporations). Of the new securities issued by banks the bulk has been debt (subordinated notes and debentures) rather than common or preferred stock.[2] In general, internal funds are more appealing as a source of capital than external funds because their cost seems very low. Retained earnings almost always look cheaper than new common stock. A new stock issue may dilute the earnings of current shareholders, but retaining earnings never will. Furthermore, there are substantial transaction costs associated with floating new debt or equity issues publicly. Retained earnings may also seem less costly than long-term debt which carries an explicit obligation to pay interest.

Raising money through new issues of common stock has become even more expensive in the last few years because bank stock prices have declined dramatically even though earnings have been growing. Bankers accustomed to seeing their shares sell for 15 to 20 times earnings in the early 1960s were dismayed to see those prices drift into the 10 to 15 times earnings range in the late 1960s and early 1970s and then plummet to the 5 to 10 times earnings range recently.[3] As stock prices

[2] "Report of Securities Issued by Commercial Banks and Holding Companies," Report No. 67, Corporate Financial Counseling Department of Irving Trust Company, New York, February 28, 1975.

[3] *Keefe Bank Stock Manual* (New York: Keefe, Bruyette, and Woods Inc., 1974). Inflation and riskier bank portfolios have been important reasons for the rising cost of new debt and equity capital. However, many bankers claim that public statements by regulators warning of capital inadequacy problems have increased the cost of funds even to very conservative banks by making investors wary of all bank securities—not just banks that had been aggressive in using leverage.

decline, the number of shares that must be sold to raise a fixed amount of new capital increases. When this occurs, the current stockholder's control of the bank is diluted and his future dividends diminish relative to what he would have received if the stock had been sold at a higher price. And each jump in equity cost has strengthened management's resolve to avoid paying the cost of raising funds with new stock issues.

Even debt capital has become more expensive in the last few years. Not long ago sound banks were able to sell their long-term obligations at an interest rate of 7 to 8 percent. However, an upward drift in rates and recent concern about bank soundness have made double-digit rates common.

CURRENT REMEDIES FOR
SPANNING THE GAP: A WEAK BRIDGE

Even though there is no universally accepted response to this problem, there have been any number of suggestions. Some have been directed toward loosening the regulatory constraint on expansion while other plans have been designed to reduce the industry's cost of capital. All of these proposals have some merit, but none constitutes a lasting solution to the problem.

Lower Capital Standards

Some effort has gone into convincing the regulatory agencies that banks don't really need all the capital that supervisors currently consider prudent. If capital standards were lowered, still more expansion could take place. Bankers point to the willingness of investors in the capital markets (until very recently) to advance debt funds to banks at interest rates nearly on a par with other high-quality corporate borrowers. This is interpreted as evidence that investors (who are the first to lose their money if banks fail) have considered banks to be good risks. If regulatory standards on capital are too conservative, reducing them would alleviate the current bind on growth. Reducing capital requirements might also enable banks to maintain the lower standard through retention of earnings. However, such a hope might be overly optimistic. A key reason that banks haven't maintained capital at the current standard through internal generation of profits is that they have been willing to sacrifice profits to achieve asset growth. If the regulator's capital constraint is relaxed without a simultaneous reexamination of the importance of maintaining profitability, the problem will just reappear in a couple of years. Asset growth will again be halted by the capital adequacy barrier, but this time it will be at an even lower standard.

More Debt

The second type of suggestion for closing the capital gap consists of plans for lowering the price that banks must pay for their capital funds. The most common proposal is that banks use more long-term debt as a substitute for equity capital. As long as debt hasn't been overused, it has a cost below that of equity and appears to be the cheapest way to raise outside capital. Debt is a particularly attractive form of capital in that it is the one form of long-term funds whose cost is a tax-deductible expense.

Yet, substituting long-term debt for new equity is also only a partial solution. Long-term debt is an inadequate substitute for equity because it has legal characteristics which are different from those of common stock. Its claim to interest is secondary to that of depositors, so it backstops their claims. But interest and principal must be repaid on time if the bank is to avoid default, and operating losses cannot be charged against debt "capital" (except in liquidation) as they can against equity capital.

Accordingly, if a bank's asset growth is financed with debt capital rather than equity, the chance of incurring a large loss that would wipe out the remaining cushion of equity capital grows. The greater the amount by which the growth of risky assets exceeds expansion of the equity cushion, the greater the risk of failure. Bondholders are also wary of this heightened risk of failure. As the investors' risks grow, the yield they demand on their investment also climbs. As a result, heavy use of "cheap" debt capital will eventually raise the cost of new equity and debt (both new and refinanced) by causing the market price of these securities to decline. This risk "spillover" reduces the cost advantage of new debt. It also hurts the financial position of the current shareholders whose investment has now dropped in value. If a bank's debt position becomes excessive by market standards, management will find that by cutting back on the use of debt the shareholders' risk will be reduced, the stock's price will tend to rise, and the overall cost of funds will be lower (even new equity issues become relatively less costly than additional debt).

New Securities

One of the problems preventing banks from using more debt capital is the poor marketability of these securities. Major banks that have market recognition are able to sell large amounts of debt at relatively low interest rates. However, smaller banks that lack this reputation aren't so fortunate. The market for their securities is normally restricted to their operating region, and borrowing costs may be higher than those of a large bank of the same risk. To overcome this disadvantage some smaller banks have borrowed debt capital from their big-city correspondents.[4] There have also been suggestions that smaller institutions use investment trusts (like mutual funds) to pool their securities. This device is intended to simplify the investor's diversification problems while providing a wider market for the securities of these banks.

Weakness in the stock and bond markets has prompted some authors to suggest that banks turn to convertible bonds for new capital. These are securities that

---

[4] This may make the smaller bank's capital position look more sound, but it hardly enhances the stability of the banking system.

can be converted into common stock if stock prices rise. Convertible bonds usually have an interest rate below that of nonconvertible debt. What's more, the price at which holders are allowed to convert their bonds into common stock can be set above the current market price of the stock. This type of security is supposed to give the issuer a cheap source of debt which will eventually be turned into equity at a better price than new stock issued right now—in a sense, the best of both worlds for the bank.

Investment trusts and convertible debt securities might be useful to a bank, but they won't make the cost of new capital substantially lower. Such a trust may improve the overall marketability of a bank's securities, making it easier for the institution to tap new sources of capital. However, an investor should be able to diversify his or her investments without the trust and has little reason other than convenience to accept a significantly lower return on pooled securities than for the individual issues.

Convertible bonds (and convertible preferred stocks) are also useful, but again they don't solve the problem. On the surface they look like a very cheap way to raise money. But this is not the case. If a bank offers a convertible bond, it may sell the securities at a low interest rate and attractive conversion price. However, it has still sold a debt issue, and debt is riskier for the bank than new equity. Holders of these bonds will only convert them to stock if the price of the bank's stock rises to a level above its conversion price in the future. If a bank really wants debt capital now and equity capital sometime in the future, it might be better off to float a bond issue initially, and then refinance it with a common stock issue later at the stock's higher price. In principle, there's no reason to expect a bank to be able to raise capital substantially more cheaply in the long run with convertible securities than with ordinary debt and stock.

Cut Dividend Payout

The high cost of new external capital has also prompted the suggestion that banks boost earnings retention by gradually cutting the proportion of earnings paid out as dividends. Retained earnings are an appealing way to build equity capital because the process doesn't create new shares which dilute earnings. The internal funds also increase the likelihood that there will be higher earnings in subsequent years.

But the suggestion that higher earnings retention be used when equity capital costs are high skips over some basic economics. If the cost of new equity is prohibitive, the cost of retained earnings is closely linked to the cost of new equity in the long run. In a world without taxes these costs would be identical except for the cost of underwriting new stock issues. Taxes make retained earnings slightly cheaper because investors whose profits are retained for reinvestment by the bank will avoid income taxes—at least until the reinvested profits produce higher dividends or until stockholders realize a capital gain on their investment. Realizing a capital gain would reduce the effective tax rate on the profits from reinvestment.

The connection between the cost of retained earnings and that of new common stock becomes clearer if we think of retained earnings as bank profits that are being reinvested within the organization for the benefit of the shareholders rather than being paid out to them in the form of dividends. Those same investors who want a very high return for investing in a new stock issue aren't likely to be happy to have their profits reinvested for them at significantly lower expected returns. If investors currently expect 15 percent as a return for investing in a bank's stock, they must feel that 15 percent is a competitive return given the risks of bank investment and the alternative uses they have for their money. If the bank can't earn enough profit on these retained earnings to give the shareholders that 15 percent return, it would make the investors better off by giving them the money as a dividend to invest as they see fit. In the long run, reinvestment of retained earnings at substandard rates will lower the bank's overall rate of return, and investors will bid down the price of the bank's stock. Therefore, reinvesting retained earnings when profit prospects don't warrant doing so is no solution to the capital problem.

Boost Earnings

The final proposal for closing the capital gap is one of speeding internal equity creation by increasing earnings margins. Greater profits would allow earnings to grow faster, equity to expand faster, and asset growth to be less impeded by capital. The proposal that banks raise their profit margins is the soundest and the most important of this crop of "solutions." It comes the closest to confronting the fundamental reason that the industry finds itself "unable" to raise adequate capital. It is also the basic component of a real solution.

THE FUNDAMENTAL PROBLEM

The problem that banks face isn't a shortage of capital but an unwillingness or inability to pay the "going rate." There is no question that capital costs are high right now. Adjusting to these rising capital costs is difficult for all businessmen— and the reaction is likely to be slow. Many bankers have delayed raising capital hoping that a future drop in market rates will reduce these capital costs.

Beyond the argument that rates may soon drop, many bank managers are simply unwilling to tolerate the dilution of earnings per share that could accompany a new stock issue (spreading the existing earnings pool over a larger number of shares). Retained earnings may have a high implicit cost, but it's a difficult cost to pinpoint. Diluted earnings, however, suggest that management may have made some errors somewhere along the line. That makes dilution a difficult path to accept (see Box).

Bankers may also be unwilling to pay the high cost of new capital for the sound economic reason that they cannot reinvest it at a sufficiently high return. They may know that they need greater earnings to justify raising additional funds yet may be unable to increase their margins because competitive pressures are too strong. Any move to raise earnings will be hard to sustain if other financial institutions don't consider themselves to be under the same pressures. If only one bank in an area raises its loan rate, its competitors will have an advantage in selling their services. In all probability the first bank will lose some of its share of the market. It's only when all banks feel the pressure to build their capital (and no one has a clear cost advantage) that profit margins can be raised successfully. Even then, banks may lose some business to other nonbank financial organizations unless those firms are under equivalent pressure to boost earnings.

In the long run, the banking industry can only pay a higher price for capital if it can pass these costs along to customers in the form of higher effective interest rates or higher fees for other services provided. The ability to pass costs along depends in greater part on whether the industry can preserve its cost advantage over (or, at least, parity with) competing suppliers of financial services. If bank loan prices can't be competitive, profit opportunities will shrink and maintaining the industry's recent growth rate will be impossible.

THE FUNDAMENTAL SOLUTION

The industry can pay the going rate for capital if it is careful to use sound methods in analyzing its cost of funds and return available on new investments. In the long run, solid financial analysis will be more effective in loosening the industry's growth constraints than plans to make bank securities more marketable. Management will also find that its own long-run interests are served by making sound financial decisions. Asset growth may be one measure of accomplishment, but consistent profitability over the long haul makes a banker's position more secure.

The Cost of Funds

One of the most basic problems that industry must confront is estimating the costs of its own sources of funds. Bank management must determine where new money is coming from, what its full cost is, and what effect decisions to change the bank's capital structure (and, thereby, its risk) will have on the cost of these funds. The cost of funds to a bank depends in part on the riskiness of its capital structure—the proportions in which it raises long-term versus short-term funds and debt capital versus equity. A bank may raise its next dollar of funds from any of several specific sources, but it must carefully maintain a balance of debt and equity as it grows over time. If this week's funds come from debt sources, they will soon have to balanced with new equity. Since increasing risk makes it impractical to expand indefinitely using only short-term borrowings, bankers must include the cost of funds from all of the sources that will eventually be tapped when they estimate the real cost of additional funds.[5] To be profitable, any in-

---

[5] A common technique for estimating a corporation's cost of new funds is the weighted average method. A business evaluates the net cost of raising additional funds from debt and equity sources by estimating the cost of each source and weighting the cost according to the proportion that those funds will represent of any new money raised. If a bank expects to finance 80 percent of its growth with short-term debt costing 4 percent after taxes and the other 20 percent of the expansion with new stock costing 12 percent, its weighted average cost of funds is $.8 \times .04 + .2 \times .12 = .032 + .024 = .056$ (5.6 percent). See Box for a more thorough explanation of this process.

WHEN WILL DILUTION OCCUR?

A common argument advanced against the sale of new stock is the concern that the stock's earnings per share (E.P.S.) will be diluted by an increase in the number of shares outstanding. This is true, and to the extent that a bank's ability to pay dividends is tied to its E.P.S., it is undesirable to dilute earnings. However, this isn't the whole story.

New equity capital does more than simply dilute the current earnings of the existing shares. The new money can be invested profitably and used as a base for expanding other liabilities. It also reduces the risk of the bank's capital structure. It is quite possible that shareholders of a bank that sells new common stock can experience a mild dilution of their earnings but be better off. They have a sounder investment because their risk is lower and the bank now has a better equity base on which to expand in the future. As a practical matter, new stock issues *almost require* dilution in the short run. Stock must be sold in large enough blocks that the flotation and underwriting cost aren't too large a proportion of the total funds raised. But the new equity will then be sufficient for further expansion of fixed-cost liabilities and the bank can releverage the earnings to their former level.

Stock Price Dip. It's almost an article of faith that new stock can't be issued after a fall in the bank's stock price without diluting earnings. Dilution may well occur, but it isn't a foregone conclusion.

Suppose the Ninth National Bank's Balance sheet is the following.

Cash	(0%)*	$ 100	Deposits	(6%)	$ 600
Bonds	(7%)	500	Borrowing	(7%)	500
Loans	(11%)	600	Capital	(20 shares	100
				@ $5 per)	
Total		$1200	Total		$1200

Assuming the bank's tax rate is 50 percent, its earnings per share would then be

revenues   − expenses = income − taxes = profit
$(0 + 35 + 66) - (36 + 35) =$ 30   −   15 $= 15/20 = \$.75$ E.P.S.

Assuming that the stock's market price is equal to its par value, this is a 15 percent return on the stockholders' investment.

Suppose this bank had some attractive investment and lending opportunities but needed additional money to expand its assets. A total of $200 could be invested as follows:

20% in bonds at 7% = .014
80% in loans at 11% = .088

.102 = 10.2% before-tax yield
5.1% after-tax yield

Suppose, also, that the bank would have to rely heavily on purchased funds and new stock to raise this money but could get it in the following way:

20% from new deposits
70% from borrowings
10% from new common stock (4 new shares).

The average cost of these marginal sources of funds (adjusted for the tax deductibility of interest) would be

Proportion		Tax-Adjusted Cost	
.2	X	$(.06 \times .5 = .03)$	= .0060
.7	X	$(.07 \times .5 = .035)$	= .0245
.1	X	$(.15)$	= .0150

$$.0455 = 4.55\% \text{ tax-adjusted cost of funds}$$

As long as funds can be raised at 4.55 percent and invested at 5.1 percent, the bank should expand.** In fact, if the bank makes this expansion its new balance sheet would be

Cash	(0%)	$ 100	Deposits	(6%)	$ 640
Bonds	(7%)	540	Borrowings	(7%)	640
Loans	(11%)	760	Capital	(24 shares	120
				@ $5 par)	
Total		$1400	Total		$1400

and the E.P.S. of the bank's stock (including the new shares) would jump to

revenues   —   expenses   = income — taxes = profit
$(0 + 37.80 + 83.60) - (38.40 + 44.80) =$ 38.20 — 19.10 = 19.10/24 =
$.796 E.P.S.

---

*The numbers in parentheses denote the effective *yield* on assets or the net cost of funds raised. Economic theory suggests that a firm should utilize a source of funds until the marginal cost of the next dollar raised from that source is exactly equal to the marginal cost of a dollar from any alternative source. If the bank described above really found that its cost of obtaining new deposits was below the cost of new short-term borrowings, it should tap that source until the marginal cost of deposits rises to the level of the cost of new borrowings.

**Bankers continually confront choices between greater return with higher risk or lesser returns with lesser risks. This analysis assumes that the bank's overall risk has not been altered by the expansion. The proportion of risk assets is up, but so is the bank's capital position. Therefore, the return expected by investors will not change.

Now suppose that inflation picks up or investors become worried about the long-run profitability of banks. The price of Ninth National's stock might drop from $5 to $4 a share. That represents a significant increase in the cost of new equity capital to the bank (15 percent to 18¾ percent), and it will now take five new shares rather than four to raise the $20 of new equity. However, the fact that these costs have risen is not sufficient reason to abandon the expansion. If profits from the new investments are high enough to cover the jump in equity costs, the bank should go ahead with its plans. If overall profits are unchanged the new E.P.S. will be ...

$$\$19.10/25 \text{ shares} = \$ .764 \text{ E.P.S.}$$

This is far less attractive than the 79.6¢ E.P.S. that the bank's shareholders would have received had the stock price remained $5 a share. But both new and old shareholders are still better off with the expansion than they would have been without it (76.4¢ versus 75¢).

In summary, an expansion that earns enough to benefit the new shareholders will automatically make the old ones better off. It's only when the new capital investment isn't profitable by the market's current standard of returns that expansion shouldn't be undertaken. Dilution will occur *only* when the wrong financial decision has been made or when the bank has exceeded the bounds of prudent leverage and has to sell more equity to get back to a safe capital structure.

vestment made by the bank should earn enough profit to pay for all the funds used to finance it.

Lending money at rates which cover only the cost of funds borrowed to make the loan will quickly lead to profit problems. The cost of the new equity that must be raised to keep risk exposure constant must also be covered in the rate charged on the loan. Otherwise, the cost of the bank's funds will rise even further. If the cost of new capital is increasing, the signal to managment should be clear: either reduce the bank's overall risk or be prepared to earn a high enough return on assets to pay for this capital. Successful operation over a long period requires that investors be given an expected return on their funds that is as high as returns available from other comparable securities. The fact that markets for the capital of smaller banks are especially imperfect doesn't alter the fact that those banks must have equity to expand and must pay whatever the "going market rate" is for that equity.

A Minimum Return

Once a bank has estimated the price it must pay for new funds it has a benchmark for judging alternative investments. A bank should only invest in loans or securities (or combinations of them) whose expected return is above the cost of the new funds required to finance them. That seems obvious. But the decision must be made on the basis of the current cost of all funds that will be raised during the next planning period rather than just the cost of a block of short-term debt which might be raised next week. It should also consider the full effect that any change in the bank's asset or liability risks will have on the cost of any funds raised. Furthermore, if the bank expects to have more funds than it needs to meet loan demand and liquidity requirements for an extended period, simply investing them in the highest yielding asset available may not be the best strategy. The investment must still yield enough to pay the full cost of these funds, or they should be returned to those who have loaned to or invested in the bank. This might be done by not replacing maturing debt issues or by paying extra dividends. In the long run, capital markets should eventually force a bank in the direction of managing its funds efficiently. (Limitations on entry into banking and imperfections in the market for bank securities may make market discipline less effective than it is in unregulated industries.)

Shrink, If Necessary

If investment prospects don't justify raising new funds, the institution shouldn't try to expand. Doing so isn't in the best interests of either shareholders or management. When the cost of funds exceeds the returns available to a bank, capital markets are giving management a signal that alternative uses for its shareholders' funds are relatively attractive. If the bank can't earn a competitive return on its equity, its stockholders can use the money for other investments. A bank that reinvests shareholder earnings when its return isn't on a par with other securities of similar risk is preventing shareholders from making better use of their own money. Eventually, the shareholders will sense this and try to sell their stock. The falling stock price will put pressure on management to correct the problem or answer to the stockholders.

The market is also signaling the bank that consumers and borrowers aren't sufficiently interested in its banking services to pay the prices that make the bank able to give investors a competitive return. Either another financial organization can provide that service at a lower cost or tastes have changed and people don't really want the service at all. Banks that can't afford to pay the going rate for funds (because they can't pass their higher costs on to their customers) should not expect to get additional money.

The Regulatory Constraint

If banks were completely unregulated and free to buy money and sell services in a competitive business environment, these market forces could resolve the "capital shortage" automatically. But the fact is, they're not free and, therefore, they do not work perfectly. The industry, in fact, is tightly regulated, and the regulations influence bank profits. Limitations on entry into the industry is an example of an implicit subsidy from Government to commercial banks. Conversely, capital adequacy constraints, reserve requirements, and portfolio limitations tend to lower bank profits. The point is not that these constraints are "wrong" or "un-just," but that they influence the profitability and competitiveness of banks vis-á-vis other financial service organizations.

Firms operating in an unregulated world have the right to raise their prices enough to compete for the higher cost equity funds—as long as their customers are willing to pay those higher prices. Banks are free to make some price adjust-ments, but they may not be able to pass on higher money costs as effectively as unregulated financial corporations. If banking agency regulations or state usury statutes inadvertently hold earnings below the level needed to raise new capital, the industry's growth would be unnecessarily curtailed.

There is no way to know, right now, whether this will be an important problem or not. Bank regulators must be vigilant in assuring that only the constraints that are necessary to promoting the financial system's stability are enforced.

CONCLUSION

Any projection of historical trends in bank growth, profits, and dividend payout practices suggests that the banking system's demand for external capital will ex-pand rapidly in the years immediately ahead. Yet the capital "gap" will probably sow the seeds of its own resolution. If banks curtail their growth because of an inability to find profitable new investments (or to circumvent the regulator's capital constraints), the least attractive investments can gradually be culled from their portfolios. By concentrating available resources on the more profitable busi-ness that remains, banks will be taking steps to build capital internally. Better profits and stronger capital positions, will cut risks, and banks will then be more able to compete for new external capital. Competition from the nonbank financial sector will remain, but these organizations must also pay high prices for additional capital. The key, however, is astute use by banks of the money available to them and prudence in raising only those funds that can be reinvested profitably. As long as the profit opportunities exist, banks will have the opportunity and the justification for raising whatever funds they need. When expected profitability is insufficient, the desire to expand must be held in check.

Regulators also face a challenge in the years ahead. They must not only protect the public's interest in its financial system but also try to keep the game "fair." The regulatory agencies can alter the competitive viability of the industries they regulate. If these industries are to serve society and their shareholders efficiently, they must be free to respond to their changing economic environment. The desire to expand banking's capital base rapidly is one development which can only be accomplished successfully if regulation doesn't prevent the industry from compet-ing for funds, investing rationally, and passing rising costs along to customers who are willing to bear them.

PART IV

ASSET–LIABILITY MANAGEMENT AND FINANCIAL FUTURES

21

Asset/Liability Management–
Part 1 Establishing a Function and
Developing a Near-Term Profit Plan*

Barrett F. Binder

What will be the most critical factor in achieving high bank performance over the next several years? The answer is unequivocal—sound asset/liability management.

Inflation, recession anxieties, adjustments in monetary policy, raw materials shortages as well as constant shocks to the economy produced by political and international events make it extremely difficult for banks to profitably allocate assets—to determine their mix and volume levels—and to match rate-sensitive assets and liabilities properly.

An instability in interest rate levels resulting from economic dislocations has combined with certain factors that have increased the competition for and raised the cost of funds that banks purchase. There has been, in addition to intensified vying with thrift institutions for deposits, sustained disintermediation resulting from greater retail depositor sophistication, inflation, the higher interest rate levels offered by money market mutual funds and other market investment options, the new financial services arrangements made by such nonbanks as Merrill Lynch, American Express, J. C. Penney, and Sears, Roebuck and the decreasing propensity to save. On the corporate side, more specialized and refined cash management services by nonbanks and the widening use of leverage by industrial concerns to insure earnings growth also have hindered the generation of core deposits. Moreover, with the phase-out of Regulation Q and therefore the increased need for banks of all sizes to purchase funds, the ability to cope with unpredictable changes in money market rates becomes more urgent.

High bank performance depends on adopting a funds management approach that will have consistent success in meeting corporate profit, growth and market

*Reprinted with permission from the *Magazine of Bank Administration*, November 1980, pp. 42-48. Copyright © 1980, by the Bank Administration Institute.

penetration objectives, insuring desired levels for liquidity and capital adequacy, and, more particularly, protecting institutions' performance against unsettled economic cycles and the resulting net interest margin fluctuations. Such an approach is asset/liability management.

This three-part series defines and describes asset/liability management, especially with respect to rate-sensitivity and interest rate risk, forecasting and scenario construction, asset allocation and credit risk, liquidity and funding, capital requirements and monitoring and control techniques.

WHAT IS ASSET/LIABILITY MANAGEMENT?

Asset/liability management is a planning, implementation and control process for matching the mix and maturities of assets and liabilities in ways that maximize net interest margin on an ongoing basis. The key concept is the coordinated or simultaneous management of both assets and liabilities. The management process works primarily by controlling the gap between rate-sensitive assets and rate-sensitive liabilities, that is, the differential between those instruments which can mature or be repriced upward or downward within the next 90 or fewer days. It also focuses on the volume and mix of these instruments, which include Fed funds and securities sold under agreements to repurchase (Repos), floating-rate loans, short-term investments, CDs over $100,000, money market CDs, Eurodollar deposits and public funds.

But, while the asset/liability management process addresses chiefly the relationship between rate-sensitive assets and liabilities, other balance sheet considerations are also crucial.

First of all, the protracted inflation that banks have been experiencing has not only caused a contraction in core deposits through internal and external disintermediation and increased costs and volatility of purchased funds. It has, in addition, contributed to the continual erosion of capital ratios, which are a constraint on asset/liability growth.

Banks have thus been caught in a difficult cycle. Internal capital formation rates have become increasingly less able to match inflation-driven asset growth rates, and raising external capital provides the only means of making up the deficiency. But upward shifts in interest rates, increased emphasis on capital adequacy and uncertainty about how the industry will cope with the elimination of Regulation Q have caused the ratios of earnings and book values to market prices to remain at discouragingly unfavorable levels. The effect has been to block equity financing plans except for occasional convertible preferred financings, dividend reinvestment programs and subscription offerings by smaller banks. Moreover, the recent inversion in the rate relationship between the intermediate- and long-term debt markets has caused banks to resist this latter type of financing.

Thus at a time of increasingly stringent monitoring of capital support of assets by regulatory authorities, rating agencies and the marketplace, the cost of capital is going up. These increased costs reduce the profits which internally generate capital, thereby further decreasing capital available for covering asset growth and for supplemental funding of loans and investments. With reduced capital and earnings comes a diminished reputation in the financial markets, primarily for larger banks, resulting in further higher costs for capital and funds. The final thrust is less chance to optimize net interest margin, which is the primary goal of asset/liability management.

The focus by bankers, therefore, should be not just on strategies for controlling the highly variable spread between borrowing and lending rates, but also on effective planning for the entire balance sheet. Most critically, bankers must determine how their institutions' overall management process should be organized, equipped and adjusted to achieve ongoing success in meeting asset/liability management objectives.

ESTABLISHING AN ASSET/LIABILITY MANAGEMENT FUNCTION

How does a bank get the asset/liability management process started? The essential requirements are the recognition of the need and top management's strong support.

Asset/Liability Management Committee   When such commitment exists, one initial step is to set up a committee which can begin to meet informally. In the case of small banks, the president and a few key officers can jointly guide and be active in loan, investment, trading account and money market decisions. For larger banks, an asset/liability management committee is usually formed, with representatives from every significant portion of the balance sheet, i.e., heads of income producing groups and funds sources. These might include the chairman and president to make high-level decisions and symbolize commitment; the chief financial officer; the controller to generate data for overall corporate profit planning activities (tax, etc.); the head of commercial loans; the head of retail loans; the head of international loans; the investment manager; the officer who coordinates funding, such as a treasurer or funds manager; an economist to give the economic, monetary and market picture; and possibly the head of credit policy supervision.

Responsibilities   The responsibilities of the asset/liability management committee usually include directing the overall acquisition and allocation of funds to maximize earnings and insure adequate liquidity; presenting recent performance as well as forecasts and budgets of loan demand and funding sources, so that the committee can assess liability and loan pricing strategies; establishing funds acquisition practices and options for the allocation of loans; monitoring earnings spread, asset/liability distributions and maturities; determining how to deal with reserve requirements for money market activities; reviewing budget variances; and, most important, developing action plans based on the causes of these variances.

Policy Issues   The committee should formalize the parameters of these strategy considerations in an asset/liability management policy statement. Furthermore, it should review this policy in relation to the overall management process, develop procedures, act as a link between line management and the corporate planning function and recommend policy changes when conditions warrant.

While all of these responsibilities are essential, the critical or basic function of the asset/liability management committee changes with market conditions. That is, currently the primary concern might be insuring sufficient liquidity. A few months down the line the focal point might shift to strategies for acquiring reasonably priced short-term money over a long period of time. Still later, the critical concern might be developing adequate capital to support earning assets growth or expansion into new lines of business.

Implementation The implementation of these policies and directives is accomplished by line managers who also give bottom-up input into asset/liability management decision making. Officers close to the borrowing customers (and their product needs) and to the money markets, respectively, use and develop funds daily, and therefore can provide practical data for forecasting volumes and interest rates. They can also furnish input regarding new customer markets and lending requirements/products, which might help the bank increase the yield on its loan portfolio.

To meet its responsibilities, the asset/liability management committee must draw some preliminary conclusions about what kind of staff support is required, what latitude should be provided for interim tactical decisions and who can make them, what variety of strategies is possible on the line level, what is an appropriate review and decision cycle and what criteria should be emphasized in measuring performance.

Information Consideration must be given to the role of automation
Requirements and outside services and expertise for providing rapid, analytically based decision and processing capabilities. One of the implications of more exacting asset/liability management is the availability of timely, continuous and detailed information from both inside and outside the bank. This requirement demands better information systems and the integration of the systems for a more coordinated decision making process, money market operations and swift rebalancing of the funds composition and asset mix.

THE INITIAL STAGES OF THE PROCESS

The first step in meeting asset/liability management responsibilities revolves around the planning function and developing a near-term profit plan. That is, banks must structure their balance sheets and anticipate the determining factors of their net interest margins—rate sensitivity, asset pricing and funding costs. They must forecast noncontrollable factors such as loan and core deposit volume and plan controllable factors, especially the investment portfolio size and mix and purchased funds volume. They must consider beforehand asset/liability rate, volume and mix effects on their interest margins.

Having an effective financial information system is the basic requirement for constructing this short-range profit plan. With the aid of such a system, banks can forecast the volumes of various asset and liability categories through analysis of their charts of accounts and average daily balance sheets. These forecasted balance sheets allow banks to determine their net sources and net uses of funds and their capability regarding cash flows, as well as to examine the growth trends of different types of loans and deposits.

With this information along with statistical projections, judgmental management inputs and *pro forma* simulations, those in charge of the asset/liability management function can establish the rates of interest expected to be earned on earning assets as well as the rates expected to be paid on interest-paying liabilities. This part of the process may involve several independent estimates of future rates, followed by a consensus opinion on these forecasts for strategy planning purposes.

The asset/liability management committee can then develop several alternative scenarios through sensitivity or "what if" analysis. These scenarios should incorporate such variables as expected loan demand, investment opportunities, core deposit growth, regulatory changes, monetary policy adjustment, and the overall state of the economy, in addition to interest rates on particular sources and uses of funds. Moreover, these scenarios should be based on some system of weighting the likelihood of possible outcomes, e.g., on the use of probability distributions. When these scenarios are completed, banks can test a number of strategies and policies against each of them for cost, profit and liquidity implications.

The next step is to divide loan, investment and deposit data into fixed- and variable-rate categories and to provide expected loan, deposit and investment maturity schedules along with appropriate maturing rates and yields. These data can be used to generate funds gap reports, which itemize variable-rate assets and variable-rate liabilities, total the item dollars of these two categories and then subtract them to determine the gap or differential. The same procedures could be followed for fixed and nonrate funds to give a picture of overall average balances for the balance sheet items.

These variable and fixed-rate data can also be formatted into interest rate sensitivity reports as well as mix/spread analyses. Reports formatted in these ways show the effects of anticipated interest rates and of the volume and mix of asset and liability items on net interest margin.

ASSET ALLOCATION

When this information and possibly further "what if" analyses are reviewed, the bank can undertake the asset allocation process. But it should not do so without careful consideration of the maturity structure, cost, and availability of funds. Looking first at the liability side is especially necessary for small banks, which have fewer and less diversified options for acquiring funds than do large institutions.

The goal of every bank in asset allocation is to maximize the percentage of and yield on earning assets with prudent management of risk. In the case of banks with an established asset/liability function, the appropriate committee can act as a judiciary body which settles various conflicts regarding loan allocation. The heads of various loan areas will each tend to seek as large an allocation as possible to optimize their respective profit results. But planned allocations must work to promote overall bank performance.

For example, a retail bank which in the past has deployed its funds in the personal and mortgage loan areas, may find a higher and more steady flow of revenue from commercial and construction loans. Of course, yields in these new areas may be influenced greatly by such factors as credit risk, state usury laws, market forces, competition, the need to lock in profitable customer relationships and, of course, volatility in interest rates. With the sharply increased rate fluctuations both in frequency and size since 1977, banks have gone shorter and much more variable-rate on their loans. This has been reinforced by the increased dependence on rate-sensitive liabilities.

Today, one of the more dramatic changes in bank asset management is occurring in fixed-income securities. Previously, investment portfolios consisting principally of government obligations were viewed as prime sources of liquidity. But ever increasing interest rates have made it difficult to liquidate securities without losses and therefore a negative impact on earnings.

As a result, many bankers are resisting the temptation to increase investment yields by purchasing longer-term issues. They believe that portfolios should be smaller, shorter and sufficiently flexible to match the fluctuating cost of liabilities (especially as Regulation Q is phased out over the next six years), unless banks can persuade the Fed that reserves can be invested in governments, all or part of which might be longer-term, or unless new variable-rate securities develop.

Yet many bankers are considering adding to their investment portfolios because some Treasury and agency security yields are attractive compared with consumer loans for which rates are limited by local usury ceilings, maturities may be longer and credit risk is greater. Moreover, a certain volume of these securities is necessary for collateralizing repurchase agreements and public funds borrowings and to maintain a good public image. Finally, it may be possible for banks to tack financial advisory services on to their investment accounts, which can generate fee income. Success in this regard depends on the extent of local urban development and fiscal soundness.

It should be noted that, since earnings and liquidity must often be balanced off against each other, asset allocation must be managed in conjunction with decisions about the most appropriate liability structure to support earning assets. Therefore, the asset/liability management committee or its smaller bank counterpart acts not only as a body for assessing interest rate projections and making judgments about the allocations of assets. It must also function as the protector of liquidity, and its responsibilities in large banks might include such diverse concerns as foreign central bank time deposits, Eurodollars, swaps for foreign currencies for foreign branches that need them, CDs, commercial paper, dealer operations and managing the daily money position.

22

Asset/Liability Management– Part 2 Management and Control of Rate Sensitivity[*]

Barrett F. Binder

When the basic operating plan for allocating assets and liabilities is in place, banks can turn their attention to its execution. The most pressing requirement concerning this phase is measuring rate-sensitivity and managing it through the "funds gap" (dollar mismatch) or the ratio of rate-sensitive assets (RSA) to rate-sensitive liabilities (RSL).

MANAGING THE GAP

There are three gap management options available to banks. First, they may maintain a ratio which, for the most part, tends to be asset sensitive or greater than 1.00. For example, if a bank has $122 million in RSA and $84 million in RSL, it has a funds gap or differential of $38 million and a ratio of 1.45.

Second, banks may hold a balanced position by allowing a portion of their rate-sensitive assets to be supported by an equal amount of rate-sensitive (purchased) funds (RSA/RSL = 1.00). In the case of this option, the assumption is that the rate spread and therefore operating earnings will exhibit the least amount of variability. This option might seem especially attractive in a time of frequent and substantial swings in rates, such as that which has existed for the past three years.

But it must be recognized that there is no perfect hedge here because assets, e.g., prime rate loans, are generally less immediately sensitive to rate changes than liabilities such as $100,000 CDs. That is, their respective rate levels do not always move in tandem because there is often a lag problem after turning points in rates.

[*]Reprinted with permission from the *Magazine of Bank Administration*, December 1980, pp. 31-35. Copyright © 1980 by the Bank Administration Institute.

Furthermore, there are also volume shifts at different phases of the rate cycle, e.g., money market certificates may be 10 percent of liabilities when market rates are around 12 percent but a much smaller percentage of liabilities when rates drop.

In fact, there are highly competitive market pressures at work on both sides of the interest differential equation at all phases of the rate cycle, possibly making the margin contribution of the second option less substantial and controllable than that of the asset-sensitive position. Moreover, a balanced position may mean a loss of market share on the loan side, for it may entail turning away fixed-rate borrowers in order to maintain the equality between RSA and RSL.

A third "gap" management option is allowing rate-sensitive liabilities to exceed rate-sensitive assets. The rationale here is that short-term instruments normally have lower interest rates than longer-term ones (which have a risk premium). Therefore a sensitivity ratio of less than 1.00 can bring in additional profits as long as the bank does not get caught in a rate change or in a phase where long-term money is available at lower rates due to a yield curve inversion, such as the situation that existed well through the first quarter of 1980.

If banks do assume, at least in part, a negative gap, they might prefer to use U. S. Government securities because these instruments are relatively easy to liquidate.

Generally, high-performance banks tend to be potentially balanced. That is, they try to maintain flexibility enough to move to an equality between RSA and RSL. But most often they are off-balance and asset-sensitive according to interest rate trends, especially in today's rising rate environment. Of course, the greater the volatility and interest rate risk, the stronger the inclination to hold a balanced position. The main concern is to have sufficient flexibility on the asset side of the balance sheet to keep pace with the rapid changes in the cost of funds. Deregulation of the liability side of the balance sheet has been happening so quickly that banks have had difficulty getting their assets repriced and changed from fixed to floating rate fast enough.

The standard strategy is as follows: The gap between RSA and RSL must be managed to expand and contract with rate cycle phases:

Rising rates	→	Widening gap
High rates	→	Widest gap
Falling rates	→	Narrowing gap
Low rates	→	Narrowest gap

For example, if a bank is entering a period of rising interest rates with inadequate capital to support volume expansion, it should increase the RSA/RSL ratio. It should raise this ratio to well above 1.00 by placing more loans on a floating-rate basis, selling real estate loans to outside investors by issuing mortgage-backed pass-through certificates, lengthening the average life of the large-CD portfolio and by shortening the average maturity of the investment portfolio account. Of course, the interest-sensitive ratio here would most likely involve a range (minimum to maximum) rather than one particular number.

An excessively wide gap at high-rate phases may maximize earnings at that time, but if not narrowed while high rates are available on fixed-rate assets, it will result in reduced earnings during a subsequent lower phase. Asset/liability strategies should be oriented toward optimizing gap relationships through a complete cycle and not maximizing at any one phase.

Thus, banks should acquire the rate-sensitive assets (through "roll-overs" or new contracts) in resalable lots, but not all at one time during the cyclical phase. Since no one has found a way to be sure that a rate cycle has either peaked or bottomed out, it is only prudent to space the acquisitions and sales over several months.

Banks should therefore pre-plan moves at predetermined market-rate (price) levels, especially because of the unpredictability of the rate cycle. They must replicate a whole series of gap ratios to see the impact of these strategies in advance.

Gap Size

It is necessary to look at the gap (dollar difference) or mismatch not only in relation to external factors such as economic changes and different phases of the rate cycle, but also in relation (%) to internal factors such as total assets, earning assets and equity.

James V. Baker, Jr., President of James Baker & Co. (Oklahoma City, Ok.), states the following percentages: "A RSA/RSL ratio of 1.6 can be exceeded if RSA/RSL is less than 15% of total assets, less than 20% of earning assets and less than 30% of equity capital."

What is a prudent rate-sensitivity ratio can also be determined by the proportion of RSA or RSL, separately, to earnings assets, total assets, total liabilities or equity. For example, if a bank only purchases 14 percent of its total funds, it can maintain a higher risk/return position than if that proportion were larger.

It should be noted in this context that looking at other banks' rate-sensitivity ratios as benchmarks may provide a very incomplete picture. Those with identical ratios of rate-sensitive assets to rate-sensitive liabilities can vary widely in the maturity mismatches between assets and funding sources or in the compositions of these two categories. The result is different margin performance.

For example, banks relying most heavily on CDs for funding, such as consumer-oriented regionals, will benefit the least during a period of declining interest rates such as the second quarter of 1980. This result occurred because many CDs did not mature in that quarter, and therefore the banks had to wait until the next two quarters to benefit fully from declining rates. Money centers and wholesale oriented regionals, which heavily use Fed funds and repurchase agreements, should benefit the most from that quarter's declining rates. These two funding sources have very short maturities and respond quickly to rate movements. Finally, even among CD-dependent banks, there may be wide discrepancies between CD maturity structures. Therefore peer group comparisons of rate-sensitivity must include the line item breakdown as well as the rate-sensitive asset and liability totals.

Other Considerations

Pricing Strategy   The rate sensitivity ratio must be managed in relation to pricing strategy. As the marginal cost of funds for most banks continues to rise and fluctuate (especially as the discount rate shows volatility over a certain level, say 11 percent), so must loan prices. The pricing trend during 1979-1980 has moved increasingly toward floating-rate commercial loans. Moreover, Citibank, N. A. has recently announced that retail customers can expect to pay a floating rate on installment loans, and that the same would be true for users of overdraft checking privileges and large preauthorized lines of credit.

Futures Contracts   As a further hedge (besides gap management) against interest rate risk and to provide stability in the margin, banks can consider the growing use of financial futures contracts. Futures and forward contracts may be used, among other purposes, as a general hedge against the interest rate exposure associated with undesired mismatches in interest-sensitive assets and liabilities. Long positions in contracts can be used in a period of falling interest rates as a hedge against funding interest-sensitive assets with fixed-rate sources of funds; short positions in contracts can be used at a time of rising interest rates as a hedge against funding fixed-rate assets with interest-sensitive liabilities. In this latter instance, where customer acceptance of variable-rate loans for instalment or mortgage borrowing is low or where such variable-rate loans are not allowed by law, banks can gain much greater latitude in their loan portfolio and thereby help themselves in keeping good customers.

At the same time, banks should note that there are certain pitfalls or at least question marks about futures hedging. First of all, a bank may have already built in a hedge by maintaining a balanced position, or a rate-sensitivity ratio equal to 1.00. A second factor is that the futures market is generally more volatile than the cash market. Therefore there is a distinct possibility that the cash price for a particular type of instrument will not move in exact tandem with its futures counterpart. This disparity, called *basis risk*, may mean the elimination of rate protection and, in fact, financial loss from the hedge.

Interest rate risk, vis-a-vis profitability, can also be hedged in the aggregate in more traditional fashion through loan portfolio diversification and employment of the investment portfolio as a counterbalance.

Measurement   It should be remembered that not only is it difficult to determine what the rate-sensitivity ratio should be at various points in the interest rate cycle. It is also hard to calculate what, in fact, this ratio is.

Banks must first decide on what is an appropriate time frame for separating rate-sensitive assets and liabilities from those which are fixed-rate. Management may wish to place in the rate-sensitivity category those instruments which mature or can be repriced upward or downward within a particular analysis period of short duration, say 90 days or less. Banks must also determine whether they will use end-of-the-analysis-period figures, or average daily balances during the period. The latter figures are usually more representative.

Furthermore, the measurement process requires a specific knowledge of what instruments are outstanding, their rates and maturity schedules, the extent of floating rate items in the portfolio and when interest rates are likely to change. Yet many banks do not have sufficiently automated financial information systems to provide the required data on a constant basis. Furthermore, instruments like demand loans are not actual assets which can be accurately quantified, but only potential assets about which it is only possible to make a rough estimate.

Asset Classification   It is not always easy to classify assets and liabilities as rate-sensitive or fixed. For example, borrowers on real estate loans, which are normally fixed, may decide to refinance their loans if rates fall substantially. Also, since the middle of the 1970s, banks have been extending a large number of capped loans. That is, in an attempt to placate corporate borrowers seeking predictability in the cost of funds, loan officers have ostensibly made prime-related loans but have stipulated that the rate cannot exceed a certain level, say 12 percent. This type of loan shows up on the books as a rate-sensitive asset, even though it has long ceased to be a floating-rate instrument. Finally, on demand or passbook savings, depositors may choose to withdraw their balances, which are usually considered fixed, and invest in higher yielding deposits.

THE LIQUIDITY FACTOR

Rate-sensitivity exposure must also be managed in relation to current and prospective liquidity levels. The close relation between these two factors exists because low liquidity and a high degree of interest rate sensitivity on the liability side mean a great risk of negative margins. For example, in a rising interest rate environment, liquidity requirements might increase because of more demand and passbook savings deposit claims presented for payment and greater demand regarding loan commitments. These requirements, not to mention the renewal or coverage of all maturing debt instruments, must be met without excessive losses from untimely bond sales.

To measure liquidity in relation to rate sensitivity, the following ratios are important:

$$\frac{\text{Liquid Earning Assets}}{\text{Volatile Funds}}$$

$$\frac{\text{Volatile Funds}}{\text{Total Earning Assets}}$$

$$\frac{\text{Liquid Earning Assets}}{\text{Total Earning Assets}}$$

To supply the correct numbers for the denominator of the first ratio and the numerator of the second, banks must determine which funds and dollar amounts are reliable and which of them are volatile, however difficult the measurement. For what is not reliable probably will not be available. By the same token, banks must define the non-liquid portion of their loan and investment portfolios (the third ratio above, or Fixed-Rate Assets/Core Deposits).

When the liquidity ratio is at or near 1.00, a bank has attained a balanced liquidity position. The difference between net liquid assets and volatile funds equals the amount of the excess or deficit liquidity position.

If liquidity is managed on the balance sheet, the manager is interested in a liquidity cushion, i.e., having more liquid assets than volatile sources of funds. If, on the other hand, liquidity is managed off the balance sheet through escape valves (such as stand-by loan participation agreements), the organization can tolerate a position of fewer liquid assets than volatile funds. The bank can be in this position and not have a problem because pre-arranged contingency options are available. One bank may have a ratio of two dollars of liquid assets for each dollar of volatile sources of funds, while another may have only 75 cents of liquid assets. Both banks may be well managed but with different liquidity policies. It is also necessary to consider pledging requirements and usage rates on the commitment portfolio when determining liquidity requirements.

Another key measure of liquidity in today's volatile interest rate environment is Large Liability Dependence. This ratio indicates the net reliance on short-term, interest-sensitive, large-denomination purchased funds to finance longer-term investment securities, and loans and leases other than broker/dealer loans. (A supplementary definition of purchased funds might also include money market certificates.) In this complex ratio, net purchased funds is the difference between gross purchased funds and temporary investments. In the gross purchased funds category are (1) CDs over $100,000, (2) deposits in foreign offices, (3) Fed funds purchased and Repos and (4) other short borrowings. Temporary investments include: (1) Fed funds sold and Repos, (2) time deposits in other banks, (3) trading account securities, (4) investment securities due in one year or less and (5) broker/ dealer loans. These assets, which are cashable items, tend to be short-term and virtually without market or credit risk. They are generally funded with similar types of liabilities. Bank analysts net temporary investments against large denomination liabilities in order to compute the "net purchased" or interest rate risky position supporting loans and investments. This net figure is divided by gross earning assets to determine the bank's reliance on what is typically its highest-cost and least dependable source of funds:

$$\frac{\text{Large Denomination Liabilities} - \text{Temporary Investments}}{\text{Loans} + \text{Investments}}$$

Put in its most practical terms, it is fair to say that liquidity, currently the most significant risk consideration in asset/liability managment, is essentially an off-balance sheet factor. That is, it involves money that a bank does not have but could obtain in one or two days if necessary.

To insure adequate liquidity, or a safe pattern of cash flows, in a fluctuating-rate environment, banks should consider the implementation of four strategies:

- Extending the maturities of liabilities, unless interest rates are heading downward.
- Diversifying sources of funds, including the development of new funding sources. Banks' ability to gain access to these sources will depend on their

earnings capacity, earnings history and stability, capital adequacy and reputation.
- Matching the maturities of assets and liabilities through this strategy causes
  a higher cost of funding assets than maturity mismatching. Each bank must
  strike its own balance in this liquidity/earnings tradeoff.
- Improving asset liquidity through the use of salable mortgage-backed pass-
  through certificates.

Banks should not depend too heavily on short-term investment securities as a
source of liquidity because such a strategy makes too much of a compromise with
profitability. That is, banks tend to acquire these assets when interest rates are
low and sell them for liquidity purposes when rates are high, thereby realizing a
suboptimal yield.

MONITORING AND CONTROL

As banks plan and deploy these asset/liability management strategies, it is critical that they monitor and perform variance analysis of interest rates, volume levels
and mix of assets and liabilities. They should conduct this activity on a continuing
basis. The actual control mechanism naturally varies among banks. But it is possible
to indicate some basic considerations.

First of all, banks should use long-range plans as a guide for profit planning.
Quarterly or more often, the board of directors along with senior asset/liability
management officers should review comparisons of actual versus planned results
from the annual profit plan. These reviews should focus on dollar, as well as percentage, variances for the quarter being examined and the year-to-date results.
Based on discernable changes in trends or patterns, the board and management
should make alterations in strategies for loan policies, bond portfolio structure
and funds acquisition in order to achieve year-end goals.

The key to the control process, however, is the budget, both on the senior management and profit center levels. Officers involved in the asset/liability management process should review budget variances with sufficient frequency so that
timely corrective action can be taken on adverse variances with regard to interest
rates, volume levels and mix of assets and liabilities. On an operating level, strategies
in reaction to contingencies often take place on a daily basis.

The three variance factors are interactive, for changes in interest rates will affect
volume levels, both in loans and investments, and in core deposits. These changes,
in turn, will necessarily produce shifts in the mix of these funds. All three factors—
rate, volume, and mix—combine to determine a bank's net interest margin dollars.
Moreover, growth in volume and shifts in mix during 1979 and the early months
of 1980 appear to have compensated for the impact on interest margin of adverse
fluctuations in rates.

Furthermore, these interrelated factors frequently conflict and depend on operating factors, managerial policies, regulatory restrictions and vagaries of the market. For example, a bank might wish to increase loan volume levels to maintain
strong growth. But at this time interest rates may be especially volatile or low,
though core deposits or short-term borrowed funds may be in greater supply. For

as Dr. Ronald L. Olson, President of Olson Research Associates, Inc., has pointed out, the rate of growth of earning assets fluctuates over rate cycles; strongest during periods of rising rates and weakest during times of declining rates. Finally, the attempt to improve the mix by switching into higher-yield assets may be thwarted because loan demand or volume is down, for mix is largely a residual factor.

Adequate flexibility should be built into the budgeting process so that variance analysis input and rolling monthly 12-month forecasts can be factored in on an on-going basis. These tools can be used to isolate the current and prospective impact of the three key factors: rate, volume and mix. In other words, if variance analysis and external indicators are used to update the budget, factors being forecast and considered uncontrollable in the short run can be adjusted.

For example, interest rate changes, when compared to volume and mix, are generally least controllable because market conditions dominate. But by being more sensitized to factors which may create rate changes through variance analysis, and if it is done far enough in advance, managers can modify the mix factor to a bank's advantage. The budget involved here might establish ranges, both in terms of dollar amounts and maturity mix, for particular assets and liabilities. That is, there would be minimum and maximum dollar amounts and percentage ranges for different maturities.

Asset/liability managers could explain these budgetary guidelines or roadmaps to the heads of various balance sheet items, thereby freeing these officers to take action to meet rate, volume and mix objectives.

Banks generally engage in two types of variance analyses: (1) actual versus planned and (2) current month's versus previous month's variance.

Controllable variances reflect the ability to manage; market related variances, while largely beyond the control of managers, do reflect their ability to adjust and react effectively; other variances indicate policy and procedural considerations. Yet the key purpose is not the variance analysis for its own sake, but to pinpoint change producing factors in order to direct corrective strategies.

It should be a guide for management action.

23

Asset/Liability Management— Part 3 Funding and Capital Management[*]

Barrett F. Binder

Though interest rate sensitivity and the matching or mismatching of asset and liability maturities have held center stage during recent years, an even more basic issue is emerging—the funding gap.

Banking is increasingly becoming a risk management business, and the greatest risk lies not simply in the competitive environment for selling loans, but also in the accessibility of funds both for shorter-term and capital purposes at a cost that gives a reasonable and consistent return on investment.

Banks should be cautioned, however, that purchasing liquidity by attracting liabilities with significantly higher interest rate levels than prevail in the market only adds to funding risk. It draws hot money at best, and the purchasing bank is voluntarily narrowing its spread. Moreover, purchased liquidity is available while a bank has adequate earnings. But if the asset side starts to yield less than the overall cost of liabilities, the smart money pulls out.

Thus, maintaining adequate liquidity requires not just off-balance sheet efforts to gain funds during emergencies, but the organized and systematic implementation of strategies such as scheduling the investment portfolio so that a portion of it is always maturing in the next 90 days. This type of approach will insure, at all possible times, that a bank has sufficient funds for loans, investments, deposit coverage, debt repayment and the expansion of service capability when they are necessary.

GUIDELINES FOR FUNDING

There are four key facets of funding and capital management: basic funding strategies with respect to cost and risk; deposit funding and customer relationship banking; purchased funds and money market operations and asset/liability management in relation to capital adequacy.

Basic Funding Strategies

Funding strategies that should be implemented vary with the size, structure, market objectives, deposit base and access to money and capital markets of the particular bank. But certain essential options can be enunciated. Banks should:

- Organize for more productive funding operations. They should give priority to having an active marketing and sales program for attracting new sources from their customer bases and elsewhere. They should determine what ideas to communicate to prospective customers, and what services to offer as inducements to attract new sources of funds. Furthermore, sales efforts should be supported by computer based marketing information tools where feasible. These capabilities, in turn, should be integral to a comprehensive liabilities processing system which includes customer cash flow position (linking assets and liabilities) and activity data and customer contact history. Finally, banks should measure, develop and monitor their market shares of purchased funds as distinct from their shares of core deposits.

- Compete for stable deposit money by building multiservice customer relationships.

- Lengthen the maturity of purchased liabilities, (including potentially fixed-rate, two- to five-year CDs and Euro-CDs for large banks), unless longer-term rates so far exceed short-term rates as to make this option infeasible. This strategy is especially effective in a rising interest rate environment and, in addition, helps control liquidity risk by reducing the amount of funds the bank has to raise on any given day in any market. The tradeoff here is between reducing interest rate risk exposure by paying a premium on longer-term CDs and other liabilities (if longer-term assets are being matched) versus higher margins but greater interest rate risk if no premium is paid.

- Diversify sources of funds by maintaining an active presence in as many money markets as possible. Smaller banks should avoid depending almost exclusively on local markets, eventually saturating them and, as a result, limiting the growth of their asset bases. Large banks should expand their funding operations along currency, country, investor and maturity lines.

- Develop, if a smaller bank, shared risk or combined borrowing arrangements with other small institutions for floating, say, CDs in the national markets, i.e., the counterpart to loan participations on the liability side. In addition to diversifying risk, this pooled approach would involve the large-dollar amounts attractive to national dealers. A correspondent or one of the participating banks might market the combined account.

Along the same lines, small banks might consider packaging $100,000 CDs with other banks for direct sale to a money market mutual funds through a larger bank correspondent. In this way, deposits which money funds have drained off can be recycled back into community banks.

- Promote buyer/seller relations and market reputation—for investor confidence enables the bank to raise the funds it needs, when it needs them, at the most reasonable rates. Banks should make themselves known in the money markets, not just by sending their annual reports but by making in-person presentations which advise dealers and brokers as to why their liability offerings are sound investments.

- Plan and arrange for contingency funding through a variety of sources before adverse market conditions can cause a crisis, e. g., maintaining unsecured Fed funds lines of credit with correspondent banks.

- Add to capital through long-term debt (if it can be considered as such, and if market rates permit), thereby strengthening the corporation's capital position.

- Have the parent company, in the case of large bank holding companies, make market borrowings to attract a broad variety of sources at more attractive rates, to gain economies of scale and to reduce trips to the market because the parent may be able to raise greater volumes of funds at any one time. By the same token, the institution should avoid double leverage, a practice whereby bank holding company parents borrow in order to meet regulator demands for more equity in the underlying banks.

- For very large banks, centralize funding operations to achieve better information processing, coordination, control, and use of money generating options. At the same time, there should be sufficient delegation of authority so that banks can stay on top of local markets and help diversify risk by reducing the impact that any one wrong decision could have on corporate earnings or liquidity.

Deposit Funding and Customer Relationship Banking

Consumer and Corporate Deposits   When the bank has established its funding guidelines, it should turn its attention to the major opportunity area for funds development—consumer and corporate deposits. The creation of money market instruments, increasing interest rates, the 1980 Monetary Control Act, the presence of nationwide NOW accounts and the emergence of more sophisticated consumers and corporate cash managers have irreversibly eroded inexpensive demand and savings balances as sources of funds.

But with the elimination of Regulation Q on the liability side and the relaxation of usury limits on the asset side, banks will be better able to compete for deposit money and still achieve reasonable interest margins.

At the same time, banks should not compete for deposit funds simply on the basis of rates. Two other factors are crucial—customer convenience through branches or electronic delivery systems and multi-service customer relationships.

Some would argue that opting for the retail market to gain deposit money is a zero sum game. For as long as interest rate ceilings prevail, disintermediation will occur (barring some precipitous drop in market rates.) Moreover, when Regulation

Q is phased out, rates on consumer deposits may be prohibitive, even if usury limits on loans are relaxed. Furthermore, banks which have a higher proportion of retail business also have greater overhead because of the high transaction levels involved and because of the labor intensiveness of branch operations. Therefore the actual cost of deposits, everything considered, may cancel the benefits of having access to this deposit money.

But the opposing and probably prevailing argument is that in an increasingly funds-scarce environment, the consistent availability of consumer deposit money may outweigh its price (within a reasonable range). Moreover, as the use of new technology delivery systems such as ATMs and POS terminals helps control personnel costs and banks price their transaction services more rationally and completely, the retail business may provide deposit funds without an undue net cost burden.

Customer
Relationships

The other critical factor in competing for deposit money—multiservice customer relationships—applies to the corporate as well as to the retail market. Commercial customers whose needs are met through cash management and information processing services as well as loan commitments, and retail customers who use ATMs and financial advisory services and who have mortgage loans are much more likely to put substantial deposits in a bank than one-service customers.

Do these relationships contribute profits as well as provide a strategic source of funds? The answer is affirmative, if the bank performs accurate customer account profitability analysis. It may be that the bank pays high rates on deposits but more than compensates with loan and/or noncredit revenue. Or the reverse may occur. The bank may deploy technology and advisory services as loss leaders (plus the inducement of loans) to bring in deposit money as long as the overall relationship is profitable.

Purchased Funds and Money Market Operations

Deposit money gained through the above strategies may help alleviate the funding gap, but this source is not enough. High and volatile interest rates will continue, and as a result will create a secular change in the dependence on purchased funds, to a point where they will, for many banks, represent more than two-thirds of total liabilities. Moreover, with the increased reliance on purchased funds required to support adequate earnings growth and the competition that is growing for these funds, a substantial risk is emerging that these funds may not be available at a profitable spread.

These factors, along with the rapidly growing variety of money market instruments, including the prospect of a global scope of operations and the introduction of foreign currencies and investment instruments, cause money market operations to be an emerging pressure point of asset/liability management.[1]

[1] "Money market" refers to all those activities of funding, daily funds management, investment and trading management and customer investment services which take place in and with domestic and international money markets. The liability portion includes Repos, CDs, Euro Deposits, Euro CDs, commercial paper (holding company), Fed funds and Bankers Acceptances.

With high rates in addition to fierce competition for money, the bank's money market operations must not only attract many more customers and the funds to avoid funding gaps, but also higher levels of productivity. The squeeze on bank earnings produced by the higher costs of purchased funds must be offset, in part, by money market efforts in widening spreads.

The bank must seek ways to increase yields on investments and minimize the cost of purchased funds while preserving adequate asset quality and acceptable levels of risk. A key to achieving these objectives will be attracting and holding, through better service, a larger and stable "retail" customer base (exclusive dependence on national markets could be very risky). Reaching these objectives will also call for an ability to handle a wider variety of financial instruments with respect to analysis, transaction processing, accounting and reporting. It will call for effective communications systems.

There are several key factors for success regarding purchase or sale transactions in the money market. One of the most important is determining what the market (not necessarily what the bank) wants regarding financial instruments. Though the bank can create or find new types of instruments to make its borrowings more attractive, the majority of money market options are fairly fixed, e.g., Repos, CDs, Fed funds and the like. Therefore the bank's best strategy is to offer a mix of borrowings geared to market conditions.

Furthermore, the bank must not only constantly strive to diversify its funding sources, but also to keep in contact with the least expensive and most dependable of these sources. That is, it should time its purchases of funds advantageously, buying them when the CD or Eurodollar yield is favorable rather than at random or only when the need arises, i.e., when the bank is strapped by loan demand and commitments (when purchase rates are usually high).

The decision of what to buy and where to sell is dominated by traders at the desk managing the bank's funds position. After adjusting for different reserve requirements, traders compare the rate on 60-day CDs with term Fed funds and 60-day Eurodollars, picking the one that costs the least.

The Fed funds trader compares the overnight rate with the Repos trader, with one-day Eurodollar funds and with the rate and yield on dealer loans, and, adjusting for reserve requirements, decides where one-day funds should be raised.

The overriding concern in buyer-seller relations is consistent presence in the money markets, even if this strategy occasionally means paying an insurance premium (buying at slightly unfavorable rates), or at least making periodic bids, to promote funds availability. Dealers and brokers are not interested in one-time deals. They do not want to take the trouble to learn about a bank if they are never going to see that institution again. The payoff for them is over time.

Whatever the strategies for tapping particular sources of funds, the overall liability composition, as has been frequently stressed in this article, cannot be managed independently of the asset mix. Banks should employ an asset/liability matching process which incorporates maturity structures, funds reliability and volatility, asset and funds types as well as consideration of the spread. For example, arbitrage assets might be matched against arbitrage funds, U. S. Government investment securities might be funded with funds acquired via repurchase agreements, short-term money market assets, including Fed funds sold, trading account assets, and short-term sub-prime loans might be funded with overnight funds, and loans might be funded with a combination of overnight funds, term purchased funds, and core deposits. Of course, for small banks, which are more heavily dependent on core deposits, the matching scheme would be quite different.

Matching may be of specific assets and liabilities, especially if they are of large dollar amounts, or of categories of these balance sheet items. The guiding requirement, again, should be managing interest rate risk and margin fluctuations. Banks should pay particular attention to maximizing rate sensitive assets, including variable rate industrial development bonds, mortgages and instalment loans, in addition to repricing assets—as a protection against deregulated volatile liabilities.

Asset/Liability Management and Capital Adequacy

Finally, funding and other asset/liability management strategies cannot be separated from capital policy considerations. This relationship exists for five principal reasons.

Asset Growth   Sufficient capital is necessary to support asset growth. It is a second line of defense (the first is the loan loss reserve) against bad loans. This factor is especially evident with respect to the great emphasis placed by the regulators on the *Capital to Assets* ratio.

But, as indicated in the first instalment of this article, internal capital formation rates have not been keeping pace with inflation-induced asset growth rates; and the floating of equity capital has come to mean material erosion of the earnings per share position of current stockholders. Therefore, banks will have to determine the following:

- Should they seek more variable but higher average earnings or more stable, uniformly growing, but lower average net interest margins and earnings? If banks are too conservative in controlling interest rate risk, margins and profits might decline to the point of generating too little capital internally, i.e., causing capital risk.

- Should banks expand their loan brokerage business, thereby reducing the proportions of total commercial and consumer loans permanently held in their portfolios? This strategy, backed by government securities and accomplished with the help of correspondent banks, would alleviate Capital/Assets problems and enhance banks' share of total loan originations.

- To what extent can sale/leaseback financing of bank plant and equipment, new sources of revenue from noninterest products and services, and mergers and acquisitions of highly capitalized banks help reduce Capital/Assets pressures?

Investors' Attitudes   The investment community believes that capital is necessary to underwrite interest rate or market risk. That is, capital should be able to cover margin losses, particularly because of the increased costs and volatility of purchased funds. Many analysts believe, for example, that First Pennsylvania Bank, N. A. in 1979 was not sufficiently capitalized to withstand the earnings volatility that its mismatched portfolio created. That failing pushed the bank into the hands of the regulators. A capital cushion might have alleviated the crisis.

The Rating Agencies   Moody's and Standard and Poor's will be increasingly more stringent in their monitoring of capital levels. Their conclusions, in turn, will affect banks' access to capital sources of funds and the availability of long-term financing.

This type of financing has become more and more necessary for supplementary funding purposes, not only because of declining core deposit growth and continued volatile market rates, but also because of holding company expansion into a broader range of activities in international, real estate, and credit card lending, mortgage banking, lease financing, consumer financing, factoring and merchant banking, as well as the capital financing requirements for anticipated nationwide banking.

Borrowing Base   Capital is closely related to asset/liability management because it is the base through which a bank can add to or reduce its shorter-term liabilities. This fact is especially the case because if the market has confidence in a bank due to its key indicators, such as good earnings and adequate capital, that bank can borrow funds as inexpensively or less expensively than its competitors. The lower cost of funds results in higher earnings and formation of capital, which improves reputation, which then reinforces the ability to borrow at the best rates available. Therefore, because capital can be used both directly to extend credit and indirectly as a base for attracting additional funds, bank funds management must consider capital needs and discretionary sources of funds at the same time.

Debt instruments sold in the capital markets, such as three-year notes, are directly related to asset/liability management because the proceeds can be used to reduce outstanding commercial paper and other short-term debt and can also be employed to fund intermediate term, fixed-rate assets (i.e., matching maturities).

Even 30-year debentures, such as a recent offering of U. S. Bancorp, Portland, Oregon, are being used for shorter-term liability coverage. Richard Nockleby, Vice President, Corporate Finance of the bank, indicated that there is very little difference in cost between intermediate and long-term debt (at least in the current interest rate environment), and the longer-term debt can give the holding company more flexibility. The bank will use the proceeds primarily to pay down commercial paper and other short-term obligations of the holding company as well as for general corporate purposes.

Quasi-Capital   Capital is related to asset/liability management because certain issues have the characteristics of both liabilities and capital, e. g., perpetual preferred stock, convertible preferred stock, convertible notes and long-term debt.

REEVALUATING FUNDAMENTAL ASSUMPTIONS

In addition to the aforementioned balance sheet connections, there are two other considerations of importance.

The first of these considerations, as indicated in the first article in this series, is that the pressure points that define asset/liability management today—interest rate sensitivity and liquidity/funds management—may not be the primary decision points in the future. The entire balance sheet and its implications for profitability, risk control, and growth must always be kept under view.

The second factor to keep in mind is that, increasingly, short-term strategies and performance results must be examined with regard to longer-term implications. Moreover, these future implications may require current decisions about capital expenditures and financing that may alter the longer-range outcomes.

For example, banks might build a financial deterioration scenario for the 1980s, assuming that they are passive and take no innovative action. In this portrayal, net income margin, because of the rising cost of funds and the competitive, downward pressure on loan prices, narrows to 2%. Furthermore, noninterest expense, insufficiently offset by noninterest income, reduces net income to zero. This situation is aggravated by rising costs of insurance and hedges due to a riskier interest rate environment, increased marketing costs resulting from intensifying competition and the costs of new technology.

This negative picture is offset to some extent by productivity gains from technology and eventually higher average spreads over purchased funds because, in the long run, all banks which survive will be forced to price their loans higher.

By recognizing that the critical decision points of asset/liability management will change over time and that strategic initiatives can effect very different outcomes, these banks could substantially improve their evolving profit positions. On a near-term level, they could charge higher commitment fees, rigorously manage their money market operations, expand their investment options, venture into new loan markets and into loan originations and develop their techniques in tax planning. For the intermediate term, they could improve their profitability analysis and improvement efforts, increase their market shares through increased distribution channels such as loan production offices (LPOs) and possibly affiliates and branches in other states, develop new products and services (particularly in the noncredit area) and implement a productivity improvement program. On a long-term basis they could modify their management techniques by employing a more structured and coordinated decision process, aided by new technology and financial techniques for the monitoring and testing of alternatives. At the same time, they could expand into international markets and enlarge their domestic base through acquisitions, branch development and/or electronic payment systems.

All of these asset/liability management strategies add up to income stabilization, asset and earnings growth, adequate liquidity and capital—and consistent high performance.

24

New Initiatives in Asset/Liability Management *

Barrett F. Binder

With today's wide and volatile swings in interest rates, banks' risk of error in matching maturities is dramatic, and so is the impact of such errors on bank earnings. Furthermore, the rising cost of core funds and progressively narrower spreads make the margin for error narrower than ever. On the other hand, narrowing spreads could mean a drying up of profits if banks do not assume and manage some degree of rate risk, or if they do not compensate through alternative sources of revenue, or both. Therefore, downside risk and upside profit opportunities must be more carefully measured and coordinated as part of asset/liability management.

Successful management of asset/liability risks and returns depends on working with four basic options: Higher asset growth (volume), increases in the yields and percentages of earning assets, attempts to selectively mismatch maturities, and accelerated development of noninterest revenue.

The first two options are constrained. Higher asset growth will put additional pressure on capital, could drive down loan quality and may not be possible in mature markets. Increasing yields and percentages of earning assets also has definite limits. Controlled mismatching and developing noninterest revenue, however, show considerable promise.

THE INTEREST RATE RISK/RETURN TRADE-OFF

While avoiding interest rate risk is desirable, it cannot be the sole consideration in determining an overall risk position. Unwillingness to accept some rate risk

*Reprinted with permission from the *Magazine of Bank Administration*, June 1981, pp. 56-64. Copyright © 1981 by the Bank Administration Institute.

389

through modest maturity mismatches could lead to increased credit risk. For example, a bank might be persuaded to book less creditworthy, higher-risk/higher-return deals, such as certain construction loans, to compensate for the opportunity cost of a balanced position. Or if a bank has priced a loan on a variable-rate basis to avoid market rate risk, and interest rates increase sharply as they have in the past, say from 14 percent to 18½ percent, the borrower's ability to pay may be adversely affected. In both of these cases, the bank has inadvertently traded interest rate risk for credit risk. Market share and capital generation risks are also part of the composite risk.

Many banks are trying to quantify these risks, integrate them on some decision or policy level, and manage them in terms of the trade-offs involved.

These banks recognize, moreover, that there is no perfectly hedged or balanced position even if they did wish to eliminate interest rate risk through this means. Rate levels for assets and liabilities do not always move in tandem or to the same degree (e. g., a 200 basis point change in liabilities vs. a 250 change in assets). Also, rate-sensitive assets are constrained by usury limits in a rising rate environment. Moreover, there are volume shifts at different phases of the rate cycle, e. g., money market certificates may be 20 percent of liabilities when market rates are around 17 percent, but a much smaller percentage of liabilities when rates drop.

Furthermore, there is a hidden bias toward asset sensitivity in a declining interest rate environment. This is due to the ability of borrowers to pre-pay or renegotiate loans. Loan levels therefore decline faster than sensitivity measures suggest.

The complementary side of this hidden bias is that there may be less core deposit volume (disintermediation) if rates go up, and thus greater liability sensitivity than anticipated in the sensitivity ratio.

Deliberate mismatching will continue to be resisted by small banks because of their more limited freedom to choose assets and liabilities. They may well prefer to restructure the mix and pricing of assets and liabilities to achieve balance. This game plan is presently justified because many still enjoy lower funds costs and a potential for wide spreads, as compared to their larger and more wholesale-oriented counterparts. But as inflationary pressures and intensifying competition for deposits bid up funding costs, the advantage will decline and the mismatching approach may become more necessary.

EXERCISING THE DELIBERATE MISMATCH OPTION

What gaps, if any, are the right ones? They vary constantly depending on the lead times necessary for implementation, the various means available for adjusting gaps when they are unfavorable, as well as on how interest rates are expected to move.

In a rising-rate environment banks may decide to maintain a ratio which, for short times, tends to be asset-sensitive or greater than 1.00. For example, if a bank has $128 million in rate-sensitive assets (RSA) and $106 million in rate-sensitive liabilities (RSL), it has a funds gap or differential of $22 million and a ratio of 1.21.

Such a mismatch might consist of an excess of flexible-rate loans, cash flows from loans and investments, short-term investments and Fed funds sold over the total of short-term large CDs, money market CDs, public funds, Fed funds purchased and Repos.

Conversely, in a declining-rate environment, banks may decide to be negatively mismatched, i.e., an RSA/RSL ratio of less than 1.00, being careful not to rely too heavily on short-term investment securities.

The banks best able to mismatch maturities deliberately and take advantage of the yield curve are those that have broadened their planning horizons. They have systematically set in place the longer lead-time initiatives necessary to restructure balance sheet pricing and mix so that they can create positions in specialty loan and deposit markets (as compared to the short-term manipulation of discretionary assets and liabilities). These banks focus their efforts on determining basic business strategy, on establishing a strong base for high performance in the future and on maintaining control of interest sensitivity and net interest margin over the two-to-five year range. In this way they provide themselves escape valves for adding or reducing assets and liabilities when mismatches are intolerable or margins have narrowed to the point of potential negative carries.

These strategic initiatives can serve as a basis for short-term, discretionary changes in rate-sensitivity, cash flows and liquidity. While loan portfolios are still largely nondiscretionary, essentially reflecting the demands of the borrower and overall economic influences, banks are attempting to gain greater control of interest rate risk. Among the principal strategies are the following:

- Growth and dominance in special market segments.
- Acquisitions of rate-sensitive assets (through "roll-overs" or new contracts) in resalable lots, not all at one time during the rate cycle, but spread out over several months.
- Reduction of fixed-rate mortgage and/or instalment loans, either by refusing to make these deals or by pricing them out of the market.
- Creating a complete spectrum of flexible-rate assets for all categories of borrowings so that actual costs can be adequately reflected in prices, though the numerical growth of such arrangements will depend on evolving consumer acceptance. These assets might include two-year balloon mortgages, instalment loans and municipal bonds and government guaranteed loans that would have flexible-rate terms.
- Making use of the futures market, especially Treasury Bill futures to hedge fixed-rate loans.
- Reducing dependence on long-term bonds (and possibly closing a negative gap by investing maturing portfolio securities in shorter-maturity government/agency or municipal bonds and arranging tax swaps when profits are strong and rates high).
- Making greater use of money market investments.
- Increasing the ability to move credit-based business on and off the balance sheet through originations, participations, leasing, money market loans and the discretionary sale of insured loans.

THE ROLE OF FUNDS MANAGEMENT

Funds management should be the primary instrument for coordinating discretionary balance sheet initiatives, especially since money market liabilities are the most controllable items on the financial statement.

To increase discretionary opportunities on the liability side of the balance sheet, many banks are consolidating their funds management operations and developing greater funds generation capabilities. They are giving priority to having an active marketing and sales program for attracting new sources from their customer bases and other non-brokered direct sources.

Some banks, in their attempts to develop new sources of direct funds, are involved in market analysis and targeting of specific prospects, such as corporations and government units and agencies, looking at individual growth potential, industry growth and cash flows, as well as the coordination of many bank business units (e.g., sensitizing loan officers to tapping customer funds pockets) to turn these prospects into funds providers.

Furthermore, many banks are developing and actively promoting a spectrum of services, especially cash management options, as an incentive to attract new sources of funds. For example, they sometimes pursue a "funnel strategy." That is, they offer money market investment services that maximize the flow of each customer's cash surpluses through the bank.

Along these lines, banks can:

- Provide and publicly promote fee-based trading services for government, agency and municipal securities; and for commercial paper, bankers acceptances, secondary market CDs and Euro CDs, and Eurodeposits.
- Offer record-keeping for a fee and, whether or not accepted as a service, maintain computer-based books of account to analyze customer cash flows more accurately.
- Monitor the total flow of surplus funds, including maturities, and manage it through sales, promotion and pricing so as to direct needed portions into bank liabilities.
- Consider setting requirements for these fee-based services, such as the opening of a NOW or corporate deposit account for new customers. This arrangement will add additional net income.

On the horizon, many banks may be supporting their funding sales efforts with computer-based marketing information tools where feasible. These capabilities, in turn, may be integral to a comprehensive liabilities processing system which includes customer cash flow position (linking assets and liabilities) and activity data and customer contact history.

Finally, banks are measuring, developing and monitoring their market shares of purchased funds as distinct from their shares of core deposits.

In the former case, they are trying to diversify their sources by maintaining an active presence in as many money markets as possible, beginning with the lower cost, less price-sensitive local and regional markets, and establishing their name in and resorting to the national markets largely as a liquidity supplement (e.g., for medium- and longer-term CDs) to fill in gaps when timing is critical and/or rates are low. In regard to core deposits, these banks are generally competing by building the types of multi-service customer relationships mentioned above.

RATE SENSITIVITY AND LIQUIDITY

A high degree of interest rate sensitivity on the liability side and low liquidity mean a great risk of negative margins. Since liquidity, especially for larger banks, will increasingly be found off the balance sheet through purchasing funds, the above-mentioned funds generation strategies take on special importance. Contractual sources of supplemental funds should be negotiated in advance with correspondents and money market participants. Refinements must be pursued in the methods of estimating both outside sources of discretionary funds (Fed funds, Repos, CDs, special borrowings, etc.) and the statistically uncertain need for funds (deposit outflows, loan commitment utilization, etc.)

A measurement tool for refining the estimates of these funding sources and needs is the following equation,

$$\text{Potential Coverage of Deposit Losses and Actual Use of Loan Commitments} = \frac{\text{Total Sources (Liquid Assets + New Borrowings)}}{\text{Estimated Withdrawals + Increased Loan Commitment Usage}}.$$

One of the advantages of this approach, especially if it includes projections out over a number of periods, comes from its focus on loan commitments. With a

Table 1   Net Interest Margin (NIM) Risk and Gap Limits

PANEL A	(A) Allowable NIM Risk for the Period	(B) Estimated Potential Interest Rate Movement	(C) Allowable Average Gap for the Period
1 month	50%	2%	100% of earning assets
1 quarter	25%	5%	20% of earning assets
6 months	15%	7%	8.5% of earning assets
1 year	5%	9%	2.2% of earning assets

$$\text{Column C} = \frac{(\text{Column A})(\text{Net Yield \%})}{\text{Column B}}$$

PANEL B	(A) Allowable NIM Risk for the Period	(B) Estimated Potential Interest Rate Movement	(C) Allowable Average Gap for the Period
1 month	50%	1%	200% of earning assets
1 quarter	25%	2%	50% of earning assets
6 months	15%	3%	20% of earning assets
1 year	5%	4%	5% of earning assets

more detailed understanding of the components and the usage potential for various customer groups, opportunities to expand commitments selectively (and increase fee income) may be seized without jeopardizing liquidity.

Liquidity risk is integral to the risk/return factors inherent in deliberate mismatching. Longer-term liabilities, for example, may provide greater liquidity but also greater interest rate risk if they support a disproportionately smaller amount of similar maturity assets. Banks must relate measures of liquidity risk—i.e., the trade-off between the cost of maintaining liquidity (maintaining lines, narrow spreads on purchased funds) and the likely costs of running out (lost asset sales, liquidation costs, etc.)—to net interest margin objectives.

MEASUREMENT AND MANAGEMENT OF RATE SENSITIVITY

The willingness of banks to be prudently mismatched and their ability to meet net interest margin (NIM) objectives depend not only on the discretion and flexibility they have built into their balance sheets, but also on the precision with which they can measure and monitor their sensitivity positions.

The sensitivity ratio RSA/RSL may be helpful in monitoring broad changes in the bank's position, but it is an inadequate benchmark by itself. Rather, the absolute size of the dollar gap (especially in relation to total or earning assets) is the crucial determinant of net interest margin stability.

If a measure of gap is available (whether for a point in time or as an average balance over a period of time, say 30 or 90 days), relating it to earning assets produces a quick indicator of earnings risk. Since this indicator provides a means for dimensioning actual risk for the bank, it can become the basis for establishing meaningful policy limits on the degree of interest rate risk the bank is willing to expose itself to beyond which contingency actions will be triggered.

For example, First National Bank, with earning assets of $5 billion, may not allow its gap to exceed $500 million as a matter of policy. In fact, during late 1980 it may have adopted an even narrower constraint of less than $200 million. The reasoning supporting this restriction could be that if a gap of $500 million exists for six months, a period during which little corrective action might be taken, the bank has a differential at risk that is 10 percent of earning assets. If a 1 percent shift in rates occurred in an unfavorable direction and was sustained for that six-month period and the bank's NIM as a percentage of earning assets is 4 percent, a 2.5 percent reduction in NIM would be experienced for six months. The general relationship involved may be expressed as

$$\begin{array}{l}\text{The percentage risk} \\ \text{to which the NIM} \\ \text{for the period is} \\ \text{exposed}\end{array} = \frac{\begin{array}{l}\text{Average gap for any period} \\ \text{as a percentage of earning} \\ \text{assets}\end{array} \times \begin{array}{l}\text{Average change in interest rates} \\ \text{for the same period compared to} \\ \text{today's level}\end{array}}{\text{Expected normal net yield on earning assets}} \times 100$$

To utilize this measurement approach from the opposite direction, a bank may decide what percentage of its NIM it is prepared to risk for any given operating period. Then, based on its judgment of how much interest rate movement it believes may occur for such a period, it can derive limits on the allowable gap for the period.

These relationships can be generalized so as to relate risk policy limits and expected interest rate variability to limits for the gap. As an example, a bank whose NIM as a percentage of earning assets (net yield) is 4 percent per annum can examine its gap curve and look for periods of various duration during which average gap exceeded the policy limits determined by estimates of interest rate variability. By comparison, in a more stable interest rate environment, policy constraints on NIM risk can translate into expanded gap limits. As an illustration, compare panels A and B in Table 1.

For First National Bank referred to above, the contraction of gap limits to $200 million (or 4 percent of earning assets) reflects a belief that interest rates could vary by 2.5 percent on average for the period (assuming the environment has become more volatile), and it wants to hold its risk to 2.5 percent of NIM.

A bank may want to limit the exposure of NIM to interest rate risk over an entire year to something less than 5 percent. At the same time, it may be willing to accept a 50 percent risk for one week, and frequently will if it has large imbalances in overnight/very short money market assets or overnight funds (Fed funds, Repos, etc.). In contrast, a policy might be set of 5 percent for all periods of time. If this policy were carried out, the actual average over a full year would be less than 5 percent. This result may be inconsistent with the achievement of desirable margins (which require management of some risk). On the other hand, such a limit may impose bounds on allowable gaps which cannot be achieved consistently. (For a bank with a 4 percent NIM yield on earning assets, the gap would have to be kept under 2 percent of earning assets if rates were expected to change by 1 percent and under only 0.4 percent of earning assets for a rate change of 5 percent.

MANAGING LINKAGES BETWEEN THE BALANCE SHEET AND INCOME STATEMENT

Management of net interest margin tends to be made difficult by including too many decision factors. But opportunities might be lost if the bank only considers interest rate risk and changes in discretionary funds. Capital adequacy, noninterest income and expense, technology needs, tax strategies and strategic choices on markets, products and bank structure all require linkage to asset/liability management.

High performing banks pay special attention to risk/return factors of net interest margin management in relation to non-interest revenue and expense. Fees are being generated directly out of deposit services, with NOW accounts accelerating this trend. Originations, commitment fees, participations, as-agent investments, debit cards and the whole family of technology-based banking services, and financial advisory services are all part of this trend and will represent a markedly expanded share of total income, as well as a hook for a relationship that could eventually meld with bank credit.

The key for banks is to exploit the reserves of credibility they hold with customers and organize the delivery of these services, build on sound long-range plans and operating capabilities, and to forestall competitors from building experience, relationships and their own credibility.

The development of capital resources is also linked to asset/liability management decisions. Not only is capital essential for supporting asset growth, funding and acquisition financing, and the underwriting of market rate and credit risk. The reverse is also true. That is, asset/liability strategies are a key determinant of capital capacity.

A trend of narrowed margins means slower internal capital growth. Therefore, it may be best to have moderate interest margin instability and higher overall earnings growth. On the other hand, margin instability may put further downward pressure on stock prices and the ability to generate capital externally. Each bank must strike its own balance between earnings risk/return on the one hand, and capital generation on the other.

The basic question is whether banks will survive the current convulsions caused by intense competition, deposit run-offs, the rising cost of funds, unpredictable interest rates and unstable margins and the prospect of interstate banking. The answer is yes, if banks establish innovative and disciplined asset/liability management.

25

Interest Rate Futures: A Challenge for Bankers[*]

Howard Keen, Jr.

Contracts for future delivery of commodities have been around for what seems time immemorial. For the most part, these have been contracts for agricultural goods such as grains and livestock. Recently, however, markets have been organized to trade contracts for future delivery of debt securities—contracts whose price goes up and down with changes in the interest rate on the underlying securities.

These interest rate futures contracts debuted in October 1975 when trading in Government National Mortgage Association (GNMA) certificates began at the Chicago Board of Trade. Since that time, futures contracts have been developed for Treasury securities (bills, notes, and bonds), commercial paper, and CDs.

Interest rate futures contracts provide an opportunity to protect against changes in market interest rates, and so they may be attractive for commercial banks. They are not without pitfalls, however, and the challenge to bankers is to get the gains they offer while avoiding the pitfalls. At the same time, bank regulators face the challenge of adopting a regulatory stance that both provides appropriate safeguards and lets banks get the most mileage out of this financial innovation.

NEW TWIST ON AN OLD IDEA

Trading in contracts for future delivery has a long history. It's reported that a futures market in rice was operating in Japan as early as 1697, and a futures transaction was recorded in England in 1826. In the United States, trading in futures

*Reprinted from the *Business Review*, November-December 1980, pp. 13-22, with permission from the Federal Reserve Bank of Philadelphia.

first took place at the Chicago Board of Trade in the 1860s. By 1880, futures contracts were being traded in wheat, corn, oats, and cotton, and as time went by, contracts for other commodities came into use. Futures trading in sugar, oats, rye, barley, eggs, and butter started about the time of World War I. Contracts for soybeans, potatoes, and copper and silver began to be traded in the 1930s, for turkeys in the 1940s, and for platinum in the 1950s. Cattle, hogs, lumber, and frozen orange juice concentrate were added to the list in the 1960s.[1]

Like contracts for other commodities, interest rate futures contracts are traded on commodity exchanges—nonprofit organizations that provide facilities for trading. An integral part of each exchange is a clearing agency or corporation. All futures contracts and related financial settlements are handled through the clearinghouse.

The exchanges and clearinghouses together establish rules governing the operations of futures markets. (Futures trading is regulated also by the Federal government through the Commodity Futures Trading Commission.) These rules standardize the contracts traded on a given exchange by stipulating precise descriptions of commodities trades, delivery methods, delivery times, requirements for security deposits (margins), frequencies of adjusting the value of contracts, and limits on daily price fluctuations. These standards are roughly similar across the several exchanges, though they differ according to the kind of security for which the contract is being traded.

Besides regulating futures trades, the clearinghouse plays a central role in every futures transaction. While futures are bought and sold by traders on the floor of the exchange (in the trading pits), the resulting contracts have the clearinghouse on one side and a trader on the other rather than traders on both sides as buyers and sellers. Buyers of futures contracts are obliged to make payment to the clearinghouse while sellers are entitled to receive payment from it. Consequently, buyers and sellers of futures contracts need not be concerned with the creditworthiness of each other but only with that of the clearinghouse. This arrangement lowers the risk of default and adds to the attractiveness of futures markets.[2]

Thus the markets for interest rate futures offer well-organized trading opportunities for prospective investors.

HEDGING CAN BENEFIT BANKERS

The real usefulness of futures markets is that they provide a relatively low-cost method for transferring the risk of unanticipated changes in interest rates. In

[1] The history of early futures trading can be found in Henry H. Bakken, "Futures Trading: Origin, Development, and Present Economic Status." Reprinted from *Futures Trading Seminar Volume III* (Madison, Wisconsin: Mimir Publishers, Inc., 1966). A listing of commodities traded on organized exchanges in the United States along with dates of initial trading is given in *Annual Report 1978* (Washington: Commodity Futures Trading Commission). A detailed treatment of interest rate futures can be found in Allan M. Loosigian, *Interest Rate Futures* (Princeton: Dow Jones and Company, 1980).

[2] Agreements for delivery in the future can also be made with *forward contracts*. The latter differ from futures contracts in that they are not usually traded on organized exchanges, lack standardized terms, can be canceled only by both transactors, and typically require no margin payments.

principle, futures can be used both to increase exposure to interest rate risk (speculate) and to reduce exposure (hedge). But because current regulations prohibit banks from speculating (see *Speculating with Interest Rate Futures*), if bankers are to find interest rate futures beneficial, it has to be as a tool for hedging.

Hedging With Interest Rate Futures

To make money, banks borrow at one rate and lend at a higher one. But changes in interest rates can complicate this seemingly simple process, especially if they're unanticipated. If borrowing costs rise relative to lending rates, earnings may be reduced. And if bank stockholders have a preference for steady income, frequent interest rate changes can cause additional problems for bank managers by creating volatility in earnings. Hedging with interest rate futures could help bankers deal with both of these problems.

A banker might find futures useful when other methods of hedging are closed off by regulation or are considered to be too costly. If rates on all of a bank's financial assets and liabilities were to adjust proportionately in line with some common rate, for example, then unexpected changes in interest rates would have no impact on that bank's earnings. An unexpected change in the common rate would raise or lower the prevailing rates on assets and liabilities by the same amount while leaving earnings unchanged. But things usually don't turn out this way. Bank assets and liabilities aren't perfectly homogeneous, and their rates don't move exactly in line with each other. At the same time, regulatory restrictions such as ceilings on interest rates restrict movement in explicit rates of certain assets and liabilities. Finally, competitive pressures might discourage a bank from issuing floating-rate loans even though its own sources of funds are sensitive to changes in rates.[3] Under such conditions bankers should consider the use of interest rate futures to protect their positions against unanticipated changes in interest rates.

Bankers can use futures for three purposes—protecting the value of a portfolio, locking in borrowing costs, and locking in the return on investments. In the first two cases, the sale of a futures contract (a short hedge) would guard against interest rates that turn out to be higher than expected, while in the third, the purchase of a futures contract (a long hedge) would protect against interest rates that turn out to be lower than expected. In each case the objective is to protect or hedge against the impact of unexpected changes in interest rates on the profitability of anticipated cash market transactions. These are transactions that involve the purchase or sale of securities for immediate delivery. The cash market position is hedged by taking an opposite position in the futures market (see *Mechanics of Trading. . . .*).[4]

[3] For a discussion of this point and a more complex example of using interest rate futures to lock in borrowing costs, see James Marvin Blackwell, "The Ramifications of Hedging Interest Rates by Commercial Banks," The University of Texas at Austin, May 1979.

[4] Hedging can be viewed from several different perspectives. Traditional theory focuses on the potential for reducing risk and probably is the view most applicable to commercial bank use of interest rate futures. Hedging also has been viewed as undertaken primarily to earn a profit from a change in the relationship of the cash and futures prices. These two approaches are combined in the framework of portfolio theory, and its

SPECULATING WITH INTEREST RATE FUTURES

A speculator is a person or firm that is willing to bear added risk for the opportunity of earning a profit. With interest rate futures, the risk that speculators are willing to bear is the risk of unexpected changes in interest rates. Speculators can make a profit if they guess correctly about rate movements; but they can lose if they guess incorrectly.

If Cash Market Rate Turns Out To Be:	Winning Strategy Would Have Been:
Below Futures Rate	Long (buy then sell)
Above Futures Rate (yield on futures contract)	Short (sell then buy)

If the actual rate is expected to be lower than the rate implied in the futures contract today, a speculator can profit from buying a contract (going long) and then selling it as the delivery date approaches. Because yields and prices move in opposite directions, an actual rate in the future that is below the futures rate today implies an increase in the value of the underlying securities and therefore an increase in the value of the futures contract itself. Thus the speculator gains as he sells the contract for more than he paid for it. Similarly, an actual rate in the future that is above the implied futures rate today will cause the price of the underlying securities and thereby the price of the futures contract to fall so that a short (sell then buy) strategy would result in a gain as the sale price is higher than the purchase price. For example:

On October 1, 1976 the implied yield in the futures contract for delivery of three-month Treasury bills in the third week of December 1976 was 5.28 percent—above the then current cash market yield of 5.04 percent. A speculator who thought that by mid-December the rate would be below 5.28 percent would take a long position in October then offset it by selling another futures contract before the delivery date in December. If the anticipation was for the rate to be above 5.28 percent, the reverse strategy could be followed.

By December 1, 1976, three-month Treasury bill yields in the cash market had fallen to 4.41 percent while yields on the December futures contract fell to 4.43 percent and its price rose by $2,125, or $25 for every basis point. The long strategy would have resulted in a gain while a short strategy would have shown a comparable loss.

Date	Cash Market	Yields Futures Market*	Futures Contract Price†
October 1, 1976	5.04%	5.28%	$986,800
December 1, 1976	4.41%	4.43%	$988,925
Change	−.63%	−.85%	$ +2,125

Strategy Results: ‡
  Long   +$2,125
  Short −$2,125

---

*Treasury bill futures are reported on an index of 100 minus the futures market yield. The index for the above was 94.72 and 95.57 on October 1 and December 1 respectively.

†Futures contract price is computed as $1 million minus (yield times $1 million times 90/360) for 90-day T-bills.

‡Ignores brokerage fees and commissions and any opportunity cost of margins.

A Short Hedge   A short hedge involves the sale of one futures contract with the intention of offsetting it later by buying another contract for the same instrument with the same delivery date. If the price of the futures contract falls, the investor gains. A futures position of this kind can be used to protect the value of a portfolio and to lock in the cost of borrowing at some future date.

Consider a mortgage banker who in June makes a commitment to buy a pool of mortgages the following January at a set price with the intention of profiting by reselling them to investors at a higher price. If the value of the mortgage pool falls by January, the banker could take a loss on this transaction. Because the prices of fixed-income securities (like mortgages) fall when their interest rates rise (and vice versa), the mortgage banker will suffer a loss if long-term interest rates increase.

To hedge his exposure to loss, the banker may want to take a position that will produce a gain in the futures market if long-term rates do rise. This could be done by selling (shorting) a GNMA futures contract in June and then buying an identical contract in January. Just as the increase in rates will reduce the value of the mortgage pool, it will lower the price of the GNMA futures contract and result in a gain for the banker, as he buys a contract for less than he sold one for earlier (Table 1).

In a similar manner, a short hedge can be used to lock in future borrowing costs. Such a strategy might be used, for example, if a fixed-rate loan of some particular maturity is to be financed by rolling over shorter term liabilities during the life of the loan. If interest rates increase, the bank would have to pay higher rates on its liabilities, but these higher rates would be offset to some degree by the gain that results from the transaction in the futures market when rates increase.

Table 1 A Short Hedge Can Protect a Portfolio Against a Rise in Rates		
	Cash Market	Futures Market
June	Mortgage banker commits to buy pool of mortgages in January to be resold to investors at that time.	Sells March GNMA futures contract.
	Long-term rates rise; the value of the pool of mortgages as well as the value of the GNMA futures contract falls.	
January	Acquires mortgage pool and resells to investors at a loss.	Buys March GNMA futures contract.
Net Result*	Loss	Gain.

*Ignores brokerage fees and commissions and any opportunity cost of margins.

Source: *Hedging Interest Rate Risks*. 1st revised edition. Chicago: Chicago Board of Trade, September 1977, p. 17.

implications for hedging differ from those of the other two alone. for a discussion of these views, see Louis H. Ederington, "The Hedging Performance of the New Futures Markets," *Journal of Finance* 34 (March 1979), pp. 157-170.

MECHANICS OF TRADING INTEREST RATE FUTURES

Suppose an individual or business firm decides in January to buy a futures contract for delivery of three-month Treasury bills two months out (in March). This would be a March futures contract. The first step is to contact a futures broker (a futures commission merchant). After deciding on acceptable bid prices and providing the broker with a security deposit, the buy order is sent to a broker on the floor of the commodity exchange. The floor broker shouts out the bid in the trading pits, and if a seller can be found, the transaction takes place. After the trade is consummated, the buyer and seller have no further dealings with each other as far as this transaction is concerned. But the buyer has an obligation to make payment (in March) to the clearinghouse while the seller is obliged to deliver securities (in March) to the clearinghouse.

Although the minimum amount for a futures contract is $100,000, buyers and sellers do not have to provide the full amount of cash or the actual securities at the time the futures contract is bought or sold. Instead, each puts up a relatively small amount of cash (margin) as a security deposit. The clearinghouse requires a minimum initial margin of between approximately $500 and $2,500, depending on the contract. At the end of each trading day, the clearinghouse adjusts the value of each outstanding contract to reflect final settlement prices for that day. This procedure, known as marking-to-market, means that gains and losses on futures contracts are computed daily.

In essence, the broker has an account with the clearinghouse and the customer has one with the broker. When the value of a contract rises, the buying broker's account with the clearinghouse is credited. If the value of a contract falls, the two accounts are reduced accordingly. And if the value falls sufficiently, it might drop below the maintenance margin at which the broker's account with the clearinghouse (and the customer's account with the broker) must be replenished (through a margin call) to restore it to the initial margin. Such daily marking of contracts to market value together with maintenance margins ensure that the minimum security deposit will be preserved.

Consider an example—the IMM's $1-million par value 90-day Treasury bill contract with initial margin of $1,500 and maintenance margin of $1,200. If the value of this contract falls by more than $300, a call for funds would occur to restore the margin to $1,500. Because each basis point (.01 percent) represents $25 for this contract ($1 million times .01 percent times 90/360 days), a rise in yield of more than 12 basis points would trigger a margin call.

Once buyers and sellers are holding futures contracts, they can satisfy their obligations by taking or making delivery of the specified securities according to the terms of delivery in the contract, or they can cancel their contract by taking an offsetting position. Buyers cancel by selling identical contracts and sellers cancel by purchasing identical contracts. Most futures contracts are terminated by cancellation, which suggests that participants use the markets for something other than locking in future sales or purchases.

A Long Hedge   In contrast to a short hedge which is used to guard against a rise in rates, a long hedge is designed to protect against a fall in rates. A long hedge entails the purchase of a futures contract with the intention of offsetting it later by selling an identical contract. This type of hedge can be used to lock in the return on an investment that is planned for a date in the future.

Suppose, for example, that on April 1 a banker anticipates that on June 1 he will receive $1 million from a maturing investment. He plans to reinvest the funds in three-month Treasury bills when the older investment matures. The yield on the bills as of April 1 is 13 percent, but the banker has a premonition that rates will fall in the meantime and he wants to hedge against such a fall. The hedging can be done by purchasing a three-month Treasury bill futures contract for delivery in June.[5] By June 1, if rates in the cash market had fallen to 12.55 percent, the investment in Treasury bills would result in an opportunity loss of $1,125. But if expected future short-term rates were to fall equally, the price of the futures contract would rise and the sale of the contract would result in an exactly offsetting gain of $1,125. The net effect would be a yield of 13 percent, since $1 million of bills could be purchased in June for a net outlay of $967,500— $968,625 less the $1,125 gain from the futures transaction (Table 2).

In the case of both short and long hedges, interest rate futures can benefit a banker by enabling him to ensure (before paying brokerage fees and commissions of about $50-$60 per hedge) either the value of a portfolio, the cost of borrowing, or the investment yield from a transaction in the future. In this way, the banker is getting an insurance policy which like any such policy reduces the risk associated with unexpected events.

Table 2   A Long Hedge Can Protect an Anticipated Investment Against Reduced Yields

	Cash Market	Futures Market
April 1	Proceeds of $1 million from maturing investment expected June 1. Banker wishes to lock in current yield of 13%. Cost of $1 million in 3-months T-bills at 13% is $967,500.*	Purchases one ($1 million) June 3 months T-bill contract for $967,000 (13.20%).
June 1	Buys $1 million of 3-months T-bills for $968,625 (12.55%).	Sells (offsets) one ($1 million) June 3-months T-bill contract for $968,125 (12.75%).
Net Result†	Opportunity loss = $1,125.	Gain = $1,125.

*The price of $1 million of 3-months T-bills in both the cash and futures markets is computed as $1 million minus (yield times $1 million times 90/360).

†Ignores brokerage fees and commissions and any opportunity cost of margins.

Source: Mark F. Polanis and David C. Fisher, "Banking on Interest Rate Futures," *Bank Administration*, August 1979, p. 39.

[5] Other methods of hedging a cash market position include use of forward contracts, standby contracts, repurchase agreements, and spot market transactions. See *Treasury/Federal Reserve Study of Treasury Futures Markets*, Volume II, May 1979, pp. 23-29 and Appendix A, pp. 5-6.

BUT THERE ARE PITFALLS

While interest rate futures provide opportunities for bankers to reduce exposure to interest rate risk, they have their pitfalls as well. Their use actually will increase risk under certain conditions, and it can result in lower earnings in some cases. Further, in the extreme case, the use of interest rate futures could jeopardize bank solvency.

Risk Can Be Higher, Earnings Lower

Although interest rate futures can help a banker to reduce exposure to adverse movements in rates, they also can increase that exposure. An increase in exposure could occur if a bank's assets and liabilities are affected equally by changes in market interest rates.[6] In this case the portfolio would be hedged already, and taking a position with futures would serve only to establish a new unhedged position. In short, the impact of interest rate futures on a bank is determined by its total balance sheet. Thus an analysis of the extent to which a bank's earnings are sensitive to interest rate changes is an absolute must if hedging is to reduce a bank's exposure to interest rate risk.

Bankers undertake a futures market hedge expecting to lock in a level of earnings from a particular investment strategy. However, the outcome may differ from their expectations. A change in earnings relative to anticipations can occur because the so-called *basis* (the cash market yield minus the futures market yield) may not be the same at the time a futures position is offset as it was when the position first was taken.[7] If a hedge is perfect, the opportunity loss in the cash market will be offset exactly by the gain in the futures market. But sometimes a gain or loss in the cash market won't be offset exactly. Thus a crucial element to the success of hedging with interest rate futures is what happens to the basis. Regardless of which direction rates in the cash market move, if the basis does not change, the loss in one market will be just matched by the gain in the other market. If futures rates don't move proportionately with cash market rates and the basis does change, however, the extent of the offset will be affected. Depending upon the size and direction of the change in basis, income could rise or fall (Table 3).

Bankers need not be completely in the dark about how a change in the basis will affect their earnings. As the delivery date of a futures contract approaches, the price of that contract and the cash market price of the underlying securities

---

[6] See George M. McCabe and Robert W. McLeod, "Regulation and Bank Trading in the Futures Markets," *Issues in Bank Regulation* 3 (Summer 1979), pp. 6-14.

[7] Although the basis usually is defined as the cash market price minus the futures market price, numerical examples typically compute the basis as the difference between the cash market yield and the futures market yield. Examples in this article follow the latter and the only point to be aware of in this regard is that when the basis increases algebraically as measured by the difference in yields, it decreases algebraically as measured by the difference in prices and vice versa. Whichever measure of the basis is used, the appropriate cash market component will be determined by the transaction to be hedged. For example, if a short hedge is undertaken to protect the value of securities held by an investor, the cash market component in the calculation of the basis would be that for securities with the same term to maturity as those in the investor's portfolio.

Table 3   A Change in Basis Will Have an Impact on a Long Hedge*

	Cash Market	Futures Market	Basis	Net Result
April 1	$967,500 (13.00%)	$967,000 (13.20%)	−.20	
		Rates Fall, Basis Unchanged		
June 1	$968,750 (12.50%)	$968,250 (12.70%)	−.20	0
	(−$1,250)	(+$1,250)		
		Rates Fall, Basis Increases		
June 1	$968,750 (12.50%)	$968,875 (12.45%)	+.05	$625
	(−$1,250)	(+$1,875)		
		Rates Fall, Basis Decreases		
June 1	$968,750 (12.50%)	$967,625 (12.95%)	−.45	−$625
	(−$1,250)	(+$625)		
		Rates Rise, Basis Unchanged		
June 1	$966,250 (13.50%)	$965,750 (13.70%)	−.20	0
	(+$1,250)	(−$1,250)		
		Rates Rise, Basis Increases		
June 1	$966,250 (13.50%)	$966,375 (13.45%)	+.05	$625
	(+1,250)	(−$ 625)		
		Rates Rise, Basis Decreases		
June 1	$966,250 (13.50%)	$965,125 (13.95%)	−.45	−$625
	($1,250)	(−$1,875)		

*Changes in the cash market yield and the basis represent average two-month changes for 90-day T-bills using figures for the first business day in each month over the period January 1976 through March 1980. Although changes in both directions are illustrated above, averages were positive for both measures.

should move toward equality. Thus the basis should be approximately zero by the last trading day of a futures contract, and this characteristic can be used to get some idea of how the basis might change.

If the basis for a June-delivery contract is −.20 on April 1, for example, a reasonably good guess is that from April 1 to the last trading day around the third week in June, the change in the basis would be +.20. An increase in the basis would add to the earnings from a long hedge and reduce those from a short hedge. This is not to say that the basis won't jump around prior to the last trading day of a contract. But recognizing that the basis should be about zero at delivery can provide a fairly good idea of how the basis will move as the delivery date approaches.

For bankers contemplating the use of interest rate futures, it's a good idea to become familiar with past behavior of the basis. Hedging substitutes basis risk for risk from the cash market, and the less volatile the change in the basis, the greater the potential for reducing risk by hedging with interest rate futures.[8] When the entire cash market position is matched with a futures position, risk can

[8] This is illustrated by Ederington, p. 161. In this article it is estimated that in the period 1976-77, some reduction in interest rate risk could have been achieved in two-week and four-week hedges with 8-percent GNMA futures and with 90-day T-bill futures, although the GNMA futures seemed to be more effective in reducing risk, especially for two-week hedges. For both GNMAs and T-bills, greater risk reduction was possible in four-week than two-week hedges. It should be noted that the relationship between the cash price of one type of security and the futures price of a different security is usually not as close as it is for similar securities. As a result, *cross hedging*—hedging a cash market position with a different security in the futures market—is considered to provide less opportunity for reducing interest rate risk than the straight hedging illustrated in the text.

be reduced if, as is typical, the volatility of the change in the basis is less than that of the change in the cash price.[9]

Hedging with interest rate futures can reduce earnings in another way by limiting any gains from unexpected changes in interest rates. Recall that the goal of the long hedge in Figure 3 is to guard against a rate of return less than 13 percent. If the banker has correctly anticipated a fall in interest rates, he'll be better off having locked in that higher rate than he would have been if he hadn't used the futures market. If rates unexpectedly rise, however, his hedge will limit the rate of return to 13 percent instead of the unhedged return of 13½ percent. Thus the possibility that hedging could limit earnings in certain instances should be viewed as part of the price for reduced exposure to loss.

Regulatory Concern

Because of these pitfalls and because relatively low required margins may make it easier for trading to take place without the authorization of top bank decision-makers, interest rate futures are a concern to regulators who are charged with maintaining the soundness of individual banks as well as the banking system.[10]

The prime concern over banks' use of interest rate futures is that it might result in insolvency. Trouble could occur, for example, if highly risky futures positions were taken or if lack of experience led to injudicious trading. In response to such concerns, Federal regulators have issued trading guidelines to the banks.

Futures positions that increase exposure to loss from interest rate changes are not to be taken (though regulators may not always find it an easy matter to distinguish speculative from hedging transactions). And a bank's participation is to take place in a prescribed manner. Involvement is to begin at the top with a bank's directors endorsing a policy on strategies, internal monitoring and control, position limits, and the like. In addition, regulations prescribe explanatory notes in financial statements to describe futures activity that materially affects a bank's financial condition. At the same time, Federal regulators plan to keep a close watch on how banks use interest rate future.

---

[9] Whether hedging reduces the variance of returns depends upon two things. One is the relative volatility of the change in the basis and that of the cash price and the other is the percentage of the cash market position that is hedged. Although traditional theory assumes this percentage to be one hundred, portfolio theory implies that the risk-minimizing percentage can be different. See Ederington.

[10] For a fuller discussion of this point, see Brian Charles Gendreau, "The Regulation of Bank Trading in Futures and Forward Markets" (Washington: Board of Governors of the Federal Reserve System, June 1979). There are additional areas of concern about interest rate futures that are not covered in this article. They include the possibility of cornering or squeezing the market, the effect on the stability of spot prices, trading of futures by uninformed users, the impact on the flexibility of Treasury debt management, adequacy of required margins, and the accounting and tax treatment of interest rate futures transactions. Many of these worries emanate from the growing popularity of financial futures in recent years and the ensuing proliferation of contracts. Concern was heightened, however, by events in the silver market earlier this year when prices plummeted and there was difficulty in satisfying calls for additional margin.

SUMMING UP

All in all, interest rate futures pose a challenge for both bankers and bank regulators. On the positive side, interest rate futures provide bankers with a convenient way to hedge their exposure to interest rate risk. At the same time, however, they have pitfalls, and some of these could lead to serious financial difficulties. For bankers the challenge is to decide how futures can be used to improve their banks' performance, while for policymakers the challenge is to provide an environment within which banks can take advantage of the benefits of interest rate futures while at the same time maintaining the soundness of the banking system. As time goes by and bankers gain more experience with interest rate futures, both they and the policymakers should find these challenges easier to meet.

26

The Use of Financial Futures in Banking*

George M. McCabe and Robert W. McLeod

In recent years, large commercial banks have increasingly relied on purchased funds such as CDs, repos, and federal funds to finance lending operations. Indeed, these large banks have become a sort of "funds broker," raising funds in one market and lending in another. As deregulation proceeds this is probably the emerging pattern for banks of all sizes in the future. This approach, widely termed "spread lending," enables the bank to make a profit as long as it maintains a positive spread between the loan rate and the rate paid on the purchased funds. However, if short-term sources of funds are financing longer-term bank loans, the usual situation in banking, an increase in interest rates could cause a narrowing of the spread or even a negative spread. Controlling this interest rate risk is one of the primary tasks of management.

APPROACHES TO MANAGING INTEREST-RATE RISK

Floating-Rate Loans

Most banks use two basic asset-liability management techniques to control interest-rate risk. The first involves floating-rate loans. With floating rates, the interest rate on a loan is tied to the bank's cost of funds or some prime rate and thus varies over the life of the loan. As the cost of funds increases, the prime lending rate should also increase, thus preserving the spread.

There are problems with floating-rate loans. One of particular concern to bankers is that there is often a lag between changes in money market conditions and changes in loan rates. Thus, during periods of rapidly rising interest rates, the spread may narrow. The major problem with floating-rate loans, though, is that they do not eliminate interest rate risk—they simply transfer the risk to borrowers. There are many bank customers, especially highly leveraged borrowers, who are reluctant to incur the risk of a floating-rate loan because of the uncertain cost effects and cash flows. Thus, most borrowers prefer fixed-rate loans with specific maturities or floating-rate loans with a cap. But banks usually charge a sizable premium for these loans. Many borrowers then seek alternative sources of funds such as other banks, insurance companies, or the public debt market.

Matching Maturities or Layering

The other technique commonly used to control the risk or variations in the spread involves matching maturities of assets and liabilities. The basic idea underlying this approach, often called "layering," is to match the maturities of assets with those of the liabilities funding the assets. Since banks typically do not associate each and every loan with a specific source of funds, matching maturities of *individual* assets and *individual* liabilities is not practical except in special cases involving very large loans. The concept of matching, or layering, usually relates to maturity categories. As such, the approach is an approximation to individual matching. The more categories, the more involved the process becomes, but the more closely variations in the spread can be controlled. An example using the simplified commercial bank balance sheet shown in Panel A of Table 1 will clarify the technique.

Table 1   Commercial Bank Balance Sheet

A. Asset and Liability Structure

Assets		Liabilities	
Investments	$1,600	Demand Deposits	$1,600
Loans	5,000	Savings Accounts	1,600
Fixed Assets	400	Certificates of Deposit	3,000
		Common Equity	800
	$7,000		$7,000

B. Breakdown by Maturity or Re-Pricing Interval

Maturity or Re-Pricing Interval	Assets	Liabilities	Net Exposed Balance
0- 90 days[a]	$1,000	$3,000	($2,000)
91-180 days	1,200		1,200
181-270 days	2,000		2,000
271-365 days	2,400		2,400
Non-interest sensitive[b]	400	4,000	(3,600)
	$7,000	$7,000	

[a]Includes floating-rate loans. In practice, loans with extended re-pricing intervals, such as adjustable rate mortgage loans, may be in other categories depending on the timing of the re-adjustment.

[b]For simplicity of exposition, it is assumed that this category includes Fixed Assets on the asset side, and all the liability accounts except CDs.

The first step is to separate the assets and liabilities in accordance with their interest rate sensitivity. In Panel B such a breakdown is shown assuming quarterly intervals and a one-year horizon.[1] The assets and liabilities are classified in terms of their maturity or re-pricing interval. On the asset side, for example, floating-rate loans that are repriced within 90 days, as well as investments and fixed-rate loans that mature within 90 days are in the first category. The remaining assets and liabilities are similarly classified. The first category, 0-90 days, represents the most interest-sensitive assets and liabilities because the returns on assets and costs of liabilities may be brought in line with market rates. If the amount of assets in this category is the same as that of liabilities the bank is in a hedged position. However, as shown in Panel B, liabilities in this category exceed assets by $2,000. This net exposed balance creates a problem. If interest rates increase, the bank would have to refinance $3,000 of liabilities (CDs) within 90 days at the higher rate but assets of only $1,000 are maturing or are subject to repricing such that the return may be increased. The bank's overall spread will narrow. If the bank "matched" maturities, or the interest rate sensitivity of assets and liabilities, its interest rate risk would be reduced.

There is some controversy among bankers as to how far to carry the matching concept. On one hand, some would argue that banking is a lending business and banks should not be involved in interest rate speculation. The bank should aim for a "matched book" and eliminate the gaps at each maturity layer. However, other bankers argue that the resulting spreads would be too thin. They believe that to be profitable the bank must mismatch. It must aim for a higher concentration of liabilities in low-cost maturities and a higher concentration of assets in high-rate maturities. Followers of this approach would deliberately mismatch when they felt the increased expected profits justified increased risk. With an upward sloping yield curve they would borrow short and lend long. One has only to recall the plight of the savings and loan industry in the early 1980s to see the risk involved with this strategy.

One could argue that the whole idea of layering or gap management is not essential to risk analysis and all that is necessary is to match the durations of the bank's assets with its liabilities. This is not sufficient. First, banks generally wish to avoid undue fluctuations in earnings. Matching durations would mean that losses in one quarter or year would be offset by profits in another. Second, there is no assurance that interest rates would not fall again, so there would be no offset. If, in our example, interest rates rose in the first quarter, the bank would roll over the $3,000 of CDs at the new higher rate with the rollover of the $1,000 of short-term assets only partially offsetting the increased costs. If interest rates now fall, the $1,200 of assets in the 91-180-day category would be rolled over at a lower rate and there would be no gain to offset the loss in the first quarter. Indeed, there may be an additional loss. So, if the bank wishes to stabilize earnings and protect itself against variations in the spread, it needs to match assets and liabilities

---

[1] In practice, the analysis may be based on closer intervals and extend beyond one year. In particular, the bank would probably want to establish a separate category for assets or liabilities that can be repriced instantaneously, e.g., by a change in the prime.

at each maturity layer. Therefore, the bank needs to shorten the maturity of its investments or loan portfolio and/or lengthen the maturity of its CD portfolio.[2]

Some Problems

In theory, matching is simple to do; in practice, there are considerable difficulties. A bank must orient its loan portfolio and loan policies to meet its customers' needs if it wishes to compete. It will find that the terms and maturity distribution of its loan portfolio are dictated by its customers' needs for funds and not its own maturity requirements. This means that any adjustments of maturities, in order to achieve matchings of assets and liabilities, must be made on the liabilities side and largely in the CD portfolio. For small banks, with limited access to the national credit markets, adjustments in the maturity distribution of their CD portfolio may be very difficult, if not impossible. Even for very large banks the thinness of the longer-term CD market makes adjustments to the maturity distribution beyond one year quite difficult and/or costly to make. As a practical matter, then, the ability to control interest rate risk through layering is limited for most banks.

USING INTEREST RATE FUTURES TO CONTROL RISK

Hedging Individual Loans

With the advent of futures markets for financial instruments, other types of risk reduction strategies have emerged. As will become clear, these strategies have several advantages over those described above. It is not the purpose here to delve into the mechanics and specifics of the interest rate futures market. Rather, this paper focuses on hedging strategy.

> *Example.*   Consider a large money center bank that wishes to make a one-year, December to November fixed-rate loan of $1 million and finance it from a series of four 90-day CDs. Further assume that 90-day Treasury bill futures contracts (TBFC) are trading as follows:[3]

[2] Actually this is too simple. Sophisticated proponents of duration would argue that duration is an instantaneous concept. Matching durations will protect the bank against a one-shot change in interest rates. Then the bank must alter its portfolio so as to match the duration of assets and liabilities at the new rates for protection against any new change in rates. A bank that varied its assets and liabilities so as to continuously match durations would be protected in real terms against interest rate risk but its accounting income would still fluctuate. A bank that was matched at each maturity layer, however, would not have to rebalance as interest rates change.

[3] There are three contracts the bank could use to hedge—the Treasury bill contract, the CD contract, or the Eurodollar contract. In general, we would expect the bank to use the CD contract if it planned to finance the loan using CDs and the Eurodollar contract if it planned to finance the loan from Eurodollar borrowings. The Treasury bill contract, however, has more volume and thus might be viewed as more liquid. The mechanics of the three contracts are similar though not identical. We have chosen to use T-bills for our examples here because the T-bill futures market is older and because T-bills are traded on a discount basis and this makes for simpler examples. Also, CD futures are traded for only four quarters in the future so it would be difficult to hedge much beyond a one-year loan without resorting to T-bill futures.

	IMM Index	Discount[4]
March	91.5	8.5%
June	91.0	9.0
September	90.5	9.5

Also, the bank can sell a 90-day CD today for an 8 percent annualized rate. The 8 percent rate is the bank's actual cost of funds for the first 90 days of the loan. Assuming for simplicity that the bank can sell CDs at the Treasury bill rate, then 8.5 percent, 9.0 percent and 9.5 percent represent market estimates of the cost of funds for future quarters. The bank can then use the futures market to reduce variations in its cost of funds. The average cost of funds will be:

December–March	8.0%
March–June	8.5
June–September	9.0
September–December	9.5
	35.0/4 = 8.75%.

With an average percentage cost of borrowing equal to 8.75 percent, the average dollar cost will be $1,000,000 × .0875 = $87,500.

Now if the bank makes the loan at an assumed spread of 100 basis points, or 9.75 percent, it should earn $10,000 in net interest margin over the term of the loan. But to lock in this profit, it must simultaneously sell three Treasury bill futures contracts (TBFC) of $1,000,000 each for delivery in March, June, and September.[5] If, as assumed, the bank can float CDs at the Treasury bill rate, then the bank is now perfectly hedged and its $10,000 profit assured.[6] This can be demonstrated by tracing our hypothetical case through the year.

Assume that interest rates are higher than anticipated when the March CDs are renewed. The going rate on CDs is now 10 percent instead of the anticipated 8.5 percent. This has increased the cost of borrowing for this three-month period from

---

[4] Treasury bills (and also CDs and Eurodollar CDs) are traded in terms of the IMM index which is 100—the annualized discount. Also the rate quoted on T-bills is a discount yield. This is identical to the cash market in T-bills but is not comparable to other types of yields. A 6 percent discount means a 90-day bill is selling for

$$\$1,000,000 \left[1 - \frac{90(.06)}{360} \right] = \$985,000.$$

The IMM publishes tables making conversions to other types of yields.

[5] There is a subtle complication here caused by the mark-to-market feature of futures contracts (discussed in footnote 7). With marking-to-market, gains or losses in the futures position occur when rates change instead of when the position is offset. Thus they can earn interest from the time rates change to the time the hedge is lifted and the hedged CD floated. This can be accounted for by matching the present discounted value of the three CDs to the implied value of the futures contracts (i.e., not to the face value of $1,000,000 but to $1,000,000 × [1 − (r/4)]. This strategy would involve increasing the size of the hedge as time passes and the present value of the CDs increase. More importantly, such precise matchings would often not be possible as T-bill, CD and Eurodollar futures are all traded in $1,000,000 contracts and so the strategy would involve fractions of futures contracts. To simplify our example we have ignored this complication.

[6] We have not discussed delivery dates in the text. T-bill futures are deliverable on a single day, the first Thursday after the third weekly Treasury bill auction in the delivery months March, June, September, and December. On this day the "short" or seller of the futures contract must deliver $1,000,000 face value of 90-day Treasury bills to the particular "long" or buyer who has been designated by the clearing corporation. The Eurodollar CD is similar in that it too has a single designated delivery date. The domestic CD contract, however, is deliverable from the 15th through the last day of the delivery month.

$21,250 to $25,000. This is $3,750 more than was anticipated. However, the increased cost of funds should be offset by the increased value of the TBFC. Since each basis point change has a value of $25, the gain in the value of the contract is 150 × $25 = $3,750. The bank's average cost of funds remains 8.5 percent.[7]

Now suppose that by June, interest rates have risen further so the CD must be renewed at 11 percent instead of the expected 9 percent. The cost of borrowing is $27,500, or $5,000 more than the expected $22,500. But the June TBFC will have increased in value by $5,000 and would be closed out to offset the increased cost of borrowing. Suppose that by September interest rates have dropped so the CD is renewed at 8 percent instead of the expected 9.5 percent. The cost of borrowing will be $20,000 or $3,750 less than the expected cost of $23,750. But now the value of the TBFC will have dropped and could only be closed at a $3,750 loss. The hedge cuts both ways.

Table 2 summarizes the bank's borrowing costs and related changes in the futures position for our example. The effect of the hedge was to protect the bank from unforeseen movements in interest rates and ensure that the bank could raise funds for the $1,000,000 loan at a known cost of 8.75 percent. The bank has made a fixed-rate loan and avoided the risk of variation in its earnings.

The above example was simplified in several ways. First, a bank clearly cannot issue its CDs at the T-bill rate. What is crucial is the spread between the bank's CD

On the delivery date the futures rate and cash rate must be the same, otherwise an astute speculator could buy the T-bill in the cash market and sell it in the futures market, or vice-versa, for a profit. As a practical matter, the cash and future rates will be very close throughout the delivery month. In other months the cash rate and futures rates may diverge somewhat so the hedge would not be perfect.

[7] An intuitive way to see this change in value of the futures contract is to ignore the mark-to-market feature of the futures contract. In January the bank sold a contract for delivery of $1,000,000 of 90-day T-bills in March at 8.5 percent. This means that in March the bank is obligated to deliver $1,000,000 face value of 90-day T-bills at 8.5 percent and receive

$$\$1,000,000 \left[1 - \frac{(.085)90}{360} \right] = \$978,750.$$

But in March, 90-day T-bills are trading at 10 percent. The bank could close its position if it wished by buying and delivering $1,000,000 of T-bills at a cost of $975,000. The difference between the two amounts, $3,750, is the gain on the contract. The International Monetary Market (IMM) achieves a similar result but by a different means. First, they note that for every basis point change in the interest rate there is a $25 change in value. Second, they mark the contract to market daily. Thus, for each basis point rise in the rate they take $25 from the long's margin and add $25 to the short's margin. By March then, the bank has gained (10 − 8.5) × 100 × $25 = $3,750. Since its contract has been marked-to-market and it has received its gain, the bank must now deliver the T-bills at the market rate of 10 percent or $975,000. There would be no advantage to doing this so it would normally just offset the contract by buying an equivalent contract.

In the domestic CD contract there is an additional complication. Bank CDs typically bear coupon interest. Thus a $1,000,000, 10%, 90-day CD will have a maturity value of (1 + .10/4) × 1,000,000 = $1,025,000. The settlement or invoice price (IP) is calculated using the maturity value (MV). For a 90-day CD,

$$IP = \left(\frac{MV}{1 + \frac{F}{4}} \right)$$

where F is the yield.

A change in yield of one basis point does not give a change in the invoice price of exactly $25. For the bank who wishes to hedge against large changes in interest rates this is trivial but it does allow for some subtle arbitrage strategies. Also, it makes CD futures somewhat more difficult to explain to boards of directors and to finance students.

Table 2   Borrowing Costs Using Interest Rate Futures

	Expected Interest Rate	Expected Cost of Borrowing	Actual Interest Rate	Actual Cost of Borrowing	Change in Value of Futures Position	Borrowing Cost Less Change in Futures Position	Hedged Interest Rate
December-March	8.0%	$20,000	8%	$20,000	None	$20,000	8.0%
March-June	8.5	21,250	10	25,000	+ 3,750	21,250	8.5
June-September	9.0	22,500	11	27,500	+ 5,000	22,500	9.0
September-December	9.5	23,750	8	20,000	− 3,750	23,750	9.5
	8.75%	$87,500		$92,500	+$5,000	$87,500	8.75%

rate and the T-bill rate. If the bank's CD rate is always one percentage point above the T-bill rate, the hedge will still be perfect. Gains and losses from futures transactions would be the same as shown in Table 3, but the bank's expected and actual cost of borrowing would be one percentage point higher. Any deviations from these expected CD costs would be offset by gains or losses in the futures position. It is only when the spread between the bank's CD rate and the T-bill rate changes that the hedge will not be perfect. This is called *basis risk*. Hedging in CD futures instead of T-bill futures may reduce but will not eliminate basis risk. The rates on CD futures are based on the CD rates of ten of the country's largest, most well-known, and safest banks. Typically, there will be a spread between the CDs of these large banks and those of smaller regional banks and this spread will vary. The basic argument for hedging is that basis risk is considerably less than the interest rate risk that is avoided by hedging. The spread between CD rates and T-bill rates does not vary nearly so much as the rates themselves. Thus, a well-conceived hedging program will greatly reduce a bank's risk.[8]

Also, the above example was phrased in terms of the bank floating 90-day CDs in the delivery months. Clearly, other maturities of CD's could be floated and in other months.[9] However, the available futures contracts are for 90-day T-bills deliverable in December, March, June, and September.[10] To the extent the CD being hedged deviates from the deliverable instrument in maturity or delivery date, the basis risk is increased. Again this risk should be considerably less than the interest rate risk borne by not hedging.

---

[8] One of the fears of those unfamiliar with futures is that their counterpart in the futures transaction will default. This is unfounded because of the clearinghouse. The precise duties of the clearinghouse vary among the exchanges but they share one essential feature. Once a futures trade has been completed they intervene between buyer and seller. Both parties' counterpart is, then, the clearinghouse. Normally, futures positions are closed out without delivery. The buyer, for example, will sell an equivalent position and the clearinghouse will then net out the position. In the case of actual delivery the clearinghouse will assign an outstanding and typically different buyer to accept delivery from the seller, but even then the clearinghouse guarantees performance. In the case of the major financial futures exchanges (the Chicago Mercantile Exchange and the Chicago Board of Trade) the clearinghouse has capital contributed by its members (most large U.S. brokerage firms). In addition, in case of severe problems, the members are liable for additional assessments. A failure in financial futures then would, of necessity, involve a collapse of a significant part of the U.S. financial system.

[9] In general, to hedge an x-day CD one needs to sell x/90th of a CD or T-bill future, *i.e.*, one third of a contract for a 30-day CD.

[10] Actually, 89- and 91-day T-bills are deliverable at a specified conversion value. For CD futures even more maturities are deliverable.

The example involved a one-year loan. T-bill futures are listed for eight quarters into the future while CD futures are listed for only four quarters. Thus a bank could hedge a loan in the manner described for only nine quarters. (The first CD does not have to be hedged.) Beyond nine quarters the bank must turn to other techniques. CDs beyond nine quarters could be hedged by a technique called *rolling the hedge forward*. This involves placing the hedge in the latest available futures contract (here the eighth) and then rolling the hedge forward quarter by quarter to the newly listed contract. This technique has been shown elsewhere to be only slightly less effective than hedging in the desired but unlisted contract.[11] However, the rates being locked in can no longer be obtained from the futures markets. They can be estimated from the term structure of interest rates, though, so the loan can still be priced. Another alternative would be to make longer-term loans at a fixed rate for nine quarters and then allow the rate to be fixed for another nine quarters at rates implied by futures rates at the end of the nine quarters.

Loan Prepayment

The previous example implicitly assumed away the problem of loan prepayments. Suppose the bank made the above loan based on a hedged cost of funds of 9.75 percent, one percentage point above the T-bill rate, and then the CD and T-bill rates fell to 8 and 7 percent, respectively. The bank has a loss on its futures position which is hopefully offset by the fixed-rate loan which is now at above-market rates. However, if the loan is now prepaid, the bank is left with just the loss on the futures contracts. The only way for the bank to fully protect itself is to require a prepayment penalty at least equal to the cost of closing out the futures position. Anything less and the bank isn't fully protected. Anything more unnecessarily penalizes the borrower.

Pricing the Loan

Once the bank has hedged the individual loan as described, the loan can be easily priced. If the bank expected its CDs to be floated at one percentage point above the T-bill rate then its cost of funds in the example for the four CDs needed to finance the loan will be about 9, 9.5, 10, and 10.5 percent, respectively. The costs may vary slightly due to changes in basis ·but the hedge insures they won't vary much. The bank can thus base its loan rate on these rates. Typically it would take the average of 9.75 percent and add on a spread which would include the bank's profit plus reimbursement for various expenses including the cost of hedging.

Hedging Costs

There are two major costs associated with hedging— commissions and margins. Commissions are nearly always less than $60 per contract per round trip (one buy and one sell to close the position). For active traders costs may be as low as $25. This is .0025 percent of the $1 million being hedged. Also, the exchange requires traders to post a margin. This is not like margins in the stock market but is more like a performance bond. At the close of trading each business day all futures positions are marked-to-market,

---

[11] George M. McCabe and Charles T. Frankle, "Rolling the Hedge Forward in the Treasury Bill Futures Market," *Financial Management*, Summer 1983, pp. 21-29.

which means that the daily gains or losses in value are added to or subtracted from the margin account. If the margin falls below specified levels, extra margin must be posted. Likewise excess margin may be withdrawn. While these additions or subtractions to the margin are in cash, the margin may be posted in interest-bearing securities and then the daily settlement made in cash. For a major bank used to large cash inflows and outflows, this should be no problem. The margin cost also is relatively small.

The Synthetic Fixed-Rate Loan[12]

Another way to accomplish the above result and avoid some of the regulatory and accounting hassles described later is to book the loan as a floating-rate loan at 2 percentage points over the T-bill rate and let the borrower do the hedging. This is referred to as a *synthetic fixed-rate loan.* By making the loan on a floating-rate basis, the bank has avoided much of the interest rate risk. Assuming a spread of two percentage points over the quarterly T-bill rate and continuing with the preceding example, the borrower would be charged 10, 12, 13, and 10 percent. The total interest cost over the year would be $112,500. The gain of $5,000 from hedging would reduce the borrower's interest cost to $107,500 or 10.75 percent. This is the same rate the bank would have charged had it charged two percentage points over its hedged, expected cost of funds of 8.75 percent.

For the *synthetic fixed-rate loan* to work well, the loan must be tied to an easily hedgeable market rate like the T-bill rate or the CD rate of the ten large U.S. banks mentioned earlier. The rate must also change every 90 days and in the delivery months. A bank's prime rate is not easily hedgeable as it is changed administratively and irregularly and is not directly tied to market rates. Also, the bank must be prepared to fund changes in the firm's margin accounts caused by the mark-to-market features of the contracts.[13]

HEDGING THE WHOLE BANK

While hedging individual loan commitments as described previously is, in general, a useful first step in managing interest rate volatility, it must be done carefully with an awareness of the exposure to interest rate fluctuations in other areas of the bank. Without this awareness there are cases where hedging can actually in-

---

[12] For another discussion of this concept see, James Kurt Dew and Terrence F. Martell, "Treasury Bill Futures, Commercial Bank Lending and the Synthetic Fixed-Rate Loan," *Journal of Commercial Banking Lending,* June 1981.

[13] In the above example, if interest rates fall, the borrower, who is also the hedger, would lose on the futures position but this would be offset by the lower interest on the loan due to the floating-rate feature. However, the gain from the lower interest rates would be spread over the life of the loan whereas, due to the mark-to-market feature of futures contracts, the entire loss would occur immediately.

crease the bank's exposure to interest rate risk. The simplest way to maintain this awareness is to view hedging and the management of interest rate risk as a bank-wide function.

Consider the bank described earlier in Panels A and B of Table 1. This bank has a severe mismatch of asset and liability maturities. To correct this in the cash markets it has to lengthen the maturity of its liabilities and/or shorten those of its assets. As discussed, this may be difficult to do in the cash markets. However, it is not particularly difficult to do in the futures markets.

For hedging purposes, we need only deal with the *net exposed balances.* The portion of assets and liabilities that are matched and netted out can be viewed as a sort of natural hedge. The $1,000 of 0-90-day interest-sensitive assets will not affect the spread because they are matched with $1,000 of the $3,000 in 0-90-day liabilities. When interest rates rise and $1,000 of the 0-90-day CDs must be rolled over at a higher rate, the $1,000 of 0-90-day assets have also matured and can be reinvested at the new rate, which would maintain the spread.[14] When there is a matching there is a natural hedge that maintains itself over time.

As can be seen in Table 1, the example bank has a net exposed liability balance (or "negative gap") of $2,000 of CDs in the maturity range of 0-90 days which it must refinance at prevailing rates. This poses a problem in maintaining a desired spread because the bank cannot reprice its 90-180-day assets of $1,200 at the same time. In other words, the bank is exposed to an interest rate squeeze on $1,200 for 90 days. The remainder of the $2,000 ($800) has to be rolled over twice before a matching, exposed asset balance can be repriced. Therefore, the bank is exposed to an interest-rate squeeze on $800 for 180 days. If the CD market were such that the bank could have issued $1,200 of 91-180-day CDs and $800 of 181-270-day CDs in place of the $2,000 in 0-90-day CDs, the bank could have avoided the problem. However, this is not necessary because the bank can achieve the same results by hedging the rollovers.

By using futures contracts with an appropriately structured hedge, the bank can effectively lock in a certain cost of funds at each rollover or renewal of CDs. In the previous example the bank would need to sell $2,000 of 90-day T-bill futures contracts with a three-month delivery date. In order to be fully covered against the risk of the spread narrowing the bank would also sell $800 of 90-day contracts with a delivery date six months from now. This is necessary because the $800 has to be rolled over into the third quarter.

An example will show how this approach will affect the spread. Assume that the bank has its assets invested at 12 percent and, as before, that CDs can be floated at the T-bill rate of 10 percent. Also assume that analysts expect rates to stay at 10 percent so T-bill futures also trade at 10 percent. However suppose interest rates on 90-day CD's and T-bills unexpectedly rise to 11 percent in the next quarter. The bank can reinvest $1,000 at 13 percent in order to maintain the spread on that portion of its assets. Without hedging the bank would have a lower spread because they would have to wait until the loans or investments in the 91-

---

[14] There will always be some mismatching within each maturity layer. Thirty-day liabilities must be rolled over before 60-day assets mature. But the extent of the problem is much less than 30-day liabilities and 360-day assets.

180- and 181-272-day categories matured before the rates could be raised. With hedging the bank would be able to maintain its spread.

As shown in Panel A of Table 3, there is no net gain or loss if the bank has hedged as described previously. The loss in the cash market due to increased cost of funds is offset by the gain in the futures market transactions. The spread has been maintained.

Another way to describe what has been done is to view the $2,000 of net exposed 90-day liability balances as having been converted through hedging into the equiv-

Table 3   Hedging the Whole Bank

A. Gain or Loss from Hedged Position

Time	Cash-Market Transactions	Offsetting Futures Market Transactions
Loan origination and flotation of first CD	Anticipated CD costs 10%, or for quarter two, $(.10/4) \times \$2,000 = \$50$	Sell $2,000 of T-bill futures contracts for delivery at beginning of quarter two for a price of $[1 - (.10/4)] \times \$2,000 = \$1,950$
	For quarter three $(.10/4) \times \$800 = \$20$	Sell $800 of T-bill futures contracts for delivery at beginning of quarter three for a price of $[1 - (.10/4)] \times \$800 = \$780$
Rollover of first exposed CD to quarter two	Actual CD cost 11% $(.11/4) \times \$2,000) = \$55$. Additional cost $= \$55 - \$50 = \$5$	Buy back $2,000 of quarter two T-bill futures for $[1 - (.11/4)] \times \$2,000 = \$1,945$ Gain $= \$1,950 - \$1,945 = \$5$
Rollover of second exposed CD to quarter three	Actual CD cost 11% $(.11/4) \times \$800) = \$22$. Additional cost $= \$22 - \$20 = \$2$	Buy back $800 of quarter three futures for Gain $= \$780 - \$778 = \$2$
	Total Net Gain (loss) $= 0$	

B. Net Exposed Balances After Hedging

Maturity or Interval	Net Exposed Balance	Asset or Liability
0 - 90 days	0	
91 - 180 days	0	
181 - 270 days	$1,200	Asset
271 - 365 days	$2,400	Asset
Non-Interest Sensitive	$3,600	Liability

Maturity or Interval	Net Exposed Balance	Asset or Liability
0 - 90 days	0	
91 - 180 days	0	
181 - 270 days	$1,200	Asset
271 - 365 days	$2,400	Asset
Non-Interest Sensitive	$3,600	Liability

alent of $1,200 of 91-180-day and $800 of 181-270-day liabilities. Hedging has effectively restructured the net exposed balances from those shown in Table 1 to those shown in Panel B of Table 3. The objective of eliminating variations in the spread by matching assets and liabilities was accomplished by hedging. The remaining interest sensitive positions are asset balances which are funded by noninterest sensitive sources of funds such as stockholders' equity and demand deposits.

Another type of problem is characterized in Panel A of Table 4. The bank has funded short-term assets with liabilities that mature in the fourth quarter and will have to be refinanced. Possible solutions to this problem are to lengthen the maturity of assets in order to match the $600 negative gap position in the fourth quarter or hedging the reinvestment of $600 of the $800 in the third quarter by purchasing T-bill futures contracts. This will essentially convert $600 of the 181-270-day funds into the equivalent of 271-365-day funds. Using either approach the bank's net exposed or gap positions would be as shown in Panel B.

REGULATORY, ACCOUNTING, AND TAX TREATMENT

Financial futures are relatively new instruments and the regulations governing their use are in a state of flux. Thus, what is said here is tentative. In general, if a bank is hedging, accountants and the Internal Revenue Service will allow it to match the financial futures contract to whatever is being hedged and treat both consistently. This will normally involve recognizing the gains or losses from the hedge at the same time the gains or losses from the cash transaction are recognized. Federal bank supervisory agencies, and in particular, the Office of the

Table 4   Changing the Net Exposed Position

A. Bank Balance Sheet by Maturity

Days to Maturity	Quarter of Maturity	Assets	Liabilities	Net Exposed Position
0 - 90	1	$1,000	$ 200	$ 800
91-180	2	1,000		1,000
181-270	3	800		800
271-365	4	600	1,200	(600)
Noninterest-sensitive		400	2,400	
		$3,800	$3,800	

B. Net Exposed Positions After Hedging

Days to Maturity	Quarter	Net Exposed Position	Asset or Liability
0- 90	1	$ 800	Asset
91-180	2	1,000	Asset
181-270	3	200	Asset
271-365	4	0	
Noninterest-sensitive		$2,000	

Comptroller of the Currency, requires futures contracts to be marked-to-market regardless of the treatment of any associated cash transaction. In our examples above, if interest rates fall, the benefits to the bank will occur in lower CD rates over some time in the future. Using mark-to-market accounting, the loss associated with contracts will occur immediately. This will result in a drop in current reported earnings and a rise in future reported earnings. It is the view of most of the accounting profession that this does not reflect the underlying economics of the situation and does not realistically reflect the nature of the hedge. As one might expect there is considerable pressure on the Comptroller to change this policy. In the meantime, banks have three options: (1) accept the unrealistic accounting; (2) require their customers to book the hedge (i.e., help create a *synthetic fixed-rate loan*); or (3) keep two sets of books, one for the regulatory agencies and one for shareholders. Options two and three seem preferable. Unrealistic accounting is never desirable. While some larger, sophisticated customers may be willing to hedge themselves, smaller customers with loans less than $1 million and less sophisticated borrowers may be unwilling or unable to do so, leaving the bank with option 3.

OTHER BANK USES OF FUTURES

In the previous discussions it was noted that some bankers deliberately mismatch the maturities of their assets and liabilities in the hope of obtaining a higher spread. The single-asset counterpart of mismatching is a technique known as *riding the yield curve.* Suppose a bank has funds deposited in a 90-day CD that it knows will be withdrawn at maturity in March. The bank can match by investing in 90-day funds at 10 percent or mismatch by investing in 180 day funds at 12 percent planning to sell the, then 90-day bill in March. The extra gain is offset by an increased risk of capital loss. The risk of this capital loss can be reduced by shorting a 90-day T-bill future. Suppose March futures are selling for 11 percent. Continuing to use discount yields this means the 90-day March bill can be purchased for $1,000,000[1 − (90 × .10)/360]   = $975,000 and the 180-day June bill for $1,000,000[1 − (180 × .12)/360]   = $940,000. By March the 180-day June bill will be a 90-day June bill. At 11 percent it should be able to be sold for $1,000,000 [1 − (90 × .11)/360]   = $972,500. If this March sale price is locked in by a hedge the bank's interest will be $972,500 − $940,000 = $32,500 instead of $25,000.[15] With these interest rates the bank can clearly proift from riding the yield curve. The problem is that arbitragers will figure this out too and will begin to buy the 180-day bill and short the futures. This will cause the rate on the 180-day bill to fall and the March futures rate to rise until there is very little profit potential left. While some banks which are very close to the markets may find profitable oppor-

---

[15] For ease of exposition we have ignored the fact that the three amounts invested are slightly different than $1,000,000.

tunities to ride the yield curve, arbitragers will usually insure that such profits are minimal or non-existent.[16]

SUMMARY

There are many ways in which financial institutions can reduce their exposure to interest rate risk. Among the more common approaches to this problem are the use of floating-rate loans and matching maturities of assets and liabilities. This paper has pointed out how the use of futures contracts can enable a financial institution to effectively reduce its interest rate risk by shifting the maturity of its net exposed asset or liability position in order to maintain a predetermined spread. Although in practice an institution may not be able to eliminate all of its risk due to variations in maturities within time periods, the significant risk reduction associated with the techniques outlined in this article are well worth the effort.

---

[16] Students of finance will recognize this as a form of the expectations theory. Basically the theory would say the 180-day rate is a geometric average of the two expected 90-day rates. For there to be a pure profit in riding the yield curve requires a liquidity premium on interest rates and normal backwardization in futures rates.

PART V

COST, COMPETITIVE, AND REGULATORY ISSUES

27

Estimating the Cost of Your Bank's Funds*

Ronald D. Watson

By the time Franklin National Bank finally succumbed in 1974, it had been assured an honored spot in modern banking theory as the textbook example of how *not* to run a bank. One of Franklin's weaknesses was the incorrect method its management used to estimate the cost of the bank's funds.[1] During a period of high interest rates, the bank consistently underestimated the cost of raising money. In fact, the cost of the money that Franklin borrowed to invest was higher than the return on the investments it was making.

Most bankers are far more sensitive to this problem than Franklin's management was, but being aware of how important it is to know the cost of money and being able to make an accurate estimate of that cost are two very different things. Making good cost estimates takes time and requires a thorough understanding of how investors make their decisions. Further, these estimates must reflect current conditions in the money markets instead of being based on costs in the past; and they must take account of the effect that the bank's choice of a capital structure may have on its cost of funds. Getting an accurate estimate of the cost of funds poses some tough computational problems, but there is no other way to find out what rate of return is required to make a profit.

THE OLD WAY: HISTORICAL AVERAGE COSTS

In the past, the most common method of estimating the cost of a bank's funds was to add together all the net expenses (interest, reserve requirements, and other

*Reprinted from the *Business Review*, May/June 1978, pp. 3-11, with permission from the Federal Reserve Bank of Philadelphia and the author.

[1] Sanford Rose, "What Really Went Wrong at Franklin National," *Fortune* (October 1974), p. 118.

expenses less service charge income) of borrowing current funds and divide the total by the amount being borrowed. This gave an historical estimate of the average return that had to be earned on assets acquired with these funds for the bank to break even in its investment activities. If the shareholders were to receive a return on the funds they supplied, a profit margin had to be added to this basic historical cost of funds estimate (see Appendix).

But historical costs can be extremely unreliable as a pricing guide if conditions are changing over time. When interest rates are rising, the average cost of funds already obtained will be below the cost of replacing those funds by new borrowing, and the bank may accept new investments it should reject. When rates are dropping, the historical cost of funds will be higher than replacement costs, and the bank may be led to set too high a standard for new investments, passing up opportunities to make profits. Historical estimates can be unreliable also when a bank's capital structure is changing. If a bank's debt is increasing faster than its equity, for example, it may come to be regarded as a riskier operation, and this perception of added risk may raise the cost of the bank's funds from all sources. It's because of drawbacks such as these that bankers have turned from historical cost estimates to some basic economic principles for generating cost estimates.

THE NEW WAY: A BIT OF THEORY

The theory behind this new cost estimating method starts from a reasonable premise—that bank managers should make investment decisions which make the bank more profitable. This theory rationalizes the rules of thumb that many bankers actually use when they look at profitability—rules such as adding in a desired long-term profit margin as they try to gauge the expected cost of funds over time.

Matching Added Costs with Added Revenues

To obtain the largest profit available, a bank should compare the expected return from an investment with the current cost of obtaining the money needed to finance that investment. If the return (in the long run) from a new loan or security doesn't exceed the probable cost of financing that asset while the bank owns it, the bank would do better not to acquire it. The added amount that would be brought in by lending one more unit of money to a borrower is the *marginal revenue*. The added amount that would be paid out to procure one more unit of loanable funds is the *marginal cost*.[2]

The use of current information in making the cost of funds estimates is extremely important. The cost of a bank's funds normally will change as market in-

---

[2] Statement of the MC = MR principle is intentionally very general, so that complications such as tied-product returns and discounted future benefits can be accommodated within the definition.

terest rates move. Some cost changes, as for CDs and Federal funds, will be highly visible, while others, as for demand deposits and savings accounts, will not be so obvious. The banker must keep abreast of both. As interest rates rise, a banker will find that other financial institutions will compete more vigorously for these funds, and the depositors themselves will make an effort to shift into the more lucrative investments. To attract and hold these funds, a bank may have to step up its advertising, resort to premiums, and expand its menu of depositor services. The result will be a higher cost to the bank for funds from these sources.

Less obvious will be the rising cost of equity funds—the bank's common stock. The target rate that a bank's management sets for returns to shareholders should be adjusted to reflect any changes in yields on other long-term investments. Investors who have the alternative of investing in long-term bonds at 8 or 9 percent with little risk must expect to receive more than that from an investment in common stock, or they will stay with the safer security. When long-term interest rates rise 1 or 2 percentage points, the return to common shareholders must move by a similar amount. In a competitive money market, the bank's shareholders always will have investment options that offer the current market rates. Even though a bank may not be selling a brand new stock issue in this high-rate environment, it still must aim to earn the competitive rate for its current owners. If it doesn't, the owners would be better off to instruct management to pay the maximum dividend possible. The stockholders then could use the extra dividends to make investments elsewhere at the higher prevailing rates.

When New Costs Don't Match Old Costs

The decision on a new investment should be made on the basis of the cost of new money. Even if a bank were lucky enough to obtain a large pool of funds at rates that are below current market levels, shareholders, who bear the risk of loss, should be the beneficiaries of this good fortune. If historical costs are used to set current loan rates, the benefits of having these relatively cheap funds will be transferred to the borrowers rather than being retained for the common stockholders. If circumstances were reversed, it's unlikely that borrowers would be willing to pay high interest rates on loans from a bank which has unusually *high* average costs. The fact that the bank had the misfortune of being stuck with large amounts of funds acquired when rates were very high wouldn't matter if cheaper sources were available elsewhere. Regardless of costs or the effect on profits available for stockholders, bankers can't charge borrowers a rate that is much higher than rates available elsewhere. So historical costs should not be considered in making today's investment decisions. Rather, the cost of an additional dollar of funds should be compared with the return that will be realized when that additional dollar is invested. So much for theory.

But how should an estimate of the marginal cost of funds be made? Although averaging historical costs is relatively easy, figuring out the full cost of a new dollar of funds is another matter—especially if it's necessary to estimate the impact that using various sources of funds will have on the cost of other sources.

MARGINAL COST ESTIMATION METHODS

Two basic options are available to the banker who is trying to make a marginal cost estimate. One is to identify the source of funds that the bank currently is using to raise new money. Once this source is identified, an estimate might be made of the cost of raising another block of these funds. This estimate of the marginal cost of a single source will serve as the *hurdle rate*—the minimum required rate of return—for any new investment of average riskiness. The other strategy is to estimate the marginal cost of each of the sources being employed within the bank. By weighting the cost of new dollars drawn from each source by the amount to be raised from that source, bankers can construct a weighted average of marginal costs. The second method sounds more complex, but it has some advantages over the first that make it worth considering.

The Marginal Cost of a Single Source

The most straightforward approach is to determine which source of funds the bank wants to use, compute its marginal cost, and use that estimate as the hurdle rate. Presumably, the source selected will be the cheapest one available to the bank. For example, if CDs are the source a banker turns to, the cost of additional dollars borrowed in that market is the relevant marginal cost. The interest rate on CDs is easy enough to determine, but this rate is only part of the real marginal cost of these funds.

Suppose a bank—for example, the hypothetical Ninth National Bank—wants to borrow $1 million for expansion. If it turns to the CD market and pays 7 percent, that interest rate is the base for the bank's cost calculations. But the job of estimating the marginal cost of this source is just beginning. The bank will incur a small cost in acquiring and repaying this money, and that cost should be included in the estimate. Also, there will be a reserve requirement against this source of funds. Any obligation to keep a portion of the borrowed money in the form of idle cash raises the effective cost of the funds. These adjustments to the basic interest cost are easy to make.

A much more difficult adjustment to the cost is the one required to compensate suppliers of other sources of funds for the added risk created by this new borrowing. Ninth National's leverage—its ratio of debt to equity—will be increased by the addition of more CD funds. Since higher leverage produces more risk for the bank, other creditors and shareholders may not be as willing to continue supplying Ninth National with funds at the same interest rates as before. Depositors whose funds are covered by deposit insurance probably won't care. But the holders of big deposits and CDs might, because they are not fully insured, and their concern could cause them to shift their funds to another bank or demand a higher return from Ninth National. In either case, the bank's cost to attract and hold such deposits is likely to rise.

The same thing will occur with the capital note holders and the common stockholders. When they sense that risks are increasing, they'll seek a higher return on their investments. The ones that presently own these securities can't automatically start charging the bank a higher rate for funds that already have been committed, but investors will demand a higher return for any new invested funds. The bank will be obliged to increase its earnings and ultimately its dividends to stockholders in order to compensate them for their higher risk. If it doesn't, the interests of the current shareholders will be harmed, and that would be inconsistent with management's obligation to run the bank in a way which enhances the shareholders' wealth (see THE SINGLE MARGINAL SOURCE CALCULATION).

In any event, it should be clear that the impact which heavy use of one source of funding has on the cost of other sources should be included in any analysis of the cost of marginal funds. This risk spillover cost is very difficult to measure, but it must be included in the calculation. Accordingly, the cost of new CD money

THE SINGLE MARGINAL SOURCE CALCULATION

Suppose the management of Ninth National is looking for another $100 and wants to raise the money by issuing CDs. It will be obliged to pay the going market interest rate for funds (say, 7 percent). It must then add to this amount several surcharges which raise the effective rate. The cost of reserve requirements on the CD funds might, for example, be 3 percent (annualized), the cost to acquire such funds 0.5 percent (annualized), and the cost of servicing the funds 0.3 percent (annualized). Using the formula

$$\text{cost of funds} = \frac{(\text{interest rate} + \text{servicing costs} + \text{acquisition costs} + \text{insurance})}{(1 - \text{reserve requirement})}$$

the explicit cost of the CD funds is found to be 0.0804 or about 8 percent.

This is only part of the job. Since the bank now is being more heavily financed with short-term borrowed funds, the risk is greater. Both the other suppliers of borrowed funds and the shareholders may wish to raise the cost of future funds they provide for this bank. This additional indirect cost must be added to the explicit cost estimate. Suppose that raising $100 of new CD funds created $.20 in added costs for other sources of funds. The *real* marginal cost of the CD funds would be estimated as their explicit cost plus the risk spillover cost:

marginal cost = 8.04 percent + 0.2 percent = 8.24 percent.

Failure to include all of these costs other than interest in the estimate will lead to a hurdle rate for new investments that understates the real cost of new funds.

can be found only after considering the direct interest cost, any acquisition and servicing costs, reserve requirements, and risk spillover costs.[3]

The same principles apply to estimating the cost of demand and time deposits (handling, acquisition, reserve requirements, and deposit insurance costs are likely to be higher than for CDs) or capital notes (risk spillover may raise the cost of the bank's CDs and uninsured deposits as well as the cost of its common stock). Similarly, the nominal, before-tax cost of new common stock may overstate its real cost because it will have the effect of reducing overall risk and is likely to lower the net cost of other debt sources.

Averaging All Marginal Costs

The other approach to calculating a bank's marginal cost is to presume that the institution will be financed during the next few months in pretty much the same way as it's being financed now. Checking and savings accounts will open and close and the bank will experience deposits and withdrawals. But as long as advertising doesn't diminish and services don't deteriorate, total dollars from each retail source will change only gradually. The bank will wind up paying the going rate to hold funds from each of these sources. Similarly, market rates (plus associated costs) will be paid for any CDs sold even if they are simply replacements for maturing issues. Finally, the bank will have to pay competitive returns for capital if it expects to keep access to these sources of funds. In short, the mix of sources doesn't change, and the bank must pay current rates for each source used (see THE AVERAGE OF MARGINAL COSTS CALCULATION).

If Ninth National is trying to calculate the overall cost of this pool of funds, it will need an estimate of the marginal cost of each source employed. That estimate must include any explicit interest payments, acquisition and servicing costs, deposit insurance, and reserve requirements. Such a calculation will be straightforward for CDs and capital notes but very difficult for demand and time deposits (even if the bank has a reliable cost accounting system). Estimating the percentage of the advertising budget that goes to keeping demand deposit levels steady or the additional advertising that would be required to increase time and savings deposits by a few percent is a very uncertain undertaking. At best it will involve a substantial amount of informed judgment.

When management is satisfied with these marginal cost estimates, an overall average can be calculated by multiplying each estimate by the fraction of the bank's funds that will be raised from this source in the near future. The weighted average will indicate the cost to the bank of buying the funds that will be used for investments or loans made during that time and it will serve as a minimum target rate of return for a new investment of average risk.

For all its complexity, this estimate has an advantage over the single-source cost estimate. With the weighted average approach there is no need to try to calculate the impact that risk spillovers have on the cost of other sources. The present level

---

[3] A more technical explanation of this calculation can be found in Ronald D. Watson, "The Marginal Cost of Funds Concept in Banking," Research Paper No. 19, Federal Reserve Bank of Philadelphia, January 1977; reprinted with revisions in the *Journal of Bank Research* 8 (Autumn 1977), pp. 136-147.

THE AVERAGE OF MARGINAL COSTS CALCULATION

Since figuring out the risk spillover costs is very difficult, the banker might prefer to calculate his explicit marginal costs for each source of funds and average those estimates to find out what the entire pool of funds presently is costing. Suppose that the bank is structured as follows:

	Added Dollars	Explicit Cost*	
Demand deposits	$ 30	.05	$1.50
Time deposits	40	.07	2.80
CDs	10	.08	.80
Capital notes	10	.09	.90
Common stock	10	.22	2.20
	$100		$8.20

The Ninth National's estimate would be: marginal cost $= \dfrac{\$8.20}{\$100.00} = 0.082$ = 8.2 percent.

*With acquisition, servicing, and reserve costs included.

of the bank's leverage risk already is reflected in the prices of its liabilities and equity securities. If the composition of the pool of funds doesn't change, the risks aren't going to change significantly. The risk spillover that each source of funds creates for the other sources is neutralized in this pooling process and need not be estimated separately. As a result, estimates of the current marginal cost of each source, averaged across all sources, will provide a correct estimate of the bank's pool of funds without further risk adjustments.

CHOOSE YOUR POISON

Both of the cost estimation methods just described have pitfalls. Calculating the marginal cost of a single source such as CDs looks easy. The interest rate is known and the reserve and handling costs are measurable. But estimating the size of the risk spillover adjustment that should be added to the other costs to get the real marginal cost is very difficult.

In addition, one of the basic principles of economic theory is that businesses should tap each source of funds until the cost of the next dollar raised from that source is the same as the cost of a dollar from each other available source. That's the way to maximize profit, since it keeps money costs as low as possible. If a bank concentrates its attention on the cost of just one source, it may lose sight of the availability of funds from other sources that are cheaper.

Computing a weighted average of marginal costs keeps a banker looking at all costs simultaneously. Estimating the marginal cost of the bank's demand and time deposits remains a sticky problem, but the uncertainties of calculating risk spillover adjustments are avoided. This method will not provide the manager with the information needed to balance the marginal cost of one source against the marginal cost of another. For that a marginal cost estimate is needed that includes the risk spillover adjustment for each type of funds used. But the banker doesn't have to worry about risk spillover adjustments when this method is used. The banker may not be getting the cheapest mix of funds, especially if a relatively cheap source of funds was overlooked; but the banker will be getting an accurate estimate of the cost of the pool of funds. In this, the banker has an advantage over his counterpart to raise funds from all of the available sources. If the real marginal costs of each source are not really equal, use of the single-source technique will produce a faulty estimate.

If both methods can give a correct answer, the calculations you make should give the same answer. If they do, you have a cost of funds estimate. If they don't, you had better try to figure out why. Do you need better data about your costs? Is the bank being financed with too expensive a mix of sources? Are the institution's costs under both calculations higher than previously thought? Has the bank been adding new business at a loss rather than a profit?

The exercise may be frustrating. It may be disturbing. But a sharp banker has to go through it if he's to do a first-rate job of managing profits.

APPENDIX

AN EXAMPLE OF HISTORICAL AVERAGE COST CALCULATIONS

Consider the case of the hypothetical Ninth National Bank. This bank gets its funds from demand and time deposits, CDs, subordinated capital notes, and common stock (see BALANCE SHEET). The full cost of each source of funds (interest and servicing cost of all funds obtained from that source) is indicated in parentheses.

NINTH NATIONAL BANK BALANCE SHEET

Cash and due	$ 100	Demand deposits	(4%)	$ 300
Investments	300	Time deposits	(6%)	400
Loans	600	CDs	(6%)	100
		Capital notes	(8%)	100
		Common stock	(20%)	100
Total	$1000	Total		$1000

Since management wants to insure that the shareholders' funds earn a return of 20 percent (10 percent after taxes if the tax rate is 50 percent), it must include this profit objective in its average cost of funds estimate.

Demand deposits	$.04 \times \$300 = \$12$
Time deposits	$.06 \times 400 = 24$
CDs	$.06 \times 100 = 6$
Capital notes	$.08 \times 100 = 8$
Common stock	$.20 \times 100 = 20$ (before taxes)
	$\$1000 \quad \$70$

$$\text{Cost of funds} = \frac{\$70}{\$1000} = 0.07 = 7.0 \text{ percent.}$$

Only if Ninth National is able to average a 7-percent return on all invested funds will it be able to pay shareholders that target 10-percent return (after taxes).

Most banks would have little trouble computing this breakeven return, and it would appear to solve the problem of estimating a cost of funds which could be used as a minimum required rate of return (hurdle rate) for new investment decisions. But, this will work only when interest rates are perfectly steady. Otherwise, using actual average costs to set the hurdle rate for new investments will give the wrong answer.

As an illustration, suppose that the inflation rate increases, and one consequence of this change is a jump in interest rates on most securities. For simplicity, let's say that all rates go up 1 percentage point. The cost of *replacing* all Ninth National's deposits, CDs, and capital funds might now be:

Demand deposits	5%
Time deposits	7%
CDs	7%
Capital notes	9%
Common stock	11% (after taxes).

The weighted average cost of a new pool of funds would be over 8 percent rather than the 7 percent that Ninth National has been paying for its funds. What happens if the bank continues to use that historical cost hurdle rate of 7 percent?

One thing that will happen is that Ninth National might be tempted to take on new loans and investments that yield only 7½%. If the bank invests in a $100 bond that yields 7½%, it will be earning $7.50 per year. But as long as the composition of the bank's sources of funds doesn't change, the cost of new funds acquired to make that investment is:

Demand deposits	.05 × $30 =	$1.50
Time deposits	.07 × 40 =	2.80
CDs	.07 × 10 =	.70
Capital notes	.09 × 10 =	.90
Common stock	.22 × 10 =	2.20
	$100	$8.10.

Since shareholders are the last to be paid, this shortfall will come out of their part of the bank's income:

$7.50	income
−5.90	cost of debt sources
1.60	earnings before taxes
−.80	taxes
$ .80	earnings after taxes.

$$\text{Return on new shareholder equity} = \frac{\$.80}{\$10.00} = 0.08 = 8 \text{ percent}.$$

This return is not high enough to pay shareholders the return of 11 percent (after taxes) that they expect from their investment in the bank's stock. The ones that are dissatisfied will want to sell their stock and its price will be forced downward. All of the shareholders will be worse off because of the incorrect investment decision.

28

The Garn–St Germain Depository Institutions Act of 1982[*]

by Gillian Garcia, Herbert Baer, Elijah Brewer, David R. Allardice,
Thomas F. Cargill, John Dobra, George G. Kaufman, Anne Marie L. Gonczy,
Robert D. Laurent, and Larry R. Mote

HISTORY LEADING TO THE ACT

In the past, the savings and loan associations (S&Ls), mutual savings banks, and credit unions that constitute the thrift industry have been in the business of credit risk, denomination, maturity, and interest rate intermediation. That is, traditionally they have purchased small denomination, short-term deposits in order to make larger, longer-term fixed rate loans. Their intention has been to profit from this intermediation by charging a higher rate on their loans than that paid on their deposits.[1] It is this maturity imbalance aspect of the thrifts' business, together with a traditional inability to revise the interest rate or other conditions of their long-term loans on the occurrence of unforeseen events, that has produced the industry's recent serious problems.

Such intermediation exposes depository institutions to three risks. The first is the traditional and recognized risk of default. Coping with this risk has remained the responsibility of management, although the current problems facing commercial banks of potential default by several domestic corporations and foreign governments are testing this responsibility.

The second risk arises from the possibility that depositors may unexpectedly withdraw their deposits and the institution may not have enough liquid assets to meet the demand; this is liquidity risk. Central banks in general—and also the Federal Home Loan Bank (FHLB) in the U.S.—have long acted as lenders-of-last-resort to limit exposure to this risk.

*Reprinted, with deletions, from *Economic Perspectives*, March/April 1983, pp. 3-31, with permission from the Federal Reserve Bank of Chicago.

[1] As Kaufman (1972) has pointed out, it is not necessary that the mortgage loan rate exceed the institution's cost of funds at every moment in time. At certain stages of the business cycle short-term rates are likely to exceed long-term rates. Then losses will be made, which must be recouped and dominated over the full term of the loan by profits made during other stages of the cycle.

The third danger occurs when market interest rates rise unexpectedly. In a world where depository institutions pay market interest rates on their liabilities, rising interest rates raise costs and put pressure on profits. This pressure is particularly acute for institutions that have made long-term loans at fixed rates, the traditional form of the mortgage contract in the United States since the 1930s. This predicament—interest rate risk—is particularly characteristic of the savings and loan industry. It has been exacerbated by an inability, in some states, to enforce due-on-sale clauses in mortgage contracts. This inability lengthens the contract beyond its expected life.

Avoiding undue exposure to this risk has remained management's responsibility. But a pervasive inability to handle interest-rate risk among savings and loan associations and mutual savings banks has caused Congress to intervene. During the past 2-3 years the position of the industry has deteriorated so severely as to provide the principal impetus for the current legislation.

Increasing pressure on thrift earnings, stemming from rising market interest rates, provided a persuasive argument for the 1966 extension of interest-rate ceilings on deposits to thrifts as well as commercial banks. The extension was intended to help thrift profitability by ensuring that their sources of low-cost funds would be channeled particularly to mortgage lending, thus sustaining demand in the housing industry. In time, however, deposit rates—fixed under Regulation Q in the face of rising market interest rates—led to the disintermediation that became a recurring problem at peaks of the interest rate cycle.

Sudden and rapid disintermediation can lead to a liquidity crisis. Liquidity crises are potentially life-threatening to depository institutions if the lender of last resort does not satisfy their liquidity needs. Then institutions are forced to sell assets. As the market value of assets has been reduced by the rise in interest rates, liquidation may not provide sufficient funds to pay off depositors and insolvency results.

One way to prevent disintermediation is to allow thrifts and banks to pay market rates on their liabilities. The problem here is that those institutions have followed customary practice and are, therefore, carrying a portfolio of fixed-rate long-term assets acquired in an earlier period at low rates, so that they may not be able to afford the higher rates. If they are forced to pay such rates in order to prevent disintermediation, profits will be sharply reduced or eliminated, as they have been in recent years. An industry with too many successive years of negative earnings cannot remain viable.

The Congress and the regulators have made a succession of attempts to alleviate these problems. During the 1960s and 1970s large depositors, having ready access to alternative instruments paying market rates, were successful in getting banks and thrifts to pay market rates on large (over $100,000) certificates of deposit, repurchase agreements, etc. It has taken much longer for the smaller saver to gain the same opportunity.

During the 1970s, however, efforts were made to prevent small-saver disintermediation. Permission was granted for financial institutions to pay rates above the low, regulated passbook savings deposit rate. In this way, a hierarchy of Regulation Q rates for time deposits of increasing maturity was created. To obtain higher rates the saver was encouraged to extend the maturity of his certificate. The intention here was to lengthen the average maturity or, more precisely, the duration of the liability portfolio, to reduce the gap between assets and liabilities and also to discourage disintermediation by placing penalties on early withdrawals.[2]

Steps Toward Ending Regulation Q

As interest rates continued their trend upward, the regulators made several concessions toward permitting market interest rates to be paid to the small saver. The first step was the short-lived 1973 introduction of the "wild-card" certificate. For a short period this allowed uncapped rates to be paid on a limited amount of long-term certificates of deposit. The second attempt, resulting from court action that overruled the regulators' objections, was an experimental permission for negotiable order of withdrawal accounts (NOWs) in the New England States. This allowed interest (at regulated rates) to be paid on transaction accounts. Money market certificates (MMCs), were introduced in June 1978. Automatic transfer accounts (ATs) followed in November 1978.

The MMC allowed Treasury-bill-linked rates to be paid on certificates of 6 months' maturity. These certificates proved very popular and had the beneficial result of reducing depository institution exposure to disintermediation. However, they encouraged depositors to place their intermediate denomination ($10,000) deposits in relatively short-term accounts. This did nothing to help the S&Ls' duration and interest rate imbalance problem. Consequently, permission was given in 1979 for a small-savers' certificate (SSC) of 4-year and later of 2½-year maturity. This concession constitutes the fifth step toward deregulating deposit rates.

The Depository Institutions and Monetary Control Act of 1980 (DIDMCA) created an interagency committee, the Depository Institutions Deregulation Committee (DIDC) to oversee an orderly phase-out of interest rate ceilings by 1986. In January 1981, NOW accounts became available nationwide in implementation of the act. Progress toward permitting market-interest-related accounts was then stalled until the spring and summer of 1982, when two medium-denomination, short-maturity (7-31 and 91 day) accounts were authorized by DIDC and rate ceilings were removed on the longest-term accounts according to a phase-out schedule adopted by the committee.

Nevertheless, the disintermediation problem remained. The money market mutual fund industry began in 1972, but it was dormant until 1978. It then began

---

[2] While the maturity imbalance in depository institutions' portfolios is easy to comprehend, research workers have found that the concept of duration provides a more precise tool for analysis. The maturity of a security refers only to the date of capital repayment. Duration, on the other hand, considers the timing of *all* payments—of both capital and interest—due on a security. Duration, then, is a weighted average time of cash flow receipt. For a further discussion of the concept, see Reilly and Sidhu [1980].

to grow rapidly, as interest rates rose, because it offered a small-denomination, no minimum-maturity, market-interest-rate vehicle to consumers. By the fall of 1982, MMMFs held $230 billion of the nation's funds.

Increased Asset Powers

Successive tinkerings with the unpopular (among small savers and academics) Regulation Q had raised depository institutions' interest costs but had eliminated neither the disintermediation nor the duration imbalance of thrifts' balance sheets. Profitability was thus jeopardized. Attention then turned, at the beginning of the 1980s, to encouraging interest responsiveness for assets as well as liabilities. While some states, such as California, already permitted their state-chartered institutions to offer variable-rate residential mortgage contracts, the regulatory agencies did not permit them for federally chartered thrifts and banks until 1979 and 1980. Even then the S&L industry position continued to deteriorate; Congressional action was needed to alleviate it.

Congressional Response to the Financial Crisis

As the decade of the 1970s closed, it was increasingly evident that the patchwork of ad hoc regulatory concessions and adjustments to Regulation Q was not succeeding. Furthermore, there were other important deterrents to depository institution profitability that lay beyond the regulators' purview. The earnings and net worth position of the thrifts, in particular, deteriorated in the high-interest-rate, accelerating-inflation, depreciating-dollar, gold, silver and commodity price-explosion environment of the winter of 1979-80. The crisis atmosphere prompted the two houses of Congress to reconcile their differences over legislation proposed during 1979 and to enact the Depository Institutions Deregulation and Monetary Control Act of 1980.[3]

DIDMCA aimed to strengthen deposit institutions' positions by permitting somewhat greater flexibility on both the asset and liability sides of their balance sheets. It was clear at the time of passage, however, that the act was not a panacea. In particular, it would take several years for the new asset powers to reduce the average maturity of the asset portfolio, to raise earnings, and to make them more responsive to rising market rates. The most immediate solution to the major S&L problem (the backlog of old, fixed, low-rate mortgages) would be a sustained drop in interest rates. Such a fall occurred in the quarter following the passage of DIDMCA, but it was short-lived and in any case not caused by the act. During the summer of 1980 rates began to rise rapidly and did not fall significantly until the late summer of 1982. In the meantime, the position of the S&L industry had deteriorated so much that it was seen as the Achilles' heel of the financial system.[4]

[3] The book, *Financial Deregulation and Monetary Control*, by Thomas F. Cargill and Gillian G. Garcia, gives the 1980 act's history, summarizes its content, and discusses its impact and the issues it leaves to be addressed.

[4] The extent of the crisis is described in Andrew S. Carron's important book, *The Plight of the Thrift Institutions* (1982).

The actual and potential failure rate of individual institutions was reminiscent of the 1930s.

Legislation often derives from the Congress' perception of a crisis. Such is a description of the process leading to the Garn-St Germain Act. Previously, different bills had been introduced into the Congress but had been stalled by the interplay between political parties and lobbying forces. As the perceived severity of the thrifts' crisis increased, political differences, were suppressed, compromises were reached, and action was taken.[5]

The resulting Garn-St Germain Act is primarily a rescue operation for the S&Ls and mutual savings banks. But the act also enlarges the options of other depository institutions. It gives regulators greater flexibility in handling crisis situations in which banks and/or thrifts cease to be viable. It provides greater equity for the small saver and is a step toward a more deregulated financial system.

THE MAIN FEATURES OF THE ACT

The 1982 act is complex, containing eight titles dealing in detail with different areas of financial reform. Minutiae will be passed over in the following discussion in order to emphasize those aspects considered most important. The discussion is divided into three sections: provisions permanently widening the sources of depository institution funds, and contributing toward the removal of interest-rate ceilings; provisions permanently expanding the uses of funds and other powers; and provisions that temporarily grant regulators emergency powers to deal with the current depository institution crisis.

The Sources of Funds

The act makes four contributions to broadening the catchment area for funds.

1. The best known provision of the Garn-St Germain Act is its authorization (in Title III) for the new money market deposit account (MMDA). The Congress, impressed by the recent rapid growth of MMMFs, amended DIDMCA to authorize depository institutions to offer an account "directly equivalent to and competitive with money market mutual funds." This account, which has been widely available since December 14, 1982, is federally insured, pays an interest rate restricted only by the discretion of the institution (on initial and average maintained balances of $2,500 or more), and has limited transaction features (six transfers per month: pre-authorized, automatic, or by telephone, of which no more than three may be by check, but unlimited personal withdrawals). On personal accounts it carries no required reserves;

---

[5] Fischer, Gentry, and Verderamo provide a succinct description of the bills that originated in the two houses of Congress and the reconcilliation process that led to the present act.

a 3-percent reserve requirement is imposed on nonpersonal accounts. If the average balance falls below $2,500, the NOW account ceiling is applicable.

This authorization is regarded as a major breach of the regulatory barriers that restrict competition for funds by depository institutions. It came as a surprise, therefore, that the DIDC acted quickly to authorize another new account, available beginning January 5, 1983. This Super NOW account is restricted to the NOW account clientele (see below), has a minimum initial and maintained average balance of $2,500, has unlimited transaction features, and unregulated interest rates (it pays a NOW rate on balances below the $2,500 level). But it carries a reserve requirement as a transactions account— presently 12 percent.

In December 1982, the DIDC requested public comment on still another proposed account. This Super MMD account would have unlimited transaction features, unregulated interest rates, and would be available to all including corporations. The new account would presumably also carry a 12-percent reserve requirement. The committee also requested comment on a proposal to accelerate the existing timetable for rate deregulation. At its March 1 meeting, however, the committee decided against further action. These matters will be reconsidered at the June 28 meeting.

2. Besides this major permission for market-interest-paying accounts, the act makes three other provisions to broaden depository institutions' ability to obtain funds. Title VII of the act permits federal, state, and local governments to hold NOW accounts. Previously these accounts had been limited to persons and to nongovernment, nonprofit organizations.

3. Federally chartered savings and loan associations are permitted to offer demand deposits to persons or organizations that have a business loan relationship with the association or that wish to receive payment due from nonbusiness customers (Title III). Previously, only commercial and mutual savings banks had been able to accept demand deposits.

4. The DIDC is required to remove by the beginning of 1984 any existing differential in the Regulation Q rate permitted to banks and thrifts (Title III). Previously, thrifts were typically permitted to offer a rate ¼ percent above that of commercial banks on most types of deposits subject to ceiling regulation.

The Uses of Funds and Other Powers

Both thrift and bank institutions benefit to some degree from the act's provisions for expanded powers. However, the powers of federal savings and loan associations and savings banks (SBs) are enhanced most by the act. Five sets of provisions are discussed below.

1. Title III authorizes federally chartered S&Ls and SBs for the first time to make overdraft loans; to invest in the accounts of other insured institutions; and importantly, to make commercial loans. The act also enhances their powers to invest in state and local government obligations; to make residen-

tial and nonresidential real estate loans; to make consumer and educational loans.[6]
2. The existing state-imposed restrictions on the execution of the due-on-sale provisions of mortgage contracts are preempted in Title II for both federal and state institutions. The preemption is delayed for certain seriously affected ("window period") loans, and is prohibited in the case of within-family property transfers.
3. Thrifts are given wide powers in Title III to alter their charters. They can convert from state to federal charter and conversely, where state law permits. They may switch between mutual and stock form and between savings and loan association and savings bank charters.
4. State banks and thrifts are empowered in Title VIII to offer the alternative, variable-rate, mortgage instruments that are permitted to their federal counterparts.
5. National banks receive some relatively minor adjustment of their powers. For example, the "safety and soundness" limitations on the size of loans made to a single borrower are relaxed. Previously, a bank could lend no more than 10 percent of its capital and surplus to any individual borrower. Now, that percentage is raised to 15 percent plus an additional 10 percent for loans secured by readily marketable collateral. However, these limitations will henceforth be applied to loans made to foreign governments and their agencies. Also, restrictions on bank real estate lending and on "insider" loans are relaxed. Banks are also permitted to charter "bankers' banks" and the scope of bank service corporation activities is broadened. However, new restrictions are placed on the large bank holding companies.

Emergency Powers

Titles I and II of the act enhance, for three years, the powers of the Federal Deposit Insurance Corporation (FDIC) and Federal Savings and Loan Insurance Corporation (FSLIC) to aid troubled banks and thrifts.[7] The agencies can aid institutions which are closed, insolvent, in default or so endangered; or where severe financial conditions exist that threaten the stability of the financial system; or in order to reduce the corporations' exposure to loss. They are empowered to take six types of action. They can issue guarantees; purchase or assume an insured institution's assets or liabilities (but, to preclude nationalization, not its common stock); make loans and contributions to and deposits in a troubled insured institution or company that will acquire it; organize charter conversions; arrange extraordinary mergers and acquisitions; and issue net worth certificates to banks and thrifts with substantial residential real estate loans.

---

[6] S&Ls now have powers to take demand deposits and to make commercial loans. These are the critical elements necessary to meet the Federal Reserve's definition of a bank. Therefore, in order for S&Ls to avoid the restrictions incumbent on that classification, the definition of a bank has been amended to exclude institutions insured by the FSLIC or chartered by the FHLBB.

[7] The act gives similar powers to the National Credit Union Administration (NCUA) to aid troubled credit unions.

The act provides a framework for both the FDIC and FSLIC to arrange emergency acquisitions of failing institutions across geographic and institutional barriers. While many opposed these powers on the grounds that they would blur the distinction between banks and thrifts and open the door to interstate banking, the regulators argued successfully that they need these provisions to avert potential crises. In some particularly hard-hit regions, it had become increasingly difficult to find merger partners that fit the old rules. In fact, during 1982, the Federal Reserve Board (FRB) and the FHLBB had already authorized both interstate and interindustry mergers, including Citicorp's controversial acquisition of Fidelity Federal Savings and Loan Association of Oakland, California.

Under the new rules the FDIC can authorize the acquisition of a large, closed commercial bank, or a closed or endangered mutual savings bank (assets over $500 million) by another federally insured institution, in-state or out-of-state. The FSLIC may exercise such powers regardless of the size of the failing thrift. Further, any qualified purchaser, including out-of-state banks, holding companies, other insured institutions, or *any* other acceptable company may submit bids for the failed thrift. Any federally insured depository institution can bid for a failed large bank. If the lowest bid comes not from an in-state, similar-type institution, all within-the-ballpark bidders may bid again. Then the corporation must attempt to minimize its risk of loss subject to the following priorities:

  i. like, in-state institutions
 ii. like, out-of-state institutions
iii. different, in-state institutions
 iv. different, out-of-state institutions
  v. among out-of-state bidders, priority is to be given to adjacent state institutions
 vi. the FSLIC, but not the FDIC, is to give priority to minority-controlled bidders when a minority-controlled thrift fails.

Provisions are made for consultation with state regulators where appropriate. The act's provisions are discussed in more detail in the sections that follow. The act's implications for S&Ls, commercial banks, and bank holding companies are examined, as well as the due-on-sale provisions, the call for a re-examination of deposit insurance, and the monetary policy implications of the new deposit instruments. A discussion of issues that remain to be addressed follows.

THE ACT'S IMPACT ON S&Ls

The preceding discussion of the savings and loan industry's problems suggests several areas where the act could help. For example, it authorizes asset portfolio changes that could reduce costs, increase earnings, and lessen exposure to risk through diversification. At the same time, the act authorizes new liability powers that will tend to increase costs, at least during the transition period.

The beneficial effects of these new powers will not be visible for several years. In the meantime it will be necessary to deal with the industry's earnings crisis. Unlike commercial banks, savings and loan associations in general were not able to overcome the problems presented by their exposure to interest-rate risk. S&Ls' asset portfolios remained heavily concentrated in mortgage loans and securities through the early 1980s. Further, until very recently, most S&Ls were forced to make only fixed-rate mortgages. Similarly, savings and loan associations have shown greater rigidity than commercial banks in their liability portfolios.

This rigidity in portfolio composition has placed a heavy burden on thrift profitability. Work by Richard Kopcke [1981] suggests that thrifts were unprofitable at various points in the 1970s, although the industry reported accounting profits during this period. Moreover, the industry's returns on assets and net worth were more volatile than that of the commercial banking industry. The situation deteriorated rapidly in 1980. During 1981 both profit measures were negative. The following sections will discuss the long-term and emergency powers in turn.

Asset Powers

Title III makes three significant and permanent changes to S&Ls' asset powers: (1) commercial lending, including commercial mortgage lending; (2) consumer lending; and (3) lending to government.

1. While the 1980 DIDMC act had given thrifts some relatively minor access to commercial lending, the present act makes radical changes in this area.[8] For example, S&Ls can henceforth invest up to 55 percent of their assets in three types of commercial loans: (i) loans secured by commercial real estate to 40 percent of assets; (ii) secured or unsecured commercial loans to 5 percent of assets; and (iii) leasing to 10 percent of assets.[9]
2. The legislation increases the 1980 act's permission to invest in consumer loans to 30 percent (from 20 percent) of assets. Further, the range of permitted activities is increased by giving a broader interpretation to the meaning of consumer loans. This category now includes inventory and floor planning loans in addition to the more traditional kinds of consumer lending. This broader interpretation might allow S&Ls to make "consumer" loans while escaping many states' usury ceilings on consumer loans (which neither the present nor the 1980 act have removed).
3. The act increases S&Ls' ability to lend to government. The 1980 act had given the industry unlimited power to invest in federal government and state and local general obligations. The present act also allows S&Ls to invest in revenue bonds.

---

[8] The 1980 act had given S&Ls powers to make loans secured by commercial real estate to 20 percent of assets. They were required to have the first lien on the assets. This requirement is now removed, so that business may now borrow against their real estate in order to purchase capital goods or finance inventory.

[9] DIDMCA gave S&Ls authority to invest up to 5 percent of their assets in construction loans. Through an error in drafting, this permission was canceled by the current act. An attempt to restore the authority died with the 97th Congress.

The Potential of   These changes offer S&Ls the opportunity to increase
Asset Diversification   net income and reduce the riskiness of that income. Net
                           income will increase for two reasons. First, there is con-
siderable variation in the efficiency of individual banks and S&Ls. Permitting S&Ls
to enter commercial and consumer loan markets will provide relatively efficient
S&Ls with an opportunity to take business away from those commercial banks
that are relatively inefficient. However, these new activities do pose some challenges for the industry. Consumer and commercial lending are considerably different from mortgage lending. Loan processing costs are higher for consumer loans,
and both consumer and commercial loans are subject to greater default risk and
are less easily resold in secondary markets.

Second, asset diversification may enable thrifts to reduce their average interest
costs. In the past, thrifts have often offered a higher interest rate than have commercial banks. This differential permitted thrifts to compensate depositors for the
lack of transactions accounts, consumer loan services, commercial loans and trust
services. When thrifts became subject to interest rate regulation, this differential
was incorporated into the Regulation Q ceilings.[10] The removal of restrictions on
thrift activities under the 1980 and current acts makes it increasingly possible for
S&Ls to offer full-service banking. This will likely decrease the differential necessary for thrifts to attract funds. At the same time, operating costs may increase as
the S&Ls move closer to full-service banking.

Regardless of the impact on expected profitability, asset diversification offers
S&Ls another advantage—the opportunity to lessen their exposure to interest rate
risk. Currently, the duration of S&L assets greatly exceeds the duration of their
liabilities. When interest rates fall unexpectedly, S&Ls are able to reap large gains.
However, when interest rates rise unexpectedly, as happened during the period
1979 to 1982, S&Ls are exposed to huge losses and possible failures. Shortening
the duration of the asset portfolio will reduce the exposure to both gains and
losses due to unexpected movements in interest rates.

Consumer resistance to variable-rate mortgages, which have been permitted to
federally chartered institutions since 1979, has made it difficult for S&Ls to reduce
the duration of their asset portfolios. The ability to make consumer and commercial loans gives S&Ls an alternative means of shortening the duration of their asset
portfolios. Consumer loans are typically fixed-rate loans, but their duration is
substantially less than that of fixed-rate mortgages. Commercial loans are typically
both short maturity and variable in rate. The result of diversification into these
new areas will be a savings and loan industry that is more effectively insulated
from unexpected movements in interest rates and hence from failure.

Barriers To   There is, however, a question whether S&Ls will take
Diversification   advantage of these diversification opportunities. State-
                           chartered institutions which have previously held asset
diversification powers have made little use of them.[11] There are several possible
reasons for this neglect, but the most important of these are tax considerations.

---

[10] These issues are discussed in greater detail in the staff working paper, Garcia et al [1983].

[11] Researchers have investigated portfolio composition in Florida, Maine, and Texas.

At present, S&Ls that hold at least 60 percent of their assets in qualified form (mainly residential mortgages, cash, and federal securities), receive favorable tax treatment. They can reduce their corporate income tax payments by retaining a proportion of their earnings in a "bad-debt" reserve. The value of the tax deduction decreases as the S&L reduces the proportion of its qualified assets below 82 percent. The advantage disappears completely when the percentage falls below 60 percent. Researchers have pointed out that assets replacing mortgages in an S&L's portfolio typically do not have sufficiently higher interest rates to overcome that tax advantage.[12] This is an important reason why thrifts may not make dramatic changes in their asset composition, for the act does not change the tax incentives for S&Ls to invest in residential mortgages.

In this regard, the authority to invest in state and local government tax-exempt securities may be important. Recent research shows that a judicious use of the new powers to diversify into consumer and commercial loans to reduce asset duration, and simultaneously into state and local securities to shelter income from taxes, may be a successful way to avoid the current tax disincentive to diversification.[13] The effectiveness of such a strategy is shown to depend on the relative yields of tax-exempt securities and taxable assets of similar risk.

The New Liability Powers

The new liability powers could benefit S&Ls in four ways. They could: (1) reduce costs (in the long run, short-term costs will likely increase); (2) increase liability duration; (3) reduce the threat of disintermediation; and (4) allow liability volume to grow. The act's contributions in these areas will be discussed in turn.

All indications are that the new money market deposit and Super NOW accounts will increase interest costs. Forecasters predict that a substantial amount of funds deposited in the new accounts will come from existing deposits already housed elsewhere in the association at lower interest costs. Further, in the short run, the new accounts will probably augment operating costs, though in the long run the ability to offer market rates will permit thrifts to reduce non-monetary compensation to customers formerly affected by Regulation Q. Consequently, at least in the near term, the new accounts are expected to raise, rather than reduce, costs. Moreover, they are not expected to increase liability maturity, because both have instant availability rather than fixed terms to maturity.

The new accounts' contribution to S&L viability is expected to come in the third and fourth areas above. That is, they can reduce any vestigial threat of disintermediation and allow the liability base to grow. Henceforth, depository institutions will be able to overcome the remainder of the disintermediation problem by paying market interest rates on both transactions and savings accounts offered to small savers. Further, the ability to compete effectively with money market mutual funds offers the chance for depository institutions to regain funds that

---

[12] See the U. S. Department of the Treasury [1980].
[13] See Garcia et al [1983].

have fled the industry over the past three years. This inflow of funds will facilitate the diversification process. It is easier for associations to shift asset composition by expanding the asset base than by selling and reinvesting existing assets. By speeding the diversification into higher yielding, shorter duration assets, the new liability powers will reduce S&L exposure to possible unexpected future increases in interest rates. They also will make possible an earlier return to profitability.

The new asset and liability powers are potentially important for the long run resolution of the thrifts' problems. This long run solution can occur, however, only if the short-term crisis is avoided. In this respect, the act's emergency provisions are important.

The Emergency Provisions

If interest rates do not remain below their average 1981 and 1982 levels, many associations (and mutual savings banks) are threatened with failure in the near future. Titles I and II of the act provide industry regulators with powers to deal with such associations should the need arise. The act authorizes regulators to purchase assets from, make deposits in, or otherwise subsidize a failing institution. It spells out guidelines for interindustry and interstate acquisitions of failing institutions, and it empowers regulators to purchase net worth certificates from an association as a way to improve its book net worth.

The depth of the thrift crisis has been ably demonstrated by Andrew S. Carron [1982] in his important book, *The Plight of the Thrift Institutions.* Carron argues that there are many troubled thrifts, and that ailing institutions are typically smaller, and rapidly growing, with above average operating costs, officer and employee compensation, interest expenses, and service costs. He argues that mergers would provide economies of scale and the elimination of managerial inefficiency for approximately half of the troubled associations. The other half, he believes, need an explicit subsidy to ensure survival.

A study of Seventh District savings and loan associations supports Carron's findings with two exceptions.[14] In 1981 in this district, the average low-profit association was larger than the average high profit association (average assets of $227 million versus average assets of $60 million). Furthermore, this study suggests that profitable associations have been able to cope with interest-rate risk only because, either through good fortune or good mangement, they were able to take advantage of interest-rate ceilings, not because they managed their assets differently. Hence, it was not clear that mergers would improve managerial efficiency. There are also reasons to believe that economies of scale would be negligible.[15]

Problems With   Prior to the act, even when it was clear that a merger
Mergers   would be beneficial, regulators were finding it increas-
                       ingly difficult to obtain merger partners in the same state
and of the same kind for failing thrifts. They needed both specific authority to

----

[14] See Brewer [1982].

[15] McNulty (1982) summarizes the literature on economies of scale in the S&L industry.

allow interstate and interindustry mergers and also greater flexibility in the types of assistance given to facilitate those mergers. The remedy to this problem was clear: Congress responded by providing the framework (described in the preceding section) for interstate and interindustry mergers and by clearly setting out its priorities in this matter.

Prior to the act, problems were also created for the regulators by the use of book rather than economic net worth as a criterion for forcing a merger. Regulators set a cut-off level for book net worth. This cut-off had been successively reduced to 4 and then 3 percent and was recently effectively near zero. With net worth below this level, regulators acted—typically by closing or merging the institution. Unfortunately, however, book net worth is not a good measure of the ultimate viability of an institution. Some institutions above the cut-off level can be recognized as doomed to ultimate failure. Their costs and revenues are such that losses will continue to deplete net worth over time. Other associations that are currently at or below the cut-off point have good chances of recovering to profitability.

Management reaction to approaching the cut-off rate is important. If managers decide that failure will ultimately happen, they can contribute to the process by appropriating remaining net worth in the form of enhanced salaries or by dissipating it on the futures market.[16]

Regulators needed a program that would allow them to distinguish between endangered institutions that were viable and those that were not. The former should be helped over their temporary problems and the latter prevented from misusing resources and exposing the FSLIC to loss.

The Net Worth Certificate Program

Where merger did not promise any benefit, the solution to the regulators' problem was less apparent. Carron had argued that an explicit cash subsidy would be necessary when dealing with severely troubled institutions. On the other hand, Congress was loath to take actions that would increase the budget deficit. The net worth certificate program emerged as a compromise solution.

Under it, the FSLIC and the FDIC are permitted to purchase net worth certificates from distressed real estate banks and thrifts in exchange for promissory notes. These certificates are treated as capital for regulatory purposes, much the way regulators treat some debenture issues or the income capital certificates previously introduced by the FSLIC. Since the coupon payment on the promissory note and the certificates are identical, no cash necessarily changes hands. Thus regulators are able to bolster the book net worth of distressed institutions, avoid the merger route, and dispense with cash outlays (unless an institution fails).

The net worth program promises a number of benefits. First, it will allow regulators to maintain a competitive financial services industry. The previous remedies, carried to their logical conclusion, would have greatly increased concentration in the industry, possibly causing a decline in competitive performance. Second, managers of economically viable institutions previously threatened with closure will have this threat reduced, improving their incentives to make good decisions and hastening the return to profitability.

[16] See Baer [1982].

Third, the net worth certificate program will permit regulators to "gamble" that interest rates, having fallen, will stay down so that cash outlays will not be necessary in either the short or long run.

A fourth potential benefit—to identify nonviable institutions and prevent management from dissipating their assets and passing losses over to the insurance agency—is more elusive. It is difficult to distinguish viable from nonviable institutions, so that it is inevitable that some unsound institutions will participate in the program. Indeed, losses from mismanagment represent the principal potential cost to the program, for the insurance agencies will eventually be forced to foot the bill.

The act attempts to deal with this problem by permitting institutions to only partially offset their losses through the net worth certificate program. For example, the program sets out guidelines that associations with net worth between 0 and 1 percent of assets can receive up to 70 percent of the previous year's losses. Associations with higher net worth up to 3 percent receive smaller percentage contributions. With losses only partially compensated, nonviable institutions will not be sustained indefinitely. Rather, they will eventually exhaust their net worth and fail. The Federal Home Loan Bank Board has chosen to supplement this discrimination process by introducing additional incentives for good management. The Board has announced that S&Ls will only be allowed to offset 20 percent of losses due to operating expenses that are more than 10 percent above the mean for similar institutions. This will give managers additional incentives to control operating expenses. Further, the act itself specifies that losses due to speculation on the futures market will not be eligible for assistance. Institutions that do not respond to these incentives will exhaust their net worth.

Will the Solution Work? If interest rates remain at their current level, the net worth certificate program and the emergency powers will likely prove adequate for the immediate thrift "crisis." Time bought in this way may allow the long run powers to work. But will they?

On a previous occasion, they did not because the interest-rate respite was too short. The 1980 DIDMC act gave depository institutions broader asset and liability powers. It was recognized at the time that these could alleviate the industry's basic problems only if interest rates did not return to levels seen in 1979. But interest rates rose again beginning in the summer of 1980 and remained high during 1981 and well into 1982, provoking a wave of failures and forced mergers. Since the summer of 1982, however, interest rates have been falling. At the time of writing (January 1983) it is hoped that interest rates will fall further and stay down. If this hope is fulfilled, then the thrift problem should be resolvable. However, the same hope accompanied the March 1980 passage of DIDMCA, and that hope was not fulfilled. If interest rates rise sharply in the near future, the act's new asset and liability powers will not be given sufficient time to improve thrifts' earnings or risk exposure. In this event, the net worth certificate and merger powers may not be sufficient to deal with the situation. Then Carron's warning would become relevant. To avoid a severe financial crisis, a direct cash outlay subsidy could then become necessary.

THE IMPACT ON COMMERCIAL BANKS

In the decades since the Second World War, commercial banks have several times reevaluated and realigned their strategies in response to opportunities or problems that faced the industry. During the first half of the century, bank policies concentrated on matching specific sources of funds to selected uses.[17] In the 1950s these policies were replaced by efforts to actively manage the asset portfolio while taking for granted the supply of funds. This supply presented no problem because interest-rate ceilings were not binding. During the 1960s emphasis shifted further, to liability management. The shift became necessary when market interest rates rose above the ceilings and disintermediation became a problem as, for example, in 1966.

As a result of these realignments the composition of both asset and liability portfolios changed dramatically.[18] Nonearning assets, such as cash and bank reserves, grew only sluggishly in dollar value while earning assets grew vigorously. The share of nonearning assets fell from 23.9 percent in 1950 to 10.5 percent in 1981. The share of Treasury securities also fell. The proportion of earning assets rose, particularly those with short duration or those paying variable rates such as commercial loans; for example, loans increased from 30.9 percent to 56.0 percent during this period.

The composition of liability portfolios also changed. Demand deposits fell from 73.8 percent in 1950 to 23.9 percent in 1981, while time and savings deposits rose—from 24.9 percent to 57.6 percent. In general, greater reliance was placed on instruments that pay market-related interest rates. For example, in 1956 only 1 percent of liabilities paid unregulated rates but by the close of 1981, 50 percent of liabilities paid market rates.[19]

The changes in composition and the growth of asset and liability portfolios enabled the banking industry to remain profitable and to avoid undue exposure to interest rate risk [Flannery, 1981]. The ratio of net income to assets varied cyclically over the period, ranging from a low of 0.66 percent in 1976-77 to a high of 0.84 percent in 1980. The return on equity rose consistently from 9.69 percent in 1960 to 11.86 percent in 1981. In the fall of 1982, the banking industry was not facing the crisis that confronted the S&L industry. This conclusion remains true for large and small banks [Flannery, 1981, and Hanweck and Kilcollin, 1982] and also, as Eisenbeis and Kwast [1982] have shown, for banks which, like S&Ls, specialize in residential real estate lending.

This does not mean that commercial banks have not faced problems. Rather, their managers and regulators provided the flexibility for the commercial banks to

---

[17] The real bills doctrine argued that deposits are essentially short-term notice accounts and hence deposit funds should be used for short-term, self-liquidating loans. For discussion of this point see Robinson [1962, pp. 93-115] or Shaw [1950, pp. 122-184].

[18] For a more detailed discussion of bank profitability and changes in bank asset and liability composition, see Garcia et al [1983].

[19] During the 1950s, Regulation Q ceilings were generally not binding. As market interest rates rose, and ceilings became binding with increasing frequency, banks devised ways to circumvent the ceilings.

evolve as necessary. At the time of the act's passage four concerns faced the industry: (1) the recently increased level and volatility of interest rates had raised exposure to interest rate risk; (2) the worldwide recession had increased actual and potential default rates on both domestic and international loans; (3) the enhanced S&L powers under DIDMCA and the current act increased the competitive ability of the S&L industry; (4) nondepository institutions were increasingly encroaching on what had traditionally been bank-reserved territory.

Nevertheless, the banks were less in need of immediate legislation than the thrifts so that much of the Garn-St Germain content is not directed specifically at the banking industry. However, the act does have important implications for commercial banks.

First and foremost, the new MMD and Super NOW accounts enable depository institutions, including banks, to compete directly with money market mutual funds. This opportunity is important to retail banks that can now offer market rates in order to retain their depositors. It is also important to small banks that had previously been unable to replace funds lost to MMMF accounts by selling large CDs to those funds. While the new accounts offer smaller banks the opportunity to assure the portfolio growth conducive to portfolio flexibility, they also raise the specter of increasing banks' interest costs and reducing their profitability, at least in the short-run. Both marketing and utilizing funds from the new accounts will provide a test of managements' skills.

Secondly, while the act significantly increases the S&L industry's ability to compete with commercial banks in asset deployment, the removal of any Regulation Q differential by January 1, 1984 will assist banks' competition for funds.

The act gives a third advantage—the ability to organize bankers' banks and a greater opportunity to utilize bank service corporations. Concurrent legislation also enables large commercial banks to invest in export trading companies. Service corporations may also provide an easier organizational answer than the formation of a bank holding company to the question of how commercial banks may take advantage of the permission to engage in limited brokerage activities granted by the Comptroller of the Currency to national banks and the Federal Reserve to state-chartered banks.[20]

Fourth, banks are given greater flexibility in lending. For example, the safety and soundness percentage limitation on national bank lending to individual borrowers is relaxed. This should assist small agricultural banks, particularly those that wish to concentrate rather than diversify their portfolios. Previously these banks have needed to organize loan participations or sales to correspondents. Henceforth they will have less need for these potentially costly resorts.

Specialization involves risk, so that the efficacy of a legislative change that encourages concentration of risk may be questioned in times of severe recession and falling commodity prices—the economic situation existing at the time of the act's passage. Further concentration of their loan portfolios could jeopardize the safety of agricultural (and other) banks. Indeed, it is the banking system's heavy exposure to losses from international loans that is responsible for the extension of the safety and soundness provisions to loans made to foreign governments and their agencies.

---

[20] This potential usage is argued by Hawke, Sweet, and Mierzewski [1982].

It is not clear, at this time of writing, whether the emergency powers contained in Titles I and II will be much utilized for commercial banks. It would appear that few real estate banks will need to utilize the capital assistance or net worth certificate programs. The merger and acquisition alternatives are likely to prove less costly to the FDIC in those cases of failure in the banking industry attributable to management error.

With regard to asset powers, commercial banks did not receive what they sought from Congress. They were not, for example, explicitly given the power to engage in full service brokerage activities nor to underwrite municipal revenue bonds, corporate bonds, or equities.

THE IMPACT ON BANK HOLDING COMPANIES

The Garn-St Germain Act has four features that will influence the activities of bank holding companies (BHCs). They are: (1) the act's emergency interstate and across-industry acquisition provisions; (2) the revisions of regulations that govern BHCs' insurance activities; (3) a relaxation of the constraints governing transactions between subsidiary banks and their holding company; and (4) an expansion of powers permitted to bank service corporations.

Interstate and Cross-Industry Acquisitions

Before the act's passage a BHC was prevented from acquiring a commercial bank in other than its home state by the Douglas Amendment to the BHCA. Further, *de facto* holding companies were prevented (until the acquisition of Scioto Savings Association of Columbus, Ohio, by Interstate Financial Corporation, Dayton, Ohio, was approved by the Federal Reserve Board in April 1982) from acquiring savings and loan associations by the Federal Reserve Board's reluctance to approve such acquisitions without explicit Congressional authorization.

The Garn-St Germain Act makes only limited progress toward deregulation in these areas. Title I, Section 116, gives the FDIC authority to seek, or to permit, interstate and/or cross-industry mergers of troubled, large, insured commercial banks and mutual savings banks. Title I, Section 123, of the act explicitly grants permission for the emergency acquisition of troubled, insured S&Ls. However, both sections order merger priorities so as to discourage mergers among different types of institutions within and across state lines. These priorities and the requirement that the FDIC limit merger assistance to commercial and mutual savings banks having $500 million assets or more will severely limit the number of acquisitions by BHCs under the act. There are, however, no such size restrictions on assisted acquisitions of S&Ls.

Insurance Activities of BHCs

Title VI of the act amends the Bank Holding Company Act by preventing BHCs from providing insurance as principals, agents, or brokers. The provision is one of the very few areas where the act works to increase restrictions rather than to promote deregulation. However, the act lists seven exceptions to the restrictions. As originally written, these exceptions held the potential for increasing the insurance activities of small BHCs. However, later amendment to the act restored Congress' intention to restrict insurance activities as *not* closely related to banking.

Other Activities of BHCs

The act allows virtually unlimited financial transactions between affiliated banks in a multi-bank holding company and liberalized collateral requirements on bank loans to affiliated companies. An exception is made to prevent the transfer of low quality assets. [See Rose and Talley, 1982.] It retains, however, the traditional separation of banking from commerce.

Bank Service Corporations

Since 1962, commercial banks have been able to form service corporations. Such corporations could, however, provide services only to commercial banks. Under the Garn-St Germain Act, bank service corporations can undertake three different categories of activity. They may render: (1) "depository institution" services; (2) those non-depository institution services that are permitted to commercial banks; and (3) other activities found by the Board of Governors to be "closely related" to banking. In this regard, the recent finding by the Federal Reserve that discount brokerage activities are both "closely related" and a "proper incident to" banking in response to the request by Bank of America to purchase Charles Schwab, opens the door for commercial banks to enter the discount brokerage (if not the underwriting) business. There are no geographical limits to the provision of such services as long as state branching laws are not violated. Further, these services may be provided to depository institutions, to nondepository institutions, and to the general public.

DUE-ON-SALE PROVISIONS

Title III-Part C ends the legal controversy that emerged in the late 1970s over the due-on-sale clause in mortgage loan contracts. The due-on-sale clause is a provision of many conventional mortgage loan contracts that gives the lender the option to declare the loan due and payable if all or part of the property securing the loan is sold or transferred before maturity. Prior to the period of rising interest rates in the 1970s, the clause was used primarily to protect the security of the loan in the event the mortgage would be transferred to a high risk borrower. During the 1970s, mortgage lenders began to employ the clause as a portfolio management tool.[21] The issue received national attention when the California Supreme Court in 1978 ruled in the case of *Wellenkamp v Bank of American et. al.* that the clause represented an "unreasonable restraint on alienation."

California courts extended the prohibition against the clause to noninstitutional lenders and interpreted the Wellenkamp decision to apply equally to state and federal institutions operating within California. Some 16 other states also had laws prohibiting the enforcement of the clause along the lines of the Wellenkamp decision. The California courts explicitly ruled that laws restricting the clause were not superseded by federal regulation. This decision set up a classic confrontation between federal and state regulatory goals.

The United States Supreme Court in June 1982 heard the case of *Fidelity Savings and Loan Association of Glendale, California v. de la Cuesta* and decided that the clause in a loan contract in favor of federally chartered institutions could be enforced despite the existence of state law to the contrary. This case was decided exclusively on the issue of federal preemption.

The act specifically carries the matter further by providing for a federal override of state-imposed restrictions on the clause. Title III-Part C of the act is relatively short; however, it will go a long way toward ending the controversy over the use of the clause in property loan contracts. The act provides for a federal override of state-imposed restrictions on the use of the clause by a broad range of lenders in real property loan contracts. The term "lender" refers to a person, financial institution, or government agency, and "real property loan" refers to a loan, mortgage, advance, or credit sale secured by a lien on real property. "Real property" is defined to include manufactured homes. The act specifies that all rights and remedies for both the lender and borrower are defined and fixed by the loan contract.

There are two important qualifications to the general federal override. First, the act defines a "window period" in which mortgage contracts created during the window period are subject for three years to any state law or ruling prohibiting the enforcement of the clause for reasons other than protecting the security of the loan. The window period covers the period from the date on which the state prohibited the clause to the date the act was enacted (October 1982). Some loan contracts created during this period are thus subject to state restrictions on the clause, if they exist, until October 1985. Second, the act forbids enforcement by federal S&Ls and savings banks in the case of property transfers to close family members. (See Fischer, 1982.)

The Supreme Court ruling and the 1982 Act are best viewed, from an economic perspective, as making significant progress toward settling a dispute over the wind-

---

[21] When setting a fixed interest rate on a mortgage, the lender must price the loan above the average cost of funds expected over the term of the loan to make a profit. As mortgages are often repaid before maturity, lenders set the interest charge according to the expected life of the mortgage. When interest rates rise unexpectedly, the life of the mortgage increases, also unexpectedly, because the borrower has an incentive to retain the mortgage. If he wishes to sell he can charge a higher price for the house if he can avoid any due-on-sale provision and pass the mortgage on to the buyer along with the house. As this situation recurred repeatedly during the 1970s, lenders sought to recoup their funds when a house was sold in order to relend the funds at a higher rate.

fall gains to owners of mortgaged properties and to windfall losses to lenders in those situations where the clause cannot be used to adjust the mortgage interest rate.

A RE-EXAMINATION OF DEPOSIT INSURANCE

At the beginning of the Great Depression, between 1929 and 1933, more than one-third of the commercial banks failed and either closed or were merged with other institutions. Thrift institutions fared only slightly better. Many of the failures occurred when large numbers of frightened depositors simultaneously attempted to withdraw their deposits. Because the cash banks hold at any one time is only a small percentage of their deposit liabilities, they were forced to sell loans and investment securities to meet withdrawals. With many more sellers than buyers, the prices of loans and securities declined sharply, and some banks were unable to pay off in full. As a result, these banks were forced into bankruptcy and many depositors experienced losses.

In 1933, the United States introduced Federal deposit insurance that guarantees depositors that they will receive the full par value of their insured deposits, up to some specified amount (presently $100,000). By any measure, deposit insurance has been a success. The number of bank failures declined from almost 4,000 in 1933 to under 100 per year immediately after its introduction. Thereafter failures rarely exceeded 10 per year until 1982. In 1982, 42 commercial banks were closed by the Federal Deposit Insurance Corporation (FDIC).

The Garn-St Germain Act requires the three federal deposit insurance agencies— the FDIC for commercial and most mutual savings banks, the Federal Savings and Loan Insurance Corporation (FSLIC) for savings and loan associations, and the National Credit Union Administration (NCUA) for credit unions—to conduct studies of the insurance system. In particular, the questions to be considered are: (1) how the current system affects bank structure and operation; (2) the possibility of depositors purchasing additional voluntary insurance; (3) the potential for private insurance; (4) basing insurance premiums on risk; (5) the implications of increased insurance coverage; (6) increased public disclosure of the financial condition of the banks; and (7) consolidating the three deposit insurance agencies. The studies are to be completed and submitted to Congress no later than April 15, 1983. Discussed briefly here are only two of these issues: risk-sensitive insurance premiums and the extent of insurance coverage.

Risk-Sensitive Premiums

By law, premiums for deposit insurance are levied on the insured depository institutions in proportion to their total deposits, even though all deposits are not insured and all institutions are not equally risky and likely to become insolvent. Thus, larger banks that tend to have a smaller proportion of insured to total deposits and more conservative banks effectively subsidize smaller and/or more risky banks. This not only appears inequitable but also encourages institutions to assume additional risk, in an attempt to reap additional rewards from the higher yields that riskier projects typically offer, at no additional insurance cost.

To discourage such behavior, the deposit insurance agencies have regulated appropriate operating behavior and monitored compliance. These constraints have interfered with the ability of the banks to provide all the services that they believe are in their best interests and it has long been suggested that the insurance premiums be related to the risk characteristics of the bank balance sheet. This would make the premiums comparable to the premium structure for most other types of insurance. Riskier banks would pay higher deposit insurance premiums than less risky banks, just as race drivers pay higher life insurance premiums than university professors.

The major barrier to introducing such premiums has been the difficulty of measuring default and interest rate risks with sufficient precision. Although difficult, recent advances, such as the ready availability of data on computers, have made quantifying risk somewhat easier and risk-sensitive premiums more feasible. In addition, because the higher premiums would discourage banks from engaging in riskier activities, shifting to a risk-sensitive premium structure would permit a significant reduction in the degree of bank regulation and supervision.

Deposit Insurance Coverage

Future changes in the percentage of deposits insured resulting from the study's proposals could have significant implications both for the likelihood of runs on banks by depositors and for the risks incurred by the banks. For example, the lower the maximum amount of the depositor's account that is insured, the greater is the number of depositors potentially imperiled by bank failures and the more likely is a widespread attempt by these depositors to withdraw their deposits in times of crisis. This may encourage runs on banks. On the other hand, with lower coverage at least some depositors, particularly larger ones, will be more careful about the banks they use. By choosing those they consider least risky, they implicitly exert pressure on all banks to avoid assuming undue risks and operate more soundly. This should reduce the need for depositors to shift their funds quickly out of the banks. Private market discipline on the risk behavior of the banks is diminished as the percentage of deposit accounts insured increases and disappears altogether when deposit accounts are insured in full.

IMPLICATIONS FOR MONETARY POLICY

The introduction of Super-NOW and money market deposit accounts poses two major problems for the Federal Reserve in its conduct of monetary policy, at least in the near term future. One problem concerns the extent to which continued emphasis on monetary aggregate growth will enable the Fed to achieve the desired impact on the economy. Another problem concerns the Fed's ability to control monetary aggregate growth.

The two problems reflect the two-stage process inherent in the present conduct of monetary policy. At the first stage, the Federal Reserve establishes ranges of growth for a set of intermediate targets that are deemed consistent with achieving desired economic goals expressed in terms of employment, inflation, and GNP. At the second stage, the Federal Reserve uses its policy instruments (the supply of reserves provided through open market operations, the discount rate, and reserve requirements) to control the set of intermediate targets. At present, these intermediate targets include various monetary and credit aggregates. Primary emphasis was given to M1 as an intermediate target until fall 1982, when emphasis was shifted to the broader aggregates because of distortions caused by the new accounts and other factors.

The two-stage process describing the current conduct of monetary policy can be summarized as the impact from reserves, R, to money, M, to GNP:

$$R \rightarrow M \rightarrow GNP.$$

Influence Over the Final Economy

The Federal Reserve's influence over the economy via use of the monetary aggregates, that is, the transmission of the effects of changing the growth rate of money to the real economy, is best understood in the context of the income velocity of circulation. Income velocity(V) measures the relationship between the level of nominal GNP and the quantity of money as a ratio. If the monetary aggregate rises faster than GNP, velocity falls. Conversely, velocity increases to the extent that GNP growth is greater than money growth. This relationship summarizes the money to GNP stage of Federal Reserve influence over the economy:

$$MV = GNP.$$

In order to maintain that influence, the Federal Reserve needs to anticipate what effect the new accounts will have on the velocities of the various monetary aggregates.

The evidence suggests that MMDAs are extremely popular, and that shifts of funds into MMDAs from non-M2 sources contributed to the recent rapid growth in M2. Thus, it is highly likely that M2 velocity in the first quarter of 1983 will be lower than it would have been without the new accounts. It is not so easy to predict what will happen to M1 velocity, however. Shifts into Super NOW accounts from non-M1 sources will raise M1 growth, while shifts into MMDAs from M1 sources will lower M1 growth. What the net impact will be is unclear. However, while Super NOW accounts have not been as popular as MMDAs, the limited evidence available suggests more funds have been shifted into M1. Thus, M1 velocity in the first quarter of 1983 may be lower than it would have been without the new accounts.

Once the transition phase is over, the Federal Reserve will be able to recognize the new velocity relationships and use them in formulating policy. In the interim, however, it will be difficult for the Fed to know, for example, whether faster growth in M2 results from a stimulative policy on its part or from an increase in the public's desired holdings of that aggregate reflected by a fall in velocity. In the latter case, holding the growth of M2 during the transition period to its previous rate would exert a depressing effect on economic activity, because the public, in order to satisfy its increased desire to hold money, would decrease expenditure levels. With this difficulty in mind, the Federal Reserve has decided to calculate the 1983 targeted growth range for M2 from a February/March average base instead of the usual fourth quarter average base, in anticipation that the bulk of the money shifts will have occurred by then. Also to allow for some further shifts, the Fed also raised the M2 growth projected for 1983.

In the past, when transactions balances earned no interest, the public's demand for the various monetary aggregates fell whenever market rates rose. This made velocity a function of interest rates. In this situation, when judging what target money growth rates to set, the Fed needed to take into account the variability in the relationship between money and income caused by changes in interest rates. Now that money holders can receive market rates without foregoing their money holdings, the interest elasticity complication in policy should be less important.[22]

Thus, after the transition period is over and the new relationships are established and recognized, it may become easier to conduct monetary policy by setting intermediate targets for money. However, the transition period is likely to be difficult. This fact has been acknowledged by the Federal Reserve in its current shift toward greater flexibility in policy implementation.

Control Over the Aggregates

Federal Reserve control of any particular monetary aggregate requires that the Fed know the relationship between its policy instruments and the aggregate to be controlled. This relationship can be summarized as

$$M = mR$$

where M is the monetary aggregate to be controlled, R is the level of reserves, and m is the multiplier. Imagine that the Federal Reserve wished to control the level of transactions balances in an ideal situation in which the following conditions prevail: transactions balances are clearly distinguishable from other deposits; all and only transactions balances are included in M1; all and only M1 components carry the same reserve requirement; and the Federal Reserve controls the supply of reserves precisely. In such a world, the multiplier relationship m between M1 and R would be known exactly and the Federal Reserve could control the quantity of M1 precisely.

In the real world, however, the multiplier relationship is not known exactly.

---

[22] In this context, the phrase "market interest rates" does not refer to Treasury bill rates. Rather, the phrase means rates that are set by market forces and are appropriate to instruments of immediate liquidity, small and easily divisible denomination, high security, substantial convenience, and no transaction cost. Such rates are expected to be *below* Treasury bill rates.

There are many ways in which the ideal situation does not quite hold. For example, reserve requirements are imposed on nonpersonal time deposits and Eurocurrency liabilities as well as on transaction accounts. In addition, reserve requirements on transactions accounts are graduated—3 percent on the first $26.3 million and 12 percent on transaction accounts above this amount at each depository institution. Further complicating this situation is the act's provision exempting the first $2 million of reservable liabilities at each institution. Moreover, the Federal Reserve's control of the supply of reserves is imprecise because other factors that are difficult to predict such as float and Treasury balances also affect the supply of reserves.

Furthermore, financial innovations have made it increasingly difficult to distinguish transactions accounts from other balances. Money market mutual funds, repurchase agreements, and other new instruments have some transactions features, for example, but are not included in M1 and are not subject to reserve requirements. The existence and growth of these instruments have complicated the Federal Reserve's conduct of monetary policy by raising questions concerning the appropriateness of the current M1 definition as a measure of transactions balances. All of these factors serve to make the multiplier relationship less predictable, thereby impairing the Fed's ability to control the monetary aggregates.

How will the latest accounts affect this situation? Because of its unlimited transactions features, the Super NOW account has been classified as a transactions account for reserve requirement purposes, and has been included in M1. Because a market rate is earned, however, it is possible that some nontransactions funds might be placed in Super NOW accounts as well. The MMDA is more difficult to classify because it has limited transactions features. Furthermore, the act mandates that MMDAs not be subject to transactions account reserve requirements. Personal (0 percent) and nonpersonal (3 percent) time deposit reserve requirements have been imposed on MMDAs, and they have been included in M2 along with other savings and small time deposits and money market mutual funds.

As the public adapts to the new accounts, funds are shifted from other sources that may be subject to different or no reserve requirements. Such shifts make predictions of the multiplier relationship more uncertain than usual. For example, balances in MMDAs have grown very rapidly, exceeding $300 billion by early March. It is difficult for the Federal Reserve to know where these funds have come from and to anticipate what effect they will have on the multiplier relationship.

Once the transition period nears completion, however, the Fed will be able to review the situation, recognize the new multiplier relationship that exists between the chosen monetary aggregate and the level of reserves, and restore its control over the quantity of money. In the meantime, however, the introduction and growth of the new accounts make monetary control more difficult.

WHAT REMAINS TO BE DONE

The thrust of the present act, the DIDMCA of 1980, and the several Congressional studies of the U. S. financial services industry before them, is toward deregulation. Together, the two acts take so large a step toward deregulation that they rival in importance the banking legislation of the 1930s, much of which they repeal.

Is Deregulation a Good Thing?

Why is it a good idea today to remove regulation initiated during the 1930s? The movement toward the deregulation of depository institutions is not an isolated phenomenon: deregulation has earlier been applied to the airline, trucking, and brokerage businesses. The generality of this process suggests that a change has taken place in the theoretical underpinnings of the regulatory impetus.

Theory of Regulation

The imposition of regulations can be justified in situations where external economies or diseconomies exist. In these cases, the actions of industry participants pursuing their own interests will not best achieve society's goals. Rather participants must be shepherded into modifying their behavior to achieve the social optimum.

The shepherding influence can be applied by a governmental authority in one of two ways. The actions giving rise to external diseconomies can be explicitly forbidden (or rationed) by regulation or they can be implicitly discouraged by imposing a tariff on unwanted behavior. Conversely, where external economies exist, society can encourage the activity either by requiring it to be done or by making it financially rewarding. Ultimately then the choice is between: (1) establishing regulations which impose hidden costs or rewards on the economy, (2) directly altering the price system to achieve the desired objective. The legislation of the 1930s adopted the first regulatory approach.

Historical Background

The regulations of the 1930s arose as a reaction to contemporary analysis of the Great Depression. It was, for instance, believed that excessive competition had weakened depository institutions and contributed to the wide-spread banking failures. In turn, bank failures spread and imposed unreasonable costs on others; that is, they carried (and still carry) external diseconomies. After the Great Depression, safety and soundness were to be insured by eliminating the opportunities for both excessive competition and concentration. In this way Regulation Q originated, placing restrictions on interest payable on savings deposits and forbidding the payment of interest on demand deposits; restrictions on portfolio composition; restraints on permitted product lines, underwriting and dealing in securities; and stringent standards to be met in chartering new entrants to the industry. While these new restrictions limited competition, the Congress relied upon longstanding limits to geographic expansion to prevent undue concentration of economic power.

These regulations have been in force since the 1930s or, in some cases, even earlier. But times have changed: higher and more volatile interest rates, greater ease of travel, and of information storage and processing, have rendered many of the old regulations obsolete and/or unduly costly to industry participants.[23] In

---

[23] The arguments for and against deregulation are discussed in greater detail by Kaufman, Mote, and Rosenblum [1982].

turn, the high incentives to avoidance have also raised the governmental costs of enforcing compliance so that a "regulatory dialectic" has developed.[24]

In this situation it has been judged time to deregulate and to replace, wherever possible, explicit decree by a system of price incentives. Nevertheless, it is appropriate to check in each instance of deregulation whether society's objectives can best be attained in this way. Further, it may be necessary henceforth to apply the antitrust laws to prevent undue concentration in the financial services industry as in others. Finally, it is necessary to know how to price the targeted activities. Recent advances in the theory of financial economics make pricing now feasible.

Progress Toward Deregulation

Taken together, the DIDMCA Act of 1980 and the current Garn-St Germain legislation constitute an enormous step toward the deregulation of the financial services industry. Nevertheless, if the direction of these acts—toward the achievement of a highly competitive, minimally regulated system—is accepted, some issues remain to be addressed.

Geographic Restrictions

Perhaps the most obvious areas in which further liberalization would be desirable—one dealt with only tangentially in the act—is the geographic confinement of commercial banking. For example, there remain geographic restrictions on branching both within and across states. Further, the Douglas Amendment to the Bank Holding Company Act prohibits interstate acquisitions of banks by bank holding companies. Given the legislation's exhortation to a "level playing field," it is odd that banks should remain more restricted than S&Ls in this regard. In general, federal laws of most states are highly restrictive, particularly where interstate banking is concerned.

The Garn-St Germain Act deals with these geographic restrictions only in its emergency powers section. Title I and II authorize the acquisition of closed or endangered insured commercial banks and thrifts by out-of-state insured institutions. These provisions expand financial institutions' interstate branching capabilities by permitting them to operate deposit-taking offices in more than one state. Clearly designed for exceptional circumstances, the sections of the act allowing limited interstate acquisitions are subject to a sunset provision calling for their repeal after three years. Thus, the act modifies the deference of federal branching law to state legislation only to a limited degree, and only temporarily, except that branches acquired under the act's emergency authority may be retained after that authority expires.

Adopted for a variety of reasons in the past, but having the primary effect of protecting narrow, parochial interests, state branching laws have Balkanized the

---

[24] The phrase "regulatory dialectic" was coined by Professor Edward J. Kane. See, for example, Kane [1981].

banking industry to a degree not experienced by any other industry. The kinds of arguments used to justify these restrictions—states' rights, the protection of small institutions, the preservation of personal service, the desire to keep money in the local community, the failure of many studies to demonstrate any clearcut superiority of branch bank performance, and so on—have been rejected as bases for protectionist legislation in most other industries. With some exceptions, students of the issue strongly favor the dismantling and eventual elimination of state geographical restrictions on branch and holding company banking. One way to achieve this objective would be to amend the National Bank Act to allow national banks to branch nationally and to repeal the Douglas Amendment to the Bank Holding Company Act.

That these restrictions have been rendered largely ineffectual—except, perhaps, in the case of deposit-gathering through local offices—by the establishment across state lines of Edge Act corporations, loan production offices, and the other, many, and various nonbank subsidiaries of holding companies, is irrelevant. The restrictions still constitute a constraint on the choice of the most efficient form of organization, a form that many banks and thrifts would choose if given the option. Anti-trust legislation could still be applied to prevent undue horizontal integration in the industry.

Chartering

Another fundamental area of regulation that neither the DIDMCA nor the current act deals with explicitly is entry. While the two acts reduce barriers to entry into specific service lines by existing institutions, except in the emergency titles they are silent on the isssue of chartering *new banks.* The traditional chartering process used by the Comptroller of the Currency, the FHLBB, and most state banking departments gave considerable weight to the financial conditions of existing institutions and the "convenience and needs of the community." It is now recognized that such an approach is basically incompatible with a competitive financial system. Therefore, the chartering agencies, within the broad range of discretion granted them by legislation, are working to adjust their entry criteria to the changing environment.

At some point, nevertheless, it may become necessary to amend the National Bank Act to liberalize further the criteria that are applied in judging bank charter applications. Asymetrically, the FHLBB has been given the necessary flexibility when chartering S&Ls and savings banks. Title III Section 311 of the act empowers the Board to create and charter S&Ls and savings banks, "giving primary consideration to the best practices of thrift institutions in the U. S." Most state governments are expected to respond by liberalizing their entry requirements for state-chartered institutions, in order to avoid giving any advantage to federally chartered institutions.

Product Line Restrictions

The original Garn bill would have liberalized restrictions on the securities activities of banks, allowing them both to underwrite all types of municipal revenue bonds and to manage money market mutual funds. These provisions were eventually dropped in one of the compromises necessary to secure passage of the act. The legislative history of the act also makes it clear that while permitting diversification, Congress wishes S&Ls to continue as major providers of funds for residential housing. In recognition of this, immediately on passage, the FHLBB withdrew its proposals to permit S&L service corporations to engage in a wide range of activities including real estate brokering, the manufacture of mobile homes, insurance underwriting, securities activities, and the operation of mutual funds.

During the pre-act hearings, commercial banks sought powers to underwrite all municipal revenue bonds and to offer full brokerage services. While the act does not explicitly grant these powers, rulings by the Comptroller of the Currency, the FDIC, and the Federal Reserve Board henceforth will enable banks, their holding companies, or service corporations, to offer limited discount brokerage services. They do not, however, have authority to act in general as dealers or underwriters. Further, William Isaac, the chairman of the FDIC, has recently questioned the legitimacy of nonbanks' (such as Sears Roebuck's and Merrill Lynch's) entrance into the banking industry. Consequently the question of competition between banks and nonbanks (and in particular the securities industry) is likely to surface again soon, and with greater urgency.

Nevertheless, the restrictions on, for example, securities activities of banks are one of the areas that need, in particular, to be carefully reconsidered in light of their original rationale, the possible inefficiencies they may create, and any advantages they provide. While such restrictions originated in the 1930s in response to abuses perceived at that time, the contribution of the securities abuses of a relatively few banks to the banking debacle of the 1930s has never been clearly isolated from that of other events occurring at the same time. The importance of these abuses—though not their egregiousness—may have been exaggerated. Moreover, there may be means short of divorcement to achieve the ends intended by the Glass-Steagall Act, means that do not sacrifice the potential efficiencies of combining banking and underwriting in the same institution.

On the other hand, it is also possible to exaggerate the benefits of such a recombination of commercial and investment banking. In the first place, the legal separation restricts entry into investment banking only by a single class of institutions—banks; all others are free to enter.

Secondly, it has not been clearly demonstrated that potential conflicts of interest arising from a bank's fiduciary relationships with two sets of clients (the company needing to raise capital and depositors) can be eliminated simply by restructuring the bank's internal operations. To the extent that this result is achieved by the erection of a "Chinese Wall," analogous to that separating bank lending and trust department activities, the synergism alleged to inhere in such a combination of activities would be lost. The benefits to be derived from commercial bank entry into municipal revenue bond underwriting appear miniscule, although this remains a point of considerable controversy.

Third, there is little or no evidence on the convenience to customers of being able to bank and carry out securities transactions at the same institution. On balance, the close matching of advantages and disadvantages suggests the need for a much more fundamental reappraisal of the Glass-Steagall restrictions than has been undertaken to date.

Depository Institution Powers

Both DIDMCA and the Garn-St Germain Act do much to expand the asset and liability powers of nonbank depository institutions, particularly in the areas of consumer and commercial lending, the offering of transaction accounts, and—since DIDC's actions in late 1982—the offering of a savings deposit instrument (almost) free of reserve requirements and interest rate restrictions and a transactions account paying market interest rates. These changes greatly lessen, but do not eliminate legally enforced specialization by depository financial institutions. To achieve complete elimination would require not only the removal of all maximum percentage restrictions on various types of assets that thrift institutions may acquire, but also the repeal or further pruning of the bad-debt deduction provisions that give savings and loan associations such an enormous incentive to concentrate on residental lending. If the country still wishes to subsidize housing construction, it would be preferable to make such subsidies direct and explicit, so that their costs can be more clearly perceived and evaluated. Here, the intention is to allow thrifts, in particular, to diversify their portfolios in order to reduce their (and, ultimately the FSLIC's) exposure to interest rate risk. However, use of these powers may at the same time increase thrift and corporation exposure to default risk. While the balance of advantage has been judged in favor of deregulation at this time, that balance may not always be so.

A less dramatic, but, as the discussion of the act's effects on savings and loan associations suggests, potentially effective way to achieve the risk-reducing benefits of diversification while continuing an emphasis on residential housing, would be to add state and local securities to the list of assets qualifying for the bad-debt deduction.

Ending Regulation Q

Interest rate deregulation, though a central purpose of DIDMCA and one pushed still farther by the Garn-St Germain Act's authorization of the new money market deposit and Super NOW accounts, is still incomplete. At the time of writing, the DIDC has called for public comment on an acceleration of the ceiling-removal process and in particular, on the extension of the MMD account to permit unlimited transactions for customers not eligible to hold Super NOWs. Until such a provision is adopted, the prohibition of interest on corporate demand deposits will continue to be circumvented by such devices as repurchase agreements, subsidized loan rates and so on. It should be noted however, that while a business market-interest-paying deposit would be useful to small business, it would not prove attractive to larger corporations. Transactions accounts carry reserve requirements. RPs do not and therefore earn a higher rate. Consequently, even though RPs must be collateralized by government securities, they may remain a preferred instrument for larger corporations. Nevertheless, such circumventions are inherently clumsy and RPs, for example, give rise to unresolved legal issues concerning ownership of the securities subject to repurchase. Moreover, they have destructive implications for the meaning and accuracy of M1 and pose at least transitional difficulties for the conduct of monetary policy.

Allowing depository institutions to set unregulated rates on their liabilities will not involve them in excessive and unsafe competition. Further, removal of Regulation Q will not more than transitionally interfere with the conduct of monetary policy. In the long run, it should facilitate monetary policy by eliminating cyclical shifts of funds from one aggregate to another as ceilings alternatively become binding and nonbinding with changes in market interest rates.

Emergency Powers

Those provisions of the Garn-St Germain Act that are clearly of a transitional nature—in particular, those authorizing the issuance of net worth certificates to troubled thrift institutions—will take some time to work themselves out. Whether the great majority of these certificates can be retired within a reasonable time is questionable at best: repayment provisions are not specified in the act. The FHLBB has, however, recently issued guidelines for repayment. The current provisions buy some time for further scrutiny of the problem, for the natural healing process to occur as assets are repaid and reinvested on better terms, or, most importantly, for interest rates to fall. Absent these events, the thrift problem will recur.

Deposit Insurance

The establishment of deposit insurance for banks and thrifts has largely removed the external diseconomy arising from runs on depository institutions. Although accounts are currently insured only to $100,000, prior to 1982 no depositor had incurred a loss as a result of a large bank failure in recent decades. Secure in this knowledge, some banks have undertaken risky operations in the past, and will again in the future. As deposit insurance premiums do not reflect risk, risk-takers expose the insurance agencies (and ultimately other depository institutions) to loss. In the past, unacceptable degrees of risk-taking have been prevented largely through regulations that preclude unacceptable behavior. As the deregulatory process successfully removes restraints on depository institution behavior, new ways must be found to forestall unacceptable behavior, possibly by pricing insurance according to risk exposure.

Conclusion

The Garn-St Germain Act takes a second, important legislative step towards the deregulatory objective of efficiency and equity set forth for the earlier DIDMCA of 1980. Neither that act, nor the current one is a panacea. Progress has been made but much remains to be done.

REFERENCES

Baer, Herbert, "An American Tragedy: The Economics of the Savings and Loan Industry," unpublished paper, June 1982.

Brewer, Elijah, "The Thrift Problem in the 7th District," unpublished paper, November 1982.

Cargill, Thomas F., and Gillian Garcia, *Financial Deregulation and Monetary Control*, Hoover Institution Press, Stanford, California, 1982.

Carron, Andrew S., *The Plight of the Thrift Institutions*, The Brookings Institution, Washington, D. C., 1982.

Eisenbeis, Robert A., and Myron L. Kwast, "The Implications of Expanded Portfolio Powers on S&L Institution Performance," unpublished paper 1982.

Fischer, L. Richard, Elizabeth G. Gentry and Petrina M. E. Verderamo, *The Garn-St Germain Depository Institutions Act of 1982: What's In It for You?*, The Consumer Bankers Association, Arlington, Virginia, 1982.

Garcia, Gillian and the Staff of the Federal Reserve Bank of Chicago, "Financial Deregulation: History and Perspective of the Garn-St Germain Depository Institutional Act of 1982," Federal Reserve Bank of Chicago, Staff Study 83-3, 1983.

Flannery, Mark J. "Market Interest Rates and Commercial Bank Profitability: An Empirical Investigation," *Journal of Finance*, Volume 36, Number 5, December 1981, 1085-1101.

Hanweck, Gerald A. and Thomas E. Kilcollin, "A Note on Bank Profitability and Interest Rate Risk." Working Paper No. 51, Board of Governors of the Federal Reserve System, July 1981.

Hawke, John D. Jr., William J. Sweet Jr., and Michael B. Mierzewski, "Revised BHC Act Offers Banks New Opportunities," *Legal Times*, December 20, 1982, pp. 17, 21-22.

Kane, Edward J., "Accelerating Inflation, Technological Innovation and the Decreasing Effectiveness of Banking Regulation," *Journal of Finance*, May 1981, 355-67.

Kaufman, George G., "The Thrift Institution Problem Reconsidered." *Journal of Bank Research*, Spring 1972.

Kaufman, George, Larry Mote, and Harvey Rosenblum, "Implications of Deregulation for Product Lines and Geographic Markets of Financial Institutions," Federal Reserve Bank of Chicago, *Proceedings of a Conference on Bank Structure and Competition*, April 1982, 7-21.

Kopcke, Richard W., "The Condition of Massachusetts Savings Banks and California Savings and Loan Associations," *The Future of the Thrift Industry*, Conference Series No. 24, Federal Reserve Bank of Boston, 1981.

McNulty, James E., "Economics of Scale: A Case Study of the Florida Savings and Loan Industry," Federal Reserve Bank of Atlanta, *Economic Review*, November 1982, 22-31.

Reilly, K., and Rupinder S. Sidhu, "The Many Uses of Bond Duration," *Financial Analyst's Journal*, July-August, 1980.

Robinson, Roland, *The Management of Bank Funds*, 2nd edition, New York, N. Y.: McGraw Hill, 1962.

Rose, John T., and Samuel H. Talley, "The Banking Affiliates Act of 1982, Amendments to Section 23A," Federal Reserve Bulletin, November 1982, 639-699.

Salamon, Julie, "Money Funds Proliferate As Assets Fall," *Wall Street Journal*, March 21, 1983, pp. 21, 25.

Shaw, Edward S., *Money, Income and Monetary Policy*, Chicago, Ill.: Richard D. Irwin, Inc., 1950.

U. S. Department of the Treasury, *Report of the Interagency Task Force on Thrift Institutions*, June 1980.

29

A New Supervisory System for Rating Banks*

George R. Juncker

The commercial banking system which serves the United States is a very diverse one. Its nearly 14,500 banks range from single-office institutions, with less than $1 million in assets and serving a limited market area, to the international banking giants with hundreds of offices located in the world's financial centers and with assets which total many billions of dollars. Federal supervision of such a diverse banking system is necessarily a complex and demanding task for the three agencies that share responsibility for seeing that the banking system is safe and sound and serves the financial needs of the nation. While all three Federal agencies have approached the analysis of bank condition in a somewhat similar way, past differences in bank rating procedures and techniques used by the agencies had complicated the task of evaluating the condition of the banking system as a whole. In May, the Federal Reserve System, the Office of the Comptroller of the Currency, and the Federal Deposit Insurance Corporation (FDIC) announced adoption of a uniform system for rating the condition of the nation's commercial banks.

The new rating system gives senior officials at the supervisory agencies a capsule summary of the condition of individual banks as well as an indication of the health of groups of banks or the overall banking system. The ratings are intended as a tool to focus attention on real and potential problems and to permit the effective allocation of supervisory resources among the banks. Federal law gives primary supervisory responsibility for the nation's 4,700 national banks to the Office of the Comptroller of the Currency. The Federal Reserve System exercises direct supervisory authority over about 1,000 banks that are chartered by state banking authorities and that are members of the Federal Reserve System. The FDIC provides Federal supervision over more than 8,700 insured, state-chartered commer-

*Reprinted from the *Quarterly Review*, Summer 1978, pp. 47-50, with permission from the Federal Reserve Bank of New York.

cial banks that are not members of the Federal Reserve System. In addition, the Federal Reserve System is charged with primary responsibilities for supervising the more than 2,000 bank holding companies in the United States with one or more commercial bank subsidiaries.

The new Uniform Interagency Bank Rating System will help ensure consistency in the way the Federal bank supervisors view individual banks within the banking system. The new rating system has two main elements.

1. An assessment by Federal bank examiners or analysts of five critical aspects of a bank's operations and condition. These are adequacy of the bank's capital, the quality of the bank's assets (primarily its loans and investments), the ability of the bank's management and administration, the quality of the bank's earnings, and the level of its liquidity.
2. An overall judgment incorporating these basic factors and other factors considered significant by the examiners or analysts, expressed as a single composite rating of the bank's condition and soundness. Banks will be placed in one of five groups, ranging from banks that are sound in almost every respect to those with excessive weaknesses requiring urgent aid.

The new rating system builds upon the foundation of earlier systems used by the three agencies. These rating systems date back to at least as early as 1926 when the Federal Reserve Bank of New York used a simple system to categorize over 900 member banks then in the Second District.[1] Each of the three Federal banking supervisors adopted its own rating system in the mid-1930s after extensive interagency discussion. These systems tended to be very complex and attempted to combine subjective judgments and quantitative standards.[2] Probably because of their rigidity and complexity, coupled with improvements in the strength and stability of the nation's economy and banking system, these rating systems began to fall into disfavor in the 1940s as simplified approaches were sought. In 1952, the Federal Reserve System and the Office of the Comptroller of the Currency agreed on the basic structure of a rating system. That system, like the new uniform system, provided for separate ratings for capital adequacy, asset quality, and management and included an overall judgment of the bank's condition.[3]

The Federal Reserve's responsibility for supervising the activities of the nation's registered bank holding companies created particular interest in the design of an improved system for rating banks which could be used by all three Federal bank regulatory agencies. The new uniform system was designed, in large part, by a group

---

[1] This rating system went by the name of MERIT. Based heavily upon management and asset quality in relation to capital, a rating of M was assigned for banks in good condition, E for satisfactory condition, R for fair, I for unsatisfactory, and T for serious.

[2] One system "scored" six characteristics—management, loans, securities, capital account, deposit growth, and earnings—and combined these numeric scores with a series of weighting factors. Judgmental inputs on factors not specifically measured were not permitted, making the resulting score difficult to interpret either as an absolute measure of conditions or even in its relationship to other scores.

[3] The Federal Reserve and the Comptroller of the Currency have used what is essentially this rating system almost continuously since it was originally adopted. The specific definitions used in that system were included in former Governor Robert Holland's testimony before the Committee on banking, Housing, and Urban Affairs, United States Senate (February 6, 1976).

headed by Eugene A. Thomas, vice president of the Federal Reserve Bank of San Francisco, working under the direction of the Federal Reserve Bank Presidents' Conference Committee on Regulations, Bank Supervision, and Legislation.

Under the new system, each performance characteristic and the composite is rated on a scale from one to five, which indicates the extent of the bank's strength or weakness. A rating of "1" indicates strength, "5" indicates a degree of weakness requiring urgent corrective actions. Thus, the strongest possible rating for a bank would be:

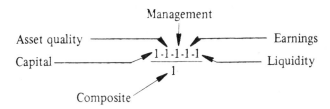

On the other hand, a rating of $\dfrac{4\text{-}5\text{-}4\text{-}5\text{-}3}{4}$ would indicate a bank with critical problems with asset quality and earnings and an overall condition that is less than satisfactory. Close supervisory attention and financial monitoring would be indicated by such a rating.

The examiner-analyst in using the new system evaluates each of the five elements of a bank's condition and the composite rating independently according to specifically defined standards. (See box for the definitions of each composite rating and the description of each performance zone as agreed upon by the three agencies.) While the five performance dimensions are somewhat interdependent, each is rated separately. Similarly, the composite is not determined by calculating an average of the separate components but rather is based on an independent judgment of the overall condition of the bank. Other factors, such as local economic conditions and prospects, trends in financial performance, and affiliation with a bank holding company, are evaluated by the examiner-analyst and incorporated into his overall assessment of the bank's condition.

Arriving at a six number representation of a bank's condition is an exercise which requires sound analytical judgment. It is admittedly an attempt to reduce to quantified terms a very complex judgmental evaluation process. A single ratio or group of ratios cannot fully or accurately describe all the underlying factors that influence a bank's past, present, or future performance. Thus, consistency in the new system depends not, for example, on rigid definitions of what constitutes adequate earnings but rather on an appreciation by the examiner-analyst of the several roles earnings play in making a bank sound and the matching of the bank's particular and peculiar situation to the agreed-upon definitions.

The first of the five performance dimensions—*capital adequacy*—gives recognition to the role that capital plays as the foundation supporting business risks within the bank. The greater the risks faced by a bank, the greater is its need for a strong capital base. In appraising these risks, the Federal supervisors review the risk "mix" of the asset portfolio as well as the skill with which management plans ahead and minimizes risks. The vitality of a bank's market area is also included in the analysis. The examiner-analyst also reviews the bank's capital-to-risk assets relationship, its

I. Composite Rating

The five composite ratings are defined as follows:

Composite 1
Banks in this group are sound institutions in almost every respect; any critical findings are basically of a minor nature and can be handled in a routine manner. Such banks are resistant to external economic and financial disturbances and capable of withstanding the vagaries of the business cycle more ably than banks with lower composite ratings.

Composite 2
Banks in this group are also fundamentally sound institutions but may reflect modest weaknesses correctable in the normal course of business. Such banks are stable and also able to withstand business fluctuations well; however, areas of weakness could develop into conditions of greater concern. To the extent that the minor adjustments are handled in the normal course of business, the supervisory response is limited.

Composite 3
Banks in this group exhibit a combination of weaknesses ranging from moderately severe to unsatisfactory. Such banks are only nominally resistant to the onset of adverse business conditions and could easily deteriorate if concerted action is not effective in correcting the areas of weakness. Consequently, such banks are vulnerable and require more than normal supervision. Overall strength and financial capacity, however, are still such as to make failure only a remote possibility.

Composite 4
Banks in this group have an immoderate volume of asset weaknesses, or a combination of other conditions that are less than satisfactory. Unless prompt action is taken to correct these conditions, they could reasonably develop into a situation that could impair future viability. A potential for failure is present but is not pronounced. Banks in this category require close supervisory attention and monitoring of financial condition.

Composite 5
This category is reserved for banks whose conditions are worse than those defined under Composite 4. The intensity and nature of weaknesses are such as to require urgent aid from the shareholders or other sources. Such banks require immediate corrective action and constant supervisory attention. The probability of failure is high for these banks.

trend, and a comparison of the bank's ratio with other banks of similar size and doing similar types of business.

An appraisal of the quality and collectibility of a bank's loans and investments has traditionally been one of the key parts of a Federal supervisory examination. The asset quality performance rating is largely based upon data on the overall quality of the assets held by the bank as developed during a supervisory examination. The new system, like earlier ones, relies heavily upon the classification of the

II.   Performance Evaluation

The five key performance dimensions—capital adequacy, asset quality, management-administration, earnings, and liquidity—are evaluated on a scale of one to five defined as follows:

Rating No. 1 indicates *strong* performance. It is the highest rating and is indicative of performance that is significantly higher than average.

Rating No. 2 reflects *satisfactory* performance. It reflects performance that is average or above; it includes performance that adequately provides for the safe and sound operation of the bank.

Rating No. 3 represents performance that is flawed to some degree; as such, is considered *fair*. It is neither satisfactory nor marginal but is characterized by performance of below-average quality.

Rating No. 4 represents *marginal* performance which is significantly below average; if left unchecked, such performance might evolve into weaknesses or conditions that could threaten the viability of the institution.

Rating No. 5 is considered *unsatisfactory*. It is the lowest rating and is indicative of performance that is critically deficient and in need of immediate remedial attention. Such performance by itself, or in combination with other weaknesses, could threaten the viability of the institution.

bank's credits into loss, doubtful, and substandard categories according to the likelihood of the bank's actually absorbing a loss on a credit.[4] Loan and investment policies, the adequacy of valuation reserves, and management's demonstrated ability

[4] The usual rule of thumb used for interpreting these classifications is that all credits classified loss will indeed represent eventual losses, 50 percent of aggregate credits classified doubtful will be charged off, as well as 20 percent of substandard classifications. Of course, actual loss experiences vary from credit to credit and bank to bank depending upon a wide variety of circumstances.

to collect problem credits would also be considered by the examiner-analyst in coming to a judgment regarding overall asset quality.

The third element in the rating evaluates the quality of a bank's corporate management including its board of directors. Management's technical competence, leadership, and administrative ability are evaluated along with the internal controls and operating procedures that have been installed. The bank's compliance with banking laws and regulations is another factor in the appraisal, as are the provisions for management succession. Judgments regarding management's willingness and ability to serve the legitimate banking needs of the community are also considered.

The strength of the bank's earnings is the fourth element in the performance rating. Here, a judgment is rendered on the adequacy of earnings to provide a sufficient return to the bank's stockholders to generate sufficient cash flows for the normal needs of borrowers, and to provide for the future needs through the development of capital. The "quality" of earnings is also analyzed, with particular attention paid to the adequacy of the bank's additions to valuation reserves and to the tax effects on net income. Peer-group comparisons and trends in earnings provide additional quantitative evidence for the rating.

The liquidity rating is based upon the bank's ability to manage its assets and liabilities in such a way as to ensure that it can meet the demands of both depositors and borrowers without undue strain. Among the factors considered in evaluating liquidity are the availability of assets readily convertible into cash, the bank's formal and informal commitments for future lending or investment, the structure and volatility of deposits, the reliance on interest-sensitive funds including money market instruments and other sources of borrowing, and the ability to adjust rates on loans when rates on interest-sensitive sources of funds fluctuate. The examiner-analyst will review the frequency and level of borrowings and include judgments of the bank's ability to sustain any level of borrowings over the business cycle or to attract new sources of funds. These judgments also include analyses of the bank's present and future access to traditional money market sources of funds and other domestic and foreign sources. The bank's average liquidity experience over a period of time, as well as its liquidity position on the examination date, would be considered. For Federal Reserve member banks, the use of the discount window is also reviewed to determine if borrowings are for other than seasonal or short-term adjustment purposes.

After analyzing the five key factors, the examiner-analyst arrives at a composite rating which summarizes the agency's overall view of the bank's condition and reflects the level of continuing supervisory attention which the bank's condition seems to warrant. A composite "1" rated bank would receive little supervisory attention between examinations, while a composite "5" bank would be subject to constant monitoring and a corrective action program developed by the bank's management and directors and accepted by its Federal supervisors.

The new rating system provides a uniform structure for use by the three Federal supervisory agencies in evaluating the condition of the nation's commercial banks. This uniformity of approach is expected to lead to more consistent and even-handed supervisory treatment. It should also enable more informed judgments regarding trends in the condition of the banking system as a whole.

30

The Withering of Capital[*]

James C. Van Horne[†]

One can hardly open the papers without reading something about a major corporation, consumer cooperatives, farmers, homebuyers, and a host of others in our society getting a boost from the government in their financing. The form of assistance varies, but the purpose is to direct the flow of savings toward some specific investment objective and/or to reduce the interest cost. These two facets define the social allocation of capital.

Recently, concern has mounted with respect to these programs. In early 1981, Congress sharply curtailed tax-exempt mortgage bond financing, and tax-exemption for such bonds ends altogether in 1983. The *Depository Institutions Deregulation and Monetary Control Act of 1980* (DIDMCA) will reduce the social allocation of capital to housing. In addition, usury laws on residential mortgages and business and agricultural loans were declared void unless prior to 1983 voters in the state specifically approve new usury laws. Finally, many politicians show signs of wanting to curb guarantees and to "reindustrialize" capital flows toward productive sectors of the economy.

While these actions and statements may indicate a partial blunting of the trends of the past two decades, the social allocation of capital in this country is far from dead. New plans are developing all the time, bringing with them new problems as well as benefits. The purpose of this paper is to examine the issues, assess their importance, and, hopefully, bring additional perspective to the social allocation of capital.

*Reprinted with permission from the *Journal of the Midwest Finance Association*, Volume 10, 1981, pp. 83-91.

†A. P. Gianinni Professor of Finance, Stanford University.

ALTERING CAPITAL FLOWS AND INTEREST RATES

Usury Laws

There are a number of ways by which a government can alter the flow of funds in the financial markets and/or the interest rate charged. One approach is to impose a ceiling on the rate of interest known as a *usury law.* Such a law limits the rate that may be charged on certain classes of consumer-related loans such as credit card loans, mortgage loans, and installment loans. In those states where they exist, usury limits on business-related loans are usually higher than those imposed on consumer loans.

Government Intermediaries

Federal, state, and local governments can form a financial intermediary, or agency, and borrow in the capital markets. The funds can then be loaned to a savings and loan association, housing authority, municipality, or other borrowers at the same rate or a slightly higher rate. In either case, the rate charged is lower than what the ultimate borrower would pay in the market. An example is the Export-Import Bank, which borrows from the Treasury at the government bond rate and then relends to foreigners purchasing U.S. products. Government sponsored agencies such as the Farm Credit Administration, the Federal Home Loan Bank and Fannie Mae borrow funds in the capital markets and relend them in support of various specified activities. Whether it be exporters, farmers, or home-buyers, a subsidy is involved because financing is at below-market rates.

Government Guarantees

Another means for socially allocating capital is the *government guarantee.* Here, the government either guarantees the debt or insures the loan against default. Recent examples include Wheeling-Pittsburgh Steel Corporation, which obtained $100 million in federal loan guarantees to finance a new steel mill, Chrysler Corporation, which obtained $1.5 billion in federal loan guarantees to sustain its operations, and New York City, perhaps the most famous of all. These examples are the most publicized of the guarantees. Virtually every department of the federal government has guaranteed and insured loan programs. The beneficiaries include such diverse groups as students, shipbuilders, grazing associations, homeowners, the Guam Power Authority, veterans, and small businesses. By 1980 there were some 200 government guaranteed or insured loan programs amounting to over $400 billion compared with less than $200 billion in the mid-1970s.

Regulations and Subsidies

Capital flows also are affected by *regulations.* Take, for example, the savings rate ceilings that have been imposed on depository institutions as well as the in-

terest rate differential that allowed savings and loan associations to pay a somewhat higher rate than commercial banks. The purpose was to direct savings to
mortgage lending institutions and stimulate housing at lower rates of interest than
otherwise would prevail. (The differential and ceilings will be eliminated by 1986
under the provisions of DIDMCA.) Yet another means for socially allocating capital
is a straight subsidy. An example of this would be a mortgage loan to a borrower
or a subsidized rate to a lender.

Tax-Exempt Financing

The federal government also affects capital flows and interest rates when it de-
crees who and what qualifies for tax-exempt financing. The advantage to the borrower is obvious—the interest cost is significantly less than if taxable bonds were
issued. While we usually think of municipal debt financing schools, sewers, public
buildings, parks and highways, this no longer is the case. Presently, only about
one-quarter of all municipal financing goes to such projects. Increasingly, tax-
exempt financing is being used to finance private projects.

Corporations issue industrial development bonds to finance plants as well as commercial structures (limited to $10 million per project). While begun in Mississippi
in the 1930s to attract industry, industrial development bonds now finance the
construction of fast food outlets, department stores, bank branches, racquet clubs
and many other private projects. Mortgage revenue bonds were the rage in 1979
and 1980. Here homebuyers were able to borrow from state housing authorities
at lower than prevailing mortgage rates because the authority issued tax-exempt
bonds. Recently, the California National Guard wooed recruits by promising them
a low interest mortgage if they would sign up. In turn, these were financed by tax-
exempt revenue bonds. Pollution control bonds, student loans, and farm loans ("Ag-
gie Bonds") are other examples of the use of tax-exempt financing of private projects. Such financing is burgeoning and now dominates the municipal securities
market.

ORIGIN AND PURPOSE

The origin of the social allocation of capital began in the 1930s not only with
industrial development bonds, but also with actuarially sound guaranteed loans to
farmers and homeowners. Not much was heard about these programs because the
volume of loans was small. Most plans to socially allocate capital in this country
were developed since the late 1960s. New plans are emerging all the time and the
listing of programs grows longer and longer. Special interest groups and politicians
see "government banks," "government guarantees," and tax-exempt financing as a
panacea for society's problems. The logic is simple. If one can somehow qualify—and the window is open rather wide—you can avail yourself of capital which
might not be available in the marketplace or available only at a significantly higher
interest rate.

Proponents of the social allocation of capital tell us that there really is no cost;
the federal or state government merely gives its backing so as to facilitate the flow

of capital to deserving projects. They point with pride to the federal government guarantee of the Lockheed loan in 1971. Not only did the company turn around to where the guarantee no longer was necessary to attract capital, but the government received a fee for its guarantee.

With the social allocation of capital we know that the housing sector, the city, the energy project, the consumer cooperative, or the corporation gains as a direct recipient. In many instances, society gains as well in that housing is built, employment in depressed areas is stimulated, pollution is reduced, hospitals are built or improved, and energy production is increased. Certainly, there are gains to society and these benefits are an inducement to those in government to continue to allow these programs to thrive. But is there really no cost?

THE COSTS REEXAMINED

Social allocation of capital has a cost. The parties not favored in the allocation formula suffer on a relative basis. The cost of channeling savings to housing falls heavily on low- and moderate-income families, and under most programs to socially allocate capital, our nation's financial markets work less efficiently in channeling funds to the most productive uses, which, in turn, hurts us all. Let us explore these contentions in greater detail, starting with the guarantee arrangement.

In the evolution of the New York City matter, the original plea was that the federal government guarantee the financial obligations of the city. Now what would have happened if this had transpired? Well, for one thing it would have made the obligations more valuable than Treasury securities. Not only would they carry the obligation of the U. S. government, but their interest would be tax-exempt as well. Imagine the windfall gain to investors. Contrast this gain with the return to a person who invests in the securities of a well-run municipality. This investor accepts a lower initial yield because the risk is lower than that of New York City. All of this is in keeping with equilibrium in financial markets according to risk and return. However, the relationship between risk and return is altered when the federal government steps in to guarantee the obligations of one borrower but not those of others.

This alteration explicitly favors a city or corporation which is not well-managed financially. If only through political pressure it is able to get the federal government to enter the scene and guarantee the securities, it will be able to borrow at a lower rate. This explains what happens to the return, but does the underlying risk go away? Of course not. It is merely shifted from the investor to the federal government and to taxpayers at large. If default should occur, the federal government will need to make good on the obligations. Where will it get the funds? Either by foregoing programs, increasing taxes, or increasing the federal debt. In addition to the future burden on taxpayers, increasing the debt may bring pressure on interest rates paid by all borrowers. Therefore, there is a cost to the guarantee, though admittedly it is a hidden one. This is the contingent or potential cost to present and future taxpayers as well as the cost to others in the financial markets.[1]

Moreover, the function of financial markets is altered. We know that this function is to efficiently channel savings in our society to the most productive investment opportunities, be they private sector investments or public sector investments with a social return. The mechanism by which funds are channeled is the tradeoff between risk and return. When a government explicitly directs funds to certain investments which, because of the risk involved, either would not be able to attract funds on their own or would be able to attract them only at a higher rate, it tampers with the workings of the marketplace.

Funds no longer flow on the basis of risk and return. One set of potential borrowers moves to the head of the line and capital is allocated to them on the basis of government decree, not by the marketplace. No longer must these borrowers justify the project's rate of return in relation to any market determined standard of efficiency. The result is that some projects are undertaken which would be rejected if the ultimate borrower had to pay the market rate to finance a project of that risk. In society as a whole, investments are undertaken which are not optimal in the sense of economic efficiency. Also, if distortions in risk-return relationships lead to less efficient financial markets, the result is that savings are allocated in our society at higher costs and/or with greater inconvenience. In turn, this has adverse implications for capital formation and for economic growth.

From this discussion, it is easy to go to the case of the federal government, or some agency thereof, borrowing in the financial markets and relending to another party. The purpose is to provide funds at a lower rate than the party—individual, city, or corporation—could obtain in the marketplace. In short, the creditworthiness of the federal government is substituted for that of the party involved. Because the former has the unique ability to print money to repay claims against it, the rate of interest is lower.

The effects of this form of socially allocating capital are much the same as before. In whole or in part the federal government absorbs the risk of default, and this risk ultimately is borne by taxpayers. In addition, other borrowers in the marketplace may be at a disadvantage. Clearly they are at a disadvantage relative to those to whom capital is allocated socially. However, they also may be at a disadvantage in an absolute sense of having to pay a higher interest rate. Again the equilibrium mechanism in the financial markets is distorted in that funds no longer flow on the basis of risk and return. These markets simply become less efficient in channeling savings to investment projects.

Turning now to government regulations which divert the flow of savings in our society away from what would occur in the marketplace, the effect is similar to that discussed earlier. In this case artificial restraints are established which bias the flow of savings toward socially desirable causes. The best known and most impor-

---

[1] For an option pricing model analysis of the value to the corporation, and cost to the government, of a guarantee, see Sossin [7]. For the average corporation the value/cost of a guarnatee is relatively small, but as market variance of a company increases beyond the average of all firms the value/cost of the guarantee guarantee, see Sossin [7]. For the average corporation the value/cost of a guarnatee is relatively small, but as market variance of a company increases beyond the average of all firms the value/cost of the guarantee and the interest cost savings to the company increases dramatically. See also Merton[4].

tant case is mortgage financing. By establishing ceilings on savings rates of mortgage lending institutions and by creating barriers to investment in alternative money market instruments, the hope was to enhance mortgage financing at rates of interest lower than what otherwise would be market-clearing rates. This, too, results in projects being undertaken that cannot be justified in terms of a market-determined cost of capital. Also, it may lessen the efficiency of financial markets with results similar to those described before. (The interest rate ceilings discussed here are in the process of being phased out.)

However, the direct cost effect was different than that mentioned earlier. Rather than falling on taxpayers in general, it fell on savers who had to accept lower interest rates on their savings than would otherwise prevail. In other words, by placing limits on the maximum rate paid and by establishing barriers to investing elsewhere, savers had to accept lower rates of interest than the market-clearing rates which would have existed in the absence of these restrictions. The problem was particularly acute during periods of rising interest rates.

Fortunately, the forces of competition are not long shackled. During the 1970s money market funds developed. These funds enable individuals to invest indirectly in money market instruments in smaller denominations than is possible with a direct investment in a Treasury bill or other money market instrument. This development is truly a financial innovation, for it filled an unmet need by giving the traditional small-scale saver an alternative.

We said before that the direct cost of socially allocating capital to mortgages falls on savers at savings institutions. More specifically, this cost falls on low- and medium-income savers who do not have alternative investments for their savings. They must accept lower savings rates than would prevail in free and competitive financial markets.[2] The recently passed DIDMCA will eventually eliminate a good deal of this opportunity cost.

Another supposed means to reduce the cost of borrowing is through usury laws. The problems here are well-known. It generally is agreed that binding ceilings on interest rates limit the supply of loans and/or give rise to certain non-interest costs such as closing fees, servicing fees, and discounts from the face value of the debt instrument—i.e., points. Inherently, the mechanisms for circumventing usury laws are less efficient than the simple use of interest rates to allocate credit.

Perhaps more important, usury laws often result in credit being rationed.[3] The larger the excess demand, the more lenders will try to upgrade the quality of their loans. Riskier loan applicants are increasingly rejected. Ironically, to the extent these applicants are low-income people, the end result may be that there is no cost of borrowing for them because they are unable to obtain credit at the ceiling rate. This occurence clearly is counter to the intentions of the framers of usury laws. The voiding of many of these laws under the DIDMCA is long overdue.

There are great incentives to get one's project qualified for tax-exempt financing. Given rational behavior, it is little wonder that tax-exempt financing of private projects has flourished. The limiting factors are only the demand for such projects and the legality of whether or not a project qualifies. Several costs are involved

---

[2] For an analysis of the opportunity cost to savers, see Pyle [6].

[3] For an empirical analysis of these laws, see Crafton [2].

with this method of social allocation. For one thing, there is a revenue loss to the federal government, as tax-exempt bonds are substituted for taxable bonds. In essence, the federal government subsidizes those private projects which qualify. Owing to certain offsets, the revenue effect is not one for one. Still the revenue loss to the government is significant, and this loss results in programs being foregone, higher taxes for others, or increases in the federal debt.

As discussed before for other methods, at the margin less productive projects are favored relative to those which can be financed only with taxable bonds. Consequently, there is an opportunity cost to society in the form of lower productivity than is possible if all private projects competed for capital on the same basis. Another consideration is that the market for municipal securities may be partially segmented on the demand side. That is, only a limited number of investors are able to take full advantage of the tax-exemption of interest income. As the overall supply of municipal securities increases, municipalities must appeal to investors in lower and lower tax brackets. As this occurs, interest rates in the municipal market rise, all other things the same. As a result, municipalities financing public projects must pay a higher interest cost than would be true if there were no tax-exempt financing of private projects. Thus, the capital costs associated with providing such traditional facilities as schools, sewers, recreational areas, and highways increases.

So far, we have covered five of the six means for socially allocating capital mentioned at the outset. The last one to be considered is the interest rate subsidy, which can be either to the borrower or to the lender. If it is deemed appropriate to socially allocate capital toward some objective, the interest rate subsidy to the borrower results in the least disruption to the financial markets and is the most equitable. For one thing, the subsidy goes directly to the party you wish to benefit. For example, the government may not wish to subsidize all borrowers in the mortgage market, but only low- to moderate-income persons.

If the market-clearing rate on a mortgage loan were 16 percent and the subsidy were 4 percent, the effective interest cost would be 12 percent. The risk-return equilibration mechanism in financial markets is not distorted. The borrower must compete for funds, but he/she knows that part of the interest cost will be picked up by the government in the form of a subsidy. In other words, financial markets are allowed to perform their function in the same manner as before and equilibrium occurs on the basis of expected risk and return. The government does not intercede directly in the marketplace. Moreover, the subsidy comes from the federal government or, more specifically, from taxpayers as a whole. It does not fall directly on low- and medium-income savers who are forced to accept lower interest rates on their savings than otherwise would prevail.

The interest rate subsidy also could go to the lender. Here the government would subsidize certain types, or categories, of loans—such as mortgages or loans to cities. A subsidy of this sort will result in a lower rate of interest on this category of loan than would otherwise prevail. However, the subsidy here is a shotgun approach in that it benefits all borrowers in a particular category. While this may be appropriate if you are trying to stimulate housing and construction overall, it is not so effective if you are trying to enable low- to medium-income individuals to purchase housing. Here a subsidy to the borrower is better.

While the subsidy is the most effective way to socially allocate capital, one should not conclude that there are no inefficiencies involved. Projects are accepted which would not be accepted if a market-determined cost of capital were employed. Thus, the subsidy shares with other methods the shortcoming of altering the risk-return acceptance criterion for projects. However, we must bear in mind that by definition the purpose is to socially allocate capital as opposed to allocating it strictly on economic grounds.

CONCLUSIONS

It is important to recognize that the cries for the social allocation of capital are increasing. The political appeal is irresistible—there seemingly is no cost, or at least the cost is so hidden as to be illusive. Without question there are unmet social needs in our society, and some of these needs may be satisfied by the social allocation of capital. The problem is that methods for socially allocating capital are seldom evaluated in their totality. Usually the benefits are readily apparent and always cited. However, the "true costs" are seldom considered. As a result, the idea often is given that the social allocation of capital is either without cost or that the costs are unimportant. As shown, however, there is a cost, not only to the government and to taxpayers, but to society as a whole in having less efficient financial markets and lower than possible productivity and economic growth.

Unfortunately, the more hidden the cost, the more tempting it is to socially allocate capital. More disturbing is the fact that usually the more hidden the cost of a method, the less efficient the process by which capital is socially allocated. The benefits of a plan to socially allocate capital must be judged in relation to the opportunity cost to taxpayers, to other borrowers, to savers, to the efficiency of financial markets, and in relation to the economic and/or social contribution foregone by the rejection of other projects. While there is little question that the decision-making process is easier if these costs are ignored, they represent the very crux of the issue. As they ultimately must be borne by society in one way or another, these costs should be analyzed at the time of a decision.

One of the problems is that social allocation of capital programs largely have gone unchecked over the years. Bringing these programs into the federal budget makes a good deal of sense. For one thing, it would cause Congress to analyze new proposals in a much more rigorous way. The present "off budget" treatment is outside the normal review and control process of the Congress. Treating programs to socially allocate capital as part of the budget process also would ensure that reasonable information was developed and that the totality of the picture was known. Centralization of information, approval, and control would result in more rational decisions being made.

In those cases where Congress or some other part of the government deems it appropriate to socially allocate capital, a strong case can be made that it be in the form of an interest-rate subsidy to the borrower. Assuming a high degree of competition between various financial instruments, the subsidy is likely to be the most effective way to socially allocate capital, provided it comes from general tax revenues. With an interest-rate subsidy, financial markets are able to perform their function more efficiently and, in the case of mortgage loans, more equitably.

Hopefully a more rational approach to the social allocation of capital will occur in the future than has occurred in the past. However, this will come to pass only if pressure is brought through the political processes.

REFERENCES

[1]   "A Guidelines Handbook on Federal Loan Guarantee Programs," Subcommittee on Economic Stabilization of the Committee on Banking, Finance and Urban Affairs, House of Representatives, 96th Congress (Washington, D.C.: U. S. Government Printing Office), February 1979.

[2]   Crafton, Steven M., "An Empirical Test of the Effect of Usury Laws," *Journal of Law and Economics,* 23 (April 1980), 135-145.

[3]   Fortune, Peter, "The Effectiveness of Recent Policies to Maintain Thrift-Deposit Flows," *Journal of Money, Credit and Banking,* 7 (August 1975), 297-315.

[4]   Merton, Robert, "An Analytical Derivation of the Cost of Deposit Insurance and Loan Guarantees: An Application of Modern Option Pricing Theory," *Journal of Banking and Finance,* 1 (June 1977), 3-12.

[5]   Penner, Rudolph G., and William L. Silber, "The Interaction between Federal Credit Programs and the Impact on the Allocation of Credit," *American Economic Review,* 62 (December 1973), 838-852.

[6]   Pyle, David H., "The Losses on Savings Deposits from Interest Rate Regulation," *Bell Journal of Economics,* 5 (Autumn 1974), 614-622.

[7]   Sossin, Howard B., "On the Valuation of Federal Loan Guarantees to Corporations," Research Paper, Columbia University (August 1979).

[8]   Van Horne, James C., *Financial Market Rates and Flows.* (Englewood Cliffs, New Jersey: Prentice Hall, 1978), Chapter 9.

Index

SYSTEMS PUBLICATIONS, INC.
P.O. BOX 318 HASLETT, MI 48840